Introduction to Financial Accounting

Second Edition

A Pearson Custom Publication

Introduction to Financial Accounting

Second Edition

Compiled from:

Financial Accounting
Fifth Edition
by Anne Britton and Chris Waterston

Financial Accounting: An Introduction
by Augustine Benedict and Barry Elliott

Financial Accounting: An Introduction
Fourth Edition
by Pauline Weetman

Financial Accounting for Decision Makers
Fifth Edition
by Peter Atrill and Eddie McLaney

Financial Accounting:
An International Introduction
Third Edition
by David Alexander and Christopher Nobes

Financial Accounting and Reporting
Thirteenth Edition
by Barry Elliott and Jamie Elliott

PEARSON
Custom
Publishing

Pearson Education Limited
Edinburgh Gate
Harlow
Essex CM20 2JE

And associated companies throughout the world

Visit us on the World Wide Web at:
www.pearsoned.co.uk

First published 2009
This Custom Book Edition © 2011 Published by Pearson Education Limited

Compiled from:

Financial Accounting
Fifth Edition
by Anne Britton and Chris Waterston
ISBN 978 0 273 71930 4
Copyright © Pearson Education Limited 1996, 2010

Financial Accounting: An Introduction
by Augustine Benedict and Barry Elliott
ISBN 978 0 273 68885 3
Copyright © Augustine Benedict and Barry Elliott 2008

Financial Accounting: An Introduction
Fourth Edition
by Pauline Weetman
ISBN 978 0 273 70340 2
Copyright © Pearson Education Limited 1996, 1999, 2003, 2006

Financial Accounting for Decision Makers
Fifth Edition
by Peter Atrill and Eddie McLaney
ISBN 978 0 273 71275 6
Copyright © Prentice Hall Europe 1996, 1999
Copyright © Pearson Education Limited 2002, 2008

Financial Accounting: An International Introduction
Third Edition
by David Alexander and Christopher Nobes
ISBN 978 0 273 70926 8
Copyright © Pearson Education Limited 2002, 2006

Financial Accounting and Reporting
Thirteenth Edition
by Barry Elliott and Jamie Elliott
ISBN 978 0 273 72332 5
Copyright © Prentice Hall International UK Limited 1993, 1999
Copyright © Pearson Education Limited 2000, 2009

ISBN 978 0 85776 032 6

Printed and bound in Great Britain by Antony Rowe.

Contents

SECTION 1
INTRODUCTION

1

What is accounting?

Objectives

By the end of this chapter you should be able to:

▶ Discuss the need for, and purposes of, accounting.

▶ Outline the nature and types of accounting.

▶ Describe the major formats in which accounting information is presented.

▶ List the users of accounting and describe their particular informational needs.

Introduction

This chapter aims to introduce the purposes and the types of accounting, and to consider who might be interested in a knowledge of accounting. Since you are reading this book, you presumably have some interest in accounting, or at least a need to study it. Nevertheless, you may not be aware of the range of activities that make up accounting, nor be quite sure about what, and who, accounting is for. In this chapter we look at these issues under three headings – the purposes, the types and the users.

If you have done some accounting before, you may be tempted to skip over this chapter. Don't. The last few years have seen a strong trend towards accounting for the spirit of transactions, rather than the letter. If you are to understand what the spirit of a transaction is, then you must be clear about the fundamental issues dealt with in this chapter.

Purposes of accounting

Before we look at the purposes of accounting, it is helpful to review briefly the contexts in which accounting occurs. In other words, we examine the different types of organisation that need accounting.

Activity 1.1

What types of organisation can you think of? Jot them down and then put a cross against any that you think have no need of accounting.

Answer

The following list of organisations covers the main types. You may have included others, or have expressed the same ones in different words.

▶ *Sole trader*. This means one person who runs a business on their own, or perhaps with a few employees. The main aim is to make a profit.

▶ *Partnership*. This is two or more people who carry on a business in common, intending to make a profit.

▶ *Limited company*. In the UK, a limited company is a legal organisation set up under the Companies Act 2006. The owners are called the shareholders, and it is run by directors, who are appointed by the shareholders. In small companies it is common for the shareholders to appoint themselves as directors. Larger companies are often public limited companies, or plcs. You will find out more about limited companies in Chapter 8.

▶ *Public sector bodies*, such as local councils or the National Health Service. Traditionally, these bodies have not existed to make a profit, but exist to provide a service.

▶ *Clubs and societies*, such as a local cricket club. Again the intention is not to make a profit but to provide services for members.

All of these organisations require some form of accounting, however simple. Our next task is to explore why this should be so.

Activity 1.2

Accounting is undertaken by organisations for a variety of reasons. What do you think they are? Jot down at least three reasons before you read on.

Answer

This is probably the most fundamental question in accountancy. Nevertheless, there are no agreed, clear answers to it. In principle, therefore, your answers are as valid as any others, but we would expect you to include some or all of the following:

1 To record what money has come into the organisation and what has gone out.

2 To help managers make decisions about how to run the organisation.

3 To tell other people about the activities and consequent profit or loss of the organisation during the past year, or other period.

4 To tell other people about the present financial state of the organisation.

5 To provide a basis for taxation.

6 To help assess whether the organisation is beneficial to society as a whole.

7 To control the organisation, by controlling the finances.

8 To provide a basis for planning future activities.

9 To support legal relationships, for example how much one business owes another.

This is not a comprehensive list: you may have listed other items, or expressed similar points in different ways. Points 2 and 8 in the list arguably overlap. However, if you look at our list and your own, you should see that the purposes are broadly of two types.

First, there are purposes that relate to the running of the business, that is, those that form a basis for decision making. In Chapter 11 you will see that part of the regulatory framework of financial accounting is a document called the 'Framework for the Preparation and Presentation of Financial Statements' (hereafter just called the Framework). This is a publication by the International Accounting Standards Board (IASB), which is itself an authoritative international group of accountants. The Framework is dealt with in more detail in Chapter 4; briefly, it states that the prime objective of financial statements is to aid decision making.

Second, there is a group of purposes that can be classified as 'stewardship'. This term means that accounting is used to keep track of what has been done with the financial resources entrusted to its managers. Historically, this was the original purpose of financial accounting, whereby managers ('stewards') had to account to the owners for their stewardship of the owners' money. The Framework is clear that stewardship is secondary to decision making as a general aim of financial accounting. This means that accounting is now less a matter of keeping track of the money, and more a matter of using the resulting information to actively manage the organisation, and for outsiders to make decisions about the organisation.

A brief history

We've seen that the primary purpose of accounting is now seen as the provision of information to help those interested in the organisation (the 'stakeholders') make decisions about it. This is a more active use of accounting information than was originally the case.

Keeping track of economic data, i.e. stewardship, has been a main purpose of accounting for many years. Modern accounting is usually dated to 1494, when one Luca Pacioli codified the accounting that had developed during the Renaissance to keep track of the increased trading that was occurring. For a long time afterwards it was still about stewardship, but early in the twentieth century a more proactive use started to be made of accounting. As we've seen, this more modern view sees accounting as primarily a way of helping us make decisions about the future, rather than simply keeping track of what happened in the past.

If this is what accounting is for, what does that imply for the present nature of accounting? Well, for one thing, it means that accounting is not just a matter of recording data, or even of processing them in an organised way. It is both these things, but an increasingly large part of accounting is concerned with subsequently presenting the resultant information to those who are interested in the welfare of the organisation. The next section looks in more detail at the consequent nature of today's accounting.

Types of accounting

Accounting can be divided very roughly into two areas, financial accounting and management accounting. Bear in mind that the division is a rather arbitrary one, and many functions in the accountancy world spread across both areas. Nevertheless, it is a distinction that is often made, and which can help to make accountancy as a whole more manageable.

Financial accounting is concerned with the recording, processing and presentation of economic information after the event to those people outside the organisation who are interested in it. By contrast, management accounting deals with similar activities, but is geared to providing information about the organisation to its managers to help them run it. In other words, the heart of the distinction is the *purpose* of the accounting, rather than what is done. This may become clearer if we look at each of the three functions of recording, processing and presentation.

Recording

All accounting requires the prior collection of raw data and their organisation into some form of structured record. In principle, this could be as crude as writing down each transaction in a single book, as it occurs. It should be obvious, however, that it would not be easy to get information out of this book. You may be aware that, in fact, almost all accounting systems across the world rely on 'double entry' **recording** in some form. This method has been so successful over the past 500 years since it was codified precisely because it is relatively easy to get information out of it. In Chapter 5 you will start to learn about this system.

Before we can start on the practicalities of recording data, however, there remains one major question to be answered.

Activity 1.3   What sorts of transaction does an accountant record? Note down at least four.

Answer   There are many kinds of transactions, and you may have noted others than those listed below, or expressed similar items in different ways.

1 Sales made.

2 Money received for the sales – remember that you don't always get paid as soon as you sell something.

3 Production materials bought.

4 Expenses incurred, for example electricity used.

5 Production materials and expenses paid for – again, we don't always pay for something as soon as we buy it.

6 Borrowing money from the bank.

7 Persuading other people to put money into our organisation.

8 Buying big items that we intend to keep, such as buildings or machinery.

Note that what accountants therefore record is almost always restricted to what can be valued reasonably objectively in money terms. In other words, if you can't attach a currency symbol, such as a £ sign, to it, accountants ignore it. Furthermore, accountants tend to focus on the organisation, rather than taking a broader societal view.

Activity 1.4	List three things about an organisation that accountants might not record, but which you would regard as useful things to be told about.

Answer	As with most of the questions raised in this chapter, there is no single, correct answer. Some of the things we consider to be currently important are:

1 The value added to the economy by the activities of the organisation.

2 The measurement and inclusion of human resources. Some football clubs, for example, include a valuation of their players in their statement of financial position (balance sheet), that is, the summary of what the organisation owns and owes. Others claim that it is impossible to say objectively what a player is worth, and so omit them from the statement of financial position. Which approach do you think gives the best picture of what the organisation owns? We think this area of accounting is one of the more interesting ones, and it is dealt with more fully in the next chapter and in Chapter 13.

3 Environmental accounting, which tries to report the impact of the organisation on the environment, perhaps in terms of tonnes of pollutants emitted, compared with previous years, other similar organisations, or standards of some sort.

4 Social accounting, which provides information about the social impact of the organisation. This could include looking at, say, the employment of minority groups, or the effect of purchasing policies, especially where supplies come from the Third World. In the UK, The Body Shop plc is one of the more notable companies already moving down this road.

The above possibilities are not part of generally accepted accounting practice at the moment. However, there are signs that this is changing. Ethical investment is a growing force in the UK, with around £9 billion invested by investment funds which claim some ethical basis. An organisation trying to attract such investment could find that providing some of the information suggested above could help. Against this, there is a view that organisations in the UK, especially limited companies, already have to provide so much information that the costs of doing so prevent them from concentrating on their core business. All we can do here is note that accounting is constantly changing, and that there are signs that it is moving towards some of the issues indicated above. This is discussed in more detail under 'The future of financial accounting' later in this chapter.

Chapter 5 will start to explore exactly how organisations record data and turn them into useful financial statements of various sorts. For the moment all we need to consider is what data should be recorded and why. To consolidate your knowledge so far, try putting a tick in the correct box in the table shown in Activity 1.5.

Activity 1.5   In conventional accounting, which of the events listed in the table would usually be recorded and which would be ignored?

	Recorded	Ignored
1 Selling one of the organisation's cars	✓	
2 Paying the wages	✓	
3 Making the tea		✓
4 Moving staff between jobs in the office		✓
5 Incurring a fine for polluting a local river	✓	
6 Paying the fine	✓	

Answer   You should have ticked the 'recorded' column for items 1, 2, 5 and 6, since all these result in objectively measurable resources coming into or leaving the organisation. On the other hand, items 3 and 4 do not change the economic relationship with the outside world, and would therefore not be recorded in a financial accounting system. You should therefore have ticked the 'ignored' column for these two.

You might expect the law to specify what records are required. In fact, in the UK the Companies Act is quite vague about exactly what records need be kept, and say only that they should be 'sufficient to show and explain' the transactions and consequent position of the company. This means that the records differ between companies, each organising the recording as it thinks best. It need not be like this. In France, for example, the *plan comptable*, that is, the government's accounting plan, specifies exactly which ledger accounts must be kept, and exactly what can and can't be recorded in each. Ledger accounts are explained in Chapter 5.

Activity 1.6   Which approach, the UK or the French, do you think is better? Why?

Answer   As usual, the answer depends on what you think accounting is for. The UK system has the benefit of flexibility, in that it allows each organisation to set up an accounting system that best suits its own circumstances and needs. If we are aiming to present information for users to make decisions about that organisation, then gearing the system to the peculiarities of the organisation is most likely to result in relevant information.

On the other hand, allowing each organisation to design a different system is unlikely to result in information that is comparably prepared and presented between organisations. Despite rules set down by the Companies Acts and by the IASB in accounting standards, lack of comparability is a major problem in the UK. We leave it to you to judge whether state control of accounting would be politically and culturally acceptable in the UK. Nevertheless, as we've seen, it is becoming the case that UK accounting is increasingly subject to international accounting standards published by the International Accounting Standards Board. Ultimately, we get the accounting that reflects our society.

Processing

Processing means turning the raw data that we have recorded into useful information that can be presented to those interested in knowing about the organisation. As we have already seen, the processing will be determined by what information we want from our accounting system, and by the underlying method of recording that we have adopted. Given these two, the processing is simply the way we turn the recorded data into the required financial information.

Beginning in Chapter 5, you will see how we not only record data but how we then process it so that we can produce the financial statements that most users of the information require. Having looked at the essential features of recording, it may help to appreciate what is involved in processing if we now turn our attention to the end product. In other words, it is time to look at the ways in which financial information is most usually presented.

Presenting

We saw above that there are very lax rules in the UK about what records need be kept and how the data in them are then processed. However, as you will see as we progress through this book, limited companies in the UK are closely governed with respect to the presentation of information to the users of the accounts. The Companies Act requires a statement of comprehensive income (income statement) and a statement of financial position (balance sheet). Furthermore, accountants' own rules, the accounting standards, also require a statement of cash flows and a statement of changes in equity.

Overall, what we have here is an accounting system, that is a series of inter-connected entities, together making up the total system. It may be best to present this idea as a diagram.

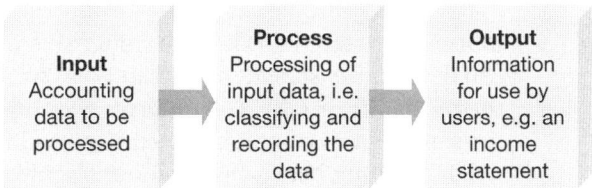

In the diagram above, the data we identified earlier as being appropriate for accounting form the input to our system. We then process this data, usually using some form of double entry bookkeeping. In practice, of course, this processing will normally be computer based. Once we've put the input data into a form that users can access to help them make decisions, we call this organised data 'information'. In financial accounting, this information takes the form of the four financial statements we listed above. We'll look at them in much more detail later in the book – indeed, you will learn to prepare them yourself – but they are so fundamental to accounting that it is worth taking a brief look at them now.

The statement of comprehensive income

This is a list of the expenses incurred by the organisation, set against its revenues, the net result being a profit if revenues are more than expenses, and a loss if the reverse is true. It covers a specific period, usually one year. Note that this used be known as the **income statement** until 2009, and before that, in the UK at least, this statement used to be known as the **profit and loss account**. Many accountants will no doubt continue to refer to the statement as an income statement or as a profit and loss account, especially for smaller companies, for a few years yet. There's more information about this change in Chapter 11.

In fact, the new **statement of comprehensive income**, as the name suggests, actually reports more than the income statement used to. Specifically, the new statement reports the trading profit, exactly as the income statement did, but then adds on a section reporting non-trading gains, such as changes in the value of our property. This is all covered in detail in Chapters 3 and 13.

The statement of financial position

This is a summary of the assets and liabilities of the organisation at a specific time. With effect from 2009, the IASB now refers to this as a '**statement of financial position**', although it was previously called the **balance sheet**, and this term is likely to be more commonly used for a while yet. In simple terms, assets are what the organisation owns and liabilities are what it owes. As you will see in the next chapter, these definitions are not strictly true, but they are good enough for a basic understanding.

The statement of cash flows

Like the statement of comprehensive income, the **statement of cash flows** covers a specific period, but it differs by listing the actual cash received and paid out. The statement of comprehensive income, by contrast, lists the amounts incurred. For example, if we sell goods for £10,000 but are paid only £8,000 immediately, with the other £2,000 to be paid to us next month, the statement of comprehensive income would record the sale of £10,000 but the statement of cash flows would record only the cash event of the receipt of £8,000. The difference will become clearer when you look at the statement of comprehensive income adjustments in Chapters 6 and 7.

For the time being, however, we should note that the statement of cash flows is usually regarded as a more reliable statement of activity in that it deals only with actual cash in and out, and those cash flows are normally an objective fact. The sale recorded in the statement of comprehensive income, by contrast, is less objective since it inherently contains an element of uncertainty. For example, in the example above, it is possible that some goods, say £1,000's worth, will yet be returned to us as unsuitable and the final sale could then be seen as only £9,000. This greater objectivity of cash flows, and hence of the statement of cash flows, has led some accountants to regard the statement of cash flows as a more useful and reliable statement than the statement of comprehensive income. You will see these differences in more detail when we look at the preparation of statement of cash flows in Chapter 10.

Statement of changes in equity

As we saw above, the statement of comprehensive income lists revenues and expenses, that is, amounts we are entitled to and have to pay, respectively, as a result of our routine operations, usually from our trading. However, organisations can also gain or lose wealth from causes other than trading.

For example, what if the value of our buildings rises – is that a gain? The gain hasn't arisen from anything we have done (except buy the building in the first place and keep it), so it presumably can't be seen as a trading gain. On the other hand, aren't we richer because the value of our building has risen, and shouldn't we then report this increase in wealth? This is exactly what a statement of changes in equity does – it reports gains and losses, including those that have arisen other than from operations, and so reconciles the opening and closing equities, i.e. the owners' stake in the business.

It may have occurred to you that all four of these statements are summaries of different aspects of the organisation, prepared for those outside the business. They therefore fall within the area of *financial* accounting. The presentation of *management* accounting information is not governed by the Companies Acts or the accounting standards. This means that management accounting statements vary between organisations. Nevertheless, most organisations of any size will produce some or all of the following, and these would normally be regarded as management accounting statements:

► A structured guess about what revenues and expenses will be in the future. This is usually called a budget.

► A comparison of the previously estimated revenues and costs with the actual revenues and costs. Such a statement allows managers to see where things have not gone according to plan, by highlighting the variances between estimated and actual figures. It is therefore sometimes known as a variance report, or variance analysis report.

► An analysis of the cost of a particular product or service provided by the organisation, showing the cost of each item that has gone into that product or service.

► An estimate of what money will come into and flow out of the organisation over the coming months. This is usually known as a cash flow forecast.

*A*ctivity 1.7

Earlier in this chapter we referred to the statement of cash flows. This is not the same thing as a cash flow forecast. To ensure that you appreciate the difference, and hence something of the difference between financial and management accounting, state the difference in your own words.

Answer

A statement of cash flows is a summary of what cash flow actually occurred during the past accounting period. It is a record of what happened, prepared primarily for those outside the business. It would therefore normally be regarded as part of financial accounting. The cash flow forecast is an educated, structured guess about what we think the cash flows will be in the next accounting period(s). It is mainly prepared for managers, to help them plan the activities of the organisation in the future. It is thus probably best classified as management accounting.

As you may have guessed from its title, this book is only about financial accounting. We will therefore not be dealing with management accounting topics any further.

Who cares anyway? The users

You should have noticed in our discussion above that what accounting is ultimately depends largely on who we think the end users will be. If, for example, you think that the information produced by the accounting process is primarily for the managers of the organisation, you would probably want to focus on recording and processing data about, say, the estimated and actual costs of products, and estimates of future revenues and costs. You could then present the resulting information to managers in the form of comparisons of estimated and actual costs for making each product.

Alternatively, if you think those with the greatest need of information about the organisation are those who work there, you might be more concerned to record and process information about changes in rates of pay, health and safety records, emission levels of toxic products, or employment of minority groups. Think for a moment about how such a perspective would change the nature of accounting.

*A*ctivity 1.8   As a way of getting to grips with the various groups who are usually held to need financial information, and why they need it, try completing the following table. To get you started, we have already filled in some of the table. Don't look ahead to the completed table which follows until you have tried this for yourself.

User group	User needs
1 Investors	Return on capital. Growth in the total value of the organisation.
2	Security of employment. Wage rates, and the share of generated wealth going to the employees, compared with owners and the Revenue.
3 Lenders	
4 Suppliers and other trade creditors	
5 Customers	
6	Tax assessments and trade statistics.
7 Public	

Answer   At this point, we should admit that we have cheated a little here, and based the list of users on the 'Framework for Preparation and Presentation of Financial Statements'. You may recall that we came across the Framework earlier, where it gave us an authoritative statement about the purposes of financial accounting. The list is very similar to other lists, notably that in the 'Statement of Principles', which was developed independently in the UK through the 1990s. The suggested user needs are our own. The completed table is as follows:

User group	User needs
1 Investors	Return on capital. Growth in the total value of the organisation.
2 Employees	Security of employment. Wage rates, and the share of generated wealth going to the employees, compared with owners and the Revenue.
3 Lenders	Ability to make repayments of capital and interest. Security, in the event of non-repayment.
4 Suppliers and other trade creditors	Credit worthiness of the organisation. Time typically taken to pay suppliers.
5 Customers	Security of supply, i.e. will the organisation still be in business next year?
6 Government and its agencies	Tax assessments and trade statistics.
7 Public	A 'catch-all' category covering local communities, pressure groups and industry watchers.

As a final point on users, note that they will not only be interested in commercial businesses. You saw at the start of this chapter that accounting is required by all organisations, not just commercial ones. We have therefore used the term 'organisations' in this chapter to cover not only businesses, but also charities, public sector organisations such as the NHS, voluntary bodies and social clubs. Each will have a different weighting of users, and different information needs.

The future of financial accounting

If nothing else, you should be finishing this chapter with the idea that accounting is a dynamic subject. This means that it is constantly changing to reflect changing practices and the requirements of competing user groups. It may be helpful to conclude this first chapter with a brief exploration of where financial accounting may be going over the next few years.

Notice what the table of users above is suggesting. A single set of financial statements has to meet all the user needs in the list above. This is an ambitious aim. Is it likely that it is achievable? If not, are we to try to satisfy all users partially, or to put the needs of some users above the needs of others? Who decides? Would it be acceptable to produce a number of financial statements, each one geared to the needs of a different user? If we did, what would happen to comparability, and who would pay for all the extra reports? You should be getting used to the idea that there are few definite answers to many of the questions in accounting, and the questions we have raised here are simply more examples of such questions. All we can suggest is that you think about them in the light of what you have learned in this chapter, and bear them in mind for later chapters.

For a specific example of how accounting is currently changing, we could take the growing area of social and environmental accounting. We touched on what is involved in this form of accounting earlier in the chapter. All we want to emphasise here is that it constitutes an extension – some would say an alternative – to existing generally accepted accounting practice. It has arisen because of changing societal concerns over the environment and over the impact of business on social issues. In turn, the more responsible and responsive businesses have reacted to the changed context by changes in their commercial practices. This is resulting in some, so far limited, changes in accounting.

Nevertheless, social and environmental accounting is not only a good example of the way financial accounting changes, but is also an increasingly important topic in its own right. What follows is therefore a brief summary of some of the main features of this new form of accounting.

It should be said to begin with that there are currently no legal or accounting rules which require such accounting. Why, then, do some companies do it? There is a complex range of views on this but we can distinguish three broad categories.

First, there are those companies, and other organisations, that do it because their core values are tied up with social and environmental concerns. They therefore regard it as important to gather and present information about their activities in these areas. It must be said that there are not many such companies in the UK, but The Body Shop and Traidcraft would perhaps fall into this category.

Second, there is a fast-growing range of companies that are entering social and environmental reporting because they foresee that such concerns are becoming an increasingly significant issue in business. In other words, while there may be some concern, as with the first group, the main motivation is more probably commercial. This is a growing group in the UK and elsewhere, and could be said to include such companies as BT, Scottish Power, Shell and CIS. In Europe, environmental reporting is strongly supported by Norsk Hydro, Daimler Benz and Volvo among others.

Third, there is a large group of companies that undertakes little or nothing in the way of social and environmental reporting.

You may have noticed that activity focuses on environmental reporting rather than social. Why this should be is an interesting question, and we can identify two possible causes. First, reporting on such environmental matters as tonnes of sulphur dioxide emitted, or kilometres of copper cable recycled, is a significant shift from traditional accounting. As we saw earlier in this chapter, the traditional approach in financial accounting has been to ignore an event unless it can be objectively measured in some unit of currency. Even so, with environmental reporting there is still a reasonably objective unit of measurement. However, this is unlikely to be the case if we are reporting on such social issues as the impact of making 500 employees redundant, or seconding 20 of our staff to work on local community projects. In other words, environmental accounting is proving technically easier than social accounting. Second, social reporting can be seen as more politically charged than identifying our impact on the physical environment – we are all green now.

Activity 1.9

Look back at the user groups we identified earlier in this chapter. Which three groups do you think would benefit most from environmental (not social) reporting? Give a couple of reasons to justify each of your choices.

Answer

This is another of those questions to which there is no unarguably correct answer. Nevertheless, our answer is:

Investors

▶ Environmental liabilities are becoming an ever-greater commercial issue. Unless they are reported, an investor is unable to fully assess the worth of the reporting company.

▶ Environmental action can prove good business sense, for example where cutting waste cuts costs.

Employees

▶ Many environmental issues have a health and safety impact, of obvious concern to an employee.

▶ Many employees want to feel that they work for an environmentally responsible employer.

Customers

▶ As more well-respected companies undertake environmental accounting, environmental responsibility can be taken as a measure of a well-run company, so helping to ensure stability of supply.

▶ Increasingly, firms are asking their suppliers to verify that what they supply comes, as far as possible, from renewable sources.

Summary

This first chapter asks what accounting is all about. We saw that it is concerned with:

▶ the recording, processing and presentation of economically measurable information

▶ the law, especially the Companies Act

▶ the international accounting standards set by the IASB.

These issues are themselves a reflection of what users want to know about the organisation. Where the users are primarily concerned about information for the internal running of the organisation, the resultant accounting systems and reporting would usually be classified as management accounting. Otherwise, it will be the subject of this book, financial accounting.

Many textbooks simply describe accounting as it is, while this chapter has tried also to suggest how accounting might be. After all, if you continue with your studies of accountancy, you will one day be one of those who will determine the nature and purposes of accountancy.

Before you can tackle such issues seriously, however, you should be competent in the existing practice of financial accounting. The rest of this book will help you achieve that competence, but always remember that all accounting is ultimately determined by the issues we have covered in this chapter.

Key terms

decision making
stewardship
recording
processing
presentation
income statement
statement of comprehensive
    income

profit and loss account
balance sheet
statement of financial position
statement of cash flows
statement of changes in equity

*S*elf-assessment questions

For each of the following questions, choose the single most appropriate answer.

1 The main purposes of financial accounting and reporting are:

 (a) for stewardship and to aid decision making, in that order.
 (b) to aid decision making and to comply with company law, in that order.
 (c) to aid decision making and for stewardship, in that order.
 (d) for stewardship, and to comply with company law, in that order.

2 The main purpose of management accounting and reporting is to:

 (a) provide information for internal decision making.
 (b) determine costs of production processes.
 (c) set budgets against which actual costs can be compared.
 (d) none of the above.

3 Which two of the following events would not normally result in an immediate accounting transaction?

 (i)   Buying goods, agreeing to pay next month.
 (ii) Selling goods for cash, payable immediately.
 (iii) Taking on a new employee.
 (iv) Announcing a new product line.

 (a) (i) and (iii)
 (b) (iv) and (i)
 (c) (ii) and (iv)
 (d) (iii) and (iv)

4 The main purpose of a statement of cash flows is to:

   (a) summarise short-term assets and liabilities at a point in time.
   (b) summarise the cash in hand at a point in time.
   (c) summarise cash paid and received over a period.
   (d) summarise cash paid and payable, and received and receivable over a period.

5 Which user group is likely to be most interested in the growth in wealth of the organi-sation, and the profit relative to the money tied up in the organisation?

   (a) lenders
   (b) Investors
   (c) Employees
   (d) None of the above

6 Accounting standards are:

   (a) broad statements of guidance on accounting practice.
   (b) effectively mandatory statements of acceptable accounting practice.
   (c) rules set out in the Companies Act governing accounting practice.
   (d) the same thing as the French *plan comptable*.

7 Social and environmental accounting is:

   (a) a mandatory part of UK financial accounting.
   (b) a possible extension to UK financial accounting.
   (c) a particular form of management accounting.
   (d) none of the above.

8 The essential difference between the UK and French systems of financial accounting is that:

   (a) The UK system specifies more precisely the form of recording and presentation.
   (b) The French system specifies more precisely the form of recording and presentation.
   (c) There is no significant difference.
   (d) They are recorded in different units of currency.

9 Match the statements listed in the left-hand column against the correct definition in the right-hand column. Note that there will therefore be two definitions that are not applicable.

Statement of comprehensive income	A summary of the environmental impacts of the organisation
Statement of financial position	A summary of liquid funds that flowed in and out of the organisation in the past year
Statement of cash flows	A summary of why the organisation has become richer or poorer during the past year
	A summary of gains and losses made by the organisation during the past year
	A summary of the assets, liabilities and capital applicable to the organisation at the end of the year

10 The IASB Framework outlines two rationales for financial accounting, namely decision making and stewardship. It suggests that accounting is done to help users make decisions (decision making) and to confirm what has happened (stewardship). Which of these two purposes do you consider to be the more important? Give reasons for your answer.

Your answer should be in the form of a short essay, of about 300 to 500 words, or at least in the form of comprehensive notes for such an essay. There is no single right answer, nor will you find the answer by looking it up in this chapter. You will have to apply the ideas and facts introduced in this chapter to formulate your own answer – indeed, requiring you to work through the issues like this is the point of this question. Our answer is at the back of the book, and is based on the Framework, and lists the main points that you should have covered.

SECTION 2
PREPARATION OF FINANCIAL STATEMENTS:
THE BALANCE SHEET AND THE INCOME STATEMENT

2

The statement of financial position

Objectives

By the end of this chapter you should be able to:

▶ List and explain the major sources and applications of funds for a commercial entity.

▶ Construct a simple statement of financial position.

▶ Outline the alternative methods of valuing assets and liabilities.

Introduction

In Chapter 1 we looked at the purposes of accounting, and saw how accounting information is conventionally presented. One of the main methods of presentation was the statement of financial position, which we saw is the new name for what has traditionally been called the balance sheet. Whatever it's called, this is a statement of the financial position of the undertaking at a specific point in time. In this chapter we look at the statement of financial position in more detail, and you will learn how to prepare one.

Before we tackle the construction of a statement of financial position, however, we need to turn our attention to where the money typically comes from and where it is spent. You discovered in the previous chapter that a statement of financial position is simply a list of the assets and liabilities of an entity. The entity must have got the assets by spending money on them, and must have got that money in the first place by incurring a liability to third parties. This should become clearer if we now examine what are more formally known as the **sources and applications of funds**.

The sources and applications of funds

The starting point is to consider where an entity gets its money from. Some entities will have unusual sources. Charities, for example, receive donations, whereas most other entities do not. Furthermore, public sector bodies, such as local authorities and the police, receive government funds. Nevertheless, we can identify some sources of funds which will be widely applicable, especially to commercial organisations.

Activity 2.1   List three sources of funds for a typical business. You may find it helpful to think about your present or past employer, or another business you know of.

Answer   Our list would include the following:

1 Money borrowed from an outsider, often a bank. Money borrowed is known as 'debt finance'.

2 Money invested by the owners. For a sole trader or a partnership this is known simply as 'capital'. For a limited company, such money is called 'share capital'.

3 Once a business is up and running it will hopefully make profits. Profit is then another source of funds, and can be used in the business as soon as it is received. The total of capital or share capital, together with such profit, is then called 'equity finance'.

4 More subtly, the credit allowed to an entity by a supplier is also a source of funds. If I agree to supply you with goods and accept payment next month, what I am effectively doing is lending you the goods for a month. Such a loan in kind is analogous to the loan in money that we listed as point 1 above.

There are thus two broad classifications of funding sources: equity (otherwise known as capital) and debt. These are both liabilities of the business because the business has an obligation to repay them eventually. Loans will have to be repaid and even the capital invested by the owners of the business will have to be repaid to them if and when the business comes to an end. Similarly, the profits ultimately belong not to the business, but to the owners, since the whole business belongs to them. The profits will therefore have to be paid by the business to the owners. In other words, the profits made in the past and retained by the business are a liability of the business.

In the meantime, the business can spend the equity and debt funds on buying a range of goods and services. Some of the things it buys will have a transitory existence, such as the labour of the workforce. The immediate benefit that comes from buying one hour of an employee's time ends at the end of that hour. Similarly, there will be nothing to show for money applied to paying the electricity bill. Note that the labour and the electricity may well have been used to produce the business's product, and any inventory (stock) of that product will have a continuing existence. The distinction we are aiming for, however, is that the labour and the electricity no longer exist as labour and electricity, but as part of the inventory value.

For comparison, some of the things the business applies its funds to will have a continuing existence. We have already seen that one such example could be inventory. Others could be, for example, buildings, vehicles or machinery. Items like this which have a continuing existence in themselves, and are of future benefit to the business, are called assets.

In Chapter 1 we defined **assets** as things we own and **liabilities** as things we owe. We can now adopt more accurate definitions, namely:

▶ The essence of an asset is the right to receive future economic benefit as a result of past transactions or events.

▶ A liability is the obligation to transfer economic benefits as a result of past transactions or events.

Both of these definitions are based on definitions in the International Accounting Standards. In Chapter 11 we will look at the significance of these standards and at how they are replacing the UK's own Financial Reporting Standards, but for the moment you only need to be aware that they are very authoritative in the world of financial accounting.

The situation we have arrived at may become clearer if we look at an activity.

Activity 2.2	A new business starts up as a limited company called Sunrise Ltd by raising £10,000 from its owners, i.e. its shareholders. It puts this money into a new bank account. What would be the asset(s) and liability(ies)?

Answer	The asset would be a bank account with £10,000 in it, and the liability would be share capital of £10,000. Remember that the share capital is a liability because it represents money that has been contributed to the company by the shareholders. It is a liability of the company to the owners, that is, the company is distinct from the owners.

Activity 2.3	Sunrise Ltd then uses £6,000 of its bank account to buy a delivery van. List the asset(s) and liability(ies) after this transaction.

Answer	The list should have been fairly easy to construct, i.e.:

Assets:	Delivery van	£6,000
	Bank account	£4,000
Liability:	Share capital	£10,000

What you may not have noticed is that you have just constructed your first statement of financial position. In other words, a statement of financial position is simply a listing of all assets and liabilities. As we saw in Chapter 1, the actual layout of the statement of financial position is presented in a specific, detailed format, especially for limited companies, but its basic nature is no more than you have just done.

Activity 2.4	Finally, Sunrise Ltd buys some inventory for £3,000 but does not yet pay for it. That is, it buys on credit from Daytime Suppliers, agreeing to pay them the £3,000 next month. List the asset(s) and liability(ies) after this transaction.

Answer   Our answer is shown below:

Assets:	Delivery van	£6,000
	Inventory	£3,000
	Bank account	£4,000
Liabilities:	Share capital	£10,000
	Creditor	£3,000

Note one very important matter – the total assets equal the total liabilities. This is not a coincidence, or just a feature of this example. It is inevitable because the liabilities are providing the funds that we are then spending on these assets. This equality is fundamental to all financial accounting, and is often expressed as the **balance sheet equation**. (We're still using the traditional term for this equation, even though the balance sheet is now more properly known as the statement of financial position.) This equation is usually set out so as to make a distinction between the capital liability and all other liabilities. This is done in order to maintain the distinction we saw earlier between equity and debt. In the case of Sunrise Ltd, for example, the equity is the share capital, while the debt is the creditor. After all, giving us goods with only a promise to pay in return could be thought of as a loan in kind.

The balance sheet equation thus becomes:

ASSETS = CAPITAL + LIABILITIES

Note that the equation can be re-expressed in a number of different ways, including:

CAPITAL = ASSETS – LIABILITIES

Bear in mind that capital can also be referred to as equity – it's one of the slightly confusing cases where accounting jargon can be imprecise, so you need to be aware of the alternatives. It is also worth noting here that this equality forms the basis of double entry bookkeeping, which we will deal with in Chapter 5.

The format of the statement of financial position

We have seen that a statement of financial position is no more than a list of assets and liabilities (including capital) at a particular point in time. However, we have also noted that there is a specific format for the statement of financial position. In the case of limited companies in the UK, this format is specified by law, in the Companies Act, which refers to the accounting standards. The next step in learning to construct a statement of financial position is therefore to apply the standard format to a list of assets and liabilities.

A few days later, on 30 June 20X6, Sunrise Ltd has the following assets and liabilities (the use of dates such as '20X6' is a standard way of expressing a generic date, commonly used in textbooks):

Assets: Delivery van £6,000; Inventory (i.e. stock of goods for sale) £3,000; Bank £500; Machinery £2,200; Debtors £700.

Liabilities: Share capital £10,000; Creditors £400; Loan repayable in five years £2,000.

The first step is to divide the assets into 'non-current assets' and 'current assets'. Non-current assets are those where the expected life, i.e. how long we think the asset will last in our business, is more than one year. (Note that 'non-current assets' is the term for such assets under the new international accounting standards; they used to be known as 'fixed assets' in the UK, and many accountants will probably continue to use the latter term for a while yet.) Current assets are then those that we do not expect to still have one year from now. This is a rather crude pair of definitions, and we will see in Chapter 8 that it will not always be valid, but is nevertheless acceptable for our present purposes.

Activity 2.5

List the non-current assets and subtotal them. Then list the current assets beneath the non-current assets, sub-total each group, and add the two subtotals.

Answer

Your answer should look like the one below. There is a number of specific points relating to our layout, which are explained below.

Non-current assets

Machinery		2,200
Delivery van		6,000
		8,200

Current assets

Inventory	3,000	
Trade receivables	700	
Bank	500	
		4,200
		12,400

Note the following points about the layout above. These are not optional issues, but matters you must normally comply with.

▶ There are two columns of figures, with the current assets being inset to provide for a sub-total for the current assets.

▶ Both the non-current and current assets are listed in reverse order of liquidity. This means that both lists start with the asset that is likely to be hardest to turn into cash. We have assumed, for example, that a van is easier and quicker to sell than machinery, and that trade receivables are more liquid than inventory. The bank account is obviously the most liquid asset and therefore comes last in the list of current assets.

▶ There is a subtotal for each group of assets.

▶ The total of all assets is double-underlined to show that the £12,400 is a final total for the first half of the statement.

The next step is to list and add up the equity and the liabilities.

Activity 2.6	Extend your statement of financial position to list the equity (capital) and the liabilities, and then total your figures, and double underline the total.

Answer	Your completed statement of financial position should now look as follows. As before, there is a number of important points relating to the layout, which are explained below.

SUNRISE LTD
STATEMENT OF FINANCIAL POSITION AS AT 30 JUNE 20X6

Non-current assets

Machinery		2,200
Delivery van		6,000
		8,200

Current assets

Inventory	3,000	
Trade receivables	700	
Bank	500	
		4,200
		12,400
Share capital		10,000

Non-current liability

Loan, repayable in five years		2,000

Current liability

Trade payables		400
		12,400

▶ The completed statement of financial position must be headed by the name of the reporting entity and the date of the statement of financial position. Remember that the statement of financial position only reports the entity's state of affairs at a single moment.

▶ The division of liabilities into current and non-current is done on the same basis as the split of assets into non-current and current. That is, current liabilities are those we expect to have cleared within a year, while non-current liabilities are those we expect to still owe one year from the date of the statement of financial position.

▶ If we subtract the current liabilities from the current assets then the net figure, £3,800 in the example above, is what is known as the **working capital** of the organisation.

▶ If we subtract the non-current liabilities (£2,000) and the current liabilities (£400) from the total assets (£12,400) it will, of course, equal the share capital or equity (£10,000). This £10,000 can be also be thought of as the **net worth**, i.e. what the organisation is worth, assuming that the statement of financial position reflects something close to the true values of assets and liabilities.

A few words about non-commercial organisations

All we've said above has assumed that the organisation we're accounting for is commercial, i.e. it is owned by one or more people who aim to make a profit from it. Where this isn't true, for example government authorities, the National Health Service, charities, or social organisations, then the format of the statement of financial position will be a little different.

The first half will often be the same as above, since most organisations will have buildings, bank accounts and other assets, even where the object of their activities is not to make a profit. However, the second half of the statement of financial position will include liabilities as before, but will not include owners' equity but, instead, the stake in the organisation held by government, trustees or members. These people don't own the organisation in the same way that shareholders own a company, but they caretake the funds so that the organisation can provide the services it was set up to provide.

In terms of the format of the statement of financial position, the capital will consist not of 'owners' equity' but of 'funds'. These may be divided into a number of individual funds, depending on the nature and needs of the organisation, but in total will constitute the funding for the net assets listed in the statement of financial position. We'll explore this further in Chapter 8.

What the statement of financial position tells the user

Having now prepared a statement of financial position, it is worth considering what it tells us. In other words, what does a statement of financial position mean? We already know that it provides a list of assets and liabilities at a particular point in time, and you saw above that the total of the statement of financial position represents, in principle, what the entity is worth. Knowing the state of affairs of an entity would obviously be a useful thing to know, but it is not necessarily true that this is what the statement of financial position tells us.

Activity 2.7   Look at the statement of financial position for Sunrise Ltd, on page 22.

1 We have included the delivery van at what we paid for it. List at least two other ways we could have valued it.

2 Note down one reason why the trade receivables may not actually result in a benefit to the business of £700.

Answer   Sorting out alternative valuations of assets, and indeed liabilities, is one of the major difficulties in financial accounting and reporting. As you have seen in the statement of financial position above, the usual practice is to record assets at what the business paid for them. This is known as the historical cost. Nevertheless, alternatives are possible, and you could have listed any or all of the following:

▶ Historical cost less an allowance for using up the asset to date. Such an allowance is called depreciation, and is dealt with in more detail in Chapter 6. This valuation is, of course, still simply a refinement of the historical cost valuation.

▶ Selling price, i.e. what the van could be sold for. This is usually called the realisable value. Normal practice when considering realisable value is to deduct any costs of sale, such as advertising. In this case the net figure is known as the net realisable value, or NRV.

▶ Replacement cost, i.e. the cost of replacing the van if, for example, it were stolen this afternoon. In a perfect market (i.e. one of zero transaction costs, perfect competition and perfect knowledge of the market by all concerned) this should be the same as the realisable value.

▶ A refinement of the replacement cost approach would be to use the cost of replacing the asset, not with another identical one, but with something that will do the same job. This may be particularly relevant in times of rapidly changing technologies, such as computing.

▶ Finally, we could take a more complex view, and say that the van's value is the economic benefit that it will bring to the business. This is in line with the definition of an asset that we looked at earlier in this chapter. Arriving at this valuation will involve estimating the additional net revenues that the business will earn because of its use of the van. Such additional net revenues will be difficult to determine, but might be the profit on the orders that we only got because we were able to deliver directly and quickly to the customer. This is conceptually and practically the most difficult approach to valuation, and we will therefore examine it more thoroughly later in this chapter and in Chapter 13.

As far as the trade receivables are concerned, their statement of financial position valuation will not turn out to be what they are worth if the debtor does not, in fact, pay us. We have, after all, previously defined the essence of an asset as being control of future economic benefit. If there is no payment, we will receive no economic benefit, and the debtor will therefore not turn out to be an asset. It should therefore not be shown as an asset in the statement of financial position, but as an expense in the statement of comprehensive income, usually described as something such as 'Bad Debt

Written Off'. We will look at expenses in the statement of comprehensive income in more detail in Chapter 3.

Alternatively, the debtor may only be expected to pay us part of what is owed, perhaps £500 of the total £700. In this latter case it would seem to be sensible, and consistent with the definition of an asset, to value the debtor in the statement of financial position at £500. The remaining £200 would then be written off as an expense.

Valuation in the statement of financial position, especially of assets, is thus a problematic area of financial accounting and reporting. The final part of this chapter therefore considers each of the suggested alternative methods of valuation in the statement of financial position more fully.

The alternative valuation methods

We have seen that the obvious way to value an asset is at what we paid for it, that is, at its historical cost. This is obviously simple and unambiguous as a method. In other words, it has the advantage of objectivity.

Activity 2.8

List at least two disadvantages that you can see with the use of historical cost as a method of valuing an asset.

Answer

The most obvious problem with historical cost is that it will gradually become more and more out of date. It will describe the value of an asset as it was several years ago. This is inappropriate when we have already said that a statement of financial position is supposed to give us a picture of the entity today. Furthermore, the higher the level of inflation then the more inappropriate the historical cost valuation will become, as the difference between today's cost and the historical cost gets wider.

Second, and more subtly, adding together assets in the statement of financial position which were bought at different dates is implicitly adding together items expressed in different £s, since the real value of the £ will fall during times of inflation. The meaning of the aggregate amount is then highly questionable.

If the deficiencies of historical cost stem from the fact that it becomes more and more out of date, perhaps we should use a current method of valuation. One possibility would be to value an asset at what it would cost today, that is its *current cost*. One way of looking at this is to say that we will value each asset at what it would cost if we were to buy it today, as a replacement for the existing asset. This is known as the replacement cost.

Activity 2.9

Which of the following statements about a method of valuing assets are true? Mark each with a T for true, or an F for false.

1 Replacement cost represents a current valuation of what the entity is worth _____
2 Replacement cost is usually simpler to determine than historical cost _____
3 Replacement cost is more objective than historical cost _____
4 Historical cost is the more true and fair valuation _____
5 Historical cost is a more useful method of valuation than replacement cost _____

Answer

Our suggested answer is set out below. Note that some of our answers are debatable, especially the last two. Whether historical cost is the more true and fair valuation or not depends on what we mean by true and fair. There is no agreed definition of this key phrase, which appears in the Companies Act as the over-riding requirement for financial statements in the UK. Nevertheless, we think that replacement cost comes closer to providing a true and fair valuation, if only because it is a better representation of the position at the statement of financial position date.

Similarly, statement 5 depends on your definition of useful – an issue that we looked at in the previous chapter. This is a very contentious statement, and our answer depends on seeing objectivity as a very important quality of accounting. We think it is because it improves the comparability and the understandability of financial accounting, as well as its reliability. We have therefore marked this question as true. However, you could think that the more up-to-date nature of replacement cost makes that valuation method the more useful.

1	Replacement cost represents a current valuation of what the entity is worth	T
2	Replacement cost is usually simpler to determine than historical cost	F
3	Replacement cost is more objective than historical cost	F
4	Historical cost is the more true and fair valuation	F
5	Historical cost is a more useful method of valuation than replacement cost	T

Replacement cost is a current valuation, but it is not the only one. **Net realisable value** is also a current valuation, one that values an asset at what it could be sold for, rather than at what it could be bought for. You might expect these two valuations to be the same, or certainly very similar. In perfect market circumstances, that is, where all buyers and sellers have the same information and competition is universal, you would be right. However, you should note that buying and selling costs, and imperfections in the market, for example through poor information being available to one party to the deal, will often mean that what we could sell for, net of selling costs, is not the same as what we could buy for.

Furthermore, you should note that using net realisable value could be held to be inappropriate to a business that has no intention of selling one or all of its assets. After all, selling all the assets would probably only be the case if the entity were being wound up. For an entity that is a going concern, replacement cost might be held to be more suitable as a method of valuation, although not all accountants would agree with this view. Going concern is a concept that we will return to in Chapter 4.

Finally, as we noted above, the economic value method is both conceptually and practically the most difficult method, and we will therefore leave a detailed exploration of that method until Chapter 13.

Statement of changes in equity

If we do decide to show a valuation other than the existing historical cost in our statement of financial position then the issue arises of reporting that change. In Chapter 1 we briefly considered the statement of changes in equity, and saw that it is, indeed, largely a summary of any gains and/or losses we may make when the value of our assets and liabilities changes. If we regard those changes as substantial and for the long term, then we could reflect such a change in a change in the valuation of the asset or liability in the statement of financial position. This would be one way to obtain a more up-to-date valuation.

For example, if we decide to reflect a rise in the value of a building from its historical cost of £300,000 to a current valuation of £400,000, then the asset side of the statement of financial position would rise by £100,000 to reflect this, and the capital side must also rise so that the statement of financial position still balances. The rise on the capital side is shown in a 'revaluation reserve' of £100,000, showing that the organisation is now richer by £100,000. This gain is not a trading gain so would not be reported as trading income, but would appear in the 'other comprehensive income' part of the statement of comprehensive income and in the statement of changes in equity, so that the gain is reported as an event of the year. We will look at the preparation of statements of comprehensive income in the next chapter, and at statements of changes in equity in more detail in Chapter 13.

Uncertainty

At this point you may be beginning to feel that there are no clear answers in accounting, and that it is not the straightforward process you thought it was. We know that this may be unsettling, and that you may be asking whether there is any point to accounting when the answer always seems to be 'it depends . . .'. Nevertheless, for better or worse, this is the position of UK accounting.

At anything above a very basic level, accounting is not a mechanistic exercise, because it has to reflect the uncertainties and complexities of the transactions it describes. We have deliberately started this book with a consideration of fundamental questions about the nature and purposes of accounting for two reasons. First, you can only learn to do good accounting if you understand why you are accounting in the way you are. Second, we think that sorting out these issues is one of the more interesting aspects of accounting.

To check your understanding of what we have covered in this chapter you should now attempt the following question. It brings together many of the points from Chapter 1 as well as from this chapter, so you will help yourself if you attempt it seriously. We have provided an answer after the question, but try not to simply read through our answer.

*A*ctivity 2.10   Dayspring Ltd undertakes the following activities in its first week of existence:

1 Starts its activities by raising £50,000 from the issue of 50,000 £1 shares, and putting this money into a new bank account.

2 Buys a workshop for £30,000, paying by cheque.

3 Buys two delivery vans for £8,000 each, paying by cheque.

4 Interviews and appoints two employees, to start work next week.

▶

5 Borrows £10,000, agreeing to repay it in one lump sum, with interest, in two years' time. Puts the money into the bank account.

6 Buys machinery for £15,000 on credit from Hartford Supplies.

7 Decides that it does not need two delivery vans, and sells one of them on credit to Sunset Garages for £8,000.

Required

There are three questions for you to deal with:

1 Prepare the statement of financial position at the end of the week. You could do this by preparing successive statements of financial positions after each relevant transaction, but this would be rather clumsy and time-consuming. For a fairly small set of transactions like this, it is probably better, therefore, to simply keep a rough record of the balance of each item. The workshop, for example, starts at £30,000 and then does not change, and so will appear in your statement of financial position at £30,000. The bank account will take more analysis.

You may find it helpful to use the Sunrise Ltd statement of financial position (page 22) as a guide to the correct layout.

2 Justify your treatment of transaction (4).

3 Suggest two groups who would probably be particularly interested in the statement of financial position you have prepared. Briefly note down why each would be interested.

Answer

Our suggested answers are set out below. Make sure that you understand all parts of them before you leave this chapter.

1   **DAYSPRING LTD**

STATEMENT OF FINANCIAL POSITION AT END OF FIRST WEEK

Non-current assets

Workshop		30,000
Machinery		15,000
Delivery van		8,000
		53,000
Current assets		
Trade receivables	8,000	
Bank	14,000	22,000
		75,000
Share capital		50,000
Non-current liability		
Loan, repayable in five years		10,000
Current liability		
Trade payables		15,000
		75,000

2 There is a number of reasons why the appointment of two employees should not be reflected in the statement of financial position. If you have done some accounting before, you may have mentioned the accruals, or matching concept. In terms of what we have covered so far in this book, you could have justified the exclusion of transaction (4) by reference to the definitions of assets and liabilities.

  We know that only assets and liabilities (including capital) appear in a statement of financial position. Does the appointment of employees to start next week result in an asset or liability as defined? An employee will normally result in future economic benefit to the business, and will in principle, therefore, be an asset. However, quantifying this benefit with reasonable objectivity will usually be impossible. In these circumstances, an employee should therefore not be recognised as an asset in a statement of financial position.

3 It is possible to make out a case for virtually any user group having some interest in the financial statements of any organisation. However, it is likely that the shareholders and the lender will be particularly interested in the statement of financial position of Dayspring Ltd, since it has substantial sums at stake in the company. Additionally, you could have made out a good case for saying that Hartford Supplies would be especially interested, given that they have effectively lent Dayspring Ltd £15,000.

Summary

This chapter has been about the statement of financial position. We have seen that it is:

▶ essentially just a listing of assets and liabilities

▶ in a specified format.

You have also prepared a simple statement of financial position for yourself. However, what ultimately determines the nature and usefulness of the statement of financial position are:

▶ the definitions of the assets and liabilities (these definitions are worth learning and remembering)

▶ the different bases on which assets and liabilities can be valued; the usual method – historical cost – is not necessarily the best basis.

In Chapter 3 we continue our review of the basic accounting statements with an exploration of the statement of comprehensive income.

Key terms

sources and applications of funds	net worth
assets	working capital
liabilities	alternative methods of valuation
balance sheet equation	replacement cost
non-current assets	net realisable value

Self-assessment questions

Select the most appropriate answer for each of the following multiple choice questions.

1 Non-current assets are:

   (a) Assets the organisation expects to keep for more than one year.
   (b) Assets worth more than £1m.
   (c) Assets that can't normally be physically moved.
   (d) Assets specified as fixed by the organisation.

2 Liabilities are:

   (a) The capital of an organisation.
   (b) The total of assets and capital.
   (c) The obligation to transfer economic resources.
   (d) The total an organisation would have to pay if it were wound up.

3 The total of a statement of financial position represents:

   (a) What the organisation would sell for if someone took it over.
   (b) The original historical cost of the assets, amended by revaluations.
   (c) The total replacement cost, net of liabilities.
   (d) What the directors believe the organisation should be valued at.

4 The difference between debt and equity is that:

   (a) Debt is what the organisation owes its shareholders and equity is what it owes government.
   (b) Debt is what the organisation owes its lenders and equity is what it owes government.
   (c) Debt is what the organisation owes its lenders and equity is what it owes shareholders.
   (d) Debt is what the organisation owes its shareholders and equity is what it owes lenders.

5 'Working capital' is the difference between:

   (a) Non-current assets and current liabilities.
   (b) Share capital and non-current assets.
   (c) Current assets and current liabilities.
   (d) Non-current liabilities and current assets.

6 'Historical cost valuation' means valuing an asset at:

   (a) What it was worth one year ago.
   (b) What it is worth at the statement of financial position date.
   (c) What it would cost to replace.
   (d) What was paid for it.

7 Mortlake Ltd owned a building that had cost £42,000 just before the end of the current accounting year on 31 December, and a vehicle bought for £13,000 at the same time. A new access road was announced on the statement of financial position date, perhaps making the building worth about £50,000 on the open market. Inventory existing at the statement of financial position date had been bought for £7,000, but had deteriorated in storage and was now valued at £6,000. Trade receivables and trade payables at the statement of financial position date were £4,000 and £5,000 respectively.

You are required to prepare the statement of financial position, including the equity figure as the amount needed to make the statement of financial position balance. For each item where there is a choice of valuation, you should briefly note down why you have chosen the valuation you have.

8 Hammerstein Ltd has a number of assets with the following details. For each asset you are required to state the most true and fair valuation, and to justify your choice. In all cases you should ignore depreciation. (Depreciation is a topic that we will deal with in Chapter 6.)

(a) A building cost £300,000 four years ago. Since then the company has spent £80,000 on an extension to the building and £45,000 on repairs. The current market price of a similar building next door is £400,000.

(b) Two cars were bought last month for use by the company's sales force. The first cost £12,000 and the second £15,000. The first was written off in an accident just after the statement of financial position date and insurance proceeds are expected to be £10,000.

(c) Computing equipment was acquired for £19,000 one year ago. The same equipment is no longer made, but could be bought for about £8,000 on the second-hand market. Equipment that would do much the same job could be bought new and would cost around £15,000.

(d) We have three trade receivables (debtors) at the statement of financial position date. The first owes £2,000 and has always paid on time in full. The second owes £700 and has disappeared. The third owes £800 and has been promising to pay for the last three months, but has so far paid nothing.

9 Prepare the statement of financial position at 31 December 20X9 for Yeovil Electronics, in each of the following situations. The capital is not given, so you should calculate it as being the figure needed to make the statement of financial position balance, in accordance with the balance sheet equation.

(a) First, the accountant has extracted the following balances from the books at 31 December, all balances being at the traditional historical cost valuation.

Premises	345,000
Plant and machinery	104,800
Inventory	67,250
Trade receivables	46,200
Bank overdraft	15,000
Trade payables	56,780
Non-current loan	120,000

Prepare the historical cost statement of financial position. ▶

(b) Second, the managers of Yeovil Electronics are concerned that the historical cost figures do not represent the 'true' worth of the company and are accordingly a poor basis for their decision making. They have therefore estimated the replacement cost of the assets and liabilities. Specifically, the balances that differ significantly from historical cost are:

Premises	480,000
Plant and machinery	95,000
Inventory	61,000
Trade payables	53,600

All other figures may be assumed to be at historical cost. Prepare a replacement cost statement of financial position.

(c) Third, the major lender has expressed a wish to wind up the company, sell the assets, and use the proceeds firstly to repay her loan of £120,000. Her estimates of what the assets would sell for and what the liabilities could be settled for are set out below. Draft a statement of financial position using these net realisable values.

Premises	450,000
Plant and machinery	40,000
Inventory	83,650
Trade receivables	44,000
Bank overdraft	15,000
Trade payables	56,780

(d) Which statement of financial position gives the most true and fair view of the state of affairs of Yeovil Electronics? Justify your decision.

3

The statement of comprehensive income

Objectives

By the end of this chapter you should be able to:

▶ List the main trading transactions.

▶ Identify major non-trading events that result in gains or losses.

▶ Prepare a simple statement of comprehensive income, including the treatment of opening and closing inventory.

▶ Account for non-commercial organisations.

Introduction

This chapter introduces the second of the main financial statements typically used in the UK, that is, the statement of comprehensive income, along with the associated statement of changes in equity. The advent of international accounting standards to the UK has resulted in changes in jargon here as well as in the statement of financial position. Specifically, what is from 2009 properly called the statement of comprehensive income used to be called the income statement, and before that was known as the profit and loss account. It's likely that all terms will be used in the UK for the immediate future.

The statement of financial position that we explored in the previous chapter tells us something about the state of affairs at a point in time, usually the last day of the accounting year. The statement of comprehensive income tells us something about what happened during that year. In its simplest form, the statement of comprehensive income is just a list of the revenues and expenses that arose during a particular period. In practice, it can be complicated. This chapter looks first at the basics of statement of comprehensive incomes, and then goes back to pick up some of the complications. In this way you should be able to grasp the essentials without being distracted by the intricacies.

Structure of the statement

The **statement of comprehensive** income has two distinct parts. The first is a summary of the trading results, usually for the past year. This is equivalent to the old income statement or profit and loss account. Indeed, for ease of reference, this part of the statement can still be called the 'income statement'.

The second part is a summary of non-trading gains and losses and this section is entirely new. A common example of the sort of thing that might go in this section could include gains and losses on revaluations of property. We saw in the last chapter that, initially at least, we normally value property at what we paid for it, i.e. at its historical cost. If we later decide to recognise the fact that our property has risen in value since we bought it, then is that a profit? The gain hasn't come from trading, and we haven't even sold the property, so it seems right not to include it with trading gains and losses. On the other hand, the rise in the value of the property has made the business richer and surely we should report that? The new statement of comprehensive income resolves this dilemma by including such gains and losses, but separately from the trading gains. This means that a typical statement of comprehensive income will be structured like this:

Revenues	1,000 ⎫	Part 1:
Cost	600 ⎬	'income statement'
Profit from trading	400 ⎭	
Gain from revaluation of property	*150* ⎫	*Part 2:*
Total comprehensive income	*550* ⎭	*'Other comprehensive income'*

As we'll see in Chapter 13, gains from revaluations of property aren't the only possible sources of non-trading gains, but they are probably the most common, so we've used them to illustrate the structure. What this structure does is show the profit or loss from trading – £400 in our example above – and then combines that with non-trading gains, to show the total increase in wealth that's arisen in the past year – £550 in the example above.

Finally, note that the rules in International Accounting Standard 1 'Presentation of Financial Statements' allow us to present the two parts of the statement separately, but in this book we'll use the combined presentation above.

Having seen that there are two distinct parts to the statement of comprehensive income, we'll explore the statement in this chapter by looking at each part in turn.

The income statement part

To recap, this part of the statement only reports trading transactions. Furthermore, bear in mind that the statement of comprehensive income as a whole does not tell us about everything that happened during the year. Specifically, it does not tell us about events that cannot be objectively quantified. This exclusion is one that we have already come across in relation to the statement of financial position.

Activity 3.1

Note down at least three specific events that will therefore not usually be included in the first, income statement, part of a statement of comprehensive income.

Answer

There are many examples that you could have chosen, but they should all be either events:

▶ the effect of which cannot be quantified with reasonable certainty, such as the employment of a new manager, or the introduction of a new manufacturing process, or

▶ which do not relate to trading, such as the purchase of an asset, or the issue of new shares (both of these would, however, be reflected in the statement of financial position instead).

So, what does go in the first, income statement part of a statement of comprehensive income? There are three distinct elements to this, and we can deal with each of these elements in turn.

The first section of the income statement part can be called the **trading account**, and it details the core trading of an organisation. For example, for a supermarket, this would deduct the cost of purchasing the goods sold from the proceeds of the sales, to calculate the profit on trading. This profit is more properly called the 'gross profit'.

Activity 3.2

Mr Tate owns a supermarket, which trades as Lowprice Supermarkets. In June, Lowprice Supermarkets buys goods from its suppliers costing £220,000, and makes sales of £300,000. Prepare the trading account.

Answer

LOWPRICE SUPERMARKETS
TRADING ACCOUNT FOR THE MONTH ENDED 30 JUNE

Sales	300,000
Cost of goods sold	220,000
Gross profit	80,000

You should note that the trading account is headed by the name of the entity, just as the statement of financial position was in the previous chapter. It is also good practice to head the trading account not only with the fact that it is a trading account, but also to specify which period it covers.

It is unlikely, of course, that the supermarket sells all the inventory it has on its shelves. ('Inventory' is accounting jargon for 'stock', introduced by the advent of international accounting standards into the UK in 2005. We'll no doubt continue to talk about 'stock' alongside 'inventory' for a few years yet, but note that 'inventory' is technically the correct term now.) There will almost certainly be a **closing inventory** of goods left over at the end of the month. This inventory represents goods that have been bought but not sold. If we are to compare the selling price of the goods sold with their cost, then we should deduct the cost of any goods not sold from the purchases' cost. This net amount, which we then deduct from sales to calculate the gross profit, is called the 'cost of goods sold' or the 'cost of sales'. These are both good names, because they accurately describe exactly what this net figure represents, i.e. the cost to Lowprice of the goods it has sold to its customers.

If, for example, the supermarket staff do a stocktake at the end of June – i.e. they physically count it – and find that there are goods left which cost Lowprice £55,000, then the trading account will look like this:

LOWPRICE SUPERMARKETS
TRADING ACCOUNT FOR THE MONTH ENDED 30 JUNE

Sales		300,000
Purchase	220,000	
Less: Closing inventory	55,000	
Cost of sales		165,000
Gross profit		135,000

Notice the technique we used above of insetting a subsidiary calculation into a left-hand column, and carrying the total out into the main, right-hand column.

Before we move on, we should look at how we cope if there was inventory at the beginning of June as well as at the end. If a stocktake at the start of June had shown an opening inventory for the month of, say, £48,000, think what must have happened to this inventory. Assuming it was neither lost nor stolen, then this inventory must have been sold during the month. In other words, it is part of the cost of sales for June, and should therefore be added to the purchases in the trading account. True, some of it might still be inventory as part of the £55,000 at the end of the month, but this does not change the fact that what has been sold should be added to the purchases.

Activity 3.3   Use the opening inventory figure of £48,000 to revise the trading account above.

Answer

LOWPRICE SUPERMARKETS
TRADING ACCOUNT FOR THE MONTH ENDED 30 JUNE

Sales		300,000
Opening inventory	48,000	
Add: Purchases	220,000	
	268,000	
Less: Closing inventory	55,000	
Cost of sales		213,000
Gross profit		87,000

In our examples above we have put a double underline under the gross profit to indicate that this is the end of the financial statement. This is correct so long as we are only preparing a trading account. Usually, however, the user of the financial statements will also want information about other expenses, such as insurance, wages, rent and so on. Such information is provided by the second section of the income statement part of the statement of comprehensive income.

Operating costs

The second section of the income statement part of the statement of comprehensive income starts where the trading account left off, that is, with the gross profit. There will then be no need to underline the gross profit, since we will construct what will effectively be a single financial statement. What is therefore happening is that the trading account presents the 'raw' profit on direct trading, and the second section shows what expenses are then paid out of the gross profit. The net result is called the 'net profit'.

Activity 3.4

Assume that the other expenses for June were wages of £32,000, insurance of £4,000, heat and light expenses amounting to £17,000, and telephone costs of £2,000. Draft the income statement part of the statement of comprehensive income for June. (You can use the same insetting technique that we saw above to provide a subtotal of the overhead expenses.)

Answer

LOWPRICE SUPERMARKETS
INCOME STATEMENT FOR THE MONTH ENDED 30 JUNE

Sales		300,000
Opening inventory	48,000	
Add: Purchases	220,000	
	268,000	
Less: Closing inventory	55,000	
Cost of sales		213,000
Gross profit		87,000
Wages	32,000	
Insurance	4,000	
Heat and light	17,000	
Telephone	2,000	
		55,000
Net profit		32,000

As we noted at the beginning of this chapter, this first look at the income statement will avoid complications. We will pick up some of the more important ones later in this chapter, and others in later chapters, particularly in Chapters 7 and 8. Nevertheless, the income statement above is valid for non-company accounting, where the net profit is simply added to the owner's capital account. For limited companies, it only remains to consider what will happen to the £32,000 profit and to report those happenings. Such a report is the third and final section of the income statement part of the statement of comprehensive income. This is traditionally referred to as the appropriation account.

The appropriation account

As the name suggests, the **appropriation account** details the various appropriations of profit. In simpler language, it lists what has happened to the profit made by the entity in the past year. There are normally only three things that can happen to the profit.

Activity 3.5   Think about who is likely to be entitled to a share of a limited company's profit, and so suggest what these three appropriations will be.

Answer   You may have expressed your ideas in different ways, but your suggestions should have fallen into the following groups:

1 *Tax*. The Revenue, or equivalent authority in other countries, will want the first slice of a limited company's profit. We will look at tax in more detail in Chapter 8.

2 *Owners' share*. In a limited company this share will be in the form of dividends – again we will look at dividends in more detail in Chapter 8. More generically, this slice of profit will more usually be called the distribution.

3 *Retained profit*. By default, this is the amount left over after the other appropriations. In a sole trader or partnership business, this amount will simply be added to the capital of the sole trader or shared out to the capitals of the partners. In a company the procedure is more formal, and the retained profit will be transferred to one or more 'reserves'. Once again, Chapter 8 will examine this transfer in greater detail.

Traditionally each of these three appropriations was subtracted in turn from the net profit. However, current practice under International Accounting Standard 1 'Presentation of Financial Statements' subtracts the tax from net profit to leave the retained profit, but the dividends are seen as what we do with the profit after tax, rather than part of the calculation of profit, so we now show them in a separate statement, the 'Statement of Changes in Equity'. We'll look at this later in this chapter.

The presentation of the appropriation account within the income statement section of the statement of comprehensive income is relatively simple. All we need to do is subtract the tax from the net profit, and we'll worry about the dividends later in the statement of changes in equity.

<table>
<tr><td>**Activity 3.6**</td><td>Assume that Lowprice Supermarkets is a limited company. It calculates its tax liability on the profit for June at £11,000. Any retained profit is to be transferred to the company's reserves. Draft the appropriation account for June.</td></tr>
</table>

Answer

LOWPRICE SUPERMARKETS LTD
APPROPRIATION ACCOUNT FOR THE MONTH ENDED 30 JUNE

Net profit before tax	32,000
Tax	11,000
Profit after tax	21,000

Statement of changes in equity

We have now seen all the elements of the income statement part of the statement of comprehensive income, but we have still to look at the associated statement of changes in equity. This is simply a summary of why the equity, i.e. the shareholders' stake, has changed during the year. We know from previous studies that equity may rise because we revise the value of our buildings upward. However, in the absence of such capital gains, the change in equity will typically be due to the profit after tax that we've just worked out, less any dividends paid out to the shareholders, so it will look like this:

LOWPRICE SUPERMARKETS LTD
STATEMENT OF CHANGES IN EQUITY FOR THE MONTH ENDED 30 JUNE

Retained earnings at 1 June	10,000
Profit after tax	21,000
Less: Dividends	(8,000)
Retained earnings at 30 June	23,000

We should now have a fair understanding of the income statement, ie the trading, part of the statement of comprehensive income. Our next step is to look at the 'other comprehensive income' part. Before we do this, however, you should try the following activity. It brings together all we have covered in this chapter, and is intended to consolidate your knowledge and understanding of the basics.

*A*ctivity 3.7

Suraya Ltd started in business on 1 January 20X7. On 31 December 20X7 the following balances were taken from the company's books, and from a final stocktake:

Sales	296,483
Heat and light	26,730
Insurance	11,978
Wages	36,389
Opening inventory	15,450
Closing inventory	16,070
Purchases	175,962
Dividend	18,400
Rent	6,397
Retained earnings balance at start of period	55,000

The tax liability on the profit for the year was estimated at £7,360. Any retained profit is to be transferred to the company's reserves.

Prepare the statement of comprehensive income and the statement of changes in equity for the year ended 31 December 20X7. The statement of comprehensive income will incorporate the trading, operating costs and appropriation sections, but the whole thing can be entitled simply 'Statement of comprehensive income'.

Answer

Your answer should look like the following. Check your answer against ours, noting not just the numbers, but also the narration in the title and in how each number is labelled. Accounting is about communication, and the words matter.

SURAYA LTD
STATEMENT OF COMPREHENSIVE INCOME
FOR THE YEAR ENDED 31 DECEMBER 20X7

Sales		296,483
Cost of sales:		
Opening inventory	15,450	
Purchases	175,962	
	191,412	
Closing inventory	16,070	
		175,342
Gross profit		121,141
Heat and light	26,730	
Insurance	11,978	
Wages	36,389	
Rent	6,397	
		81,494
Net profit before tax		39,647
Tax		7,360
Profit after tax		32,287

We can now draft the statement of changes in equity.

SURAYA LTD
STATEMENT OF CHANGES IN EQUITY
FOR THE YEAR ENDED 31 DECEMBER 20X7

Retained earnings balance at 31 December 20X6	55,000
Profit for the period	32,287
Less: Dividends	(18,400)
Retained earnings balance at 31 December 20X7	68,887

Other comprehensive income

Having arrived at the net trading profit, the remainder of the statement of comprehensive income is relatively brief. All we need to do is list any gains that come from non-trading sources. There are a few of these, but we'll consider just two:

▶ gains from revaluing non-current assets

▶ gains on holding foreign currency.

We'll look at revaluations of non-current assets in more detail in Chapter 13, but, for now, we can simply add any such gains to the trading profit. Gains and losses on foreign currency are a bit more complex to deal with.

Let's say we place £1,000 on deposit at a bank, but we choose the Paris branch of a French bank. The deposit will presumably be held in euros, so our £1,000 is changed into euros at whatever the exchange rate is at the time, say €1.20 = £1, so €1,200. Note that our asset is then no longer £1,000 (although that's how it's recorded in our books) but €1,200. When we next prepare a statement of financial position we need to include this asset, of course, at its current value. Remember that the asset is now €1,200, so we need to include it at the current sterling equivalent. If the exchange rate is now, say, €1.10 = £1, then the sterling equivalent will be 1,200/1.10 = £1,091. In other words, we've made a gain of £91 simply by holding our money in a foreign currency. This isn't a trading gain so we report it in the 'other comprehensive income' part of the statement of comprehensive income.

Example 3.1

Harper Industries Ltd has calculated its net profit after tax as £200,000. During the year it revalued its non-current assets from £420,000 to £550,000. Finally, it bought an investment in Germany costing £60,000, but which is held in euros. At the date of purchase the exchange rate was €1.25 = £1, but at the accounting year end the rate has moved to €1.20 = £1. We are required to prepare extracts from the statement of comprehensive income.

There are three elements to be reported, namely the trading profit from the income statement part (200,000), the gain on the revaluation of the non-current assets (550,000 – 420,000 = 130,000), and the gain on exchange. Since we spent £60,000 at €1.25 = £1, we must hold 60,000 × 1.25 = €75,000. At the new exchange rate this will be worth 75,000 /1.20 = £62,500, so we've gained £2,500. The relevant extract from the statement of comprehensive income will therefore be:

Example 3.1
continued

Net profit after tax	200,000
Gain on revaluation of non-current assests	130,000
Gain on exchange	2,500
Total comprehensive income	332,500

The rest of this chapter is now concerned with three refinements which you need to be aware of before we leave the statement of comprehensive income. These are inventory valuation, non-trading organisations, and the particular presentation of statements of comprehensive income for limited companies.

Inventory valuation

We have seen how the purchases figure has to be adjusted by adding on the opening inventory and deducting the closing inventory to arrive at the cost of the sales figure. However, we have not yet given any thought to where the inventory figure came from, other than to say it resulted from a stocktake.

A stocktake involves counting all the inventory items that we hold at a particular time. While this will give us the number of each inventory line we hold, it will not attach a value to that number. Counting the inventory of bags of sugar held by Lowprice Supermarkets at the end of June, for example, will tell us that we have, say, 60 bags in stock, but not what each is worth. There is a number of different bases of **inventory valuation** that we could use, such as:

▶ *Historical cost*, that is, what Lowprice Supermarkets paid for each bag.

▶ *Replacement cost*, that is, what it would cost Lowprice to buy the inventory again today. This will often be more than the historical cost, especially when prices are rising quickly.

▶ *Net realisable value*, which is what Lowprice could sell each bag of sugar for, less any immediate costs of sale. In these circumstances, this would be the selling price on the shelf, and would normally be more than either cost above.

We shall see in Chapter 13 that there are other bases of valuation, and we will look at the relative merits of each in that chapter. For the moment we can take a pragmatic approach, and all we need to know is what International Accounting Standard 2 (IAS 2) 'Inventories' says. In Chapter 11 we shall examine the nature and purposes of such accounting standards, but note for now that their regulations should be followed when preparing financial statements. IAS 2 specifies that inventory should be valued at 'the lower of cost and net realisable value'.

As with the bags of sugar in Lowprice Supermarkets, the lower of these alternatives will normally be cost. Net realisable value will only be lower in relatively rare cases, such as when the inventory has gone out of fashion, or is close to its sell-by date. In such circumstances the owner might be prepared to sell for less than he or she paid for it, in order to be able to sell it.

However, this is not the end of the matter, because identifying what we paid for the inventory, that is, its historical cost, is not always straightforward. Look, for example, at the following case.

Lowprice Supermarkets had the following transactions in bags of sugar during June:

1st	Bought 300 bags from the supplier for 60p each
14th	Sold 160 bags for 95p each
19th	Bought 100 bags for 65p each
26th	Sold 200 bags for 95p each

If we now try to work out the profit on our trading in sugar, we must follow through the sales transactions. The first sale was of 160 bags at 95p, i.e. £152, and the cost of this sale is clearly 160 bags at the 60p we paid for them, i.e. £96. There was thus a gross profit of £56 on the first sale.

The sales value of the second batch of sales is also fairly easy to calculate, that is, 200 bags at 95p, i.e. £190. However, the cost of these sales is problematic. Have we now sold the remaining 140 bags from those we bought on 1 June, and 60 from those bought on 19 June? If so, the cost of sales will be 140 at 60p plus 60 at 65p, i.e. £123.

One way to decide which batch of purchases is being sold for any given sale is to consider the physical reality. Normal supermarket practice would be to sell the older inventory first, so that they are not left with inventory past its sell-by date. In other words, the first inventory that came in is the first to go out. This method is called 'first in, first out', usually abbreviated to 'FIFO'. In our example above, this is what we did, which resulted in a cost of sales of £123. FIFO is widely used in practice, largely because it does reflect normal inventory rotation practice.

Alternatively, have we sold all the 100 bought on 19 June and thus 100 from those left from the batch bought on 1 June? In this case, the cost of sales will be 100 at 65p plus 100 at 60p, i.e. £125. This is certainly not a large difference from the other calculation of £123, but replicated over all product lines in the supermarket it is clear that we potentially have a significantly different cost of sales figure, and hence a different gross profit reported. Notice that, if we adopt a FIFO approach, any inventory left over is assumed to be from the later delivery.

Some traders, however, do not deal in inventory which has a short sell-by date, but do have inventory which is difficult to handle. An example would be a steel stockholder, dealing in girders, RSJs and so on. When a new delivery arrives from the steel mill, the stockholder is unlikely to move the existing inventory to store the new delivery underneath the old. When he then sells to a customer, he will usually take the steel from the top of the pile, and will thus be selling the newer inventory. In other words, the last inventory that came in is the first to go out. An inventory system that rests on this model is known as 'last in, first out', or 'LIFO'. This is the approach implicitly adopted by the second alternative in our example above, and resulted in a cost of sales of £125.

However, there's a major problem with LIFO, in that IAS 2 'Inventories' does not allow it as a valuation method. Rightly or wrongly, the view taken is that examples such as the steel one above are relatively rare in practice, so as LIFO will not normally reflect practice, it is not permitted. Accordingly, we'll say no more about LIFO.

There is, however, one more possibility for our inventory valuation. Consider the position of a garage that takes a new delivery of petrol into a tank already part full from a previous delivery. When a customer draws off a few litres what she takes will be a mixture of the old and new inventory. Neither FIFO nor LIFO will now be wholly appropriate – what we need is a mixture, to reflect the mixture that has been taken as the cost of sales. This third method is called average cost, abbreviated to AVCO, and calculated as follows.

Suppose customers in Lowprice Supermarkets could help themselves to sugar from the total inventory, and took some of the old delivery and some of the new. The sales on 14 June must have been from the inventory bought on 1 June for 60p, since we had no other inventory at that time. The cost of sales must therefore have been 160 at 60p, i.e. £96 again. However, the sale on 26 June of 200 is now deemed to come partly from the 140 bags remaining from those delivered on 1 June (cost 60p), and partly from the 100 delivered on 19 June (cost 65p). The way to work out the average cost to Lowprice of the bags sold on 26 June is:

140 bags at 60p	=	84
100 bags at 65p	=	65
240		149

The average cost of each bag sold on 26 June must therefore have been 149/240, i.e. 62p. This would then be the AVCO valuation of the remaining inventory of 40 bags, so that the closing inventory under AVCO would be shown in the trading account at 40 times 62p, i.e. £25, to the nearest £.

Activity 3.8

Anne, a trader, had the following dealings during August in her only item of inventory. There was no opening inventory.

1st	Bought 40 for £28 each
5th	Bought 25 for £30 each
10th	Sold 50 for £45 each
21st	Bought 30 for £32 each
27th	Sold 35 for £45 each

Draft the trading account for the month, assuming:

▶ a FIFO basis of inventory valuation

▶ an AVCO basis of inventory valuation.

Answer

We have used a tabular layout for our answer, which we think allows for a better comparison of the methods.

	FIFO		AVCO	
Sales		3,825		3,825
Purchases	2,830		2,830	
Closing inventory	320		309	
Cost of sales		2,510		2,521
Gross profit		1,315		1,304

Notice that the sales and purchases figures do not alter. What gives the different gross profit figure is the different inventory valuation. Under FIFO the remaining ten items are valued at £32, since the earlier inventory has been sold and what is left as the closing inventory is priced at what came in last. Under AVCO, the closing inventory is calculated like this:

Sale on 10 August		
40 at £28	=	1,120
25 at £30	=	750
65		1,870

Cost of sale = 50/65 × 1,870 = 1,438
Inventory remaining = 15/65 × 1,870 = 432

Sale on 27 August		
15 at average cost, as above	=	432
30 at £32	=	960
45		1,392

Cost of sale = 35/45 × 1,392 = 1,083
Inventory remaining = 10/45 × 1,392 = 309

We thus have two bases on which we can arrive at a cost for our inventory, and the question that should occur to you is which one is right? As you may be beginning to suspect by now, the answer is that there is no single right choice. It would seem reasonable to choose the method that best reflects our inventory management in practice, using FIFO, for example, where strict inventory rotation is a feature of our business. Many businesses do, in fact, use FIFO. However, it is important to note that many accountants would argue that the accounting treatment need not necessarily reflect the physical reality – certainly, there is no obligation for it to do so, either in law or in any accounting standard. Hence, there is no absolutely correct method, but bear in mind that IAS 2 no longer allows the use of LIFO, as it argues that the inventory value under this method is unlikely to bear a reasonable relationship to actual costs incurred in the period.

Non-commercial organisations

So far in this chapter we have been looking at organisations whose aim is to trade for a profit. While this will be true of the great majority of organisations for whom accounts are prepared, it is not universal. Some organisations exist for more fundamental purposes. Examples are charities, social clubs and religious bodies.

Such organisations will not usually prepare a statement of comprehensive income, because they typically do not trade, and because a financial statement that reports on the profit or loss is inappropriate for bodies that do not aim at a profit. There are two possible alternatives to the statement of comprehensive income for such bodies. These are the 'receipts and payments account' and the 'income and expenditure account'.

The **receipts and payments account** is, in fact, sometimes also used for reporting the activities of very small trading organisations, but is more often found in non-trading bodies. As the name suggests, it is simply a list of what money has been received and what has been paid out. In other words, at its simplest, it is just a summary of the bank account. There will thus be no inventory adjustment, such as we have just looked at above for the trading account. Nor will there be any of the other adjustments that we will come across in Chapter 6, and which are involved in the preparation of a commercial statement of comprehensive income.

The receipts and payments account for an athletics club might look like this:

MOORTOWN ATHLETICS CLUB
RECEIPTS AND PAYMENTS ACCOUNT
FOR THE MONTH ENDED 31 JANUARY

Subscriptions from members		120
Life memberships		45
		165
Rent of clubhouse	75	
Publicity	10	
Travel	20	
Furnishings	40	
		145
Excess of receipts over payments		20

The 'subscriptions from members' is a typical source of funds for a non-profit-making organisation. It will usually cover the whole of the forthcoming year. 'Life memberships' may be a feature of some clubs. They represent lump sums paid by members which entitle them to life membership without paying any further subscriptions.

Notice also that the payments include a non-current asset, 'furnishings'. Everything, including non-current assets that would normally be shown separately in the statement of financial position, is included in the receipts and payments account.

By contrast, an **income and expenditure account** is prepared using all the adjustments, such as the inventory adjustment, that are used in preparing the statement of comprehensive income. The difference between the income and expenditure account and the statement of comprehensive income is one of terminology. The former title seems more appropriate than the latter when the statement is reporting on a non-profit-making organisation. In all other respects an income and expenditure account is identical to a statement of comprehensive income.

If, for example, Moortown Athletics Club decides to prepare an income and expenditure account instead of a receipts and payments account, it will use exactly the same techniques that a commercial organisation would use to prepare a statement of comprehensive income. It will therefore need to determine its trade receivables, trade payables and inventory, and to distinguish between capital and revenue items.

Activity 3.9 | Suppose that the subscriptions from members of the Moortown Athletics Club (see above) are for the year to 31 December, but were all received in January, and that the rent of the clubhouse was paid in January for the first three months of the calendar year. There is a stock of publicity materials left at the end of January valued at £5. Amend the receipts and payments account above to turn it into an income and expenditure account. To do this, you will need to adjust the cash flows by the amounts outstanding in order to arrive at the amount that relates to January alone. Life memberships are awkward because they relate to an uncertain future period, i.e. the lives of the relevant members. It will therefore often be regarded as acceptable for the club to account for these wholly in the period when they are received.

You may find this a difficult activity, but, as always, do try it before you look at the answer.

Answer

MOORTOWN ATHLETICS CLUB
INCOME AND EXPENDITURE ACCOUNT
FOR THE MONTH ENDED 31 JANUARY

Subscriptions from members (£120/12 months)		10
Life memberships		45
		55
Rent of clubhouse (75/3 months)	25	
Publicity (10 – 5)	5	
Travel	20	
Furnishings	40	
		90
Excess of expenditure over income		35

Our answer above includes calculations of the adjustments we have made. Make sure you at least understand the answer before you move on. Notice that the cash surplus reported by the receipts and payments account indicated a positive view of the club's finances, but the income and expenditure account gives a very different view of its financial health. This is primarily because the income and expenditure account allows for the fact that the subscriptions received in January will have to last the club for the whole year.

Limited companies

This is a topic that we will deal with in more detail in Chapter 8. However, if you have seen any statement of comprehensive income published by limited companies, you may have noticed that they do not look exactly like the one you prepared for Lowprice Supermarkets. This is because the Companies Act, in conjunction with the international accounting standards, specifies a more aggregated layout, where the expenses are grouped, not by 'purpose' as we have done (cost of sales, heat and light, insurance, wages, rent), but by 'function'. The three broad functional areas that are specified are:

▶ cost of sales

▶ selling and distribution expenses

▶ administration expenses.

There are other changes, as we will see in Chapter 8, but this regrouping of expenses is perhaps the most striking. For now, all you need to be aware of is the different presentation of the statement of comprehensive income imposed by the law. Note that it is purely a matter of different presentation – the final net profit will be exactly the same, whichever method of presentation is used.

Information technology and accounting

Before we leave the statement of comprehensive income and the statement of financial position that we considered in the previous chapter, it is worth briefly looking at the role of information technology in all this accounting. It is a topic that we will return to in more detail in Chapter 15, but has become so central to accounting that we should introduce it before moving on.

All the accounting that you have done in the past couple of chapters has been manual, that is, you used pen and paper to keep track of changes to the bank account, summarise the expenses in the statement of comprehensive income, and so on. In practice much or all of this work tends to be done using computers. This should not be surprising given that you have seen that accounting is largely concerned with recording and summarising routine transactions. Since computers are good at dealing with large numbers of well-defined routine events, accounting has used computers since the earliest days of information technology.

Recording the purchase of inventory for £3,000 on credit from Daytime Suppliers, as Sunrise Ltd did in Chapter 1, for example, would be a very typical transaction. In a manual system, we would record the asset as inventory and also record our liability towards Daytime. This implies two entries, and we may forget one, or enter one twice, or enter both but for the wrong amount. In Chapter 5 we will look at how this works in more detail and at how we can control for such errors, but for now note that the possibility of such errors is inherent in manual systems. If uncorrected, the inventory and/or the creditor figure that we report in the statement of financial position would be wrong.

In a computer-based system the entry of the inventory purchase will require us also to record the liability towards Daytime. In other words, the software will not let us record the transaction at all unless we record both aspects for the same amount. This is not fool-proof – we could record both the inventory and the liability at £300 instead of £3,000, for example, but it is an improvement.

Perhaps more importantly, information technology is able to sort and extract the information we want from very large amounts of data extremely quickly. This means that more, and more flexible, information can be extracted from the data that we already hold.

These are all issues that we will return to in Chapter 15. For now, all you need be aware of is that accounting usually relies heavily on information technology, even though the exercises in this book inevitably require you to use a manual approach.

Activity **3.10** List three advantages for a business having its accounting carried out using information technology. (There are a couple inherent in what we have said above, but try to come up with at least one other for yourself.)

Answer

1 Accounting software can impose a certain amount of control on the accuracy and completeness of our accounting.

2 Information can be extracted both more quickly and in a wider variety of formats than would usually be possible with a manual system.

3 Computer-based systems can reduce the overall level of understanding of accounting required by staff, and so reduce training costs.

4 Business partners, including our auditors, expect to be able to exchange data with us so that, for example, they can place orders with us through the internet.

Summary

This chapter has introduced you to what is usually just called the statement of comprehensive income. You have seen that it is actually made up of two parts, that is:

▶ an income statement reporting trading results

▶ other comprehensive income, which reports non-trading results, such as gains from revaluations of non-current assets.

In turn, we broke the income statement down into three elements, namely:

▶ the trading account

▶ the operating costs account

▶ the appropriation account.

Each of these parts has been examined in turn, and you have now covered the essentials of financial reporting, specifically:

▶ a simple statement of comprehensive income, including an inventory adjustment

▶ a simple statement of financial position in the previous chapter

▶ some of the problems surrounding the question of how to value inventory, distinguishing between, and calculating, the FIFO, LIFO and AVCO bases.

One of the points that has hopefully struck you is that each of these inventory valuation bases results in a different profit figure. Furthermore, we saw in Chapter 2 that there is a number of different ways to value assets, and each results in a different statement of financial position being reported. There is obviously a problem looming here, which is the range of possible accounting results from given data. Before looking at any more of the techniques of accounting, we will therefore look in some detail at what theory of accounting has been developed to help us tackle this problem. The next chapter is therefore concerned with the concepts and characteristics of accounting.

Key terms

statement of comprehensive income
trading account
closing inventory
opening inventory
appropriation account

statement of changes in equity
inventory valuation
receipts and payments account
income and expenditure account
information technology

Self-assessment questions

1 The following details relate to the trading activities of Anarkhi Ltd for its first year of trading, to 30 June:

Purchases	531,946
Sales	794,062
Wages	218,470
Transport	54,475
Rent and insurance	30,775
Tax	3,900

All purchases may be considered as part of cost of sales. All other costs should be allocated 40% to cost of sales, 40% to selling and distribution expenses, and 20% to administration expenses.

Anarkhi Ltd uses the FIFO method of inventory valuation. On 23 June there was no trading inventory. During the last week of the year, inventory transactions were:

5,000 units delivered at £12 each
2,000 units delivered at £13 each
3,000 units sold at £19 each

You are required to draft the statement of comprehensive income for the year, adopting the Companies Act format as far as possible. You will need to calculate the value of the closing inventory and to allocate the expenses as listed above to their Companies Act categories before you can construct the statement of comprehensive income.

2 This question requires you to prepare an statement of comprehensive income, but then also brings in the preparation of the associated statement of financial position. In this way it aims to integrate your study of Chapters 2 and 3. Note that any retained profit you calculate in the statement of comprehensive income should appear in the statement of financial position as 'Reserves', included immediately after share capital.

Use the following balances of Tayside Glass Ltd to prepare an statement of comprehensive income for its first year of trading, which ended on 31 March 20X9 and the associated statement of financial position at that date. You will first need to identify which items relate to the statement of comprehensive income and which to the statement of financial position.

Sales	80,007
Purchases	62,419
Trade receivables	1,215
Trade payables	1,630
Rent	4,600
Telephone	627
Delivery van	4,000
Wages	9,650
Share capital	10,000
Light and heat	1,629
Office expenses	1,127
Bank – positive balance	370
Shop fittings	6,000

There was no opening inventory, since this was the first year of trading. The closing inventory was valued at £4,200.

3 Marsden Computing buys end-of-range computers and sells them to the general public at monthly auctions. Its transactions for the past three months have been as follows (on 1 January it held 20 computers which had cost £550 each):

January Bought 300 computers at £550 each and sold 260 for £700 each
February Bought 240 computers at £650 each and sold 280 for £700 each
March   Bought 300 computers at £600 each and sold 290 for £680 each.

Prepare the trading account for the three-month period, assuming

(a) a FIFO inventory valuation method

(b) an AVCO inventory valuation method.

4 Hambleton Players is a cricket club which exists primarily to play cricket but incidentally carries out some fund-raising activities. As accountant for the club, outline the arguments for producing a receipts and payments account, compared with the arguments for preparing an statement of comprehensive income, to report the activities of the club for the past year.

Section 3
The Double Entry System
of Recording Transactions and the Trial Balance

4

Concepts and characteristics

Objectives

By the end of this chapter you should be able to:
- ▶ Outline the generally accepted concepts and conventions of financial accounting.
- ▶ Explain the four major characteristics of financial reporting.

Introduction

At this stage, it is worth taking stock of where we have got to. Chapter 1 explored the nature and uses of accounting, and then Chapters 2 and 3 looked at the two major statements conventionally used in financial accounting, that is, the statement of financial position (previously known as the balance sheet) and the statement of comprehensive income. One of the points that should have struck you is that accounting is far from being the exact science many people believe it to be.

In particular, we have already seen how both the statement of financial position and the statement of comprehensive income can vary according to the basic assumptions we make about how and what we should measure. For example, statements of financial position would look very different if all companies did what some football clubs currently do, and showed the value of their employees – the players, valued at their transfer fees – on the statement of financial position. Again, we saw in the previous chapter that the gross profit will vary if we change our assumptions about inventory rotation, and use FIFO instead of AVCO as a basis of inventory valuation. As you will see as we work through this book, there are many other examples.

What we seem to have in accounting is a situation where the statement of financial position and the statement of comprehensive income, taken together, present a different picture of the state of affairs and the performance of an entity, respectively, depending on what fundamental assumptions we make. In other words, the economic health of an entity can apparently vary not only with the reality of economic changes, but also with how we choose to account for that reality. How, then, can any user place any reliance on the financial statements?

The approach that accountants in many countries, including the UK, have chosen as their way forward is a two-stage technique:

▶ to agree on explicit underlying assumptions, and then

▶ to develop accounting practices that are consistent with those generally accepted assumptions, and hence lead towards 'a true and fair view'.

We have come to accept this approach in the UK as being so obviously correct that it can be hard to think of any alternative. However, it is instructive to look at what, say, the French approach has been. The French approach is to specify in great detail exactly what sort of transactions go under each heading or account, and then to further specify how those accounts shall be presented. The set of rules that specify these headings and presentations is known as the *plan comptable* – the plan of accounts. There is thus, for example, no choice about whether to use FIFO or AVCO, since the single, 'correct' method is laid down in the *plan comptable*.

The French equivalent of the UK idea of a true and fair view is the *image fidèle*. A rough translation would be 'faithful picture', and it is notable that the French first specified the 'plan', as the way to produce accounts, and only subsequently imposed the aim of an *image fidèle*. In other words, the attainment of an *image fidèle* is not central to French accounting in the same way as the attainment of 'a true and fair view' is central to UK accounting.

---

*A*ctivity 4.1

Complete the following table, by making at least one entry under each heading. You may find it helpful to think in terms of the relative disadvantages of the UK system, rather than of the relative advantages of the French system. You will be addressing much the same issues.

	UK approach	French approach
Relative advantages		

Answer

Any answers to this activity will be a matter of debate, but our views are that the UK approach has advantages in terms of relevance. By allowing some choice of method, it can be argued that UK accounts can be prepared according to methods which are geared to the particular needs of the entity, rather than being geared to a mythical 'national average' entity. Furthermore, it may be that the need to consider the most appropriate treatment of a given accounting issue, rather than to simply follow the specified treatment, results in a more lively and participative accounting profession.

On the other hand, the French approach does have the key benefit of consistency. All entities will, in principle at least, treat the same item in the same way, so improving comparability between the accounts of different entities. In addition, the prescription of practice should result in less debate and therefore in faster preparation, and faster will mean cheaper.

You may have had your own, equally valid, ideas. We hope so, because, as you have just seen, accounting in the UK is ultimately determined by some minimum agreement on fundamental underlying assumptions. If you have no ideas then you can't engage in this fundamental debate. The rest of this chapter presents the current state of the more important parts of this debate. It is divided into two main sections. The first part, concepts, covers fairly well-established ideas. The second part, characteristics, deals with more recently developed thinking about what makes a set of financial statements 'good' – whatever that means.

Concepts and policies

To reiterate, concepts are the underlying ideas of accounting. They have usually been implicit and understood as a common culture of accounting, rather than being made explicit, even though we have seen above how important they are. Given that such underlying theoretical principles can radically change the view the financial statements give of an entity, it should be obvious that preparers and users of those statements should be very clear about the particular principles that have been applied to any given set of statements. Requiring such an explicit declaration of the accounting practices they result in for a given entity is a large part of the purposes of International Accounting Standard 8 (IAS 8), 'Accounting Policies, Changes in Accounting Estimates and Errors'.

We will consider the nature and authority of accounting standards in more detail in Chapter 11, but for the moment you need only be aware that they are generally held to be effectively mandatory in almost all cases. At the heart of IAS 8 is the assumption that all financial statements will be consistent with a few basic, specified principles, known as the concepts. Linked to this, International Accounting Standard 1 (IAS 1) 'Presentation of Financial Statements' highlights two concepts, going concern and accruals, as being pervasive. In other words, these two ideas are held to be so important that they should underpin all accounting.

You should note that this is a change from the UK position before 2001, when the standard in force was SSAP 2 'Disclosure of accounting policies', which specified four basic concepts, namely going concern and accruals again, but also consistency and prudence. What has happened to the latter two is an instructive story, and one that we will consider later in this chapter.

IAS 8 is concerned that the accounting policies it uses should be both explicitly stated and appropriate for the organisation to achieve a true and fair view. Policies are defined as 'the specific principles, bases, conventions, rules and practices applied by an entity in preparing and presenting financial statements'. Put simply, policies are how an organisation chooses to account for transactions and events given the range of different methods available to it. We have already seen that an organisation has some choice in how it accounts for inventory, for example. However, this is not an entirely free choice, since IAS 8 requires that the accounting an organisation chooses should be based on a few basic policies, principally, as we have seen, going concern and accruals, but also realisation. It is therefore time to turn our attention to a more detailed consideration of the ideas of accounting.

Going concern

There is an assumption that the business will continue to operate for the foreseeable future. The application of this policy could make a difference, for example when we consider asset valuations. We have seen that the usual basis is historical cost, but if the entity is no longer a going concern and will be wound up, it is arguably more appropriate to value the assets at selling price, since they will soon be sold.

Accruals (or matching)

When preparing the statement of comprehensive income, revenue and profits are matched with the associated costs and expenses incurred in earning them (known as accruals or matching). This means that revenues and expenses are recognised when they are incurred, rather than when the related cash is received or paid. A sale will thus be accounted for when the contract is agreed, and not when the goods or services are paid for.

Realisation

Realisation is an idea that we touched upon in Chapter 3 when we explored the two parts of the statement of comprehensive income. We saw then that one of the critical differences is that the first, trading, part of the statement of comprehensive income deals only with transactions that are realised; that is, ones where the money has changed hands, or is almost certain to do so in the near future, whereas the second 'other comprehensive income' part deals with unrealised transactions. This is an increasingly important issue in accounting, and we will return to it later in this chapter under 'Revenue recognition'.

The characteristics of good accounting

The question which then arises is how do we select and apply these policies in practice? If there is a range of possible accounting policies, how can we judge which represent good accounting? Certainly, the policies we choose should be in line with the three concepts above, but that could still leave us with a range of possible policies from which to choose. In other words, what are the characteristics of good accounting? This question is dealt with in the 'Framework for the Preparation and Presentation of Financial Statements', which specifies four such characteristics, namely relevance, reliability, comparability and understandability. We'll explore the nature and authority of this 'Framework' later in the chapter and in more detail in Chapter 11; for now simply note that it is a formal codification, by the International Accounting Standards Board, of the ideas we've been discussing in this chapter.

Briefly, relevance asserts that good financial information is information which is relevant to helping users to make decisions about the organisation being reported on. Reliability is essentially a matter of freedom from bias and material error. Comparability simply means that accounting policies should normally be the same from one year to the next, and ideally also between organisations, so that comparisons aren't distorted by different methods of accounting. Finally, understandability makes the seemingly obvious point that financial information should be understandable by users. However, we shall see when we look at the Framework that it isn't always that simple.

Activity 4.2

In the list below, two definitions are given. Identify which definition relates to which two of the three policies we explored above, i.e. accruals, going concern and realisation.

A The non-cash effects of transactions and other events to be reflected, as far as is possible, in the financial statements for the accounting period in which they occur.

B The information provided by financial statements is usually most relevant if prepared on the hypothesis that the entity is to continue in operational existence for the foreseeable future.

Answer

The correct answer is that A is an extract from the definition of accruals, and B from that for going concern.

In addition to the well-established ideas outlined above, there is also a number of implicit ideas that are generally accepted. You will find that these are referred to both in books and, less commonly, in practice, so it is worth being aware of them.

Consistency concept

There should be consistency of treatment of like items within each accounting period and from one period to the next. In other words, once you have chosen an accounting treatment, you should stick with it from one year to the next. The key reason for this is to promote comparability, which we identified above as a key characteristic. That is, it helps the user to make comparisons over time, and so to pick out useful trends. Having decided, for example, to value our buildings at historical cost, rather than at, say, replacement cost, consistency requires that we will normally continue to adopt historical cost for the buildings.

Prudence concept

In the UK tradition of accounting, prudence was regarded as one of the major ideas. In recent years it has been significantly downgraded, so that it is now simply one approach to help achieve the characteristic of reliability.

When we have to choose between two or more accounting treatments of an economic event, prudence dictates that we should always aim to show a treatment free from bias and/or the result we would like to present. The logic is that explicitly avoiding overstatement under conditions of uncertainty results in more reliable accounting. For example, we saw in Chapter 3 that inventory is valued at the lower of cost and net realisable value, rather than at the normal selling price. The justification for this lower valuation has been the prudence concept. Note that prudence doesn't mean erring on the low side, but it does mean not erring on the high side.

Separate valuation

This concept is best explained by an example:

> Assume that A has sold goods on credit to B worth £600, so that, in A's books, B shows up as a trade receivable for £600. Meanwhile, B has sold goods on credit to A for £400. In A's books, B also therefore appears as a trade payable for £400. No agreement has been made about setting off one amount against another.
> What should we show in A's statement of financial position in relation to B?

You could argue that we should simply show the net trade receivable of £200 as a current asset. However, there is a counter-argument that holds that showing just the net trade receivable does not give a full picture of the total situation, and thus does not give a true and fair view. After all, in the absence of an explicit agreement between A and B to legally set off the £400 against the £600, the position is that B must pay the full £600. This being so, the correct presentation in A's statement of financial position would be to show a trade receivable of £600 and a trade payable of £400. In other words, the trade receivable and the trade payable should be separately valued, and disclosed as such.

Business entity

We have come across this concept already, in relation to capital in the statement of financial position. The business has an identity and existence distinct from the owners, so that the business can and should record an amount owing to its owner, i.e. the capital. Transactions of a business are recorded as they affect the business, not as they affect the owner.

Duality

Again, we have already seen this concept in action, when we looked at sources and applications of funds in Chapter 2. In relation to any one economic event, two aspects are recorded in the accounts, that is, the source of funds and the related applications. The balance sheet equation is an application of the duality concept. In Chapter 5 we will see that it also underpins double entry bookkeeping.

Monetary measurement

Only those events and situations that can be reasonably objectively measured in money terms are recorded. This means, for example, that 'happy and skilled workforce' is not an asset that you will see on a statement of financial position, even though most managements routinely say that their workforce is the company's greatest asset, and it may even be true. It does not appear because the value of this asset cannot normally be objectively quantified.

Objectivity

This concept is obviously closely linked to money measurement. More generally, however, and more formally, it is a required attribute of accounting that competent individuals working independently should arrive at the same or very similar measures of given economic events or situations.

Historical cost

The usual method of arriving at an objectively agreeable quantification of an event is to value it at what the item in question cost. This is known as its historical cost. It has the huge advantage over any other system of being simple and relatively objective, but we will see in Chapter 13 that it has its own problems, especially in times of significant inflation.

Materiality

A small mistake in the financial statements of an entity will not invalidate those statements. They should still be usable by anyone interested in the entity. However, the key issue is obviously what we mean by 'small'. The concept of materiality applies the test of whether the financial statements still show a true and fair view, and are still of use to users. If the answer is yes, then the error is not material, and we need not spend time and resources trying to find and correct it. If, on the other hand, the mis-statement, or even the total omission, of an item would result in the financial statements as a whole not showing a true and fair view, then that item would be regarded as material. Such an error would have to be corrected if the statements are to comply with the Companies Act 2006 and show a true and fair view.

The materiality of an item is related to the size of the entity. The omission or mis-statement of a £10,000 item would probably not be material in the financial statements of Tesco, but would almost certainly be very material in the financial statements of a one-person business. Note that materiality can be measured against size, as suggested above, but occasionally it may be more appropriate to measure it against profits. If, for example, the profits of Tesco were only £20,000, then a £10,000 item could, perhaps, be considered material.

*A*ctivity 4.3 Sam and Louise had £800, out of which they purchased a second-hand van for £500. All their other assets are to be ignored. They estimated that the van will have a life of about another 20,000 miles. Sam and Louise started a light removals business, but were involved in an accident on their first day, and damaged a bicycle. Sam promised to pay for the damage and the rider said he thought the bike could be repaired for between £60 and £100.

▶

At the end of their first day, Sam and Louise were offered £600 for the van. They were also paid £50 cash for a job they did in the morning and £70 for the afternoon's job, payable next week. During the day, they had travelled 50 miles.

List Sam and Louise's assets and liabilities at the start and end of the first day and hence say how much better, or worse, off they are since they started. More importantly, in doing so, clearly indicate which accounting ideas justify your calculations.

This is an important activity, drawing together much of what we have covered so far in this book, so try to do it, and do it conscientiously.

Answer

Given that the ideas involved in any answer to this question are so open ended, what follows should not be regarded as the definitive answer, but rather as a reasonable response that covers all the main points that should be made.

		Relevant ideas
Opening position		
Asset		
Cash	800	*Money measurement*
Liability		
Capital	800	*Business entity*
Closing position		
Assets		
Van	500	*Historical cost, materiality, reliability, prudence*
Trade receivables	70	*Accruals*
Cash	350	*Money measurement*
	920	
Liabilities		
Owing for bicycle	100	*Accruals, reliability*
	820	
Capital		
Opening position	800	*Business entity*
Increase in wealth	20	*Going concern*
	820	

What our answer sets out is both the opening and closing statement of financial positions. Notice how the increase in wealth has been calculated by determining the difference between the opening capital position and what the net result of the assets and liabilities tells us must be the closing value of the business. Another way to view this increase in wealth is as the net income for the period. In other words, what we have done above is to calculate the net profit without preparing a statement of comprehensive income. We do not have the detail about revenues and expenses that the statement of comprehensive income provides, but it is an alternative way to calculate profit. This is an idea that we will return to in Chapter 13.

In terms of the concepts that we have listed above, there is a number of points to be made. First, both the opening and the closing cash positions depend on their validity as measures of wealth on the basic assumption that we can measure anything by attaching a number of £s to it. In other words, the whole exercise rests on the money measurement concept.

Second, the valuation of the van is more of a problem. The usual basis would be to value it according to what we paid for it, i.e. at its historical cost, but there are other possibilities. We could, for example, decide that a more relevant and useful valuation would be what we were offered for it, that is, £600. Would this value be any less logical or reasonable than using the old cost? If not, the implication is that the conventional choice of historical cost is at least partly arbitrary. If, on the other hand, the choice of historical cost is more logical and reasonable than any other, we should be explicit about why we believe this. As we saw before, a major advantage of historical cost is its relative objectivity, and the inherent prudence arguably enhances the reliability of the measurement.

Third, this is not the only issue in relation to the valuation of the van, there is also the question of depreciation. This a topic that we will cover in more detail in Chapter 6, but note that if the van is going to be of benefit for 20,000 miles, the accruals concept would suggest that we should allocate some of the cost of £500 against the day's profits. The question of how much benefit can be answered by saying that we have presumably had 50/20,000ths of the benefit, since we have travelled 50 miles out of a total usable mileage of 20,000. Using the historical cost value of £500, this works out to a depreciation charge for the period of £1.25, which hardly seems worth bothering with. In more formal terms, we can invoke the convention of materiality to justify ignoring any charge for the using up of the value of the van, at least for one day.

Fourth, accruals and realisation could be used to justify the inclusion of the amount due for the afternoon's work, that is, the trade receivable of £70.

Fifth, the adoption of prudence would guide our valuation of the trade payable, since showing £100 as being outstanding is a more reliable treatment than only showing £60. Showing £60 would result in a lower total for liabilities and would arguably therefore be an overstatement of our position, contrary to prudence. Further, the amount has not yet been paid, but we conventionally allow for it since it relates to this accounting period. The formal justification for making such allowances is, of course, the accruals concept.

Sixth and finally, the net effect of applying all these concepts and conventions to the opening and closing valuations of Sam and Louise's business is to report an increase in wealth of £20. Unless they withdraw this profit, it will be carried forward to finance their business in future periods. The implication is that we are assuming that the business is a going concern.

This has been a discursive answer to a fairly short activity. However, we have been concerned to demonstrate how even simple accounting practice rests explicitly on fundamental assumptions, usually known as the concepts or principles, or just the ideas, of accounting. If we change the ideas, we will get different accounting. To look in more detail at how the ideas work through into practical accounting, we need to consider estimation and measurement bases.

Accounting estimation and measurement bases

In the conventional understanding of the conceptual framework, estimation builds on the policies, and measurement bases then build on the estimation. Estimation is concerned with how the policies can be applied to economic transactions and events in order to attach a number of £s to an accounting item. For example, the accounting policy of accruals applied to inventory implies that we should allow for opening and closing inventory in the calculation of gross profit. However, this still leaves the question of how to value that inventory, and estimation is the particular method that we select. As we saw in the previous chapter this could be FIFO or AVCO, and our particular choice is then our estimation technique.

To continue the example, we have decided to apply the policy of accruals and so chosen to allow for inventory in the profit calculation, and have further chosen, say, FIFO as the estimation technique for inventory. There remains just one final step before we have an amount to enter into the statement of comprehensive income for the inventory adjustment, and that is to measure the value on our FIFO basis. The final step is thus to select the measurement basis.

We already know that there are alternative measurement basis such as historical cost, replacement cost and net realisable value. We choose one of these, and then stick with it to provide consistency and hence comparability, and this choice is our measurement basis.

Accounting practice is thus determined by the policies the entity chooses. If it had chosen different policies then the practices would have been different, and the statement of comprehensive income and statement of financial position would present a different view of the entity. If users are to be able to make allowances for differing policies between entities they are looking at, then they must at least know what the policies are. Finally, therefore, IAS 8 requires that the accounting policies and associated estimation techniques should be disclosed as a note to the financial statements. If we change the estimation basis then the figures will change, of course, so IAS 8 also requires explicit disclosure of any such change.

Revenue recognition

This is a topic that we have touched on earlier, especially in relation to the realisation concept. That introduced the idea that we should only take account of revenues and expenses when the associated cash flow has happened, or at least become reasonably certain. However, this is not always easy to apply in practice and the idea has recently been developed into the broader area of revenue recognition.

There has been an international accounting standard, IAS 18 'Revenue Recognition', in the area for a number of years. The standard starts with a consideration of what we mean by revenue, and asserts that it is an inflow of economic benefits arising from ordinary activities. This seems like an obvious definition, but note two points about it. First, the reference to economic benefits is an echo of the definition of an asset, that is, the revenue associated with it is what makes an asset worth something. Second, revenue only arises from ordinary activities, so selling a major asset, for example, is not revenue.

This leads on to the next major issue which is how we measure the amount of the revenue. The approach adopted is to take the fair value of the consideration received. In other words, the value of revenue is not the value to us of what we gave up, but the value of what we received from our customer.

So far this all appears to be fairly obvious and you may be wondering why we need an accounting standard on such a simple topic. However, the recognition and measurement of revenue is not always so simple. For example, consider the following activity.

*A*ctivity 4.4

Markham Publishing plc sells books to bookshops worth £200,000 just before the accounting year end. The agreement is that any book not sold may be returned to the publisher. None are returned in this accounting year, but past experience is that about 10% will be returned next year. The right of return expires after two years. Is the revenue to be entered in this year's Markham statement of comprehensive income £200,000 or £180,000 or something else?

Answer

The approach adopted by the standard setters is that one of two accounting policies will be appropriate, depending on the circumstances. (The fact that there is no right way to deal with this situation is an indication that revenue recognition is not as simple a topic as it first appears.) One policy would be to recognise £180,000, being the books sold that are likely to stay sold, that is, to allow for returns as best we can given the inherent uncertainty.

The other policy put forward by the standard setters is to only recognise the sale after the possibility of any returns has expired. This would imply not recognising any revenue until two years have passed. This latter approach might be considered inappropriate in the circumstances, and the decision about which policy to adopt would rest on a consideration of the policies and characteristics set out in IAS 8 and which we explored earlier in this chapter. Ultimately, we would have to decide, as always, which of the alternatives produces the most true and fair view. In other words, there's no single correct answer, and we would have to assess how sure we are of our estimate that about 10% of books will be returned. Only if we have evidence from prior experience that our estimate is sound should we account for sales of £180,000. If we have little idea of returns then it would probably be best not to recognise any revenue until the situation becomes more certain, presumably next year.

A true and fair view

As a final element in our survey of the ideas of accounting we should consider a true and fair view. This phrase comes from the Companies Act, and is the over-riding legal requirement for financial statements in the UK, that is, they must show a 'true and fair view'. The phrase is not then defined in the Act so is implicitly left to accountants to define in practice. It is held to be achieved primarily through adherence to the accounting standards, which implies that the ideas we have considered in this chapter do have legal impact.

The 'Framework'

To give it its full title the 'Framework' is properly called The Framework for the Preparation and Presentation of Financial Statements. We introduced it earlier in this chapter, where we noted that it is a codification of many of the ideas of accounting that we've been considering. It can be seen as the International Accounting Standard Board's attempt at a conceptual framework for accounting. Alternatively, we could regard it as a standard for setting standards, in that it provides guidance on what constitutes good accounting.

It is divided into a number of sections, each dealing with a specific theoretical topic. The next page or so explores each of these sections in some detail.

First, the Framework deals with who are the users of financial information. This is a topic that we considered back in Chapter 1, so we needn't consider it again here. Second, the Framework goes on to address the question of why we do accounting. Again, this is something we explored back in Chapter 1, where we decided that it's primarily 'decision usefulness' – the main purpose of accounting is to help users make decisions about the organisation.

The Framework then goes on to consider the characteristics of good accounting. We've already touched on these, but they're such an important issue that we'll leave them for now and explore them as a separate topic later in this chapter, under the 'Characteristics' heading.

The next part of the Framework identifies and defines the basic building blocks of financial accounting. These are identified as being assets, liabilities, equity, gains and losses, and contributions from, and distributions to, owners. These classifications will be familiar to you from our exploration of the statement of financial position in Chapter 2. The significance of their formal declaration in the Framework is that they now define the scope of financial accounting. All items that appear in financial statements must fall into one of the specified categories. The question of whether a key employee should be shown as an asset of the company in the statement of financial position, for example, should be answered, at least partly, by reference to the definition of an asset in this part of the Framework. In such a case, the issue would be whether the employee represents 'future economic benefit' controlled by the company, since that phrase is the heart of the definition of an asset. Presumably, the answer would be yes, given that it is likely that the net revenues generated by such a key employee would exceed the cost of his or her wages. However, the question does not rest there, because the material in the framework on elements has to be seen alongside the issue of recognition.

Accordingly, the framework goes on to deal with the circumstances in which these elements should be recognised in the financial statements. It should come as no surprise to find that it requires items to be recognised only if they are elements as defined. We have already accepted that our key employee probably fits the definition of an asset. However, the framework also imposes the further condition that the element must also be capable of being objectively quantified. In other words, we need to be able to objectively quantify the 'future economic benefit' that our employee represents. One approach could be to sum the net revenues after wages costs that the employee will bring in during his or her time with the company.

Activity 4.5	Briefly, note down at least one practical problem that you foresee with such an approach to valuation. As always, you will learn more and faster if you think about the issue raised in the activity than if you simply skip ahead to the answer.

Answer	Our view is that the main problem is the uncertainty inherent in any estimate of future revenues and expenses. It would be highly questionable, for example, whether our guesses about the net revenues or the number of years the employee will stay with us will turn out to be accurate. If we cannot objectively quantify an element, then the Framework requires that we do not recognise it, that is, we should not include it in the financial statements. More subtly, such an approach to valuation is not historical cost, and we have already seen that historical cost is the most widely used and accepted method of valuation. If we use some estimate of future value for an employee, and historical cost for another asset, such as a building, it is hard to see what the total of the two assets represents or means. We looked at valuation problems in Chapter 2, and will return to the topic in greater depth in Chapter 13. In the meantime, the Framework goes on to address the issue of valuation.

Specifically, the next section of the Framework deals with the alternative bases on which we could quantify financial items. So far we have only looked seriously at historical cost, but we will explore other possibilities in Chapter 13. As you may be beginning to realise from the brief discussion above, valuation is a complex topic.

Finally, the last main topic dealt with by the Framework is an exploration of capital maintenance. This means looking at what we understand by the 'wealth' or 'net worth' of an organisation. It's something we touched on back in Chapter 2, and something that we'll return to in Chapter 13.

In the rest of this chapter we will consider the characteristics in more detail, that is, the conventional wisdom on what constitutes good accounting. This topic therefore represents guidelines for everything else we do in this book.

The characteristics

As we briefly saw earlier in this chapter, the Framework identifies the qualitative characteristics of good financial reporting as relevance, reliability, comparability and understandability.

Activity 4.6 Write two sentences of your own to define each of the characteristics, 'relevance' and 'reliability'. In other words, what do you think these words mean in accounting terms?

Answer Our answer is based closely on the Framework, which says that the relevance of financial information is primarily related to its predictive role, that is, the extent to which the information helps users to predict the organisation's future and so to make decisions about it. For example, the attempt by a potential investor to predict future profitability and dividend levels will be at least partly based on the financial statements. Relevance also relates to the use of financial information to confirm past predictions, e.g. about returns on a particular capital project.

In relation to reliability, the Framework asserts that reliability of financial information is deemed to be achieved by producing information that has a series of characteristics. There are five of these, but most should already be familiar from your studies earlier in this book.

1 *Faithful representation*. This consists of valid description, free from error, although it should be taken together with a suitable 'choice of aspect', i.e. a decision of which properties of a transaction we should disclose. Achievement of faithful representation also depends on the idea of 'substance over form'.

2 *Substance over form*. Briefly, this idea says that where there's a difference between the strict form of the legal position and the economic substance of an event then we should always account for the substance rather than the form. This is a very important, and quite complex, idea in accounting, and so we'll consider it as a topic in its own right later in this chapter.

3 *Neutrality*. The information presented must be free from bias. There is a very close link here to the prior concept of objectivity.

4 *Prudence*. This principle is restated. While we should aim to reflect an unbiased view of an event or transaction, in accordance with neutrality, under conditions of uncertainty it will be helpful to select a prudent view of the possible outcomes.

5 *Completeness*. The more complete the information is the better, but the benefits of completeness should be weighed against the costs of the time and money needed to prepare full information.

Activity 4.7 The other characteristics are comparability and understandability. Repeat the previous activity, this time jotting down a couple of your own sentences to define each of these terms.

Answer Once again, our answer draws heavily on the points made in the Framework. Specifically, the achievement of comparability implies the presentation of financial information in a consistent way from one year to the next, and between enterprises. One important feature of this will be the disclosure of and adherence to accounting policies. The presentation of comparative figures for the previous year will also help to achieve this characteristic.

Understandability requires a prior consideration of who the users of the information are held to be. The presentation of the information should then be such that those users will normally be able to make substantial use of that information. It will, however, be acceptable to assume that users are reasonably well-informed about basic accounting and economic matters.

Finally, the Framework insists that all the above characteristics are subject to a minimum threshold of quality. The main consideration here is materiality, which provides a cut-off point for the disclosure or non-disclosure of particular events. Furthermore, you should bear in mind that in the UK everything in the Framework is subject to the over-riding legal requirement to show a true and fair view.

Activity 4.8

Global Trading is currently preparing its annual report and accounts. As its name suggests, it is a very big enterprise, with very complex accounting procedures and reports. Currently, it publishes an statement of comprehensive income and a statement of financial position. The directors are considering a proposal to produce a more simplified set of financial statements, either in addition to, or even instead of, the usual, more complex statements. One possibility, for example, would be to produce simply a summary of monies in and out of the bank account.

Taking each of the four characteristics in turn, assess whether the proposal is sound. You may ignore any legal requirements.

Answer

As with many of the questions in this fundamental area of accounting, there is no single correct answer. However, we think the following suggested answer covers most of the main points.

Relevance

The Framework says that relevance rests on whether the financial statements are of significant use for predicting or confirming economic events. Whether the proposal improves relevance depends on who the users are, and what they want to predict or confirm. A lender, for example, would probably find a summary of cash movements relevant, since he or she would be concerned about the ability of Global Trading to make repayments. A shareholder, on the other hand, would probably be most concerned about the profit made, and would accordingly find the statement of comprehensive income more relevant, and the proposal would therefore not be as sound.

Reliability

This characteristic is to be judged according to faithful representation, substance over form, neutrality, prudence and completeness. These points seem to be as valid for either approach to accounting, but they at least do not suggest that the proposal should be rejected on the grounds of reliability. Indeed, in terms of neutrality (objectivity) the proposal could be seen as positive, in that the amounts passing through the bank account are a more objective measure of events than, say, the measure of profit. In terms of completeness, the provision of the suggested statement in addition to existing statements is likely to be positive. Note, however, that provision of an extra statement will take time, so delaying the publication of the statements and so making them more out of date.

▶

Understandability

A summary of monies in and out of the bank account will probably be understandable to a wider group of users than will a conventionally complex set of financial statements. On these grounds the proposal seems sound. However, we need to balance this against the difficulties we have already noted in relation to relevance and reliability. Arguably, it is more important that the accounts be 'right' than that they be understandable.

Comparability

This refers to a user's ability to make comparisons both with Global Trading's own accounts in previous years, and with the accounts of other similar companies. Comparability with previous years will be poor, unless the company retrospectively prepares a similar cash summary for those years. This is possible, but would be expensive. Comparability with other companies will only be possible if other companies produce a similar statement.

Overall, it is not possible to make a clear recommendation to the directors, without knowing more about the circumstances. What we can say is that the four characteristics seem to provide criteria by which we can start to judge the validity of both current and proposed accounting practices.

Substance over form

You'll remember that the idea of 'substance over form' is part of how we achieve reliability. It's a fundamental part of the conceptual framework so we've separated it out here to deal with it as a topic in its own right.

In essence, the idea says that there can be a difference between the economic substance of a transaction – what's really happening – and the strict legal form. An example is probably the best way to explain how the idea works. If we buy a car and use it in our business then there's no difference. The economic substance is that the car is our asset, since we receive any economic benefits associated with its use. Similarly, since we bought the car the legal form is also that its our car. However, compare this with the situation where we lease the car for most or all of its expected life.

We will again physically have the car, we'll use it to earn economic benefits for our business, we'll control who can drive it, and we'll pay for the running costs. In substance, it appears to be our asset, and so we'll presumably show it in our statement of financial position. However, legally the car doesn't belong to us, but belongs to the lease company. Accordingly we shouldn't show it in our statement of financial position. There's a conflict between what the economic substance of the lease suggests we do and what the legal form suggests is the correct accounting. The concept of substance over form says that in those situations where we have such a conflict then we account according to the economic substance rather than the legal form. In this case we would therefore show the car in our statement of financial position, and then depreciate it, even though it belongs to someone else. Note that the idea of substance over form applies to all accounting, not just to leases. It's therefore a very powerful idea in accounting.

Summary

This chapter has dealt with three topics:

▶ the concepts of accounting, the most important of which are set out in the Framework, complemented by IAS 1 and IAS 8

▶ IAS 8, which sets up a structure of policies for determining accounting practice in a reasonably coherent way

▶ the Framework, which attempts a definition of what constitutes good accounting. In other words, it provides a target for all our accounting to aim at.

This chapter concludes the first part of this book. So far, we have explored the nature of accounting, looked at the two main statements by which accounting reports to the outside world, and started to look at some of the theoretical underpinning to accounting. We will return to the theory in Chapter 13. In the meantime, however, we should turn our attention to the everyday practicalities of accounting. Chapter 5 therefore starts our study of double entry bookkeeping.

Key terms

concepts	characteristics
going concern	measurement bases
accruals	revenue recognition
matching	true and fair view
realisation	

Self-assessment questions

Select the most appropriate answer for each of the following multiple choice questions.

1 The assumption that an organisation will continue to operate indefinitely is a fair description of which concept?

(a) Accruals
(b) Going concern
(c) Consistency
(d) Prudence

2 The concept of materiality implies that an organisation will:

(a) Only account for items which don't affect the overall view gained from its accounts.
(b) Not account for non-current assets which are due to be sold in the next accounting year.

▶

(c) Only account for non-current assets and those current assets costing more than £1,000.

(d) Not account for items which don't affect the overall view gained from its accounts.

3 The concept of money measurement means:

(a) Accounts cost a material amount of money to prepare.

(b) Only items that can be objectively measured in money terms are accounted for.

(c) Accounts are only ever prepared in one currency.

(d) Items in accounts are recorded at the amount of money they originally cost.

4 The recognition that an organisation is distinct from its owners is a fair description of which concept?

(a) Duality

(b) Separate valuation

(c) Business entity

(d) Objectivity

5 The concept of realisation means that:

(a) Items are accounted for in the period in which the associated cash flow occurs.

(b) Items are recognised when the directors realise that a cost has been incurred.

(c) Items are accounted for when only they can be objectively measured.

(d) Items are recognised when the associated cash becomes reasonably certain of being received or paid.

6 'The International Accounting Standards Board (IASB) should spend less time on developing a vague set of principles and more time on specifying clear accounting practices.' To what extent do you agree with this statement?

As in the self-assessment question for Chapter 1, you should justify your response and construct your answer as an essay of 300 to 500 words, or as comprehensive notes for such an essay. Again, we have provided feedback as a list of points that you should have covered.

7 Back in Chapter 1 we asked you to identify the relative merits of the UK and French approaches to financial reporting. To recap, the French system is based on the *plan comptable*, a specification of exactly which accounts must be kept to record which transactions and how those details are then to be presented in the statement of comprehensive income and in the statement of financial position. This can be contrasted with the less directed approach used in the UK and outlined in this chapter.

For each of the characteristics of good accounting that you have now explored (relevance, reliability, comparability and understandability), suggest one reason to prefer the UK system and one reason to prefer the French system. You may like to set out your answer as a table – we have.

8 Outline the purposes and main features of the Framework for the Preparation and Presentation of Financial Statements. Your answer should be in the form of an essay of around 500 words, briefly covering both the content and the purposes of the Framework.

5

The double entry system

Objectives

By the end of this chapter you should be able to:
- ▶ Identify the need for a system of double entry.
- ▶ Relate the duality concept to this system.
- ▶ Prepare ledger accounts.
- ▶ Balance off ledger accounts.
- ▶ Extract a trial balance and understand its importance within the system.
- ▶ Prepare simple statements of comprehensive income (income statements) and statements of financial position (balance sheets) from a trial balance.

Introduction

This chapter is intended to introduce you to the basics of the double entry bookkeeping system that was codified by Luca Pacioli in the fifteenth century. As an accountant you may not be involved in the actual recording within the double entry bookkeeping system as this is carried out by bookkeepers or indeed a computer. You must, however, understand the system as you, as an accountant, will be called on to ensure the system is operating effectively and to complete year-end entries to enable relevant and reliable financial statements to be prepared for an organisation.

The need for a double entry system

You have seen in previous chapters that it is possible to construct a statement of financial position (a balance sheet), to show the position of a business at a point in time, and a statement of income to identify the profitability of a business for a period of time. How did you do this? Refresh your memory with the following activity.

Activity 5.1

Mr Bean intends to set up in business as an antiques dealer. He places £20,000 of his own money into a business bank account then purchases items for resale for £12,000 and a van for £5,000. He rents a shop for £3,600 per annum paying the first monthly instalment of rent. At the end of his first month of trading he is able to identify the fact that he has sold for cash two items, one costing £2,000 for £3,500, and one costing £500 for £800.

Draw up the statement of financial position for Mr Bean as at the end of the first month's trading and a statement of comprehensive income for the period.

Answer

MR BEAN
STATEMENT OF FINANCIAL POSITION (BALANCE SHEET) AS
AT END OF FIRST MONTH

Non-current assets		
Van		5,000
Current assets		
Inventory	9,500	
Bank	7,000	16,500
		21,500
Capital		
Opening	20,000	
Profit	1,500	21,500

MR BEAN
STATEMENT OF COMPREHENSIVE INCOME STATEMENT
FOR THE PERIOD ENDED FIRST MONTH

Sales	4,300
Cost of sales	2,500
Gross profit	1,800
Rent	300
Net profit	1,500

How did you construct the above? Probably by doing calculations on a piece of paper to arrive at sales, cost of sales, inventory and bank figures.

Would the above have been as simple though if Mr Bean had made 100 sales during the month? Obviously the answer is no. Thus you have identified that there is a need for a record of all Mr Bean's transactions that will enable a statement of financial position and a statement of comprehensive income to be drawn up at the end of any given period. We have dealt here with a sole trader business, that of Mr Bean. However, all types of organisations, companies both private and public limited (plcs), partnerships, charities, public sector, use double entry bookkeeping to record their transactions.

Double entry system – duality

You learnt in Chapter 4 about the concept of duality.

Activity 5.2   Identify for Mr Bean the duality involved in the introduction of his capital into the business and the purchase of his van.

Answer   This was fairly straightforward. In the first case you created a liability of capital and the asset of bank, in the second you reduced the asset of bank and created an asset of van. There was a dual effect of each transaction to maintain the accounting equation:

$$\text{ASSETS} = \text{CAPITAL} + \text{LIABILITIES}$$

Double entry system – account

When you calculated the bank figure in Activity 5.1 you made a list of additions to and subtractions from the bank probably similar to the following:

Additions		Subtractions	
Capital	20,000	Van	5,000
Sale 1	3,500	Purchases	12,000
Sale 2	800	Rent	300
	24,300		17,300

Additions were sources of funds to the business and subtractions applications of those funds from the business.

The above can be represented as an **account** in a **double entry** system as follows:

BANK ACCOUNT

Capital	20,000	Van	5,000
Sale 1	3,500	Purchases	12,000
Sale 2	800	Rent	300

The left-hand side of this account is referred to as the debit side (debit means 'to give' – I give (place) £20,000 to the bank account); the right-hand side as the credit side (credit means to receive – I receive £5,000 from the bank to buy a van).

This bank account has enabled you to make a very neat recording of Mr Bean's dealings with the bank but has not recorded the *duality* of the above transactions. Looking at the transaction of purchasing the van, you have credited the bank account with £5,000, so to comply with duality it would seem reasonable to suggest that you should debit another account with £5,000.

Thus:

VAN ACCOUNT

Bank	5,000		

Complete the duality for the other transactions in the bank account.

Answer

PURCHASES ACCOUNT

Bank	12,000		

RENT ACCOUNT

Bank	300		

SALES ACCOUNT

		Bank sale 1	3,500
		Bank sale 2	800

CAPITAL ACCOUNT

		Bank	20,000

The pattern of the above accounts is that of *double entry*. For each transaction we have made a debit and a credit entry for the same amount, the description (narrative) referring always to the other double entry account.

Using your knowledge of the duality concept, the accounting equation and with reference to the double entry accounts used above you should be able to complete the following activity without too much trouble.

Activity 5.4

Complete the following table:

Account	Transaction	Entry to account
Asset	Addition	Debit
Asset	Subtraction	(a)_____
Liability	Addition	(b)_____
Liability	(c)_____	Debit
Capital	(d)_____	Credit
Capital	Subtraction	(e)_____
Expense	Addition	(f)_____
Expense	Subtraction	(g)_____
Income	Addition	(h)_____
Income	(i)_____	Debit

Answer

The missing entries are as follows:

(a) Credit, (b) Credit, (c) Subtraction, (d) Addition, (e) Debit, (f) Debit, (g) Credit, (h) Credit, (i) Subtraction.

Fairly easy we know, but we hope you thought about the activity rather than just following the pattern.

Activity 5.5

The following question is similar to Activities 5.1 and 5.3 and completing the question will ensure that you have understood the concepts so far.

Miss Coffee intends to set up in business as a retailer of ladies' high-class fashion. She places £40,000 of her own money into a business bank account and then purchases a car for £8,000 and inventory for £25,000. She rents property at £12,000 per annum paying the first month's rental. At the end of the first month of trading she is able to identify that she has sold inventory worth £2,000 for £5,000 and paid sundry expenses of £500.

Draw up the statement of financial position for Miss Coffee as at the end of the first month's trading and a statement of comprehensive income for the period together with the double entry accounts for the period.

Answer

MISS COFFEE
STATEMENT OF FINANCIAL POSITION AS AT END
OF FIRST MONTH

Non-current assets		
Car		8,000
Current assets		
Inventory	23,000	
Bank	10,500	33,500
		41,500
Capital		
Opening		40,000
Profit		1,500
		41,500

MISS COFFEE
INCOME STATEMENT OF COMPREHENSIVE FOR THE PERIOD
ENDED FIRST MONTH

Sales		5,000
Cost of sales		2,000
Gross profit		3,000
Rent	1,000	
Sundry expenses	500	1,500
Net profit		1,500

BANK ACCOUNT

Capital	40,000	Car	8,000
Sales	5,000	Rent	1,000
		Purchases	25,000
		Sundry	500

RENT ACCOUNT

Bank	1,000	

SUNDRY ACCOUNT

Bank	500	

SALES ACCOUNT

		Bank	5,000

CAR ACCOUNT

Bank	8,000	

CAPITAL ACCOUNT

		Capital	40,000

PURCHASES ACCOUNT

Bank	25,000	

Activity 5.6   This question is provided for extra practice. Mr Pickup sets up in business as a website designer. He places £25,000 of his own money into a business bank account and then purchases a computer for £2,500 and a car for £10,000. He rents a small office for £6,000 per annum and buys some furniture and other equipment for the office costing £2,200. At the end of the second month of trading Mr Pickup is able to identify that he has sold several website designs for a total of £7,500, he has paid two months' rent on the office and he has paid other expenses of £850.

Draw up the statement of financial position for Mr Pickup as at the end of the second month of trading and a statement of comprehensive income for the period together with the double entry accounts for the period. Note that there will be no cost of sales figure in this example as Mr.Pickup is not buying goods to sell on or manufacture and sell on. It is his own intellectual knowledge that he is selling in the form of his website designs.

Answer

MR PICKUP
STATEMENT OF FINANCIAL POSITION AS AT END OF
SECOND MONTH

Non-current assets

Car	10,000	
Computer	2,500	
Furniture and equipment	2,200	14,700

Current assets

Bank		15,950
		30,650

Capital

Opening		25,000
Profit		5,650
		30,650

MR PICKUP
INCOME STATEMENT OF COMPREHENSIVE FOR THE
PERIOD ENDED SECOND MONTH

Sales		7,500
Cost of sales		0
Gross profit		7,500
Rent	1,000	
Sundry expenses	850	1,850
Net profit		5,650

BANK ACCOUNT

Capital	25,000	Car	10,000
Sales	7,500	Rent	1,000
		Computer	2,500
		Equipment	2,200
		Sundry	850

RENT ACCOUNT

Bank	1,000	

SUNDRY ACCOUNT

Bank	850	

SALES ACCOUNT

		Bank	7,500

CAR ACCOUNT

Bank	10,000		

CAPITAL ACCOUNT

		Capital	25,000

COMPUTER ACCOUNT

Bank	2,500		

EQUIPMENT ACCOUNT

Bank	2,200		

Credit transactions

So far the transactions you have dealt with for Mr Bean have all involved cash as one side of the double entry.

A lot of business is carried out by the use of **credit transactions**. For example Mr Bean, when he acquired £12,000 of goods, could well have paid only £5,000 immediately and bought the rest on credit. When Mr Bean bought the £7,000 of goods on credit he will eventually have to pay the creditor the amount owed. He will therefore need to create an **accounts payable** account.

We account for this in the double entry system as follows:

PURCHASES ACCOUNT

Cash	5,000		
Creditor	7,000		

CASH ACCOUNT

		Purchases	5,000

CREDITOR ACCOUNT

		Purchases	7,000

Similarly, sales may be made on credit and a debtor would be created, and Mr Bean will need to use an **accounts receivable** account. Note that the accounts payable (the creditor) is a liability of the business and the accounts receivable (the debtor) an asset. It is also customary to maintain separate accounts for each account receivable (debtor) and each account payable (creditor) in the double entry system. You will see how these separate accounts are summed and verified by the use of control accounts in

Chapter 14. For now we will use a separate accounts payable for each creditor and accounts receivable for each debtor.

To help reinforce your understanding of the double entry system a full example is provided below for you to work through as a self-check of understanding. The suggested answer is provided at Activity 5.9 so if you feel fairly confident in respect of your understanding so far you could wait and complete Activities 5.7 and 5.9 together. By the way, it is normal in the double entry system to enter the date against each entry made. The place where double entry accounts are recorded is generally known as a ledger. This ledger is divided into sub-ledgers:

▶ Accounts payable (creditors) ledger – where we record the suppliers accounts (from whom we have purchased supplies)

▶ Accounts receivable (debtors) ledger – where we record the customers accounts (to whom we have made sales)

▶ Nominal ledger or impersonal ledger – where everything else is recorded.

We will return to this division of the ledger in Chapter 15.

Worked example of double entry

Activity 5.7

Enter the following transactions in the ledgers of A. Bate, maintaining separate bank and cash accounts.

			£
March	3	Bate placed £20,000 in a business account	
	3	Bought car for £8,000, paying by cheque	8,000
	4	Bought goods on credit from Hall	6,350
	5	Paid cheque for office expenses	340
	5	Paid cheque for car insurance	195
	8	Cashed a cheque for cash	600
	9	Cash received for sales	2,345
	12	Sold goods on credit to White	1,645
	14	Paid wages in cash	250
	18	Cash received for sales	300
	20	Banked excess cash	
	24	Bought goods on credit from Dunn	1,895
	25	Cheque received from White	850
	26	Cash sales	400
	27	Paid wages in cash	250
	28	Sold goods on credit: White	600
		Black	750
	29	Cash sales	250
	30	Cheque sent: Hall	5,500
		Dunn	1,500
	31	Paid all cash into bank	

<table>
<tr><td>*Answer*</td><td>The answer to the above is contained in the answer to Activity 5.9 but we suggest you carry out the exercise now and check your answer later.</td></tr>
</table>

Balancing off accounts

You have now learnt how to record business transactions in the books but you also need to know the following data at the end of a period:

▶ what the cash balance is

▶ what the total value of sales is that has been made

▶ how much is owed to the creditors on the accounts payable account

▶ how much debtors owe the business shown on the accounts recoverable account

▶ what the total of expenses is.

To do this we need to balance off the accounts. Looking back at the bank account we derived for you after Activity 5.2 we had:

BANK ACCOUNT

Capital	20,000	Van	5,000
Sale 1	3,500	Purchases	12,000
Sale 2	800	Rent	300

The left-hand side of this account (the debit) totals £24,300 and the credit side (the right) £17,300. The difference is £7,000, the balance at the bank you identified at Activity 5.1, an asset. You should also have noticed that the van, another asset of the business, appeared in its double entry account as a debit which implies that the asset of £7,000 at the bank has to appear as a debit.

The 'balancing off' takes place as follows:

BANK ACCOUNT

Capital	20,000	Van	5,000
Sale 1	3,500	Purchases	12,000
Sale 2	800	Rent	300
		Balance carried down	7,000
	24,300		24,300
Balance brought down	7,000		

To check whether you understand what we did to balance the bank account try the next activity.

Activity 5.8	Identify the sequence that occurred to balance off the above bank account.

Answer	You should have identified a sequence similar to the following:

1 Add up both sides and identify the difference.
2 Enter the difference on the side with the smaller total (the credit side here).
3 Enter the totals for both sides – which are now identical.
4 Complete the double entry in respect of (2) by entering the same figure on the opposite side (in this case the debit side) below the totals.

This balance brought down of £7,000 debit is the balance of cash at bank, an asset of the business. Again it is normal to enter the date in the accounts when balancing off the accounts, the carried-down date being that of the end of the period and the brought-down date that of the start of the next period.

The rest of the accounts for Mr Bean are balanced as follows:

VAN ACCOUNT

Bank	5,000	Balance carried down	5,000
Balance brought down	5,000		

PURCHASES ACCOUNT

Bank	12,000	Balance carried down	12,000
Balance brought down	12,000		

RENT ACCOUNT

Bank	300	Balance carried down	300
Balance brought down	300		

SALES ACCOUNT

		Bank	3,500
Balance carried down	4,300	Bank	800
	4,300		4,300
		Balance brought down	4,300

CAPITAL ACCOUNT

Balance carried down	20,000	Bank	20,000
		Balance brought down	20,000

Notice that when there is only one entry in an account there is no need to enter the total for each side. It is also customary to abbreviate brought down and carried down to b/d and c/d respectively. 'Balance' can also be abbreviated to 'bal'.

Activity 5.9	Balance off all the accounts for Activity 5.7

Answer	The answer below is that for Activities 5.7 and 5.9.

CAPITAL ACCOUNT

Bal c/d	20,000	Bank	20,000
		Bal b/d	20,000

OFFICE EXPENSE ACCOUNT

Bank	340	Bal c/d	340
Bal b/d	340		

CAR ACCOUNT

Bank/loan	8,000	Bal c/d	8,000
Bal b/d	8,000		

INSURANCE ACCOUNT

Bank	195	Bal c/d	195
Bal b/d	195		

LOAN ACCOUNT (note 2)

Balance c/d	5,000	Car	5,000
		Bal b/d	5,000

WAGES ACCOUNT

Cash	250		
Cash	250	Bal c/d	500
	500		500
Bal b/d	500		

PURCHASES ACCOUNT

Hall	6,350		
Dunn	1,895	Bal c/d	8,245
	8,245		8,245
Bal b/d	8,245		

SALES ACCOUNT

		Cash	2,345
		White	1,645
		Cash	300
		Cash	400
		White	600
		Black	750
Bal c/d	6,290	Cash	250
	6,290		6,290
		Bal b/d	6,290

ACCOUNT RECEIVABLE (DEBTOR) – WHITE

Sales	1,645	Bank	850
Sales	600	Bal c/d	1,395
	2,245		2,245
Bal b/d	1,395		

ACCOUNT RECEIVABLE (DEBTOR) – BLACK

Sales	750	Bal c/d	750
Bal b/d	750		

ACCOUNT PAYABLES (CREDITOR) – HALL

Bank	5,500	Purchases	6,350
Bal c/d	850		
	6,350		6,350
		Bal b/d	850

ACCOUNT PAYABLES (CREDITOR) – DUNN

Bank	1,500	Purchases	1,895
Bal c/d	395		
	1,895		1,895
		Bal b/d	395

BANK ACCOUNT

Capital	20,000	Car	3,000
Cash	2,995	Office	340
White	850	Insurance	195
Cash	400	Cash	600
		Hall	5,500
		Dunn	1,500
		Bal c/d	13,110
	24,245		24,245
Bal b/d	13,110		

CASH ACCOUNT

Bank	600	Wages	250
Sales	2,345	Bank (note 1)	2,995
Sales	300	Wages	250
Sales	400	Bank (note 1)	400
Sales	250		
	3,895		3,895

Note 1   At this point the cash account had to be totalled to identify the balance that was then paid into the bank.

Note 2   As the cost of the car was £8,000 but only £3,000 was paid in cash the remaining £5,000 is identified as a loan.

The example we have given above consists of very few sales and purchases but in an actual business or indeed any type of organisation there are likely to be many sales and purchases in a day. For most businesses it is impossible to write up every sale as we have here into the sales ledger but, for now, in our simple examples, we will continue to use the method above. You will see in Chapter 14 how we deal with multiple sales and purchases to minimise the entries in the ledgers.

Trial balance

The double entry system follows the duality concept – for every debit there is an equal credit – thus if the system has been carried out correctly the *total debit balances* should equal the *total credit balances*. This check on the operation of the system is known as a **trial balance**.

TRIAL BALANCE FOR MR BEAN AS AT (PERIOD END DATE)

	Dr	Cr
Sales		4,300
Capital		20,000
Van	5,000	
Purchases	12,000	
Rent	300	
Bank	7,000	
	24,300	24,300

Activity 5.10 Construct the trial balance in respect of Activity 5.7.

Answer

TRIAL BALANCE AS AT 31 MARCH (A. BATE)

	Dr	Cr
Capital		20,000
Bank	13,110	
Office expenses	340	
Car insurance	195	
Car	8,000	
Wages	500	
Loan		5,000
Purchases	8,245	
Sales		6,290
Accounts payable (creditors):		
Hall		850
Dunn		395
Accounts receivable (debtors):		
White	1,395	
Black	750	
	32,535	32,535

Use of trial balance

If the totals of the trial balance agree, it does not necessarily prove that the books are correct. What it will prove is that you have entered an equal debit for every credit and that the accounts have been added correctly, but there are several errors that could have been made that the trial balance will not identify. It is also worth remembering that the trial balance is not part of the double entry system itself.

Activity 5.11 The following errors have been made in the books of Mr Bean. Identify those errors that the use of a trial balance will reveal and those it will not.

1 The sales account has been incorrectly added.

2 The purchase of goods on credit was entered in the relevant accounts payable (creditor) account but not the purchases account.

3 Wages paid of £92 was debited as £92 to the wages account but as £29 credit to the bank account.

4 The sale of goods for £100 on credit was not entered in the books at all.

5 An electricity bill was correctly credited to the bank account but the debit entry was made to the office expenses account not the electricity account.

6 Goods for £50 were bought on credit and entered in the books as purchases account debit £5 account payable (creditor) account credit £50. Sales made of £50 cash were entered in the cash account as debit £50 but as £5 to the credit of the sales account.

7 A loan made to Mr Bean of £1,000 from Mr Atkinson was debited to the loan account and credited to the bank account.

Answer

A little thought and you should have been able to identify that the trial balance will reveal the following types of error:

▶ Incorrect additions in an account as per item 1.
▶ Posting (entering) one side only of the double entry as per item 2.
▶ Entering a different amount in the debit side than the credit side, for example debit £92 credit £29 as per item 3.

but will not reveal the following:

▶ An entry completely missed as per item 4.
▶ An entry in a wrong account but the double entry still maintained as per item 5.
▶ Where errors cancel each other as per item 6.
▶ Entries where the double entry is completely the wrong way around as per item 7.

Statement of comprehensive income

At the very beginning of this chapter you were able to construct a statement of comprehensive income and a statement of financial position for Mr Bean (see Activity 5.1).

You did this by identifying the expenses to match with the income in the statement of comprehensive income and identifying the assets and liabilities at the end of the period and recording these in the statement of financial position. In effect you made use of the accounting equations:

$$\text{PROFIT} = \text{INCOME} - \text{EXPENSES USED UP}$$
$$\text{ASSETS} = \text{CAPITAL} + \text{LIABILITIES} + \text{PROFIT}$$

If we regard CAPITAL and PROFIT in the above equation as owner's EQUITY it is possible to write this second equation as:

$$\text{ASSETS} = \text{EQUITY} + \text{LIABILITIES}$$

The statement of comprehensive income can be treated as part of the double entry system and we can transfer expenses and income to it maintaining the principles of double entry. This would result in a statement of comprehensive income in what is known as 'horizontal format'. This is not the normal format that is used. The normal format is 'vertical format'. We identified this vertical format for you in Chapter 3 and we will return to it again later in this chapter. Whatever format is used, horizontal or vertical, they are still part of the double entry system. We must be careful though that we only transfer that expense used up in generating the income – the accruals or matching concept. Refer back to Chapter 4 here to refresh your memory on the accruals concept. In particular we must be careful how much of the purchase expense we transfer.

Mr Bean, in Activity 5.1, had not sold all of the goods he bought, in fact he has only sold goods costing £2,500. He therefore has goods remaining of £9,500 which is not recorded as yet in the double entry system. This figure of inventory could have been ascertained in one of two ways:

1 By counting the goods remaining in the shop and valuing them at the cost Mr Bean paid.

2 By reducing the figure of purchases, each time a sale is made, by the purchase price of that item sold.

When a business has several sales within a period the easiest method is to count inventory at the end of the period (refer back to Chapter 3 for how we did this).

This inventory figure is then entered in the books by the means of a closing inventory account and the statement of comprehensive income is used to calculate the cost of goods sold. The following demonstrates this. Note we have used a horizontal format for the income statement below.

SALES ACCOUNT

Income statement	4,300	Balance b/d	4,300

PURCHASES ACCOUNT

Balance b/d	12,000	Income statement	12,000

RENT ACCOUNT

Balance b/d	300	Income statement	300

CLOSING INVENTORY ACCOUNT

Income statement	9,500		

INCOME STATEMENT

Purchases	12,000	Sales	4,300
Gross profit c/d	1,800	Closing inventory	9,500
	13,800		13,800
Rent	300	Gross profit b/d	1,800
Net profit c/d	1,500		
	1,800		1,800
		Net profit b/d	1,500

Did you understand what we did here?

Activity 5.12   Identify the sequence carried out above to arrive at the net profit figure of £1,500. For example, the sequence will start:

▶ Transfer balance on sales account to the statement of comprehensive income by debiting sales account and crediting the statement of comprehensive income.

Answer

Your sequence should have been similar to the following:

▶ Transfer balance on sales account to the statement of comprehensive income by debiting sales account and crediting the statement of comprehensive income.
▶ Transfer balance on purchases by crediting this account and debiting the statement of comprehensive income.
▶ Enter closing inventory in the ledgers by debiting closing inventory account and crediting the statement of comprehensive income.
▶ Balance off the statement of comprehensive income but call the balance Gross Profit, i.e. difference between sales and cost of goods sold.
▶ Transfer balance on rent account to the statement of comprehensive income.
▶ Balance off the statement of comprehensive income again calling balance Net Profit.

Let us see if you can do all this now.

Activity 5.13

Given that the closing inventory as at 31 March in Activity 5.9 for A. Bate is £4.500, draw up a statement of comprehensive income using horizontal form for the month ended 31 March.

Answer

STATEMENT OF COMPREHENSIVE INCOME
FOR THE MONTH ENDED 31 MARCH

Purchases	8,245	Sales		6,290
Gross profit c/d	2,545	Closing inventory		4,500
	10,790			10,790
Office expenses	340	Gross profit b/d		2,545
Car insurance	195			
Wages	500			
Net profit c/d	1,510			
	2,545			2,545
		Net profit b/d		1,510

Format of the statement of comprehensive income

In Chapter 3 we discussed the format of the statement of comprehensive income. The above statement of comprehensive income would normally be written as follows:

Sales		6,290
Purchases	8,245	
Less closing inventory	4,500	3,745
Gross profit		2,545
Office expenses	340	
Car insurance	195	
Wages	500	1,035
Net profit		1,510

This is known as a vertical statement of comprehensive income. It is perceived as being easier for users to understand, and avoids the need to insert 'carried down' and 'brought down' figures. From this point on we suggest you always use the vertical format for the statement of comprehensive income.

Balance remaining in the books

Having constructed a statement of comprehensive income for Mr Bean it is possible at this point to extract another trial balance as follows:

	Dr	Cr
Capital		20,000
Inventory	9,500	
Van	5,000	
Bank	7,000	
Net profit		1,500
	21,500	21,500

Again just a minor leap in imagination and the above could be written as follows:

STATEMENT OF FINANCIAL POSITION AS AT 31 MARCH

Assets		
Non-current assets		
Van		5,000
Current assets		
Inventory	9,500	
Bank	7,000	16,500
Total assets		21,500
Equity		
Capital		20,000
Profit		1,500
Total equity		21,500

Thus the balances remaining in the books, after having extracted a statement of comprehensive income, form a statement of financial position. The statement of financial position records the position of the business at a specific point in time. It is presented in a format that represents the equation we gave you earlier:

$$ASSETS = EQUITY + LIABILITIES$$

Activity 5.14

Draw up the statement of financial position for the information contained in Activities relating to A. Bate after the extraction of the statement of comprehensive income as at 31 March.

Answer

The statement of financial position should look as follows:

STATEMENT OF FINANCIAL POSITION AS AT 31 MARCH

Assets			
Non-current assests			
Car			8,000
Current assets			
Inventory		4,500	
Accounts receivable			
(debtors):			
White	1,395		
Black	750	2,145	
Bank		13,110	19,755
Total assests			27,755
Equity and liability			
Equity			
Capital			20,000
Profit			1,510
Profit			21,510
Non-current liabilities			
Loan		5,000	
Current liabilities			
Accounts payable			
(creditors):			
Hall	850		
Dunn	395	1,245	
Total liabilities			6,245
Total equity and liabilities			27,755

To practice preparing a statement of financial position using the accepted format try the following activity.

Activity 5.15

TRIAL BALANCE AS AT 31 MARCH FOR R. BELL

	Dr	Cr
Capital		45,000
Premises	150,000	
Vehicles	22,000	
Loan		130,000
Profit		15,000
Accounts receivable	4,300	
Accounts payable		5,200
Inventory	9,800	
Bank	8,700	
Cash	400	
	195,200	195,200

Answer

The statement of financial position should be as follows:

STATEMENT OF FINANCIAL POSITION AS AT 31 MARCH FOR R. BELL

Assets		
Non-current assets		
Premises	150,000	
Vehicle	22,000	172,000
Current assets		
Inventory	9,800	
Accounts receivable	4,300	
Bank	8,700	
Cash	400	23,200
Total assets		195,200
Equity and liabilities		
Equity		
Capital	45,000	
Profit	15,000	60,000
Non-current liabilities		
Loan	130,000	
Current liabilities		
Accounts payable	5,200	
Total liabilities		135,200
Total equity and liabilities		195,200

Summary

This chapter has introduced you to the double entry system of accounting. Within it we:

▶ have identified the need for the system when a business has several transactions to account for

▶ saw that it was based upon the concept of duality

▶ have taken you through the workings of the ledgers

▶ have balanced them off

▶ have extracted a trial balance

▶ have learnt that the statement of comprehensive income was in fact part of the double entry system and that income and expense accounts were cleared by being transferred to the statement of comprehensive income, recognising that the concept of matching must be applied, and

▶ have illustrated the matching concept within the context of cost of sales.

The remaining balances in the ledgers then formed a statement of financial position at the end of the financial period. The two main statements extracted from all this double entry, the statement of comprehensive income and the statement of financial position, have also been written in what is regarded as a 'user friendly' manner, i.e. vertical format. The statement of financial position format also reflected the equation assets = equity + liabilities

All this has been rather 'long winded' and the accounts take time to enter up. However, practice makes perfect, so we have provided several questions below.

Key terms

double entry	ledger
account	balance off
credit transactions	trial balance
accounts payable	closing inventory account
accounts receivable	

Self-assessment questions

1 On 1.4.20X1 H. Britton commenced a business dealing in subaqua equipment. He paid £20,000 into the business bank account and the following transactions took place during the month of April.

1st	From previous owner bought shop £8,000, fixtures and fittings £5,000 and stock £4,000, paying by cheque £17,000	
2nd	Withdrew cash from bank for shop use	500
	Paid for stationery and other incidentals	175
3rd	Sold goods for cash	450
4th	Sold goods on credit to A. Britton	650
5th	Cash sales	250
	Wages paid in cash	160
8th	Bought goods for resale on credit from R. Sevier	950
	A. Britton returned faulty goods	100
9th	Cash sales	340
	Paid sundry expenses in cash	80
10th	Sold goods on credit to R. Sewell	440
11th	Returned goods to R. Sevier	230
12th	Cash sales	340
	Wages paid in cash	160
	Paid excess cash into bank	
15th	Sold goods on credit to S. Boatman	260
16th	Bought goods for resale from P. Ocean	1,500
17th	Paid cheque on account to R. Sevier	500
	Received cheque on account from A. Britton	400
18th	Cash sales	550
	Office expenses paid in cash	60
19th	Paid wages in cash	160
22nd	S. Boatman paid on account by cheque	50
	Paid P. Ocean by cheque	900
	Cash sales	850
24th	Wages paid in cash	160
	Office expenses paid in cash	50
	Withdrew cash for personal use	400
25th	Paid excess cash into bank account	

Inventory on hand 30 April cost £3,500

Required
(a) Record the above transactions in the ledger accounts of H. Britton, maintaining separate cash and bank accounts and separate accounts for returned goods.
(b) Balance off the ledger accounts as at 30 April and extract a trial balance.
(c) Prepare the statement of comprehensive income for the month ended 30 April and close off all revenue and expense accounts.
(d) Prepare a statement of financial position as at 30 April.

2 On 1.6.X1 D. Alex commenced a business dealing in IT software. He paid £50,000 into the business bank account and the following transactions took place during the first week of June.

1 June	Purchased premises for £25,000 from previous owner, including £6,000 for furniture and fittings
	Purchased inventory for £10,000 and further furniture and fittings £2,000
	All transactions above were completed by cheque

2 June	Withdrew cash from bank for shop use	400
	Paid for sundry incidentals	90
	Sold goods for cash	300
	Sold goods on credit to Roberts	100
3 June	Bought goods for resale on credit from Davids	600
	Sold goods for cash	550
4 June	Sold goods for cash	400
	Sold goods on credit to Richards	350
	Paid office expenses in cash	70
5 June	Received cheque from Roberts	60
	Paid cheque on account Davids	250
	Sold goods for cash	200
	Sold goods on credit Martin	480
	Bought goods for cash	250
	Paid all excess cash into bank	
6 June	Stock on hand at cost	9,500

Required

(a) Record the above transactions in the ledger accounts of D. Alex maintaining separate cash and bank accounts.

(b) Balance off the ledger accounts as at 5 June X1 and extract a trial balance.

(c) Prepare the statement of comprehensive income for the week ended 5 June X1 and close off all revenue and expense accounts.

(d) Prepare the statement of financial position as at 5 June X1.

3 Explain why businesses have a need for a system of double entry accounting/bookkeeping.

4 Complete the following:

The double entry system of accounting is based on the concept of ......

5 What is the accounting equation?

6 A debit balance b/d on a double entry account is:

(a) an asset or expense
(b) a liability or income?

7 Explain the need for a trial balance.

8 What types of errors will the trial balance not reveal?

9 The following trial balance has been extracted from the ledgers of Narn as at 31 March 200X.

	Dr (£)	Cr (£)
Sales		79,000
Purchases	32,000	
Inventory 1st April 200W	2,700	
Salaries and wages	15,600	

Heating and lighting	3,600	
Rent	10,400	
Other expenses	2,300	
Fixtures and fittings	5,600	
Vehicles	10,900	
Motor expenses	4,500	
Trade receivables	6,600	
Trade payables		5,700
Capital injection by Narn		15,000
Bank and cash	5,500	
	99,700	99,700

Required

Prepare the income statement and the balance sheet for Narn as at 31 March 200X given that inventory at 31 March 200X was £4,200.

10 In the trial balance given at question 9 the following issues were discovered.

▶ An item of sale had been correctly entered in the cash ledger but had been entered in the sales account as at £4,500 instead of £5,400.

▶ A debtor had been entered on the ledgers as owing £2,300 instead of £3,200. The sale had been correctly entered in the ledgers.

▶ The bookkeeper had failed to record an office expense of £450 in the ledger although the item had been entered in the cash account.

▶ The bookkeeper had debited £225 to the bank account instead of crediting it.

Required

Correct the trial balance of Narn as at 31 March 200X and redraw the income statement and balance sheet.

.

Chapter 8

The journal and correction of errors

In this chapter

We will learn of:	and will be able to:
■ the journal as an important book of prime entry	■ journalise transactions which have no other prime entry
■ the style of presenting journal entries	■ correct accounting errors
■ the Suspense account and correction of errors	■ place and eliminate a balance in a Suspense account

8.1 The need for a journal

We saw in Chapter 3 that postings to the ledgers are only made after transactions have been recorded in one of the books of prime entry. The books of prime entry met so far are the Cash Book in Chapter 2 and the various day books for sales, purchases and returns in Chapter 5.

For all non-cash transactions the prime entry was once made in a single book known as the *journal*. The word 'journal', in French, merely means a daily record or diary. However, as the number of transactions grew, specialised journals were needed to record the prime entry of transactions such as purchases, sales, and their returns. It is not uncommon to refer to them as Sales Journal, Purchases Journal and so on.

Today it is customary to regard the journal (or General Journal to distinguish it from the specialised ones) as a book of prime entry for first recording any transaction which cannot be recorded in the Cash Book or in any of the specialised journals.

Activity 8.1 The books of accounts

a) What are the books of prime entry you are familiar with so far and what is entered in each?

b) What are the main books of account and why are they referred to as that?

c) What are the subsidiary books of account and why are they so regarded?

8.2 Transactions usually journalised

The act of recording a transaction in a journal is referred to as journalising. The transactions which are journalised are those for which a specialised book of prime entry has not been set aside. A journal entry is prepared in order to show the account that has been debited, the account that has been credited and the reason for the transaction. As it is used for making entries in the ledgers it will also show the page (or folio) in the ledgers to which postings were made. It is important that each journal entry should be authorised by a responsible person because it is the means by which the ledger balances can be changed.

The transactions typically recorded in the (general) Journal include the following:

1. Opening entries made when starting a business
2. Acquisition or disposal of non-current assets on credit terms
3. Transfers between ledger accounts and the correction of errors
4. Year-end adjustments such as accounting for closing inventory (Chapter 6) and adjustments for accruals, pre-payments, depreciation and bad debts (Chapter 7)
5. Reversal of cash discount (we will meet this in Chapter 9)
6. Closing entries – i.e. either closing the nominal accounts when balances are transferred to the Income Statement to determine the profit or loss for the year or closing all the accounts when the business is closed down.

8.3 The style of presenting a journal entry

In accounting the word journalising means that there is an instruction from the accountant authorising entries to be made in the ledgers. In order to make the entries, information is required as to the date, the accounts to be debited and credited, the folios for cross-referencing the ledger accounts, the amounts and the reason for making the entries.

The following is an example journalising the acquisition of a motor vehicle on credit for £18,000 from Belgravia Garages:

Date	Voucher	Particulars		F	Debit	Credit
20X7					£	£
11.2	D721	Motor Vehicles a/c	Dr		18,000	–
		To Belgravia Garages a/c			–	18,000
		Being acquisition of a vehicle on three month credit term				

We can see from this that the Journal is another subsidiary book providing the information required for the double entry, e.g. to debit the Motor Vehicle account with £18,000 and credit the Belgravia Garages account.

Where the accounting for a single transaction involves more than a pair of ledger accounts, rather than making several journal entries, a *composite journal entry*, as shown below, may serve the purpose. Observe the use of the word sundries on the first line of the journal entry. This is because, if there is more than one account which has to be debited it is conventional to start the journal entry with the word 'sundries' and to identify the accounts that should be debited by naming them after naming the account to be credited. If the debits as well as the credits are to be made in more than one account, the first two lines of the journal entry conventionally will read Sundries Dr To Sundries.

		£	£
Sundries Dr			
To General Stores a/c		–	30,000
Furniture a/c		10,000	
Motor Vehicles a/c		15,000	
Computer a/c		5,000	
Being acquisition of assets			

We will now consider the first three of these types of transaction, namely, Opening entries made when starting a business, the acquisition or disposal of non current assets on credit terms and transfers between ledger accounts and the correction of errors.

8.4 Journal entries for opening new books of account

If a person commences business with his capital in the form of cash, the amount of cash would be recorded in the Cash account (the prime entry) and posted from there to the Capital account. If, on the other hand, the capital introduced includes non-cash assets then an entry is required in the Journal from which postings will be made to the ledgers.

Let us assume, for example, that Patrice Kemal started business on 1 January 20X7 and introduced capital consisting of cash £18,000 and furniture £10,000. The cash would be entered in the Cash Book and posted to the Capital account. The non-cash items would be recorded in a journal and the entry would be as follows:

Particulars	Folio/Page	Debit	Credit
Furniture Dr		£10,000	
To Capital			£10,000
Being assets introduced as Capital by Kemal			

If there is more than a single non-current asset, e.g. Kemal also brought in a car valued at £20,000, then practice varies in the way the journal entry is prepared. One way is to have a separate journal entry:

Particulars	Folio/Page	Debit	Credit
Motor car Dr		£20,000	
To Capital			£20,000
Being assets introduced as Capital by Kemal			

Alternatively there could be a composite entry:

Particulars	Folio/Page	Debit	Credit
Furniture Dr		£10,000	
Motor car		£20,000	
To Capital			£30,000
Being assets introduced as Capital by Kemal			

The Capital account would then appear as follows:

Capital account

			£
		Cash a/c	18,000
		Journal	30,000
			48,000

Having posted the cash from Cash account to the Capital account, the journal entry shown above is posted so that the Capital account reports the whole of the capital introduced.

Activity 8.2 The capital introduced consists of assets and a liability

Dave Porter commenced business introducing as capital his car valued at £30,000, furniture valued at £12,000, £25,000 in cash as well as a bank loan of £10,000.

Required: Prepare a journal entry for the capital introduced at commencement of business.

8.5 Journal entry to account for acquisition of an asset on credit terms

Non-current assets acquired on credit terms also need to be journalised to authorise the debit in the asset and the credit in the supplier's account. If the invoice for the asset acquired on credit terms is included in the Purchases Day Book, the credit entry will be made in the supplier's account (which is correct) but the debit entry will be made in the Purchases account (which is incorrect).

Activity 8.3 Acquisition of an asset on credit terms

a) Why is it an error to record the acquisition of an asset on credit terms in the Purchases Day Book?

b) Acquired from Electroplastics Ltd, on credit terms, a photo-copying machine for £80,000 and consumables such as toners and ribbons for £2,400. Show the prime entry for this transaction.

8.6 Journal entries for transfers between accounts

Bearing in mind that a journal entry will be used only for making a prime entry for transactions which cannot be entered in any other book of prime entry, let us inquire into the prime entry needed for the following transactions. Raymond, the Procurement Manager, left for Japan with £50,000, to buy a machine. Upon his return he refunds £2,300 along with the voucher shown on the right. The prime entries, both for cash paid to Raymond

	£'000
Cost of machine	38,500
Travel expenses	9,200
Cash refund	2,300

and cash refunded by him would be in the Cash Book. For clearing the remainder of the amount advanced to Raymond a journal entry, as shown on the right, is needed.

		£'000	£'000
Sundries	Dr		
To Raymond's advance		–	47,700
Machinery a/c		38,500	
Travel Expenses a/c		9,200	
Being transfers			

8.7 Correction of errors

An accounting entry, if wrong, is not allowed to be corrected by rubbing it out or using correcting fluid. Instead, any correction needs to follow the normal double entry rules with an appropriate debit and credit. The prime entry for such corrections is made in the Journal.

As we studied in Chapter 4.9, there are different types of accounting error. We shall now consider the Journal entry that may be needed to correct accounting errors:

8.7.1 Error of omission

An error of omission is where a transaction is not recorded at all in accounts. No journal entry would be required unless it related to the acquisition of a non-current asset which would normally be recorded in the Journal. If it were 'say' a purchase invoice, then the invoice would be simply entered into the Purchase Day Book and posted in the normal way.

8.7.2 Error of duplication

An error of duplication is where the same transaction has been entered twice. If the same invoice had been entered twice then a journal entry would be required. If a debtor has been debited twice because a copy invoice was entered into the Sales Day Book for the second time, then there would be need for a reversing entry crediting the debtor's account and debiting the Sales account.

It is important that this should be by a journal entry and properly authorised to avoid the risk that cash is being collected from the debtor and misappropriated with the misappropriation being concealed by a journal entry cancelling the debt.

8.7.3 Error of commission

An error of commission is where the correct amount is posted to an incorrect account of the same class – e.g. posting to Stationery account instead of Purchases account where both are expense accounts. This is a common error which can also occur when the wrong customer is debited, perhaps when customers have similar names, e.g. if a sale of £6,500 to Joe Nathan had been posted in error to Jim Nathan.

The correcting journal entry would be as follows:

Joe Nathan's a/c	Dr	£6,500	–
To Jim Nathan's a/c		–	£6,500
Being correction of error in posting			

The credit in Jim's account removes the error, while the debit in Joe's account makes him the debtor for the goods he has received.

8.7.4 Error of principle

An error of principle is where the correct amount is posted to an incorrect account of a different class – e.g. posting the cost of fuel to Motor Vehicles account – i.e. an expense being posted to an asset account and treated as capital expenditure. This affects both the Income Statement and Balance Sheet and, if material, could have a significant effect on the net profit for the year.

The journal adjustment is simply to transfer the balance from one account to another. For example, if the fuel cost has been debited to the Motor Vehicles account then the journal entry would be to debit Fuel account and credit the Motor Vehicles account. As this transfer affects the profit it is important that the journal entry should be properly authorised by a senior person.

Activity 8.4 Correction of error

An invoice for £24,000 from Carmart Ltd for an office vehicle has been entered in the Purchases Day Book.

Required: Set out the journal entry for correcting this error.

8.7.5 Entry error

An entry error is where a wrong amount is entered. Typical entry errors include the omission of a zero, e.g. £490 is entered as £49, and transposition errors, e.g. £490 is entered as £940.

These errors are corrected by a journal entry authorising a double entry into the ledgers. If, for example, an invoice for office supplies had been journalised as £49 rather than £490 then a journal entry would increase the amount entered in the Office Supplies account by debiting £441 and increase the amount in the creditor's account by crediting £441. It is important that such a journal entry is authorised by a responsible person to avoid the risk that a creditor is artificially created and then paid through the Cash Book for supplies that had not been received.

8.8 Alternative approaches to error correction

If the accounting error is more complicated than one which requires merely a transfer from one account to another, there are two alternative means of correction. To illustrate let us assume that a credit sale of £18,400 to Rick Jones has been entered as £8,400 in the Sales Journal (first error) and posted to Rob Jones (second error). The simplest way of correcting this error is first to reverse the incorrect entries recording the sale (making the first journal entry on the right) and then

Sales a/c	Dr	£8,400	
To Rob Jones a/c			£8,400
Being correction of error			

Rick Jones a/c	Dr	£18,400	–
To Sales a/c		–	£18,400
Being correction of error			

account for the sale correctly (see the second journal entry). A quicker way is to combine these two journal entries, focusing (see the third journal entry) on correcting the balances in each of the three accounts.

Rick Jones a/c	Dr	£18,400	–
To Rob Jones a/c		–	£8,400
Sales a/c		–	£10,000
Being correction of error			

8.9 The need for journal entries to be authorised

A journal entry could well be used to cover misappropriations. For example, having mis-appropriated the amount received from a customer, the balance in that customer's account could be transferred by a journal entry to either a nominal account (e.g. staff training) or to the account of another customer whose balance is to be written off as irrecoverable. Therefore, every journal entry requires to be authorised by a responsible manager.

8.10 Suspense account

8.10.1 Why is a Suspense account opened?

Suspense is associated with uncertainty. It might simply be that it is not clear where an item should be posted, e.g. cash might have been received but it is not clear at the time who has sent it and who should be credited and it would, therefore, be put into a Suspense account until this is known.

When the totals of the two sides of a trial balance are not equal and the reason for the inequality is uncertain, the trial balance is made to balance by inserting the amount of the difference in a *Suspense account*. The intention is to make the totals on either side of the trial balance equal when the newly set up Suspense account balance is also listed on it. When, upon detecting the cause (or probably causes) of the difference, the uncertainty is resolved, the amount placed in the Suspense account is transferred to the appropriate ledger account.

8.10.2 Accounting entries to set up and eliminate a Suspense account balance

A journal entry is required to place the difference in a Suspense account and a further journal entry when errors are detected and rectified and, as we will see, not all of them consist of a pair of matching debits and credits.

To illustrate, let us assume that a cheque for £300 received from customer Ted Smith had been entered in the Cash account but had not been posted to the customer's account. The result would be that the credit side of the Trial Balance would be £300 less than the debit side. To correct this imbalance, until its cause is investigated and remedied, £300 is placed on the credit side of a Suspense account which is then included in the list of credit balances in the Trial Balance. A posting is made to the Suspense account when authorised by the following journal entry:

To Suspense a/c		–	£300
Being trial balance difference placed in suspense			

This journal entry, unlike those met with so far, requires only a single credit entry to be made. This is because, if a matching debit entry is also made in another account, the trial balance will again become imbalanced. When, in due course, the cause of the imbalance (failure to post to the credit of the customer) is detected, a second journal entry is required authorising the transfer of the amount placed in the Suspense account to the credit of the customer Ted Smith's account:

Suspense a/c	Dr	£300	–
To Ted Smith's a/c		–	£300
Being correction of error			

A similar treatment is required if there are errors in the totals posted to the Nominal Ledger accounts. For example, let us assume that amounts recorded in the Sales Day Book have been overcast by £300 showing a total of £7,838 instead of £7,538 as follows:

Sales Day Book Date: 7th May 20X5			
Invoice	Customer	F	Amount
			£
G712	Sally Davies	L85	1,468
G713	Joe Brooks	L46	945
G714	Peter Folly	L68	3,250
G715	Mike Brown	L77	1,875
	Sales a/c	L12	7,838

We know from our double entry knowledge that this total would have been posted to the credit of the Sales account in the Nominal Ledger. As the individual invoices would have been posted to the debit of the four trade receivable accounts, it follows that when the total trade receivables figure is entered in the trial balance the total debits will be £300 less than the total credits. Until we have identified the error causing the imbalance on the Trial Balance, the difference of £300 is entered into the Trial Balance on the debit side to cause it to balance. The journal entry would be as follows:

Suspense a/c	Dr	£300	–
Being difference in trial balance placed in suspense			

8.10.3 Eliminating items from the Suspense account

When, in due course, the over-casting of the Sales Day Book is detected, another journal entry would be necessary to authorise the transfer of the debit balance from the Suspense account to the Sales account, closing the Suspense account and reducing to the correct amount (£7,538) the balance in the Sales account. The journal entry would be as follows:

Sales a/c	Dr	£300	–
To Suspense a/c		–	£300
Being correction of an overcast on folio xx of the Sales DB			

Activity 8.5 Placing and eliminating a balance in the Suspense account

A copy sales invoice to Jim Wallace for £24,000 has been posted to the customer's account as £42,000.

Required: Prepare journal entries to:
a) Place in a Suspense account the resulting difference in the trial balance.
b) Eliminate the Suspense account balance upon the error being detected and corrected.

8.11 What do we do if we are unable to identify the reason for the error?

Where there is a difference on the Trial Balance, it is necessary to obtain the information needed to complete the posting, e.g. the name of the debtor who sent the cheque. It is, in principle, unacceptable to include the Suspense account as an entry in the Income Statement or Balance Sheet. A Suspense account balance signals the existence of accounting errors and the failure to detect and correct them. Hence, financial reports such as the Income Statement and the Balance Sheet should not be prepared until the balance in a Suspense account has been cleared.

However, in rare circumstances, there may arise a need to present the financial reports while the Suspense account balance remains uncleared. In such circumstances a Suspense account balance, if a debit, may be reported among assets and, if a credit, included on the capital and liabilities side of the Balance Sheet. This is not, of course, a satisfactory situation and every step should be taken to clear the balance as quickly as possible.

The worst case scenario is when the Suspense account balance is transferred to the Income Statement by adding it to an expense, if a debit, or deducting from an expense, if a credit. This can result in anyone looking at the accounts being unaware that this has happened with the danger that, whilst the amount may appear insignificant in itself, it could be the net effect of several significant errors.

8.12 Recalculation of profits after correcting errors

Errors of commission, such as the one where sales were posted to a wrong customer, would not affect the profit or loss reported in the Income Statement or its overall financial position reported on the balance sheet. On the other hand, other errors, such as the failure to post a supplier's invoice to the creditor's account, will result in the liability being understated. Similarly, the over-casting of the Sales Day Book would have resulted in the sales (i.e. income) being over-stated. Hence, in such cases, when errors are detected and rectified, the reported performance and position will require amendment.

Activity 8.6 Correcting errors and recalculating profit

For the year ended 31st December 20X7 Tim Blunt reported a gross profit of £184,500 and a net profit of £79,800. The trial balance failed to balance and a Suspense account has been opened. Subsequently, the following accounting errors were detected:

1. A page in the Purchases Day Book had been added as £144,800, instead of £114,800.

2. £4,500 paid to Molly Poe, a trade creditor, has not been posted to her account.

3. Three months' rent of £6,000, remaining unpaid, has not been accounted for.

Required:
a) Set out the journal entries needed to correct the errors.
b) Show the Suspense account.
c) Calculate the revised gross profit and net profit for the year ended 31 December 20X7.

Summary

- The journal is another subsidiary book of accounts. It was once the only book of prime entry but is now used for making prime entry for any transaction which cannot be recorded in any other book of prime entry.

- A Suspense account would be unnecessary, unless the trial balance fails to balance but, should it become necessary, a journal entry is needed to set it up and another to eliminate it.

Suggested answers to activities

8.1 The books of account

a)
Prime entry books:	What they record:
Cash Book	All cash transactions
Purchases Day Book	Credit purchases
Sales Day Book	Credit sales
Purchases Returns Day Book	Returns of credit purchases
Sales Returns Day Book	Returns of credit sales
Journal	All other transactions

b) Main books of account:
Cash Book and the ledgers
These alone record transactions on double entry basis and hence these alone are listed in a trial balance.

c) Subsidiary books of account:
The four day books and the journal

8.2 Capital consists of assets

Sundries Dr	£	£
To Sundries		
Motor Vehicles a/c	30,000	–
Furniture a/c	12,000	–
Capital a/c	–	32,000
Bank Loan a/c	–	10,000
Being assets and liability introduced as capital		

8.3 Acquisition of an asset on credit terms

a) If the invoice for acquiring an asset is recorded in the Purchases Day Book, the individual entry will be posted to the credit of the supplier's account (which is correct); but the corresponding debit will be made in the Purchases account rather than the asset account. This is because the periodical total of the Purchases Day Book is debited to the Purchases account.

8.3 continued

b) Journal entry:

Sundries	Dr		
To Electroplastics Ltd a/c		–	£82,400
Office Equipment a/c		£80,000	–
Stationery a/c		£2,400	–
Being acquisition on credit terms of a photocopy machine and its software			

8.4 Correction of error

Motor Vehicles a/c	Dr	24,000	–
To Purchases a/c		–	£24,000
Being correction of error			

The invoice for £24,000, recorded in the Purchases Day Book would have been debited to the Purchases Account, and requires transfer to the Motor Vehicles account.

8.5 Placing and elimination of a Suspense account balance

a) To place the TB difference in Suspense

To Suspense a/c	–	£18,000
Being a credit shortfall in the Trial Balance placed in a Suspense account		

b) To eliminate the amount placed in suspense:

Suspense a/c	Dr	£18,000	–
To Jim Wallace a/c		–	£18,000
Being correction of error			

8.6 Correcting errors and recalculating profit

a) Journal entries:

1	Suspense a/c	Dr	£30,000	–
	To Purchases a/c		–	£30,000
	Being correction of error			
2	Molly Poe's a/c	Dr	£4,500	–
	To Suspense a/c		–	£4,500
	Being correction of error			
3	Rent a/c	Dr	£6,000	–
	To Rent Accrued a/c		–	£6,000
	Being correction of error			

b) Suspense Account

Journal 1	30,000	Balance b/f	25,500
		Journal 2	4,500
	30,000		30,000

c)

Impact on:	Gross profit	Net profit
As reported	£184,500	£79,800
Journal entry 1	£30,000	£30,000
Journal entry 2	–	–
Journal entry 3	–	(£6,000)
Revised profits	£214,500	£103,800

Multiple choice questions

Journal entries

8.1 Which of the following statements is incorrect? In the double entry accounting system maintained manually, a journal entry:

a) Should be substantiated by appropriate voucher and authorised at a proper level

b) Is needed only in the absence of other suitable book of prime entry for the transaction

c) Should always consist of a single debit entry matched by a corresponding credit entry

d) Should always have an explanation for the entries

8.2   The journal entry to account for the acquisition on credit of factory machinery from Millet plc should require which of the following?

a) Debit Machinery account, credit Cash account

b) Debit Factory account, credit Millet plc account

c) Debit Machinery account, credit Millet plc account

d) Debit Millet plc account, credit Machinery account

8.3   Iain Blake commenced business introducing as his capital furniture worth £21,000, a car valued at £30,000 and £48,000 in cash. The journal entry for recording this would require:

a) Debit in the Cash account, credit in the Capital account

b) Debit in the three asset accounts, including cash and a credit in the Capital account

c) Debit in the two asset accounts other than cash and a credit in the Capital account

d) No journal entries

8.4   The prime entry for the acquisition of a cash book, ledgers and a journal for £240 from W. Smith Ltd on credit would be in the:

a) Purchases Day Book

b) Journal

c) Cash Book

d) None of the above

Correction of errors

8.5   If an amount paid for servicing vehicles has been posted in error to Motor Vehicles account the journal entry necessary to correct this error should require which of the following?

a) Debit Cash account, credit Motor Vehicles account

b) Debit Vehicle Maintenance account, credit Motor Vehicles account

c) Debit Motor Vehicles account, credit Vehicle Maintenance account

d) Debit Vehicle Maintenance account, credit Cash account

8.6   A repayment of £15,000 has been posted to Jerry Blake's loan account, whereas £3,000 of this amount was paid as interest on the loan. To correct this error the journal entry would require:

a) Debit Interest on Loan account, credit Jerry Blake's Loan account with £3,000

b) Debit Interest on Loan account, credit Jerry Blake's Loan account with £15,000

c) Debit Cash account, credit Jerry Blake's Loan account with £3,000

d) Debit Jerry Blake's Loan account, credit Interest on Loan account with £3,000

8.7   If a credit sale of £15,400 to Peter Smith had been entered in the Sales Day Book as £14,500, the journal entry for correcting the error should require which of the following?

a) Debit Peter Smith's account, credit Sales account with £900

b) Debit Cash account, credit Sales account with £900

c) Debit Peter Smith's account, credit Sales account with £15,400

d) Debit Sales account, credit Peter Smith's account with £900

8.8   The invoice relating to the acquisition on credit of an office equipment for £24,500 from Globe Ltd was entered in the Purchases Journal. To correct this error which of the following needs to be done?

a) Journal entry: Debit Office Equipment a/c and credit Globe Ltd a/c with £24,500

b) Journal entry: Debit Globe Ltd a/c and credit Office Equipment a/c with £24,500

c) Journal entry: Debit Office Equipment a/c and credit Purchases a/c with £24,500

d) No journal entry is needed

8.9   A sale of £7,800 to Peter Blowes has been posted to Paul Blowes. To correct this the journal entry should require which of the following?

a) Debit Sales account, credit Paul Blowes account with £7,800

b) Debit Peter Blowes account, credit Sales account with £7,800

c) Debit Sales account, credit Paul Blowes with £15,600

d) Debit Peter Blowes account, credit Paul Blowes account with £7,800

8.10   Inquiries undertaken after the failure of the trial balance to balance revealed that the difference was wholly due to carrying down the Cash account balance of £74,800 as £47,800. No Suspense account was set up. To correct this error which of the following courses of action is necessary?

a) No journal entry: Debit Cash account with £27,000

b) Journal entry: Debit Cash account, credit Suspense account with £27,000

c) Journal entry: Debit Suspense account, credit Cash account with £27,000

d) Journal entry: Debit Cash account, credit Sales account with £27,000

8.11   A sale to Roy Rogers for £21,400 has been posted to the customer's account as £24,100. The trial balance failed to balance but the difference has not been placed in a Suspense account. The journal entry for correcting this error should require which of the following?

a) Debit Sales account, credit Roy Rogers' account with £2,700

b) Credit Roy Rogers' account with £2,700 (with no corresponding second entry)

c) Debit Suspense account, credit Roy Rogers' account with £2,700

d) Debit Roy Rogers' account, credit Suspense account with £2,700

Suspense account

8.12   Which of the following errors will cause the trial balance to fail to balance?

a) Recording a sales invoice for £5,600 as £6,500 in the Sales Journal

b) Failing to record a purchase invoice for £54,000 in the Purchases Journal

c) Recording in the Purchases Journal an invoice for acquiring an asset for £60,000

d) Adding up the Returns Inwards Journal as £11,400 instead of £12,600

8.13   Identify whether you agree (yes) or disagree (no) with the following definitions:

	x: yes	y: no
a) Error of omission – not entered in any book of prime entry		
b) An entry error – wrong amount entered in the appropriate book of prime entry		
c) Duplication error – a transaction entered twice in a book of prime entry		
d) Error of commission – posted to the correct side of the wrong account of same class		
e) Error of principle – posted to the correct side of the wrong account of another class		
f) Double entry error – not posted or posted to the wrong side		
g) Transposition error – figures in an amount switched around when entering/posting		
h) Compensating error – an error which does not disturb the trial balance		

8.14 Which of the following will disturb the balancing of the trial balance?

   a) Entering a wrong amount in a book of prime entry

   b) Posting to an asset account instead of an expense account

   c) Entering an acquisition of an asset, on credit terms, in the Purchases Day Book

   d) Error in adding up a book of prime entry

8.15 If the only accounting error is each of those stated below, identify the amount of the trial balance difference which will be placed in a Suspense account:

   a) A page in the Purchases Journal was added as £34,680, instead of £36,480

x	Dr 3,640
y	Cr 1,800
z	Dr 1,800

   b) £4,200 paid to solicitors for conveyancing a property has been written off as legal expenses instead of being added to the cost of the property

x	Dr 4,800
y	None
z	Cr 2,400

   c) £2,400, being the pre-paid portion of insurance, was brought forward from the previous year as a credit balance in the nominal account

x	Dr 4,800
y	None
z	Cr 2,400

   d) £218,400 paid to a supplier has been posted to the supplier's account as £214,800

x	Cr 3,600
y	Dr 3,600
z	Dr 218,400

   e) A sale of £13,600 was recorded in the Sales Journal as £3,600 and posted to Guy Bernard, the customer, as £6,300

x	Dr 2,700
y	Dr 12,700
z	Cr 2,700

   f) The recovery of staff loan by deducting from salary at the rate of £300 per month for nine months in the year, has not been accounted for

x	Cr 2,700
y	Dr 2,700
z	None

   g) The year-end trial balance records the balance of £116,200 in the Sales Returns account as a credit balance

x	Dr 116,200
y	Dr 232,400
z	Cr 232,400

8.16 In each of the following questions the difference in trial balance has been placed in a Suspense account. If the only error subsequently detected is the one identified below, the correcting journal entry should require:

   a) An invoice for £16,500 from Ken Bros, for goods purchased for sale, was not posted to Ken Bros' account.

      w) Debit Purchases account, credit Ken Bros with £16,500

      x) Debit Purchases account, credit Ken Bros with £33,000

      y) Debit Ken Bros, credit Suspense account with £16,500

      z) Debit Suspense account, credit Ken Bros with £16,500

b) £12,500 received from customer Sally Peter was posted to the debit of her account.

   w) Debit Suspense account, credit Cash account with £12,500

   x) Debit Suspense account, credit Sally Peter's account with £12,500

   y) Debit Sally Peter's account, credit Cash account with £12,500

   z) Debit Suspense account, credit Sally Peter's account with £25,000

c) Cash book balance of £132,600 has been carried forward from one folio to the next as £123,600

   w) Journal entry: Debit Cash account, credit Suspense account with £123,600

   x) Journal entry: Debit Cash account, credit Suspense account with £9,000

   y) Journal entry: Debit Suspense account, credit Cash account with £9,000

   z) No journal entry: Debit Cash account, credit Suspense account with £9,000

d) Pre-paid rent of £12,000 has been brought down as a credit balance in the Rent account

   w) Debit Rent account with £24,000

   x) Debit Suspense account, credit Rent account with £24,000

   y) Debit Rent account, credit Suspense account with £12,000

   z) Debit Rent account, credit Suspense account with £24,000

e) A sale of £4,200 to David Smith was recorded in the Sales Journal as £2,400 and posted to Derek Smith as £240.

   w) Debit Derek, credit David £4,200

   x) Debit David £4,200, credit Sales £1,800, credit Derek £240, credit Suspense £2,160

   y) Debit Sales £2,400, debit David £2,160, credit Suspense £2,160, credit Sales £1,800

   z) Debit David £2,400, debit Suspense £2,160, credit Sales £2,400, credit Derek £240

f) A credit note for £640 issued to a customer Alex Bell has been recorded in the Return Inwards Journal as £460 and posted to the debit of Alex Bell's account.

   w) Debit Return inwards £180, debit Suspense £460, credit Alex Bell £640

   x) Debit Suspense £920, debit Return inwards £180, credit Alex Bell £1,100

   y) Debit Return Inwards £640, debit Suspense £460, credit Alex Bell £1,100

   z) Debit Suspense £920, debit Return Inwards £180, credit Alex Bell £1,100

g) A cheque for £4,650 drawn in the name of Phil Sawyer, a supplier, has been recorded in the Cash Book as £465, but not posted to Phil's account.

   w) Debit Phil Sawyer £4,650 to Suspense account £4,650

   x) Debit Phil Sawyer £465, credit Suspense £465 (£4,185 will be posted from the Cash Book)

   y) Debit Phil Sawyer £4,650, credit Cash Book £4,185, credit Suspense account £465

   z) Debit Phil Sawyer £4,650, debit Suspense account £465, credit Cash Book £5,115

8.17 The difference in the year-end trial balance was placed in a Suspense account. Subsequent inquiries revealed the following errors.

i) Sales account total has been added as £128,500 instead of £138,500

ii) Return inwards of £3,200 was not posted to the customer

iii) Carriage inwards amounting to £6,500 was listed as a credit balance

Upon correction of all of them the Suspense account was fully eliminated. What was the amount placed in suspense?

a	£200 Dr	
b	£200 Cr	
c	£6,700 Dr	
d	£6,700 Cr	

8.18 Credit side of the trial balance was £11,200 lower than the debit side. The difference was placed in Suspense. The correction of which of the following errors will reduce the Suspense account balance?

a) A cash sale of £3,400 has been posted as £4,300

b) A credit purchase of £2,150 has not been posted to the customer

c) Stationery acquired on credit terms for £340 has been recorded in the Purchases Journal

d) A credit note for £900 from a supplier has not been entered in Returns Outwards Day Book

The impact of error corrections on performance and position

8.19 An invoice of £54,500 for goods was posted to the supplier's account as £5,450. The resulting difference in trial balance was placed in a Suspense account and then adjusted with Sundry expenses account. The impact of correcting this would be:

	Gross profit	Net profit	Net assets	
a	−£54,500	−£54,500	−£54,500	
b	−	−£49,050	−£49,050	
c	−£56,400	−£49,050	+£49,050	
d	−£49,050	−£49,050	+£49,050	

8.20 £12,000 received from a credit customer was posted to the debit of the customer's account. The resultant difference in the trial balance was placed in a Suspense account and then that balance transferred to Sundry expenses. The impact of correction would be:

	Gross profit	Net profit	Net assets	
a	−	−£24,000	−£24,000	
b	−£12,000	−£12,000	−£12,000	
c	+£12,000	+£12,000	+£12,000	
d	−£24,000	−£24,000	−£24,000	

8.21 When reporting the profit and year-end position for 20X5 a business did not take into account:

i) Cost of goods lost by fire £56,400

ii) Related insurance claim admitted at £45,000

The impact of correcting these errors would be:

	Gross profit	Net profit	Net assets	
a	+£56,400	+£56,400	+£56,400	
b	−	+£45,000	+£45,000	
c	+£56,400	+£45,000	+£45,000	
d	+£56,400	−£11,400	+£45,000	

8.22 After financial statements for 20X5 were prepared it is discovered that credit notes for £4,000 issued by suppliers have not been accounted for. The impact of correcting this error would be:

	Gross profit	Net profit	Net assets	
a	−	−£4,000	−£4,000	
b	+£4,000	−	−£4,000	
c	+£4,000	+£4,000	+£4,000	
d	−£4,000	−£4,000	−£4,000	

8.23 When reporting the performance for 20X6 and its position at the end, a business failed to take account of £45,000 for goods removed by the owner and building depreciation of £18,000. The impact of correcting these errors would be:

	Gross profit	Net profit	Net assets	
a	+£45,000	+£27,000	+£18,000	
b	−£45,000	−£63,000	−£63,000	
c	+£63,000	+£45,000	+£45,000	
d	+£63,000	+£63,000	+£63,000	

General

8.24 The working capital (or net current assets) of a business is:

    a) The capital introduced by the proprietor at commencement of business

    b) Current assets less current liabilities

    c) Capital plus liabilities which are not expected to be paid within a year of the balance sheet date

    d) Non-current assets plus current assets less current liabilities

8.25 Which of the following statements is correct? If a business acquires a vehicle for £36,000, making a down payment of £15,000 and undertaking to pay the remainder a year later:

    a) Net assets will increase by £36,000

    b) Net assets will increase by £21,000

    c) Net assets will not change

    d) Net assets will decrease by £21,000

8.26 If, as at the commencement of an accounting period, the account named below has a balance as stated in respect of each, what would that balance represent:

Amount payables	Amount receivable	Unused expense
x	y	z

    a) Trade Creditors account – a credit balance

    b) Rent account – a debit balance

    c) Stationery account – a debit balance

    d) Accrued Expenses account – credit balance

    e) Insurance account – debit balance

    f) Trade Debtors account – a debit balance

    g) Salaries account – a credit balance

    h) Rent Receivable account – debit balance

    i) Staff Loan account – a debit balance

8.27 Which of the following should be the first action when making a prime entry for a transaction?

    a) Enter the transaction in the appropriate book of prime entry

    b) Decide on the ledger account to be debited and the one to be credited

    c) Post the transactions to the appropriate ledger accounts

    d) Study the voucher to identify the nature of the transaction

8.28 The amount paid by a business as premium on the owner's life insurance is accounted as:

    a) Debit Drawings account, credit Cash account

    b) Debit Insurance account, credit Cash account

    c) Debit Capital account, credit Cash account

    d) Debit Insurance account, credit Accruals account

8.29 Shown on the right is an extract of the year-end trial balance. At which of the following points of the accounting process has the trial balance been extracted?

	Debit	Credit
Machinery a/c	£580,000	–
Provision for depreciation	–	£312,600
Depreciation a/c	£84,200	–

a) At the beginning of the accounting period ☐

b) On the last day of the accounting period prior to making any year-end adjustments ☐

c) On the last day of the accounting period prior to writing off depreciation for the year ☐

d) On the last day of the accounting period after writing off depreciation for the year ☐

8.30 When the trial balance extracted from the books of Kevin Enterprises at the year-end failed to balance, the difference was placed in a Suspense account. Identify the amount that would have been placed in suspense as a result of each of the following errors:

x	y	z

a) A folio in the Purchases Journal has been under-cast by £1,800

Dr 3,640	Cr 1,800	Dr 1,800

b) £4,200 paid for conveyancing has been written off instead of capitalising

Dr 4,800	None	Cr 2,400

c) £2,400 pre-paid insurance has been brought forward from the previous year as a credit balance.

Dr 4,800	None	Cr 2,400

d) £218,400 paid to a supplier was posted to the supplier as £214,800

Dr 3,600	Cr 3,600	Dr 218,400

e) A sale of £13,600 was recorded in the Sales Journal as £3,600 and posted to the customer's account as £6,300

Cr 2,700	Dr 2,700	Dr 12,700

f) The recovery of staff loan at £300 per month for nine months in the year has not been accounted for

None	Cr 2,700	Dr 2,700

Answers to multiple choice questions

8.1: c   8.2: c   8.3: c   8.4: b   8.5: b   8.6: a   8.7: a   8.8: c   8.9: d   8.10: a   8.11: b   8.12: d   8.13a: x   8.13b: x   8.13c: x
8.13d: x   8.13e x   8.13f: x   8.13g: x   8.13h: x   8.14: d   8.15a: z   8.15b: y   8.15c: x   8.15d: y   8.15e: z   8.15f: z   8.15g: y
8.16a: z   8.16b: z   8.16c: z   8.16d: z   8.16e: x   8.16f: x   8.16g: x   8.17: b   8.18: b   8.19: b   8.20: a   8.21: d   8.22: c
8.23: a   8.24: b   8.25: c   8.26a: x   8.26b: z   8.26c: z   8.26d: x   8.26e: z   8.26f: y   8.26g: x   8.26h: y   8.26i: y   8.27: d
8.28: a   8.29: d   8.30a: z   8.30b: y   8.30c: x   8.30d: x   8.30e: x   8.30f: x

Progressive questions

PQ 8.1 Opening the books of a retail outlet

Sheila West commenced a retail outlet introducing as part of her capital furniture worth £36,000, motor vehicle £24,000, inventory £48,000 and cash £4,000. She expects the business to also take over her bank loan of £12,000.

Required: Set out the prime entry for accounting for this transaction.

PQ 8.2 Correction of errors

The audit of the books of Collin Drake, a dealer in word processors, during the year to 30th April 20X7 revealed the following errors and omissions:

i)   A sale invoiced to Sue Robert at £14,200 was recorded in the Sales Journal as £12,400.

ii) A purchase invoice of £16,450 from Tex Bros was omitted from the Purchases Journal.

iii) An invoice of £400, again from Tex Bros but this time for stationery, was listed in the Purchases Journal.

iv) £11,500 received in respect of a debt written off in the previous year, was credited to the Sales account.

v)   £16,000 paid on 1st August 20X5 for office equipment was posted to the Stationery account. Such equipment is usually depreciated at 10% per annum using the straight-line method.

vi) Included in Rent and Rates account is £2,000 paid as property tax on Collin's private residence.

Required: Set out the journal entries necessary to rectify each of the above errors.

PQ 8.3 Impact of error corrections on reported profit

The draft financial statements of Collin Drake, prior to detection and correction of the errors stated in PQ (8.2), reported, for the year ended 30th April 20X7, a gross profit of £976,800 and a net profit of £172,400.

Required: Identify the impact the correction of errors would have on these figures.

PQ 8.4 More correction of errors

The following accounting errors were detected in the course of the annual audit:

i)   £16,000, the cost of furniture acquired for office use from Smiths Ltd, has been recorded in the Purchases Day Book.

ii) £1,050 paid for servicing vehicles has been posted to Motor Vehicles account.

iii) £6,400 received from Bob Martin, a credit customer, has been posted in error to the Sales account

iv) A sale of £9,400 to Joe Budd has been recorded in the Sales Journal as £4,900 and posted to Jill Budd.

Required: Set out journal entries necessary for correcting the errors.

PQ 8.5 Journal entries to account for transactions

During the year ended 30th June 20X7 Jeremy Transport Ltd entered into the following transactions:

i)   Bob Salmon, a customer experiencing cash flow problems, hands in his vehicle valued at £15,000 in part settlement of the amount of £18,000 due from him. The company agreed to waive the remainder of the debt.

ii) £12,000 was paid to repair a vehicle. It was agreed that 50% of the cost of repair should be deducted from the salary of the foreman whose negligence had caused the damage. Accordingly, from November 20X6, for eight months the foreman was paid a salary of £2,400 per month instead of £3,000 per month. The part recovery of the repair bill and the amount yet to be recovered need to be accounted for.

iii) A vehicle acquired at a cost of £28,000 and written down to £15,000 was taken over by the owner for personal use.

Required: Set out the journal entry necessary to account for each of the above transactions.

PQ 8.6 Trial balance difference placed in a Suspense account (1)

When the trial balance extracted from the books of Darwin Stores on 31st March 20X7 failed to balance, the difference was placed in a Suspense account. Subsequent inquiries confirm the imbalance to have arisen because of the following errors:

i)   A sale of £9,600 to Sally Brown was not posted to the customer.

ii) A monthly total of the Return Inwards Journal had been posted to the nominal account as £12,400 instead of £21,400.

iii) A credit note issued for £1,200 to Peter Collins, a customer, recorded in the Return Inwards Journal has been posted to the debit of the customer's account.

iv) The balance of £4,250 in the Return Outwards account was stated in the trial balance as a debit balance.

Required:
a) The journal entries for correcting the errors.
b) The Suspense account.
c) Explain how you dealt with error (iv).

PQ 8.7 Trial balance difference placed in a Suspense account (2)

The trial balance extracted from the books of City Grocers on 31.3.20X7, failed to balance. The difference was placed in a Suspense account. Since then the following errors have been detected:

i)   A folio in the Purchases Day Book has been cast as £214,600 instead of £213,400.

ii)   £800 paid to Lal Jason, a supplier, has not been posted to his personal account.

iii) A daily total in the Sales Returns Day Book of £1,700 was not posted to the nominal account.

iv)   £120 paid for stationery was posted to Office Equipment account.

v)   £4,000 paid as rent was posted as £400.

vi)   £360 paid for advertising was posted as £630.

vii) £3,000 received from Mike Shane, a customer, was posted to the debit side of his personal account.

viii) £4,200, the total of Return Outwards Day Book was debited to the Sales Returns account in the nominal ledger.

ix)   A sale of £6,250 to Joe Rogers was recorded as £2,650 and posted to Jill Rogers as £265.

x)   Pre-paid rent amounting to £6,000 was brought forward from the previous year as a credit balance in the nominal account.

xi)   Accrued rent amounting to £3,000 at the year-end is reported in the trial balance as a debit balance.

xii) A balance of £3,000 in the Commission received account is not listed in the trial balance.

Required:
a) Set out the journal entries necessary for correcting each error.
b) On the basis that the correction of the above errors eliminates the whole balance placed in suspense, show the Suspense account.

PQ 8.8 Correcting errors through the Suspense account

Subsequent investigation reveals the following points.

i)   An office computer was purchased for £1,500 during the year and was debited to the Purchase account rather than an Office Equipment account. No depreciation is to be charged on the computer in its first year in the business.

ii)   An invoice for goods received from a supplier Easy Ltd, for £800 has been mislaid and no entry has been made.

iii) A payment of £220 for sundry expenses has been entered correctly in the Cash Book but posted as £20.

iv)   The total of the Purchases Returns Journal of £1,000 has not been posted to the Nominal Ledger. Correct entries have been made in the individual accounts in the Sales Ledger.

v)   £500 received from a customer, has been correctly entered In the Cash Book but has not been posted.

Patrick has produced the following draft trial balance as at 31 March 20X7:

	£	£
Sales		47,200
Purchases	11,600	
Opening inventory	1,800	
Sundry expenses	6,200	
Motor vehicle	4,300	
Accum. depn – vehicle		2,600
Receivables & payables	3,600	2,000
Cash at bank & in hand	400	
Capital		7,300
Premises	28,000	
Suspense a/c	3,200	
	59,100	59,100

vi) The total of the Sales Returns Journal of £3,200 has not been posted to the General Ledger but correct entries have been made in the individual accounts in the Sales Ledger.

vii) £1,300 paid to a supplier, correctly entered in the Cash Book, has not been posted.

viii) The cost of inventory as at 31 March 20X7 was £2,400.

ix) Equipment is to be depreciated by £300 and Motor vehicles by £400. Ignore depreciation of premises.

Required: (a) Journal entries to correct the errors (b) Show the Suspense account (c) Income Statement for the year ended 31 March 20X7 and (d) Balance Sheet as at that date.

PQ 8.9 A question from AAT

When Debbie Brown extracted her trial balance at March 2007 she found that it did not agree. She opened a Suspense account, prepared her Income Statement and drew up her Balance Sheet as stated on the right. Subsequent checking of her records revealed the following errors which when corrected eliminated the Suspense account:

i) A cheque for £260 for acquiring a new display stand on 31st March 2007 has been entered correctly in the Cash Book but posted to Shop Fittings account as £200.

ii) A credit note from XY Ltd for £60 has been entered in the Return Outwards Day Book but posted to XY's account as £66.

iii) Bank charges £21 appearing in the Cash Book is not posted.

iv) An invoice for £139 for sales to Thompson, correctly entered in the Sales Day Book, was posted to Thompson as £193.

v) A debit balance of £223 in Smith's account at 31.3.2007 was carried down as £253 and included in the trial balance at that figure.

Required:
a) Journal entries necessary to correct the errors.
b) The Suspense account.
c) Statement of revised profit for the year.
d) The corrected balance sheet as at 31st March 2007.

Balance sheet as at 31 March 2007		
	£	£
Non-current assets:		
Shop fittings	1,500	
Accum depn	(300)	1,200
Delivery van	3,200	
Accum depn	(800)	2,400
Current assets:		
Inventory	2,917	
Trade receivables	2,154	
Cash and bank	1,223	6,294
Total assets		9,894

	£	£
Capital 1 April 2006	7,500	
Profit for the year	5,497	
Drawings	(5,000)	7,997
Trade payables		1,888
Suspense a/c		9
		9,894

PQ 8.10 A question from CIMA

After calculating net profit for the year ended 31 March 20X7 WL has the following trial balance:

A Suspense account was opened for the difference in the trial balance. Immediately after the production of the trial balance the following errors were detected:

	£	£
Land and building at cost	10,000	–
Building – depreciation at 31.3.20X7	–	2,000
Plant at cost	12,000	
Plant – depreciation at 31.3.20X7	–	3,000
Inventory	2,500	–
Trade receivables	1,500	–
Bank	8,250	–
Trade payables	–	1,700
Rent pre-paid	400	–
Wages accrued	–	300
Capital a/c	–	19,400
Profit for the year ended 31 March 20X7	–	9,750
	34,650	36,150

i) A Payables account had been debited with £300 sales invoice (which had been correctly recorded in the Sales account).

ii) The Heat and Light account had been credited with £150 paid for gas.

iii) G. Gordon has been credited with a cheque for £800 received from another customer G. Goldman.

iv) The Insurance account contained a credit entry for insurance pre-paid of £500, but the balance had not been carried down and was hence omitted from the above trial balance.

v) Purchase Returns had been over-cast by £700.

Required:
a) Prepare journal entries to correct each of the above errors.
b) Open the Suspense account at 31 March 20X7 and enter the relevant corrections.
c) Recalculate the net profit for the year to 31 March 20X7.
d) Prepare a revised balance sheet as at 31 March 20X7.

PQ 8.11 A question from ACCA

Chi Knitwear Ltd is an old-fashioned firm with a handwritten set of books. A trial balance is extracted at the end of each month, and an Income Statement and a balance sheet are computed. This month, however, the trial balance will not balance, the credits exceeding the debits by £1,536. You are required to help and after inspection of the ledgers discover the following errors:

i) A balance of £87 on a customer's account has been omitted from the schedule of debtors, the total of which was entered as Trade receivables in the trial balance.

ii) A small piece of machinery purchased for £1,200 had been written off to repairs.

iii) The receipt side of the Cash Book had been undercast by £720.

iv) The total of one page of the Sales Day Book had been carried forward as £8,154, whereas the correct amount was £8,514.

v) A credit Note for £179 received from a supplier has been posted to the wrong side of his account.

vi) An electricity bill for the sum of £152, not yet accounted for, is discovered in a filing tray.

vii) Mr Smith, whose past debts to the company had been the subject of an allowance for doubtful debts, at last paid £731 to clear his account. His personal account has been credited but his cheque has not yet passed through the Cash Book.

Required:
a) Write up the Suspense account.
b) Set out the journal entries correcting the errors.

PQ 8.12 A trader with rental income

Jill Grey operates the Town Shop from premises leased for ten years from 1.1.20X3 paying £200,000 for the period. The upper floors of the premises contain two flats. Jill occupies one and has let out the other at £250 per week. She has also invested cash surplus to immediate requirements in Savings Certificates.

The year-end trial balance of the shop appears as shown on the right. You are informed as follows:

i)   Inventory taken on 7th January 20X8 reveals the cost of unsold goods in hand as £282,000 and unused stationery as £3,000. During the seven days after 31 December 20X7 purchases amounted to £11,000, sales (at cost plus 40%) amounted to £28,000, and stationery has been acquired for £1,000.

ii) A debt of £8,000 is to be written off and the allowance for doubtful debts adjusted to cover 10% of the amount outstanding.

iii) Salary and electricity of £18,000 and £3,000, respectively, remain unpaid as at 31 December 20X7.

iv) Jill estimates that a tenth of the cost of the lease may be allocated to each flat and depreciates furniture at 10% per annum using the reducing balance method.

v)   One third of the cost of electricity and gas is to be recovered from Jill.

vi) Interest of £4,000 earned on savings certificates is yet to be accounted for.

Required: Prepare the Income Statement for the year ended 31 December 20X7 and the Balance Sheet as at that date.

Trial Balance as at 31.12.20X7		
	£'000	£'000
Lease of shop premises	120	–
Furniture at cost	200	–
Depreciation – 31.12.20X6	–	30
Inventory – 31.12.20X6	248	–
Sales	–	1,424
Investments (saving certificates)	45	–
Electricity & gas	21	–
Rent received a/c	–	15
Postage & telephone	14	–
Purchases	987	–
Receivables & Payables	148	267
Salaries	302	–
Advertising	44	–
Stationery	16	–
Allowance for doubtful debts	–	11
6% Loan from Jack Grey	–	300
Carriage inwards	24	–
Capital a/c	–	200
Cash & bank balance	78	–
	2,247	2,247

PQ 8.13 Elimination of the Suspense account to finalise accounts

The trial balance stated on the right was extracted from the books of Joe's Retail on the last day of its accounting period, having placed in a Suspense account the amount by which it failed to balance. Subsequent inquiries revealed the following:

i)   A page of the Sales Journal was under-cast by £30,000.

ii) Goods included in purchases at £24,000 were not included in the inventory because they remained in transit on the day of the count.

iii) £12,000 paid as sales commission was posted as £21,000.

iv) One month's rent of £3,000, pre-paid as at 1st July 20X6, has been brought forward in the Rent account as a credit balance.

v)   Salary and rent amounting to £36,000 and £6,000, respectively, remain unpaid as at 30th June 20X7.

vi) Goods costing £16,000 removed by Joe for his own use have not been accounted for.

Required:

a) Journal entries to correct the errors and making adjustments.

b) The Income Statement for the year ended 30th June 20X7 and the Balance Sheet as at that date.

Trial Balance as at 30.6.20X7		
	£'000	£'000
Non-current assets	2,460	–
Accum depn	–	1,640
Depreciation	369	–
Rent	24	–
Salaries	476	–
Sales	–	2,872
Cash & bank	133	–
Inventory – 30.6.20X7	416	–
Sales commission	78	–
Receivable/payables	396	509
Cost of sales	1,708	–
Advertising	84	–
Drawings	115	–
Telephone/postage	28	–
Stationery	17	–
Capital	–	1,250
Suspense a/c	–	33
	6,304	6,304

PQ 8.14 Post Balance Sheet elimination of Suspense account balance

Mackie Stores proceeded to finalise its accounts for the year ended 31.12.20X7, by placing the difference in the trial balance in a Suspense account and reporting the Suspense account balance on the balance sheet which appears as shown on the right. Since then the auditors have been able to detect the following errors:

i) £17,000, being the cost of goods returned to suppliers, was posted to the credit of the supplier's account.

ii) £24,000 paid for advertising has been posted as £42,000.

iii) £58,000 paid to suppliers had not been posted.

iv) £48,000 paid for carriage inwards was posted to carriage outwards account.

v) £14,000, being the cost of goods removed for personal use by the proprietor, has not been accounted for.

Mackie Stores has reported a gross profit of £758,000 for the year ended 31st December 20X7.

Balance Sheet as at 31.12.20X7			
	Cost	Depn	£'000
Non-current assets	640	(280)	360
Current assets:			
Inventory		546	
Trade receivables		396	
Suspense a/c		74	
Cash & bank		54	1,070
			1,430

	£'000	£'000
Capital	750	
Net profit for the year	198	
Drawings	(50)	898
Current liabilities:		
Trade payables	498	
Accrued expenses	34	532
		1,430

Required:
a) Set out the journal entries to rectify the errors detected by the auditors, bearing in mind that Income Statement has been prepared already.
b) Ascertain the corrected gross profit and net profit for the year ended 31st December 20X7.
c) Set out the amended balance sheet as at 31st December 20X7.

SECTION 4
THE FINAL ACCOUNTS OF SOLE TRADERS

Non-current (fixed) assets

REAL WORLD CASE

New stores

During the period we opened ten stores adding 37,000 square feet of net retail space. Two stores were relocated. At the period end, total selling space was 562,000 square feet (2004: 525,000 square feet), of which 33,750 square feet opened in the 26 weeks to 29 January 2005. Ottakar's traded from 131 stores at the period end. Of these, 38 stores covering 280,000 square feet are in our Lifestyle format which includes a coffee shop, and comprises some 50% of our total selling space – a net increase of three stores (2004: 35 stores covering 260,700 square feet).

Former Hammicks stores

In April 2003 we acquired 24 stores from Hammicks Bookshops Limited. We have now traded for a full year from these stores and we are pleased with their progress. Sales and gross margins are growing to an expected level as buying practices and product sales mix become integrated with the rest of the business.

Current strategy

At the period end, Ottakar's traded from 131 branches nationwide and is the UK's second largest specialist chain behind Waterstone's. The book market is undergoing considerable change with the expansion of specialist chains such as Ottakar's and established penetration by the supermarkets and the Internet. The market is valued at some £2.5bn (source: Book Marketing Limited) and Ottakar's believes it has an 8% share of this market. The market is growing at an annualised rate of 3 to 5% (source: Book Marketing Limited) spurred on by a new level of consumer interest in books galvanised by film and other media. Over the years Ottakar's will continue to pursue its PRISM strategy comprising physical expansion, range development, innovation, staff welfare and margin growth.

Consolidated balance sheet

	Note	29 January 2005 £000	31 January 2004 Restated £000
Fixed assets			
Intangible assets	10	**674**	722
Tangible assets	11	**33,882**	30,552

Notes to the financial statements

	Freehold Land and Buildings £000	Short Leasehold Land and Buildings £000	Fixtures and Fittings £000	Office Equipment £000	Motor Vehicles £000	Total £000
Net book value						
At 29 January 2005	–	**4,832**	**23,310**	**5,733**	**7**	**33,882**
At 31 January 2004	367	5,178	19,741	5,262	4	30,552

Source: Ottakar's Annual Report 2005, pp. 5, 8, 25, 34.

Discussion point

1 Why is it important for the company to give descriptive information about the investment in fixed assets?

2 What is the largest fixed asset category by net book value?

Contents

Learning outcomes

After studying this chapter you should be able to:

- Define a non-current (fixed) asset and apply the definition.
- Explain the recognition conditions that are applied to tangible non-current (fixed) assets, intangible non-current (fixed) assets and non-current (fixed) asset investments.
- Explain users' needs for information about non-current (fixed) assets.
- Describe and explain the non-current (fixed) asset information provided in annual reports of companies.
- Evaluate the usefulness of published information about non-current (fixed) assets.
- Explain the nature of depreciation.
- Calculate depreciation, record the effect on the accounting equation and report the result in financial statements.

Additionally, for those who choose to study the Supplement:

- Record non-current (fixed) assets and depreciation in ledger accounts.

8.1 Introduction

If you have progressed through Chapters 1 to 7 you are now familiar with the accounting equation and the analysis of transactions or events using that equation. You know what is meant by the terms asset, liability, revenue, expense and ownership interest. You are aware of the structure of the primary financial statements and the way in which they seek to provide information which is relevant and reliable.

This chapter starts a new phase of the text which will help you to develop a critical awareness of some of the component items in the financial statements. Chapters 8 to 12 progress through the main sections of the balance sheet. Inevitably, they also cover relevant aspects of the income statement (profit and loss account) and the cash flow statement because transactions involving the balance sheet will sometimes have an effect in the other financial statements.

It is important at this stage not to become so enthusiastic for the intricacies of accounting procedures as to lose sight of the importance of user needs, which were set out in Chapter 1. That chapter set out, in section 1.2, the structure of most conceptual frameworks, which provides a sequence for each of Chapters 8 to 12, as follows:

- What are the principles for defining and recognising these items?
- What are the information needs of users in respect of the particular items?
- What information is currently provided by companies to meet these needs?
- Does the information show the desirable qualitative characteristics of financial statements?
- What are the principles for measuring, and processes for recording, these items?

That analysis is applied to non-current (fixed) assets in this chapter.

8.2 Definitions

The following definition of an asset was provided in Chapter 2.

Definition

> An **asset** is a resource controlled by the entity as a result of past events and from which future economic benefits are expected to flow.[1]

The following definitions explain the nature of tangible and non-tangible non-current assets. The word 'tangible' means 'able to be touched'. So 'intangible' means 'not able to be touched'.

Definitions

> A **non-current asset** is any asset that does not meet the definition of a current asset.[2] Non-current assets include tangible, intangible and financial assets of a long-term nature. These are also described as **fixed assets**.[3]
>
> **Tangible non-current (fixed) assets** are assets that have physical substance and are held for use in the production or supply of goods or services, for rental to others, or for administrative purposes on a continuing basis in the reporting entity's activities.[4]
>
> An **intangible asset** is an identifiable non-monetary asset without physical substance.[5]

These definitions are taken from different sources because the definitions have been developed and discussed at different times for different purposes. The IASB and the UK ASB have both spent many years in discussion over the subjects of accounting for tangible and intangible non-current assets because these are complex matters.

8.2.1 Examples of non-current (fixed) assets

The following is a sample of the non-current (fixed) assets found in company balance sheets.

Tangible non-current (fixed) assets

- Land and buildings owned by the entity
- Buildings leased by the entity
- Plant and equipment (owned or leased)
- Vehicles (owned or leased)
- Office equipment
- Assets under construction
- Telecommunications network
- Airport runways
- Water pipes and sewers
- Oil and mineral reserves.

Intangible non-current (fixed) assets

- Newspaper titles and publishing rights
- Patents
- Trade marks
- Goodwill purchased
- Brand names purchased.

Investments

- Long-term investments in subsidiary companies
- Long-term investments in other companies.

That sample was taken from only 10 annual reports of leading companies. Looking at more companies would soon extend the list considerably. The potential variety and the likelihood of encountering something new is one reason why definitions are essential.

8.2.2 Cost of a non-current (fixed) asset

There is one issue which is not as straightforward as it seems. That is the question of measuring the cost of a non-current (fixed) asset. When a toffee manufacturer buys a new toffee-shaping machine, the purchase price will be known from the supplier's invoice and the manufacturer's catalogue, but should the costs of delivery and installation be added to the amount recorded as the asset cost? When an insurance company buys a new head office, the purchase price will be shown in the contract, but should the legal costs be added to the amount recorded as the asset cost? When a new head office building is under development and interest is being paid on the funds borrowed to finance the development, should the interest paid on the borrowed funds be added to the cost of the development as part of the asset value?

The answer in all three cases is 'yes', although the third example causes greatest discussion and debate. The general principle is that the cost of a non-current (fixed) asset is the purchase price or the amount spent on its production together with any other expenditure incurred in bringing the non-current (fixed) asset to working condition for its intended use at its intended location.

Definition The **cost** of a non-current (fixed) asset is the purchase price or the amount spent on its production together with any costs directly attributable to bringing the non-current (fixed) asset to working condition for its intended use at its intended location.

8.2.3   Repairs and improvements

There are sometimes problems in deciding whether a payment for a repair to a non-current (fixed) asset should be treated as an expense of the business or an asset. The key lies in the words of the definition of an asset and the phrase *future economic benefits*. If the payment relates to some act which merely preserves the existing life of the asset and the existing expectations of benefit from the asset, then the payment is treated as a repair and reported as an **expense**. The asset of cash decreases and there is a decrease in the ownership interest caused by the expense.

If the payment relates to some act which significantly extends the useful life of the asset, or increases the future economic benefit expected from the asset, then the payment is treated as an **improvement** and reported as an asset. It may be reported as a separate asset but, more usually, the amount will be added to the cost or value recorded for the asset which has been improved. The asset of cash decreases and is replaced by an asset of improvements. There is no effect on the ownership interest.

The following are examples of improvements and repairs.

Improvements

- Extensions to a building which increase the operating capacity of the business.
- A new roof which gives a building an extra ten years of life.
- A new engine for a delivery van which is more powerful than the existing engine and allows faster delivery in hilly districts.
- Renewing the fittings and interior decoration of a hotel to attract international visitors instead of the traditional local customers.

Repairs

- A new roof, required because of storm damage, which will keep the building weatherproof for the remainder of its estimated life.
- A new engine for a delivery van which replaces an existing damaged engine.
- Redecorating inside a building to preserve the existing standards of cleanliness and appearance.

Activity 8.1

Imagine you are the owner of a big hotel in the centre of town. Make a list of the items you would expect to include in your business balance sheet as non-current (fixed) assets. Make a list of the types of repair which would be classed as 'improvements'. Use the definition of a non-current (fixed) asset to show that your list includes items which are correctly classified.

8.3   Recognition

This section outlines the recognition issues faced in reporting non-current assets in the separate categories of tangible assets, intangible assets, and investment assets.

8.3.1   Tangible non-current (fixed) assets

Tangible non-current (fixed) assets are those items which can be touched, seen or heard and meet the conditions set out in the definition of a non-current (fixed) asset. **Recognition** by reporting in the balance sheet presents no problem where the future benefit can be identified and the cost of the asset can be measured. (Look back to section 2.5 for an explanation of recognition.) The evidence of cost is usually a purchase invoice. Some tangible non-current (fixed) assets are recorded at a valuation made subsequent to the purchase. Revaluations are discussed in Chapter 12.

As the list in the previous section indicates, there is considerable variety in tangible non-current (fixed) assets. The common feature is that they all have a limited life expectancy. They may wear out, be used up, go out of fashion, break down or be sold for scrap. Whatever the reason, the effect is the same and is called **depreciation**. Users have many questions to ask about tangible non-current (fixed) assets, such as:

● What kinds of tangible fixed assets are in use?
● How old are they?
● How has the company measured the depreciation?
● Where is the depreciation recorded?

Answering those questions will take up most of the remainder of this chapter.

8.3.2 Intangible non-current (fixed) assets

An intangible non-current (fixed) asset is an item which meets the definition of a non-current (fixed) asset but has no physical substance. It cannot be touched, seen or heard. The evidence of its existence is the benefit flowing from it. For many years, items such as patents, trade marks and licences to manufacture products have been bought and sold between companies. The purchase has been recorded as a non-current (fixed) asset and depreciated over the estimated life of the patent, trade mark or licence. The estimated life is decided by law (for patents and trade marks) or by legal contract (for licences). The depreciation of intangible non-current (fixed) assets is usually referred to as **amortisation** (in which you may recognise the French word *mort* meaning *death*).

The intangible non-current (fixed) asset which has attracted most accounting-related comment in recent years has been the brand name of a company's product. When a company works over many years to develop the reputation of its product, that reputation creates an expected future benefit for the company and meets the definition of an **asset** as set out in Chapter 2. However, the generally held view is that it should not be recognised in the balance sheet because it fails the **recognition** test of Chapter 2. The conventional argument is that there is no measurable **cost** of the reputation gained by the brand name and the value cannot be measured with reliability.

That is the generally held view which was challenged in the mid-1980s by a number of leading companies. Some had bought other companies which had developed brand names. The new owners argued that they were buying the other company purely because of the quality of the brand name and they wanted to show that brand name in the new balance sheet. They had a reasonable argument because they had paid a price in the market and could show the cost of the brand name acquired. Other companies who had developed their own brand names did not want to be left behind and so paid expert valuers to calculate a value for their home-grown brands. A new professional specialism of brand valuation gained prominence and the experts claimed they could measure the value of a home-grown brand with reliability.

The companies which reported brand names in the balance sheet argued that the brand had a long life and did not require amortisation. This argument gave them the advantage of expanding the balance sheet without the disadvantage of amortisation appearing in the income statement (profit and loss account).

The IASB has issued a standard, IAS 38, covering accounting for intangible assets. Internally generated brand names must *not* be recognised as intangible assets. This rule applies to similar assets such as publishing titles, customer lists, or newspaper titles. Purchased brand names or trade marks or patents may be reported in a balance sheet if they meet the conditions for recognition. Recognition requires that it is probable that the expected economic benefit will flow to the entity, and the cost of the asset can be measured reliably.

If the intangible asset has a finite life it must be amortised over its useful life. The method of amortisation must reflect the pattern of use of the asset.

Activity 8.2

A company which has manufactured a well-known brand of brown bread for many years has decided that the brand name is so well known that it should appear in the balance sheet. Write down two arguments in favour of this, to be made by the company's finance director, and two arguments against, which will appear in a newspaper article.

8.3.3 Investments

Investments exist in many different forms but the essential feature is an ability to generate future economic benefits so that the wealth of the owner increases. This increase in wealth may arise because the value of the investment increases, or may arise because the investment creates income for the owner in the form of a distribution such as interest paid or dividends. Companies may hold investments for a variety of reasons. A non-current (fixed asset) investment is one which is held for long-term purposes, such as shares in another company which has close trading links with the investing company.

The number of shares held may be such as to give direct control of the investment or may be of a lesser amount which indicates a long-term relationship, without direct control, in a similar line of business.

Non-current (fixed) asset investments may be held so that resources are available to meet a long-term obligation, such as the payment of pensions. Such non-current (fixed) assets are normally found in the balance sheets of insurance companies or pension funds, rather than in the balance sheet of the company employing staff.

The features which make investments different as non-current (fixed) assets are the importance of the increase in value of the investment itself and the fact that they are not used in the production or service process. Both features require a different kind of accounting treatment from that given to other non-current (fixed) assets. Those special treatments are advanced accounting matters and will not be dealt with in any detail in this text. What you should look for in accounts is the existence of non-current (fixed) asset investments and the information provided about them. The questions users will ask are: 'How well is this investment keeping up its value?' and 'How important is the income from this investment to the overall profit of the company?'

8.4 Users' needs for information

Activity 8.3

Before you read this section, make a list of the information about non-current (fixed) assets which would be useful to you if you wished to learn more about a specific company. Then read the section and compare it with your list. How far-thinking are you in respect of accounting information?

Analysts who write reports for professional and private investors have a particular interest in the non-current (fixed) assets because these are the base from which profits are generated. They want to know what types of assets are held, how old they are and what plans the company has for future investment in non-current (fixed) assets.

The analysts also want to know about the impact of the depreciation charge on the profit of the year. They are aware that detailed aspects of calculations of depreciation may vary from one year to the next and this may affect the comparability of the profit amounts.

To estimate the remaining life of the assets, analysts compare the accumulated depreciation with the total cost (or value) of the non-current (fixed) assets. If the accumulated depreciation is relatively low, then the non-current (fixed) assets are relatively new. Other companies in the industry will be used for comparison. The analysts also compare the depreciation charge for the year with the total cost (or value) of the assets and expect to see a similar relationship from one year to the next. A sudden change will cause them to ask more questions about a change in the basis of calculation.

8.5 Information provided in the financial statements

In Chapter 7 the balance sheet of Safe and Sure plc was presented. The balance sheet showed a single line of information on tangible non-current (fixed) assets. This section shows how that single line becomes understandable when read in conjunction with the notes to the accounts, the statement of accounting policy and the finance director's review.

8.5.1 Balance sheet

	Notes	Year 7 £m	Year 6 £m
Non-current assets			
Tangible assets	2	137.5	121.9

8.5.2 Notes to the balance sheet

In the notes to the balance sheet there is considerably more information:

Note 2 Tangible non-current assets

	Land and buildings £m	Plant and equipment £m	Vehicles £m	Total £m
Cost or valuation				
At 1 January Year 7	28.3	96.4	104.8	229.5
Additions at cost	3.9	18.5	37.8	60.2
On acquisitions	0.3	1.0	0.7	2.0
Disposals	(0.6)	(3.1)	(24.7)	(28.4)
At 31 December Year 7	31.9	112.8	118.6	263.3
Aggregate depreciation				
At 1 January Year 7	2.2	58.8	46.6	107.6
Depreciation for the year	0.5	13.5	19.2	33.2
On acquisitions	0.1	0.7	0.6	1.4
Disposals	(0.2)	(2.8)	(13.4)	(16.4)
At 31 December Year 7	2.6	70.2	53.0	125.8
Net book value at 31 December Year 7	29.3	42.6	65.6	137.5
Net book value at 31 December Year 6	26.1	37.6	58.2	121.9

Analysis of land and buildings at cost or valuation

	Year 7 £m	Year 6 £m
At cost	10.4	7.1
At valuation	21.5	21.2
	31.9	28.3

The majority of the group's freehold and long-term leasehold properties were revalued during Year 5 by independent valuers. Valuations were made on the basis of the market value for existing use. The book values of the properties were adjusted to the revaluations and the resultant net surplus was credited to the revaluation reserve.

Analysis of net book value of land and buildings

	Year 7	Year 6
	£m	£m
Freehold	24.5	21.0
Leasehold:		
Over 50 years unexpired	2.1	2.4
Under 50 years unexpired	2.7	2.7
	29.3	26.1

If the revalued assets were stated on the historical cost basis the amounts would be:

	Year 7	Year 6
	£m	£m
Land and buildings at cost	15.7	14.5
Aggregate depreciation	(2.2)	(1.9)
	13.5	12.6

It is clear from the extensive nature of note 2 to the balance sheet that tangible non-current (fixed) assets are regarded as important by those who regulate the information. All companies present a detailed note of this kind because the information is required by IAS 16, *Property, Plant and Equipment*.

8.5.3   Statement of accounting policy

In addition the company is required, by the accounting standard IAS 1, *Presentation of Financial Statements*, to disclose its significant accounting policies. For this company the wording of the accounting policy statement is as follows:

Freehold and leasehold property
Freehold and leasehold land and buildings are stated either at cost or at their revalued amounts less depreciation. Full revaluations are made at five-year intervals with interim valuations in the intervening years, the most recent being in Year 0.

Provision for depreciation of freehold land and buildings is made at the annual rate of 1% of cost or the revalued amounts. Leasehold land and buildings are amortised in equal annual instalments over the periods of the leases subject to a minimum annual provision of 1% of cost or the revalued amounts. When properties are sold the difference between sales proceeds and net book value is dealt with in the income statement (profit and loss account).

Other tangible non-current (fixed) assets
Other tangible non-current assets are stated at cost less depreciation. Provision for depreciation is made mainly in equal annual instalments over the estimated useful lives of the assets as follows:

4 to 5 years   vehicles
5 to 10 years   plant, machinery and equipment

8.5.4   Operating and financial review

There is also a comment in the finance director's report, as a contribution to the operating and financial review:

Capital expenditure
The major items of capital expenditure are vehicles, equipment used on customers' premises and office equipment, particularly computers. Disposals during the year were mainly of vehicles being replaced on a rolling programme.

Activity 8.4

*Find the annual report of a company of your choice. This may be through access to the website, or by requesting a printed copy of the annual report through the website **www.ft.com**, or by using the free annual reports offer on the London Stock Exchange page of the Financial Times.*

In the annual report find the information that corresponds to the extracts from Safe & Sure given in section 8.5. What are the similarities and differences? What do you learn about the non-current (fixed) asset base of your chosen company?

8.6 Usefulness of published information

Here is David Wilson to explain how useful he sees the information provided by companies about their tangible non-current (fixed) assets. If you look back to Chapter 4 you will see that he was about to visit the company and had made a preliminary list of questions. He has now made the visit and has a better understanding of what is reported in the balance sheet. He talks to Leona in a break at a workout session.

DAVID: *I told you that in making my review before visiting the company I looked closely at the type of tangible non-current (fixed) assets held and the estimated useful life. I also checked that the depreciation period and method of calculation had not changed from previous years.*

As I was making a site visit I took the opportunity to look at the various non-current (fixed) assets. This is a group of companies, expanding by acquisition of other companies, and each acquisition brings in more land and buildings. Some of these assets are recorded at valuation rather than original cost. The company has to review the valuation on a regular That is quite a common practice and I have confidence in the firm of valuers used.

Plant and equipment has an aggregate depreciation of £70.2m which is 62% of the cost of the assets at £112.8m. It seems to me that must be saying that the plant and equipment is more than half-way through its estimated life. The finance director wasn't too enthusiastic about this interpretation. He pointed out that when another company is acquired the non-current (fixed) assets may be quite old and have to be brought into the group balance sheet, but once they are in group control there is a strict policy of evaluation and replacement. He views the depreciation policy as being at the prudent end of the spectrum, so the realistic life remaining might be marginally over half, but discretion and the fast-moving nature of the industry requires an element of caution. He called in the plant manager who showed me the replacement schedules for plant and equipment for the next three years. It certainly reassured me that risk of obsolescence is probably not a serious worry. I also met the vehicle fleet supervisor who showed me similar replacement schedules for the vehicles.

I saw how the vehicle fleet is managed so that every vehicle is idle for the minimum time. Each vehicle is assigned to a group of cleaning operatives, whose shifts are scheduled so that the vehicle's use is maximised. Plant and equipment are the responsibility of area managers who have to look after security, maintenance and efficiency of usage. I thought it was all really quite impressive.

The depreciation charge for the plant and equipment in Year 7 is £13.5m which is 12% of the cost of £112.8m and suggests an estimated life of just over eight years is being applied. That is within the range of five to ten years stated as the company's accounting policy. I think the wording 'five to ten years' is too vague. Using five years would double the depreciation charge compared with ten. I tried to pin down the finance director so that I can get a good figure for my forecast but all he would say was that there is no reason to suppose there are any unusual features in the amount in the accounts. The depreciation charge for vehicles is £19.2m which is 16% of the cost of £118.6m. That suggests an estimated life of just over six years is being applied. I asked the finance director how that squared with the accounting policy statement of estimated useful lives of four to five years for vehicles. He did seem to sigh a little at that point but was quite patient in explaining that there are some fully depreciated vehicles still in use (because they are quite prudent in their estimates of depreciation) and so the depreciation charge is not the 20% to 25% I was looking for. I'll need to think about that one but I might move my estimate for next year closer to 20%.

You asked me how this company's information measures up to the qualitative characteristics (set out in Chapter 4). Relevance I would rate highly, because there is plenty of information in the notes which I can use to ask questions about the effective use of non-current (fixed) assets and the impact on income statement (profit and loss account) through the depreciation charge. Reliability, faithful representation and neutrality are qualities I leave to the auditors. Prudence is something which seems to come out strongly in conversation with the finance director. The detailed schedule of assets which I saw suggests that completeness is not a problem. Comparability is fine because there are amounts for the previous year and the standard format allows me to make comparison with other companies in the industry. Understandability is perhaps more of a problem than I thought. Those fully depreciated assets caught me out.

LEONA: *Well, I have now heard you admit that there is some value in having auditors. Shall I tell you how much you have missed? You could have asked more searching questions about the way in which they measure the cost of plant and equipment. Does it include delivery charges and installation costs? You could have asked whether a technical expert inside the company estimates and reviews the asset lives used, or whether the finance director makes a guess. Did you ask whether they are perhaps verging on being over-prudent so that surprises come later when the depreciation charge is less than expected? You could have asked how the interim valuations are carried out. These are all questions we ask as auditors so that you may treat the information as being reliable and a faithful representation.*

Hopefully you now have a feeling for the information provided by companies on tangible non-current (fixed) assets and how it is used by the professional investor. The nature and recording of depreciation is now explained.

8.7 Depreciation: an explanation of its nature

Activity 8.5

Before you read this section, write down what you think 'depreciation' means. Then read the section and compare it with your initial views. Depreciation is a very subjective matter and there are different views of its purpose, so your answer may be interesting even if it does not match the text. You should consult your lecturer, tutor or other expert in the area to understand why your perceptions may be different.

Definitions[6]

Depreciation is the systematic allocation of the depreciable amount of an asset over its useful life.

The **depreciable amount** is the cost of an asset, or other amount substituted for cost, less its residual value.

Residual value is the estimated amount that an entity would currently obtain from disposal of the asset, after deducting the estimated cost of disposal, if the asset were already of the age and in the condition expected at the end of its useful life.

The asset may be an item of plant or equipment which is wearing out through being used. It may be a payment made by a company for the right to become a tenant of a property. That payment purchases a lease which reduces in value through the passage of time. The asset may be a computer system which becomes out of date in a very short space of time because of obsolescence. It may be a machine which produces goods for which demand falls because of changing market conditions.

The definition shows that depreciation is a device used in accounting to allocate (spread) the cost of a non-current (fixed) asset over its useful life. The process of spreading cost over more than one accounting period is called **allocation**.

In terms of the accounting equation, the useful life of the non-current (fixed) asset is being reduced and this will reduce the ownership interest.

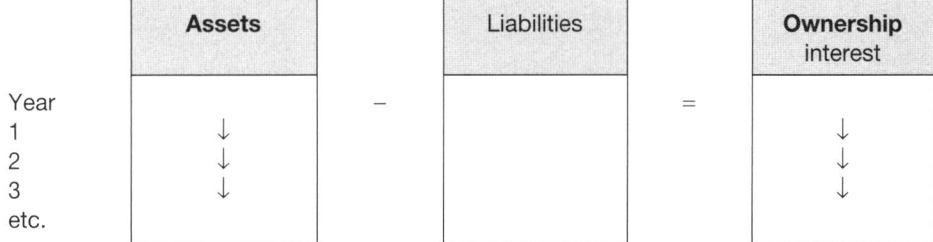

As the asset becomes older, the depreciation of one year is added to the depreciation of previous years. This is called the **accumulated depreciation** or **aggregate depreciation**. The accumulated depreciation at the end of any year is equal to the accumulated depreciation at the start of the year plus the depreciation charge for that year.

Deducting the accumulated depreciation from the original cost leaves the **net book value**. The net book value could also be described as the cost remaining as a benefit for future years.

Showing the effect of depreciation by use of arrows and the accounting equation is relatively easy. Deciding on the amount of depreciation each year is much more difficult because there are so many different views of how to calculate the amount of asset used up in each period.

8.7.1   Calculation of depreciation

Calculation of depreciation requires three pieces of information:

1 the cost of the asset;
2 the estimated useful life; and
3 the estimated residual value.

The total depreciation of the non-current (fixed) asset is equal to the cost of the non-current (fixed) asset minus the estimated residual value. The purpose of the depreciation calculation is to spread the total depreciation over the estimated useful life.

The first point at which differences of opinion arise is in the estimation of the useful life and residual value. These are matters of judgement which vary from one person to the next.

Unfortunately the differences do not stop at those estimates. There is also no agreement on the arithmetical approach to spreading the total depreciation over the useful life. Some people are of the opinion that a non-current (fixed) asset is used evenly over time and that the depreciation should reflect the benefit gained from its use. Others argue that the non-current (fixed) asset declines in value most in the early years and so the depreciation charge should be greater in earlier years.

8.7.2   Straight-line method

Those who are of the opinion that a non-current (fixed) asset is used evenly over time apply a method of calculation called straight-line depreciation. The formula is:

$$\frac{\text{Cost} - \text{Expected residual value}}{\text{Expected life}}$$

To illustrate the use of the formula, take a non-current (fixed) asset which has a cost of £1,000 and an estimated life of five years. The estimated residual value is nil. The calculation of the annual depreciation charge is:

$$\frac{£1,000 - \text{nil}}{5} = £200 \text{ per annum}$$

The depreciation rate is sometimes expressed as a percentage of the original cost. In this case the company would state its depreciation policy as follows:

Accounting policy:
Depreciation is charged on a straight-line basis at a rate of 20% of cost per annum.

Exhibit 8.1
Pattern of depreciation and net book value over the life of an asset

End of year	Depreciation of the year (a) £	Total depreciation (b) £	Net book value of the asset (£1,000 − b) £
1	200	200	800
2	200	400	600
3	200	600	400
4	200	800	200
5	200	1,000	nil

Exhibit 8.2
Graph of net book value over Years 1 to 5, for the straight-line method of depreciation

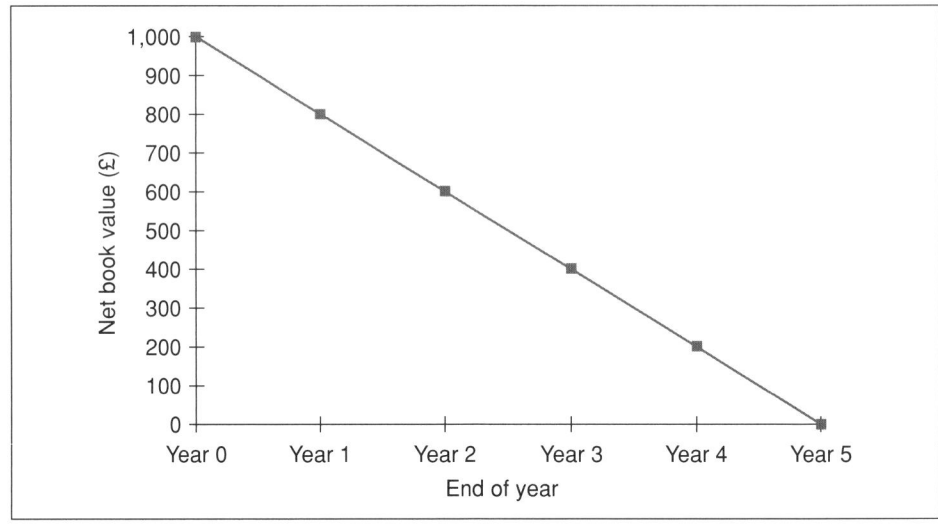

The phrase 'straight-line' is used because a graph of the net book value of the asset at the end of each year produces a straight line. Exhibit 8.1 sets out the five-year pattern of depreciation and net book value for the example used above.

Exhibit 8.2 shows a graph of the net book value at the end of each year. The graph starts at the cost figure of £1,000 when the asset is new (Year 0) and reduces by £200 each year until it is zero at the end of Year 5.

8.7.3 Reducing-balance method

Those who believe that the asset depreciates most in earlier years would calculate the depreciation using the formula:

Fixed percentage × Net book value at the start of the year

Take the example of the asset costing £1,000. The fixed percentage applied for the reducing-balance method might be as high as 50%. The calculations would be as shown in the table in Exhibit 8.3.

You will see from the table in Exhibit 8.3 that under the reducing-balance method there is always a small balance remaining. In this example, the rate of 50% is used to

Exhibit 8.3
Calculation of reducing-balance depreciation

Year	Net book value at start of year (a) £	Annual depreciation (b) = 50% of (a) £	Net book value at end of year (a – b) £
1	1,000	500	500
2	500	250	250
3	250	125	125
4	125	63	62
5	62	31	31

Exhibit 8.4
Graph of net book value over Years 1 to 5, for the reducing-balance method of depreciation

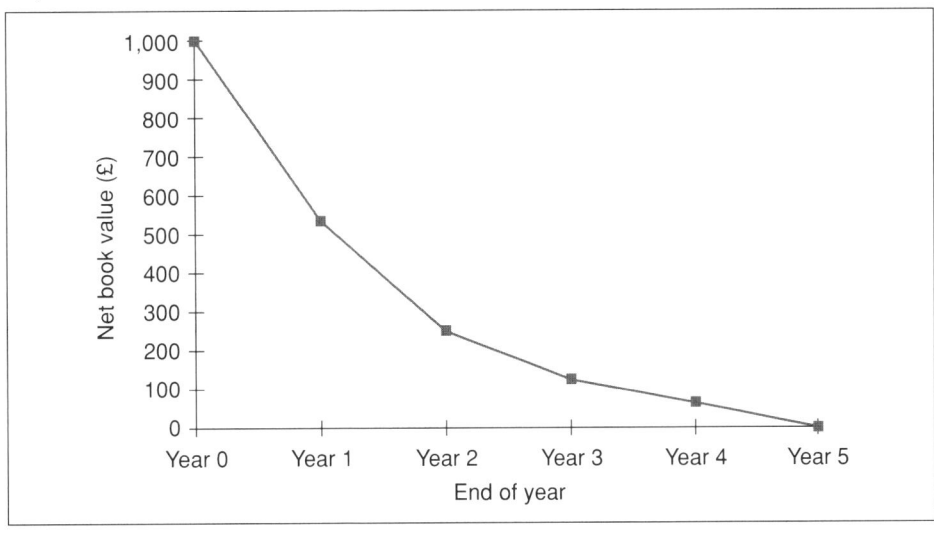

bring the net book value to a relatively small amount. The formula for calculating the exact rate requires a knowledge of compound interest and may be found at the end of the Supplement to this chapter. For those whose main interest is in understanding and interpreting accounts it is not necessary to know the formula, but it is useful to be aware that a very much higher percentage rate is required on the reducing-balance method as compared with the straight-line method. As a useful guide, the reducing-balance rate must be at least twice the rate of the straight-line calculation if the major part of the asset is to be depreciated over its useful life.

A graph of the net book value at the end of each year under the reducing-balance method is shown in Exhibit 8.4. The steep slope at the start shows that the net book value declines rapidly in the early part of the asset's life and then less steeply towards the end when most of the benefit of the asset has been used up.

8.7.4   Which method to choose?

The separate recording of asset at cost and accumulated depreciation is accounting information provided in many countries. The UK practice at a general level is consistent with the IASB standard. Country-specific factors may lead to differences in matters of detail such as the choice of depreciation method or the estimated life of non-current (fixed) assets. In some countries, the depreciation expense in the accounting income statement (profit and loss account) must match that used for the purposes of calculating taxable profit. This may encourage the use of the reducing-balance method, giving a higher expense (and so a lower profit) in the early years of the asset's life. In the UK there are separate rules in tax law for calculating depreciation, and so this has no effect on accounting profit.

The choice of depreciation method should be based on the expected pattern of usage of the asset. If the usage is evenly spread then the straight-line method is appropriate. If the usage is heaviest in early years then the reducing-balance method is the best representation of the economic activity. In practice, it is found that most UK companies use straight-line depreciation. In some other countries, particularly those where tax rules and accounting laws are closely linked, the reducing-balance method is commonly observed. So it appears that there are different international practices that may reflect different conditions in the respective countries. David and Leona discuss the problem.

DAVID: *The choice of depreciation method may have a significant impact on reported profit. Companies that are actively investing in non-current (fixed) assets will do so in the expectation of increased profits. However it may take some time for such profits to emerge. If, in the meantime, there is a relatively high charge to income statement (profit and loss account) through reducing-balance depreciation, profits may fall in the short term. In contrast the use of straight-line depreciation will have a less dramatic impact on reported profit immediately following the new investment, so the company avoids a dip in profits.*

LEONA: *I can't accept that as a valid argument to give to the auditor. I ask the company what the pattern of usage is. If the company tells me that the asset produces benefit evenly over its useful life, I can accept straight-line depreciation. If, on the other hand, I hear that the asset is more productive in its early years of life, I expect to see reducing-balance depreciation.*

DAVID: *Well let me try your social conscience. I came across a case of a UK company that had been taken over by a German parent company. The UK company had always used straight-line depreciation and was making small profits each year. The parent company had always used reducing-balance depreciation and so changed the accounting method of the UK subsidiary. Small profits turned into large losses and the parent company said that there would have to be a reduction in the workforce to cut costs. The employee representatives said that nothing had changed except that the accountants had redefined the game. They blamed the accountants for the resulting job losses and increased unemployment.*

LEONA: *My role is confined to giving an opinion on the accounting information. If a particular accounting process is detrimental to the public interest then it is the job of government to legislate.*

Activity 8.6   *Consider the discussion between David and Leona. Do you share the concern of the employee representatives as described by David? Do you agree with Leona that the economic impact of accounting information is not a problem for the auditor? What is your view on the social responsibility attached to financial reporting?*

8.7.5   Retaining cash in the business

Suppose that the policy of the owner is to take all the available profits as drawings for personal use. Take a company that has fee income of £120,000 and pays wages and other costs of £58,000. If the company did not recognise the expense of depreciation the owner's drawings could be as high as £62,000. Suppose now that depreciation of non-current (fixed) assets is calculated as £10,000. The net profit after depreciation becomes £52,000. The owner can still see £62,000 in the bank account but knows £10,000 of that amount represents using up non-current (fixed) assets. Leaving the £10,000 in the bank will allow the business to save cash for asset replacement. The owner should withdraw no more than £52,000.

It is often said that depreciation limits the amount of profits available for cash drawings by the owner and encourages saving for asset replacement. However there is nothing to stop the business spending the £10,000 on some purpose other than replacement of non-current (fixed) assets. We can only say that cash withheld from shareholders *may* be used to replace assets at the end of the asset life.

8.8 Reporting non-current (fixed) assets and depreciation in financial statements

This section moves step by step through the recording process. First, it looks at a situation of straight-line depreciation with no residual value for the asset. Then it takes in the additional complication of an estimated residual value.

8.8.1   Straight-line depreciation, no residual value

When a retail company wants new premises, it must either buy a shop or rent one. Renting is referred to as **leasing**. When the rent agreement is signed, the tenant may pay an agreed price for the privilege of having the lease. This is called the initial payment for the lease. It is paid in addition to the annual rental payment. The initial payment to acquire the lease provides a benefit of occupation for the entire period of the lease and so is a non-current (fixed) asset. Because the lease has a known life, it must be depreciated.

On 1 January Year 2 Electrical Instruments purchased a three-year lease of a shop for a payment of £60,000. Using the straight-line method of depreciation the amount of depreciation each year will be calculated on a straight-line basis as £20,000 (one-third of the cost of the lease). The income statement (profit and loss account) will report this amount as an expense in each of the three years of the lease. The balance sheet will show on one line the original cost of £60,000 and, on a second line, the accumulated depreciation to be subtracted at the end of each year.

The financial statements over the period of three years will show the following information relating to this lease:

Income statement (profit and loss account) (extract)			
Year ended 31 December	Year 2	Year 3	Year 4
	£000s	£000s	£000s
Depreciation expense	(20)	(20)	(20)

Balance sheet (extract)			
At 31 December	Year 2	Year 3	Year 4
	£000s	£000s	£000s
Lease at cost	60	60	60
Less accumulated depreciation	20	40	60
Net book value	40	20	nil

8.8.2   Straight-line depreciation with a residual value

In the case of Electrical Instruments the lease had no residual value. Take now the example of The Removals Company which commences business on 1 January Year 2 by paying cash for a van costing £60,000. It is estimated to have a useful life of three years and is estimated to have a residual value of £6,000. On 31 December Year 2 the owner calculates annual depreciation of the van as £18,000, using the formula:

$$\frac{Cost - Estimated\ residual\ value}{Estimated\ life}$$

During each year of operating the van, the company collected £120,000 in cash from customers and paid £58,000 in cash for drivers' wages, fuel and other running costs.

These transactions and events may be summarised using the accounting equation and a spreadsheet similar to that used in Chapter 5 (Exhibit 5.3). In Exhibit 8.5 there is a spreadsheet for the first year of the use of the van by the company. The assets section of the spreadsheet has three columns, one of which is for cash but two of which are for the van. The two columns for the van keep a separate record of the original cost and the accumulated depreciation. The original cost is the positive part of the asset but the accumulated depreciation is the negative part of the asset. Taking the accumulated depreciation from the original cost leaves the net book value. That is the amount of cost not yet amortised which acts as a measure of the benefit remaining in the asset for the future. In Exhibit 8.6 the information collected together by Exhibit 8.5 is presented in the form of a balance sheet and an income statement (profit and loss account).

Exhibit 8.5

Spreadsheet analysing transactions and events of The Removals Company into the elements of the accounting equation

	Transaction or event	Assets			Ownership interest	
		Van at cost	Accumulated depreciation of van	Cash	Capital contributed or withdrawn	Profit = revenue minus (expenses)
Year 2		£	£	£	£	£
1 Jan.	Owner contributes cash			60,000	60,000	
1 Jan.	Purchase furniture van	60,000		(60,000)		
All year	Collected cash from customers			120,000		120,000
All year	Paid for wages, fuel, etc.			(58,000)		(58,000)
31 Dec.	Calculate annual depreciation		(18,000)			(18,000)
	Totals	60,000	(18,000)	62,000	60,000	44,000

└──── 104,000 ────┘   └──── 104,000 ────┘

Exhibit 8.6

The Removals Company: Balance sheet at end of Year 2 and Income statement (profit and loss account) for Year 2

The Removals Company
Balance sheet at 31 December Year 2

	£
Non-current (fixed) assets	
Furniture van at cost	60,000
Accumulated depreciation	(18,000)
Net book value	42,000
Current assets	
Cash	62,000
Total assets	104,000
Ownership interest	
Ownership interest at the start of the year	nil
Capital contributed during the year	60,000
Profit of the year	44,000
	104,000

The Removals Company
Income statement (profit and loss account)
for the year ended 31 December Year 2

	£	£
Revenue		
Fees for removal work		120,000
Expenses		
Wages, fuel and other running costs	(58,000)	
Depreciation	(18,000)	
		(76,000)
Net profit		44,000

Exhibit 8.7

Spreadsheet analysis of transactions of The Removals Company, Year 3

	Transaction or event	Assets			Ownership interest		
		Van at cost	Accumulated depreciation of van	Cash	Ownership interest at start of year	Capital contributed or withdrawn	Profit = revenue minus (expenses)
Year 3		£	£	£	£	£	£
1 Jan.	Amounts brought forward at start of year	60,000	(18,000)	62,000	104,000		
All year	Collected cash from customers			120,000			120,000
All year	Paid for wages, fuel, etc.			(58,000)			(58,000)
31 Dec.	Calculate annual depreciation		(18,000)				(18,000)
	Totals	60,000	(36,000)	124,000	104,000		44,000

└────── 148,000 ──────┘ └────── 148,000 ──────┘

Exhibit 8.8

The Removals Company: Balance sheet at end of Year 3 and Income statement (profit and loss account) for Year 3

The Removals Company
Balance sheet at 31 December Year 3

	£
Non-current (fixed) assets	
Furniture van at cost	60,000
Accumulated depreciation	(36,000)
Net book value	24,000
Current assets	
Cash	124,000
Total assets	148,000
Ownership interest	
Ownership interest at the start of the year	104,000
Profit of the year	44,000
	148,000

The Removals Company
Income statement (profit and loss account)
for the year ended 31 December Year 3

	£	£
Revenue		
Fees for removal work		120,000
Expenses		
Wages, fuel and other running costs	(58,000)	
Depreciation	(18,000)	
		(76,000)
Net profit		44,000

8.8.3 Continuing to use the non-current (fixed) asset

So far, the accounting entries have related to the first year of the business so that there was no need to ask any questions about the position at the start of the period. To show the full impact of the progressive depreciation of the asset, the spreadsheet and financial statements are now presented for Year 3. Exhibit 8.7 sets out the spreadsheet and Exhibit 8.8 sets out the financial statements. It is assumed that for Year 3 the amounts of cash collected from customers and the amounts paid in cash for running costs are the same as for Year 2. No further capital is contributed by the owner and no new vans are acquired.

The first line of the spreadsheet in Exhibit 8.7 shows the position at the start of the year. The asset columns show the amounts as they were at the end of the previous year. The ownership interest shows the amount resulting at the end of the previous year, as seen in the Year 2 balance sheet. The columns for revenue and expenses are empty at the start of the year, awaiting the transactions and events of Year 3.

8.8.4 Disposing of the non-current (fixed) asset

During Year 4 the amounts of cash received from customers and cash paid for running costs are the same as they were in Year 3. Exhibit 8.9 sets out the spreadsheet for the transactions and events.

Exhibit 8.9
Spreadsheet analysis of transactions of The Removals Company, Year 4

	Transaction or event	Assets			Ownership interest		
		Van at cost	Accumulated depreciation of van	Cash	Ownership interest at start of year	Capital contributed or withdrawn	Profit = revenue minus (expenses)
Year 4		£	£	£	£	£	£
1 Jan.	Amounts brought forward at start of year	60,000	(36,000)	124,000	148,000		
All year	Collected cash from customers			120,000			120,000
All year	Paid for wages, fuel, etc.			(58,000)			(58,000)
31 Dec.	Calculate annual depreciation		(18,000)				(18,000)
	Totals	60,000	(54,000)	186,000	148,000		44,000

⌐———— 192,000 ————⌐   ⌐———— 192,000 ————⌐

Now suppose that the van is sold for £6,000 in cash on the final day of December Year 4. The spreadsheet contained in Exhibit 8.9 requires further attention, the additional accounting impact of the sale being seen in Exhibit 8.10.

Exhibit 8.10

Spreadsheet analysis of transactions of The Removals Company, Year 4, including sale of non-current (fixed) asset

	Transaction or event	Assets			Ownership interest		
		Van at cost	Accumulated depreciation of van	Cash	Ownership interest at start of year	Capital contributed or withdrawn	Profit = revenue minus (expenses)
Year 4		£	£	£	£	£	£
1 Jan.	Amounts brought forward at start of year	60,000	(36,000)	124,000	148,000		
All year	Collected cash from customers			120,000			120,000
All year	Paid for wages, fuel, etc.			(58,000)			(58,000)
31 Dec.	Calculate annual depreciation		(18,000)				(18,000)
31 Dec.	Van disposal	(60,000)	54,000	6,000			
	Totals	nil	nil	192,000	148,000		44,000

└────── 192,000 ──────┘   └────── 192,000 ──────┘

The disposal of the van must be analysed in stages:

1 collecting cash;
2 transferring ownership of the vehicle;
3 removing the vehicle from the accounting records.

When the vehicle is removed from the record, two columns must be reduced to zero. These are the *van at cost* column and the *accumulated depreciation* column. The van at cost column shows the original cost of £60,000 and the accumulated depreciation shows the amount of £54,000 which has to be deducted to show the amount of the net book value. The asset of cash increases by £6,000. In terms of the accounting equation:

Assets		–	Liabilities	=	Ownership interest
	£		no change		no change
Increase in cash	6,000				
Decrease van:					
At cost	60,000				
Accumulated depreciation	(54,000)				
	6,000				

The resulting balance sheet and income statement (profit and loss account) are shown in Exhibit 8.11.

Exhibit 8.11

The Removals Company: Balance sheet at end of Year 4 and Income statement (profit and loss account) for Year 4

The Removals Company Balance sheet at 31 December Year 4	
	£
Non-current (fixed) assets	nil
Current assets	
Cash	192,000
Total assets	192,000
Ownership interest	
Ownership interest at the start of the year	148,000
Profit of the year	44,000
	192,000

The Removals Company Income statement (profit and loss account) for the year ended 31 December Year 4		
	£	£
Revenue		
Fees for removal work		120,000
Expenses		
Wages, fuel and other running costs	(58,000)	
Depreciation	(18,000)	
		(76,000)
Net profit		44,000

8.8.5 Selling for a price which is not equal to the net book value

The previous illustration was based on selling the van for £6,000, an amount equal to the net book value. Suppose instead it was sold for £9,000. There is a gain on disposal of £3,000. This gain is reported in the income statement (profit and loss account).

Assets		–	Liabilities	=	Ownership interest
	£				
Increase cash	**9,000**				
Decrease van:			no change		**Increase by £3,000**
At cost	60,000				
Accumulated depreciation	(54,000)				
	6,000				

If the amount of the gain or loss on disposal is relatively small, it may be deducted from the depreciation charge. In that situation the income statement (profit and loss account) would appear as shown in Exhibit 8.12 where bold printing highlights the difference when compared with the income statement (profit and loss account) in Exhibit 8.11. If the gain or loss is **material** it will be reported separately.

Exhibit 8.12
Income statement (profit and loss account) for Year 4 when proceeds of sale exceed net book value of non-current (fixed) asset

The Removals Company **Income statement (profit and loss account)** **for the year ended 31 December Year 4**		
	£	£
Revenue		
Fees for removal work		120,000
Expenses		
Wages, fuel and other running costs	(58,000)	
Depreciation (18,000 – 3,000)	**(15,000)**	
		(73,000)
Net profit		47,000

8.8.6   A table of depreciation expense

To test your understanding of the impact of depreciation you may wish to use a table of the type shown in Exhibit 8.13. It shows that, whatever the proceeds of sale of the asset, the total expense in the income statement (profit and loss account) will always be the same but the amount of expense each year will vary.

Exhibit 8.13
Table of depreciation charge

(a) A van cost £60,000, was estimated to have a useful life of three years and a residual value of £6,000. It was sold for £9,000 on the last day of Year 3. Net profit before depreciation is £62,000.

Year	Net profit before depreciation	Depreciation expense of the year	Net profit after depreciation	Cost less accumulated depreciation	Net book value
	£	£	£	£	£
1	62,000	18,000	44,000	60,000 – 18,000	42,000
2	62,000	18,000	44,000	60,000 – 36,000	24,000
3	62,000	15,000	47,000	60,000 – 54,000	6,000
Total depreciation charge		51,000			
Total reported net profit			135,000		

Proceeds of sale exceed net book value by £3,000. This gain is deducted from the depreciation expense of £18,000 leaving £15,000 as the expense of the year.

(b) A van cost £60,000, was estimated to have a useful life of three years and a residual value of £9,000. The annual depreciation was calculated as £17,000. The van was sold for £9,000 on the last day of Year 3. Net profit before depreciation is £62,000.

Year	Net profit before depreciation	Depreciation expense of the year	Net profit after depreciation	Cost less accumulated depreciation	Net book value
	£	£	£	£	£
1	62,000	17,000	45,000	60,000 – 17,000	43,000
2	62,000	17,000	45,000	60,000 – 34,000	26,000
3	62,000	17,000	45,000	60,000 – 51,000	9,000
Total depreciation		51,000			
Total reported net profit			135,000		

Net book value equals proceeds of sale so the depreciation charge of Year 3 is the same as that of previous years.

If you compare the two tables (a) and (b) you will see that:

- total depreciation over the three years is the same in both cases;
- total net profit after depreciation over the three years is the same in both cases;
- annual depreciation in Years 1 and 2 is lower in table (b);
- net profit after depreciation in Years 1 and 2 is higher in table (b);
- net book value of the asset at the end of Years 1 and 2 is higher in table (b);
- the depreciation charge in Year 3 is higher in table (b);
- the net profit after depreciation in Year 3 is lower in table (b).

This is an example of what is referred to in accounting as an **allocation** problem (a 'sharing' problem). The expense is the same in total but is allocated (shared) differently across the years of the asset's life. As a result, there are different amounts in the income statement (profit and loss account) for each year but the total profit over the longer period is the same.

8.8.7   Impairment

An asset is impaired when the business will not be able to recover the amount shown in the balance sheet, either through use or through sale. If the enterprise believes that impairment may have taken place, it must carry out an **impairment review**. This requires comparison of the net book value with the cash-generating ability of the asset. If the comparison indicates that the recorded net book value is too high, the value of the asset is reduced and there is an expense in the income statement (profit and loss account).[7]

The impairment test may be applied to intangible non-current (fixed) assets such as goodwill, in order to justify non-amortisation. If no impairment is detected it may be argued that the asset has maintained its value and so amortisation is not necessary. If there has been impairment of the historical cost net book value, then the loss in asset value becomes an expense for the income statement (profit and loss account).

8.9 Summary

- A **non-current asset** is any asset that does not meet the definition of a current asset.[8] Non-current assets include tangible, intangible and financial assets of a long-term nature. These are also described as **fixed assets**.
- **Tangible non-current (fixed) assets** are assets that have physical substance and are held for use in the production or supply of goods or services, for rental to others, or for administrative purposes on a continuing basis in the reporting entity's activities.
- **An intangible asset** is an identifiable non-monetary asset without physical substance.
- Users need information about the cost of an asset and the aggregate (accumulated) depreciation as the separate components of net book value. Having this detail allows users to estimate the proportion of asset life remaining to be used. This information will be reported in the notes to the balance sheet.
- Users also need information about the accounting policy on depreciation and its impact on the reported asset values. This information will be found in the notes to the accounts on accounting policies and the notes. There may also be a description and discussion in the Operating and Financial Review, including a forward-looking description of intended capital expenditure.

- **Depreciation** is estimated for the total life of the asset and then allocated to the reporting periods involved, usually annual reporting. No particular method of depreciation is required by law. Preparers of financial statements have to exercise choices. Companies in the UK commonly use straight-line depreciation. An alternative is reducing-balance depreciation. This is found more commonly in some other countries. Choice of depreciation method affects the comparability of profit.

Further reading

The following standards are too detailed for a first level course but the definitions sections may be helpful.

IASB (2004) IAS 38, *Intangible Assets*, International Accounting Standards Board.

IASB (2004) IAS 16, *Property, Plant and Equipment*, International Accounting Standards Board.

QUESTIONS

The Questions section of each chapter has three types of question. 'Test your understanding' questions to help you review your reading are in the 'A' series of questions. You will find the answers to these by reading and thinking about the material in the book. 'Application' questions to test your ability to apply technical skills are in the 'B' series of questions. Questions requiring you to show skills in problem solving and evaluation are in the 'C' series of questions. A letter [S] indicates that there is a solution at the end of the book.

A   Test your understanding

A8.1   State the definition of a non-current (fixed) asset and explain why each condition is required. (Section 8.2)

A8.2   Explain the categories: (Section 8.2.1)

(a) tangible non-current (fixed) assets;
(b) intangible non-current (fixed) assets; and
(c) non-current (fixed) asset investments;

and give an example of each.

A8.3   What do users of financial statements particularly want to know about non-current (fixed) assets? (Section 8.4)

A8.4   What type of information would you expect to find about non-current (fixed) assets in the financial statements and notes of a major UK listed company? (Section 8.4)

A8.5   State the definition of depreciation. (Section 8.7)

A8.6   What is meant by **accumulated depreciation** (also called **aggregate depreciation**)? (Section 8.7)

A8.7   What information is needed to calculate annual depreciation? (Section 8.7.1)

A8.8   What is the formula for calculating straight-line depreciation? (Section 8.7.2)

A8.9   How is reducing-balance depreciation calculated? (Section 8.7.3)

A8.10 How does depreciation help to retain cash in a business for asset replacement? (Section 8.7.5)

A8.11 Why does the net book value of a non-current (fixed) asset not always equal the proceeds of sale? (Section 8.8.5)

A8.12 Why is depreciation said to cause an **allocation** problem in accounting? (Section 8.8.6)

A8.13 How should the cost of a non-current (fixed) asset be decided? (Section 8.2.2)

A8.14 [S] What are the matters of judgement relating to non-current (fixed) assets which users of financial statements should think about carefully when evaluating financial statements?

A8.15 What is meant by **impairment**? (Section 8.8.7)

B Application

B8.1 [S]
On reviewing the financial statements of a company, the company's accountant discovers that expenditure of £8,000 on repair to factory equipment has been incorrectly recorded as a part of the cost of the machinery. What will be the effect on the income statement (profit and loss account) and balance sheet when the error is corrected?

B8.2
On 1 January Year 1, Angela's Employment Agency was formed. The owner contributed £300,000 in cash which was immediately used to purchase a building. It is estimated to have a 20-year life and a residual value of £200,000. During Year 1 the agency collects £80,000 in fee income and pays £60,000 in wages and other costs. Record the transactions and events of Year 1 in an accounting equation spreadsheet. (See Exhibit 8.5 for an illustration.) Prepare the balance sheet at the end of Year 1 and the income statement (profit and loss account) for Year 1.

B8.3
Assume that fee income and costs are the same in Year 2 as in Year 1. Record the transactions and events of Year 2 in an accounting equation spreadsheet. Prepare the balance sheet at the end of Year 2 and the income statement (profit and loss account) for Year 2.

B8.4
Angela's Employment Agency sells the building for £285,000 on the final day of December Year 3. Record the transactions and events of Year 3 in an accounting equation spreadsheet. (See Exhibit 8.9 for an illustration.) Assume depreciation is calculated in full for Year 3.

B8.5
Explain how the accounting equation spreadsheet of your answer to question **B8.4** would alter if the building had been sold for £250,000.

B8.6
On 1 January Year 1, Company A purchased a bus costing £70,000. It was estimated to have a useful life of three years and a residual value of £4,000. It was sold for £8,000 on the last day of Year 3.

On 1 January Year 1, Company B purchased a bus also costing £70,000. It was estimated to have a useful life of three years and a residual value of £7,000. It was sold for £8,000 on the last day of Year 3.

Both companies have a net profit of £50,000 before depreciation. Calculate the depreciation charge and net profit of each company for each of the three years. Show that over the three years the total depreciation charge for each company is the same. (See Exhibit 8.13 for an example.)

C Problem solving and evaluation

C8.1 [S]
The Biscuit Manufacturing Company commenced business on 1 January Year 1 with capital of £22,000 contributed by the owner. It immediately paid cash for a biscuit machine costing £22,000. It was estimated to have a useful life of four years and at the end of that time was

estimated to have a residual value of £2,000. During each year of operation of the machine, the company collected £40,000 in cash from sale of biscuits and paid £17,000 in cash for wages, ingredients and running costs.

Required

(a) Prepare spreadsheets for each of the four years analysing the transactions and events of the company.
(b) Prepare a balance sheet at the end of Year 3 and an income statement (profit and loss account) for that year.
(c) Explain to a non-accountant how to read and understand the balance sheet and income statement (profit and loss account) you have prepared.

C8.2 [S]

The biscuit machine in question **C8.1** was sold at the end of Year 4 for a price of £3,000.

Required

(a) Prepare the spreadsheet for Year 4 analysing the transactions and events of the year.
(b) Prepare the balance sheet at the end of Year 4 and the income statement (profit and loss account) for Year 4.
(c) Explain to a non-accountant the accounting problems of finding that the asset was sold for £3,000 when the original expectation was £2,000.

C8.3 [S]

The Souvenir Company purchased, on 1 January Year 1, a machine producing embossed souvenir badges. The machine cost £16,000 and was estimated to have a five-year life with a residual value of £1,000.

Required

(a) Prepare a table of depreciation charges and net book value over the five-year life using straight-line depreciation.
(b) Make a guess at the percentage rate to be used in the reducing-balance calculation, and prepare a table of depreciation charges and net book value over the five years using reducing-balance depreciation.
(c) Using the straight-line method of depreciation, demonstrate the effect on the accounting equation of selling the asset at the end of Year 5 for a price of £2,500.
(d) Using the straight-line method of depreciation, demonstrate the effect on the accounting equation of disposing of the asset at the end of Year 5 for a zero scrap value.

Activities for study groups

Turn to the annual report of a listed company which you have used for activities in previous chapters. Find every item of information about non-current (fixed) assets. (Start with the financial statements and notes but look also at the operating and financial review, chief executive's review and other non-regulated information about the company.)

As a group, imagine you are the team of fund managers in a fund management company. You are holding a briefing meeting at which each person explains to the others some feature of the companies in which your fund invests. Today's subject is *non-current (fixed) assets*. Each person should make a short presentation to the rest of the team covering:

1 the nature and significance of non-current (fixed) assets in the company;
2 the asset lives stated in the accounting policies for depreciation purposes;
3 the asset lives estimated by you from calculations of annual depreciation as a percentage of asset cost;
4 the remaining useful life of assets as indicated by comparing accumulated depreciation with asset cost;
5 the company's plans for future investment in non-current (fixed) assets.

Notes and references

1. IASB (1989) *Framework for the Preparation and Presentation of Financial Statements, para 49(a)* 6.
2. IASB (2004) IAS 1 para. 57.
3. IASB (2004) IAS 1 para. 58 permits the use of alternative descriptions for non-current assets provided the meaning is clear.
4. ASB (1999) FRS 15, *Measurement of Tangible Fixed Assets*, para. 2.
5. IASB (2004) IAS 38 *Intangible Assets*, para. 8.
6. IASB (2004) IAS 16, *Property, Plant and Equipment*, para. 6.
7. There remain international differences on the precise method of estimating cash-generating ability. There are detailed rules in IAS 38 but these are beyond a first-level text.
8. IASB (2004) IAS 1 para. 57.

Chapter 7

Accruals, pre-payments, depreciation and bad debts

In this chapter

We will learn how to:

- account for accrued and pre-paid expenses
- account for depreciation of non-current assets
- account for bad debts and doubtful debts

and will be able to:

- adjust expenses for accruals and pre-payments
- adjust for deferred income
- measure and account for depreciation and bad debts

7.1 The accruals concept

Income and expenses are usually accounted for applying the *accruals concept*.

7.1.1 Income applying the accruals concept

Income is accounted for in the accounting period in which it is earned, even if not fully received until after end of the period. For illustration let us assume that:

- a trader's cash sales in the year were £400;
- credit sales were £100 of which £60 has been received.

The sales reported in the Income Statement will be £500 although a part of it may not have been received by the end of the year. The amount (£40) yet to be received is recognised as earned within the period on the basis that it is recoverable, if necessary, by due legal process.

7.1.2 Expenses applying the accruals concept

Expense is accounted for to the extent it is incurred in the accounting period even if a portion of it remains unpaid at the period end. For illustration let us assume that:

- a trader's gross profit for the year is £300,000;
- his expenses for which he has already paid are £290,000;

- the £290,000 includes salaries paid of £160,000 but does not include the last month's salary amounting to £16,000 which is still unpaid.

If the unpaid salary is ignored, on the premise that it has not yet been paid, the trader will be able to report a net profit of (£300,000 – £290,000) = £10,000. The underlying concept is one of matching economic resources used with the benefit obtained from their use, i.e. include all the goods and services that have been consumed to achieve the sales for the year. In accounting terminology, making such an adjustment, is referred to as applying the accruals concept and, in the above example, would reduce the profit of £10,000 to a loss of £6,000.

7.2 Accrued expense

To report the correct amount of profit in an accounting period, the whole of the income earned in that period needs to be matched with the whole of the expense incurred in the earning process, irrespective of whether the expense has been paid for by the end of that period. If such matching is not done a business could report improved profit by merely delaying payments.

To illustrate, let us assume that having agreed to pay rent at £1,000 per month, only eight months' rent had been paid by the end of the year, so that the Rent account would report a balance of £8,000 posted to it from the Cash Book. In order to account for the full expense incurred in the year, an additional £4,000 needs to be debited to the Rent account and credited to a liability account which may be named Rent Payable account or Rent Accrued account. In practice it is common to make the credit entry in a single composite liability account named *Accrued Expenses account* instead of opening a separate account for recording the liability relating to each type of expense. The ledger accounts would be as follows:

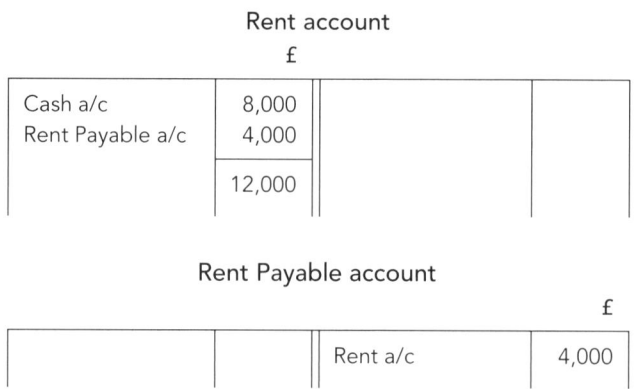

The £12,000 in the Rent account, reporting the whole expense for the period, would be transferred to the Income Statement and the credit balance of £4,000 in the Rent Payable account would be shown as a current liability in the balance sheet. Rather than opening a separate liability account, it is common practice to carry down the unpaid portion as a credit balance in the expense account. In that case the Rent account would appear as shown below:

Rent account

	£		£
Cash a/c	8,000	Income Statement	12,000
Balance c/d	4,000		
	12,000		12,000
		Balance b/d	4,000

The only difference is that the current liabilities appears as a credit balance on the Rent account instead of appearing as a credit balance in a separately named account.

Activity 7.1 The need for the accruals basis of accounting

Upon completing her first year in business as a hair-dresser, Sally Peters reports a profit of £1,470 as shown on the right. However, she has not taken into account three months' rent outstanding and £500 salary remaining unpaid to her assistant.

Required: Prepare a revised Income Statement and explain why unpaid expenses cannot be ignored.

Earnings from hairdressing	£18,500
Rent (£1,000 per month)	(£9,000)
Assistant's salary	(£5,500)
Advertising	(£1,800)
Telephone	(£460)
Profit	£1,740

7.3 Pre-paid expenses

In order to calculate the correct profit earned in a year it is necessary to match the income earned in that year with the expense relating to that year. If an amount paid in the year is expected to bring economic benefit in the following year, an appropriate proportion of the payment should be recognised as an asset at the year-end. In the balance sheet such assets are referred to as pre-paid expenses or pre-payments. The effect of the adjustment is to reduce the amount of the expense that is listed as a balance in the Trial Balance which results in a lower amount being reported as expense in the Income Statement.

For illustration, let us assume that the business entered into a rental agreement to pay £24,000 per year and that at the commencement of business on 1st January 20X7 it actually paid an amount of £30,000. This would mean that only £24,000 of the balance in the Rent account is an expense for the year. The excess of £6,000 would be an asset as at the year-end, representing the right of the business to continue occupation of the premises for a further three months after 31st December 20X7. The rent would be accounted for as follows:

Rent account

	£		£
Cash a/c	30,000	Pre-paid Rent a/c	6,000
		Balance c/d	24,000
	30,000		30,000
Balance b/d	24,000	Income Statement	24,000

Pre-paid Rent account

	£		
Rent a/c	6,000		

The pre-paid rent would be reported in the balance sheet as *pre-paid expenses* under the heading current assets. As with the Rent accrued, it is also possible to make all the entries in the Rent account and bring down a debit balance of £6,000 on that account as the current asset.

Activity 7.2 Accounting for expenses accrued and pre-paid

Expenses reported on the year-end trial balance as at 31 December 20X7 includes those listed on the right. Additionally salary £24,500 and advertising £8,400 remain unpaid at the year-end, whereas rates have been paid for five quarters at £1,200 each.

Salaries	£128,600
Advertising	£21,800
Rates	£6,000

Required: Identify the amounts at which each expense should be stated on the Income Statement and any related asset or liability to be shown on the balance sheet.

7.4 Deferred income

We have seen above that expenses incurred but not paid are included in the Income Statement and reported as current liabilities in the Balance Sheet. Similarly, income received but not earned is described as Deferred income and is reported in the balance sheet as a liability, if it is expected to qualify for treatment as income in the next year.

To illustrate, let us assume that, having agreed upon a rent of £2,000 per month, a landlord has actually received £36,000. In the landlord's books the Rent account would report a credit balance of £36,000 posted to it from the Cash Book. Since only £24,000 of this amount would have been earned in the accounting period and should be regarded as income for the period, the balance of £12,000 should be removed from the income account (by a debit entry) and posted to the credit of a deferred income account which may be named *Rent Received in Advance account*. The accounts will then appear as follows:

Rent Receivable account (income)

	£		£
Rent Received in Advance	12,000	Cash a/c	36,000

Rent Received in Advance account (liability)

	£		£
		Rent Receivable a/c	12,000

Activity 7.3 Is deferred income a liability?

In the case of the landlord referred to above it has been suggested that the rent received in advance for next year should be treated as if it were a liability. The landlord challenges this treatment pointing out that a liability is an obligation to pay, whereas he has no intention to repay the rent even if the tenant should leave the premises by the year-end.

What then is the justification for transferring the unearned portion to a liability account?

7.5 Depreciation and the straight-line method of measurement

Apart from land, all other non-current assets will not last for ever, no matter how well they are looked after. Accountants refer to this as an asset having a finite economic life – some short and others long. The payment for any non-current asset should be viewed as a payment for a bundle of services that an asset is expected to provide over its economic life. The services provided by the asset generate income and the income should be matched against an appropriate portion of the cost of the asset for determining profit.

For example, let us assume that a motor vehicle is acquired for £20,000, it is expected to be in use for four years and is expected to be disposed of thereafter for £2,000, this being known as the *scrap value*. This means that the four years use of the vehicle costs (£20,000 – £2,000) = £18,000. This amount is referred to as the *depreciable cost* of the asset.

If we use the most simple method, a fourth of the depreciable cost of the vehicle (£4,500) should be regarded as an expense in each of the four years. The portion of the depreciable cost of any non-current asset treated as an expense in an accounting period is known as *depreciation*. The simple method we have applied to measure depreciation is known as the *fixed instalment system* or the *straight-line method*. This is because in each of the four years of the asset's use the same amount (i.e. £4,500) is regarded as the expense.

Activity 7.4 Measurement of depreciation

a) What is depreciation?

b) What information do you require to determine the amount of the cost of an asset to be regarded as depreciation in an accounting period?

c) If a vehicle costing £30,000 is expected to be used for four years and to be sold as scrap for £6,000 at the end of the four years, how much depreciation will be expensed in its first year of use, applying the straight-line method for the measurement?

d) John acquired a car for £20,000 and uses it to provide a taxi service. He reports his profit in the first year as £21,800 without depreciating his vehicle. Why do you think he should depreciate his vehicle?

7.5.1 How do we know what method a company is using for measuring depreciation?

Companies in their Annual Report state their accounting policy for depreciation. The following is an extract from the 2005 Annual Report of Modelo Continente, S.G.P.S., S.A.:

Tangible assets
Depreciation is provided on a straight line basis, as from the date the asset is first used, taking into consideration the estimated useful life for each class of assets. The depreciation rates used correspond to the following estimated useful lives:

	Years
Buildings	50
Basic equipment	10 to 15
Transport equipment	5
Tools and containers	4
Fixture and fittings	10
Other tangible assets	5

Maintenance and repair costs related to tangible assets are recorded directly as costs in the year they are incurred.

Note that the number of years will naturally vary according to the type of asset – in Modelo Continente ranging from four years for tools and containers to 50 years for the buildings. The number of years will also vary from company to company. For example, Tesco plc assumes an economic life for their buildings of 40 years and 3 to 10 years for plant, equipment, fixtures & fittings and motor vehicles whereas Sainsbury plc assumes an economic life of 50 years for buildings and 3 to 15 years for fixtures, equipment and vehicles.

7.6 Accounting for depreciation

There are two methods to account for depreciation. One is to account by crediting and so reducing the balance in the asset account, the other is to make the credit in a separate *Accumulated Depreciation account.*

7.6.1 Accounting for depreciation through the asset account

Depreciation may be accounted for by removing £4,500 from the asset account by a credit entry and recording it as an expense in an account named the *Depreciation of Motor Vehicles account* by a debit entry. The accounts will then appear as follows:

Motor Vehicles account

	£		£
Balance b/f	20,000	Depreciation a/c	4,500
		Balance c/d	15,500
	20,000		20,000
Balance b/d	15,500		

Depreciation of Motor Vehicles account

	£		£
Motor Vehicles a/c	4,500	Income Statement	4,500
	4,500		4,500

At the end of the accounting period the balance in the Depreciation of Motor Vehicles account will be transferred as an expense of £4,500 to the Income Statement and the balance in the Motor Vehicle account will be reported as an asset of £15,500 in the balance sheet, being the value to which the asset has been written down by the year-end. This is known either as the *written down value* (often abbreviated to wdv) or, more frequently, as the *net book value* (abbreviated to nbv).

This process of accounting for depreciation, when repeated over the next three years, will write down the asset to its estimated scrap value of £2,000.

7.6.2 Accounting for depreciation through a separate Accumulated Depreciation account

Company law requires non-current assets to be reported on the balance sheet at cost rather than at their net book value. To facilitate this, depreciation is accounted for by a debit entry in the Depreciation account (expense) and a credit entry, not in the asset account, but in an account which is named *Accumulated Depreciation of Motor Vehicles account* or *Provision for Depreciation of Motor Vehicles account*. The accounts concerned would therefore appear as follows:

Motor Vehicles account

	£			
Balance b/f	20,000			

Depreciation of Vehicles account

	£			£
Accumulated Depreciation a/c	4,500		Year 1 Income Statement	4,500

Accumulated Depreciation account

			£
		Depreciation a/c	4,500

The Depreciation account with the debit balance records the expense, whilst the one with the credit balance holds the credit entry which would otherwise have been made in the Motor Vehicle account.

In the Balance Sheet at the end of the first year the Accumulated Depreciation account is shown as a deduction from the cost appearing in the Motor Vehicle account.

Balance Sheet as at the end of the period . . .	
	£
Motor vehicle at cost	20,000
Less: Accumulated depreciation	(4,500)
Net book value	15,500

In the following accounting periods the process will be repeated with a debit to a Depreciation account which is then transferred to the Income Statement and a credit to the Accumulated Depreciation account which accumulates the annual charges and appears in the Balance Sheet as a deduction from the Motor Vehicles account. The ledger accounts and balance sheet entries would be as follows:

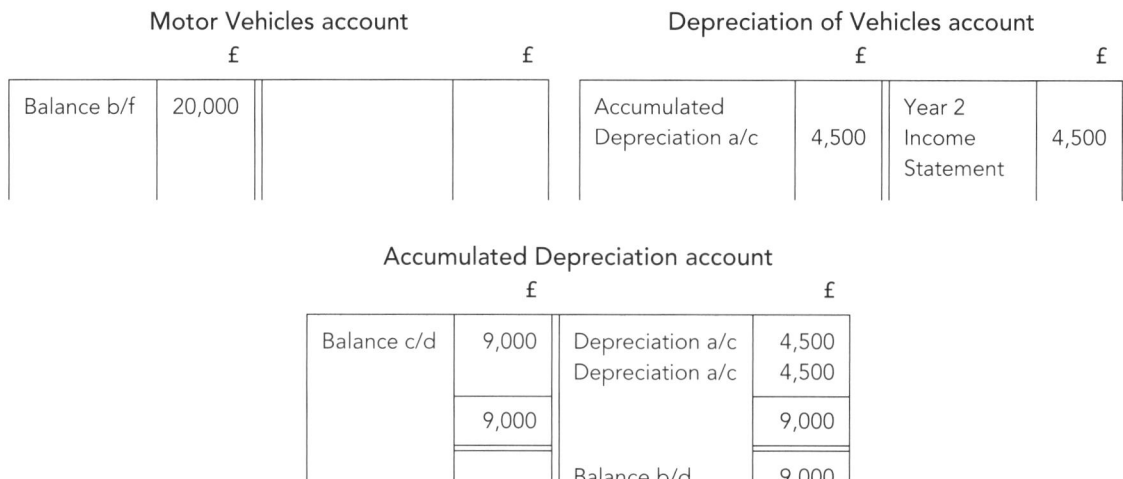

The balance sheet would appear as follows at the end of the second year:

Balance Sheet as at the end of the period . . .	
	£
Motor vehicle at cost	20,000
Less: Accumulated depreciation	(9,000)
Net book value	11,000

Activity 7.5 Accumulated depreciation using the straight-line method

A machine acquired on 1 January 20X3 for £180,000 is expected to be used for ten years and the scrap is expected to realise £20,000. The depreciation is to be calculated using the fixed instalment method.

Required: Show how the machine will be reported on the Balance Sheet as at 31st December of each year from 20X3 to 20X8.

7.7 When an asset is in use for less than the whole accounting period

When an asset is used for less than a whole year, it is depreciated for the nearest number of months of use. For example, if a vehicle depreciated at 20% per annum using the straight-line method is acquired for £20,000 three months prior to the end of the accounting period, depreciation is calculated as £20,000 × 20% × 3/12 months = £1,000.

Activity 7.6 Accounting for depreciation using the straight-line method

As at 1 January 20X7, Paula Confectioners own several machines acquired at a total cost of £480,000 and written down by that date to £218,400. On 1st April 20X7 they acquired another machine for £160,000. They depreciate machinery at 10% per annum, using the straight-line method with proportionate depreciation in the year of acquisition.

Required: Show the depreciation expensed in the year ended 31 December 20X7 and how the machinery will be reported on the balance sheet as at that date.

It is usual to time apportion when answering examination questions. However, in practice, a business may decide that it is more practical to account for depreciation for the whole year in the year of acquisition and account for no depreciation in the year of the asset's disposal.

There are also occasions when an asset may have been acquired during an accounting period but not used immediately. For example, assuming that the accounting period ends on 31st December and a building was acquired and ready for use from 1st March but was not occupied until 1st May, depreciation of the building for that period should be calculated for the ten months it could have been used, although it was used only for eight. It is a requirement of IAS 16[1] *Property, Plant and Equipment* that a non-current asset should be depreciated, not for the period for which it was used, but for the period it was available for use.

7.8 Reducing balance method of measuring depreciation

Alternatively, the depreciation to be written off an asset may be measured as a percentage, not of the cost, but of the written down value at the beginning of an accounting period. This is known as the *Reducing balance method*, because the amount written off in each successive year is a given percentage of a progressively reducing amount.

For example, if a vehicle is acquired for £20,000 and it is proposed to depreciate it annually at 20% using the Reducing balance method, the first year's depreciation would be £4,000 (20% of £20,000). The depreciation for the second year would be calculated at 20% of £16,000 (i.e. the written down value at commencement of second year).

Activity 7.7 The accumulated depreciation using the reducing balance method

A machine acquired on 1st January 20X5 for £300,000 is to be depreciated at 20% per annum using the Reducing balance method.

Required: Show amount of the depreciation in each of the first four years and how the machine would be reported in the balance sheet at the end of each year.

Since the amount written off in each period is the same percentage of a progressively reducing amount, the percentage used has to be almost double that used in the fixed instalment method. Whereas, when using the straight-line method the asset is written down to nil (or a scrap if one is anticipated), the reducing balance method will never completely eliminate the asset from the books of account because in every successive year only a percentage of whatever balance remaining in the asset account is written off as depreciation.

Activity 7.8 **Accounting for depreciation using the reducing balance method**

As at 1st January 20X7, Kite Metalwork owns machinery acquired for £720,000 and written down to £384,800 by that date. The business acquired another machine on 1st August for £120,000. Depreciation is calculated at 25% per year using the reducing balance method, with proportionate depreciation in the year of acquisition.

Required: Show the entries in the asset account and the Accumulated Depreciation account for the year ended 31 December 20X7.

7.9 Sum-of-the-year's digits method of measuring depreciation

This method attaches weights to each year of the asset's economic life. The weight depends on the asset's economic life remaining at the commencement of each year. For example, if an asset acquired on 1.1.20X6 is expected to have an economic life of four years, the weights attached to each of these four years 20X6, 20X7, 20X8 and 20X9 would be 4 : 3 : 2 : 1 respectively and the sum of these weights (referred to as digits) would be 10. Accordingly the depreciation written off in 20X6 would be 4/10 of the asset's depreciable cost.

To illustrate, let us assume that an asset costing £20,000 has a four-year life:

Year	Remaining life	Depreciation in the year	Depreciation (£)
20X6	4 years	4/10 × (Cost – Scrap value)	8,000
20X7	3 years	3/10 × (Cost – Scrap value)	6,000
20X8	2 years	2/10 × (Cost – Scrap value)	4,000
20X9	1 year	1/10 × (Cost – Scrap value)	2,000
	10 years	Sum of the years' digits	

This is a method that provides for accelerated depreciation with £8,000 depreciation in the first year whereas under the straight-line method this would be £5,000 (£20,000/4).

7.10 Bad debts and allowance for doubtful debts

Amounts due from customers are assets and reported in the Balance Sheet as debtors described as Trade receivables provided there is a reasonable assurance that the amount is recoverable, even if it is necessary to resort to the legal process. At the end of each accounting period the trade receivable balances are, therefore, reviewed to see if there is a reasonable expectation that each of the debtors will pay in full. If there is no reasonable possibility of obtaining payment then the debt is regarded as bad. If there is some possibility of obtaining payment then the debt is regarded as doubtful. We will now explain how to account for both types of debt.

7.10.1 Accounting for bad debts

If it is decided that the debt is irrecoverable, then it ceases to be an asset and is reclassified as an expense. The accounting entries needed to record this are a credit in the account recording the asset and a debit in an expense account named *Bad Debts*.

Assuming that the debt in question is one due from Jim Gee, the accounts involved will appear as:

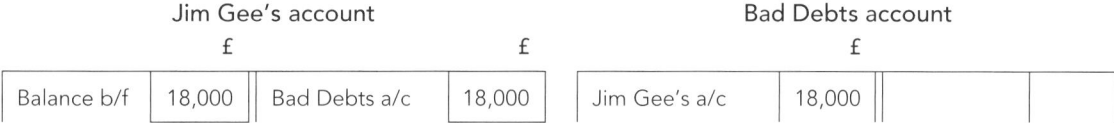

Jim Gee's account				Bad Debts account	
	£		£		£
Balance b/f	18,000	Bad Debts a/c	18,000	Jim Gee's a/c	18,000

The above entries close Jim Gee's account and show the loss as a debit balance in a Bad Debts account, which at the end of the accounting period will be transferred to the Income Statement.

7.10.2 Accounting for doubtful debts – specific provisions

The situation is not always so clear-cut that a debt can be definitely assumed to be irrecoverable and immediately treated as a loss. In real life there could be debts that are probably irrecoverable and where it would be premature to close the debtor's account, as we have done with Jim Gee, until all efforts have been made to obtain payment, e.g. making a personal telephone request, sending a solicitor's letter, applying to the court for an order. Whilst these steps are being taken the debtor's account should remain open but it should be recognised that there might be a loss and it would be prudent to provide for this in the Income Statement.

The way that the possibility of a loss is recognised in accounting is to create an *allowance for doubtful debts*. In the same way as we avoided having to credit the Motor Vehicles account, when we depreciated the asset we avoid crediting the customer's account when recording that debt as not recoverable. The credit entry is made in an account which is named 'Allowance for doubtful debts'.

Let us assume that Jim Gee's debt might not be recoverable, in which case the anticipated loss could still be accounted for by debiting the Bad Debts account. However, the credit is not to Jim Gee's account, but to an Allowance for Doubtful Debts account, as follows:

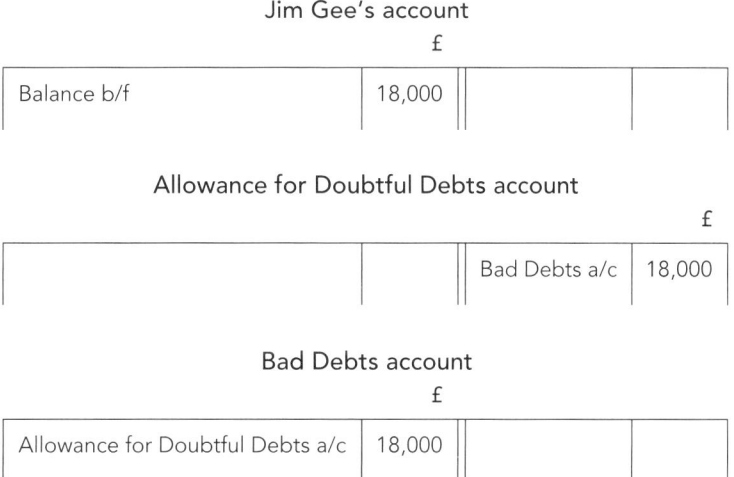

Jim Gee's account

	£		
Balance b/f	18,000		

Allowance for Doubtful Debts account

			£
		Bad Debts a/c	18,000

Bad Debts account

	£		
Allowance for Doubtful Debts a/c	18,000		

At the end of the year the debit balance on the Bad Debts account is transferred to the Income Statement and the credit balance on the Allowance for Doubtful Debts account is shown as a deduction from trade receivables in the Balance Sheet, as follows:

Balance Sheet as at the end of the year		
	£	£
Jim Gee's a/c	18,000	
Allowance for doubtful debts	(18,000)	–

What if Jim Gee settles his account in the next accounting period?

If, having set up an allowance in one year, contrary to expectation Jim Gee settles in the following year, there would then be no need for the Allowance. Accordingly the Allowance no longer needed is treated as an income in the second year and credited to that year's Income Statement.

Allowance for Doubtful Debts account

	£		£
(Year 2) Income Statement	18,000	(Year 1) Bad Debts a/c	18,000

What if, as expected, Jim's debt proves irrecoverable?

If in due course it is no longer worth pursuing Jim Gee, the credit balance in the Allowance account is transferred to the credit of Jim Gee's account, closing both accounts.

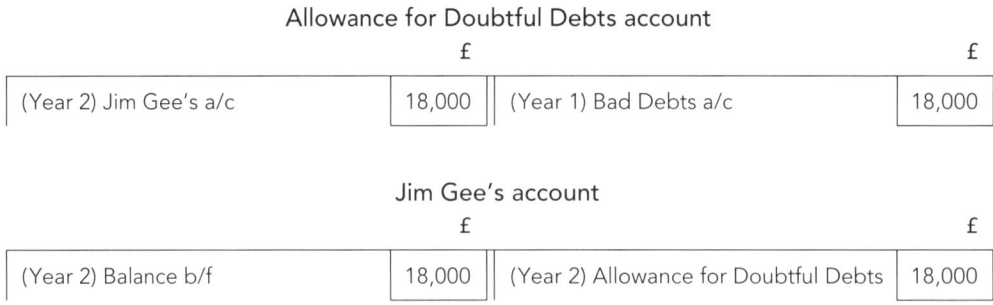

Allowance for Doubtful Debts account

	£		£
(Year 2) Jim Gee's a/c	18,000	(Year 1) Bad Debts a/c	18,000

Jim Gee's account

	£		£
(Year 2) Balance b/f	18,000	(Year 2) Allowance for Doubtful Debts	18,000

We used the case of Jim Gee to illustrate settling up an Allowance with regard to a specific debt. This is known as a *specific allowance*.

7.10.3 Accounting for doubtful debts – general allowance

A business is often unable to identify the specific debts that are likely to become irrecoverable but may be able to make a good estimate based on past experience, e.g. past experience might indicate that say 5% of trade receivables might become bad. It is common practice to base the estimate of the allowance required on an age analysis of debtors outstanding. For example, experience might indicate that no allowance is required to be made in respect of debts that are less than 30 days old (particularly if that is the agreed credit term), but that an allowance of 2% should be made on trade receivables outstanding for 30 to 60 days and 5% on those outstanding for more than 60 days. Such an allowance is referred to as a *general allowance*.

To illustrate, let us assume that Fresh Fish Supplies allows its customers 30 days' credit. As at the year-end, on 31st December 20X7, the accountant has analysed the trade receivables as follows:

Trade receivables	Date payment was due	% allowance based on past experience
£70,000	31.1.20X8	–
£35,000	31.12.20X7	2%
£10,000	30.11.20X7	5%
£115,000		

The amount to be reported in the Income Statement for the year ended 31st December 20X7 as bad debts would be 2% of £35,000 and 5% of £10,000 = £1,200. On the balance sheet as at 31st December 20X7 the trade receivables will be reported as follows:

Balance Sheet as at 31.12.20X7	
	£
Current assents: Trade receivables Allowance for doubtful debts	115,000 (1,200)
	113,800

Activity 7.9 Accounting for doubtful debts

Trade receivables reported in the books of J&B Watersports as at 31 December 20X5 amounted to £208,500. An analysis of the number of days debts had been outstanding showed the following:

Days outstanding	
Within 30 days	£124,500
Between 31 & 60 days	£62,400
Beyond 60 days	£21,600

After a review of all of the trade receivable balances, it was decided that an amount of £3,600 outstanding for more than 60 days was definitely irrecoverable. Experience indicated that an allowance should be made of 2% of amounts outstanding for between 31 and 60 and 5% of amounts outstanding for more than 60 days.

Required: Calculate the amount to be written off as bad debts in the Income Statement and show how trade receivables will be reported in the Balance Sheet as at 31 December 20X5.

7.11 Annual adjustment of the allowance for doubtful debts to account for doubtful debts in subsequent years – general allowance

The same procedure is adopted each year to determine the amount that should appear as the balance on the Allowance for Doubtful Debts account and an adjusting debit or credit is made to the Income Statement. If the allowance needs to be increased there will be a charge to the Income Statement and if the balance on the allowance is greater than required, there will be a credit to the Income Statement.

For example, let us assume that Fresh Fish Supplies calculates that it needs a allowance of £2,250 at the end of the following year. This is £250 more than the existing allowance which will therefore need to be increased by transferring this amount out of the Income Statement as an expense. The entries in the Allowance account will be as follows:

Allowance for Doubtful Debts account

	£		£
20X7 Balance c/d	2,250	20X6 Income Statement	2,000
		20X7 Income Statement	250
	2,250		2,250
		20X7 Balance b/d	2,250

In the Balance Sheet at 31 December 20X7 the balance of £2,250 would be deducted from the trade receivables total. If the allowance required at the end of 20X7 had been £1,500 then the entries would have been reversed, as follows:

Allowance for Doubtful Debts account

	£		£
Income Statement	500	20X6 Income Statement	2,000
20X7 Balance c/d	1,500		
	2,000		2,000
		20X7 Balance b/d	1,500

Activity 7.10 Adjusting the allowance for doubtful debts

The year-end trial balance reports trade receivables at £438,000 and the allowance for doubtful debts at £12,500. It is decided that a debt of £18,000 should be written off and the allowance adjusted to cover 5% of outstanding debts.

Required: Set out the Trade Receivables account and the Allowance for Doubtful Debts account, indicating the expense written off in the Income Statement and the asset reported in the Balance Sheet.

Summary

■ Results of the operations in each accounting period are determined on the basis of the accruals concept, i.e. income is accounted for when it is earned (even if yet to be received) and expenses are accounted for when a commitment is made (even if part remains unpaid at the end of the accounting period).

■ Any income received but yet to be earned by the end of the accounting period, is regarded as deferred income and treated as if it were a liability at the end of the accounting period.

■ Expenses include:
  ■ depreciation which is an appropriate portion of the depreciable cost of non-current assets;
  ■ bad debts which are trade receivables not expected to be recovered;
  ■ doubtful debts which are trade debts which may not be recovered.

■ The straight-line, reducing balance and sum of the years' digits are methods that may be used for measuring depreciation.

Reference

1 IAS 16 *Property, Plant and Equipment*, revised 2003, effective 1.1.2005, London, International Accounting Standards Board.

Suggested answers to activities

7.1 The need for the accruals basis of accounting

For correctly reporting operating results for an accounting period expenses should be accounted for on an accruals basis, i.e. not at the amount paid but at the amount incurred. If unpaid expenses are ignored, as Sally did, the result will be as follows:

a) The expense will be understated – hence the operating results over-stated (in her case reporting a profit instead of a loss).
b) The liability (commitment to pay) is not reported on the Balance Sheet.

Income Statement for the year ended . . .	
	£
Earnings from hairdressing	18,500
Rent	(12,000)
Staff salary	(6,000)
Advertising	(1,800)
Telephone	(460)
Net loss for the year	(1,760)

7.2 Accounting for expenses accrued and pre-paid

In the Income Statement:

Salaries: 128,600 + 24,500 = £153,100

Advertising: 21,800 + 8,400 = £30,200

Rates: 6,000 – 1,200 = £4,800

In the Balance Sheet:

As current asset:

Pre-paid rent £1,200

As current liabilities:
Salary accrued: £24,500
Advertising accrued: £8,400

7.3 Is deferred income a liability?

Irrespective of the landlord's intentions, the rent relating to the period after the year-end should be regarded as unearned and therefore accounted for as deferred income. Such deferred income is treated as if it were a liability.

7.4 Measurement of depreciation

a) Depreciation is the amount of the depreciable cost (i.e. the cost less the amount of scrap recoverable) of a non-current asset, allocated to each accounting period in a systematic and appropriate manner.

b) Information needed to determine depreciation:
   i) the cost of the asset;
   ii) estimated scrap value at the end of its life;
   iii) estimated useful economic life.

c)

Cost of vehicle	£30,000
Scrap value	(£6,000)
Depreciable cost	£24,000

Depreciation = 24,000/4 years = £6,000

d) Why John should depreciate his vehicle:
   - Unless an appropriate portion of the asset's cost is matched with the income generated by the asset the profit will be exaggerated.
   - Continuing to report the vehicle in the balance sheet year after year at the amount at which it was acquired will not fairly reflect the resource available to the entity at each point.
   - Depreciating the vehicle reduces the amount of profit which John would feel entitled to draw out of the business. Hence corresponding resources are automatically retained within the business so that it becomes possible to replace the asset at the end of its useful life, except where inflation spoils the situation.

7.5 The Accumulated Depreciation account

Balance Sheet as at 31 December						
	20X3	20X4	20X5	20X6	20X7	20X8
	£'000	£'000	£'000	£'000	£'000	£'000
Machine at cost	180	180	180	180	180	180
Accumulated depreciation	(16)	(32)	(48)	(64)	(80)	(96)
Written down value	164	148	132	116	100	84

7.6 Accounting for depreciation using the straight-line method

Depreciation expense:

10% of £480,000	£48,000
10% of £160,000 × 9/12 months	£12,000
	£60,000

Balance Sheet as at 31 December 20X6:

Machinery at cost (480,000 + 160,000)	£640,000
Accum depreciation (261,600[a] + 60,000)	(£321,600)
Written down value	£318,400

Note: a) Accumulated depreciation on 1.1.20X6 = 480,000 − 218,400 = £261,600.

7.7 The accumulated depreciation using the reducing balance method

1.1.20X5: Cost	£300,000
20X5 Depreciation	(£60,000)
1.1.20X6: WDV	£240,000
20X6 Depreciation	(£48,000)
1.1.20X7: WDV	£192,000
20X7 Depreciation	(£38,400)
1.1.20X8: WDV	£153,600
20X8 Depreciation	(£30,720)

Balance Sheet as at 31 December				
	20X5	20X6	20X7	20X8
	£	£	£	£
Machinery at cost	300,000	300,000	300,000	300,000
Accum depn	(60,000)	(108,000)	(146,400)	(177,120)
Written down value	240,000	192,000	153,600	122,880

Note: Each year's depreciation is calculated at 20% of the written down value at commencement of that year.

7.8 Accounting for depreciation using the reducing balance method

Accumulated depreciation on 1.1.20X7: 720,000 − 384,800 = £335,200.

Depreciation in 20X7:

25% of (£720,000 − £335,200)	£96,200
25% of (£120,000 × 5/12 months)	£12,500
	£108,700

	Machinery account				
		£			
1.1	Balance b/f	720,000			
1.8	Cash a/c	120,000			
		840,000			

			Accumulated Depreciation on Machinery account		
					£
			1.1	Balance b/f	335,200
			31.12	Depreciation	108,700
					443,900

7.9 Allowance for doubtful debts:

Income Statement	
	£
Written off	3,600
2% of 62,400	1,248
5% of 21,600 − 3,600	900
	5,748

Balance Sheet as at 31.12.20X5	
	£
Trade Receivables (208,500 − 3,600)	204,900
Less: Allowance for doubtful debts	(2,148)
	202,752

7.10 Adjusting the provision for doubtful debts

Trade Receivables account					Allowance for Doubtful Debts account				
	£		£			£			£
Balance b/f	438,000	Bad debts	18,000		Bad debts	18,000	Balance b/f		12,500
		Balance c/d	420,000		Balance c/d	21,000ᵃ	Income Statement		26,500
	438,000		438,000			39,000			39,000
Balance b/d	420,000						Balance b/d		21,000

Bad debt expense in the Income Statement:	£26,500

On the balance sheet	
Trade receivables	£420,000
Less: Allowance for doubtful debts	(£21,000)
	£399,000

Note:
a) The balance c/d in the Allowance account is calculated at
5% of trade receivables (£420,000) = £21,000.

Multiple choice questions

Accruals and pre-payments

7.1 Which of the following is correct? Where accounting records are maintained on an accruals basis:
   a) Income should be accounted for only when received
   b) Expenses should be accounted for only to the extent they have been paid for
   c) Income should be accounted on an accruals basis and expenses on a payments basis
   d) Income and expenses relating to the accounting period should be fully accounted for even if income is still to be received and expenses have yet to be paid.

7.2 An accrued expense amounting to £18,000 was overlooked when ascertaining the profit for the year. The effect of this error is that:
   a) Net profit is overstated and liability understated
   b) Net profit as well as liability are overstated
   c) Net profit is not affected but liability is understated
   d) Net profit as well as liability are understated

7.3 Expenses relevant to the accounting period which remain unpaid by period end should be:
   a) ignored until they are paid for in the next period
   b) included in the Income Statement with expenses paid and shown as a liability in the balance sheet
   c) deducted from amount already paid and shown as a liability in the balance sheet
   d) included in the Income Statement with expenses paid and shown as an asset in the balance sheet

7.4 Staff salary remaining unpaid as at the year-end should be accounted for as:

a) Debit Staff salary account and credit Cash account

b) Debit Staff salary account and credit Salary accrued account

c) Debit Salary accrued account and credit Staff salary account

d) Debit Pre-paid Salary account and credit Staff salary account

7.5 As at 1st January 20X5 salary outstanding was £128,400. During the year ended 31st December 20X5 £598,800 was paid as salary and as at 31st December 20X5 salary amounting to £142,900 remained unpaid. What is the salary expense to be written off in the Income Statement for the year?

a	£584,300	
b	£598,800	
c	£613,300	
d	£741,700	

7.6 Rent pre-paid as at the commencement of the year was £8,000. Having agreed to pay rent at £4,000 per month, the business was able to pay during the year only £28,000. The position at the year-end is:

a) Rent accrued £20,000

b) Rent pre-paid £12,000

c) Rent accrued £12,000

d) Rent pre-paid £4,000

7.7 Rent paid for eight months up to 28th February 20X6 amounts to £32,000. Since then rent has been increased by 20%. The rent written off as expense in the Income Statement for the year ended 30th June 20X6 and stated as accrued on the balance sheet as at that date would be:

	Expense	Accrued	
a	£48,000	£16,000	
b	£51,200	£19,200	
c	£38,400	£6,400	
d	£57,600	£25,600	

7.8 The monthly rent for business premises was £4,000. At 1st January 20X5 three months' rent was in arrears. £44,000 was paid as rent during the year to 31st December 20X5. What will appear as rent accrued on the Balance Sheet as at 31 December 20X5?

a	£8,000	
b	£12,000	
c	£16,000	
d	£24,000	

7.9 Camilus pays rent regularly quarterly in advance on 1st March, 1st June, 1st September and 1st December. Annual rent, agreed at £180,000, has been increased to £240,000 from 1st July 20X5. An additional £10,000 was paid on 1st July 20X5. The amount to be expensed in the year to 31.12.20X5 and reported as pre-paid as at that date would be:

	Expense	Pre-paid	
a	£240,000	£60,000	
b	£180,000	£70,000	
c	£210,000	£55,000	
d	£210,000	£40,000	

7.10 Romulus pays rent regularly quarterly in arrears on 31st March, 30th June, 30th September and 31st December. Annual rent, agreed at £240,000, was increased to £300,000 from 1st July 20X5. The amount to be expensed in the year to 31st August 20X6 and reported as accrued as at that date would be:

	Expense	Accrued	
a	£200,000	£60,000	
b	£240,000	£50,000	
c	£250,000	£50,000	
d	£290,000	£60,000	

7.11 The year-end trial balance as at 31st March 20X5 reports a debit balance of £9,800 in the Insurance account. This figure includes £6,000 paid on 1st January 20X5 as insurance for the year ended 31st December 20X5. Ascertain the amount to be charged in the Income Statement as insurance for the year ended 31st March 20X5.

a	£5,300	
b	£6,000	
c	£9,800	
d	£15,800	

7.12 A transporter's trial balance at year-end on 31 December 20X5 lists the balance in Motor Vehicle Maintenance account as £216,500. This amount includes £27,000 paid on 1 August 20X5 for servicing the fleet of vehicles over the next three years from that date. The amounts to be expensed in 20X5 and reported as pre-paid as at the year-end are:

	Expense	Pre-payment	
a	£216,500	£27,000	
b	£189,500	£27,000	
c	£193,250	£23,250	
d	£239,750	£23,250	

7.13 If an accrual as at year-end of £1,500 was treated as a prepayment, the net profit for the year would be:

a) understated by £1,500

b) overstated by £1,500

c) overstated by £3,000

d) understated by £3,000

7.14 A loan of £30,000 at 6% interest per year, was given to a member of staff, in the previous year. No interest has been received during the year. The accounting entries for accruing interest income are:

a) Debit Cash account and credit Interest Earning account

b) Debit Staff Loan account and credit Interest Earning account

c) Debit Interest receivable account and credit Interest Earning account

d) Debit Interest receivable account and credit Staff Loan account

7.15 A retailer paid £75,000 as rent and treated the whole amount as expense for the year, overlooking the fact that the amount was for a five year period commencing from the beginning of that year. The effect of this error would be:

a) Net profit and current liabilities will be understated by £75,000

b) Net profit and current assets are understated by £75,000

c) Net profit and current assets are understated by £60,000

d) Net profit and current assets are overstated by £60,000

7.16 After reporting the profit for the year it is found that £13,200 of stationery reported as an asset by the year-end had in fact already been fully used. The effect of the correction of this error would be:

a) The gross profit as well as net profit would both increase by £13,200

b) The gross profit and net profit would both decrease by £13,200

c) The gross profit would decrease by £13,200 but net profit would remain unchanged

d) The gross profit will remain unchanged but net profit will decrease by £13,200

Deferred income

7.17 A business earns income by renting out properties. During the year ended 31 December 20X6 it received £38,400 as rent. This amount includes £5,400 received as advance for 20X7. During 20X7 it received £34,500 as rent and a third of this amount relates to 20X6. The financial statements for the year ended 31 December 20X6 should report:

	Rental income	Rent in arrears	
a	£38,400	None	
b	£49,900	£11,500	
c	£44,500	£11,500	
d	£49,900	£11,500	

7.18 A business sublets three apartments in its office premises, each at £500 per month. During the year ended 30 June 20X6 it received £18,500 as rent. This includes rent received in advance on one apartment for six months to 31 December 20X6. What is the effect on the current assets and deferred income as at 30th June 20X6?

	Current asset	Deferred income	
a	£18,500	None	
b	£2,500	£3,000	
c	None	None	
d	£3,000	£2,500	

7.19 In addition to the information stated at 7.18 above, you are informed that as at 30 June 20X5 rent in arrears was £2,500 and rent received in advance £1,500. Identify the related current asset and deferred income as at 30th June 20X6.

	Current asset	Deferred income	
a	£3,500	£3,000	
b	£2,500	£3,000	
c	£3,000	£2,500	
d	£500	None	

7.20 Stated below is information relating to rental income of a business. During the year to 31 December 20X6 £74,500 was received as rent. The rental income for the year ended 31 December 20X6 would be:

As at 31st December	20X5	20X6
Rent received in advance	£4,500	£6,000
Rent in arrears	£18,000	£24,000

a	£43,000	
b	£70,000	
c	£79,000	
d	£106,000	

7.21 A part of office premises has been sublet. The rent agreed at £9,000 per year, until 31st March 20X5, has been increased to £12,000 per year since then. Rent is regularly received half yearly in advance on 1st October and 1st April. Items appearing in the financial statement for the year ended 31st December 20X5 would be:

	Income	Deferred income	
a	£11,250	£3,000	
b	£10,500	–	
c	£12,000	£2,250	
d	£9,000	£3,000	

Depreciation – the concept and accounting

7.22 The most compelling reason for accounting for depreciation is:

a) To write down the non-current asset to its disposable amount by the end of the accounting period

b) To build up resources for the purpose of replacing the non-current asset

c) To match a portion of the depreciable cost of the asset against the income generated by it

d) Because it is a requirement of company law

7.23 Which of the following describes the balance in the Accumulated Depreciation account?

a) A liability account

b) Depreciation expense written off in an accounting period

c) The cumulative sum of all depreciation expenses from the date of asset's acquisition to the present date

d) None of the above

7.24 Accumulated depreciation should be shown on the balance sheet:

a) As a current liability

b) As a deduction from current assets

c) As part of owner's equity

d) As a deduction from the cost of corresponding non-current assets

7.25 What do you understand when one refers to the net book value of a non-current asset?

a) The cost of the asset

b) The cost less accumulated depreciation up to the date of reporting in the balance sheet

c) The cost of the asset less the amount expensed as depreciation in the current period

d) The current worth of the asset

7.26 Which of the following would you include within the cost of sales:

a) Depreciation of vehicles

b) Depreciation of furniture

c) Depreciation of office equipment

d) Depreciation of machinery used in the manufacture of goods for sale

7.27 A wholesale dealer who uses his fleet of vehicles for delivering his goods to customers, reports his net profit for the year without accounting for depreciation of his vehicles. The effect is:

a) Gross profit as well as net profit are overstated

b) Gross profit is not affected but net profit is overstated

c) Gross profit as well as net profit are understated

d) Gross profit is not affected but net profit is understated

7.28 Joe Pickard, a shoe maker, reports his profit without accounting for depreciation of machinery. As a result:

a) Gross profit as well as net profit are overstated

b) Gross profit is not affected but net profit is overstated

c) Gross profit as well as net profit are understated

d) Gross profit is not affected but net profit is understated

Depreciation – the straight-line method

7.29 A trader depreciates his vehicles at 20% per annum using the straight-line method with time apportioned depreciation in the year of acquisition. In addition to the fleet acquired in previous years for £180,000, he acquired a vehicle on 1 May 20X5 for £60,000. Calculate depreciation for the year ended 31 December 20X5.

a	£12,000
b	£36,000
c	£44,000
d	£48,000

7.30 A manufacturer owns three machines – the first acquired on 1.1.20X1 for £110,000, the second on 1.7.20X3 for £90,000 and the third on 1.10.20X5 for £130,000. He expects to use each machine for ten years and realise the scrap for £10,000. Using the straight-line method, calculate the depreciation for the year ended 31.12.20X5.

a	£12,000	
b	£21,000	
c	£30,000	
d	£33,000	

7.31 Speedlink owns three trucks acquired as stated on the left. They expect to use each truck for five years. Their scrap value is 10% of the cost. Their policy is to write off the depreciable cost equally over the five years of each truck's economic life. Calculate the depreciation to be written off in the year ended 31st December 20X5.

Date	Cost
1.7.20X0	£48,000
1.1.20X2	£36,000
1.4.20X5	£60,000

a	£18,900	
b	£19,380	
c	£21,600	
d	£22,320	

7.32 A firm owns a fleet of vehicles acquired at a total cost of £264,800. Accumulated depreciation up to the beginning of the current year is £112,400. Vehicles are depreciated at 20% per annum using the straight-line method. The written down value of the vehicles by the end of the current year would be:

a	£52,960	
b	£99,440	
c	£152,400	
d	£211,840	

7.33 A builder owns three cranes, particulars of which are stated on the right. As at 31 December year 5 these are reported on the balance sheet at £99,000. The cranes are depreciated at 20% per annum, using the straight-line method and calculating depreciation for the months of use. Crane B was sold on 30 June year 6. The depreciation for year 6 would be:

a) £19,800
b) £23,000
c) £32,000
d) £36,000

Crane	Acquired	Cost
A	1.4 Year 1	£60,000
B	1.7 Year 3	£40,000
C	1.10 Year 5	£80,000

7.34 An extract of the year-end trial balance is shown on the right. A new machine had been acquired for £180,000 on 1st September 20X5. Machinery is depreciated at 10% of cost with time apportioned depreciation in the year of acquisition. The financial statements for the year ended 30th June 20X6 will report:

Trial balance as at 30th June 20X6		
	£'000	£'000
Machinery at cost	860	–
Accum depn to 30.6.20X5	–	216

	Depreciation	Written down value
a	£83,000	£561,000
b	£86,000	£561,000
c	£86,000	£558,000
d	£64,400	£579,600

Depreciation – the reducing balance method

7.35 A firm owns a fleet of vehicles acquired at a total cost of £480,000. Accumulated depreciation up to the beginning of the current year is £212,400. Vehicles are depreciated at 25% per annum using the reducing balance method. The written down value of the vehicles by the end of the current year would be:

a	£66,900	
b	£147,600	
c	£200,700	
d	£267,600	

7.36 A trader depreciates his vehicles at 40% per annum using the reducing balance method, with time apportioned depreciation in the year of acquisition. In addition to vehicles acquired on 1 July 20X5 for £180,000, he acquired a vehicle on 1 May 20X6 for £60,000. His depreciation for year ended 31.12.20X6 will be:

a	£59,200	
b	£73,600	
c	£81,600	
d	£83,200	

7.37 Gateway owns three trucks acquired as stated on the left. They depreciate their trucks at 25% per year, using the reducing balance method and time apportioning the year of acquisition. What will be the depreciation to be written off in the Income Statement for the year ended 31st December 20X6?

Date	Cost
1.7.20X3	£48,000
1.1.20X4	£36,000
1.4.20X6	£60,000

a	£22,219	
b	£25,126	
c	£25,969	
d	£36,000	

7.38 A builder owns three cranes, particulars of which are stated on the right. The cranes are depreciated at 25% per annum using the reducing balance method, time apportioning in the year of acquisition and disposal. Crane B was sold on 30th June year 6. The depreciation for year 6 would be:

Crane	Acquired on	Cost
A	1.4 Year 4	£80,000
B	1.7 Year 5	£40,000
C	1.9 Year 6	£60,000

a) £21,563

b) £23,750

c) £25,000

d) £31,563

7.39 An extract of the year-end trial balance is shown on the right. A new machine had been acquired for £180,000 on 1st September 20X5. Machinery is depreciated at 25% on reducing balance method with time apportioned depreciation in the year of acquisition. The financial statements for the year ended 30th June 20X6 will report:

Trial balance as at 30th June 20X6		
	£'000	£'000
Machinery at cost	920	–
Accum depn to 30.6.20X5	–	424

	Depreciation	Written down value
a	£112,750	£383,250
b	£116,500	£379,500
c	£157,750	£338,250
d	£161,500	£514,500

Depreciation – the sum of the years' digits method

7.40 A machine acquired for £180,000 on 1st January 20X3 is expected to have an economic life of five years and a residual value of £30,000. The machine is depreciated using the sum of the years' digits method. The depreciation for the year ended 31 Dec. 20X6 would be:

a	£10,000	
b	£20,000	
c	£24,000	
d	£30,000	

7.41 A machine was acquired for £160,000 on 1st July 20X2 and another for £200,000 on 1st January 20X5. The economic life of each machine is estimated at four years and the residual value 10% of cost. Machinery is depreciated using the sum of the years' digits method. The depreciation for the year to 31 Dec. 20X6 would be:

a	£54,000	
b	£62,000	
c	£61,200	
d	£68,400	

Bad and doubtful debts

7.42 When preparing its financial statements, if a business deliberately under-estimates the allowance required to cover doubtful debts, it would be:

   a) overstating its performance and understating its liability

   b) overstating its performance as well as its liability

   c) overstating its performance and understating its assets

   d) overstating its performance as well as its assets

7.43 A trade debt of £12,400 is to be written off as bad and the allowance for doubtful debts increased from £38,200 to £41,900. The amount to be written off against the profit for the year as bad and doubtful debts would be:

a	£8,700	
b	£12,400	
c	£16,100	
d	£54,300	

7.44 A trade debt as at 30th June 20X5 amounted to £418,400. The Allowance for doubtful debts brought forward as at 1st July 20X4 was £18,800. The proprietor decided that a debt of £3,400 should be written off and the allowance adjusted to cover 5% of trade receivables as at 30th June 20X5. Calculate the expense for the year.

a	£1,450	
b	£3,400	
c	£5,350	
d	£20,920	

7.45 Trade receivables as at 1st April 20X5 were £382,400. During the year ended 31st March 20X6, sales and sales returns amounted to £859,600 and £18,400, respectively. £659,800 was received from credit customers and £8,200 was written off as bad. An allowance for doubtful debts is maintained at 4% of debts outstanding. Calculate the expense written off in the year to 31 March 20X6.

a	£8,200	
b	£6,928	
c	£15,128	
d	£22,224	

7.46 Trade receivables as at 1 January 20X5 were £474,500. During the year ended 31 December 20X5, sales and sales returns amounted to £728,400 and £11,500, respectively. £752,200 was received from credit customers and £9,800 was written off as bad. An allowance for doubtful debts is maintained at 3% of debts outstanding. Calculate the expense written off in the year to 31 December 20X5.

a	£8,447	
b	£9,800	
c	£11,153	
d	£22,682	

7.47 As at 31 Dec. 20X5 trade debtors were £1,238,740 and the Allowance for doubtful debts was £39,420. £29,460 of trade debts have been written off already in the year. The age analysis debtors and percentage allowance usually provided are stated on the right. The bad debts expensed in the year to 31 December 20X5 would be:

Period outstanding	Amount	Allowance
Over 90 days	£12,800	100%
Over 60 days	£84,200	10%
Over 30 days	£279,400	5%
Within credit term	£862,340	0%

a) £4,230

b) £25,230

c) £33,690

d) £35,190

7.48 The year-end trial balance includes those stated on the right. Another debt of £12,400 should be written off and the allowance adjusted to 4% of debts outstanding. Ascertain the amount to be written off as bad debts in the year:

	Dr	Cr
Trade receivables	£284,075	–
Allowance for doubtful debts	–	£16,240
Bad debts	£11,600	–
Bad debt recoveries	–	£5,800

a) £1,227

b) £12,827

c) £18,627

d) £23,573

General

7.49 Which of the following would be the transaction which decreases both the assets and the liabilities?

a) A vehicle was acquired paying £32,000

b) A loan of £25,000 was settled

c) Goods were purchased for sale from Orlando Ltd for £12,800

d) Received a cheque for £5,850 from a credit customer

7.50 A balance sheet would show pre-payments as:

a) Current liabilities

b) Current assets

c) Non-current assets

d) A deduction from the capital

7.51 On its Balance Sheet a business would report as a current liability the amounts:

a) it intends to repay within one year of the balance sheet date

b) it intends to pay immediately after the date of the Balance Sheet

c) it intends to pay as early as possible but not later than a month after the Balance Sheet date

d) it hopes to repay one day

7.52 Prior to preparing the balance sheet as at 31 December 20X6 adjustments are needed for:

a) Stationery remaining unused by the year-end of £5,400

b) Rent income account includes £6,000 relating to the period after the year-end

c) A loan given to an employee is reported at £4,500 after wrongly crediting to that account an amount of £200 received as interest on the loan

d) As at the year-end salary accrued and insurance pre-paid amount to £22,500 and £4,800 respectively

After making the above adjustments the Balance Sheet as at 31 December 20X6 would report additional:

	Current asset	Current liability
a	£14,900	£22,500
b	£9,500	£33,900
c	£28,500	£14,900
d	£10,400	£28,500

Progressive questions

PQ 7.1 The impact of every transaction on account balances

The following are lists of accounts balances extracted from the books of a trader at nine different points on the same day. You are to assume that the shift from one point to the next was caused by a single transaction. You are required to identify that transaction:

	Point 1	Point 2	Point 3	Point 4	Point 5	Point 6	Point 7	Point 8	Point 9
	£	£	£	£	£	£	£	£	£
Non-current asset	40,000	40,000	40,000	40,000	40,000	40,000	40,000	40,000	40,000
Less: Depreciation	(8,000)	(8,000)	(8,000)	(8,000)	(8,000)	(8,000)	(8,000)	(8,500)	(8,500)
	32,000	32,000	32,000	32,000	32,000	32,000	32,000	31,500	31,500
Inventory	18,000	21,000	16,000	16,000	16,000	16,000	16,000	16,000	16,000
Trade receivables	15,000	15,000	23,000	18,200	18,200	18,200	18,200	18,200	18,200
Cash and bank	4,500	4,500	4,500	9,300	7,300	7,100	7,100	7,100	7,000
	69,500	72,500	75,500	75,500	73,500	73,300	73,300	72,800	72,700
	£	£	£	£	£	£	£	£	£
Capital	50,000	50,000	50,000	50,000	50,000	50,000	50,000	50,000	50,000
Add: Net profit	14,000	14,000	17,000	17,000	17,000	16,800	16,500	16,000	16,000
Less: Drawings	(4,000)	(4,000)	(4,000)	(4,000)	(4,000)	(4,000)	(4,000)	(4,000)	(4,100)
	60,000	60,000	63,000	63,000	63,000	62,800	62,500	62,000	61,900
Trade payables	6,500	9,500	9,500	9,500	7,500	7,500	7,500	7,500	7,500
Accrued expense	3,000	3,000	3,000	3,000	3,000	3,000	3,300	3,300	3,300
	69,500	72,500	75,500	75,500	73,500	73,300	73,300	72,800	72,700

Required: Identify each transaction and the amount involved.

PQ 7.2 Period-end adjustments

The year-end trial balance of Bill Renton, extracted as at 31 December 20X7 includes the items shown with related information on the right.

Item	Amount	Further information relating to each item
1. Purchases	£214,500	Goods costing £14,500 remain unsold at the year-end
2. Stationery	£3,600	Stationery costing £600 remains unused at the year-end
3. Rent	£15,000	Annual rent for 20X7 is agreed at £12,000
4. Salaries	£22,800	Staff salaries of £2,200 remained unpaid at the year-end
5. Vehicle	£18,000	Depreciation of vehicles is estimated at 20% of cost

Required: Show how each of them will appear on the Income Statement for the year ended 31st December 20X7 and the Balance Sheet as at that date.

PQ 7.3 Payments in advance and in arrears

Mod Shoes prepares its financial statements annually up to 31 December. It moved into its current premises on 1st November 20X6 agreeing a rental of £24,000 per year.

Required: Set out the Rent Account of the business for the year ended 31st December 20X7, on each of the following alternative bases:

a) rent is paid quarterly (i.e. every three months) in advance, beginning with 1st November 20X6;
b) rent is paid quarterly in arrears, the first payment being made on 31st January 20X7.

PQ 7.4 Relations between payments and expense in a new business

Information tabulated on the right relates to a business which commenced this year.

Required: Fill in the blanks in the grid with appropriate figures.

Account	During the current year:		As at the year-end:	
	Payments	Expense	Pre-payment	Accrual
a) Vehicle Maintenance	£135	£160	–	
b) Insurance	£500		–	£125
c) Salaries		£2,600	–	£55
d) Rates		£260	£95	–
e) Telephone	£290		–	£80

PQ 7.5 Relations between payments and expense in a continuing business

Information stated on the right is in respect of a business which commenced several years ago.

Required: Fill in the blanks with appropriate figures.

	Balance sheet as at 31.12.20X6		During the year ended 31.12.20X7		Balance sheet as at 31.12.20X7	
	Asset	Liability	Payment	Expense	Asset	Liability
a) Rent	£400	–	£1,600	£1,600		–
b) Fuel	–	–	£855		£155	–
c) Office equipment	£8,000	–	–			–
d) Motor vehicles	£5,500	–	£2,500			–
e) Salaries	£300	–	£6,200		–	£400
f) Insurance	–	£300		£1,200	–	£200
g) Telephone	£160	–		£420	£100	–

Office equipment and motor vehicles are depreciated at 20% and 25% per annum respectively, using the straight-line method.

PQ 7.6 Accounting for expenses on an accruals basis

In his balance sheet as at 1st June 20X6, Albert, a retailer, reported rent accrued at £400, while insurance pre-paid and rates pre-paid were reported at £360 and £350, respectively. During the year ended 31st May 20X7 the following payments were made:

Date	Item	Amount	Period covered
11.7.20X6	Rent	£600	Three months to 30 June 20X6
24.9.20X6	Insurance	£1,200	One year to 30th September 20X7
3.10.20X6	Rates	£700	Six months to 28th February 20X7
14.11.20X6	Rent	£800	Four months to 31st October 20X6
16.3.20X7	Rent	£800	Four months to 29th February 20X7
8.4.20X7	Rates	£800	Six months to 31st August 20X7

Required: Post these payments to appropriate accounts in the ledger, make the year-end adjustments and identify how each item will be reported in the Income Statement for the year ended 31st May 20X7 and the balance sheet as at that date.

PQ 7.7 A question from ICSA

Whatmore College rents a photocopy machine from City Equipment Ltd agreeing to:

i) pay an agreed rental annually in advance on 1st January and in addition pay three pence per copy taken;

ii) meet the copy charges by paying £5,000 per quarter in arrears on 31st March, 30th June, 30th September and 31st December.

As at 1st May 20X2 annual rental paid in advance amounted to £8,000 while copy charges owed was £1,245. As from 1st January 20X3 the annual rental has been increased to £15,000. During the year ended 30th April 20X3, the number of photocopies taken was 710,400. Assuming that the college maintains a single account for City Equipment, recording both rentals paid in advance and amount payables for copies taken, set out the City Equipment account for the year ended 30th April 20X3.

PQ 7.8 Accounting for income on an accruals basis (1)

The accruals basis, in relation to income, means that income is recognised in each accounting period, not in accordance with the amount received in the period, but in accordance with the amount earned in the accounting period.

Required: Fill in the blanks of the grid with appropriate figures.

	Balance sheet as at 31.12.20X6		During the year ended 31.12.20X7		Balance sheet as at 31.12.20X7	
	Asset	Liability	Receipts	Income	Asset	Liability
a) Commission earnings	£50	–	£565		£35	–
b) Interest receivable	£100	–	£900	£1,000		
c) Rent receivable	–	£150	£1,300		£100	–
d) Commission earnings	£120	–	£1,600		–	£250
e) Interest receivable	£100	–	£1,300	£1,500		–
f) Rent receivable	£500	–		£6,000	–	£500

PQ 7.9 Accounting for income on an accruals basis (2)

Free Range Stores make up accounts to 31 December each year. Premises used by them have an apartment which is rented out to university students at £2,000 per quarter. Particulars of rent received from students have been tabulated on the right.

Cash received during year 20X6		Cash received during the year 20X7	
Amount	in respect of the period	Amount	in respect of the period
£2,000	1.1.20X6 to 31.3.20X6	£2,000	1.10.20X6 to 31.12.20X6
£2,000	1.4.20X6 to 30.6.20X6	£2,000	1.1.20X7 to 31.3.20X7
£2,000	1.7.20X6 to 30.9.20X6	£2,000	1.4.20X7 to 30.6.20X7
		£2,000	1.7.20X7 to 30.9.20X7
		£2,000	1.10.20X7 to 31.12.20X7
		£2,000	1.1.20X8 to 31.3.20X8

Required: Calculate for each of the two years, 20X6 and 20X7 the amounts that should be reported as rental income in the Income Statement and as asset or liability in the Balance Sheet.

PQ 7.10 Bad debt recoveries

As at 1st April 20X6 Ronan's trade debts amounted to £186,500 and his transactions with his customers during the year ended 31 March 20X7 are stated on the right. Ronan maintains a 4% allowance for doubtful debts. The amount stated as cash received from customers includes £4,300 received from Maggie Fish whose debt had been written off as bad in the previous accounting period.

Credit sales	£528,400
Bad debts written off	£8,400
Return inwards	£19,200
Cash received from customers	£471,600

Required:
a) Explain how the amount received from Maggie Fish should be accounted for.
b) Set out the Allowance for Doubtful Debts account showing the amount to be written off as bad debt.

PQ 7.11 Allowance for Doubtful Debts account over several accounting periods

Rupert Bear's trade debts amounted to £345,500 on 1.1.20X5. Further particulars are stated on the right. He always maintains an Allowance for doubtful debt at 5% of the debts outstanding at the year-end.

	20X5	20X6	20X7	20X8
Trade debts as at 31 December	£412,500	£368,400	£548,500	£512,800
Bad debts written off in the year	£18,400	£11,800	£17,650	£14,400

Required: Show the Allowance for Doubtful Debts account showing the amount he would expense as bad debts in each of the four years.

PQ 7.12 Annual adjustment of allowance for doubtful debts

Alex Smith operates a retail business, permitting his customers one month's credit, and maintaining an allowance for doubtful debts calculated as stated in the last column of the table shown below. An allowance for doubtful debts was reported on 1 January 20X6 at

Age of receivables	As at 31.12.20X6	As at 31.12.20X7	As at 31.12.20X8	Percentage allowance
One month	£210,000	£312,500	£418,500	0%
30 to 45 days	£45,000	£75,000	£64,500	3%
46 to 60 days	£28,000	£30,000	£22,000	5%
61+ days	£15,000	£20,000	£10,000	10%

£2,400. Receivables reported as outstanding for more than 61 days, as at 31 December 20X6 includes £4,000 which was written off in 20X7 and similarly, the corresponding amount reported as at 31 December 20X7 includes £1,500 written off in 20X8.

Required: Make the necessary entries in the Allowance for Doubtful Debts account maintained by Alex for each of the three years to December 20X8.

PQ 7.13 A basic question from trial balance to balance sheet

Chrys Lunt, a trader in business for several years, has extracted the year-end trial balance from his books of account as shown on the right. He informs you as follows:

i) Goods costing £72,400 remain unsold at the year-end

ii) Salaries amounting to £13,160 and Rent of £6,000 remain unpaid as at 31 December 20X7.

iii) A trade debt of £4,400 should be written off and an allowance set up at 5% of debts outstanding.

iv) Depreciation is to be written off motor vehicles and furniture at 20% and 5% per annum respectively, using the straight-line method.

Required:
Prepare the Income Statement for the year ended 31 Dec. 20X7 and set out the Balance Sheet as at 31 Dec. 20X7.

Trial Balance as at 31 December 20X7		
	£	£
Motor vehicle at cost	150,000	–
Furniture at cost	48,000	–
Accumulated depreciation:		
Motor vehicles	–	80,000
Furniture	–	16,800
Inventory – 31 Dec 20X6	52,500	–
Purchases	326,850	–
Sales	–	532,750
Returns inwards	7,250	–
Trade receivables	64,800	–
Trade payables	–	34,250
Salaries	48,540	–
Rent	18,000	–
Other expenses	22,680	–
Capital account	–	80,000
Cash & bank	5,180	
	743,800	743,800

PQ 7.14 Proprietor's personal expenses

Bill Hardy Retail extracted the Trial Balance at the end of the first year as shown on the right. You are informed as follows:

i) As at 30 June 20X7:
   inventory costing £120,000 remains unsold
   stationery costing £3,000 remains unused
   salary £6,000 and electricity £1,000 remain unpaid

ii) Rent for office premises has been agreed at £1,500 per month.

iii) Interest is payable on City Bank Loan at 10% per annum.

iv) Motor vehicles and furniture are to be depreciated at 20% and 10% per annum respectively, using the reducing balance method.

v) A trade debt of £12,000 should be written off as bad and an allowance set up for doubtful debts at 5% of debts outstanding.

vi) Sundry expenses, reported on the trial balance includes £15,000 paid as school fees for Bill Hardy's daughter.

Required:
Prepare the Income Statement for the year ended 30th June 20X7 and a Balance Sheet as at that date.

Note: The amounts in the trial balance are listed under £'000 which means that each amount has been rounded off to the nearest thousand pounds.

Trial Balance as at 30 June 20X7		
	£'000	£'000
Motor vehicles	420	–
Depn – vehicles	–	80
Stationery	12	–
Sales	–	950
Advertising	46	–
Bank a/c	36	
Staff loans	15	–
Salaries	65	–
Purchases	725	–
Rent	24	–
Sundry expenses	32	
Trade receivables	172	–
Trade payables	–	119
Furniture	150	–
Depn – furniture	–	30
Heat & light	19	–
Cash account	3	–
City Bank loan	–	150
Staff welfare	10	–
Capital account	–	400
	1,729	1,729

PQ 7.15 Focus on closing inventory

Tony Lamb deals in alarm clocks of a standard make and model. He buys the clocks for £40 each and sells them for £60. The year-end trial balance appears as shown on the right. You are informed as follows:

i)   No accounting entry has been made with regard to 500 alarm clocks distributed free as part of sales promotion.

ii) Motor vehicles are depreciated at 20% per annum on straight-line method and furniture at 10% p.a. using the reducing balance method.

iii) The loan obtained from Tina Small, on 1.11.20X6 at 10% per year, is not repayable until 31.10.2012.

iv) Rent for office premises is agreed at £2,000 per month.

v)   Following expenses remain unpaid as at 30 June 20X7:
     Salaries £6,000
     Audit fees £3,000

vi) A debt of £4,000 is to be written off and the Allowance for doubtful debts adjusted to cover 5% of remaining trade receivables.

vii) An inventory taken on 7th July 20X7 shows that there are 1,830 alarm clocks in the warehouse. Between 1st and 7th of July Purchases and Sales were £2,000 and £1,200, respectively. Any difference in the number of alarm clocks should be regarded as those taken over by Tony for distribution among members of his family.

Required: Show your calculation of alarm clocks taken over by Tony and prepare the Income Statement for the year ended 30th June 20X7 and the Balance Sheet as at that date.

Trial Balance as at 30 June 20X7		
	£'000	£'000
Motor vehicles	180	–
Furniture	90	–
Provision for depreciation:		
Motor vehicles	–	60
Furniture	–	30
Inventory – 30.6.20X6	120	–
Purchases	640	–
Sales	–	990
Salaries	72	–
Stationery	12	–
Advertising	39	–
Postage	8	–
Sales commission	5	–
Loan to manager	10	–
Trade receivables	204	–
Trade payables	–	134
Loan from Tina Small	–	150
Light & heat	12	–
Rent	30	–
Allowance for doubtful debts	–	5
Carriages outward	9	–
Cash & bank balance	18	–
Capital – Tony Lamb	–	80
	1,449	1,449

PQ 7.16 Trial balances extracted on same date at different stages of accounting

Mike Russell commenced business on 1 January 20X6 with a capital in cash of £100,000. On the same date he acquired some furniture for £10,000 and a vehicle for £20,000. Sales during the year on credit terms amount to £492,000 and he received £458,000 from his credit customers. His payments during the year to 31 December 20X6 are summarised as follows:

To trade payables	£436,000	Salaries and wages	£48,000
Postage and telephone	£1,000	Lighting and heating	£2,000
Sales commission	£4,000	Rent	£15,000
Staff welfare	£3,000	Advertising	£9,000

Trade payables as at 31st December 20X6 amount to £29,000.

Required:
a) Account for the above transactions, extracting a trial balance as at 31.12.20X6.
b) Account for the closing inventory of £78,000, find the cost of goods sold and extract a second trial balance immediately thereafter.

c) Account for the following year-end adjustments, extracting another trial balance after making the adjustments:

> Mike expects to use his furniture and vehicle for five years and wishes to depreciate both using the straight-line method. He reports that as at 31st December 20X6 he owes £4,000 as salaries and £1,000 for heating; while the rent for the shop premises has been agreed at £1,000 per month.

d) Prepare an Income Statement for the year ended 31.12.20X6 and a balance sheet as at that date.

PQ 7.17 Another trial balance to balance sheet question

The year-end trial balance of a retailer is shown on the right. You are informed as follows:

i) Cost of goods in hand on 30 June 20X7 was £72,000.

ii) Non-current assets are to be depreciated using the straight-line method, time apportioning for the months of use. The vehicles acquired on 1st October 20X6 are expected to have a 20% scrap value after five years use. Furniture, acquired on 1st July 20X6, is expected to be used for ten years with negligible scrap value.

iii) A debt of £5,000 is to be written off and an allowance for doubtful debts set up at 5% of remaining trade receivables.

iv) Rent has been agreed at £3,000 per month. A third of the premises is used personally by the owner of the shop.

v) £12,000 salary remains unpaid as at 30th June 20X7.

vi) Loan obtained from Brown on 1 August 20X6 carries interest at 12% per annum and is repayable by 31st July 20X9.

Required: Prepare the Income Statement for the year ended 30th June 20X7 and the balance sheet as at that date.

Trial Balance as at 30.6.20X7		
	£'000	£'000
Motor vehicles	50	–
Furniture	40	–
Purchases	348	–
Sales	–	590
Salaries	78	–
Rent	40	–
Interest paid to Brown	3	
Receivables/Payables	45	27
Inventory – 1 July 20X6	42	–
Stationery	12	–
Carriage inwards	14	–
Postage	7	–
Capital account	–	90
Business rates	12	–
Telephone	9	–
Loan from Brown	–	60
Cash book	67	–
	767	767

PQ 7.18 Preparing a business forecast

On 1 January 20X8, Sally Sobers submits a business plan to her bank seeking financial assistance. Her plan is to buy ceramic vases, print decorative designs on them and sell them to the retail trade. She requires a printing machine, which would cost £10,000, and may be used for five years. She intends to buy 10,000 vases in the first year, and step up the purchases each year by 5,000 vases more than the previous year's quantity, during the next three years. The current purchase price per vase is £30, but the price is expected to increase by £5 per vase in each of the next three years. She expects to sell not less than 8,000 vases in the first year, 14,000 in the second and 18,000 in the third. Her selling price per vase will be £40 in the first year, £45 in the second and £50 in the third. She estimated that the overhead would remain at £4 per vase in each of the three years. This does not include depreciation of machine, which is to be calculated using the straight-line method. The cost of inventory on hand at the end of each year is to be calculated on the First In First Out cost flow assumption.

Required: Prepare for Sally a forecast of her business performance in the three years commencing on 1 January 20X8 assuming that all her expectations were met and ignoring interest on any finance expected from the bank.

PQ 7.19 ACCA adapted

You are given the balances on 1 January 20X6 as stated on the left and further information of transactions in 20X6 as stated on the right:

Trade receivables	£10,000
Allowance for doubtful debts	£400

Sales for the year on credit terms	£100,000
Sales returns during the year	£1,000
Receipts from customers in the year	£90,000
Bad debts written off	£500
Discounts allowed to customers	£400

At the end of year 20X6 the allowance for doubtful debts is required to be 5% of trade receivables, after making a specific allowance for a debt of £200 from a customer who has gone bankrupt.

Transactions in 20X7 were as follows:

Sales in the year (90% on credit)	£100,000
Sales returns (90% relating to credit customers)	£2,000
Receipts from credit customers	£95,000
Offset against amount due to a supplier[a]	£3,000
Bad debt written off in the year	£1,500
Discounts allowed to customers[b]	£500

Notes:
a) An amount due from a customer set off from what is owed to the same party reported as a supplier.
b) A reduction of amount receivable from a customer as an incentive to obtain early payment.

At the end of 20X7 the allowance for doubtful debts is still required to be 5% of of trade receivables.

Required: Set out the Trade Receivables account and the Allowance for Doubtful Debts accounts for the years ended 31st December 20X6 and 20X7.

Chapter 10

Control accounts

In this chapter

We will learn of:
- Control accounts and their usefulness

and will be able to:
- prepare Control accounts
- reconcile a Control account balance with the sum of corresponding individual balances

10.1 Introduction to Control accounts

Trade receivables are reported as a current asset and trade payables are reported as a current liability in the balance sheet at the end of an accounting period. It is important, therefore, that a business takes steps to ensure the accuracy of these figures. One such step is the preparation of a Control account to confirm that the total of the sales ledger balances and the total of the purchases ledger balances are accurate.

10.1.1 What is a Control account?

A Control account is one which records the total of what may be a large number of individual ledger account balances. If we consider trade receivables, for example, there may be numerous accounts, perhaps thousands, for individual debtors in the Trade Receivables Ledger, each reporting the amount receivable from a particular debtor whereas a Trade Receivables Control account will have a single balance equalling the sum of all the individual debtors' balances.

10.1.2 Why are Control accounts used?

The need for writing up Control accounts was appreciated when business entities, dealing with a large number of individual debtors (and creditors), found that extraction of a trial balance became too laborious and time consuming, because they had to extract and add up balances from a large number of personal accounts. This is particularly the case if a business is preparing a trial balance on a monthly or quarterly basis. As a solution to this they decided to maintain just one account to record in total the transactions with all debtors and, similarly, another to record in total those with all creditors. These became known as *Control accounts*.

10.1.3 Why is the account called a Control account?

It is called a Control account if the information that is entered in the account is provided by different people. For example, in the case of trade receivables it would be necessary for the Sales figure, the Cash figure and the list of balances to be under the control of three different people. If that were the case, then the manager could be reassured that the amounts appearing in the Sales Day Book and the Cash Book had been posted to individual ledger accounts. It does not, of course, prove that an error of commission has not been committed and a posting made to a wrong debtor account, only that the total sales and total cash received have been posted to accounts in the Sales Ledger.

10.1.4 Can a Control account replace the individual personal ledger accounts?

The maintenance of a Trade Receivables Control account does not mean that the maintenance of individual accounts for each debtor can be dispensed with. Without the individual accounts the amount receivable from each debtor could not be ascertained and the cash collected.

10.1.5 Control accounts may have different names

In practice you might find that a Control account is called differently in different businesses and in different computer accounting packages, e.g. a Control account maintained in respect of the credit customers might be known as a Trade Receivables Control account or a Debtors Control account or a Sales Ledger Control account or a Sold Ledger Control account; the corresponding one maintained for suppliers might be known as a Trade Payables Control account or a Creditors Control account or a Purchases Ledger Control account or a Bought Ledger Control account.

10.2 | The steps for writing up a Control account

We have seen why a Control account is prepared. Now let us go through the steps required to prepare such an account using the following Mike Otherton illustration.

10.2.1 Mike Otherton illustration

Let us assume that Mike wishes to write up a Trade Receivables Control account starting on 1st May 20X5. Mike will proceed as follows:

■ **Step (1):** Obtain from the Trade Receivables Ledger clerk a list of amounts receivable from every one of his credit customers as at 1st May 20X5:

Trade receivables as at 1 May 20X5	
	£
Mat Robert	1,000
Ivy Samuel	1,250
Rita Timothy	5,200
	7,450

■ **Step (2)**: Obtain from the Sales Day Book clerk the total credit sales made in the month of May 20X5:

Sales Day Book May 20X5	
	£
Mat Robert	6,000
Ivy Samuel	4,150
Rita Timothy	9,050
	19,200

■ **Step (3)**: Obtain from the cashier particulars of all amounts received in May 20X5 from the credit customers. This information will be readily available if the Cash Book has analysis columns.

Extract from the Cash Book	
	£
Mat Robert	900
Ivy Samuel	1,250
Rita Timothy	3,000
	5,150

■ **Step (4)**: Use the information obtained from each of the above three steps to prepare a Trade Receivables Control account:

Trade Receivables Control account

	£		£
Balance b/f	7,450	Cash	5,150
Sales	19,200	Balance c/d	21,500
	26,650		26,650
Balance b/d	21,500		

Note that each total has come from three members of staff who should be independent of each other.

10.3 A Control account balance corroborates the accuracy of individual balances

In the meantime the Trade Receivables Ledger clerk would have continued to post from the Cash Book and Sales Day Book to the individual debtor accounts in the ledger, as below:

Mat Robert's account

	£		£
Balance b/f	1,000	Cash a/c	900
Sales DB	6,000	Balance c/d	6,100
Balance b/d	6,100		

Ivy Samuel's account

	£		£
Balance b/f	1,250	Cash a/c	1,250
Sales DB	4,150	Balance c/d	4,150
Balance b/d	4,150		

Rita Timothy's account

	£		£
Balance b/f	5,200	Cash a/c	3,000
Sales DB	9,050	Balance c/d	11,250
Balance b/d	11,250		

The ledger clerk would prepare a list of the balances:

List of customers as at 31 May 20X5	
	£
Mat Robert	6,100
Ivy Samuel	4,150
Rita Timothy	11,250
	21,500

If the list total (£21,500) is the same as the control total (£21,500), then Mike is entitled to assume that the postings made by the ledger clerk are complete.

10.4   What are the benefits of writing up Control accounts?

There are several benefits such as:

1. It confirms the accuracy of the work of those writing up numerous personal accounts of individual customers and suppliers if the total of all ledger balances is the same as the Control account balance.

2. It is quicker to prepare a trial balance because a single figure for total debtors and total creditors is available instead of having to balance off and add together the balances in the accounts of a large number of individual debtors and creditors.

3. It enables the tracing of errors by localising the error, if possible, to one of the subsidiary ledgers so that there is no need to check all the accounts in full when looking for an error. For example, if a Trial Balance balances when it includes the balance in the Trade Receivables Control account, but does not when the total of individual debtors' balances is substituted, this is an indication that the initial search for the error should concentrate on the Trade Receivables Ledger.

10.5   Control accounts may be part of or may be outside the double entry system

10.5.1   Control accounts outside the double entry system

A Control account may be written up purely on a memorandum basis. Memorandum means as a note to help memory. The individual accounts written up for each customer would be part of the double entry system. What this means is that one of the pair of entries recording credit sales is in the account written up for the customer concerned and so would be one of the pair of entries recording each amount received from them. In the meantime, a Control Account (shown below in a vertical format) is written up for the purpose of ascertaining the total amount receivable from all customers on any date. If this total matches the sum of the amounts reported as receivable from each individual customer, as reported in the Trade Receivables Ledger, the accuracy of both may be assumed.

Memorandum Trade Receivables Ledger Control account		
20X5		£
1.5	Balance b/f	7,450
	Sales in May	19,200
		26,650
	Cash received in May	(5,150)
31.5	Balance c/d	21,500

10.5.2   Control accounts as part of the double entry system

Where the Control account is treated as part of the double entry system, the debit entries accounting for sales and the credit entries for amounts received are made in the Control account rather than in the individual account of each customer. Entries still have to be made in the individual debtor's ledger accounts which are maintained on a memorandum basis and are, of course, needed to keep track of the amounts receivable from each customer (and payable to each supplier). Note that these entries are outside the double entry system and some businesses recognise this by actually renaming the Trade Receivables Ledger as a Trade receivables register.

10.6 | Trade Receivables Ledger Control account

A Trade Receivables Ledger Control account would contain entries for all of the transactions that normally occur with a customer. The following is presented as a *pro forma*, i.e. as a sample:

Pro forma Trade Receivables Ledger Control account

Balance b/f	xx	Balance b/f #	x	
Sales (on credit)	xxx	Cash/cheques	xxx	
Dishonoured cheques	xx	Discounts allowed	x	
Discount (reversed)	xx	Sales returns	x	
		Bad debts w/off	x	
		Set off by contra ##	x	
Balance c/d #	x	Balance c/d	xx	
Balance b/d	xx	Balance c/d #	x	

Note: Items marked # and ## are explained on page 236.

We have already explained the accounting treatment in the ledgers of sales, cash/cheques, dishonoured cheques, discount allowed, bad debts and discount reversed and Activity 10.1 requires each of these to be dealt with in a Control account.

Activity 10.1 Trade Receivables Ledger Control account balance

Jerry Smith's trade debtors as at 1 January 20X7 totalled £12,000 and his transactions in the next two months were as follows:

	January	February
Cash sales	£1,500	£2,400
Credit sales	£15,500	£18,600
Returns by credit customers	£200	£540
Settlement discount allowed	£160	£210
Collection from credit customers	£13,650	£16,250
Reversal of discount allowed	£40	–
Bad debts written off	£240	£180
Recovery of debt written off in 20X4	–	£80

Required: Ascertain the balance he would carry down in his Trade Receivables Ledger Control account as at 31.1.20X7 and 28.2.20X7.

There are two items in the *pro forma* Control Account that require explanation:

1. The first (marked #) indicates that a customer is in credit – this could occur for a number of reasons, e.g. there may have been an over-payment or a credit allowed for defective goods returned after the customer has paid in full.

2. The second (marked ##) indicates that there has been a set off by contra – a business may possibly purchase goods from the same party to whom it also sells. For example, if we name that party John and assume that John is reported as a debtor (in the Trade Receivables Ledger) for £10,000 and a creditor (in the Trade Payables Ledger) for £4,000, it is likely that we would receive only the net amount of £6,000 from John in full settlement. To account for the settlement we have to offset £4,000 remaining in the Trade Receivables Ledger against the corresponding credit balance in the Trade Payables Ledger.

Activity 10.2 Writing up the Trade Receivables Ledger Control account

You are given the following information:

The balances in customer's accounts as at 1 March 20X7 were:	
Debit balances	£148,650
Credit balances	£14,200

The totals for March 20X7 were:	
Sales Day Book	£984,050
Sales Returns Day Book	£62,450
Discount column (in Cash Book receipt side)	£11,600
Receipts from credit customers	£846,240

Information from the Journal in March 20X7 showed:	
March 20X7	
Bad debts written off	£12,460
Discount reversed	£1,200
Offset by contra	£22,660

Balance in the Trade Receivables Ledger on 31 March 20X7:	
Credit balance	£24,280

Required: Prepare the Trade Receivables Ledger Control account for the month of March 20X7.

10.7 Trade Payables Ledger Control account

In order to write up a Trade Payables Ledger Control account the following information is required:

1. The opening credit balance brought forward: this is obtained by extracting a list of balances, at commencement of the period, from the Trade Payables Ledger.

2. Any opening debit balance brought forward: this is also obtained by extracting a list of balances, at commencement of the period, from the Trade Payables Ledger.
3. Credit purchases: from periodic totals of the Purchases Day Book.
4. Purchases returns: from periodic totals of the Returns Outward Day Book.
5. Payments to suppliers: by analysing the payment side of the Cash Book.
6. Discount received: from periodic totals of the Discount column on the payment side of the Cash Book.

A *pro forma* Control account is as follows:

Pro forma Trade Payables Control account

Balance b/f	x	Balance b/f	xx
Cash/cheque	xxx	Purchases (credit)	xxx
Purchase returns	x		
Discount received	x		
Set off by contra	x		
Balance c/d	xx	Balance c/d	x
Balance b/d	x	Balance b/d	xx

Activity 10.3 Trade Payables Ledger Control balance

Carmen owes her suppliers £224,200 on 1 March 20X7. Her transactions include those stated below:

	March	April
Purchases for cash	£11,500	£8,600
Purchases on credit	£286,400	£296,800
Payments to credit suppliers	£256,200	£288,500
Returns to credit suppliers	£12,500	£9,600
Cash discount earned	£11,200	£5,400

Required: Ascertain the Trade Payables Ledger Control account balances as at 31 March and 30 April 20X7.

Activity 10.4 Writing up a Trade Payables Ledger Control account

You are given the following information:

Balances in suppliers' accounts as at 1 July 20X7:	
Debit balances	£11,450
Credit balances	£214,840

Totals for July 20X7:	
Purchases Day Book	£627,550
Purchases Returns Day Book	£22,340
Discount column (Cash Book receipt side)	£42,800
Payments to suppliers	£586,750

Journal information:	
Offset by contra	£22,660

Balance in the Creditors' Ledger on 31 July 20X7:	
Debit balance	£5,160

Required: Prepare the Trade Payables Ledger Control account for the month ending 31 July.

| 10.8 | What action is required if a Control account balance fails to match the sum of individual balances? |

When a Control account balance fails to match the sum of the list of individual account balances, the error could be in either the Sales Ledger or the Control account, as follows.

1. Sales Ledger balances:
   - a posting error to a ledger account;
   - a casting error in an individual debtor account;
   - an error extracting a ledger balance onto the list of debtors;
   - an error casting the list.

2. The Control account:
   - an error in the amount entered from the cash account or day books;
   - a casting error.

If the Control account balance does not reconcile to the total of the list of balances, either might be incorrect. For example, if the Trial Balance balances when the Control account balance is included but not when the sum of the individual accounts is included, it would not necessarily mean that the error is in determining the individual account balances. Perhaps it could be that there has been an error in casting the Sales Day Book – this would mean that the Control account balance would be wrong and yet the Trial Balance would balance with the Control account balance included.

Activity 10.5 Reconciliation with Control account

Simon's year-end trial balance (with other items summarised) is as follows:

Trial Balance as at 30.6.X5		
	£'000	£'000
Purchases/Sales	632	984
Trade Receivables Ledger Control	216	–
Trade Payables Ledger Control	–	156
All other item balances	2,944	2,652
	3,792	3,792

Although the Trial Balance was in balance, the sum of the individual debtors and creditors, amounting to £203,000 and £147,000 respectively, failed to match the Control account balances. Further enquiry established that:

1. a page in the Sales Day Book has been added as £18,600 instead of £14,600;

2. £9,000 offset by contra between the Trade Receivables Ledger and the Trade Payables Ledger is not reflected in the Control accounts.

Required:
a) Prepare a reconciliation of Control account balances with the sum of individual debtors accounts and creditors accounts.
b) Show journal entries to correct any error(s).
c) Prepare a revised trial balance including in it the revised Control account balances.

10.9 Control accounts for other assets and liabilities

We have learned the use of a Trade Receivables Ledger Control account to control debtors and a Trade Payables Ledger Control account to control creditors and to produce totals quickly for use in a Trial Balance. We can apply the same principle to other assets and liabilities, e.g. non-current assets and inventories. For example, a Motor Vehicles account would report the total cost of all vehicles remaining in use. Each vehicle would be recorded in a Motor Vehicles Register with particulars such as:

1. The make and model
2. The registration number
3. The chassis number
4. Engine capacity
5. The cost and improvements
6. Who keeps custody
7. Supplier's particulars
8. Any guarantee/warranty
9. Mileage particulars
10. Service history
11. Major repairs
12. Insurance particulars

The sum of the cost of each vehicle stated in the register should equal the balance in the Motor Vehicles account.

Summary

- Trade receivables are reported in the balance sheet as current assets.
- Trade payables are reported in the balance sheet as current liabilities.
- A Control account is a means for a business to check that the amounts reported in the balance sheet are accurate.
- The information entered into a Control account should come from different people who are independent of each other if it is to be relied on as evidence that the balance sheet figures are accurate.
- Control accounts may be written up either within the double entry system or outside it (on a memorandum basis).
- Control accounts are useful for speedily preparing a trial balance, checking on the accuracy of balances extracted from a set of ledger accounts and for isolating errors to a particular ledger.
- Though usually identified with the Trade Receivables Ledger and Trade Payables Ledger, the Control accounts are used also to account for other assets and liabilities.

10.1 Trade Receivables Ledger Control account balance

**Trade Receivables Ledger
Control account – January 20X7**

	£		£
Balance b/f	12,500	Returns	200
Credit sales	15,500	Discount allowed	160
Discount reversed	40	Cash received	13,650
		Bad debts	240
		Balance c/d	13,790
	28,040		28,040

**Trade Receivables Ledger
Control account – February 20X7**

	£		£
Balance b/f	13,790	Returns	540
Credit sales	18,600	Discount allowed	210
		Cash received	16,250
		Bad debts	180
		Balance c/d	15,210
	32,390		32,390

10.2 Trade Receivables Ledger Control account

Trade Receivables Ledger Control account

	£		£
Balance b/f	148,650	Balance b/f	14,200
Sales	984,050	Sales returns	62,450
Discount allowed – reversal	1,200	Discount allowed	11,600
		Cash Book	846,240
		Bad debts written off	12,460
		Creditors Ledger – contra	22,660
Balance c/d	24,280	Balance c/d	188,570
	1,158,180		1,158,180
Balance b/d	188,570	Balance b/d	24,280

10.3 Trade Payables Ledger Control account balance

Trade Payables Ledger Control account – March 20X7			
	£		£
Cash – paid	256,200	Balance	224,200
Return outward	12,500	Purchases	286,400
Discount received	11,200		
Balance c/d	230,700		
	510,600		510,600

Trade Payables Ledger Control account – April 20X7			
	£		£
Cash – paid	288,500	Balance b/f	230,700
Return outward	9,600	Purchases	296,800
Discount received	5,400		
Balance c/d	224,000		
	527,500		527,500

10.4 Writing up a Trade Payables Ledger Control account

Trade Payables Ledger Control account			
	£		£
Balance b/f	11,450	Balance b/f	214,840
Purchase returns	22,340	Purchases	627,550
Discount received	42,800		
Cash book	586,750		
Drs Ledger contra	22,660		
Balance c/d	161,550	Balance c/d	5,160
	847,550		847,550
Balance b/d	5,160	Balance b/d	161,550

10.5 Reconciliation with control account

a) Reconciliation of the Control account balances with the sum of the individual personal account balances:

	Trade Receivables Ledger (£'000)	Trade Payables Ledger (£'000)
Balances in the Control accounts	216	156
Casting error in the Sales Day Book	(4)	–
Failure to record the amount offset by contra	(9)	(9)
Sum of the individual personal account balances	203	147

b) Journal:

Sales a/c	Dr	£4,000	–
To Trade Receivables Ledger Control a/c		–	£4,000
Being correction of error			
Trade Payables Ledger Control a/c	Dr	£9,000	–
To Trade Receivables Ledger Control a/c		–	£9,000
Being correction of error			

c) Revised Trial balance (summarised) as at 30 June 20X7:

	£'000	£'000
Purchases/Sales	632	980
Trade Receivables Ledger Control a/c	203	–
Trade Payables Ledger Control a/c	–	147
All other items	2,944	2,652
	3,779	3,779

Multiple choice questions

Items in a Control account

10.1 The information for preparing a Control account is obtained from:

a) the Cash Book

b) the Ledger

c) the books of prime entry

d) the General Journal

10.2 Which of the following will not appear in the Trade Receivables Ledger Control account?

a) Amounts received from credit customer

b) Cash sales

c) Credit Sales

d) Bad debts written off

10.3 Which of the following will not appear in the Trade Payables Ledger Control account?

a) Discount allowed

b) Credit purchases

c) Returns outwards

d) Amounts paid to trade payables

10.4 The periodical totals of the Returns Inwards Day Book is:

a) Debited to the Trade Receivables Ledger Control account

b) Credited to the Trade Receivables Ledger Control account

c) Debited to the Trade Payables Ledger Control account

d) Credited to the Trade Payables Ledger Control account

10.5 The periodical totals of the Discount Column on the receipt side of the Cash Book is:

a) Debited to the Trade Payables Ledger Control account

b) Credited to the Trade Payables Ledger Control account

c) Credited to the Trade Receivables Ledger Control account

d) Debited to the Trade Receivables Ledger Control account

10.6 Offset by contra is accounted for by:

a) A debit in the Trade Payables Ledger Control and a credit in the Trade Receivables Ledger Control accounts □

b) A debit in the Trade Receivables Ledger Control and a credit in the Trade Payables Ledger Control accounts □

c) A combination of entries stated in (a) above as well as in (d) below □

d) A debit and a credit respectively in the account of the particular customer appearing in the Trade Receivables Ledger and in the Trade Payables Ledger. □

Preparing a Trade Receivables Ledger Control account

10.7 As at 1 August 20X7 the Trade Receivables ledger had £216,400 debit balances and £11,450 credit balances. Credit sales in August were £582,550 and sales returns £31,600. £498,200 has been received from credit customers. Identify the debit balance by the month-end assuming that the only additional information provided was as stated in each of the following alternative scenarios.

a) Discount allowed was £14,400 and credit balances by month-end were £19,750.

x) £166,600

y) £254,750

z) £263,050

b) £235,000 of the amount received from trade receivables were net of 6% cash discount, and £14,800 of the amount received from customers was in respect of a debt written off as bad in the previous month – credit balances in the Sales Ledger by the month-end was £9,240.

x) £266,740

y) £267,640

z) £281,540

c) A trade debt of £9,500 was written off as bad in August and a cheque for £14,100 received from a customer is returned dishonoured by the bank. Upon receipt of this cheque the customer had been allowed 6% cash discount. Discount allowed in the month was £9,400 and credit balances in the Trade Receivables Ledger by the month-end was £7,200.

x) £261,000

y) £261,900

z) £270,400

d) In August £11,500 was offset by contra, £4,840 was allowed as cash discount and £2,100 was written off as bad. Credit balances in the Trade Receivables Ledger by the month-end were £14,200.

x) £253,460

y) £258,290

z) £276,450

Writing up a Trade Payables Ledger Control account

10.8 During October 20X7, purchases, purchases returns and amounts paid to suppliers were £728,450, £11,200 and £682,500 respectively. As at 1st October a list of Trade Payables Ledger balances included £149,550 credit balances and £7,400 debit balances. Identify the total of credit balances in the Trade Payables Ledger, by the month-end, assuming that the only additional information provided is as stated in each of the following alternative scenarios.

a) Payments to trade payables include £280,250 paid taking advantage of 5% cash discount offered by the suppliers and by the month end the debit balances in the Purchases Ledger amounted to £5,200.

   x) £176,900

   y) £167,350

   z) £182,100

b) During the month of October offset by contra amounted to £15,800, while by the month-end the debit balances in the Trade Payables Ledger amounted to £8,700.

   x) £169,800

   y) £161,100

   z) £201,400

10.9 Place a tick in one of the following grids to identify which of the four alternatives is the correct analysis of the side in which the items listed below will appear in a Trade Receivables Ledger Control account:

i) Cash sales	v) Reversal of discount allowed	ix) Offset by contra
ii) Credit sales	vi) Receipts from credit customers	x) Return inwards
iii) Discount allowed	vii) Allowance for doubtful debts	xi) Return outwards
iv) Carriage inwards	viii) Recovery of bad debt previously written off	xii) Bad debt written off

	On the debit side	On the credit side	On neither side	
a	i, ii, iv	iii, viii, vi, ix, x	v, vii, xi, xii	
b	ii, v	iii, vi, vii, ix, x	i, iv, viii, xi, xii	
c	ii, v	iii, vi, ix, x, xii	i, iv, vii, viii, xi	
d	ii, v, viii	iii, iv, vi, vii, ix, xi	i, x, xii	

Focus on the concept

10.10 Which of the following statements relating to Control account is correct?

   i) Control account is always written up on a memorandum basis

   ii) Control account is part of the double entry system

   iii) If a Control account is maintained the individual customers' accounts need not be

   iv) Customer's accounts may be written up on double entry basis or outside it

a	i, ii & iv	
b	ii, iii & iv	
c	ii & iv	
d	iii & iv	

10.11 Which of the following would be a normal reason for a credit balance appearing in the Trade Receivables Ledger?

   i) A customer may occasionally be also a supplier

   ii) A customer could have returned some goods after paying for them

   iii) A customer may have paid without realising his cash discount entitlement

   iv) Offset by contra exceeded the amount receivable from that customer

a	ii & iii	
b	i & ii	
c	iii & iv	
d	ii & iv	

10.12 Which of the following would be valid reasons for writing up Control accounts?

   i) It becomes possible to expedite the preparation of trial balances

   ii) It could be part of the company's internal control system

   iii) It is fashionable to write up Control accounts

   iv) It would become possible to localise any error to one of the subsidiary ledgers

a	ii, iii & iv	
b	i, ii & iii	
c	i, ii & iv	
d	i, iii & iv	

10.13   If the Trade Receivables Ledger Control account balance differs from the sum of individual receivable balances:

a) Control account balance has to be the correct amount receivable from customers

b) Sum of the individual balances has to be the correct amount receivable from customers

c) Neither amount may be the correct amount receivable from customers

d) Control account balance would be correct if the trial balance balances when it is included in it

Reconciliation of sum of individual balances with Control Account balance

10.14   The sum of the debit balances extracted from the Trade Receivables Ledger is different from the debit balance carried down in the Trade Receivables Ledger Control account. Inquiries revealed the following errors. Identify, by placing a tick in the appropriate grid, whether the correction of the error would involve (x) an adjustment to the sum of the list of Receivable balance or (y) an adjustment to the Control account balance or (z) adjustments to both.

List	Control	Both
x	y	z

a) A trade debt has been omitted from the list

b) A customer with a credit balances has been listed as a debit balance

c) A folio of the Sales Day Book was added as £214,500 instead of £254,500

d) A debt regarded as irrecoverable has not been written off

e) £1,400 received from a customer has been posted to the debit of his account

f) Debt collection fees recovered from a customer are not recorded in the Control account

g) A Returns Inwards Day Book folio was added as £9,450 instead of £9,400

h) A sale of £12,400 was posted to the customer as £1,240

i) An invoice for £16,000 was recorded as £1,600 in the Sales Day Book

j) A dishonoured cheque has been posted to the credit of the customer's account

k) A credit note received from a supplier has been entered in the Sales Day Book

l) A customer's account balance was extracted as £2,480, instead of £3,480

10.15   If a Trial Balance balances when the Trade Receivables Ledger Control account balance is included in it and does not when the sum of the list of customers' account balances is included, it would be obvious that the error is in:

a) The individual customers' accounts in the Sales Ledger

b) The Trade Receivables Ledger Control account

c) Either the Trade Receivables Ledger Control account or the individual accounts of the Trade Receivables Ledger

d) Neither the Trade Receivables Ledger Control account nor the individual customers' accounts

10.16 As at 31st March 20X7 the Trade Receivables Ledger Control account balance was reported as £296,400 and this did not agree with the sum of the individual customers' balances. The following errors were discovered.

i)   A dishonoured customer's cheque for £4,500 has been posted to the credit of the customer's account

ii) Return inwards day book was added as £17,600 instead of £27,600

iii) A copy sales invoice of £42,800 has been recorded as £24,800 in the day book

iv) £11,500 offset by contra is entered on the debit side of the Control account

a	£263,400
b	£290,400
c	£292,900
d	£281,400

Identify the trade receivables as at 31st March 20X7.

10.17 Sum of the individual customers' balances, as at 30th September 20X7, was £492,800. This did not agree with the balance in the Trade Receivables Ledger Control account. The following errors have been discovered.

i)   Total of the discount column on the receipt side of the Cash Book was over-cast by £1,800

ii) A sales invoice for £8,200 was not entered in the Sales Day Book

iii) £5,400 offset by contra is not recorded in both Personal Ledger Control accounts

iv) A cheque for £3,000 received from a customer has been debited to his account

a	£495,000
b	£493,200
c	£498,000
d	£489,600

Identify the trade receivables as at 30th September 20X7.

10.18 The Trade Receivables Ledger Control account balance, as at 30th June 20X7, was £412,500. This did not agree with the sum of individual customers' balance. The following errors have since been discovered.

i)   A copy debit note for £900 sent with goods returned to a supplier was entered in the Sales Journal

ii) £40 carriage outwards has been debited in error to the customer's account

iii) A sales invoice for £1,750 has not been posted to the customer's account

iv) Return inwards journal has been under-cast by £3,000

a	£409,410
b	£407,700
c	£407,750
d	£410,790

Identify the sum of the individual customers' balances as found before correction.

10.19 Which of the following errors will not cause the Trade Receivables Ledger Control account balance to disagree with the sum of the list of individual ledger balances?

i)   A credit note for £900 issued to a customer has not been entered in the Returns Inwards Journal

ii) A sales invoice for £6,400 has been posted to the customer as £4,600

iii) The customer's list includes a credit balance of £1,800 as a debit balance

iv) The discount column on the receipt side of Cash Book has been over-cast by £1,400

v)   £350 discount allowed to a customer has been posted to his account as £35

a	ii only
b	ii & iii
c	i only
d	iii & iv

Correction of error

10.20 The difference in trial balance was placed in a Suspense account and subsequently, upon correction of the following errors, the Suspense account balance was fully cleared.

   i)   £380, the weekly total of the discount column on the payment side of the Cash Book, has been posted to the debit of Discount Allowed account

   ii) £12,450 off set by contra was incorrectly debited to the Trade Receivables Ledger Control account and credited to the Trade Payables Ledger Control account

   iii) A supplier's credit note for £4,800 has not been posted

   iv) Bank charges amounting to £24 have not been accounted for

   The balance placed in suspense would have been:

a	£4,040 Dr
b	£4,420 Dr
c	£5,180 Cr
d	£5,560 Cr

Reconciliation of personal ledger balances

10.21 Sheila, a cosmetics retailer, buys her supplies from Eumigs. As at 1st April Sheila owed Eumigs £29,450. She has received two invoices from Eumigs for purchases during April for £54,550 and £48,500. Another invoice from Eumigs and a remittance of £80,640 by Sheila are in transit as at 30th April. When making the remittance Sheila took into account a cash discount of 4%. A monthly statement received from Eumigs shows the amount due from Sheila as £155,800. Identify the amount Shiela owes Eumigs as at 30th April.

a	£23,300
b	£71,800
c	£75,160
d	£155,800

10.22 Raymond, a dealer in motor spares, received a statement from his supplier Sedan plc reporting the balance to be paid as £179,500, whereas Raymond's own Trade Payables Ledger reports an amount owing of £98,440. Inquiries reveal

   i)   A remittance of £45,000 by Raymond is still to be received by Sedan

   ii) Raymond is yet to receive an invoice for £32,500 from Sedan

   iii) Raymond is not aware that Sedan has refused a cash discount of £560 because the cheque did not reach him within the stipulated time

   How much is the discrepancy remaining to be investigated?

a	£3,000
b	£3,560
c	£4,120
d	£12,500

General

10.23 Which of the following is an appropriate description of current assets?

   a) Assets which are readily convertible into cash

   b) Assets intended to be used or converted into cash prior to the next balance sheet date

   c) Assets which are not fixed to the ground (like buildings)

   d) Assets capable of motion (such as motor vehicles)

10.24 Which of the following would not be listed among current assets on a balance sheet?

   a) Trade receivables

   b) Opening inventory

   c) Closing inventory

   d) Pre-paid expenses

10.25 Which of the following would not be an appropriate description of working capital?

a) Current assets minus current liabilities

b) Capital employed in a business minus the amount tied down in non-current assets

c) The amount of business resources available to finance the day to day operations

d) The amount of capital introduced by the owner to carry on with the business operations

10.26 Simple Simon's capital at commencement of the year was £234,500 and by the year-end was £258,400. Identify the profit he made in the year, in each of the following alternative scenarios.

a) He drew £3,000 per month for his household expenses:

x) £12,100

y) £23,900

z) £59,900

b) His drawings were £2,000 per month plus an additional £3,500 during Christmas:

x) £3,600

y) £27,500

z) £51,400

c) His drawings were £2,500 per month, but he introduced £10,000 as additional capital during the year:

x) £40,000

y) £43,900

z) £53,900

10.27 Determine the amount of current assets and current liabilities that will result as at 31st December 20X7 from all of the following adjustments.

i) The Rent Income account includes £3,600 received as rent for four months from 1st December 20X7

ii) The debit balance in the Insurance account includes £9,600 paid for the year ending 31st March 20X8

iii) A supplier's invoice for stationery amounting to £800 is yet to be received

iv) Telephone bill for £1,240, received on 2nd January 20X8 and yet to be accounted for, includes £600 rental for the year to 30 June 20X8

	Current asset	Current liability	
a	£300	£4,740	
b	£3,900	£2,700	
c	£2,700	£3,500	
d	£2,400	£4,440	

10.28 On 1st January 20X7 Paul borrowed £60,000 from his friend Peter agreeing to re-pay the amount in five equal instalments commencing from 1st January 20X8. Ignore interest. How will the amount owed to Peter be reported in Paul's Balance Sheet as at 31st December 20X7?

a) £60,000 as a non-current liability

b) £60,000 as a current liability

c) £12,000 as a current liability and £48,000 as a non-current liability

d) £18,000 as a current liability and £48,000 as a non-current liability

10.29 Stated below is a list of accounting documents each identified by a letter stated in front. State in the grid on the right the appropriate identifying letter to name the document being described:

a) invoice   b) receipt   c) statement   d) credit note   e) cash sales memo   f) voucher

i) Document sent to customers every month to confirm the transactions during the month

ii) A written acknowledgement of amount received

iii) One or more written evidence of transactions accounted for

iv) A note to inform a customer that his account has been credited with any returns

v) The evidence usually available to support a cash purchase

vi) A document advising the customer that his/her account has been debited

Answers to multiple choice questions
10.1: c   10.2: b   10.3: a   10.4: b   10.5: c   10.6: a   10.7a: z   10.7b: x   10.7c: x   10.7d: x   10.8a: y   10.8b: x   10.9: c
10.10: c   10.11: a   10.12: c   10.13: c   10.14a: x   10.14b: x   10.14c: y   10.14.d: z   10.14e: x   10.14f: y   10.14g: y
10.14h: x   10.14i: z   10.14j: x   10.14k: z   10.14l: x   10.15: c   10.16: d   10.17: a   10.18: b   10.19: c   10.20: a
10.21: b   10.22: a   10.23: b   10.24: b   10.25: d   10.26a: z   10.26b: z   10.26c: y   10.27: d   10.28: c   10.29i: c
10.29ii: b   10.29iii: f   10.29iv: d   10.29v: e   10.29vi: a

Progressive questions

PQ 10.1 A question from AAT

The financial year of The Better Trading Company ended on 30 November 20X7. You have been asked to prepare a Total Receivables account and a Total Payables account. You are able to obtain the following information for the financial year from the books of original entry:

Sales: Cash	£344,890	Refunds given to cash customer	£5,070
Credit	£268,187	Balance in the Sales Ledger set off against	
Purchases: Cash	£14,440	the balance in the Purchases Ledger	£70
Credit	£496,600	Bad debts written off	£780
Receipts from credit customers	£250,570	Increase in the provision for bad debts	£90
Payments to suppliers on credit	£403,970	Credit notes issued to credit customers	£4,140
Discounts allowed	£5,520	Credit notes received from credit suppliers	£1,480
Discounts received	£3,510		

According to the audited financial statements for the previous year, receivables and payables as at 1st December 20X6 were £26,555 and £43,450, respectively.

Required: Draw up the relevant total accounts.

Note: A Total account is another name for a Control account.

PQ 10.2 Trade Receivables Ledger Control and Trade Payables Ledger Control accounts

The following information relates to the personal accounts of a trader during March 20X7:

	£
Cash purchases	62,400
Credit purchases	264,600
Carriage inwards	102,450
Carriage outward	412,200
Paid to suppliers	198,500
Return inwards	26,450
Return outwards	11,500
Cash sales	102,450
Credit sales	412,200
Bad debts	3,800
Settlement discount allowed to customers	15,950
Settlement discount received from suppliers	9,450
Receipts from customers	368,500
Dishonour of cheques received from customers	6,650
Reversal of discount allowed to customers	350
Debt collection expense charged to customers	150
Debt recovered by contra offset	15,500
Interest charged on a customer who persistently overstepped credit period	225

	Trade Receivables Ledger balances:		Trade Payables Ledger balances:	
As at 1st March 20X7	Debit balance	£348,250	Debit balance	£9,400
	Credit balance	£16,200	Credit balance	£225,700

	Trade Receivables Ledger balances:		Trade Payables Ledger balances:	
As at 31st March 20X7	Credit balance	£17,200	Debit balance	£11,500

Required:
a) The Trade Receivables Ledger Control account.
b) The Trade Payables Ledger Control account.

PQ 10.3 Wrongly drafted Sales Ledger Control account

A newly qualified accountant has drafted the Sales Ledger Control account for March 20X7 as shown as follows:

Sales Ledger Control account

20X7	£	20X7	£
1.3. Balance b/f	422,400	1.3. Balance b/f	18,500
Cash sales	64,500	Bank – cheques received	399,500
Credit sales	482,750	Bad debts written off	5,400
Discount allowed	4,200	Discount received	1,800
Purchase ledger contra	17,400	Return inwards	3,850
		Cheques dishonoured	1,200
31.3. Balance c/d	3,800	31.3. Balance c/d	564,800
	995,050		995,050

Each amount shown in the account, other than the closing balance of £564,800 is correct.

a) Re-draft the Sales Ledger Control Account correctly.

b) The list of individual customer's balances extracted as at 31 March 20X7 totalled £467,300 which did not match the Control account balance. The following errors have since been found:

   i) A folio of the Sales Day book has been overcast by £1,000

   ii) A credit balance of £3,800 in a customer's account has been included in the list as a debit balance.

   iii) A customer's cheque for £300 which has been dishonoured has been entered in the individual customer's account as a credit.

Required: Reconcile the total of the list of balances with the Control Account balance.

PQ 10.4 Reconciliation of Control account balance with sum of the list of individual balances

As at 31st May 20X7 the Trade Receivables Ledger Control account debit balance was £408,900, whereas the sum of the individual trade receivables accounts was £407,360. Investigations revealed the following errors:

i)   The discount column on the receipt side of the cash book was added as £2,850 instead of £1,750.

ii) A cheque for £3,500 received from Betty Brown has been posted to the debit of her personal account.

iii) £4,840 receivable from John Brass, regarded as irrecoverable, has not been written off.

iv) £7,950 due from Sam Black, set off by contra, is not recorded in the Control account.

v)   A folio of the Sales Day Book has been added as £28,800 instead of £23,800.

vi) Any difference between the two sets of balances has arisen because of a credit balance in Mary Ratner's account had been listed as a debit balance in the list of customers' balances.

Required: Set out a reconciliation of the two sets of balances.

PQ 10.5 Reconciliation of Trade Payables Control account balance with individual balances

In the books of Morden Textiles, the Trade Payables Ledger Control account reports as at 31.12.20X7 a credit balance of £326,200 and a debit balance of £4,500. The list of individual trade payables balances extracted from the Trade Payables Ledger on the same date shows credit balances totalling £333,600 and debit balances of £2,800. The following errors have been identified since then:

i)   A debit balance of £1,700 in a supplier's account has been listed, in error, as a credit balance.

ii) A credit note received from a supplier for £3,600 is still to be accounted for.

iii) A contra entry of £8,200 with the Sales Ledger is posted to the credit side of Trade Payables Ledger Control account.

iv) A Returns Outwards Day Book folio is added as £43,000 instead of £40,000.

v)   The remainder of the error arose from the failure to post a payment to the supplier's account.

Required: Prepare a reconciliation of purchase ledger balances with those in the Control account.

PQ 10.6 Part of a question from ACCA

The following errors have been discovered:

i)   An invoice for £654 has been entered in the Purchases Day Book as £456.

ii) A prompt payment discount of £100 from a supplier has been completely omitted from the books.

iii) Purchases of £250 had been entered on the wrong side of the supplier's account in the Purchases Ledger.

iv) No entry had been made to record an agreement to contra an amount of £600 owed against an amount of £400 receivable from the same party.

v)   A credit note of £60 had been entered as if it was an invoice.

Required: State the numerical effect on the Purchases Ledger Control account balance of each of the above errors.

PQ 10.7 Another question from ACCA

The Sales Ledger Control account of C Ltd is on the right. A list of individual customer balances at the month-end shows debit balance as £54,468.59 and credit balance as £520.80.

The following facts have now been discovered:

Sales Ledger Control account

	£		£
Balance b/d	70,814.16	Balance b/d	1,198.73
Sales	54,738.36	Sales returns	2,344.39
Dishonour of cheque	607.15	Cash book	68,708.27
Debt collection fees	108.81	Contra	378.82
		Bad debts	474.16
Balance c/d	1,194.26	Balance c/d	54,358.37

1) No entries have been made in the Sales Ledger for the debt collection fees and bad debts written off.

2) The Sales Day Book has been over-added by £500.

3) The Sales Returns Day Book has been under-added by £10.

4) A credit balance of £673.46 has been taken as a debit balance when listing the customer balances.

5) The account of a customer who settled by contra was debited with £378.82.

6) A debit balance on a customer's account of £347.58 has been stated in the list as £374.85.

7) The dishonoured cheque had been entered in the sales ledger as a credit of £601.75.

Required:
a) Correct the Sales ledger control.
b) Reconcile the corrected Control balances with the sum of the individual balances.

PQ 10.8 Another question from ACCA

A trial balance has an excess of debits over credits of £14,000 and a Suspense account has been opened to make it balance. It is later discovered that:

i)   the discounts allowed balance of £3,000 and the discount received balance of £7,000 have been entered on the wrong side of the trial balance.

ii) The Creditors Control account balance of £233,786 has been included in the trial balance as £237,386.

iii) An invoice of £500 had been omitted from the Sales Day Book.

iv) The balance on the current account with the senior partner's wife has been omitted from the trial balance.

Required:
a) Set out how you would make the necessary corrections.
b) Show the Suspense account, assuming that the corrections eliminated the balance placed in it.

PQ 10.9 A question from paper (3) CAT

At 30 November 20X4 the balance on the Receivables Control account in Elizabeth's General Ledger was $39,982. The total of the list of balances on the customers' personal accounts was $39,614. Elizabeth discovered the following errors:

i)   an invoice for $288 was entered correctly in the General Ledger, but no entry was made in the personal ledger.

ii) a payment of $1,300 was accepted in full settlement of a balance of $1,309. No entry was made to record the discount.

iii) A credit note issued to a credit customer for $120 was incorrectly treated as an invoice.

iv) An addition error on a personal account meant that the balance was understated by $27.

v) A customer had lodged a payment of $325 directly to Elizabeth's Bank account. The balance in the personal account was adjusted, but no entry was made in the General Ledger.

vi) An invoice for $644 was posted as £466 in the General Ledger.

vii) A credit balance of $47 on a customer's account was treated as a debit balance.

Required:
a) The Receivables Control account, including the necessary correcting entries.
b) Prepare a reconciliation of Control account balance with sum of the list of balances.
c) State the correct receivables balance for inclusion in final accounts and indicate where it should be reported on the balance sheet.

PQ 10.10 Reconciliation of Control account balance with sum of individual balances (1)

Bruce Stationers maintains a Trade Receivables Ledger Control account in the Real Ledger and has organised the Sales Ledger on a self-balancing basis. On 31st March 20X7, the Sales Ledger Control account (in the Nominal Ledger) showed a debit balance of £346,800 and a credit balance of £16,200. These do not agree with the sum of the balances extracted from the individual accounts in the Sales Ledger. Subsequent inquiries reveal as follows:

i) A sale of £12,400 has been posted to the customer in the Sales Ledger as £21,400.

ii) The January 20X7 total of the Sales Day Book has been added as £116,400 instead of £114,800.

iii) The dishonour of a cheque for £6,800 has been posted to the credit of the customer's account.

iv) A credit balance of £2,800 in a customer's account has been listed as a debit balance in the list of balances.

v) The Discount column, on the Receipt side of the Cash Book, has been added as £21,600 instead of £22,200.

vi) A payment of £160 for delivering goods to a customer's residence has been posted in error to the customer's account (as well as the Control account) instead of the Delivery Expense account in the Nominal Ledger.

vii) £2,600 written off as bad debt has not been entered in the Control account.

viii) Because of a casting error when balancing a customer's account, £26,700 is reported as receivable from that customer whereas the correct amount should be £29,700.

ix) A debt collecting expense of £650 incurred in obtaining judgement against a trade receivable remains unpaid. This item is still to be charged to the customer in the Sales Ledger and to be included in the Control account.

x) The recovery of £7,200 in respect of debts written off in the previous year has been posted to the credit of the Control account.

xi) The recovery of a debt of £8,200 by off-set contra is yet to be recorded in either of the Control accounts.

xii) A 5% settlement discount, claimed by a customer from whom a cheque for £4,275 was received, although approved, is still to be accounted for.

Required: Prepare a reconciliation of the sales ledger balances with the balances in the Control account, identifying the sum of the individual sales ledger balances prior to embarking on the reconciliation.

PQ 10.11 Reconciliation of Control account balance with sum of individual balances (2)

Camberwell Ltd's Trade Receivables Ledger Control account balances as at 31st March 20X8 were as stated in the box on the right, whereas the sum of the individual account balances in the Trade Receivables Ledger was £717,840.

Debit balances	£748,250
Credit balances	£8,200

Inquiries revealed the following:

i) The Sales Returns Day Book has been overcast by £800.

ii) £4,900 offset by contra, though recorded in the personal ledgers, was not posted to the Control accounts.

iii) A sales invoice for £19,810, though recorded in the Sales Day Book, has not been posted.

iv) £3,200, being the daily total of the discount column on the receipt side of the Cash Book, has not been posted to the Control account.

v) A customer's account balance has been carried down as £15,400 whereas it should have been £18,400.

vi) A debt write off of £4,500 was entered in neither the customer's account nor the Control account.

vii) A credit balance of £8,200 in the Trade Receivables Ledger has been included in the list as a debit balance.

viii) A customer's balance omitted from the list accounts for the difference.

Required: Set out a reconciliation of the Trade Receivables Ledger Control account balance with the sum of individual ledger balances.

PQ 10.12 Another question from ACCA

a) An inexperienced bookkeeper has drawn up a trial balance for the year ended 30 June 20X7 as shown on the right.

Required: Draw up a corrected trial balance, debiting or crediting any residual error to a Suspense account.

b) Further investigation of the Suspense account ascertained in (a) above, reveals the following errors:

i) Goods bought from J Jones amounting to £13 have been posted to his account as £33.

ii) Furniture which has cost £173 has been debited to the General Expenses account.

iii) An invoice from Suppliers Ltd for £370 has been omitted from the Purchases account, but credited to Suppliers Ltd account.

iv) Sales on credit to A Hope Ltd for £450 have been posted to the Sales account, but not to the Sales ledger.

v) The balance on the Capital account has been incorrectly brought forward in the ledger and should have been £4,291.

vi) An amount of £86 received from A Blunt, a customer, in settlement of his account has been treated as a cash sale.

vii) Discount allowed has been under-totalled by £35.

	Dr	Cr
	£	£
Allowance for doubtful debts	200	
Bank overdraft	1,654	
Capital		4,591
Trade payables		1,637
Trade receivables	2,983	
Discount received	252	
Discount allowed		733
Drawings	1,200	
Office furniture	2,155	
General expenses		829
Purchases	10,923	
Returns inwards		330
Rent & rates	314	
Salaries	2,520	
Sales		16,882
Inventory as at 1st July 20x6	2,418	
Accum depn – furniture	364	
	24,982	24,982

Required: Prepare journal entries correcting each of the above errors and write up the Suspense account.

7

Preparation of statement of comprehensive income and statement of financial position from trial balance and adjustments

Objectives

By the end of this chapter you should be able to:

▶ Prepare a statement of comprehensive income from a trial balance after taking account of several adjustments.

▶ Prepare a statement of financial position from a trial balance after several adjustments.

Introduction

This chapter aims to bring together your knowledge of Chapters 5 and 6 so that you can prepare statements of comprehensive income and statements of financial position at the period end of a business after taking account of all the period-end adjustments necessary to the ledger accounts. These period-end adjustments will ensure that the final statements prepared will be in accordance with concepts and conventions of accounting that were identified in Chapter 4. Use will be made of the extended trial balance technique in compiling these final statements. At this stage we are still only dealing with accounts of a sole trader business.

First, though, a recap of Chapters 5 and 6:

▶ Ledger accounts are required for all assets, liabilities, expenses and income within a business.

▶ These ledger accounts are written up using double entry – the duality concept.

▶ At a period end, ledger accounts are balanced.

▶ Expense and income accounts are transferred to the statement of comprehensive income which is a double entry account.

▶ Any other balances remaining in the ledgers are shown on a statement of financial position.

▶ To prepare accounts in accordance with accounting concepts and conventions several adjustments need to be made to the ledger accounts before transfers are made to the statement of comprehensive income.

▶ These adjustments take account of accruals and prepayments so that expenses used up are matched to the revenue they generate.

▶ Adjustments are required for bad debts and provision for bad debts to comply with prudence and accepted accounting practice.

▶ A depreciation adjustment for non-current assets that are used up in generating revenue is also required.

This chapter will consist of two examples that will demonstrate adjustments required to the ledgers at the period end, the extraction of a trial balance at this stage, and the preparation of a statement of comprehensive income and statement of financial position for the period. Work through these examples carefully as you will then be expected to complete a similar activity yourself. Our examples will conclude with a technique called an extended trial balance, which is a working paper from which the adjustments to the double entry accounts will be made. This speeds up the process of producing a statement of comprehensive income and a statement of financial position without having to wait for all the ledger accounts to be adjusted. This can be a useful technique for students in examinations. Remember that in Chapter 6, Activity 6.14, we asked you to prepare non-current asset adjustments without using ledger accounts. Note that the ledgers will eventually have to be amended for the period-end adjustments whether or not we use an extended trial balance.

Extended example

Example 7.1

The following trial balance was extracted from the ledgers of a sole trader, Mai Wong, as at 31.12.X5:

	Dr	Cr
Sales		45,000
Purchases	15,000	
Inventory 1.1.X5	2,300	
Wages	5,200	
Office expenses	900	
Heating and lighting	850	
Telephone	450	
Rent	2,200	
Fixtures and fittings	7,550	
Vehicles	8,500	
Provision for depreciation 1.1.X5:		
Fixtures and fittings		755

Example 7.1
continued

Capital		8,805
Accounts receivable	1,300	
Accounts payable		1,150
Insurance	650	
Motor expenses	210	
Drawings	10,400	
Bank and cash	200	
	55,710	55,710

The following **period-end adjustments** are required:

▶ Office expenses to be accrued, £50.

▶ Heating and lighting to be accrued, £150.

▶ Rent paid in advance, £200.

▶ Insurance paid in advance, £80.

▶ Fixtures and fittings to be depreciated at 10% of cost and vehicles 20% of cost.

▶ An item of fixtures was sold during the year for £90. The item had been bought on 1.1.X3 for £120. The sale proceeds were credited to the sales account.

▶ Closing inventory is valued at £1,950.

▶ £90 of the motor expenses relates to items for Mai Wong's own use.

Show the adjustments necessary to the ledger accounts to account for the above and the transfers to the statement of comprehensive income for the year.

OFFICE EXPENSES ACCOUNT

31.12.X5	Balance b/d	900			
31.12.X5	Balance c/d (1)	50	31.12.X5	Statement of (2)	950
				comprehensive	
		950		income	950
			1.1.X6	Balance b/d (1)	50

Entry 1 is the accrual of £50 for the year and the corresponding carry-down of the balance to the following year.

Entry 2 shows the charge to the statement of comprehensive income for the year, which is the £900 cash paid plus £50 accrual. This accrual is to ensure matching of expenses used up to the revenue generated.

HEATING AND LIGHTING ACCOUNT

31.12.X5	Balance b/d	850			
31.12.X5	Balance c/d (1)	150	31.12.X5	Statement of	1,000
				comprehensive	
				income	
		1,000			1,000
			11.X6	Balance b/d	150

Example 7.1
continued

RENT ACCOUNT

31.12.X5	Balance b/d	2,200	31.12.X5	Statement of comprehensive income	2,000
			31.12.X5	Balance c/d	200
		2,200			2,200
1.1.X6	Balance b/d	200			

INSURANCE ACCOUNT

31.12.X5	Balance b/d	650	31.12.X5	Statement of comprehensive income	570
			31.12.X5	Balance c/d	80
		650			650
1.1.X6	Balance b/d	80			

The above three accounts show similar entries to those for office expenses.

FIXTURES AND FITTINGS ACCOUNT

31.12.X5	Balance b/d	7,550	31.12.X5	Sale	120
			31.12.X5	Balance c/d	7,430
		7,550			7,550
1.1.X6	Balance b/d	7,430			

Here we have shown the 'write-out' from the asset account of the fixtures sold. The corresponding debit entry will be shown in the sale of fixtures account. A similar write-out needs to be made in the provision for depreciation account for fixtures and fittings. The depreciation previously provided on the fixtures sold will have been £120 × 10% for two years, that is, £24.

PROVISION FOR DEPRECIATION OF FIXTURES ACCOUNT

31.12.X5	Sale	24	31.12.X5	Balance c/d	755
31.12.X5	Balance c/d	1,474	31.12.X5	Statement of comprehensive income (1)	743
		1,498			1,498
			1.1.X6	Balance b/d	1,474

Entry 1 is the depreciation for the current year calculated on the remaining assets of £7,430 after the sale of £120. A corresponding entry will be made in the statement of comprehensive income.

Example 7.1
continued

The sale of fixtures account will appear as follows:

SALE OF FIXTURES ACCOUNT

31.12.X5	Fixtures	120	31.12.X5	Depreciation	24
			31.12.X5	Sales (1)	90
			31.12.X5	Statement of comprehensive income	6
		120			120

Entry 1 is the transfer of the sale proceeds of the fixtures which had been included in the sales account. The transfer of £6 to the statement of comprehensive income represents a loss on sale of the asset. The sales account will need amending as follows:

SALES ACCOUNT

31.12.X5	Sale of fixtures	90	31.12.X5	Balance b/d	45,000
31.12.X5	Statement of comprehensive income	44,910			
		45,000			45,000

The charge for depreciation on the vehicles also needs calculating and entering into the accounts: depreciation for the year 20% × £8,500 = £1,700.

PROVISION FOR DEPRECIATION OF VEHICLES ACCOUNT

31.12.X5	Balance c/d	1,700	31.12.X5	Statement of comprehensive income	1,700
			1.1.X6	Balance b/d	1,700

The motor expenses account also needs amending as £90 of these expenses related to Mai Wong's own use. This £90 is treated as drawings of Mai Wong.

MOTOR EXPENSES ACCOUNT

31.12.X5	Balance b/d	210	31.12.X5	Drawings	90
			31.12.X5	Statement of comprehensive income	120
		210			210

The accounts for purchases, inventory 1.1.X5, wages and telephone will all be transferred to the income statement and an account for closing inventory opened as follows:

Example 7.1
continued

CLOSING INVENTORY ACCOUNT

31.12.X5 Statement of comprehensive income	1,950	

The income statement will now appear as follows:

STATEMENT OF COMPREHENSIVE INCOME FOR THE YEAR ENDED 31.12.X5

Sales		44,910
Opening inventory	2,300	
Add purchases	15,000	
	17,300	
Less closing inventory	1,950	15,350
Gross profit		29,560
Wages	5,200	
Office expenses	950	
Heating and lighting	1,000	
Rent	2,000	
Insurance	570	
Depreciation: Fixtures	743	
Vehicles	1,700	
Telephone	450	
Motor expenses	120	
Loss on sale	6	12,739
Net profit		16,821

All balances now remaining in the ledgers are entered in the balance sheet as follows:

STATEMENT OF FINANCIAL POSITION AS AT 31.12.X5

	Cost	Depreciation	Net book value
ASSETS			
Non-current assets			
Fixtures and fittings	7,430	1,474	5,956
Vehicles	8,500	1,700	6,800
	15,930	3,174	12,756
Current assets			
Inventory		1,950	
Accounts receivable		1,300	
Rent prepaid		200	
Insurance prepaid		80	
Bank and cash		200	3,730
TOTAL ASSETS			16,486
EQUITY AND			
LIABILITIES			

Example 7.1
continued

Equity			8,805
Add profit		16,821	
Less drawings		10,490	6,331
			15,136
Current liabilities			
Accounts payable		1,150	
Office expenses accrued		50	
Heat and light accrued		150	1,350
TOTAL EQUITY AND LIABILITIES			16,486

Adjusting the ledger accounts as shown above is very time consuming but has to be done by a business if it keeps double entry records. Many businesses will use computerised ledgers. We will look at these in Chapter 15. The process of adjusting the ledgers for both computerised and manual systems can be controlled by the use of an extended trial balance – a worksheet. The worksheet for the example above would appear as follows:

	Trial balance		Adjustments		Statement of comprehensive income		Balance sheet	
	Dr	Cr	Dr	Cr	Dr	Cr	Dr	Cr
Sales		45,000	90			44,910		
Purchases	15,000				15,000			
Inventory	2,300				2,300			
Wages	5,200				5,200			
Office	900		50		950			
Heating and lighting	850		150		1,000			
Telephone	450				450			
Rent	2,200			200	2,000			
Fixtures and fittings	7,550			120			7.430	
Vehicles	8,500						8,500	
Depreciation, furniture and fittings		755	24	743				1,474
Capital		8,805						8,805
Accounts receivable	1,300						1,300	
Accounts payable		1,150						1,150
Insurance	650			80	570			
Motor	210			90	120			
Drawings	10,400		90				10,490	
Bank	200						200	
	55,710	55,710						
Accruals				200				200
Prepayments			280				280	
Depreciation, furniture and fittings				743	743			

Example 7.1 continued

Depreciation, vehicle	1,700		1,700				
Profit on sale	6		6				
Provision for depreciation, vehicle				1,700			1,700
Closing inventory	1,950					1,950	
Statement of comprehensive income		1,950		1,950			
Net profit				16,821			16,821
	5,083	5,083	46,860	46,860	30,150	30,150

This worksheet has been constructed as follows:

▶ The first two columns, headed trial balance, are simply a listing of the income, expenses, assets and liabilities from the question trial balance.

▶ The third and fourth columns, headed adjustments, take account of all the period end adjustments:

   ▶ Office expenses – debit 50, credit accruals 50.

   ▶ Heating and lighting – debit 150, credit accruals 150; accruals balance is now 200.

   ▶ Rent – credit rent 200, debit prepayments 200.

   ▶ Insurance – credit insurance 80, debit prepayments 80; prepayments balance now 280.

   ▶ Fixtures and fittings sale – debit sales 90, credit sales account 90. Write out the cost of the fixtures sold by crediting fixtures asset account 120, debiting sale account 120. Write out depreciation accrued on the item sold by debiting provision for depreciation 24 (two years depreciation at 12 per year), crediting sale account 24. Now balance the sale account and you are left with a debit balance b/d of 6 which is profit on sale.

   ▶ Depreciation on fixtures and fittings – the extended trial balance now shows a debit of 7,550 and a credit of 120. The overall debit is 7,430. Depreciation is provided on this at 10% by crediting provision for depreciation 743 and debiting depreciation charge 743.

   ▶ Vehicles only has a debit balance showing in the extended trial balance so far of 8,500, so the depreciation charge is 20% × 8,500 = 1,700 which is credited to provision for depreciation and debited to provision charge.

   ▶ Closing inventory needs entering, so debit closing inventory account, 1,950. Credit statement of comprehensive income.

   ▶ The last adjustment is to account for the personal drawings of Mai Wong by crediting motor expenses 90, then crediting drawings 90.

▶ Columns five and six show the transfers of balances on income and expense ledgers after the adjustments have been made to the statement of comprehensive income.

▶ Columns seven and eight show the assets and liabilities and capital and reserves tranferred to the statement of financial position.

Example 7.1 continued

▶ As each pair of columns is completed we check the extended worksheet by totalling the columns and the pairs should be equal. If they are not, then a mistake will have been made somewhere in the worksheet and this must be corrected.

Look at this extended trial balance carefully and follow all the adjustments made and the entries into the statement of comprehensive income and statement of financial position. You may find this method of drawing up the final accounts useful for examinations. The extended trial balance technique lends itself to computer spreadsheet applications.

The following activity is similar to Example 7.1 but only uses the extended trial balance technique not the ledgers.

Activity 7.1

The following trial balance was extracted from the ledgers of a sole trader Sue Chong as at 31.12.X8.

	Dr	Cr
Sales		95,500
Purchases	42,500	
Sales returns	4,500	
Inventory 1.1.X7	13,700	
Salaries	9,700	
General expenses	1,700	
Rent and rates	6,200	
Insurance	1,700	
Heating and lighting	4,300	
Plant and equipment	15,000	
Vehicles	12,000	
Vehicle expenses	1,700	
Capital		15,500
Drawings	13,200	
Accounts receivable	3,200	
Accounts payable		3,750
Bank		5,000
Cash	670	
Provision for depreciation:		
Plant and equipment		6,000
Vehicles		4,320
	130,070	130,070

The following period-end adjustments are required:

1 General expenses to be accrued, £90.

2 Heating and lighting to be accrued, £250.

3 Rent paid in advance, £400.

4 Rates paid in advance, £70.

5 Plant and equipment to be depreciated on a straight line basis assuming a useful life of four years and a residual value at the end of the useful life of £3,000.

6 Vehicles to be depreciated 20% reducing balance method.

7 An item of plant was purchased by the use of a loan for £15,000 on 1.1.X8. The loan carries interest at 5% per annum and the plant has a useful life of five years, no residual value and a straight line method of use. The loan is repayable 31.12.Y2. No entries have been made in the ledgers or the trial balance of Sue Chong for this purchase or any aspect of the loan.

8 Closing inventory is valued at £12,500.

Prepare the extended trial balance and the statement of comprehensive income for the period ended 31.12.X8 and the statement of financial position as at that date.

Answer   Extended trial balance for Sue Chong for the period ended 31.12.X8

	Trial balance		Adjustments		Statement of income		Statement of financial position	
	Dr	Cr	Dr	Cr	Dr	Cr	Dr	Cr
Sales		95,500				95,500		
Purchases	42,500				42,500			
Sales returns	4,500				4,500			
Inventory	13,700				13,700			
Salaries	9,700				9,700			
General expenses	1,700		90		1,790			
Rent and rates	6,200			400 +70	5,730			
Insurance	1,700				1,700			
Vehicle expense	1,700				1,700			
Heating and lighting	4,300		250		4,550			
Plant and equipment	15,000		15,000				30,000	
Vehicles	12,000						12,000	
Capital	15,500		15,500					
Drawings	13,200						13,200	
Accounts receivable	3,200						3,200	
Accounts payable		3,750						3,750
Bank		5,000						5,000
Cash	670						670	
Prov dep P and E		6,000		6,000				12,000
Prov dep veh		4,320		1,536				5,856
Accruals				340				340
Prepayments			470				470	
Closing inventory			12,500				12,500	
Statement of comprehensive income				12,500		12,500		
Loan				15,000				15,000

Dep P and E		6,000		6,000			
Dep veh		1,536		1,536			
Loan interest accrual			750				750
Loan interest expense		750		750			
Net profit				13,844			13,844
	130,070	130,070	36,596	36,596	108,000	108,000	72,040	72,040

STATEMENT OF COMPREHENSIVE INCOME FOR THE PERIOD ENDED 31.12.X8

Sales		95,500
Less sales returns		4,500
		91,000
Opening inventory	13,700	
Purchases	42,500	
	56,200	
Closing inventory	12,500	43,700
Gross profit		47,300
Salaries	9,700	
General expenses 1,700+90	1,790	
Rent and rates 6,200 – 400 – 70	5,730	
Insurance	1,700	
Heating and lighting 4,300+250	4,550	
Vehicle expenses	1,700	
Depreciation plant and equipment (15,000 – 3,000)/4 + 15,000/5	6,000	
Depreciation vehicles (12,000 – 4,320)×20%	1,536	
Loan interest 15,000×5%	750	33,456
Net profit		13,844

STATEMENT OF FINANCIAL POSITION AS AT 31.12.X8

	Cost	Depreciation	NBV
ASSETS			
Non-current assets			
Plant and equipment	30,000	12,000	18,000
Vehicles	12,000	5,856	6,144
	42,000	17,856	24,144
Current assets			
Inventory		12,500	
Accounts receivable		3,200	
Prepayments		470	

Cash	<u>670</u>	16,840
TOTAL ASSETS		40,984
EQUITY AND LIABILITIES		
Equity		
Capital	15,500	
Less drawings	<u>13,200</u>	2,300
Profit		13,844
		16,144
Non-current liabilities		
Loan		15,000
Current liabilities		
Accounts payable	3,750	
Accruals 90+250+750	1,090	
Bank	<u>5,000</u>	9,840
TOTAL EQUITY AND LIABILITIES		40,984

So far we have dealt with year-end account preparation for a sole trader, but the same process applies when preparing a statement of comprehensive income and statement of financial position from a trial balance and making adjustments for any type of business or organisation. Try the following activity which deals with the transactions of a club.

*A*ctivity 7.2   From the following trial balance relating to the position of a tennis club as at 31 March 200X, draw up the income and expenditure account (similar to the statement of comprehensive income) and the statement of financial position as at that date.

	Debit	*Credit*
Clubhouse at cost	54,700	
Accounts payable		3,300
Accounts receivable	2,200	
Inventory 31 March 200X	1,080	
Gross profit on bars, etc.		1,240
Furniture and fittings	7,600	
Bank and cash	5,600	
General expenses	760	
Insurance	1,200	
Heating and lighting	780	
Subscriptions to the club		10,100
Accumulated fund 1 April 200W		
(similar to capital)		19,470
Provision for depreciation:		
Clubhouse		38,290
Furniture and fittings		1,520

| | 73,920 | 73,920 |

The following information is also available:

▶ The insurance paid for the year only relates to the first six months of the period.

▶ Heating and lighting of £230 needs to be accrued.

▶ Clubhouse is depreciated 10% on cost and furniture and fittings 20% on cost.

Answer

INCOME AND EXPENDITURE ACCOUNT FOR THE PERIOD ENDED 31 MARCH 200X

Subscriptions		10,100
Gross profit		1,240
		11,340
Insurance (1,200 + 1,200)	2,400	
Heating and lighting (780 + 230)	1,010	
General expenses	760	
Depreciation: Clubhouse	5,470	
Furniture and fittings	1,520	11,160
Surplus		180

STATEMENT OF FINANCIAL POSITION AS AT 31 MARCH 200X

ASSETS

Non-current assets		
Clubhouse (54,700 − 5,470 − 38,290)	10,940	
Furniture and fittings (7,600 − 1,520 − 1,520)	4,560	15,500
Current assets		
Inventory	1,080	
Accounts receivable	2,200	
Bank and cash	5,600	8,880
TOTAL ASSETS		**£24,380**

EQUITY AND LIABILITIES

Equity		
Accumulated fund 1 April 200X		19,470
Surplus		180
		19,650
Current liabilities		
Accounts payable	3,300	
Accurals (1,200 + 230)	1,430	4,730
TOTAL EQUITY AND LIABILITIES		24,380

Summary

This chapter has combined your learning from Chapters 5 and 6. You should now be able to:

▶ prepare an income statement and balance sheet from a trial balance after making several adjustments at the period end to this trial balance for a business and a club.

We also illustrated the technique of an extended trial balance which is, in fact, a worksheet to control the adjustments within the ledger accounts. It can, however, be a useful tool to use in an examination.

We have only provided four self-assessment questions in this chapter as you will find plenty of practice in preparing statements of comprehensive income and statements of financial position in Chapter 8. You may like to attempt to do the exercises at the end of the chapter using an extended trial balance but note that we have not provided the answers in that way.

Key terms

extended trial balance	period-end adjustments

Self-assessment questions

1 The following trial balance was extracted from the books of Rodney, a sole trader, as at 31.12.X5:

	Dr	Cr
Capital 1.1.X5		15,500
Drawings	4,660	
Accounts receivable and payable	6,530	5,210
Sales		71,230
Purchases	29,760	
Inventory 1.1.X5	4,340	
Rates	800	
Heat and light	2,650	
Wages	8,250	
Bad debts	230	
Provision for bad debts		280
General expenses	2,340	
Motor expenses	3,240	
Premises at cost	30,000	
Fixtures and fittings	8,000	
Vehicles	12,000	

▶

Provision for depreciation 1.1.X5:		
Premises		2,400
Fixtures and fittings		1,600
Vehicles		5,400
Bank	820	
Loan		12,000
	113,620	113,620

The following matters have not been taken into account in the preparation of the above trial balance:

▶ Inventory 31.12.X5 £4,870.

▶ Light and heat due 31.12.X5 £120, general expenses due £80.

▶ Depreciation is to be provided for the year as follows:

Premises – 2% on cost

Fixtures and fittings – 10% on cost

Vehicles – 20% reducing balance.

▶ A further bad debt of £130 is to be written off and the bad debts provision is to be at 5% of debtors after the write-off.

▶ The loan interest of £600 has not been paid for the year.

You are required to prepare a statement of comprehensive income for the year ended 31.12.X5 and a statement of financial position as at that date.

2 The following trial balance was extracted from the books of ATEC as at 31.12.X9:

	Dr	Cr
Sales		53,500
Purchases	29,200	
Inventory 1.1.X9	5,400	
Office expenses	150	
Electricity	700	
Salaries and wages	12,100	
Rates	600	
Telephone	280	
Other expenses	120	
Premises	30,000	
Rents received		550
Equipment	12,000	
Vehicles	12,000	
Provisions for depreciation:		
Premises		4,200
Equipment		8,400
Vehicles		3,000
Drawings	16,000	

Accounts receivable and payable	4,800	5,200
Provision for bad debts		90
Capital 1.1.X9		46,500
Bank		2,000
Cash	90	
	123,440	123,440

The following matters have not been taken into account in the preparation of the above trial balance:

▶ inventory as at 31.12.X9 £6,200

▶ accruals required as at 31.12.X9

　－ electricity　　　　　　　£230

　－ salaries and wages　　　£230

　－ telephone　　　　　　　£90

▶ rents receivable are £50 per month as from 1.1.X9

▶ the business commenced 1.1.X2 and depreciation has been provided on a straight line basis for premises and equipment since that date except for the current year for which no depreciation charge has yet been made

▶ vehicles are depreciated at 25% reducing balance and were purchased 1.1.X8

▶ no sales of non-current assets have been made prior to 1.1.X9. On 1.7.X9 part of the premises, cost £15,000, was sold for £25,000. These sale proceeds have been credited to the capital account

▶ drawings includes the purchase of a second-hand van for £5,000 on 1.2.X9. This van is used solely for business purposes

▶ bad debts to be written off as at 31.12.X9 amount to £120 and bad debts provision is to be set at 25% of accounts receivable after writing off bad debts

▶ depreciation is to be provided on the basis of a full year's charge in the year of purchase of the asset but none in the year of sale of the asset.

You are required to prepare a statement of comprehensive income for the year ended 31.12.X9 and a statement of financial position as at that date.

3 The following balances have been extracted from the accounting records of Celia, a sole trader, as at 31 March 20X8.

Sales	295,500
Sales returns	1,800
Purchases	154,500
Purchase returns	750
Accounts receivable	49,250
Accounts payable	32,180
Provision for bad debts	1,970
Plant and equipment	92,000
Plant and equipment depreciation provision 1.4.20X7	36,800
Vehicles	15,000

Vehicles depreciation provision 1.4.20X7	6,000
Drawings	19,750
General expenses	16,750
Wages	32,500
Rent and rates	12,000
Loan repayable 2015 carrying 8% interest per annum	25,000
Bank	12,175
Inventory 1.4.20X7	18,000
Capital	10,000
Retained profits 1.4.20X7	15,525

The following information is also available:

▶ The provision for doubtful debts is to be adjusted to 2% of accounts receivable

▶ Depreciation is to be provided for the year to 31.3.2008 at the following rates:

    – Plant and equipment 20% on cost

    – Vehicles 25% reducing balance

▶ Wages of £700 are to be accrued at 31.3.20X8

▶ Rent of £400 has been prepaid as at 31.3. 20X8

▶ The interest on the loan needs to be accrued for the year

▶ The inventory at 31.3.20X8 has been valued at £18,750. This includes damaged inventory items of £2,000 that are expected to be sold for £600.

Prepare the statement of comprehensive income for the year ended 31.3.20X8 and a statement of financial position as at that date for Celia.

4 From the following balances relating to the accounts of a small football club as at 31 March 20X8 draw up the income and expenditure account and the statement of financial position as at that date.

Club house at cost	25,000
Accounts receivable	1,200
Accounts payable	990
Inventory 31 March 20X8	550
Gross profit on bars, etc.	5,600
Gross profit on events	8,200
Furniture and fittings at cost	3,400
General expenses	2,300
Insurance	500
Heat and light	2,200
Subscriptions to the club	12,300
Accumulated fund 1 April 20X7	8,400
Provision for depreciation as at 1 April 20X7:	
Clubhouse	1,000
Furniture and fittings	340
Bank and cash	1,680

The following information is also available:

▶ The insurance paid only amounts to that for the first nine months of the year.

▶ Subscriptions due totaling £2,300 have not been paid to the club.

▶ Heating and lighting of £450 needs to be accrued.

▶ The local DJ, who provided the entertainment at several of the events run by the football club, has recently submitted his invoice for £2,800. This amount has not been included in the accounts payable.

▶ It is estimated that 1% of the accounts receivable as at 31 March 20X8 may not be paid.

▶ Depreciation for the year is to be provided as follows: premises straight line useful life 25 years with no residual value, furniture and fittings straight line useful life 10 years with no residual value.

SECTION 5
INCOMPLETE RECORDS

Chapter 20

Incomplete records

In this chapter

We will learn:

■ to deal with incomplete records and single entry situations

■ the four rules that help in such situations

and will be able to:

■ either estimate the profit/loss

■ or prepare financial statements in an incomplete record situation

20.1 The approach to an incomplete records situation

Accountants use the expression *incomplete records* to refer to a situation where the accounting records, which had been maintained on proper double entry basis, have been partly destroyed (e.g. by fire, flood or deliberate action) so that it is no longer possible to extract a trial balance. An alternative situation where a trial balance cannot be extracted because accounting records were not maintained on the double entry system is referred to as *single entry*.

The approach to preparing the financial statements depends on the extent of the information that is available.

20.1.1 Not sufficient information to prepare an Income Statement and Balance Sheet

The only thing possible in these circumstances is to estimate the profit or loss for the accounting period by comparing the owner's equity at the commencement of the period with that at the end. This is where we make use of the accounting equation Assets – Liabilities = Equity (see Chapter 4). If the owner's equity at commencement was £400,000 and it has become £600,000 by the end, the inference is that the business has made a profit of £200,000 (£600,000 – £400,000). The inference will be correct provided, during the period, the owner has not removed any business assets for personal use or introduced additional capital. If we assume further that the owner's drawings in the period were £36,000 and additional capital introduced was £50,000, the revised estimate of profit will be:

Equity at end – Equity at commencement + Drawings – Capital introduced =   Profit
£600,000   –   £400,000   + £36,000 –   £50,000   = £186,000

Activity 20.1 **Where information is inadequate**

The tax authorities seek your assistance to estimate the profit made in the year ended 31st December 20X7 by a retail shop belonging to Chris Jones. They inform you as follows:

i) Chris has no source of income other than from his shop.

ii) Considering the style and standard of living Chris' living expenses should be at least £1,500 per month.

iii) The assets and liabilities of the shop have been ascertained as stated on the right.

iv) In June 20X7 Chris Jones introduced as additional capital £20,000 left to him by his late uncle.

	31.12.20X6	31.12.20X7
	£	£
Non-current assets at WDV	180,000	215,000
Inventory at cost	284,200	326,600
Trade receivables	16,500	21,400
Cash & bank balance	11,400	26,800
Trade payables	(165,800)	(158,500)

20.1.2 Sufficient information to prepare an Income Statement and Balance Sheet

If, on the other hand, we have more information so that, rather than estimate the profit, we are able to prepare the financial statements, then we approach the situation as follows:

- **Step 1:** Prepare a *statement of affairs* as at the commencement of the accounting period, identifying the capital at that date. A statement of affairs, like a balance sheet, lists the assets and liabilities with the difference representing the owner's capital. In accounting, the term balance sheet is used only where accounting records have been maintained on a double entry basis.

- **Step 2:** Post the information to appropriate ledger accounts. This means that the records are then on a double entry basis.

- **Step 3:** Account, by a pair of matching entries (i.e. on the double entry basis) for every transaction and event you have been able to identify.

20.1.3 Almost sufficient information to prepare an Income Statement and Balance Sheet

There may be occasions when, after making use of all information, there remains a need to make estimates for certain of the items. This means a further step:

- **Step 4:** Make guesses as best as you can to finalise the Income Statement and Balance Sheet.

20.2 Four rules to remember

When dealing with an incomplete record situation remember four rules:

1. There are four classes of accounts as shown in the diagram on the right.
   - An account of the two classes on the left always has a debit balance.
   - An account of the other two classes always has a credit balance.

Debits	Credits
Asset	Liability
Expense	Income

2. Unless it has been stated otherwise always assume that:
   - purchases and sales of goods for sale are on credit terms,
   - acquisition/disposal of assets are on cash terms.
3. Take good care to identify whether the information provided is:
   - a payment or expense (e.g. amount of rent paid or the rent payable for the period),
   - a receipt or income (e.g. the amount of income collected or the whole income earned).
4. When less than full information has been provided adopt the crossword puzzle mentality –
   - identify how many letters (amounts) are needed to complete the word (account),
   - make a guess only after all clues (information) provided have been fully used.

20.3 Illustration of how the four rules work

Let us illustrate the application of the four rules, assuming that the assets and liabilities of Tim's Retail, at commencement of the period, are reported as follows:

As at 30th June 20X6	£
Non-current assets	400
Inventory at cost	120
Trade receivables	210
Cash	20
Trade payables	(190)

Step 1 is taken by presenting the information in the form of a statement of affairs identifying the capital at that date:

Statement of affairs as at 30th June 20X6	£
Non-current assets	400
Inventory	120
Trade receivables	210
Cash	20
Trade payables	(190)
Capital as at 30.6.20X6	560

Step 2 is to open the six accounts needed to report these balances, remembering the first rule that the first four accounts, reporting assets, will each have a debit balance and the Trade Payables account and Capital account will each have a credit balance.

Let us now assume that the additional information given with regard to Tim's Retail is as follows:

During the year ended 30th June 20X7	
	£
Non-current assets bought	100
Purchases	300
Rent for the year	60
Payment for other expenses	80
As at 30th June 20X7:	
Non-current assets	450
Inventory at cost	190
Trade receivables	285
Cash in hand	30
Trade payables	210
Rent accrued	15

Step 3 is to account for this information applying double entry rules. When doing this we have to bear in mind the second rule that, unless otherwise told, the non-current assets are acquired for cash (credit Cash account and debit Non-Current Asset account); whereas purchases are made on credit terms (debit Purchases account and credit Trade Payables account).

Remember also the third rule which requires clarification on whether the information provided is of an expense or payment for the expense. For example, with regard to rent, the information is on the expense in the year, accounted for by a debit in the Rent (expense) account and credit in a Rent (liability) account. With regard to other expenses, on the other hand, the information is of cash paid, to be accounted by a credit in the Cash account and a debit in Other Expenses account. The year-end balances will need to be carried down in the respective ledger account, remembering that closing inventory is accounted for by a credit in the Income Statement and a debit in an Asset account which will appear on the balance sheet.

This brings us to Step 4 which is to fill in the blanks in each account, making guesses as best as possible. For example, in the case of the Non-Current Asset missing item, the amount may be guessed easily as depreciation of £50. This can be done with equal ease also in the case of Trade Payables account as a cash payment of £280.

Non-Current Asset account				Trade Payables account			
	£		£		£		£
Balance b/f	400	?	?	?	?	Balance b/f	190
Cash a/c	100	Balance c/d	450	Balance c/d	210	Purchases	300
	500		500		490		490
Balance b/d	450						
						Balance b/d	210

The Rent account missing figure would again be a cash payment of £45 to complete the ledger account. In the case of Trade receivables guessing becomes impossible because there are two missing items.

Rent (liability) account

	£		£
?	?	Rent (expense)	60
Balance c/d	15		
	60		60
		Balance b/d	15

Trade Receivables account

	£		£
Balance b/f	210	?	?
?	?	Balance c/d	285
Balance b/d	285		

One of these can be found (as £515 received from customers) by completing the Cash account. When this information is included in the Trade Receivables account we can identify the other missing item as credit sales for the year of £590.

Cash account

	£		£
Balance b/f	20	Non-current asset	100
?	?	Other expense	80
		Payables	280
		Rent	45
		Balance c/d	30
	535		535
Balance b/d	30		

Trade Receivables account

	£		£
Balance b/f	210	Cash a/c	515
?	?	Balance c/d	285
	800		800
Balance	285		

We now have all of the information that we require to prepare the Income Statement and Balance Sheet for the year ended 30 June 20X7 as follows:

Income Statement for the year ended 30.6.20X7		
	£	£
Sales		590
Inventory	120	
Purchases	300	
Inventory	(190)	230
Gross profit		360
Rent	60	
Depreciation	50	
Other expenses	80	190
Net profit		170

Balance Sheet as at 30.6.20X7		
	£	£
Non-current assets		450
Current assets:		
Inventory	190	
Trade receivables	285	
Cash in hand	30	505
		955
	£	£
Capital	560	
Profit	170	730
Current liabilities:		
Trade payables	210	
Rent accrued	15	225
		955

Activity 20.2 Preparing financial statements from incomplete records

Simon lists his assets and liabilities as shown below on the right and provides the following information:

i) Drawings by Simon £40,000

ii) Payments to suppliers £1,731,600

iii) Receipts from customers £2,160,000

iv) Paid salaries £180,000

v) Paid for other expenses £154,800

Required: Prepare Simon's Income Statement for the year ended 31st December 20X7 and the Balance Sheet as at that date.

	1.1.20X7	31.12.20X7
	£	£
Non-current assets	96,400	112,800
Accum depn	(24,600)	(32,400)
	71,800	80,400
Inventory	234,500	252,800
Trade receivables	43,200	46,800
Bank balance	2,160	?
Trade payables	97,200	109,800

Activity 20.3 The need to distinguish between payments and expenses

Betty Harrow assumed duties as accountant of a retail shop, Tongdean, on 7th January 20X8. The owner of the shop provides her with the following information:

i) The shop's assets and liabilities includes those shown on the right.

ii) During the year ended 31st December 20X7:
- Purchases were £486,200.
- Rent was payable at £3,000 per month.
- Salaries paid was £72,000.
- Other expense paid £16,400.
- Proprietor's drawings were £200 per week.
- Depreciation written off was £32,000.
- Non-current assets, written down to £60,000 were sold for £48,000.

	31.12.20X6	31.12.20X7
	£	£
Non-current assets at WDV	240,000	284,000
Inventory at cost	112,400	138,200
Trade receivables	136,800	164,600
Cash & bank balance	12,600	15,400
Trade payables	62,500	77,800

iii) As at 31st December 20X7 salary (£8,000) and other expenses (£3,000) remain unpaid, while one month's rent had been pre-paid.

Required: Prepare the financial statements for the year ended 31st December 20X7.

Summary

- Incomplete records refer either to a situation where accounting records are partly lost or one where accounting records have not been maintained on the double entry system.
- Where information is not sufficient to prepare an income statement and balance sheet, estimates of profit and loss may be made.
- When dealing with an incomplete records situation compliance with certain procedural rules may help.

Suggested answers to activities

20.1 Where information is inadequate

	31.12.20X6	31.12.20X7
	£	£
Non-current assets	180,000	215,000
Inventory	284,200	326,600
Trade receivables	16,500	21,400
Cash & bank	11,400	26,800
Trade payables	(165,800)	(158,500)
Capital	326,300	431,300

Capital as at 31 December 20X7	£431,300
Capital as at 31 December 20X6	(£326,300)
Increase in capital in the year	£105,000
Add: Drawings @ £1,500 × 12 months	£18,000
Less: New capital introduced	(20,000)
Estimated profit in the year	£103,000

20.2 Preparing financial statements from incomplete records

Income Statement for the year ended 31.12.20X7		
	£	£
Sales		2,163,600
Inventory	234,500	
Purchases	1,744,200	
Inventory	(252,800)	(1,725,900)
Gross profit		437,700
Salaries	180,000	
Expenses	154,800	
Depn	7,800[b]	(342,600)
Net profit		95,100

Balance Sheet as at 31.12.20X7		
	£	£
Non-current assets		112,800
Accum depn		(32,400)
		80,400
Current assets:		
Inventories	252,800	
Receivables	46,800	
Cash & bank	39,360	338,960
		419,360

	£	£
Capital	254,460	
Net profit	95,100	
Drawings	(40,000)	309,560
Current liabilities:		
Payables		109,800
		419,360

Workings:

Statement of affairs as at 31.12.20X6	
	£
Non-current asset	96,400
Accum depn	(24,600)
	71,800
Inventory	234,500
Receivables	43,200
Cash/bank	2,160
Payables	(97,200)
Capital[a]	254,460

Cash account

	£		£
Balance b/f	2,160	Drawings	40,000
Receivables	2,160,000	Payables	1,731,600
		Salaries	180,000
		Expenses	154,800
		Non-current asset	16,400
		Balance[a]	39,360
	2,162,160		2,162,160
Balance b/d	39,360		

Trade Receivables account

	£		£
Balance b/f	43,200	Cash book	2,160,000
Sales[a]	2,163,600	Balance c/d	46,800
	2,206,800		2,206,800
Balance b/d	46,800		

Trade Payables account

	£		£
Cash book	1,731,600	Balance b/f	97,200
Balance c/d	109,800	Purchases[a]	1,744,200
	1,841,400		1,841,400
		Balance b/d	109,800

Non-Current Asset account

	£		£
Balance b/f	96,400		
Cash book[a]	16,400	Balance c/d	112,800
	112,800		112,800
Balance b/d	112,800		

Notes:
a) Balancing figures
b) Accum depn: 32,400 − 24,600 = £7,800

20.3 The need to distinguish between payments and expenses

Income Statement for the year ended 31.12.20X7

	£	£
Sales		727,300
Inventory	112,400	
Purchases	486,200	
Inventory	(138,200)	(460,400)
Gross profit		266,900
Salaries[b]	80,000	
Rent[c]	36,000	
Asset disposal[e]	12,000	
Expenses[d]	19,400	
Depn	32,000	(179,400)
Net profit		87,500

Balance Sheet as at 31.12.20X7

	£	£
Non-current assets		284,000
Current assets:		
Inventory	138,200	
Receivables	164,600	
Pre-paid rent	3,000	
Cash & bank	15,400	321,200
		605,200

	£	£
Capital	439,300	
Net profit	87,500	
Drawings	(10,400)	516,400
Current liabilities:		
Payables	77,800	
Salary accrued	8,000	
Expense accrued	3,000	88,800
		605,200

Workings:

Statement of affairs as at 31.12.20X6

	£
Non-current asset	240,000
Inventory	112,400
Receivables	136,800
Cash/bank	12,600
Payables	(62,500)
Capital[a]	439,300

Cash account

	£		£
Balance b/f	12,600	Rent	39,000
Disposal	48,000	Salary	72,000
Receivable[a]	699,500	Expenses	16,400
		Drawings	10,400
		Non-current asset	136,000
		Payables	470,900
		Balance c/d	15,400
	760,100		760,100
Balance b/d	15,400		

Trade Receivables account

	£		£
Balance b/f	136,800	Cash book	699,500
Sales[a]	727,300	Balance c/d	164,600
	864,100		864,100
Balance b/d	164,600		

Trade Payables account

	£		£
Cash book[a]	470,900	Balance b/f	62,500
Balance c/d	77,800	Purchases	486,200
	548,700		548,700
		Balance b/d	77,800

Non-Current Asset account

	£		£
Balance b/f	240,000	Disposal	60,000
Cash book	136,000	Depn	32,000
		Balance c/d	284,000
	376,000		376,000
Balance b/d	284,000		

Notes:
a) Balancing figures
b) Salaries: 72 + 8 = £80
c) Rent: 39 paid – 3 pre-paid = £36 expense
d) Expense: 16.4 + 3 = £19.4
e) Loss on asset disposal: 60,000 – 48,000 = £12,000

Multiple choice questions

Estimation of profit or loss

20.1 The owner's capital in a business was £340,000 on 30th June 20X8 and £215,000 a year earlier. In each of the following independent scenarios, given the stated amount of proprietor's drawings and capital introduced within the year, estimate the profit (P) or loss (L)

a) Drawings during the year was £3,000 per month

b) During the year, no drawings; capital introduced was £9,000

c) Drawings were £40,000 and capital introduced £20,000

d) Drawings were £24,000 and capital introduced £150,000

x	y	z
£125,000 P	£161,000 P	£89,000 P
£116,000 P	£125,000 P	£134,000 P
£185,000 P	£165,000 P	£145,000 P
£1,000 L	£251,000 P	£149,000 P

20.2 Rupert owns a retail shop, but does not maintain any accounting records. The tax inspector prepared a Statement of Affairs for him on 30th June 20X7 establishing his capital on that date as £426,500. Carrying out a similar exercise one year later, his capital in the business was established as £596,800. Further inquiries reveal that (i) he has no other source of income, (ii) he must be spending not less than £2,000 per month on living, (iii) he educates his son at Harvard spending on average £1,000 per month (iv) he paid £40,000 in the year for a private car, selling the old one for £8,000. What is your estimate of his business profit in the year?

a	£246,300
b	£170,300
c	£238,300
d	£226,300

Focus on identifying the sales revenue

20.3 Trade receivables as at 30th September 20X6 was £24,800 and a year later £42,400. Identify the sales revenue during the year ended 30th September 20X7, taking into account the following additional information provided in each of the following independent scenarios:

a) The amount received from credit customers was £59,500

b) Amount received £52,800, debts written off £400 and sales returns £500

c) Sales received £49,400, cheques dishonoured £200, discount allowed £100

d) £55,680 was received from customers taking 4% cash discount

x	y	z
£41,900	£59,500	£77,100
£71,300	£70,400	£70,800
£66,900	£67,300	£66,700
£75,507	£75,600	£73,280

20.4 The cash and bank balance of a shop on 31st December 20X7 and a year prior to that were £11,200 and £14,500 respectively. During the year ended 31st December 20X7 £4,800 was paid out in cash and £39,500 by cheque. Trade receivables were £41,500 on 31st December 20X7 and £39,900 a year prior to that date. Taking into consideration the additional information provided in each of the following independent scenarios, identify the sales revenue in 20X7.

a) £3,000 was received from disposal of a non-current asset

b) £1,200 due from a customer was offset by contra

c) Drawings, not included in the cash payments, was £300 per month

d) A debt of £400 was written off and the allowance for doubtful debts increased by £300

x	y	z
£39,600	£46,200	£45,600
£50,400	£41,400	£43,800
£46,200	£42,900	£52,800
£43,300	£43,000	£42,700

20.5 Jerry, the owner of a retail shop, does not maintain proper accounting records. He seeks your assistance to calculate his sales revenue for the year. He always banks his daily takings, only leaving a float of £100 to meet incidental expenses and after taking £20 per day for household expenses. Miscellaneous expenses paid in cash, recorded in his diary, amounted to £26,640. He makes other payments always by cheque and the total cheque payments in the year amounted to £595,400. His bank balance at the beginning of the year was £29,400 and at the end £41,800. His trade receivables were £18,400 at the beginning of the year and £22,900 at the end. What was his sales revenue in the year?

a	£646,240	
b	£646,340	
c	£638,860	
d	£638,960	

20.6 Morning Bakers have prepared a summary of their bank statement for the year ending 30 June 20X8 as shown on the left. Deposits not cleared were £15,500 on 1.7.20X7 and £9,500 a year later. Cheques not presented for payment amounted to £27,400 on 1.7.20X7 and £3,000 a year later. All payments are always made by cheque and sales are always strictly on a cash basis. Identify the sales for the year.

Balance on 1.1	£72,450
Lodgements	£184,240
Cheques drawn	(£112,900)
Balance – 31.12	£143,790

a	£190,240	
b	£178,240	
c	£184,420	
d	£181,240	

20.7 In an attempt to identify the sales revenue in 20X7 of Pauline's hardware store, you have prepared a summary of her bank statements as shown below on the left. Bank lodgements not cleared were £3,900 on 1.1.20X7 and £7,200 on 31.12.20X7. A cheque for £500 in payment of December rent is yet to be presented for payment. Pauline makes all her payments by cheque, apart from small incidental payments (amounting to £4,280 in the year) paid out of a petty cash imprest of of £300. Her trade receivables were £19,400 as at 1st January and £22,700 as at 31st December. Identify her sales revenue for 20X7.

Balance on 1.1	£24,580
Lodgements	£492,650
Cheques drawn	(£428,900)
Balance – 31.12	£88,330

a	£495,950	
b	£499,250	
c	£503,530	
d	£7,580	

20.8 Trade payables of Brixton Corner were £248,450 on 30th September 20X8 and £195,900 a year prior to that date. Payments to suppliers in the year to 30th September 20X8 were £794,700. The cost of inventory on 1st October 20X7 was £98,400 and a year later was £112,250. Identify the sales revenue for the year, in each of the following independent scenarios:

a) Sales prices were set to achieve a gross profit ratio of 10%

b) Sales were always made at cost plus 20%

c) Sales were made at cost plus a third

d) Sales were usually made at cost plus 20%; but sales invoiced at £194,400 during the summer were subject to a special discount of 10%.

x		y		z	
£926,000		£916,740		£931,975	
£1,000,080		£1,016,700		£1,059,063	
£1,129,667		£1,041,750		£1,111,200	
£784,080		£978,480		£1,000,080	

Focus on identifying purchases

20.9 Particulars relating to a General Store are stated below on the left. The cash takings during the year ended 30th June 20X8 were £594,800. The sales are made at cost plus 10%. A trade debt of £300 was written off. Identify the amount of purchases in the year ended 30th June 20X8.

a	£607,900	
b	£553,200	
c	£608,200	
d	£605,000	

As at 30th June	20X7	20X8
Trade receivables	£49,800	£59,700
Inventory	£39,200	£42,400

20.10   Payments to suppliers during the year to 30th September 20X8 were £486,780, taking advantage of 5% cash discount offered by suppliers. Taking note of the information in the box on the left, identify the amount of purchases in the year.

a	£498,180	
b	£546,858	
c	£523,800	
d	£503,304	

As at 30th September	20X7	20X8
Trade payables	£54,500	£65,900

20.11   Cash takings from customers during the year were £524,800. The trade receivables at the commencement of the year and at end were £84,700 and £94,500 respectively. The cost of inventory on hand was £39,800 at the commencement and £42,400 at the end. Identify the purchases during the year, in each of the following independent scenarios:

   a) Sales were at cost plus 50%

   b) Gross profit ratio is 25% and carriage inwards amounted to £24,000

   c) Sales were at cost plus 20% and bad debts written off £3,000.

   d) Gross profit ratio is 50% but goods costing £5,000 were lost in a fire

x	y	z
£359,000	£269,900	£537,200
£513,200	£446,350	£379,550
£540,200	£448,100	£432,680
£542,200	£364,000	£274,900

20.12   A summary of a retailer's bank statements identified that, during the year, cheques for £948,500 have been drawn in the name of suppliers. However, cheques drawn in the name of suppliers, not presented to the bank were £42,400 at the beginning and £59,200 at the end of the year. Trade payables were £214,600 at the beginning and £159,400 at the end of the year. Cash discounts received amounted to £9,400. Identify the amount of purchases during the year.

a	£876,500	
b	£885,900	
c	£902,700	
d	£919,500	

Focus on expenses

20.13   Payments during the year of £21,900 for insurance include an amount of £5,400 paid for a year ending four months after the balance sheet date. At the beginning of the year insurance pre-paid was £900. What is the insurance expense in the year?

a	£17,400	
b	£510	
c	£21,000	
d	£19,200	

20.14   According to the bank statement summary for the year, cheques for £14,800 have been drawn in the name of the landlord. However, a landlord's cheque for £1,200 had not been presented for payment at the beginning of the year and another for £2,800 at the year-end. Rent accrued at the beginning of the year was £3,600 and at the end £2,800. What is the year's rent expense?

a	£12,400	
b	£15,600	
c	£17,200	
d	£14,000	

20.15   Browns have rented a photo-copying machine from Whites. The contract is that, besides the monthly rental of £1,200, further payments will be calculated at 3p per copy made. As at 1st April 20X7 rental of £3,000 had been paid in advance; while £2,298 was owed in respect of copies made. During the year ended 31st March 20X8, Browns have paid to Whites £7,200 as rental and £8,978 for copies made. According to meter readings 302,800 copies have been made. Calculate the amount owed to White at 31st March 20X8.

a	£18,121	
b	£21,721	
c	£17,746	
d	£17,371	

Focus on non-trading income

20.16 In addition to its trading activities a business earns substantial amounts as rent, particulars of which are stated on the left. Rent received during 20X8 was £54,800. Identify the rental income it should report in its Income Statement for the year 20X8.

	31.12.20X7	31.12.20X8
	£	£
Rent received in advance	9,800	5,400
Rent in arrears	21,500	32,600

a	£27,600
b	£93,700
c	£15,900
d	£70,300

20.17 On 1st August 20X7 a business invested £400,000 in a fixed deposit account earning interest at 6% per annum. Identify the amount of interest income to be reported in the Income Statement of the business for the year ended 31st March 20X8.

a	£18,000
b	£16,000
c	£24,000
d	£12,000

20.18 Shown on the left is a summary of rent received by a business from sub-letting three suites of its office premises.

Suites	Date received	Amount	Period relating to
A	9.4.20X7	£2,700	Three months to 30.4.20X7
B	11.5.20X7	£4,800	Six months to 30.6.20X7
C	21.8.20X7	£12,000	One year to 31.7.20X7
A	7.10.20X7	£5,400	Six months to 31.10.20X7
C	12.12.20X7	£12,000	One year to 31.12.20X8

Identify the amount that should be included as rental income in the year ended 31st March 20X8 and as an asset or liability on the balance sheet as at that date.

	Income	Liability	Asset
a	£36,900	–	£11,700
b	£32,400	£4,000	£11,700
c	£36,400	–	£11,700
d	£32,400	£4,000	£15,700

Focus on non-current assets

20.19 The non-current assets of a business were reported at a written down value of £548,000 at the year-end and at £472,400 a year prior to that. Depreciation in the year was £51,600. Assets costing £60,000, written down to £21,200 had been sold in the year for £18,000. Identify cost of assets acquired in the year.

a	£144,800
b	£186,800
c	£148,400
d	£2,400

20.20 Non-current assets have been reported on balance sheets of a business as shown below on the left. An asset costing £40,000, written down to £28,000, was sold in the year for £20,000. What is the cost of non-current assets acquired during the year?

	31.3.20X7	31.3.20X8
	£	£
Non-current assets at cost	524,000	578,000
Accumulated depreciation	98,600	112,200

a	£40,000
b	£94,000
c	£74,000
d	£82,000

20.21   Non-current assets have been reported on the balance sheets as shown below on the left. A new asset had been acquired for £120,000 and depreciation of £38,000 written off. An asset was disposed of for £10,000. Identify the gain (G) or loss (L) on the disposal. The following information was available at 30 September 20X8:

As at 31st December	20X7	20X8
Non-current assets at cost	£498,000	£594,000
Accumulated depreciation	£74,200	£98,600

a	£14,000 L
b	£14,000 G
c	£400 L
d	£400 G

20.22   During the year land had been revalued and the surplus reported in a Revaluation Surplus account and an asset costing £80,000, written down to £38,000 had been sold for £40,000. Identify the cost of any non-current assets acquired during the year ending 30th September 20X8.

	30.9.20X7	30.9.20X8
	£	£
Non-current assets at cost	595,000	924,000
Accumulated depreciation	84,400	97,200
Revaluation surplus	–	120,000

a	£289,000
b	£409,000
c	£329,000
d	£249,000

Focus on missing inventory/cash

20.23   Shown below on the left is an extract of the year-end trial balance as at 30th June 20X8. Sales are always made at cost plus 25%. The cost of inventory as at 30.6.20X8 is found to be £54,000. What is the cost of inventory missing?

Inventory as at 30.6.20X7	£78,000	–
Sales	–	£490,000
Purchases	£398,000	–

a	£30,000
b	£84,000
c	£108,500
d	£54,500

20.24   The balance sheet of a newsagent as at 30th June 20X7 reported trade receivables as £79,400 and the balance at bank as £59,400. Daily takings are required to be banked intact and all payments made by cheque. Total of all counterfoils of cheques issued in the year amounts to £394,200. Extract from the year-end trial balance as at 30th June 20X8 is shown on the left. Sales are always effected at cost plus 20%. Cost of inventory on 30 June 20X8 was £62,500. You have been invited to identify the amount of any cash defalcation in the year ended 30th June 20X8.

Inventory as at 30.6.20X7	£48,200
Purchases	£349,400
Bank balance	£11,800
Trade receivables	£81,200

a	£447,920
b	£65,520
c	£134,920
d	£53,720

Answers to multiple choice questions
20.1a: y   20.1b: x   20.1c: z   20.1d: x   20.2: c   20.3a: z   20.3b: x   20.3c: x   20.3d: y   20.4a: x   20.4b: z   20.4c: x   20.4d: y   20.5: a   20.6: b   20.7: c   20.8a: x   20.8b: x   20.8c: z   20.8d: y   20.9: b   20.10: c   20.11a: x   20.11b: z   20.11c: y   20.11d: z   20.12: d   20.13: c   20.14: b   20.15: a   20.16: d   20.17: b   20.18: b   20.19: c   20.20: b   20.21: c   20.22: a   20.23: a   20.24: d

Progressive questions

PQ 20.1 Scenarios when financial statements can or cannot be prepared

The assets and liabilities of a retail shop owned by John Ross have been ascertained as stated on the right.

	31.12.20X7	31.12.20X8
	£	£
Non-current assets at WDV	240,000	284,000
Inventory at cost	112,400	138,200
Trade receivables	136,800	164,600
Cash and bank balance	12,600	15,400
Trade payables	62,500	77,800

Scenario (a):
Assuming that no more information is available with regard to this business estimate the profit made in 20X6.

Scenario (b):
Make a revised estimate of the profit John Ross earned from this shop if, in addition to the above information, you have been able to ascertain as follows:

i) John Ross has no income other than from this shop.
ii) Considering his style of living John Ross must be spending not less than £200 week as household expenses.

Scenario (c):
In addition to the information provided in scenario (a), you have been able to ascertain the following information.

i) Purchases in the year 31st December 20X8 amounted to £486,200.
ii) Non-current assets have been acquired during the year for £60,000.
iii) A diary maintained by John Ross reveals that he has drawn £200 per week to meet his household expenses and has made the payments stated on the right.

Rent	£24,000
Salaries	£48,800
Other expenses	£16,400

Required: Prepare the Income Statement of the retail shop for the year ended 31st December 20X8 and the Balance Sheet as at that date.

PQ 20.2 A basic question on incomplete records

Simon shows his assets and liabilities as stated on the right. Transactions during the year to 31.12.20X8 were as follows:

	1.1.20X8	31.12.20X8
	£	£
Non-current assets	96,400	112,800
Accum depreciation	(24,600)	(32,400)
	71,800	80,400
Inventory	234,500	252,800
Trade receivables	43,200	46,800
Bank balance	2,160	?
Trade payables	97,200	109,800

i) Drawings by the proprietor £40,000.
ii) Payments to suppliers £1,731,600.
iii) Receipts from customers £2,160,000.
iv) Paid salaries £180,000.
v) Paid for other expenses £154,800.

Required: Prepare Simon's
a) summarised Cash Book;
b) Income Statement for the year ended 31st December 20X8 and Balance Sheet as at that date.

PQ 20.3 Incomplete records with goods also taken by sole trader

Dick Barton is a sole trader who makes all business payments by cheque. All takings, including cash sales, are paid into the bank account.

A summary of the bank statements for year is shown on the right.

Required: The Income Statement for the year ended 30 April 20X8 and the Balance Sheet as at that date.

Bank summary:	£		£
Balance at 1.5.20X7	1,200	Trade payables	49,600
Trade receivables	63,120	General expenses	12,620
Cash sales	20,000	Rent	4,000
		Drawings	15,000
		Fixtures	750

Assets and liabilities	30.04.20X7	30.04.20X8
	£	£
Trade receivables	3,800	5,860
Trade payables	3,320	4,250
General expenses owed	620	930
Inventory at cost	4,350	6,200
Fixtures (net)	1,200	1,500
Rent prepaid	300	500

PQ 20.4 Involving cash and bank transactions

Balance Sheet as at 31 December 20X6	
	£
Tangible assets	180,000
Accum depn	(72,000)
	108,000
Inventory	112,000
Receivables	21,400
Bank balance	12,800
Cash in hand	300
Payables	(32,500)
Capital	222,000

Since submitting her last Balance Sheet as shown below on left to the Tax Department, Stella Norris has lost the services of her book-keeper. From a diary of cash payments made by her and by summarising her bank statements for the year ended 31 December 20X7, she identifies the payments made in the year as follows:

	Cash	Bank
To suppliers	£12,800	£144,400
As office rent	–	£10,000
Salary to shop assistants	–	£22,000
Office cleaning		
Other miscellaneous expenses	£720	£1,500
A vehicle acquired on 1st July 20X7	£940	£2,850
	–	£18,000

She states that she regularly takes £200 per week from the till for personal expenses. Her policy is to depreciate the tangible non-current assets, including the new vehicle, at 20% per annum, using the straight-line method and time apportioning the depreciation expense. As at 31 20X7 she reports her current assets and liabilities as stated on the left.

Assets/liabilities as 31.12.20X7	
Inventory	£142,800
Receivables	£48,400
Bank balance	£18,500
Cash in hand	£400
Payables	£49,800

Required: On the basis of the information provided by Stella, prepare for her:
a) a summarised two column Cash Book recording the year's transactions
b) the Income Statement for the year ended 31 December 20X7 and
c) the Balance Sheet as at 31 December 20X7

PQ 20.5 Involving acquisition and disposal of non-current assets

Jeane's Shop provides you with the following information:

Transactions during the year ended 31.3.20X8:

i) Furniture acquired for £16,200 and written down to £5,400 was scrapped in the year.

ii) A vehicle acquired for £54,000 was sold during the year for £30,000 making a gain of £8,000.

iii) Sales, amounting to £846,200 in the year yielded a gross profit ratio of 25%.

iv) Expenses incurred in the year include:
- bad debts £2,100;
- depreciation on furniture £4,200;
- administration/selling expenses £68,200.

v) No record has been maintained of amounts drawn from time to time by Jeane.

Net assets as at:	31.3.20X7	31.3.20X8
	£	£
Furniture at cost	36,400	54,200
Depreciation	(18,200)	?
Motor vehicles	124,000	132,400
Depreciation	(86,800)	(68,400)
Inventory	154,500	216,800
Trade receivables	216,400	254,200
Cash & bank	16,200	9,600
Trade payables	208,300	245,900
Accrued expense	16,400	32,500

Required:
a) Statement of Affairs as at 1st April 20X7.
b) The Income Statement for the year ended 31.3.20X8 and the Balance Sheet as at that date.

PQ 20.6 A question from ACCA paper 1.1 – December 2005

Aim is a sole trader who does not keep a full set of accounting records. An analysis of his bank transactions is shown below on the left. Aim's other assets and liabilities were as stated below on the right:

	Receipts	Payments
	$	$
Overdraft 1 July 2004	–	32,400
Cash banked	418,200	–
Disposal of motor van	4,500	–
Payment for purchases	–	316,300
New van (bought 1.1.2005)	–	22,000
Rent and general expenses	–	49,200
Drawings	–	80,400
Overdraft on 30 June 2005	77,600	–
	500,300	500,300

	30.6.2005	30.6.2004
	$	$
Shop fittings (cost $45,000)	?	35,000
Motor van (cost $18,000)	–	4,000
New motor van	22,000	–
Trade receivables	48,600	44,700
Trade payables	24,200	19,600
Inventories	63,200	58,900
Owing for rent and expenses	13,000	12,500

Notes:
i) Before banking the cash received from customers Aim made payments listed on the right.
ii) Aim depreciates motor van and shop fittings, on the straight-line basis (assuming no residual value), at 20% and 10% per year, respectively, depreciating for the full year in the year of purchase and not depreciating in the year of disposal.

Wages	$74,000
Purchases	$13,700
Expenses	$7,400

Required: Prepare Aim's Income Statement for the year ended 30 June 2005.

PQ 20.7 Another question from ACCA paper 1.1 – December 2004

Bob is a sole trader who does not maintain complete accounting records. The following information is available:

Asset/liability	30.9.2003	30.9.2004
	$	$
Inventory	38,000	46,000
Receivable	119,200	125,000
Pre-paid	2,400	2,600
Payables	68,100	77,100
Accruals	3,900	4,600

Bank summary

	£		£
Balance	20,500	Purchases	408,100
Deposits	12,900	Expenses	89,400
Customers	519,400	Drawings	30,000
		Balance	25,300
	552,800		552,800

Cash summary

	£		£
Balance b/f	300	Banked	12,900
Sales	79,000	Purchases	14,200
		Expenses	4,100
		Drawings	47,900
		Balance	200
	79,300		79,300

Bob has taken away goods from inventory for his personal use but has kept no records of their cost. Bob always fixes his selling prices by adding 50% to the buying price of goods. There is no wastage.

Required: Prepare Bob's Income Statement for the year ended 30 September 2004; calculate the cost of goods taken by Bob.

PQ 20.8 Where a two column Cash Book is needed

Bruce Drake requests your assistance to prepare the financial statements of his business for the year ended 30th June 20X8 and has provided you with the following information:

i) The shop's assets and liabilities include those stated on the right.

ii) Motor vehicles acquired for £28,000 and written down to £12,000, were sold for £9,000.

iii) Bruce always banks his takings at close of business every day, leaving a float of £500.

iv) Rent is agreed at £2,000 per month. Bruce and his family occupy a third of the premises.

v) A fire in May 20X8 destroyed a substantial amount of inventory. An insurance claim has been agreed at £30,000.

vi) Payments made in the year, recorded by Bruce in a diary, are summarised as shown on the right.

vii) The business always effects its sales consistently at cost plus a third.

Required:

a) Record these transactions in a two column Cash Book.

b) Prepare the Income Statement for the year ended 30th June 20X8 and the Balance Sheet as at that date.

	30.6.20X7	30.6.20X8
	£	£
Motor vehicles at WDV	82,000	106,000
Office equipment at WDV	24,500	28,400
Inventory at cost	142,400	96,500
Trade receivables	98,500	118,400
Pre-paid insurance	1,200	?
Balance at bank	21,300	19,700
Trade payables	68,600	114,200
Salaries accrued	18,200	15,600

	In cash	By cheque
	£	£
For purchases	12,400	662,800
Rent	–	30,000
Salaries and wages	3,600	108,500
Motor vehicles	–	60,000
Office equipment	–	16,000
Living expenses – family	3,400	14,200
Other admin/distribution expenses	7,800	44,600
Insurance – year to 30.9.20X8	–	6,000

PQ 20.9 Adopt the crossword puzzle mentality

Rick Alderman owns a shop. Because of a recent bereavement he has neglected to maintain full accounting records. To prepare the financial statements for the year ended 31st December 20X7 he has gathered the following information:

i) The total of administrative expenses and distribution cost, other than depreciation, was reported as £214,500 during the year ended 31st December 20X6. The corresponding amount for the current year is expected to be 20% more.

ii) The assets and liabilities of the shop were as stated on the right.

iii) Apart from new furniture acquired on 1st October 20X7, the other furniture was all acquired when the business started on 1st January 20X5. Furniture is depreciated at 10% per annum using the straight-line method.

iv) Rick has no other source of income and he draws from the business £400 per week as living expenses.

v) Sales are always effected at cost plus 50%.

	31.12.20X6	30.12.20X7
	£	£
Furniture at cost	240,000	300,000
Inventory at cost	426,400	316,500
Trade receivables	48,200	64,400
Pre-paid rent	6,000	–
Cash & bank	38,600	55,200
Trade payables	185,200	212,600
Accrued expenses	12,600	17,800

Required: Prepare the Income Statement for the year ended 31st December 20X7 and the Balance Sheet as at that date.

PQ 20.10 Incomplete record involving bank reconciliation

John Dyson is in business trading wholesale in consumer durables. He purchases from reputable suppliers and sells at a price calculated to yield a profit margin of 25% on cost. His accounts are in a state of disarray and you have been assigned the task of preparing the financial statements for the year ended 30th September 20X8. You have been able to obtain from his auditors the balance sheet as at 30th September 20X7 as appearing on the right. Your investigations reveal:

i) Unpaid invoices for supplies as at 30.9.20X8 amount to £196,700.

ii) Trade receivables as at 30.9.20X8, confirmed by circularising each of the debtors, was £168,500.

iii) Non-current assets are depreciated at 20% per annum using the reducing balance method.

iv) Cost of inventory as at 30.9.20X8 was £284,600.

v) John always banks the whole of his takings, only maintaining a float of £300, and has summarised the payments made out of this float as follows:
   - Paid to suppliers £12,400
   - For other expenses £9,600
   - Drawings £11,800

Balance Sheet as at 30.9.20X7			
	Cost	Accum depn	WDV
Furniture	60,000	(24,000)	36,000
Equipment	45,000	(10,400)	34,600
Inventory		242,600	
Trade receivables		312,400	
Bank balance		51,600	
Cash in hand		300	606,900
			677,500

		£	£
Capital		312,500	
Profit for the year		98,600	
Drawings		(11,800)	399,300
Current liabilities:			
Trade payables		245,400	
Accrued expenses		32,800	278,200
			677,500

vi) Bank statements for the year have been summarised as shown on the right. Uncleared deposits were £17,500 on 30th September 20X7 and £24,400 a year earlier. A cheque for £46,800 drawn in favour of a supplier on 27th September 20X8 was not presented to the bank for payment until a week later.

	£		£
Balance – 1.10.20X7	27,200	Purchases	724,500
Bank lodgement	962,300	Rent	36,000
		Salaries and wages	88,400
		Furniture – 1.1.20X8	80,000
		John's life insurance	15,000
		Other expenses	27,400
		Balance – 30.9.20X8	18,200
	989,500		989,500

vii) Analysis of bank statements in October 20X8 reveal that £24,400 of payments made in that month were for expenses (not suppliers) relating to the period up to 30th September 20X8.

Required: The Income Statement for the year ended 30th September 20X8 and the Balance Sheet as at that date.

SECTION 6
ACCOUNTING PRINCIPLES, CONCEPTS AND POLICIES APPLIED TO ACCOUNTING FOR INVENTORIES

Chapter 6

Inventories, profit margin and gross profit ratio

In this chapter

We will learn of:	and will be able to:
■ year-end inventory	■ account for goods remaining unsold by the end of the year
■ cost of goods sold	
■ profit margin and the gross profit ratio	■ match sales income with the cost of goods sold
	■ calculate profit margin and gross profit ratio

6.1 Reporting unsold purchases as an asset

It is unrealistic to assume, as we have until now, that all goods purchased for sale would have been sold by the end of the accounting period. The reality is that some will remain unsold and would need to be accounted for as an asset, referred to as *inventory*. Inventory is an asset because it is within the control of the business and is expected to generate future economic benefit when it is sold in a future accounting period.

6.1.1 Accounting for inventory

To illustrate the accounting, let us assume that in 20X6 a trader, Binary Bill, purchased ten computers at £1,000 each and only seven of them were sold at £1,500 each by the year-end. His Sales account would report an income of £10,500 (£1,500 × 7) whilst the Purchases account would report £10,000, being the cost of all ten computers.

At the end of the year there would need to be a transfer out of the Purchases account of £7,000 to a Cost of Goods Sold account to record the expense and a transfer of £3,000 to an Inventory account to record the asset consisting of the three unsold computers.

6.1.2 Ledger accounts illustrated

After transferring the cost of the three computers remaining unsold, the accounts would appear as follows:

Purchases account

	£		£
Cash a/c	10,000	Cost of Goods Sold a/c	7,000
		Inventory a/c	3,000

Inventory account

	£		
Purchases a/c	3,000		

The cost of goods sold (expense) is then transferred to the Income Statement and compared with the sales (income) of £10,500 to reveal a gross profit of £3,500, i.e. a gross profit of £500 on each of seven computers.

Cost of Goods Sold account

	£		£
Purchases a/c	7,000	Income Statement	7,000

Sales account

	£		£
Income Statement	10,500	Cash a/c	10,500

6.1.3 Income Statement vertical presentation

The information contained in the ledger accounts would be presented as follows:

Income Statement of Binary Bill for the year ended 31 December 20X6		
	£	£
Sales		10,500
Less:		
Purchases	10,000	
Less: Closing inventory	3,000	
Cost of goods sold		(7,000)
Gross profit		3,500

The cost of goods sold is matched with the sales (income) of £10,500 to reveal a gross profit of £3,500, i.e. a gross profit of £500 on each of seven computers.

Note how important it is to get an accurate figure for the year-end closing inventory. If the stock-taker had omitted one of the computers the cost of goods sold would have been £8,000 and the net profit £2,500, i.e. it would have been reduced by almost 30% – similarly, if the stock-taker had made a mistake and included an additional computer, the cost of goods sold would have been reduced and the net profit increased by almost 30%. Any error in the inventory figure would also result in the inventory reported in the balance sheet being inaccurate.

For most classroom exercises and examination purposes it is quicker and usual to use the vertical Income Statement approach to arrive at the cost of goods sold. The ledger entries have been illustrated to show how the transactions would be recorded in practice in a manual or computer system. You will also find that an understanding of the ledger entries will also be helpful in later chapters when dealing with the correction of accounting errors.

Activity 6.1 Accounting for inventory

An extract from the year-end Trial Balance of a trader, Sid Street, is shown on the right. The cost of inventory remaining unsold at the year-end was £8,250.

Required: Ascertain the gross profit made in the year ended 31 December 20X7 using the Income Statement in its vertical format.

Trial Balance as at 31 December 20X7		
	£	£
Sales	–	54,800
Purchases	42,400	–
Returns inwards	3,940	–
Returns outwards	–	1,850

6.2 Goods lost or disposed of otherwise than by sale

In order to report the gross profit accurately the sales (income) should be matched correctly with the cost of goods actually sold. If goods have been lost or used for other purposes (say issued for charity or distributed free as part of a sales promotion exercise) then the cost of such goods should be removed from the Purchases account and transferred to appropriately named expense accounts. This then leaves the Purchases account with only the cost of goods actually sold.

Let us assume that in the Binary Bill illustration (in Section 6.1 above) it is discovered that there are only two computers on hand at the year-end and one has been lost. The gross profit reported in the Income Statement should still remain at £3,500 (7 × £500) and we achieve this by making the following entries to show the cost of goods sold remaining at £7,000 and the lost computer being treated as an expense of £1,000 and deducted from the gross profit:

Sales (7 @ 1,500)		£10,500
Purchases (10 @ £1,000)	£10,000	
Less:		
Inventory (2 @ £1,000)	(£2,000)	
Goods lost (1 @ £1,000)	*(£1,000)*	(£7,000)
Gross profit		£3,500
Goods lost (1 @ £1,000)		*(£1,000)*

The ledger accounts would be as follows:

Purchases account					Inventory account			
	£		£			£		
Cash a/c	10,000	Cost of Goods Sold a/c	7,000		Purchases a/c	2,000		
		Inventory a/c	2,000					
		Goods lost a/c	1,000					

The cost of goods sold (expense) is then transferred to the Income Statement and compared with the sales (income) of £10,500 to reveal a gross profit of £3,500, i.e. a gross profit of £500 on each of seven computers.

Cost of Goods Sold account				
	£			£
Purchases a/c	7,000	Income Statement		7,000

Goods Lost account (an expense)				
	£			£
Purchases a/c	1,000	Income Statement		1,000

If the computer that has been lost is not accounted for as shown above, the cost of goods sold would be reported as £8,000 and incorrectly include the cost of the lost computer.

Activity 6.2 Accounting for inventory disposal other than by way of sale

An extract from the year-end trial balance of a trader is shown on the right. The cost of inventory remaining unsold by the year-end is £8,000. Goods costing £250 had been issued for charity.

Required: Ascertain the gross profit and the net profit for the year ended 31 December 20X7.

Trial Balance as at 31 December 20X7		
	£	£
Sales	–	54,800
Purchases	42,400	–
Returns inwards	3,940	–
Return outwards	–	1,850
Expenses	11,840	–

6.3 Goods removed for personal use by the proprietor

In many businesses the proprietor may take some of the goods that had been purchased by the business for personal use, e.g. a restaurant owner taking food that had been bought for the restaurant or a garage owner taking petrol or diesel for personal use. The accounting practice in such cases is for the proprietor to be charged for the goods at cost by transferring their cost from the Purchases account to the Drawings account.

6.4 Accounting for closing and opening inventory

Inventory remaining unsold at the end of an accounting period is usually referred to as *closing inventory* in the Income Statement. It is available for sale in the next period when it is re-termed *opening inventory* in the next year's Income Statement.

For example, if in addition to the three computers in inventory at the commencement of the second year (20X7), 15 more are purchased at £1,000 each, the cost of 18 computers available for sale in 20X7 would be reported in two different accounts, i.e. £3,000 in the Opening Inventory account and £15,000 in the Purchases account.

6.4.1 Accounting treatment if all inventory is sold during the year

If all of the 18 computers were sold in 20X7, the balance on the Opening Inventory account and the balance on the Purchases account would both be transferred to a Cost of Goods sold account and the total £18,000 transferred to the Income Statement.

6.4.2 Accounting treatment if some of the inventory is unsold at the end of the accounting period

Let us assume that two computers (costing £2,000) remain unsold at the end of 20X7. This means that the cost of goods sold in 20X7 is (£3,000 + £15,000 – £2,000 =) £16,000 and this is the amount to be transferred to the Income Statement (or Trading account).

6.4.3 What are the accounting entries if we know that the computers in the opening inventory have been sold?

In some businesses we are able to identify exactly the items that have been sold, e.g. any business that sells a product with an identification number such as a car, caravan, computer or washing machine. If, therefore, we can be certain that those remaining unsold were those purchased in 20X7, then the accounting entries would be as follows:

1. Transfer to a Cost of Goods Sold account (which is then transferred to the Income Statement) the whole of the balance (£3,000) in the Opening Inventory account and £13,000 of the balance in the Purchases account to make £16,000.

2. Transfer to a Closing Inventory account the £2,000 remaining in the Purchases account which will then be reported in the Balance Sheet as an asset.

6.4.4 What are the accounting entries if we do not know that the computers in the opening inventory have been sold?

In many businesses, however, we cannot identify the exact items that were sold, e.g. a builders merchant – where the business may not always know whether the goods remaining in hand at the end of a year were those purchased in that year or in the previous year or a combination of both. In those circumstances the accounting entries made are as follows:

1. Transfer to the Income Statement the whole of the balances in both the Opening Inventory account and in the Purchases account.

2. Transfer back from the Income Statement (crediting that account) to the Closing Inventory account (debiting that account) the cost of the goods remaining unsold at the year-end.

The following illustrates the entries that would appear in the ledger accounts, but in normal classroom activity it is more usual to calculate the cost of goods sold using an Income Statement presentation.

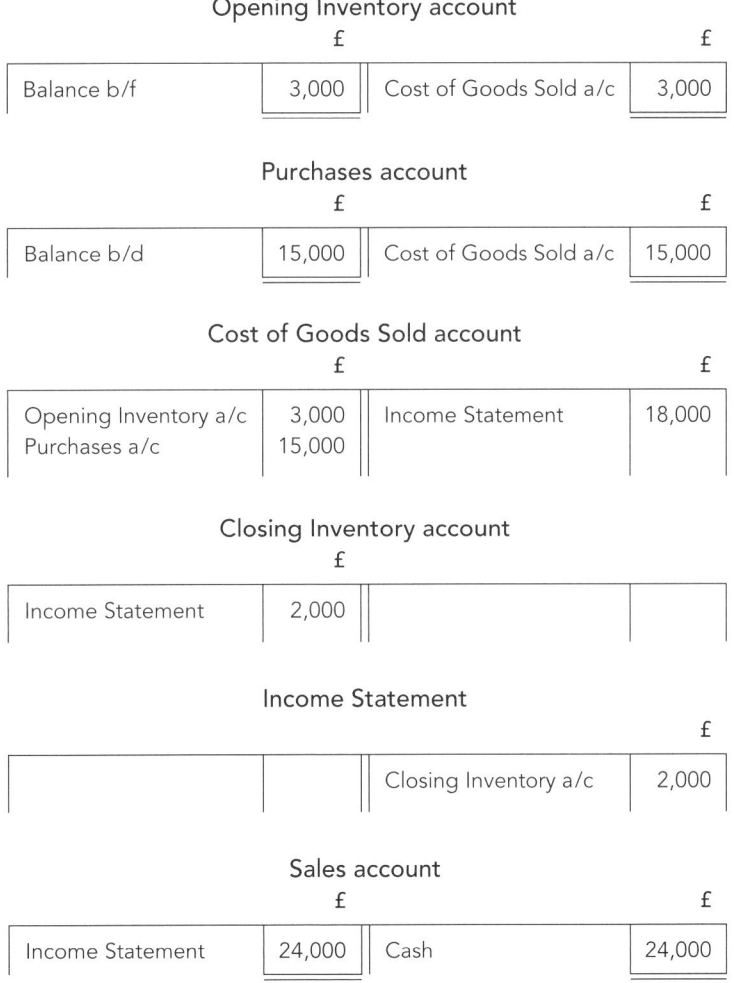

Opening Inventory account

	£		£
Balance b/f	3,000	Cost of Goods Sold a/c	3,000

Purchases account

	£		£
Balance b/d	15,000	Cost of Goods Sold a/c	15,000

Cost of Goods Sold account

	£		£
Opening Inventory a/c	3,000	Income Statement	18,000
Purchases a/c	15,000		

Closing Inventory account

	£		
Income Statement	2,000		

Income Statement

			£
		Closing Inventory a/c	2,000

Sales account

	£		£
Income Statement	24,000	Cash	24,000

6.4.5 The Income Statement presentation

There are various formats that can be used for the Income Statement – treating it either as a ledger account format with a debit and credit side or in vertical narrative style format. Using the ledger account format, the Closing inventory could be shown credited to the Income Statement as follows:

Income Statement for the year ended 31 December 20X7				
	£			£
Opening inventory	3,000	Sales		24,000
Purchases	15,000	Closing inventory		2,000
	18,000			
Gross profit c/d	8,000			
	26,000			26,000

Or, in order to highlight the cost of goods sold the credit entry to the Income Statement of the closing inventory is usually shown as a deduction on the debit side as follows:

Income Statement for the year ended 31 December 20X7				
	£			£
Opening inventory	3,000	Sales		24,000
Purchases	15,000			
	18,000			
Less: Closing inventory	(2,000)			
Cost of goods sold	16,000			
Gross profit c/d	8,000			
	24,000			24,000

Or, if the Income Statement is prepared in vertical narrative style format rather than ledger account format, the presentation would be amended as follows:

Income Statement for the year ended 31 December 20X7		
	£	£
Sales		24,000
Less:		
Opening inventory	3,000	
Purchases	15,000	
	18,000	
Less: Closing inventory	2,000	
Cost of goods sold		(16,000)
Gross profit		8,000

Activity 6.3 Accounting for opening and closing inventory

An extract from the year-end trial balance is shown on the right. Unsold inventory at the year-end is £39,580. Goods costing £4,200 were issued free for advertising purposes, while goods costing £500 have been lost.

Required: Set out the Trading account (Income Statement) for the year ended 31 December 20X7.

Trial Balance as at 31 December 20X7		
	£	£
Sales	–	214,800
Purchases	164,560	–
Inventory – 1.1.20X7	29,420	–
Return inwards	1,120	–
Expenses	42,840	–

6.5 Expenses included within cost of sales

We have so far only included the invoiced price (after trade discount) of goods to be sold as an expense in arriving at the gross profit figure. There are, however, certain other expenses that are treated as part of the cost of goods sold which will reduce the amount of the gross profit. These include the *transport costs* or delivery costs incurred in bringing the goods into store and the cost of bringing goods sold to a *saleable condition* and *saleable location*. Let us consider some of such expenses.

6.5.1 Transport costs

Accountants refer to the cost of transporting the goods as *carriage*. The expense of transporting the goods to the place of business is referred to as *carriage inwards* and is regarded as part of the cost of sales. Hence, if a computer sold for £1,500 was purchased for £1,000 and £25 was paid for carriage inwards the total cost of sales would be £1,025 and the gross profit (£1,500 – £1000 – £25 =) £475. On the other hand, the cost of delivering the goods to the customer is referred to as the *carriage outwards* and it is regarded as a selling expense and so is included within the expenses that are deducted from gross profit when calculating the net profit.

6.5.2 Costs of bringing to saleable condition

Any expense incurred on bringing the goods sold to the *condition* in which they are sold is included as part of cost of sales. For example, a dealer in second-hand vehicles will include within his cost of sales not only the purchase price of the vehicle but also all other expenses such as the cost of spares, repairs, painting and wages incurred on bringing the car to the condition in which it is sold. If the dealer also uses non-current assets such as a paint baking equipment when respraying, there would also be an amount included for the depreciation of that equipment.

6.5.3 Costs of bringing to saleable location

Any expense incurred on bringing the goods sold to the *location* from where they are sold is included as part of the cost of sales. For example, a dealer in imported goods will include in his cost of sales not only the price paid to the overseas supplier and the transport costs but also all other expenses incurred in bringing the goods to the location from which they are sold. Such expenses include insurance, import duty and the like.

Activity 6.4 The cost of goods sold

Rebecca imports dolls from Taiwan and hand paints them before selling them in the UK. Her inventory of dolls as on 1st January 20X7 had been purchased at a cost of £42,500 while her inventory by the year-end had cost her £107,300. Her sales in the year to 31 December 20X7 were £394,500. In July 20X7 she had gifted to charity dolls costing £12,800. Her expenses in 20X7 are listed on the right. She informs you that 75% of salary and wages was paid to those directly engaged in hand painting the dolls.

Salaries and wages	£28,800
Advertising	£29,450
Purchase of dolls	£184,250
Materials for improving dolls	£11,820
Rent	£12,000
Import duty	£27,540
Freight and insurance	£16,950
Telephone & postage	£5,825
Carriage outwards	£7,650
Packing for delivery	£7,845

Required: Calculate her gross profit and net profit for the year ended 31 December 20X7.

6.6 The task of finding the quantity and cost of closing inventory

Ideally, a trader should know the cost of goods as he sells them and hence the cost of what remains at the end of each accounting period. This certainly would be the case when the item sold is of a high value and individually identifiable by say a serial number or description, e.g. a motor car, computer, valuable item of jewellery. It is possible in these situations to match the cost of sales with the sales and to identify the items still unsold at the year-end.

Let us illustrate this situation by referring to a trader who sells yachts. Assume that his transactions in the year were as follows:

Date of purchase	The item purchased	Serial number	Cost price (£)	Date of sale	Sale price (£)	Profit (£)
3.1.20X7	Yacht	SK100	100,000	30.10.20X7	189,000	89,000
14.3.20X7	Yacht	PV300	58,000	28.9.20X7	69,000	11,000
26.7.20X7	Yacht	XR251	102,000	–	–	–

The performance for the year and the position at the end of the year will be as shown below.

Income Statement for the year to 31.12.X7			Balance Sheet as at 31.12.X7	
	£	£		£
Sales		258,000		
Cost of sales:				
SK100	100,000		Inventory	
PV300	58,000	(158,000)	(XR251)	102,000
Gross profit		100,000		

However, inventories often consist of so many different small value items that are bought at different times in the year and at varying prices meaning that the task of identifying the actual individual cost of the items sold and the ones remaining unsold may be difficult or not cost-effective. For example, the inventory held by a general store could range from perishable foodstuffs such as milk and bread to non-perishables such as canned foods to household products such as toiletries and cleaners with each of the items stocked in a variety of brand names, sizes and packaging and prices. In these circumstances a business entity has to use one of the many methods available, firstly to ascertain the quantity of goods remaining unsold at year-end and secondly to ascertain, as best as possible in the circumstances, the cost of these goods. Major retailers with point of sale computing do, of course, find it cost-effective because the real-time recording informs their restocking requirements.

6.7 Ascertaining unsold goods by taking physical inventory

The common method of identifying unsold goods at the end of an accounting period is by taking a physical inventory count (i.e physically counting and listing each item) on that date or, more commonly, a convenient day close to it such as the following weekend when business is closed or slower.

We have seen that an error with the inventory count has a direct impact on the gross profit figure which is increased or decreased £ for £ of the error. This means that there need to be proper controls over the actual counting process. For example, every location where inventory is held has to be identified, the counters need to be sufficiently experienced to recognise the inventory that they are counting and the recording of quantities should be on pre-numbered inventory sheets. The quantity will then be priced, and it is important to assess the condition of the inventory to see if any need to be priced below their invoice cost because, for example, they are damaged, out of date or shop soiled.

The quantity counted often requires adjustment for the following:

1. Items that have been included in the purchases figure on the receipt of an invoice but which are not physically on the premises, e.g. goods might be in transit, there might be an unexpected production hold up at the manufacturers.

2. Items might belong to the business but not have been included when the inventory was counted, e.g. items in the custody of customers (on approval or sale or return basis) or with third parties like agents or consignees. Such items should be included in the closing inventory.

3. Items might have been sold and a sales invoice issued and posted to the Sales account but the items still remain on the premises and have been included in the count by the

counters. The cost of these items should be deducted from the results of the inventory (because it is necessary to include the cost of these items in the cost of sales).

4. Items of expense stock (such as stationery or packing material) may have been incorrectly included within the count and treated as inventory for resale. The cost of these items will need to be adjusted against the appropriate head of expense.

6.8 Valuing the closing inventory

Closing inventory is valued at cost or net realisable value unless for any reason, such as being shop soiled, the business does not expect to be able to sell an item to recover its cost. Companies in their Annual Report state their accounting policy for inventories. The following is an extract [www.reckittbenckiser.com] from the Reckitt Benckiser Annual Report and Financial Statements 2005:

Inventories
Inventories are stated at the lower of cost or net realisable value. Cost comprises materials, direct labour and an appropriate portion of overhead expenses (based on normal operating capacity). Net realisable value is the estimated selling price less applicable selling expenses.

Cost is easily determined for high-value items such as cars but, where this information is not available on an item by item basis, we need to adopt an alternative. The alternative is to assume a cost flow, often arbitrarily, to associate the costs paid during the year with the units remaining unsold at the end of the year. There are many such cost flow assumptions in use, though the common ones are the 'first in first out' (FIFO), 'simple average cost' and 'weighted average cost'.

Because there is a choice of cost flow assumption, companies in their Annual Report state their accounting policy for inventories and may adopt different cost bases for different inventories. For example, the J Sainsbury plc 2006 Annual Report [www.j-sainsbury.co.uk] stated:

Inventories
Inventories are valued at the lower of cost and net realisable value. Inventories at warehouses are valued on a first-in, first-out basis. Those at retail outlets are valued at calculated average cost prices. Cost includes all direct costs and other appropriate attributable costs incurred in bringing inventories to their present location and condition.

Let us use the case of Samuel, a builder's merchant, to illustrate the alternative cost flow assumptions that could be made to associate cost with the units remaining unsold. Samuel's purchases and sales of sand in 20X7 are as follows:

Purchases				Sales			
Date 20X7	Quantity in tonnes	Unit cost per tonne (£)	Total cost (£)	Date 20X7	Quantity in tonnes	Unit price per tonne (£)	Total sale (£)
1.1	100	10	1,000	4.2	90	30	2,700
17.4	400	20	8,000	26.5	310	35	10,850
28.6	1,200	25	30,000	14.9	450	40	18,000
11.10	100	35	3,500	5.11	200	40	8,000
	1,800		42,500		1,050		39,550

The unit cost per tonne has increased substantially during the year and the amount of profit for the year depends on the unit cost he uses to value the 750 tonnes of sand remaining unsold at the year-end. There is no single correct answer because there is no way he could identify the actual cost of the pile in hand. All that can be done in the circumstance is to make a cost flow assumption or apply an average. We will discuss the FIFO and LIFO assumptions and the average cost method.

6.8.1 First in first out (FIFO)

FIFO is by far the commonest cost flow assumption adopted in the UK and many other countries. This is not so for some countries, e.g. Germany, Italy, South Africa and some countries of South America. FIFO assumes that the inventory is sold in the sequence in which it was purchased with the result that the unit price of items remaining unsold is presumed to be the most recent invoiced price.

There are some businesses where inventory rotation is important and FIFO is a realistic assumption, e.g. businesses dealing in perishables (like fruits, vegetables and eggs) and date marked processed food. The assumption is that the business would ensure that early purchases are sold before their expiry dates. Continuing with the Samuel example, the FIFO valuation of the 750 tonnes of sand would apply the latest prices which were paid on 28 June and 11 October and would be calculated as follows:

Cost of closing inventory			
Tonnes	Bought on	Unit cost (£)	Cost (£)
650	28.6.X7	25	16,250
100	11.10.X7	35	3,500
750			19,750

Trading account for the year ended 31.12.20X7		
	£'000	£'000
Sales		39,550
Purchases	42,500	
Less: Inventory	(19,750)	(22,750)
Gross profit		16,800

The advantages of using FIFO include the following:

1. The assumed sequence of inventory movement may reasonably reflect reality.
2. The balance sheet will report inventory at values which, being the latest paid, may approximate those currently prevailing.
3. The method is acceptable to the tax authorities.

The disadvantages of using FIFO include the following:

1. The expense (cost of goods sold) charged to the Income Statement is based on outdated prices and, if prices are rising, the cost charged against sales revenue will not reflect the cost of replacing the item sold.
2. If the whole of the profit calculated on this assumption were to be distributed there would be insufficient funds retained to replace the same number of items sold.

6.8.2 Last in first out (LIFO)

This time it is assumed that the goods move out in the reverse order of their arrival. Hence, the items remaining unsold are presumed to be ones which arrived the earliest and the cost of the items remaining unsold would be assumed to be the earliest price paid.

This method is used in the USA but has been discouraged in the UK because LIFO does not provide the fairest approximation to actual cost. The LIFO assumption of the sequence of inventory movements might well apply to a business such as Sam's where one could imagine Samuel piling up sand as it arrived so that the latest lot to arrive would probably be on top and likely to be sold first.

If Samuel opts to make this assumption he would value the closing inventory as follows:

Cost of closing inventory			
Tonnes	Bought on	Unit cost (£)	Cost (£)
100	1.1.'X7	10	1,000
400	17.4.'X7	20	8,000
250	28.6.'X7	25	6,250
750			15,250

Trading account for the year ended 31.12.20X7		
	£'000	£'000
Sales		39,550
Purchases	42,500	
Less: Inventory	(15,250)	(27,250)
Gross profit		12,300

The main advantage of LIFO is:

■ Profit reported on this assumption is more accurate because the prices at which goods are matched with sales revenue will be closer to the date of the sales.

The disadvantages of this method are as follows:

1. The most serious disadvantage is that, as the unit price increases, the value of inventory in the Balance Sheet becomes ever further removed from contemporary market prices.

2. The assumption is often not in keeping with the sequence of inventory movements in real life.

3. Detailed records are needed of the unit prices which may be many years old.

4. Company Law[1] requires accounts to be prepared in accordance with accounting standards which do not permit the use of this method. It is also not acceptable to the UK tax authorities.

6.8.3 Average cost (AVCO)

AVCO is not based on a cost flow assumption. It is a compromise between FIFO and LIFO and shares to a lesser extent the advantages and disadvantages of both. This method makes no assumption regarding the sequence in which the goods move. Instead, it values the unsold units at the average of the various prices paid.

Simple average cost

If Samuel opts for simple average cost he will value 750 tonnes remaining unsold at the average of the four different prices he paid in the year, without taking into account the quantities purchased at each of these prices. The average would be £22.50 per tonne ((£10 + £20 + £25 + £35)/4). The closing inventory of 750 tonnes @ £22.50 would amount to £16,875.

Weighted average cost

If Samuel opts, instead, for the weighted average cost, he would calculate the average of various prices paid for purchases by weighting the price by the quantity purchased at that price. The cost per tonne will then be £23.61 (£42,500/1,800 tonnes). The closing inventory of 750 tonnes @ £23.61 would amount to £17,708.

Under each of these methods Samuel's performance will be reported as follows:

Using simple average cost

Trading account for the year ended 31.12.20X7		
	£'000	£'000
Sales		39,550
Purchases	42,500	
Less: Inventory	(16,875)	(25,625)
Gross profit		13,925

Using weighted average cost

Trading account for the year ended 31.12.20X7		
	£'000	£'000
Sales		39,550
Purchases	42,500	
Less: Inventory	(17,708)	(24,792)
Gross profit		14,758

Activity 6.5 Finding the cost of closing inventory

At the beginning of the year Charlotte had 12 ladies' garments purchased at £45 each. Her purchases in the year are listed on the right. She sold 55 garments during the year at £90 each.

Units	Unit price
30	£50
40	£60

Required: Report her performance and position for the year, valuing unsold inventory using (a) FIFO, (b) LIFO, (c) simple average cost and (d) weighted average cost.

6.8.4 IAS 2[2] *Inventories* requirement on cost flow assumption

IAS 2 *Inventories* requires inventory to be valued using the specific cost attributable to each item. The cost flow assumptions for associating costs to the items remaining unsold is only allowed by IAS 2 when the items are interchangeable (the Standard uses the word fungible). In such circumstances, where the use of cost flow assumption is permitted, IAS 2 approves only FIFO and the weighted average cost.

6.9 What comprises the cost of inventory?

Under IAS 2 the cost of inventories should include:

1. **All costs of purchase.** In addition to the invoiced price, this includes import duty, transport, handling and other costs directly attributable to purchase, and after deducting trade discounts and rebates.

2. **The costs of conversion.** In addition to direct labour cost, this includes production overheads (both fixed and variable) systematically allocated to finished goods. The fixed overheads (the expenses that do not increase as production increases) should be allocated on the basis that production is operating at normal activity and the variable overheads based on the actual output.

3. **Other costs incurred in bringing the inventories to their present location and condition.** IAS 2 gives guidance on some of the expenses that should not be included within the cost of inventory. These include administrative overheads, selling costs, abnormal waste and interest costs.

6.10   Goods with customers on a sale or return basis

As a sales promotion technique it is possible that a business may have delivered some goods to customers allowing them a specified time to decide whether they wish to retain the goods or return them. So long as customers make up their mind before the end of the accounting period there would be no accounting problem – those that have been retained will have been accounted for as sold and those returned would have been included within closing inventory.

It might be, however, that the business has treated the goods as sold and included in the Sales account and Trade Receivables Ledger even though they are still with customers and within the returnable period. In such a case, the Sales account and Trade Receivables Ledger account entries need to be reversed and the cost of these goods included within closing inventory.

Activity 6.6 Goods with customers on approval basis

Henry, dealing in hover lawn mowers, provides you with an extract from his accounts as stated on the right. He reports that:

Opening inventory	£960
Purchases	£6,720
Sales	£8,100
Receivables	£2,700
Expenses	£590

i)   He buys each unit at £240 and sells them at £300.

ii) He has five units in hand at the year-end.

iii) Three units which are with customers on an approval basis are within the returnable period but have been accounted for as sold.

Required:

a) Explain the adjustment that would need to be made to the balances to record the reversal of the entries made for the goods that are out on approval.

b) The Income Statement.

6.11   Valuing closing inventory at net realisable value

An asset should not be reported on the balance sheet at a value in excess of the future economic benefit it is expected to generate. Accordingly, it is a requirement of IAS 2 *Inventories* that inventory should be reported as an asset at the lower of cost or *net realisable value* (NRV). Net realisable value is the price at which the item is expected to be sold less any expenses bringing it to a condition in which it can be sold.

To illustrate, let us assume that Robert deals in laptop computers, buying them at £1,000 each and selling them at £1,500 each. At the end of the financial year he had the following inventory:

	Laptops
Opening inventory	4
Purchases	12
Sales	(10)
Closing inventory	6

An Income Statement would be as follows if each laptop could be sold for more than £1,000 which was the cost price:

Sales (10 units @ £1,500)		£15,000
Opening inventory	£4,000	
Purchases	£12,000	
Closing inventory	(£6,000)	
Cost of ten laptops sold		(£10,000)
Gross profit (£10 units @ 500)		£5,000

Let us assume, however, that one of the laptops has been dropped and damaged. A decision would need to be made whether it was unsaleable or whether it would have to be sold at less than its normal price. If saleable it is necessary to estimate any costs to be incurred in rectifying the damage and then how much it could be sold for. If we assume that its repair would cost £150 and it could then be sold for £900, then its net realisable value would be £750.

IAS 2 requires that the damaged laptop should be included in the inventory at its net realisable value of £750. The Income Statement would then be adjusted and appear as follows:

Sales (10 units @ £1,500)		£15,000
Opening inventory	£4,000	
Purchases	£12,000	
Closing inventory	(£5,750)	
Damaged laptop account	(£250)	
Cost of ten laptops sold		(£10,000)
Gross profit (£10 units @ £500)		£5,000
Damaged laptop account		(£250)

Note that the loss of £250 (£1,000 less £750) has been removed from the Inventory account to an appropriately named expense account which will, along with other expenses, be deducted from the gross profit to arrive at the net profit.

This is the normal accounting treatment, but there may be circumstances where there is no need to write down the closing inventory to its lower net realisable value, e.g. if the items concerned are intended to be incorporated into a product which itself can be realised at or above its cost[2].

Activity 6.7 Value of closing inventory where items have NRV lower than cost

Shown on the right is a part of the year-end trial balance of a dealer in office coolers. The cost of Closing inventory is ascertained at £298,000. This figure includes at £54,000 the cost of two cooler units used as display models. These two units, if reconditioned at a cost of £500 each, may be sold as shop soiled at £15,000 each. Sales commission on selling these two units would be payable at 10%.

Trial Balance as at 30th June 20X7		
	£'000	£'000
Inventory as at 1.7 20x6	214	–
Sales	–	980
Purchases	648	–
Carriage inwards	21	–
Other expenses	224	–
Carriage outwards	38	–
Sales commission at 5%	49	–

Required: Set out the Income Statement for the year and the value at which the inventory should be reported on balance sheet at the year-end.

When carrying out a comparison of cost with net realisable value it is not acceptable for this to be done for the inventory taken as a whole. The comparison should be done either for each item in the inventory or for groups of fungible (interchangeable) items of inventory. The aim of this requirement, known as the *non-aggregation rule*[1], is to avoid an anticipated loss on some items remaining unsold being offset against a gain expected on other items.

Activity 6.8 Comparison of cost with NRV of fungible groups

The year-end inventory of Reyney's Electronics consists of the following items:

Model of television	Units held unsold	Unit cost	Unit sale price
PYE 28" Colour	320 sets	£380	£450
SATCHI 28" Colour	106 sets	£320	£375
GODWIN 25" Colour	85 sets	£175	£160
SELKIRK 15" Colour	64 sets	£190	£150

Required: State the value at which the inventory should be reported in the year-end balance sheet.

6.12 Profit margin and gross profit percentage

One of the main business objectives is to make a profit.

6.12.1 The profit margin

The targeted profit is often set by adding to the cost price a percentage known as the *profit margin*. For example, if Richard purchased a computer for £1,000 and added a profit margin of 25% (25% of £1,000 = £250) he would fix his selling price as £1,250. Bear in mind that the profit margin is calculated by reference to the cost.

6.12.2 The gross profit percentage

When he sells the computer for £1,250, by comparing the sales income with the cost of sales Richard would report a gross profit of £250 (£1,250 – £1,000). The *gross profit percentage* compares the gross profit with sales. Hence Richard's gross profit percentage is £250/£1,250 × 100 = 20%. It is important to remember that the gross profit is compared with the cost to report a profit margin and with sales to report a gross profit percentage or ratio.

6.12.3 Relationship between profit margin and gross profit percentage

It is useful to observe the relationship between the profit margin and the gross profit percentage. We have seen that Richard's profit margin was 1/4th of cost, whereas his gross profit ratio is 1/5th of sales. The following table further illustrates the relationship:

If profit margin is		gross profit ratio is
1/2 of cost price	=	1/3 of sale price
1/3 of cost price	=	1/4 of sale price
1/4 of cost price	=	1/5 of sale price
1/5 of cost price	=	1/6 of sale price
2/10 of cost price	=	2/12 of sale price
3/10 of cost price	=	3/13 of sale price
6/10 of cost price	=	6/16 of sale price

The relationship shows that if X buys a unit for £30 and adds on a profit margin of a third, selling it for £40, his gross profit ratio would be a fourth; if Y buys a unit for £50 and adds on a profit margin of a fifth, selling it for £60, his gross profit ratio would be a sixth and if Z buys a unit for £70 and adds on a profit margin of 2/7th, selling it for £90, his gross profit ratio would be 2/9th.

Activity 6.9 A furniture dealer estimates closing inventory

Sally sells second-hand furniture at a price set at 20% above cost. The year-end trial balance appears as stated on the right. She did not take a year-end inventory but reports that she has removed for own use inventory costing £7,000 and has given free to her old school's library furniture costing £15,000.

Required: Prepare Sally's Income Statement for the year ended 30th September 20X6 and her Balance Sheet as at that date.

	£'000	£'000
Inventory – 1st Oct. 20X5	228	–
Staff salary	34	–
Sales	–	900
Rent	48	–
Purchases	688	–
Non-current assets	180	–
Cash & bank	12	–
Capital	–	300
Drawings	10	
	1,200	1,200

Summary

- A portion of goods purchased for sale may remain unsold and will need to be treated as an asset named inventory at the end of each accounting period.
- The inventory brought forward from the previous period, referred to as opening inventory and recorded in a separate account, together with purchases in the current period, net of closing inventory and cost of goods disposed of otherwise than by sale, would constitute the cost of goods sold.
- All expenses in placing the goods sold in the condition in which they are sold and in the location from which they are sold should be included as part of the cost of goods sold.
- It is common for a business to ascertain its unsold goods at period-end by conducting a physical inventory; when this does not take place on the last day of the period appropriate adjustments are required.
- In the absence of precise information on the cost of goods remaining unsold, provided the goods are interchangeable, a business has to make a cost flow assumption of either FIFO or weighted average cost.
- Inventory, when reported as an asset, should be stated at cost or lower net realisable value.
- Profit margin relates profit to cost of goods sold; whereas the gross profit percentage relates profit to sales and there is a clear relationship between them.

References

1 Companies Act (2006), Sections 395 and 403, London, The Stationery Office.
2 IAS 2 *Inventories*, revised 2003, effective 1.1.2005, London, International Accounting Standards Board.

Suggested answers to activities

6.1 Accounting for inventory

	£	£
Sales		54,800
Less: Returns inwards		(3,940)
		50,860
Purchases	42,400	
Less: Returns outwards	(1,850)	
	40,550	
Less: Closing inventory	(8,250)	
Cost of goods sold		(32,300)
Gross profit for the year		18,560

The answers to both questions are set out in Income Statement format (rather than as Trading and Profit and Loss accounts).

6.2 Inventory disposal

	£	£
Sales		54,800
Less: Returns inwards		(3,940)
		50,860
Purchases	42,400	
Less: Returns outwards	(1,850)	
	40,550	
Less: Charity issue	(250)	
closing inventory	(8,000)	
Cost of goods sold		(32,300)
Gross profit for the year		18,560
Expenses	11,840	
Charity	250	(12,090)
Net profit for the year		6,470

6.3 Accounting for opening and closing inventories

Trading and Profit and Loss account for the year ended 31 December 20X7					
	£	£		£	£
Opening inventory a/c		29,420	Sales	214,800	
Purchases		164,560	*Less*: Returns inwards	(1,120)	213,680
		193,980			
Less: Closing inventory	(39,580)				
Inventory for advertising	(4,200)				
Inventory lost	(500)	(44,280)			
Cost of goods sold		149,700			
Gross profit c/d		63,980			
		213,680			213,680
Expenses		42,840	Gross profit b/d		63,980
Advertising (goods issued free)		4,200			
Goods lost		500			
Net profit c/d		16,440			
		63,980			63,980
Capital a/c		16,440	Net profit b/d		16,440

6.4 The cost of goods sold

	£	£
Sales		394,500
Less:		
Inventory – 1.1.20X7	42,500	
Purchases	184,250	
Freight & insurance	16,950	
Import duty	27,540	
Improvement material	11,820	
Salaries & wages – 75%	21,600	
Inventory – 31.12.20X7	(107,300)	
Goods to charity	(12,800)	
Cost of goods sold		(184,560)
Gross profit		209,940
Less: Salaries & wages	7,200	
Rent	12,000	
Telephone/post	5,825	
Advertising	29,450	
Carriage outwards	7,650	
Packing	7,845	
Charity	12,800	(82,770)
Net profit		127,170

6.7 Value of closing inventory where items have NRV lower than cost

	£'000	£'000
Sales		980
Inventory – 1.7	214	
Purchases	648	
Carriage inwards	21	
Inventory 30.6	(298)	(585)
Gross profit		395
Other expenses	224	
Carriage outwards	38	
Sales commission	49	
Loss – shop soiled[a]	28	(339)
Net profit		56

Sale price of damaged goods (15,000 × 2)	£30,000
Less: reconditioning expenses (500 × 2)	(£1,000)
Less: sales commission @ 10% of 30,000	(£3,000)
Net realisable value	£26,000

[a] Closing inventory: 298,000 – 28,000 = £270,000

6.5 Finding the cost of closing inventory

	FIFO		LIFO		Simple average		Weighted average	
	£	£	£	£	£	£	£	£
Sales		4,950		4,950		4,950		4,950
Inventory	540		540		540		540	
Purchases	3,900		3,900		3,900		3,900	
Closing inventory	(1,620)		(1,290)		(1,395)		(1,462)	
Cost of goods sold		(2,820)		(3,150)		(3,045)		(2,978)
Gross profit		2,130		1,800		1,905		1,972

6.6 Goods with customers on approval basis

The sales would need to be reduced by 900 as it curently includes an amount that could be returned. The receivables also need to be reduced by 900 as the person holding the goods has not agreed to actually buy them and would be unwilling to pay until deciding to do so. The following journal entry is the normal format used by accountants to record the bookkeeping entries that would be made, and we will be explaining journal entries in detail in Chapter 8.

Journal:		Dr	Cr
Sales a/c	Dr	900	–
To Receivables		–	900
Being sales remaining on approval			

Income statement for the year ended . . .		
	£	£
Sales		7,200
Opening inventory	960	
Purchases	6,720	
Closing inventory	(1,920)	(5,760)
Gross profit		1,440
Expenses		(590)
Profit for the year		850

Inventory: 5 in own custody plus 3 with customers = 8 × 240 = £1,920.

6.8 Comparison of cost with NRV of fungible groups

Valuation of inventory at cost or lower net realisable value						
Model	Units	Unit cost	Unit sale price	Total at cost	Total at sale price	Lower of cost or NRV
PYE 28″	320	£380	£450	£121,600	£144,000	£121,600
SATCHI 25″	106	£320	£375	£33,920	£39,750	£33,920
GODWIN 25″	85	£175	£160	£14,875	£13,600	£13,600
SELKIRK 25″	64	£190	£150	£12,160	£9,600	£9,600
TOTAL				£182,555	£206,950	£178,720

6.9 A furniture dealer estimates closing inventory

Income Statement for the year ended 30.9.20X6		
	£'000	£'000
Sales		900
Inventory – 1.10	228	
Purchases	688	
Drawings	(7)	
Gift to school	(15)	
Inventory – 30.9	(144)	
Cost of sales		(750)
Gross profit		150
Gift to school	15	
Rent	48	
Staff salary	34	(97)
Net profit		53

As the profit margin is a fifth of cost, the gross profit percentage is a sixth of sales resulting in a gross profit of £150,000. This means that the cost of goods sold was (£900,000 – £150,000) = £750,000. The cost of closing inventory is arrived at by removing the cost of goods sold (£750,000) from the cost of opening inventory plus purchases less the cost of goods taken away for own use by the proprietor and the cost of furniture gifted to the school library.

Balance Sheet as at 30 September 20X6	
	£'000
Non-current assets	180
Inventory	144
Cash & bank	12
	336

	£'000
Capital	300
Profit for the year	53
Less: Drawings	(10)
Furniture taken	(7)
	336

Multiple choice questions

Inventory and cost of sales

6.1   A trader reports opening inventory at £122,800, purchases for the year at £824,700 and closing inventory at £154,200. During the year goods costing £24,800 were lost, others costing £12,500 had been removed for own use by the proprietor and some costing £10,000 were gifted to charity. What is the cost of sales?

a	£758,500	
b	£746,000	
c	£770,800	
d	£783,300	

6.2   Which of the following expenses would you regard as part of the cost of goods sold?

    a) Advertising the goods for sale

    b) Insurance and freight on importing goods for sale

    c) Packing the goods for delivery to customers

    d) Insurance of goods in the warehouse against fire and theft

6.3   If carriage inwards amounting to £57,800 is included as part of carriage outwards the impact of the error would be:

    a) Gross profit as well as net profit will be understated

    b) Gross profit will be overstated but net profit unaffected

    c) Gross profit as well as net profit will be overstated

    d) Gross profit as well as net profit will not be affected

6.4   How would you account for the goods removed for own use by the proprietor?

    a) Credit Sales account, debit Drawings account with the sale price of the goods

    b) Credit Purchases account, debit Drawings account with the cost price of the goods

    c) Credit Opening Inventory account, debit Drawings Account with cost price of the goods

    d) Credit Trading account, debit Drawings account with the cost price of the goods

6.5   If closing inventory is accounted for as £240,000 instead of £180,000:

    a) Gross profit and net profit would both be understated

    b) Gross profit will be overstated and net profit understated

    c) Gross profit will be overstated but net profit correctly reported

    d) Gross profit as well as net profit will be overstated

6.6   Which of the following will result from a failure to account for goods removed by the proprietor for own use?

    a) Both net profit and the Capital account balance at year-end will be understated

    b) It would not make any difference to the net profit for the year or the Capital account balance

    c) Net profit will remain the same but the closing balance in the Capital account will be overstated

    d) Net profit will be under-stated but the closing balance in the Capital account will not change

6.7 If goods lost are not accounted for:

a) Gross profit as well as net profit will be overstated

b) Gross profit and net profit will be understated

c) Gross profit will be under-stated but net profit will be correctly reported

d) Gross profit will be over-stated but net profit will be correctly stated

6.8 Which of the following is incorrect? The cost of sales is:

a) Opening inventory + purchases – closing inventory

b) Opening inventory + purchases + carriage inwards – closing inventory

c) Opening inventory + purchases + carriage outwards – closing inventory

d) Sales – return inwards – gross profit

6.9 Having reported its financial performance in the year a business finds that goods costing £74,500 removed by the owner have not been accounted for. The effect of correcting this error would be:

a) No change in gross profit and net profit

b) Gross profit increases by £74,500 and net profit increases by the same amount

c) Gross profit increases by £74,500; but no change in net profit

d) Gross profit as well as net profit decrease by £74,500

6.10 On the basis of the information provided on the right a business reported the gross profit for the period as £34,000 and net profit as £14,000. Since then it has been discovered that closing inventory is in fact £280,000. The effect of correcting this error is:

Opening inventory	£354,000
Purchases	£712,000
Sales	£900,000
Closing inventory	£200,000

a) Gross profit as well as net profit remain unchanged

b) Gross profit decreases by £80,000 and net profit remains unchanged

c) Gross profit increases by £80,000 and net profit remains unchanged

d) Gross profit as well as net profit increase by £80,000

6.11 Which of the following statements is incorrect?

a) Carriage inwards is included in the Income Statement as part of cost of sales

b) Carriage outwards is shown in the Income Statement as a deduction from gross profit

c) Gross profit is the difference between purchases and sales

d) Net profit is gross profit less all expenses other than those included in the cost of goods sold

6.12 A retailer of designer menswear reports as stated on the right. The closing inventory includes £30,000 being the cost of 200 pairs of trousers damaged in storage. If repaired at a cost of £40 each, the trousers may be sold for £100 a pair. The gross profit for the year and the inventory value in the year-end balance sheet would be:

Opening inventory	£184,800
Purchases	£752,400
Sales	£858,600
Closing inventory	£248,200

a) Gross profit £101,000 and inventory value £248,200

b) Gross profit £169,600 and inventory value £230,200

c) Gross profit £83,000 and inventory value £230,200

d) Gross profit £83,000 and inventory value £248,200

6.13 The year-end trial balance of a trader includes the balances stated on the right. 75% of carriage is for delivering goods to customers. The cost of closing inventory has been ascertained to be £185,000. However, it includes damaged goods at their cost price of £36,000. If repaired at a cost of £1,800 these goods could be sold for £15,000. Calculate the gross profit for the year and the value at which closing inventory should be reported on the year-end balance sheet:

Opening inventory	£128,000
Purchases	£594,000
Sales	£790,000
Carriage	£84,000

a) Gross profit £162,000 and inventory value £162,200

b) Gross profit £139,200 and inventory value £162,200

c) Gross profit £162,000 and inventory value £185,000

d) Gross profit £139,200 and inventory value £198,200

Delayed physical inventory

6.14 A wholesale merchant sets his selling prices at cost plus 20%. His accounting period ended on 31st March 20X6. A physical inventory count took place on 5th April and the inventory valuation at that date was £482,800. Assuming that the remainder of information is as stated in each of the following alternative circumstances, ascertain the cost of closing inventory as at 31 March:

a) Purchases and sales, during the five days after 31st March, were £78,400 and £58,800 respectively. The cost of packing material at £4,500, the cost of unused stationery at £800 and the cost of parts bought for vehicle maintenance at £124 have all been included in the inventory.

w	£457,776	
x	£458,576	
y	£507,024	
z	£447,976	

b) During the five days after 31st March:
Purchases were £84,200, but goods costing £5,400 did not arrive till 7th April; sales were £95,700, but goods invoiced for £4,500 were not delivered to customers until 6th April.

w	£480,000	
x	£489,800	
y	£485,600	
z	£487,500	

c) Purchases and sales during the five days after 31st March were £79,400 and £105,300 respectively. An inventory sheet total has been carried forward from one sheet to another as £342,800 instead of £324,800. Forty-eight units of an item were stated as £300 each whereas the real cost of these items was £300 per dozen.

w	£443,250	
x	£477,500	
y	£459,950	
z	£522,350	

d) Purchases and sales, during the five days after 31st March, were £82,400 and £97,200 respectively. As at 31st March goods invoiced to customers at £37,350 were with customers, on approval. A third of these goods were returned by the customers on 4th April.

w	£460,650	
x	£502,150	
y	£504,950	
z	£512,525	

Identifying the cost of inventory

6.15 Which of the following statements would be contrary to IAS 2 Inventories requirements?

a) Inventory should be reported at the lower of cost or net realisable value

b) Unless the items in inventory are interchangeable cost flow assumptions cannot be used

c) The LIFO cost flow assumption cannot be used even when items in inventory are interchangeable

d) The cost of the inventory may include an appropriate portion of office expenses

6.16 Roger, dealing in second-hand pianos of different makes and models, uses the FIFO cost flow assumption to ascertain the cost of unsold inventory. This would be wrong because:

a) This is not the practice used by others in the trade

b) Cost flow assumptions may be used only when the items in the inventory are interchangeable

c) The profit for the accounting period will be over-stated

d) It is not possible to sell each piano in the sequence in which they were purchased

6.17 If a supermarket uses LIFO cost flow assumption to ascertain the cost of closing inventory which of the following reasons would an auditor have for disapproving of this?

i) Use of LIFO is not permitted by IAS 2 *Inventories*	a	i, ii, iii	
ii) In times of rising prices LIFO under-states inventory on the balance sheet	b	ii, iii, iv	
iii) Other supermarkets do not use LIFO cost flow assumption	c	i, iii, iv	
iv) In times of rising prices LIFO under-states profit	d	i, ii, iv	

6.18 Which among the following expenses may be included as part of the cost of closing inventory?

i)	Factory staff salary	ii)	Machinery depreciation	iii)	Sales commission	iv) Raw materials used
v)	Accounting expenses	vi)	Office rent	vii)	Stationery	a	i, ii, iii, ix, xii
viii)	Interest paid	ix)	Sales commission	x)	Direct labour	b	i, ii, iv, x, xi, xv
xi)	Factory rent	xii)	Advertising	xiii)	Postage	c	ii, vii, xi, x, xi
xiv)	Bad debts	xv)	Import duty	xvi)	Discount allowed	d	i, iv, vi, x, xi, xv

6.19 Sophie deals in DVD players of the same make and model. At the commencement of the year on 1st January she held 40 units purchased for £30 each. She sells each unit for £60. Her sales in the year amounted to £12,000. Her purchases during the year are stated on the left. Ascertain the cost of closing inventory on each cost flow assumption stated on the right.

March	90 units @ £40	
May	80 units @ £45	
July	30 units @ £50	

	FIFO	Weighted average
a	£1,950	£1,650
b	£2,000	£2,400
c	£1,950	£2,400
d	£2,000	£1,650

Profit margin and gross profit percentage

6.20 Stated on the right is information in respect of a wholesale merchant. The cost of closing inventory has been ascertained as £198,600. What is his:

Opening inventory	£142,400
Purchases	£596,200
Sales	£675,000

x	y	z
20%	25%	50%
20%	25%	50%

a) Profit margin (as a percentage),

b) Gross profit percentage.

6.21 A trader reports his sales in 20X5 as £548,700. What would be his gross profit in each of the following independent circumstances?

	x	y	z
a) His gross profit percentage is 25%	£182,900	£137,175	£109,740
b) Selling prices are cost plus 25%	£182,900	£137,175	£109,740
c) Selling prices are cost plus 20%	£91,450	£109,740	£137,175
d) Selling prices are cost plus 40%	£365,800	£219,480	£156,771

6.22 A retail trader fixes his sale price by adding 25% to the cost of every item purchased. He provides you with the information relating to 20X5 as stated on the right.

Opening inventory	£284,400
Purchases	£842,800
Sales	£985,500

x	y	z
£305,950	£388,075	£338,800
£55,950	£138,075	£88,800

a) What should his closing inventory be?

b) If his closing inventory was only £250,000 what is the cost of goods lost?

6.23 A retail trader fixes his sale price by adding a third to the cost of every item purchased. He provides you with the information relating to 20X5 as stated on the right. He suspects his sales staff of misappropriating cash takings. The extent of misappropriation is:

Opening inventory	£152,800
Purchases	£746,200
Sales	£985,800
Closing inventory	£68,300

a) £91,350

b) £121,800

c) £1,107,600

General

6.24 Which of the following would be the transaction which decreases both the assets and the liabilities?

a) A vehicle was acquired for £32,000

b) A loan of £25,000 was repaid

c) Goods were purchased for sale from Orlando Ltd for £12,800

d) Received a cheque for £5,850 from a credit customer

6.25 Which of the following would not be listed in a balance sheet as part of current assets?

a) Trade receivables

b) Opening inventory

c) Closing inventory

d) Bank balance

6.26 Which of the following is *not* a current asset?

a) Trade Receivables

b) Trade Payables

c) Bank balance

d) Inventory

6.27 On its Balance Sheet a business would report as a current liability the amounts:

a) it intends to repay within one year of the balance sheet date

b) it intends to pay immediately after the date of the Balance Sheet

c) it intends to pay as early as possible but not later than a month after the Balance Sheet date

d) it hopes to repay one day

6.28 The accounting entries for stationery remaining unused by the year-end are:

a) Debit Inventory account, credit Stationery account

b) Debit Stock of Stationery account, credit Stationery account

c) Debit Stationery account, credit Cash account

d) Debit Capital account, credit Stationery account

6.29 If the daily total of the Sales Day Book has been stated as £112,400 instead of £122,400 the effect would be:

a) Trial balance will remain in balance

b) The credit side of the trial balance will exceed the debit side by £10,000

c) The debit side of the trial balance will exceed the credit side by £10,000

d) The debit side of the trial balance will exceed the credit side by £20,000

6.30 An extract of the year-end trial balance is shown on the right. The inventory figure is the closing inventory figure. What has happened then to the opening inventory?

	Debit	Credit
Cost of goods sold	£348,694	–
Sales	–	£542,965
Closing inventory	£74,850	–

a) There has been no inventory brought forward from the previous year

b) It has been included within the amount of cost of goods sold

c) It has been removed by the owner for personal use

d) It has been stolen

6.31 Which of the following is *not* acceptable as an explanation for a fall in gross profit ratio?

a) Reduction in profit margin as a sales promotion strategy

b) Error in ascertaining the amount and cost of closing inventory

c) Failure to account for goods removed by proprietor or disposed of otherwise than by sale

d) Shifting from LIFO to FIFO in times of rising prices

6.32 In relation to reporting inventory on the balance sheet which of the following statements is incorrect?

a) Comparison of cost with NRV should be done for each item or groups of fungible items

b) The NRV is found by deducting from the selling price any expected trade discount and cash discount

c) An item of inventory need not be written down to NRV if it is not intended for sale

d) The requirement to report inventory at NRV is to ensure that an asset is not reported on the balance sheet at an amount higher than the future economic benefit expected to flow from it.

6.33 Which of the following pairs of accounts will never appear together in the same trial balance?

a) Opening Inventory account and Closing Inventory account

b) Sales account and Return Inwards account

c) Cash account and Bank account

d) Purchases account and Returns Outwards account

6.34 In the system of accounting as used in the UK which of the following is not recorded in an account?

a) Loss of goods bought for sale

b) Goods removed by the owner for own use

c) Cash discount

d) Trade discount

6.35 IAS 2 *Inventories* requires year-end inventory to be reported at the lower of cost or net realisable value. Which of the following is the correct definition of net realisable value?

a) The price at which the unsold inventory could be sold

b) The price at which the unsold inventory was purchased

c) The price at which unsold inventory could be sold less expenses of selling them

d) The price at which unsold inventory could be sold plus expenses of selling them

Answers to multiple choice questions
6.1: b   6.2: b   6.3: b   6.4: d   6.5: d   6.6: d   6.7: c   6.8: c   6.9: b   6.10: d   6.11: c   6.12: b   6.13: a   6.14a: z   6.14b: w
6.14c: y   6.14d: x   6.15: a   6.16: b   6.17: d   6.18: b   6.19: a   6.20a: y   6.20b: x   6.21a: y   6.21b: z   6.21c: x   6.21d: z   6.22a: z
6.22b: z   6.23: b   6.24: b   6.25: b   6.26: b   6.27: a   6.28: b   6.29: c   6.30: b   6.31: d   6.32: b   6.33: a   6.34: d   6.35: c

Progressive questions

PQ 6.1 The effect of ignoring closing inventory

On completion of his first year's business as a dealer in fashionware, Bernard has prepared his financial statements as on the right. His attention is drawn to his failure to take account of unsold fashionware costing £112,000 which remained on hand on 31st December 20X7.

Required: Prepare an amended Income Statement for the year ended 31 December 20X7 and a Balance Sheet as at that date, taking account of unsold inventory.

Income Statement for the year ended 31.12.20X7	
	£'000
Sales	640
Purchases	(516)
Gross profit	124
Expenses	(94)
Profit	30

Balance Sheet as at 31.12.20X7	
	£'000
Non-current assets	240
Loan to staff	15
Cash & bank	75
	330
	£'000
Capital	300
Profit	30
	330

PQ 6.2 Where physical inventory may be lower than expected

Jerry Noel retails computer software, fixing his selling price consistently at cost plus a third. The results of his trading transactions during the year ending 31.12.20X7 have been reported as shown on the right. On the basis of a physical inventory he has ascertained his unsold goods as at 31.12.20X7 as £546,000.

Inventory – 1.1.20X7	£324
Purchases	£4,620
Sales	£5,840
Return inwards	£124
Return outwards	£76

Required:

a) Explain whether Jerry has any reason to be unhappy with the results of his year-end inventory.

b) Identify the reasons which may have caused the results of inventory taken at year-end to be different from what the figure should have been as at 31.12.20X7.

PQ 6.3 Purchase invoice yet to be accounted for

Chris Day, a retailer, extracted the year-end trial balance as shown on the right. He informs you as follows:

i)   All expenses relating to the period have been paid in full.

ii) Included within other expenses is £11,400 paid for transporting goods to the shop.

iii) The goods were received but the purchase invoice for £22,500 has not been recorded in the Purchases Day Book because the invoice was not received until 4th January 20X8.

iv) The cost of inventory in hand on 31 Dec. 20X7, including the goods referred to in (iii) above, was £242,600.

v)   Goods costing £450 removed by Chris Day for his own use have not been accounted for.

Required: Prepare the Income Statement for the year ended 31 December 20X7 and the Balance Sheet as at that date.

Note: Ignore depreciation.

Trial balance as at 31 December 20X7		
	£	£
Non-current assets	180,000	–
Sales	–	563,200
Drawings	18,000	–
Inventory – 31.12.20X6	146,800	–
Trade receivables	98,500	–
Trade payables	–	64,200
Staff salary	24,800	–
Other expenses	29,400	–
Cash and bank	11,700	–
Purchases	418,200	–
Capital	–	300,000
	927,400	927,400

PQ 6.4 Identifying the inventory included in a trial balance

The year-end trial balance of Barlow Garments is shown on the right. You are informed as follows:

i)   Barlow Garments has paid in full all expenses relating to the year.

ii) Goods costing £54,000 issued free for sales promotion purposes and others costing £12,000 taken by Mr Barlow for his own use have yet to be accounted for.

iii) The cost of goods remaining unsold at year-end was £592,000.

iv) Ignore depreciation.

Required:

a) Make the accounting entries necessary for identifying the cost of goods sold and extract a trial balance at that point.

b) Make the accounting entries necessary for identifying the gross profit and extract another trial balance at that point.

c) Prepare an Income Statement for the year ended 31 December 20X7 starting with gross profit and a Balance Sheet as at that date.

d) When not identified with a date next to it, how would you know whether inventory stated in a trial balance is opening inventory or closing inventory?

Trial balance as at 31 December 20X7		
	£'000	£'000
Non-current assets	910	–
Inventory – 31.12.20X6	412	–
Purchases	3,248	–
Sales	–	4,845
Drawings	148	–
Carriage inwards	112	–
Salaries and wages	288	–
Rent	150	–
Return inwards	125	–
Return outwards	–	96
Trade receivables	495	–
Trade payables	–	326
Other expenses	165	–
Cash & bank	14	–
Capital	–	800
	6,067	6,067

PQ 6.5 The need to revise the value of closing inventory

Refer to the information stated in respect of Barlow Garments in PQ (6.4) above. When ascertaining the cost of closing inventory at £592,000, the following errors have been made:

i) The inventory includes 400 party frocks at their cost of £40 each. These frocks have a defect. It would cost £3 per frock to remedy the defect and thereafter each of them can be sold for only £28.

ii) The inventory includes 480 casual shirts at £100 each; whereas these shirts cost £100 per dozen.

Required: Prepare a revised Income Statement for the year ended 31 December 20X7 and the Balance Sheet as at that date, making appropriate corrections of the errors identified.

PQ 6.6 Possible reasons for a fall in gross profit ratio

The City Emporium sells many different products. Though their turnover for the year was marginally better than that of the previous year, the gross profit ratio was significantly lower. Identify reasons which may have caused this.

PQ 6.7 A trader takes inventory after the year-end date (1)

Hanson Stores finalises its accounts on 31st March 20X7, but was unable to do a physical inventory until 6th April 20X7. Inventory was then physically counted and entered onto inventory sheets. Every item on the inventory sheets was then priced at cost. The total value of inventory on hand, at cost price, was determined as £216,400. You have ascertained as follows:

i) Adjustments required for movements between the year-end and the date of the inventory:
    Between 1.4. 20X7 and the time of inventory, purchases amounted to £48,400, sales to £74,100 and sales returns to £2,100. The figure of sales referred to includes goods invoiced at £6,000 but which were not delivered to customers until 8.4.20X7 which was after the time inventory was taken. Hanson Stores fixes sales price to achieve a profit margin of 50% on cost.

ii) Adjustment required for errors in taking inventory:
    ■ A sub-total of £156,500 has been carried forward from one inventory sheet to the next as £165,500.
    ■ Inventory sheets include at £1,600 the cost of packing material and at £2,800 that of unused stationery.

iii) Adjustment required for inventory held by third parties at the time of the inventory was taken:
    ■ Certain goods costing £164,400 included within purchases in the year to 31.3. 20X7, were not cleared from the bonded warehouse until the second week of April 20X7.

iv) Adjustment required for inventory held by customers:
    ■ Inventory with customers on sale or return basis on 31 March 20X7 had been pro forma invoiced to them (as usual at cost plus 50%) for £5,400. A third of these goods had been returned by 6th April and the rest retained by customers. (A pro forma invoice is a sample invoice – no sale is recognised until the customer confirms retention of goods or passing of return deadline.)

v) Adjustment required for items expected to be sold at or below cost:
    ■ Included in the Inventory sheets at cost of £14,400 are certain shop soiled items which are expected to be sold at only £12,000 and subject to the payment of sales commission of 5%.

Required: Determine the value of inventory to be included in the Income Statement for the year ended 31st March 20X7 and the Balance Sheet as at 31st March 20X7.

PQ 6.8 A trader takes inventory after the year-end date (2)

The financial year of Ladybird Ltd ends on 31 December. In order to avoid interference with trading, the inventory count for the year ended 31 December 20X7 was carried out on 8th January 20X8 when the inventory on the company's premises, at cost, amounted to £117,567. The following further information is available:

i) Selling prices in 20X7 yielded a gross profit of 25% on sales. On and after 1st January 20X8, they were determined by adding 20% to the cost of goods sold.

ii) Sales in the month of December 20X7 not dispatched until early in 20X8, amounted to £2,800. These goods were all dispatched during the period 1–8 January with the exception of goods sold for £80, which were not dispatched until 10th January.

iii) Sales for the period 1–8 January 20X8 amounted to £19,590 of which goods sold for £2,700 were not dispatched until after 9th January.

iv) Purchases for the period 1–8 January 20X8 amounted to £14,685, and all the goods were received within the same period.

v) Goods purchased on 31 December 20X7 for £150 and entered in the books on that date were not received until 10th January 20X8.

Required: Ascertain the amount at which the inventory should be included in the annual accounts made up to 31 December 20X7.

PQ 6.9 A manufacturer's inventory taken after the year-end

Furniture Mart manufactures and retails household and office furniture and accounts for sales at the point the furniture is ready for delivery. It prepares accounts annually up to 30th June. On the basis of an inventory conducted on 5th July 20X7, Furniture Mart ascertained that its unsold goods in hand on that date was £865,200. You are provided with the following information:

i) On the inventory sheets 1,200 sets of furniture rollers have been valued at £20 per set whereas they cost £20 per dozen.

ii) Sales during the first five days of July amounted to £144,000, though a third of these were not delivered to the customer until 6th July. Sales are effected at cost plus a third.

iii) Purchases during the five days to 5th July amounted to £200,000, but only 25% of this was delivered by the time of the inventory.

iv) Wood, for which £75,000 was paid on 18th June 20X7 and accounted for as purchases in the year, was not received at Furniture Mart until 6th July.

v) Included in the inventory sheet at its cost of £15,000 are brass cabinet hinges, the market value of which has since gone down by 20%. These hinges are intended for making cabinets.

vi) Four hundred pieces of office shelves, included in the stock sheets at cost of £300 each, are no longer in fashion and cannot be retailed at more than £225 a piece.

vii) A dining room suite, made to a customer's order at an agreed price of £6,000, has been included in the inventory sheets at its cost of £4,800. To abide by the recent change in legislation, the suite cannot be delivered to the customer until it is re-upholstered in non inflammable material and that is expected to cost £1,500.

Required: Determine the inventory to be reported on the balance sheet as at 30th June 20X7.

PQ 6.10 A question from ACCA

After stock taking for the year ended 31 May 20X6 had taken place the closing inventory of Cobden Ltd was aggregated to a figure of £87,612. During the course of the audit that followed the undernoted facts were discovered:

i) Some goods stored outside had been included at their normal cost price of £570. They had, however, deteriorated and would require an estimated £120 to be spent to restore them to their original condition, after which they can be sold for £800.

ii) Some goods had been damaged and were now unsaleable. They could, however, be sold for £110 as spares after repairs estimated at £40 had been carried out. They had originally cost £200.

iii) One stock sheet had been over-added by £126 and another under-added by £72.

iv) Cobden Ltd had received goods costing £2,010 during the last week of 20X6, but because the invoices did not arrive until June 20X6 they have not been included in inventory.

v) A stock-sheet total of £1,234 had been transferred to the summary sheet as £1,243.

vi) Invoices totalling £638 arrived during the last week of May 20X6 (and were included in purchases and in creditors) but, because of transport delays, the goods did not arrive until June 20X6.

vii) Portable generators on hire from another company at a charge of £347 were included at this figure in inventory.

viii) Free samples sent to Cobden by various suppliers had been included in inventory at the catalogue price of £63.

ix) Goods costing £418 sent to customers on sale or return basis had been included in inventory at their selling price of £602.

x) Goods sent on sale or return basis to Cobden had been included in the inventory at the amount payables (£267) if retained. No decision to retain has been made.

Required: Ascertain the inventory to be included in the balance sheet as at 31st May 20X6.

PQ 6.11 A question from Edexcel, London Examinations – GCSE

The sixth formers at the Broadway School run a tuck shop business. They began trading on 1 December 20X6 and sell two types of chocolate bar, Break and Brunch. Their starting capital was a £200 loan from the School Fund. Transactions are for cash only. Each Break costs the sixth form 16p and each Brunch costs 12p. 25% is added to the cost to determine the selling price. Transactions during December are summarised below:

December 6: Bought five boxes of Break, each containing 48 bars, and three boxes of Brunch, each containing 36 bars.

December 20: The month's sales amounted to 200 Breaks and 90 Brunches.

Required:
a) Record the transactions in the Cash, Purchases and Sales accounts (all calculations must be shown).
b) On December 20 (the final day of term) a physical inventory-taking showed 34 Breaks and 15 Brunches in stock. Calculate the value of closing inventory and prepare an Income Statement to report the gross profit/loss for the month of December 20X6.
c) Explain the number of each item that should have been in stock.

PQ 6.12 Cost flow assumptions to find the cost of inventory

Unicombs deal in personal computers of a standard make and model. During the year ended 31.12.20X7 they made their purchases at different prices; but they retailed them consistently at £1,200 per unit until 1.10.20X7 when they increased the sale price by 10%. An inventory of 320 units was reported in their balance sheet on 31.12.20X6 at £128,000. Particulars of their purchases and sales in the year ended 31st December 20X7 are as follows:

Purchases			Sales in 20X7	
Date	Units	Unit cost (£)	Month of sale	Units
16.2.20X7	600	725	Jan to March	620
7.4.20X7	800	850	April to June	860
11.7.20X7	1,200	957	July to Sept	920
5.10.20X7	1,000	1,050	October to Dec	810

Required:

a) Determine the cost of inventory held on 31.12.20X7 on each of the following alternative cost flow assumptions: (i) FIFO, (ii) LIFO, (iii) simple average cost, (iv) weighted average cost.

b) Trace the effect of each of the above cost flow assumptions on the company's performance and position.

PQ 6.13 A question from CIMA

DEX Stores sells three different types of product. The business is made up of three different departments each having its own manager who is responsible for buying/selling a particular type of product. The owner determines the pricing policy and fixes the sale price adding to the cost a percentage of profit as stated →

The takings during April 20X5 were ————————→

The opening stock on 1 April 20X5 at cost as ——→

Inventory at cost on 3 May 20X5 ————————→

	Department A	Department B	Department C
	40%	25%	100%
	£18,725	£11,750	£147,000
	£4,200	£7,800	£22,500
	£3,700	£8,100	£21,600

Transactions that occurred between end of April and 3rd May 20X5:

	Department A	Department B	Department C
Sales	£420	£250	£1,500
Purchases	–	£1,500	–
Returns inwards	–	–	£300
Returns outwards	£270	–	£800
Purchases during April 20X5 amounted to ——→	£14,200	£8,400	£74,000

The owner has recently become concerned that the gross profit shown by the accounts does not reconcile with these percentages profit mark-ups and suspects that some of the stock may be stolen.

Required:

Calculate a) the value of stock on 30 April 20X5, b) the extent to which the owner's suspicions are justified.

PQ 6.14 A question from ACCA

a) IAS 2 *Inventories* requires inventory to be valued at the lower of cost of net realisable value. How would you arrive at the cost of finished goods in a manufacturing company?

b) Information stated on the right relates to Unipoly, manufacturer of can openers, for the year ended 31st May 20X7. There are 250,000 units of finished goods at the year-end. You

Direct material cost of can opener per unit	£1
Direct labour cost of can opener per unit	£1
Direct expenses cost of can opener per unit	£1
Production overheads per year	£600,000
Administrative overheads per year	£200,000
Selling overheads per year	£300,000
Interest payments per year	£100,000

may assume that there were no finished goods in hand at the start of the year and that there was no work in progress. The normal annual level of production is 750,000 can openers, but in the year ended 31 May 20X7 only 450,000 were produced because of labour dispute.

Required: Calculate the cost of finished goods stock in accordance with IAS 2.

PQ 6.15 Delayed inventory count

Hendon Traders, with a year end of 31 December 20X7, were able to identify the cost of unsold inventory as £412,850 on 6 January 20X8. The following information is provided:

a) Sales within the six days to 6 January, at cost plus 25%, were £128,400. £42,000 of these goods had, however, been returned by 6 January.

b) Purchases within the same six days were accounted for in the book of prime entry at £74,800. £800 of these goods did not arrive until 7 January. Further invoices for £12,400 received after 6 January, were for goods that had been delivered before that date.

c) Goods invoiced to customers at £40,000 (at cost plus 25%), though in the hands of customers, were within the returnable period permitted to them of two weeks. The delivery as well as the invoicing of these goods had taken place prior to 31 December 20X7.

d) One of the sheets in which inventory was listed has stated the total as £94,800 instead of £84,800 and on another sheet the cost of 48 items had been stated at £15 each whereas they actually cost £15 per dozen.

e) The inventory sheets include packing material acquired at a cost of £3,000 and spare parts for machine maintenance acquired at a cost of £4,000.

f) Inventory includes 18 items at their cost of £900 each. These items, however, were shop-soiled and were expected to be sold for £400 each after their condition has been restored at a cost of £50 each.

Required: Identify the cost of inventory to be reported on the balance sheet as at 31 December 20X7.

PQ 6.16 Inventory valuations – FIFO, LIFO and AVCO

Matthew Eagle buys and sells wet suits. Inventory is counted at the end of every month. On 1 January 20X1 50 wet suits were in the inventory which had cost £30 each.

The first quarter's transactions are stated on the right. No other transactions took place during the three-month period. Each wet suit sold for £50 throughout the three months.

Required:

a) Calculate the inventory valuation at 31 January and 31 March 20X1 using each of the following methods of inventory valuation:
   i)   FIFO
   ii) LIFO
   iii) AVCO

   (All calculations are to be maintained to two decimal places)

b) State which two methods of valuation in (a) are acceptable under IAS 2 explaining why the third method is unacceptable.

c) Calculate the gross profit for the three months ended 31 March 20X1 using the two methods of stock valuation in (a) which are acceptable under IAS 2.

Date	Purchases of sweaters	Sales of sweaters
Jan 8	–	30
Jan 10	100 at £30.00 each	–
Jan 12	–	30
Jan 15	–	50
Jan 21	120 at £30.50 each	–
Jan 23	–	30
Jan 28	–	60
Feb 1	–	20
Feb 5	–	30
Feb 14	150 at £31.00 each	–
Feb 20	–	40
Feb 23	–	60
Mar 1	–	30
Mar 4	120 at £31.50 each	–
Mar 10	–	50
Mar 14	–	30
Mar 19	–	40
Mar 23	100 at £32.00 each	–
Mar 27	–	60
Mar 30	–	60

SECTION 7
THE CONCEPTUAL FRAMEWORK OF ACCOUNTING

Chapter 4

Ensuring the quality of financial statements

2004/05 Group highlights

		Reported basis	At constant exchange rates[1][2]
Like for like sales		up 5.0%	
Sales	£1,614.4m	up 0.6%[2]	up 7.8%
Operating profit	£218.9m	up 4.1%[2]	up 11.3%
Profit before tax	£210.3m	up 5.3%[2]	up 12.1%
Earnings per share[3]	8.2p	up 9.3%[2]	up 15.5%
Dividend per share	3.0p	up 20.0%	
Return on capital employed[3]	26.5%	up from 25.9%[2]	
Gearing[3]	11.3%	down from 11.8%[2]	

(1) See page 29 for reconciliation to Generally Accepted Accounting Principles ('GAAP') figures.
(2) 2000/01 to 2003/04 restated for the implementation in 2004/05 of the amendment to FRS 5, 'Application Note G – Revenue Recognition'.
(3) Earnings per share, return on capital employed and gearing are defined on page 130.
(4) 53 week year.

Introduction

The key drivers of operating profitability are the:

- rate of sales growth,
- balance between like for like sales growth and sales from new store space,
- achieved gross margin,
- level of cost increases experienced by the Group,
- level of net bad debt charge relating to the in-house credit card in the US, and
- movements in the US dollar to pound sterling exchange rate, since the majority of the Group's profits are generated in the US and the Group reports in pounds sterling.

Source: Signet Group plc Annual Report and Accounts 2005, inside cover and p. 24.

Discussion points

1 How does the company present the information it regards as most relevant to the needs of readers?

2 The group provides information 'at constant exchange rates' to eliminate the effects of exchange rate fluctuations. How relevant is this information to the needs of users?

Learning outcomes

After studying this chapter you should be able to:

- List and explain the qualitative characteristics desirable in financial statements.
- Explain the approach to measurement used in financial statements.
- Explain why there is more than one view on the role of prudence in accounting.
- Understand and explain how and why financial reporting is regulated or influenced by external authorities.
- Be aware of the process by which financial statements are reviewed by an investor.

4.1 Introduction

The previous chapter used the accounting equation as a basis for explaining the structure of financial statements. It showed that design of formats for financial statements is an important first step in creating an understandable story from a list of accounting data.

The objective of financial statements is to provide information about the financial position, performance and changes in financial position of an entity that is useful to a wide range of users in making economic decisions.[1]

Information about financial position is provided in a **balance sheet**. Information about performance is provided in an **income statement** (profit and loss account).[2] Information about changes in the cash position is provided in a **cash flow statement**. These three statements were explained in outline in Chapter 3. Information about changes in financial position is also provided in a separate statement, described in Chapter 12. Notes to the financial statements provide additional information relevant to the needs of users. These notes may include information about risks and uncertainties relating to assets, liabilities, revenue and expenses.[3]

4.2 Qualitative characteristics of financial statements

The IASB *Framework* sets out qualitative characteristics that make the information provided in financial statements useful to users. The four principal qualitative characteristics are:

- understandability
- relevance
- reliability
- comparability.[4]

The principal qualitative characteristics of relevance and reliability have further sub-headings, as follows:

- relevance
  - materiality
- reliability
  - faithful representation
  - substance over form
  - neutrality
  - prudence
  - completeness.

Each of these characteristics is now described.

4.2.1 Understandability

It is essential that the information provided in financial statements is readily **understandable** by users.[5] Users are assumed to have a reasonable knowledge of business and economic activities and accounting, and a willingness to study the information with reasonable diligence. Information on complex matters should not be omitted from financial statements merely on the grounds that some users may find it difficult to understand.

4.2.2 Relevance

Information has the quality of **relevance** when it influences the economic decisions of users by helping them evaluate past, present or future events or confirming, or correcting, their past evaluations.[6]

Information has a predictive role in helping users to look to the future. Predictive value does not necessarily require a forecast. Explaining unusual aspects of current performance helps users to understand future potential. Information also has a confirmatory role in showing users how the entity has, or has not, met their expectations.[7]

Materiality

Information is **material** if its omission or misstatement could influence the economic decisions of users taken on the basis of the financial statements. Materiality depends on the size of the item or error judged in the particular circumstances of its omission or misstatement.[8]

The IASB *Framework* takes the view that materiality is a cut-off point in deciding whether information is important to users. The description of an item may make it material. The amount of an item may make it material.

For example, the balance sheet of a business shows inventories of raw materials and inventories of finished goods as two separate items. That is because the users of financial statements are interested in the types of inventory held as well as the amount of each. The risks of holding raw materials are different from the risks of holding finished goods. However the inventory of finished goods is not separated into the different types of finished goods because that would give too much detail when the risks of holding finished goods are relatively similar for all items.

4.2.3 Reliability

Information has the quality of **reliability** when it is free from material error and bias and can be depended upon by users to represent faithfully what it either purports to represent or could reasonably be expected to represent.[9]

Information may be relevant but so unreliable that it could be misleading (e.g. where a director has given a highly personal view of the value of an investment). On the other hand, it could be reliable but quite non-relevant (e.g. the information that a building standing in the centre of a major shopping street was bought for 50 guineas some 300 years ago).

Faithful representation

Faithful representation is important if accounting information is to be reliable. Faithful representation involves the words as well as the numbers in the financial statements. Sometimes it may be difficult for the managers of an entity to find the right words to describe a transaction and convey the problems of making reliable measurement. In such cases it will be important to disclose the risk of error surrounding recognition and measurement.[10]

Substance over form

If information is to meet the test of faithful representation, then the method of accounting must reflect the **substance** of the economic reality of the transaction and not merely its **legal form**.

For example, a company has sold its buildings to a bank to raise cash and then pays rent for the same buildings for the purpose of continued occupation. The company carries all the risks and problems (such as repairs and insurance) that an owner would carry. One view is that the commercial substance of that sequence of transactions is comparable to ownership. Another view is that the legal form of the transaction is a sale. The characteristic of substance over form requires that the information in the financial statements should show the commercial substance of the situation.[11]

Neutrality

The information contained in financial statements must be **neutral**. This is also described as being 'free from bias'. Financial statements are not neutral if, by the selection and presentation of information, they influence the making of a decision or judgement in order to achieve a predetermined result or outcome.[12]

This condition is quite difficult to enforce because it has to be shown that the entity producing the financial statements is trying to influence the decisions or judgements of all members of a class of users of the information. It would be impractical to know the decision-making process of every individual user.

Prudence

The preparers of financial statements have to contend with uncertainty surrounding many events and circumstances. The existence of uncertainties is recognised by the disclosure of their nature and extent and by the exercise of **prudence** in the preparation of the financial statements. Prudence is the inclusion of a degree of caution in the exercise of the judgements needed in making the estimates required under conditions of uncertainty, such that gains and assets are not overstated and losses and liabilities are not understated.[13]

Completeness

It almost goes without saying that information cannot be reliable if it is not **complete**. The information in financial statements must be complete, within the bounds of materiality and cost. An omission can cause information to be false or misleading and thus to lack reliability and relevance.[14]

4.2.4   Comparability

Comparability means that users must be able to compare the financial statements of an enterprise over time to identify trends in its financial position and performance. Users must also be able to compare the financial statements of different enterprises to evaluate their relative financial position, performance and changes in financial position.[15] Financial statements should show corresponding information for the previous period.[16]

Consistency

This concerns the measurement and display of the financial effect of like transactions and other events being carried out in a consistent way throughout an entity within each accounting period and from one period to the next, and also in a consistent way by different entities.[17]

However, the need for **consistency** should not be allowed to become an impediment to the introduction of improved accounting practices. Consistency does not require absolute uniformity.[18]

Disclosure of accounting policies

This is another important aspect of **comparability**. **Disclosure** means that users of financial statements must be informed of the accounting policies employed in the preparation of financial statements. Managers must also disclose changes in accounting policies and the effect of those changes.[19]

Exhibit 4.1
UK ASB: Relationships of the qualitative characteristics of financial information

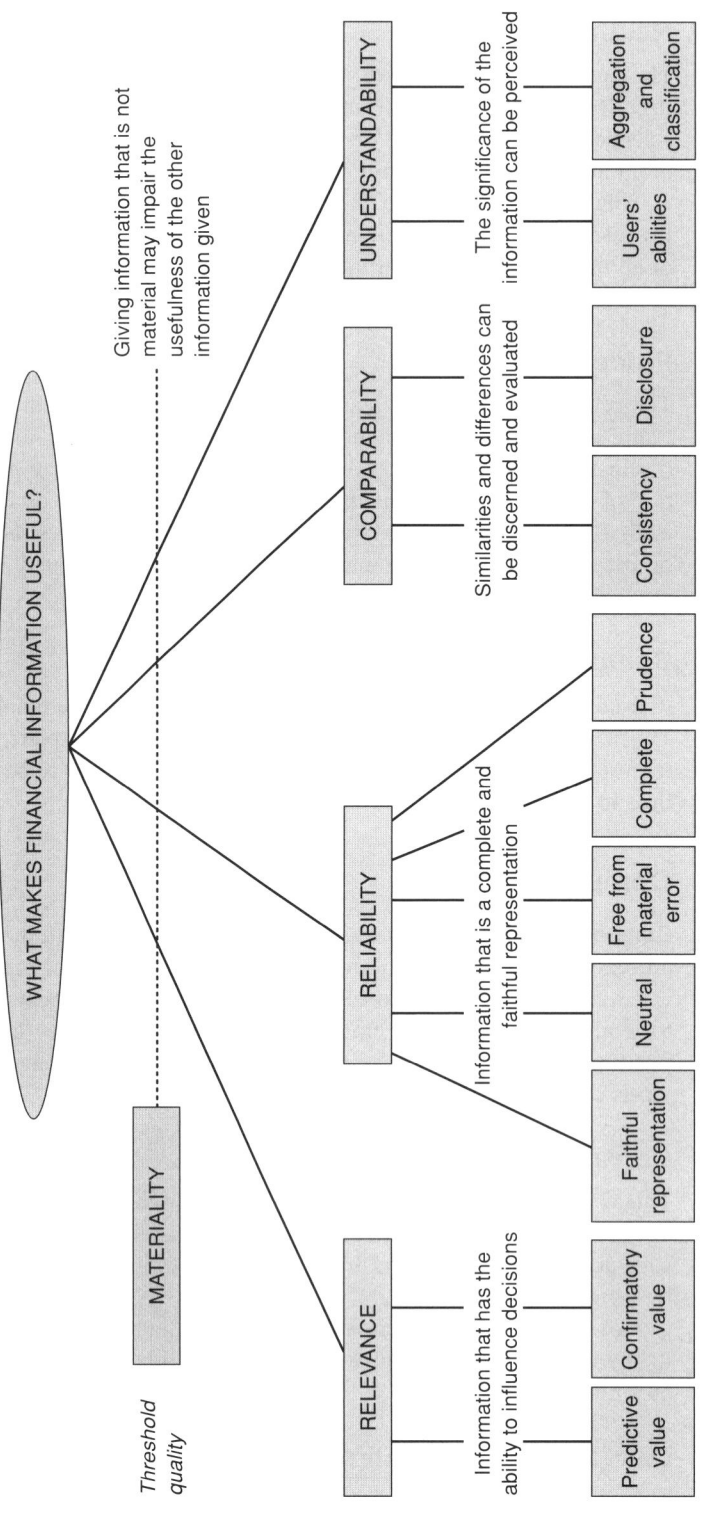

Source: ASB (1999), *Statement of Principles for Financial Reporting*, p. 34. Reproduced with the permission of the Accounting Standards Board.

The annual report of a company will usually have a separate section headed 'Accounting policies'. It will be located immediately after the primary financial statements, leading into the detailed notes to the accounts. The statement of accounting policies is essential reading for any user of the annual report.

4.2.5 Constraints on relevant and reliable information

Relevance and **reliability** are twin targets which may cause some tension in deciding the most appropriate way to report accounting information. There is a trade-off between relevance and reliability when it comes to ensuring that information is delivered in a timely manner so that it is still relevant, and when it comes to deciding whether the costs of producing further information exceed the benefits.

Timeliness

If information is provided in a timely way, the reliability may be less than 100% because some aspects of a transaction are not yet complete. If reporting is delayed until all aspects of a transaction are known then the relevance may be less than 100% because investors have become tired of waiting. The balance of **timeliness** is achieved by considering how best to serve the needs of users in making economic decisions.[20]

Benefit and cost

The benefits derived from information should be greater than the costs of providing it. The analysis is complicated because the benefits fall mainly on the users, while the costs fall mainly on the provider. It is important for standard-setters to consider the benefits and costs as a whole.[21]

4.2.6 UK ASB

The UK ASB's representation of the relationships between the various qualitative characteristics is set out in Exhibit 4.1.[22]

In many ways the ideas of the UK ASB reflect those of the IASB which were written ten years earlier. However during that ten-year period the ASB had time to benefit by thinking about ways of clarifying some aspects of the IASB's ideas. One difference in presentation is that the ASB suggests that materiality is a test to be applied at the threshold of considering an item. If any information is not material, it does not need to be considered further.

Activity 4.1

Look back to Exhibit 4.1. Is there any aspect of that diagram which came as no surprise to you? Is there any aspect of that diagram which was a surprise to you? Having read the explanations in this section, do you hold the same surprise that you did at the outset? With the benefit of hindsight, can you explain why you were surprised or not surprised? Has this analysis caused you to modify your own objectives for what you hope to learn from this book?

4.3 Measurement in financial statements

You have seen in Chapter 2, sections 2.5 and 2.8, that the recognition of assets and liability requires reliability of measurement. You have seen in Chapter 3 the methods of presentation of accounting information containing numbers that represent measurement. We now need to know more about the accounting measurement principles that establish reliability and about the disclosure of information that allows users of financial statements to understand the measurement process.

The accounting measurement principles that are most widely known in the UK are found within the Companies Act 1985:[23]

- going concern
- accruals
- consistency
- prudence.

The IASB *Framework* describes the accrual basis and going concern as 'underlying assumptions' in the preparation of financial statements. It describes **prudence** as a 'constraint' on relevance and reliability. Consistency is an aspect of comparability.

4.3.1 Going concern

Definition

> The financial statements are normally prepared on the assumption that an entity is a **going concern** and will continue in operation for the foreseeable future. Hence, it is assumed that the entity has neither the intention nor the need to liquidate or curtail materially the scale of its operations; if such an intention or need exists the financial statements may have to be prepared on a different basis and, if so, the basis used is disclosed.[24]

The UK Companies Act statement on **going concern** is rather like a crossword clue, in being short and enigmatic. It states: 'The company shall be presumed to be carrying on business as a going concern.' More guidance is needed on measurement.

For companies applying UK accounting standards there is guidance in FRS 18. It requires an entity to prepare its financial statements on a going concern basis unless the entity is being liquidated or has ceased trading, when a 'break-up' valuation may be more appropriate. On a forced sale, very little is obtained for the assets of a business. If the company is still operating but the directors are aware of conditions that cast doubts on the company's ability to continue as a going concern, they should disclose those uncertainties. They must take into account all available information about the 'foreseeable future'.

If the company is staying in business then the directors are allowed to use valuations that reflect continuity. They do not have to report 'break-up' values, which are values for immediate sale of assets. Investors are probably quite happy when the company is continuing as a going concern. They will be more concerned about the risk that it will not continue. For that reason, the directors are required to make a statement in their report to confirm that the business remains a 'going concern' for the foreseeable future. There is no readily available definition of 'foreseeable future' but the guidance given in the UK to directors and auditors points towards considering a period of 12 months from the balance sheet date.

4.3.2 Accruals (also called 'matching')

Definition

> Under the **accruals** basis, the effects of transactions and other events are recognised when they occur (and not as cash or its equivalent is received or paid) and they are recorded in the accounting records and reported in the financial statements of the periods to which they relate.[25]

The IASB explains that financial statements prepared on the accruals basis are useful for stewardship purposes because they report past transactions and events but are also helpful to users for forward-looking information because they show obligations to pay cash in the future and resources that represent cash to be received in the future.

The UK Companies Act explains the accruals concept as a requirement that all income and charges (i.e. expenses) relating to the financial year shall be taken into account, without regard to the date of receipt or payment.

The word 'accrue' means 'to fall due' or 'to come as a natural result'. If, during a year, a company sells £100m of goods but collects only £80m from customers, it records sales as £100m in the profit and loss account. The cash yet to be collected from customers is reported as an asset called 'debtor' in the balance sheet. If, during the year, it uses electricity costing £50m but has only paid £40m so far, it records the expense of £50m in the profit and loss account. The unpaid electricity bill is reported as a liability called 'accruals' in the balance sheet.

The idea of matching is also used in applying the idea of accruals. Matching has two forms, matching losses or gains against time and matching expenses against revenue. Time matching occurs when a gain or loss is spread over the relevant period of time, such as receiving interest on a loan or paying rent on a property. Matching of revenues and expenses occurs when costs such as labour are matched against the revenue earned from providing goods or services.

4.3.3 Consistency

Consistency is described in the IASB *Framework* as an aspect of comparability (see section 4.2.4). The UK Companies Act requires that accounting policies shall be applied consistently within the same accounts and from one period to the next.

4.3.4 Prudence

The Companies Act does not define prudence but uses the word prudent in relation to measurement. It requires that the amount of any item shall be determined on a prudent basis, and in particular:

(a) only profits realised at the balance sheet date shall be included in the profit and loss account; and

(b) all liabilities and losses which have arisen or are likely to arise in respect of the financial year shall be taken into account, including those which only become apparent between the balance sheet date and the date on which it is signed by the board of directors.

The UK ASB has said that decisions about recognition of income or assets and of expenses or liabilities require evidence of existence and reliability of measurement. Stronger evidence and greater reliability of measurement are required for assets and gains than for liabilities and losses.[26]

4.3.5 Realisation

There is no clear statement of the conditions that will make a profit **realised**. It is not specifically defined in the IASB system. It is an example of an idea that is so widely used that it appears to be almost impossible to explain. If you turn to a dictionary you will find 'realise' equated to 'convert into cash'. The accounting standard FRS 18[27] confirms that it is the general view that profits shall be treated as realised when evidenced in the form of cash or other assets whose cash **realisation** is reasonably certain. However, the standard avoids linking realisation to 'prudence', explaining that a focus on cash does not reflect more recent developments in financial markets. Evidence of 'reasonable certainty' in such markets does not necessarily require cash. It is based on confidence in the reliable operation of the market.

Take a piece of paper having two wide columns. Head the left-hand column 'My thoughts on measurement in accounting' and head the right-hand column 'What the book tells me about measurement'. Fill in both columns and then exchange your paper with a fellow student. Discuss with each other any similarities and differences in the left-hand column and relate these to your personal views and prior experience. Discuss with each other any similarities and differences in the right-hand column and evaluate the extent to which different people see books differently. Finally, discuss with each other the extent to which reading this section has changed your views on measurement as a subject in accounting.

4.4 Views on prudence

The Companies Act makes an explicit link between prudence and realisation that reflects UK accounting practice when the Companies Act was written. The IASB's *Framework* avoids mentioning realisation and describes prudence in terms of 'a degree of caution'.[28] From the UK ASB, the standard FRS 18 acknowledges the meaning of realisation but breaks the link between realisation and prudence.[29] Because FRS 18 is relatively new, it is not possible to say whether it will change the entrenched conservatism of accounting practice which tends towards understatement on grounds of caution. Where does that leave the student of accounting who wants to understand the meaning of prudence?

The most important message for students of accounting (and for many practitioners) is contained in the IASB's *Framework*:[30]

> *. . . the exercise of prudence does not allow . . . the deliberate understatement of assets or income, or the deliberate overstatement of liabilities or expenses, because the financial statements would not be neutral and, therefore, not have the quality of reliability.*

Why are there different views on understatement and overstatement, depending on the item being reported? Here is your first chance to use the accounting equation to solve a problem:

Assets	minus	**Liabilities**	equals	**Capital contributed/withdrawn** plus **Profit**

Profit			equals	**Revenue** minus **Expenses**

Ask yourself what will happen to profit in the accounting equation if the amount of an asset is increased while the liabilities and the capital contributed remain the same. Then ask yourself what will happen to profit in the accounting equation if the amount of a liability is decreased while the assets and the capital contributed remain the same. Next ask yourself what will happen to profit if revenue is overstated. Finally ask yourself what will happen to profit if expenses are understated.

Assuming that capital contributed/withdrawn remains constant, overstating assets will overstate profit. Understating liabilities will overstate profit. Overstating revenue will overstate profit. Understating expenses will overstate profit.

Examples

A market trader buys £100 of stock on credit, promising to pay the supplier at the end of the day. The trader sells three-quarters of the stock at a price of £90 and takes the rest home to keep for next week's market. At the end of the day the trader has £90 in cash, one-quarter of the stock which cost £25, and owes £100 to the supplier. How much profit has the trader made? The answer is that the profit is £15 (£90 received for the sale of stock less the cost of the items sold, £75, being three-quarters of the stock purchased). The accounting equation is:

Assets minus **Liabilities** at the end of the period	equals	**Ownership interest at the start of the period** plus **Capital contributed/ withdrawn** plus **Revenue of the period** minus **Expenses of the period**
stock £25 + cash £90 – liability £100	equals	nil + nil + revenue £90 – expenses £75
£15	equals	£15

1 Supposing the trader 'forgets' part of the liability and thinks it is only £84 owing, rather than £100. The assets remain at stock £25 + cash £90, which equals £115. The liability is now thought to be £84 and therefore the equation becomes:

£25 + £90 – £84	equals	nil + nil + revenue £90 – expenses £75 + [?] £16 [?]
£31	equals	£31

For the equation to be satisfied there must be a total of £31 on both sides. The total of £31 is therefore written in. The recorded profit is still only £15, calculated as revenue £90 minus expenses £75, so there is a 'hole' amounting to £16 on the right-hand side of the equation. The accounting equation has to balance so the extra £16 is written in, surrounded by question marks, on the right-hand side. It is assumed on the right-hand side that the trader has either forgotten to record revenue of £16 or has recorded too much expense, so that the amount appears to represent an unexplained profit. Thus *understating a liability will overstate profit*. That favourable news might mislead a competitor or investor. It might be bad news when the Inland Revenue demands tax on profit of £31. Also there is the unpaid supplier who may not be entirely patient when offered £84 rather than £100.

2 Supposing instead that the trader 'forgets' there is some unsold stock left. The only recorded asset would be the cash at £90 and there would be a liability of £100. This gives negative net assets of (£10) and, because the accounting equation has to balance, suggests that there is a 'forgotten' expense of £25 on the right-hand side. The equation then becomes:

£90 – £100	equals	nil + nil + £90 – £75 – [?] £25 [?]
(£10)	equals	(£10)

This would cause the Inland Revenue to ask a lot of questions as to why there was no record of stock remaining, because they know that omitting stock from the record is a well-tried means of fraudulently reducing profits and therefore reducing tax bills. *Understating an asset will understate profit.*

These two examples have illustrated the meaning of the warning that deliberate understatement or overstatement is not acceptable. The general message of prudence is: *avoid overstating profit*. In down-to-earth terms, don't raise the readers' hopes too high, only to have to tell them later that it was all in the imagination.

4.5   Regulation of financial reporting

Because the external users of accounting information do not have day-to-day access to the records of the business, they rely on the integrity and judgement of management to provide suitable information of a high quality. But will the management be honest, conscientious and careful in providing information? In an ideal world there should be no problem for investors in a company because, as shareholders, they appoint the directors and may dismiss them if dissatisfied with the service provided. However, the world is not ideal. Some companies are very large and they have many shareholders whose identity changes as shares are bought and sold. Over the years it has been found that regulation is needed particularly for financial reporting by companies. The general regulation of companies in the UK is provided by parliamentary legislation, through the Companies Act 1985.

However since 2005 the regulation of financial reporting by UK companies has taken two separate routes depending on the type of company.

The group financial statements of listed companies must comply with the IAS Regulation set by the European Commission. The IAS Regulation takes precedence over the relevant sections of the Companies Act. The IAS Regulation was issued in 2002, requiring listed group financial statements from 2005 to apply approved International Financial Reporting Standards, IFRS (previously called International Accounting Standards, IAS). The UK government subsequently permitted individual companies and non-listed groups to choose to apply IFRS. Any companies not taking up this choice must continue to apply the relevant sections of the Companies Act and follow the accounting standards set by the UK Accounting Standards Board (ASB). Other organisations that are not companies (such as sole traders, partnership, public sector bodies) have to look to the regulations that govern their operations to decide which accounting guidance to follow.

So how can we tell which accounting system has been applied in any situation? Look first for the audit report, if there is one. That will include a paragraph starting 'In our opinion'. In that paragraph the auditors will specify the accounting system on which their opinion is based. If there is no auditors' report, look for the Note on Accounting Policies. There will usually be a paragraph stating the accounting system that has been applied.

4.5.1   The IAS Regulation

In 2002 the European Commission issued the *IAS Regulation* which took effect from 1 January 2005. Its purpose is to harmonise the financial information presented by public listed companies in order to ensure a high degree of transparency and comparability of financial statements. The Regulation is relatively short but has been extended and clarified by a trail of subsequent documents. The European Commission publishes all documents on its website[31] in the languages of all Member States but that is more detail than is necessary for a first year course.

A Regulation is directly applicable in Member States. It has a higher status than a Directive, which is an instruction to Member States on the content of their national laws. Before the Regulation was issued, the company law of Member States was harmonised by following the Fourth and Seventh Directives on company law. Companies in Member States did not need to know the Directives because the national company law applied the Directives. Now that the IAS Regulation is directly applicable, Member States must ensure that they do not seek to apply to a company any additional elements of national law that are contrary to, conflict with or restrict a company's compliance with IASs.

The Commission decides on the applicability of IFRS within the Community. It is assisted by an Accounting Regulatory Committee and is advised by a technical group called the European Financial Reporting and Accounting Group EFRAG.[32] The tests for adoption of IFRS are that the standards:

(a) do not contradict specific principles of the Fourth and Seventh Directive,
(b) are conducive to the European public good, and
(c) meet the criteria of understandability, relevance, reliability and comparability required of financial information needed for making economic decisions and assessing the stewardship of management.

A standard that is adopted is said to be **endorsed**. If a standard is awaiting endorsement, or is rejected, it may be used as guidance if it is not inconsistent with endorsed standards. If a rejected standard is in conflict with adopted standards, it may not be used. When the European Commission first announced the endorsement process there were fears expressed that this would be used to create 'European IFRS' by selecting some IFRS and rejecting others. The Commission's reply was that the EU cannot give its powers to a body (the IASB) that is not subject to EU jurisdiction, and it is necessary for the EU to endorse standards as part of its duty in setting laws for Member States.

4.5.2 UK company law

Companies Act 1985

The Companies Act 1985 sets many rules for investing in and operating companies. Parts of the Act cover the information presented in financial statements. For companies and other organisations that do not follow the IAS Regulation, the Companies Act 1985 prescribes formats of presentation of the balance sheet and profit and loss account. Companies must select one of the permitted formats. It also prescribes methods of valuation of the assets and liabilities contained in the balance sheet, broadly expecting that normally these items will be recorded at their cost at the date of acquisition, subject to diminutions in value since that date. Some other approaches to valuation are permitted, but these are carefully regulated and are subject to requirements for prudence, consistency and an expectation that the business is a going concern (i.e. will continue for some time into the future). The UK legislation places strong emphasis on the requirement to present a **true and fair** view in financial statements.

Since the early 1980s company law on financial reporting has been harmonised with that of other Member States in the EU through the Fourth and Seventh Directives of the EU (*see* Chapter 7).

The directors are responsible for the preparation of company accounts. Exhibit 4.2 sets out the statement made by directors of one major public company regarding their responsibilities in these matters. This type of statement will be found in the annual reports of most of the large listed companies. It is regarded as an important aspect of giving reassurance to investors and others that there is a strong system of corporate governance within the company. It is also intended to clarify any misunderstandings the shareholders may have about the work of directors as distinct from the work of the auditors (*see* below).

The Companies (Audit, Investigations and Community Enterprise) Act, 2004 made changes intended to improve the reliability of financial reporting, the independence of auditors and disclosure to auditors. In particular it required a statement to be inserted in the directors' report confirming that there is no relevant information that has not been disclosed to the auditors. The role of the Financial Reporting Review Panel was strengthened by giving it new powers to require documents. HM Revenue and Customs was authorised to pass information about companies to the FRRP.

Exhibit 4.2

Statement of directors' responsibilities as expressed in the annual report of a public limited company

---

Statement of directors' responsibilities

Company law requires the directors to prepare accounts for each financial year which give a true and fair view of the state of affairs of the company and of the group and of the profit or loss and cash flows of the group for that period. In preparing these accounts, the directors have adopted suitable accounting policies and then applied them consistently, made judgements and estimates that are reasonable and prudent, followed applicable accounting standards and adopted the going concern basis.

The directors are responsible for ensuring that the company keeps proper accounting records which disclose with reasonable accuracy at any time the financial position of the company and enable them to ensure that the accounts comply with the IAS Regulation/Companies Act 1985. They are also responsible for safeguarding the assets of the company and taking reasonable steps for the prevention and detection of fraud and other irregularities.

Company Law Reform

A major inquiry into proposals for modernising company law, starting in the late 1990s,[33] led to a final report in 2001 which made recommendations to government. The government then issued a series of consultation documents leading in March 2005 to a White Paper[34] and draft legislation for further consultation. Changes in company law are usually slow, so it takes time for recommended changes to be put into action. Some changes are implemented ahead of others.

At the heart of the Company Law Review was the idea 'think small first'. This reflected a concern that company law has grown by being written for the larger company and then 'slimmed down' for the smaller company. This has tended to leave too great a burden on small companies. Focusing first on the small company should reduce the risk of excessive burden. Disclosure by small companies is described in outline in Chapter 7.

The government indicated that its law reform would also deal with a new EU Directive on audit. Audit is described further in section 4.5.11.

4.5.3 The Financial Reporting Council

The Financial Reporting Council (FRC)[35] describes itself as the UK's independent regulator for corporate reporting and governance. It is recognised in its regulatory role by the Department of Trade and Industry. The government effectively delegates responsibility to an independent body but maintains close interest in the strategy and operations of the FRC.

The FRC's aim is to promote confidence in corporate reporting and governance. To achieve this aim it sets itself five key objectives, in promoting:

- high quality corporate reporting
- high quality auditing
- high standards of corporate governance
- the integrity, competence and transparency of the accountancy profession
- its effectiveness as a unified independent regulator.

The FRC is one regulator but it has a wide range of functions:

- setting, monitoring and enforcing accounting and auditing standards
- statutory oversight and regulation of auditors
- operating an independent investigation and discipline scheme for public interest cases
- overseeing the regulatory activities of the professional accountancy bodies
- promoting high standards of corporate governance.

There are five operating bodies (subsidiaries of the FRC) to carry out these functions.

- Accounting Standards Board
- Auditing Practices Board
- Professional Oversight Board For Accountancy
- Financial Reporting Review Panel
- Accountancy Investigation & Discipline Board.

Each one of these is now described.

4.5.4   UK Accounting Standards Board

Traditionally, professions in the UK have been expected to regulate their own affairs and control their members. The accounting profession satisfied this expectation between 1970 and 1990 by forming the Accounting Standards Committee (ASC) and requiring members of each professional body to apply accounting standards or face disciplinary action. Over a period of years there was growing dissatisfaction with this pure self-regulatory model because the disciplinary aspects appeared to be applied only rarely and the existence of potential conflicts of self-interest was pointed to by some critics as weakening the standard-setting process. Consequently, in 1990 the purely self-regulatory approach was abandoned in favour of an independent regime having statutory backing, but retaining some self-regulatory features. The independent standard setting body was created as the Accounting Standards Board (ASB).

Since 1990 the ASB has published Financial Reporting Standards (FRSs) setting standards of practice which go beyond the requirements of company law in particular problem areas. In the period from 1970 to 1990 the standards set by the ASC were called Statements of Standard Accounting Practice (SSAPs). Those SSAPs which remained valid were adopted by the ASB and are gradually being replaced. SSAPs and FRSs collectively are referred to as 'accounting standards'. The Accounting Standards Board (ASB) is recognised as a standard-setting body under the Companies Act 1985.

The UK ASB is gradually harmonising its standards with those of the IASB so that eventually all companies will apply the same accounting standards, irrespective of whether they present financial statements under the IAS Regulation or the Companies Act. Until that happens there will continue to be some differences between ASB standards and IASB standards but in general this need not be of concern in a first year of study.

The ASB collaborates with accounting standard-setters from other countries and the IASB both in order to influence the development of international standards and in order to ensure that its standards are developed with due regard to international developments.

The ASB has up to ten Board members, of whom two (the Chairman and the Technical Director) are full-time, and the remainder, who represent a variety of interests, are part-time. ASB meetings are also attended by three observers. Under the ASB's constitution, votes of seven Board members (six when there are fewer than ten members) are required for any decision to adopt, revise or withdraw an accounting standard. Board members are appointed by a Nominations Committee comprising the chairman and fellow directors of the Financial Reporting Council (FRC).

The Accounting Standards Board is independent in its decisions on issuing standards. Before doing so the Board consults widely on all its proposals.

4.5.5 Auditing Practices Board

The Auditing Practices Board (APB) was established in April 2002, and replaces a previous APB which had been in place since 1991. APB is a part of the Financial Reporting Council. The APB is committed to leading the development of auditing practice in the UK and the Republic of Ireland so as to establish high standards of auditing, meet the developing needs of users of financial information and ensure public confidence in the auditing process.

4.5.6 Professional Oversight Board for Accountancy

The Professional Oversight Board for Accountancy (POBA) contributes to the achievement of the Financial Reporting Council's own fundamental aim of supporting investor, market and public confidence in the financial and governance stewardship of listed and other entities by:

- independent oversight of the regulation of the auditing profession by the recognised supervisory and qualifying bodies;
- monitoring the quality of the auditing function in relation to economically significant entities;
- independent oversight of the regulation of the accountancy profession by the professional accountancy bodies.

4.5.7 Financial Reporting Review Panel

When the Accounting Standards Board was established in 1990 it was felt to be important that there was a mechanism for enforcing accounting standards. An effective mechanism had been lacking in the previous process of setting standards. Accordingly the Financial Reporting Council established a Financial Reporting Review Panel (FRRP) which enquires into annual accounts where it appears that the requirements of the Companies Act, including the requirement that annual accounts shall show a true and fair view, might have been breached. The FRRP has the power to ask companies to revise their accounts where these are found to be defective. If companies do not voluntarily make such a revision, the FRRP may take proceedings in a court of law to require the company to revise its accounts. These powers are contained in the Companies Act 1985 and delegated to the FRRP by the Secretary of State for Trade and Industry. So far the FRRP has not found it necessary to resort to legal action, having found its powers of persuasion were sufficient.

The Financial Reporting Review Panel (FRRP), (referred to as 'the Panel') considers whether the annual accounts of public companies and large private companies comply with the requirements of the Companies Act 1985, including applicable accounting standards. The Panel does not offer advice on the application of accounting standards or the accounting requirements of the Companies Act 1985.

The Panel can ask directors to explain apparent departures from the requirements. If it is not satisfied by the directors' explanations it aims to persuade them to adopt a more appropriate accounting treatment. The directors may then voluntarily withdraw their accounts and replace them with revised accounts that correct the matters in error. Depending on the circumstances, the FRRP may accept another form of remedial action – for example, correction of the comparative figures in the next set of annual financial statements. Failing voluntary correction, the Panel can exercise its powers to secure the necessary revision of the original accounts through a court order. The FRRP has enjoyed a long and successful record in resolving all cases brought to its attention without having to apply for a court order. The Panel maintains a legal costs fund of £2m for this purpose. Also, if the case concerns accounts issued under listing rules, the Panel may report to the Financial Services Authority.

4.5.8 Accountancy Investigation and Discipline Board

The Accountancy Investigation and Discipline Board (AIDB) is the independent, investigative and disciplinary body for accountants in the UK. It has up to eight members. The AIDB is responsible for operating and administering an independent disciplinary scheme ('the Scheme') covering members of the major professional bodies.

The AIDB will deal with cases which raise or appear to raise important issues affecting the public interest in the UK and which need to be investigated to determine whether or not there has been any misconduct by an accountant or accountancy firm.

4.5.9 Committee on Corporate Governance

The Committee on Corporate Governance works to satisfy the FRC's responsibility for promoting high standards of corporate governance. It aims to do so by:

- maintaining an effective Combined Code on Corporate Governance and promoting its widespread application;
- ensuring that related guidance, such as that on internal control, is current and relevant;
- influencing EU and global corporate governance developments;
- helping to promote boardroom professionalism and diversity; and
- encouraging constructive interaction between company boards and institutional shareholders.

4.5.10 The Financial Services Authority

Under the Financial Services and Markets Act 2000, the Financial Services Authority (FSA) is a single regulator with responsibility across a wide range of financial market activity. It is required to maintain confidence in the UK financial system, to promote public understanding of the financial system, to secure protection for consumers and to reduce the scope for financial crime. The FSA is an independent, non-governmental body and receives no funds from government. It reports annually to Parliament through the Treasury.

The FSA regulates listing of companies' shares on the UK stock exchange. The work is carried out by a division called the UK Listing Authority (UKLA). When a company first has its shares listed, it must produce a prospectus, which is normally much more detailed than the annual report. The regulations covering the content of a prospectus are set by the UKLA. Once a company has achieved a listing, it must keep up with ongoing obligations under the Listing Rules, which includes providing accounting information to the market in the annual report and press releases. Details of the Listing Rules are not necessary for first-year study but if you are interested you can read them on the FSA's website: www.fsa.gov.uk.

4.5.11 Auditors

The shareholders of companies do not have a right of access to the records of the day-to-day running of the business, and so they need someone to act on their behalf to ensure that the directors are presenting a true and fair view of the company's position at a point in time and of the profits generated during a period of time. To achieve this reassurance, the shareholders appoint a firm of auditors to investigate

Exhibit 4.3
Sample audit report

INDEPENDENT AUDITOR'S REPORT TO THE SHAREHOLDERS OF XYZ PLC

We have audited the group financial statements of (name of entity) for the year ended . . . which comprise the Group Income Statement, the Group Balance Sheet, the Group Cash Flow Statement, the Group Statement of Change in Shareholders' Equity and the related notes. These group financial statements have been prepared under the accounting policies set out therein.

We have reported separately on the parent company financial statements of (name of entity) for the year ended and on the information in the Directors' Remuneration Report that is described as having been audited.

Respective responsibilities of directors and auditors
The directors' responsibilities for preparing the Annual Report and the group financial statements in accordance with applicable law and International Financial Reporting Standards (IFRSs) as adopted for use in the European Union are set out in the Statement of Directors' Responsibilities.

Our responsibility is to audit the group financial statements in accordance with relevant legal and regulatory requirements and International Standards on Auditing (UK and Ireland). We report to you our opinion as to whether the group financial statements give a true and fair view and whether the group financial statements have been properly prepared in accordance with the Companies Act 1985 and Article 4 of the IAS Regulation. We also report to you if, in our opinion, the Directors' Report is not consistent with the group financial statements, if we have not received all the information and explanations we require for our audit, or if information specified by law regarding director's remuneration and other transactions is not disclosed. We review whether the Corporate Governance Statement reflects the company's compliance with the nine provisions of the 2003 FRC Combined Code specified for our review by the Listing Rules of the Financial Services Authority, and we report if it does not. We are not required to consider whether the board's statements on internal control cover all risks and controls, or form an opinion on the effectiveness of the group's corporate governance procedures or its risk and control procedures.

We read other information contained in the Annual Report and consider whether it is consistent with the audited group financial statements. The other information comprises only [the Directors' Report, the Chairman's Statement, the Operating and Financial Review and the Corporate Governance Statement]. We consider the implications for our report if we become aware of any apparent misstatements or material inconsistencies with the group financial statements. Our responsibilities do not extend to any other information.

Basis of audit opinion
We conducted our audit in accordance with International Standards on Auditing (UK and Ireland) issued by the Auditing Practices Board. An audit includes examination, on a test basis, of evidence relevant to the amounts and disclosures in the group financial statements. It also includes an assessment of the significant estimates and judgments made by the directors in the preparation of the group financial statements, and of whether the accounting policies are appropriate to the group's circumstances, consistently applied and adequately disclosed.

We planned and performed our audit so as to obtain all the information and explanations which we considered necessary in order to provide us with sufficient evidence to give reasonable assurance that the group financial statements are free from material misstatement, whether caused by fraud or other irregularity or error. In forming our opinion we also evaluated the overall adequacy of the presentation of information in the group financial statements.

Opinion
In our opinion:
the group financial statements give a true and fair view, in accordance with IFRSs as adopted for use in the European Union, of the state of the group's affairs as at . . . and of its profit[loss] for the year then ended; and the group financial statements have been properly prepared in accordance with the Companies Act 1985 and Article 4 of the IAS Regulation.

Registered auditors' Address
Date

the company's financial records and give an opinion on the truth and fairness of the financial information presented. Exhibit 4.3 sets out the wording of a typical audit report to the shareholders of a public company. There are some words and phrases in this report which will become more familiar as you progress through the text. These include 'historical cost convention' (Chapter 14), 'revaluation of certain fixed assets' (Chapter 12) and 'accounting policies' (introduced in Chapter 3 but mentioned again at various points).

You will note that the auditors do not look at all the pages of the annual report. The earlier part of the annual report is important to the companies in setting the scene and explaining their businesses. These earlier pages are reviewed by the auditors to ensure that anything said there is consistent with the information presented in the audited financial statements. You will also note that the auditors have their own code of practice, referred to as International Standards for Auditing (ISAs). The ISAs are prepared by the International Auditing and Assurance Standards Board (IAASB) which operates under a body called the International Financial Accounting Committee (IFAC). The standards are then adopted by national standard setters. In the UK the national standard setter is the Auditing Practices Board (APB) which is one of the arms of the Financial Reporting Council.

What surprises some readers is the phrase 'reasonable assurance that the accounts are free from material misstatement'. The auditors are not expected to be totally certain in their opinion and they are only looking for errors or fraud which is material. The meaning of the word 'material' has proved difficult to define and it tends to be a matter left to the judgement of the auditor. The best guidance available is that an item is material if its misstatement or omission would cause the reader of the annual report (shareholder or creditor) to take a different decision or view based on the financial statements.

4.5.12   The tax system

Businesses pay tax to HM Revenue and Customs (as the tax collecting agent of the government) based on the profits they make. Sole traders and partnerships pay income tax on their profits while companies pay corporation tax. There are differences in detail of the law governing these two types of taxes but broadly they both require as a starting point a calculation of profit using commercial accounting practices. The law governing taxation is quite separate from the law and regulations governing financial reporting, so in principle the preparation of financial statements is not affected by tax matters. That is very different from some other countries in the EU where the tax law stipulates that an item must be in the financial accounting statements if it is to be considered for tax purposes. Those countries have an approach to financial reporting which is more closely driven by taxation matters.

In the UK the distinction may be blurred in practice in the case of sole traders because HM Revenue and Customs is the main user of the financial statements of the sole trader. Similarly, tax factors may influence partnership accounts, although here the fairness of sharing among the partners is also important. The very smallest companies, where the owners also run the business, may in practice have the same attitude to tax matters as does the sole trader or partnership. For larger companies with a wider spread of ownership, the needs of shareholders will take priority.

4.5.13   Is regulation necessary?

There are those who would argue that all this regulatory mechanism is unnecessary. They take the view that in a market-based economy, competitive forces will ensure that those providing information will meet the needs of users. It is argued that investors will not entrust their funds to a business which provides inadequate information. Banks will not lend money unless they are provided with sufficient information to answer their questions about the likelihood of receiving interest and eventual repayment of the loan. Employee morale may be lowered if a business appears non-communicative regarding its present position and past record of performance. Suppliers may not wish to give credit to a business which appears secretive or has a reputation for producing poor-quality information. Customers may be similarly doubtful.

Against that quite attractive argument for the abolition of all regulations stand some well-documented financial scandals where businesses have failed. Employees have lost their jobs, with little prospect of finding comparable employment elsewhere; suppliers have not been paid and have found themselves in financial difficulties as a result. Customers have lost a source of supply and have been unable to meet the requirements of their own customers until a new source is found. Those who have provided long-term finance for the business, as lenders and investors, have lost their investment. Investigation shows that the signs and warnings had existed for those who were sufficiently experienced to see them, but these signs and warnings did not emerge in the published accounting information for external use.

Such financial scandals may be few in number but the large-scale examples cause widespread misery and lead to calls for action. Governments experience pressure from the electorate and lobby groups; professional bodies and business interest groups decide they ought to be seen to react; and new regulations are developed which ensure that the particular problem cannot recur. All parties are then reasonably satisfied that they have done their best to protect those who need protection against the imbalance of business life, and the new practices are used until the next scandal occurs and the process starts over again.

There is no clear answer to the question 'Is regulation necessary?' Researchers have not found any strong evidence that the forces of supply and demand in the market fail to work and have suggested that the need for regulation must be justified by showing that the benefits exceed the costs. That is quite a difficult challenge but is worth keeping in mind as you explore some of the more intricate aspects of accounting regulation.

Activity 4.4	*Look back through this section and, for each subheading, make a note of whether you were previously aware that such regulation existed. In each case, irrespective of your previous state of knowledge, do you now feel a greater or a lesser sense of confidence in accounting information? How strong is your confidence in published accounting information? If not 100%, what further reassurance would you require?*

4.6 Reviewing published financial statements

If you look at the annual report of any large listed company you will find that it has two main sections. The first part contains a variety of diagrams and photographs, a statement by the chairman, a report by the chief executive and, in many cases, an Operating and Financial Review which may extend to a considerable number of pages. Other aspects of the business, such as its corporate governance and environmental policy, may also be explained. This first part is a mixture of unregulated and broadly regulated material. There are many sources of influence on its contents, some of which will be explained in later chapters of this book.

The second part contains the financial statements, which are heavily regulated. As if to emphasise this change of status, the second part of the annual report will often have a different appearance, perhaps being printed on a different colour or grade of paper, or possibly having a smaller print size. Appendix I to this book contains extracts from the financial statements of a fictitious company, Safe and Sure plc, which will be used for illustration in this and subsequent chapters.

Relaxing after a hard workout at the health club, David Wilson took the opportunity to buy Leona a drink and tell her something about Safe and Sure prior to a visit to the company's headquarters to meet the finance director.

DAVID: *This is a major listed company, registered in the UK but operating around the world selling its services in disposal and recycling, cleaning and security. Its name is well known and its services command high prices because of the company's reputation gained over many years. Basically it is a very simple business to understand. It sells services by making contracts with customers and collects cash when the service is performed.*

In preparation for my visit I looked first at the performance of the period. This company promises to deliver growth of at least 20% in revenue and in profit before tax so first of all I checked that the promise had been delivered. Sure enough, at the front of the annual report under 'Highlights of the year' there was a table showing revenue had increased by 22.4% and profit before tax had increased by 20.4%. I knew I would need to look through the profit and loss account in more detail to find out how the increases had come about, but first of all I read the operating review (written by the chief executive) and the financial review (written by the finance director). The chief executive gave more details on which areas had the greatest increase in revenue and operating profit and which areas had been disappointing. That all helps me in making my forecast of profit for next year.

The chief executive made reference to acquisitions during the year, so I knew I would also need to think whether the increase in revenue and profits was due to an improvement in sales and marketing as compared with last year or whether it reflected the inclusion of new business for the first time.

In the financial review, the finance director explained that the business tries to use as little working capital as possible (that means they try to keep down the current assets and match them as far as possible with current liabilities). I guessed I would need to look at the balance sheet to confirm that, so I headed next for the financial statements at the back of the annual report, pausing to glance at the auditors' report to make sure there was nothing highlighted by them as being amiss.

The financial statements are quite detailed and I wanted a broad picture so I noted down the main items from each in a summary format which leaves out some of the detail but which I find quite useful.

4.6.1   Income statement (profit and loss account)

Safe and Sure plc
Summary income statement (profit and loss account) with comparative figures

	Notes	Year 7 £m	Year 6 £m
Continuing operations			
Revenue		714.6	589.3
Cost of sales		(491.0)	(406.3)
Gross profit		223.6	183.0
Expenses and interest		(26.1)	(26.0)
Profit before tax		197.5	157.0
Tax on profit		(62.2)	(52.4)
Profit for the period from continuing operations		135.3	104.6
Discontinued operations			
Loss for the period from discontinued operations		(20.5)	(10.0)
Profit for the period attributable to ordinary shareholders		114.8	94.6

DAVID: *It is part of my job to make forecasts of what the next reported profit of the company is likely to be (i.e. the profit of Year 8). This is March Year 8 now so there are plenty of current signs I can pick up, but I also want to think about how far Year 7 will be repeated or improve during Year 8. A few years ago I would have made a rough guess and then phoned the finance director for some guidance on whether I was in the right area. That's no longer allowed because the Financial Services Authority tightened up the rules on companies giving information to some investors which is not available to others, especially where that information could affect the share price.*

One easy way out is for me to collect the reports which come in from our stockbrokers. Their analysts have specialist knowledge of the industry and can sometimes work out what is happening in a business faster than some of the management. However, I like to form my own opinion using other sources, such as trade journals, and I read the annual report to give me the background structure for my forecast. The company has helpfully separated out the effect of continuing and discontinued operations, which helps me in making a forecast.

When I meet the finance director next week I'll have with me a spreadsheet analysing revenue and profit before tax – so far as I can find the data – by product line and for each of the countries in which the company trades. I'll also ask the following questions:

1 *Although the revenue has increased, the ratio of gross profit to revenue on continuing operations has increased only very slightly, from 31.1% in Year 6 to 31.3% in Year 7. That suggests that the company has increased revenue by holding price rises at a level matching the increase in operating costs. I would like to see the company pushing ahead with price rises but does the company expect to see a fall in demand when its prices eventually rise?*

2 *The tax charge on continuing operations has decreased from approximately 33% to 31.5%, slightly higher than the rate which would be expected of UK companies. I know that this company is trading overseas. You say in your financial review that the tax charge is 30% in the UK and rates on overseas profits will reduce, so am I safe in assuming that 30% is a good working guide for the future in respect of this company?*

3 *With all this overseas business there must be an element of foreign exchange risk. You say in your financial review that all material foreign currency transactions are matched back into the currency of the group company undertaking the transaction. You don't hedge the translation of overseas profits back into sterling. You also say that using Year 6 exchange rates the Year 7 profit, including the effect of the discontinued operations, would have been £180.5m rather than the £177.0m reported. That seems a fairly minimal effect but are these amounts hiding any swings in major currencies where large downward movements are offset by correspondingly large upward movements?*

4 *Your increase in revenue, comparing £714.6m to £589.9m, is 21.1% which is meeting the 20% target you set yourself. However, elsewhere in the financial statements I see that the acquisitions in Year 7 contributed £13.5m to revenue. If I strip that amount out of the total revenue I'm left with an increase in respect of activities continuing from Year 6 which is only 19%. When the scope for acquisitions is exhausted, will you be able to sustain the 20% target by organic growth alone?*

4.6.2   Balance sheet

DAVID: *Looking at the balance sheet, this is a fairly simple type of business. It is financed almost entirely by equity capital (shareholders' funds), so there are none of the risks associated with high levels of borrowings which might be found in other companies.*

Again, I have summarised and left out some of the details which aren't significant in financial terms.

Safe and Sure plc
Summarised balance sheet (with comparative amounts)

	Notes	Year 7 £m	Year 6 £m
Non-current assets			
Intangible assets		260.3	237.6
Tangible assets		137.5	121.9
Investments		2.8	2.0
Taxation recoverable		5.9	4.9
		406.5	366.4
Current assets			
Inventories (stocks)		26.6	24.3
Amounts receivable (debtors)		146.9	134.7
Six-month deposits		2.0	–
Cash and cash equivalents		105.3	90.5
		280.8	249.5
Current liabilities			
Amounts payable (creditors)		(159.8)	(157.5)
Bank overdraft		(40.1)	(62.6)
		(199.9)	(220.1)
Net current assets		80.9	29.4
Total assets less current liabilities		487.4	395.8
Non-current liabilities			
Amounts payable (creditors)	9	(2.7)	(2.6)
Bank and other borrowings	10	(0.2)	(0.6)
Provisions	11	(20.2)	(22.2)
Net assets		464.3	370.4
Capital and reserves			
Shareholders' funds		464.3	370.4

DAVID: *By far the largest non-current (fixed) asset is the intangible asset of goodwill arising on acquisition. It reflects the fact that the group has had to pay a price for the future prospects of companies it has acquired. Although the company reports this in the group's balance sheet, and I like to see whether the asset is holding its value from the group's point of view, I have some reservations about the quality of the asset because I know it would vanish overnight if the group found itself in difficulties.*

The other non-current assets are mainly equipment for carrying out the cleaning operations and vehicles in which to transport the equipment. I've checked in the notes to the accounts that vehicles are being depreciated over four to five years and plant and equipment over five to ten years, all of which sounds about right. Also, they haven't changed the depreciation period, or the method of calculation, since last year so the amounts are comparable. Estimated useful lives for depreciation are something I watch closely. There is a great temptation for companies which have underperformed to cut back on the depreciation by deciding the useful life has extended. (Depreciation is explained more fully in Chapter 8.)

I think I might ask a few questions about working capital (the current assets minus the current liabilities of the business). Normally I like to see current assets somewhat greater than current liabilities – a ratio of 1.5 to 1 could be about right – as a cushion to ensure the liabilities are met as they fall due. However, in this company the finance director makes a point of saying that they like to utilise as little working capital as possible, so I'm wondering why it increased from £29.4m in Year 6 to more than £80m in Year 7. There appear to be two effects working together: current assets went up and current liabilities went down. Amounts receivable (trade debtors) increased in Year 7 in absolute terms but that isn't as bad as it looks when allowance is made for the increase in revenue.

Amounts receivable in Year 7 are 20.6% of continuing revenue, which shows some control has been achieved when it is compared with the Year 6 amount at 22.8% of revenue. My questions will be:

1 *Mostly, the increase in the working capital (net current assets) appears to be due to the decrease in bank borrowing. Was this a voluntary action by the company or did the bank insist?*

2 *The second major cause of the increase in the working capital is the increase in the balance held in the bank account. Is that being held for a planned purpose and, if so, what?*

3 *The ratio of current assets to current liabilities has increased from last year. What target ratio are you aiming for?*

I always shudder when I see 'provisions' in a balance sheet. The notes to the financial statements show that these are broadly:

	£m
For treating a contaminated site	12.0
For restructuring part of the business	4.2
For tax payable some way into the future	4.0
Total	20.2

I shall want to ask whether the estimated liability in relation to the contaminated site is adequate in the light of any changes in legislation. I know the auditors will have asked this question in relation to existing legislation but I want to think also about forthcoming legislation.

I am always wary of provisions for restructuring. I shall be asking more about why the restructuring is necessary and when it will take place. I want to know that the provision is sufficient to cover the problem, but not excessive.

The provision for tax payable some way into the future is an aspect of prudence in accounting. I don't pay much attention unless the amount is very large or suddenly changes dramatically. (An explanation of deferred taxation is contained in Chapter 10.)

4.6.3   Cash flow statement

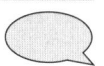

DAVID: *Cash is an important factor for any business. It is only one of the resources available but it is the key to survival. I've summarised the totals of the various main sections of the cash flow statement. 'Net cash' means the cash less the bank borrowings.*

Safe and Sure plc
Summary cash flow statement (with comparative amounts)
Consolidated cash flow statement for the years ended 31 December

	Notes	Year 7	Year 6
		£m	£m
Net cash from operating activities		143.0	116.3
Net cash used in investing activities		(98.3)	(85.3)
Net cash used in financing activities		(10.2)	(46.4)
Net increase/(decrease) in cash and cash equivalents*		34.5	(15.4)

What I'm basically looking for in the cash flow statement is how well the company is balancing various sources of finance. It generated £143m from operating activities and that was more than sufficient to cover its investing activities in new fixed assets and acquisitions. There was also enough to cover the dividend of £29.5m, which is a financing activity but that was partly covered by raising new loan finance. This is why the cash used in financing activities is only £10.2m. I come back to my earlier question of why they are holding so much cash.

Activity 4.5   *Read David's explanation again and compare it carefully with the financial statements. It is quite likely that you will not understand everything immediately because the purpose of this book as a whole is to help you understand published financial statements and we are, as yet, only at the end of Chapter 4. Make a note of the items you don't fully understand and keep that note safe in a file. As you progress through the rest of the book, look back to that note and tick off the points which subsequently become clear. The aim is to have a page full of ticks by the end of the book.*

4.7 Summary

The objective of financial statements is to provide information about the financial position, performance and changes in financial position of an entity that is useful to a wide range of users in making economic decisions.

The four principal qualitative characteristics, as described by the IASB *Framework*, are:

- understandability
- relevance
- reliability
- comparability.

Relevance and **reliability** are twin targets which may cause some tension in deciding the most appropriate way to report accounting information.

The accounting measurement principles that are most widely known in the UK are found within the Companies Act 1985:

- going concern
- accruals
- consistency
- prudence.

Prudence in accounting means exercising a degree of caution when reporting assets, liabilities and profits. Overstatement of assets causes the overstatement of profit. Understatement of liabilities causes the overstatement of profit. Prudence requires avoiding overstating profit but also avoiding deliberate understatement of profit.

Regulation of financial reporting in the UK comes from several sources.

- The IAS Regulation requires all listed groups of companies to prepare financial statements using the system of the International Accounting Standards Board (IASB system). Other companies may choose to follow the IASB system.
- Companies that do not follow the IASB system must comply with UK company law.
- The Financial Reporting Council regulates accounting and auditing matters under the authority of UK company law.
- The Financial Reporting Council oversees the UK Accounting Standards Board which sets accounting standards for companies that are complying with UK company law.
- The Financial Reporting Review Panel takes action against companies whose annual reports do not comply with the relevant accounting system (IASB or UK company law).
- The Financial Services Authority regulates a wide range of financial service activities including the London Stock Exchange. It sets Listing Rules for companies listed on the Stock Exchange.
- Auditors give an opinion on whether financial statements present a true and fair view of the profit or loss of the period and the state of affairs at the end of the period. They are professionally qualified accountants with auditing experience who are members of a recognised professional body.

● The UK tax system charges corporation tax on company profits. Her Majesty's Revenue and Customs (HMRC) start with the accounting profit in calculating the amount of tax payable but there are some special rules of accounting for tax purposes.

Further reading

IASB (1989), *Framework for the Preparation and Presentation of Financial Statements*, International Accounting Standards Board.

Paterson, R. (2002), 'Whatever happened to Prudence?', *Accountancy*, January, p. 105.

The website of the Financial Reporting Council explains the methods and nature of regulation of financial reporting and the accountancy profession: www.frc.org.uk

QUESTIONS

The Questions section of each chapter has three types of question. 'Test your understanding' questions to help you review your reading are in the 'A' series of questions. You will find the answers to these by reading and thinking about the material in the book. 'Application' questions to test your ability to apply technical skills are in the 'B' series of questions. Questions requiring you to show skills in problem solving and evaluation are in the 'C' series of questions. A letter [S] indicates that there is a solution at the end of the book.

A   Test your understanding

A4.1   Explain what is meant by each of the following: (section 4.2)

(a) relevance;
(b) reliability;
(c) faithful representation;
(d) neutrality;
(e) prudence;
(f) completeness;
(g) comparability;
(h) understandability; and
(i) materiality.

A4.2   Explain the accounting measurement principles of each of the following: (section 4.3)

(a) going concern;
(b) accruals;
(c) consistency;
(d) the concept of prudence.

A4.3   Explain why companies should avoid overstatement of assets or understatement of liabilities. (section 4.4)

A4.4   Explain the responsibilities of directors of a company towards shareholders in relation to the financial statements of a company. (section 4.5.2)

A4.5   Explain the impact on financial statements of each of the following: (section 4.5)

(a) company law;
(b) the International Accounting Standards Board; and
(c) the UK tax law.

A4.6   Explain how the monitoring of financial statements is carried out by each of the following: (section 4.5)

(a) the auditors; and
(b) the Financial Reporting Review Panel.

B Application

B4.1 [S]
Explain each of the following:

(a) The IAS Regulation
(b) The Financial Reporting Council
(c) The Auditing Practices Board

B4.2 [S]
Explain any two accounting measurement principles, explaining how each affects current accounting practice.

B4.3 [S]
Discuss the extent to which the regulatory bodies explained in this chapter have, or ought to have, a particular concern for the needs of the following groups of users of financial statements:

(a) shareholders;
(b) employees;
(c) customers; and
(d) suppliers.

C Problem solving and evaluation

C4.1
Choose one or more characteristics from the following box that you could use to discuss the accounting aspects of each of the statements 1 to 5 and explain your ideas:

- relevance
- reliability
- comparability
- understandability
- materiality
- neutrality
- completeness
- prudence
- faithful representation

1 Director: 'We do not need to tell shareholders about a loss of £2,000 on damaged stock when our operating profit for the year is £60m.'
2 Shareholder: 'I would prefer the balance sheet to tell me the current market value of land is £20m than to tell me that the historical cost is £5m, although I know that market values fluctuate.'
3 Analyst: 'If the company changes its stock valuation from average cost to FIFO, I want to hear a good reason and I want to know what last year's profit would have been on the same basis.'
4 Regulator: 'If the company reports that it has paid "*commission on overseas sales*", I don't expect to discover later that it really meant bribes to local officials.'
5 Director: 'We have made a profit on our drinks sales but a loss on food sales. In the Notes to the Accounts on segmental results I suggest we combine them as "food and drink". It will mean the annual report is less detailed for our shareholders but it will keep competitors in the dark for a while.'

C4.2
Choose one or more accounting measurement principles from the following box that you could use to discuss the accounting aspects of each of the problems 1–5 and explain your ideas.

- going concern
- accruals
- consistency
- prudence.

1 Director: 'The fixed assets of the business are reported at depreciated historical cost because we expect the company to continue in existence for the foreseeable future. The market value is much higher but that is not relevant because we don't intend to sell them.'
2 Auditor: 'We are insisting that the company raises the provision for doubtful debts from 2% to 2.5% of debtor amount. There has been recession among the customer base and the financial statements should reflect that.'

3 Analyst: 'I have great problems in tracking the depreciation policy of this company. It owns several airports. Over the past three years the expected useful life of runways has risen from 30 years to 50 years and now it is 100 years. I find it hard to believe that the technology of tarmacadam has improved so much in three years.'

4 Auditor: 'We have serious doubts about the ability of this company to renew its bank overdraft at next month's review meeting with the bank. The company ought to put shareholders on warning about the implications for the financial statements.'

5 Shareholder: 'I don't understand why the company gives a profit and loss account and a cash flow statement in the annual report. Is there any difference between profit and cash flow?'

Activities for study groups

Continuing to use the annual reports of a company that you obtained for Chapter 1, look for the evidence in each report of the existence of the directors, the auditors and the various regulatory bodies.

In your group, draw up a list of the evidence presented by companies to show that the annual report has been the subject of regulation. Discuss whether the annual report gives sufficient reassurance of its relevance and reliability to the non-expert reader.

Notes and references

1. IASB (1989), *Framework*, para. 12.
2. *Ibid.*, para. 20.
3. *Ibid.*, para. 21.
4. *Ibid.*, para. 24.
5. *Ibid.*, para. 25.
6. *Ibid.*, para. 26.
7. *Ibid.*, paras. 27–8.
8. *Ibid.*, paras. 29–30.
9. *Ibid.*, para. 31.
10. *Ibid.*, paras. 33–4.
11. *Ibid.*, para. 35.
12. *Ibid.*, para. 36.
13. *Ibid.*, para. 37.
14. *Ibid.*, para. 38.
15. *Ibid.*, para. 39.
16. *Ibid.*, para. 42.
17. *Ibid.*, para. 39.
18. *Ibid.*, para. 41.
19. *Ibid.*, para. 40.
20. *Ibid.*, para. 43.
21. *Ibid.*, para. 44.
22. ASB (1999), *Statement of Principles*, p. 34.
23. Companies Act 1985, sch. 4, paras. 10–14.
24. IASB (1989), *Framework*, para. 23.
25. IASB (1989), *Framework*, para. 23.
26. ASB (1999), Appendix III, paras. 21–3.
27. ASB (2000), Financial Reporting Standard 18 (FRS 18) *Accounting Policies*, Accounting Standards Board, para. 28.
28. IASB (1989), *Framework*, para. 37.
29. ASB (2000), Appendix IV, paras. 12 to 20.
30. IASB (1989), *Framework*, para. 27.
31. http://europa.eu.int/comm/internal_market/accounting/index_en.htm
32. www.efrag.org/
33. Details can be found on the website of the Department of Trade and Industry, www.dti.gov.uk/cld/review.htm
34. Company Law Reform, March 2005, Cm. 6456, DTI.
35. www.frc.org.uk/

Chapter 14

The conceptual framework for accounting

In this chapter

We will learn of:

- how to identify the stakeholders in a business entity
- the main areas of interest each group has and their information needs
- the assumptions made when preparing financial statements
- the working rules applied when preparing financial statements
- the qualitative characteristics information in financial statements should possess
- the definition of the main elements in financial statements

14.1 Financial reports

The financial reports are used by a business to communicate information on the financial effect of its activities to external users. They are intended to meet the common information needs of a wide range of users and include:

- financial statements such as the Income Statement, the Balance Sheet and the Cash Flow Statement, including explanatory notes;
- narrative reports such as the Chairman's Statement, Directors' Report and Operating and Financial Review.

Limited companies, the commonest form of business organisation, are legally required to make the reports available to shareholders and to members of the public as documents of public record, filed with the Registrar of Companies.

The format of these reports, as well as their content, is specified in Company Law. There has been a growing increase in the content as government has reacted on an *ad hoc* basis, e.g. requiring political donations and charitable donations to be included and an ever-increasing amount of detail on directors' remuneration. Each additional disclosure has been designed usually to deal with shortcomings identified by investigations into company failures or to deal with matters of public concern such as the level of directors' remuneration.

It has been recognised by the accounting profession that there is a need for a proactive approach[1] to disclosure requirements. As part of this approach it is now appreciated that the financial reports could be made more meaningful if their contents and format of presentation were to be determined, after considering the following:

1. Who are the different parties (known as *stakeholders*) with a legitimate claim for information?
2. What are the main areas of interest that each of those parties has?
3. Which items of information will be of relevance to those areas of interest?
4. What are the qualitative characteristics which these parties will expect of the information provided to them?
5. Which vehicles will prove most effective for communicating the identified information?

Activity 14.1 Limitations of financial statements

There is a view that traditional financial statements prepared by business entities are inadequate for communicating fully the financial performance and financial position of business entities. State with reasons whether you agree with this view.

14.2 Identification of the stakeholders

The *stakeholders* are parties who have a legitimate claim for information from profit-oriented entities. They have been identified in the *Framework*[1] as follows:

1. **Investors** being those who have provided or intend to provide risk capital.
2. **Lenders** (present and prospective) being the providers of loan capital.
3. **Suppliers** being providers of goods/services on credit.
4. **Employees** whose financial security and prospects are entwined with those of the entity.
5. **Customers** who expect to be served as well as serviced by the entity.
6. **Government** and its agencies whose interest is usually met by special purpose reports.
7. **The public** whose welfare is affected by the activities of the entity.

14.3 Main areas of stakeholder interest

The main areas of interest to a range of stakeholders may be identified as follows:

1. **Discharge of stewardship**: In a limited company, although the resources of the entity are owned usually by numerous shareholders, the management of those resources (the stewardship) is entrusted to a few directors. The divorce of ownership from management places the management in a *fiduciary* (position of trust) relationship with the owners and hence with a responsibility to account to the owners for:
   ■ protection, proper application and efficient use of the resources;
   ■ achieving returns on the resources that are acceptable to the owners.
2. **Profitability** of the entity's activities: the profit expected by the shareholders is affected by the type of commercial risk. For example, in a retail business there might be

an expectation of steady growth and customer satisfaction is important, whereas in a pharmaceutical business there might be long periods of low profits, or even losses, whilst new products are being developed. In the long term profitability is paramount because losses erode the capital base of the entity and may, in time, jeopardise its very existence. Profitability is one of the measures used for assessing stewardship.

3. **Liquidity** provides the means to settle debts and to achieve financial adaptability. It is gauged on the basis of the ability of the business to:
   - meet its bills as and when they fall due;
   - have the resources to avail itself of profit-making opportunities.

Financial adaptability is the entity's ability to take effective action to alter the amount and timing of its cash flows so that it can respond to unexpected needs or opportunities, e.g. being able to finance a long period of product development. If liquidity is weak then this will:
   - raise alarm bells with suppliers and loan creditors with regard to the credit worthiness of the entity;
   - mean incurring higher costs on any borrowing;
   - mean missing out on profit making opportunities;
   - mean that shareholders will have to invest more capital to provide the necessary funds.

4. **Solvency** is the ability of the entity, in the event it is wound up, to meet in full all claims on its resources. If the entity is a limited liability company then lenders need to be careful because the shareholders only have an obligation to contribute the amount they agreed to pay for their shares. If the company runs out of funds the lenders and suppliers to whom the company owes money could be in danger of not being paid.

5. **National goals and public welfare obligations** can impact on an entity in its aim to maintain customer loyalty, social image and a conducive operating environment. For example:
   - national goals include pressures for regional development, non-discrimination employment policies and ethical standards such as anti-bribery and corruption legislation;
   - public welfare which may be advanced by protecting the environment, providing employment, conserving foreign exchange holdings, improving the standard of living and so on.

6. **Employee welfare** encourages staff morale and productivity, from e.g. benefiting from employee suggestions to avoiding industrial action at the other extreme. The extent to which an entity secures the welfare of its staff may be gauged not only on the basis of remuneration levels but also taking into account other aspects of interest to employees, such as the following:
   - rate of staff turnover;
   - training and staff development facilities and promotional prospects;
   - work ethics, office atmosphere, grievance redress and staff motivation;
   - debt relief, medical facilities, retirement benefits;
   - participation in the management process.

Activity 14.2 **Economic decisions based on information in financial reports**

It is claimed that a range of stakeholders depend on financial reports to make crucial economic decisions. Identify two such economic decisions the shareholders have to make.

14.4 The information needs of all stakeholders are not the same

The objective of financial reports is to provide information that is useful to those for whom they are prepared. The same set of financial reports is expected to satisfy the information needs of a variety of stakeholders we have identified above. The problem is that their interests do not always coincide. For example:

1. A supplier considering an entity's application for credit would find the annually prepared financial statements and reports inadequate for the purpose and would have to fall back on reports of Credit Protection Agencies.

2. A bank, placed in similar circumstances, would find it necessary to insist on additional information such as management reports, budgets and monthly cash flow forecasts.

3. The information needs of different stakeholders may even be in conflict, for example, a bank may prefer the borrower's balance sheet to be prepared on a breakup value basis in order to assess the security for the loan; an investor, on the other hand, is more interested in one prepared on a going concern basis.

Activity 14.3 Areas of stakeholder interest

Fill in the words Potentially, Very and Highly in the following grid to state your opinion of the extent of interest each identified group of stakeholders would have in the specified areas:

Stakeholders	Stewardship	Profitability	Liquidity	Solvency	Employee welfare	National goals
1. Investors						
2. Lenders						
3. Suppliers						
4. Employees						

The reports that companies publish annually are expected to provide sufficient information for all stakeholders to make informed economic decisions. However, as we have seen, different groups of stakeholders need to make different decisions, and the information they need for the purpose is not the same. The International Accounting Standards Board (IASB) considers, however, that there is a degree of overlap in the information requirements of the different groups to the extent that all of them are interested, to varying degrees, in an entity's:

- financial performance as seen in the Income Statement;
- financial position as seen in the Balance Sheet;
- ability to generate cash and respond to unexpected needs and opportunities.

In view of this overlap the IASB has assumed that, if an entity satisfies the information needs of shareholders, then the information needs of other stakeholders will also be satisfied. Other groups of stakeholders should be aware of this assumption so that, when making their decisions, they would regard the information in financial statements only as a broad frame of reference against which to identify more specific information they should obtain.

14.5 Underlying assumptions when preparing financial statements

When preparing financial statements the following underlying assumptions are made:

1. Separate entity.
2. Accruals including matching.
3. Going concern.
4. Money measurement.
5. Stable value of money.

14.5.1 Separate entity

When accounting for transactions, it is assumed that the entity in respect of which the accounting records are maintained is separate from (i) its owner or owners and (ii) from other entities owned by the same person(s). For example, looked at from the point of view of the business entity, the capital contributed by the owner is a liability and is accounted for as such, whereas from the point of view of the one who contributed it, the capital would be an asset. In a strictly legal sense this assumption is true only with regard to limited companies which, on incorporation, are recognised as separate entities not only distinct from but also having rights against those who own it. Without such a clear demarcation, which incorporation provides, it is difficult to identify the thin line dividing the resources and activities of the entity from those of its owner, although it is necessary for both accounting and tax purposes.

14.5.2 Accruals including matching

The *Framework*[1] requires that the effect of transactions and other events should be recognised, recorded and reported in financial statements when they occur and not when corresponding cash is received or paid. The *Framework*[1] explains that financial statements prepared on an accruals basis inform users not only of past transactions involving payments and receipts of cash but also of obligations to pay cash in future and resources that represent cash to be received in the future.

14.5.3 Going concern

The financial statements are prepared on the assumption[1] that the entity will continue in operational existence for the foreseeable future and that there is no intention or necessity to close down the business or to significantly curtail the scale of its operations. It is on the basis of the assumption that the entity will remain a going concern that a non-current asset continues to be reported at depreciated historical cost, even if its realisable value is lower. Those responsible for preparing financial statements are required to satisfy themselves that there are no problems affecting the ability of the entity to continue. For example, it is usual to consider:

- adequacy of both working and long-term capital;
- operational prospects such as the size of the order book, market share, market trends and intensity of competition;
- availability of resources including raw material, man-power and know-how.

However, financial statements prepared on an assumption of going concern may not be adequate for evaluating aspects such as the security available to a lending bank which may also have to consider prospects of a forced realisation of assets in the event of an emergency.

Activity 14.4 **The going concern assumption**

Unless expressly stated otherwise, financial statements are assumed to have been prepared on the premise that the entity will remain in the business as a going concern for the foreseeable future.

Required: Explain how assets and liabilities are valued and reported on the basis of the assumption that the entity will continue at the current scale of operation for the foreseeable future.

14.5.4 Money measurement

An entity's transactions can be accounted for in physical terms, without necessarily involving money values. The assets of an entity could be expressed, for example, as consisting of x acres of land, y tons of coal and z bales of textiles. The advantage of comparing physical quantities over time is that it is clear whether there has been a growth or decline, e.g. an acre of land remains the same in extent today as it was centuries ago. The disadvantage of measuring in physical terms, however, is that the physical values cannot be aggregated so as to identify the total wealth of an entity in a single figure. For example, receivables, payables and cash cannot be aggregated with physical measures such as acres. Without aggregation, using a common unit of measurement such as the £, it is not possible to compare different entities or the same entity over time.

For these reasons accountants measure assets and liabilities in terms of money. Money values, when established by market transactions, are traditionally accepted as objective and reliable for reporting an entity's performance and position. The disadvantage is that any transaction or event, which cannot be measured in terms of money, is not accounted for in the financial statements. This has been increasingly realised by the accounting profession and has led to companies providing more narrative comment in their annual financial reports.

Activity 14.5 **Business information which money cannot measure**

Accountants measure everything they account for in money terms. Accordingly they assume that what is not measurable in terms of money need not be accounted for. They are aware, however, of significant areas which cannot be measured in terms of money and yet are of interest to those to whom accounting reports are intended.

Required:
a) Identify some business information which money cannot measure, but which may be important to the successful running of a business.
b) Explain how such information is communicated to those interested in it.

14.5.5 Stable value of money

Accountants in each country use their national currency as the yardstick for measuring transactions and events for the purpose of accounting. We in the UK use the pound sterling. This gives rise to problems such as the following:

1. Whereas physical measures (e.g. acres) remain a stable measure over time, monetary measures do not. A pound sterling today is worth less than 66% of its value 10 years ago and around 20% of its value 30 years ago.

2. Each asset does not always have a constant money value over time. For example, because of limitation in supply, land has increased in money value over time.

3. Measurements made in money are distorted by variations in exchange rate. For example, a machine bought from Japan 20 years ago may be worth much more today because of the appreciation of the exchange value of the Japanese Yen.

Yet money remains the yardstick of accounting measurement because it provides the only means of aggregating non-current assets, current assets and current liabilities and making possible comparisons over time and between entities. Accountants have to choose whether to assume that money is stable in value or to adjust all of the figures in the financial statements to take account of the changes in value. Rather than do this, they have made the assumption that the value of money remains constant over time.

On the basis of this assumption, the financial statements seem to imply that an entity earning £20 million this year has performed better than when it earned £19 million a year earlier and that an entity X with net assets of £100 million is better resourced than an entity Y with £90 million. Neither of these assertions may be valid if, because of inflation, the value of money has diminished. For example:

■ if there is an inflation of 10%, the earning this year of £20 million is worth only (£20 × 100/110) = £18.18 million in terms of last year's money values, so that the performance this year is worse;

■ if the entity Y acquired most of its assets in 1960, when the Retail Price Index was 12.5, and has the same £ amount of assets in 20X7 as the entity X which acquired its assets in 20X4 when the Retail Price Index was 163, then clearly entity Y is far better resourced than entity X.

A variation in the value of money, therefore, not only distorts comparison over time and with other entities, but also inhibits performance reporting as well as position reporting. For example, performance reporting is bound to be distorted to the extent that earnings measured in terms of current (lower) monetary units are compared with expense at least some of which (like depreciation of assets and opening inventory) is measured in monetary units of a prior period. Position reporting is distorted as well because the assets reported on a historical cost basis will be stated at different money values that prevailed at the time each of them was acquired.

Accountants are fully conscious that measurements are distorted by changing values of their unit of measurement. The distortion is of course greater in times of more pronounced inflation. That is why the accounting profession tends to intensify its efforts at finding a solution to the problem during periods of accelerated inflation, as was the case in the 1970s when they actively searched for ways of accounting for price level changes. Currently inflation is low and there is little pressure to take it into account.

Activity 14.6 Alternative to historical cost accounting

Accounting on the basis of historical cost is valid only if it is assumed that the value of money remains constant over time. This constraint would be overcome if accounting uses current values rather than historical costs.

Required: Explain the reluctance to record accounting information using current values.

14.6 Working rules

There are a number of working rules that are followed when accounting for transactions to be reported in financial statements. These are:

1. Time interval rule.
2. Realisation rule.
3. Historical cost rule.
4. Valuation rules.
5. Non-aggregation rule.

14.6.1 Time interval rule

In the distant past, the accounts for voyages and trade across the seas, were based on *the venture concept* and prepared only when the venture was completed and all of the merchandise had been sold. This meant that there was no need to make estimates such as how long the non-current assets would last and the value of inventory. At the present day, however, stakeholders require information with greater frequency. This is achieved by following the time interval rule which requires accounting information to be provided to stakeholders at regular intervals – in the UK the Companies Act 2006 requires companies to publish their financial reports annually.

This rule means that entities must prepare accrual-based financial statements and match income with its associated costs. The calculation of accrued income and expense can be a simple arithmetical calculation, e.g. measuring rent accrued, or it might involve making estimates with regard to incomplete transactions. For example, an estimate is required when deciding if inventory should be valued at cost or net realisable value and an estimate is required of the expected economic life and scrap value of plant and equipment when measuring depreciation.

14.6.2 Realisation rule

The realisation rule requires that income should not be recognised in the Income Statement until it has been realised. In accounting, realisation requires all uncertainties relating to the earning process to have been substantially resolved. The ideal and prudent approach would be to define income as realised when:

1. The product is finished so that there is no uncertainty as to its readiness for sale.
2. The sale has been agreed so that there is no uncertainty as to whether a buyer can be found and on the sales price.
3. The sale proceeds have been received.

If realisation in the form of cash were a necessary condition for accounting for income, then credit sales would not be accounted for as income. In practice the last condition that the sales proceeds should have been received is relaxed and considered to have been satisfied if there is a reasonable assurance of receiving it. Consequently, credit sales are regarded as income and give rise to an asset (referred to as trade receivables) provided there is reasonable certainty that the cash will be received. We saw in Chapter 7 that an Allowance for doubtful debts is created and deducted from the profit if there is not reasonable certainty.

Why is it important that income should be realised?

In the UK Company Law states that only profits realised by the balance sheet date should be included in the Income Statement and that distribution to shareholders can only be made out of realised profits. The thought underlying this is that the rule ensures that the entity should be able to pay dividends without reducing its operational capacity, i.e. there should be cash or access to cash from the year's profits.

Activity 14.7 **Realisation rule inhibits performance reporting**

Two sisters, Tessa and Vanessa, commenced separate businesses on 1.1.20X6 each with capital of £50,000 in cash. On that day each invested their whole capital in 50,000 ordinary shares of £1 each at par. By 31st December 20X6 these shares were quoted on the London Stock Exchange at 120p per share. Tessa sold her shares on that date but Vanessa held on to hers expecting the shares to go up even further.

Required:
a) Set out the Balance sheet of the business activity of each sister as at 31st December 20X6.
b) State whether you regard Vanessa's performance in the year as poorer than Tessa's.

A major problem with the realisation rule is the determination of the precise point at which income may be regarded as having been realised. Professionals, such as solicitors, who are usually not permitted by rules of professional etiquette to sue their clients for professional fees, have regarded their fee income as earned only when received in cash. A club or association may also adopt the same attitude. It is important to note that the point at which the income may be regarded as realised, though critical to accounting, may not always be clear. The practice in this area has still not been standardised in the UK.

14.6.3 Historical cost rule

The historical cost (actual amount paid) is the time hallowed method accountants have always used to measure the resources of an entity as well as the expenses. The value is based on the amount actually paid and, being established by an arm's length market transaction, it is objective, verifiable in that the amount can be checked and reliable. Reliable is a qualitative characteristic that is explained further below (Section 14.8). Since this rule has been applied over the years, profit reported on this basis is generally understood and accepted.

The shortcomings of accounting on the historical cost rule should, however, be admitted.

Resources are not reported at their current worth

The balance sheet, reporting resources at their historical cost, fails to reflect the current value of the resources available to the entity. There is a further problem as the amounts stated on a balance sheet become meaningless because assets are stated at costs paid at different times when money values, depending on the inflation rate, may have been different. There has been an attempt to get over this by allowing companies to revalue their non-current assets on a regular basis. This is permitted by the Companies Act[2] which in 1981 introduced the *alternative accounting rule* permitting assets to be accounted at the market value rather than cost. However, not all companies take advantage of this and continue to include non-current assets in their balance sheet at cost.

Resources may be omitted from the Balance Sheet

It is not usual to include the value of employees on the balance sheet unless a payment has been made e.g. by football clubs.

Performance is not accurately reported

This occurs because the Income Statement matches current period's earnings against expenses, some of which might have been incurred at an earlier date when money may have had a different value. The extent of the mismatch depends on the level of inflation and the time gap between the payment and the use of assets. In addition, it does not recognise the loss suffered through holding monetary assets (such as receivables and bank balance) while prices are rising and causing an erosion in the purchasing power of such assets.

14.6.4 Valuation rules

Some of the valuation rules adopted by accountants are as follows:

1. Non-current assets are valued at cost less depreciation at the balance sheet date (see Chapter 7).
2. Inventory is valued at the lower of cost and net realisable value (see Chapter 6).
3. Trade Receivables are valued at their expected cash realisable value (see Chapter 7).
4. A liability is stated at the amount of cash or cash equivalent which is considered to be necessary to fully discharge the obligation existing at the balance sheet date.

14.6.5 Non-aggregation working rule

This rule (referred to in Section 6.11) applies when, with regard to assets such as inventory, cost is compared with realisable value for determining which is lower. The rule, stated in the Companies Act of 1985[2], demands that the comparison should be done separately for each individual asset or for groups of fungible (meaning interchangeable) assets.

Activity 14.8 IASB's underlying assumptions

We have come across many accounting concepts, of which some are assumptions we make and others are rules we comply with when accounting for transactions. However, IASB's Framework has named two as underlying assumptions.

Required:
a) What are these two underlying assumptions?
b) Why are they identified as underlying assumptions?

14.7 Capital maintenance

Profit is regarded as the return on the capital invested by the owner of a business. However, if the profit is not correctly measured and the proprietor draws out the whole of the profit from the business, a part of such drawings may represent repayment to him of the capital invested.

For example, assume that Dave, who owns a taxi business, invested a capital of £20,000 to buy a vehicle with an estimated economic life of five years. If he measures his annual profit without depreciating the vehicle and draws out the whole of the profit year after year, at the end of the five years he would need to invest another £20,000 to buy another vehicle. What this means is that the amount of his annual drawing included in part a repayment to him of the capital he invested in the business.

If, on the other hand, he were to provide for depreciation at 20% of the cost annually, he would have reduced the amount of the annual profit by £4,000 and not taken out this amount as drawings. As a result he would have, by the end of the vehicle's economic life, retained within the business £20,000 (£4,000 × 5) and so maintained the money capital of £20,000 available for re-investment. This is known as *maintenance of money capital*.

If the value of money remains unchanged during this period and the price of vehicles remains unchanged, £20,000 would be sufficient to replace the vehicle. This means that his business can continue to operate at the same capacity as before. In that case he would have maintained his real capital as well. On the contrary, if the price of vehicles increased during the period, £20,000 may only be sufficient to buy a smaller vehicle. This means that while his money capital is maintained, his real capital (i.e. the operating capacity of the business) is not.

14.8 Qualitative characteristics of information in financial statements

The accountant's aim is to produce financial statements that present a *fair view* of the financial performance during an accounting period and the financial position on the last day of that period. The ultimate test on whether to include accounting information in a financial statement is, therefore, whether the inclusion of the information is necessary in order to achieve a true and fair view.

The *Framework*[1] suggests that the financial statements would convey a true and fair view if they are prepared in accordance with accounting standards and if the information they contain possesses identified qualitative characteristics which make the statements useful. To place them in a proper perspective the qualitative characteristics identified in the *Framework* may be structured[3] as follows:

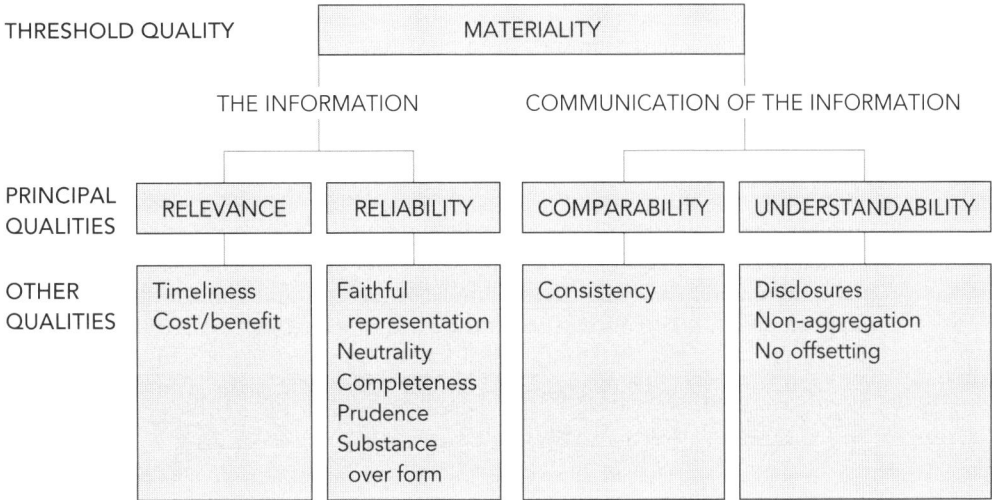

Materiality. In accounting materiality means assessing information's significance to the stakeholders. Information is regarded as material if, by nature or amount, it is significant for those who have to make decisions. For shareholders it is information that could influence decisions such as whether to buy, retain or sell shares in a company. There are many situations where accountants have to exercise their discretion with regard to materiality, for example:

1. Deciding whether to capitalise an item as an asset or write it off as an expense, e.g. is it an asset if a company has spent £5,000 on tools? The answer would be influenced by the size of the company being Yes if preparing the financial statements of a carpenter and No if preparing the financial statements of a multinational company.

2. Deciding whether to report an item separately because of its size, e.g. should bad debts of £10,000 be separately disclosed or included in the selling expenses? Again, it depends on the size of the organisation and other factors such as comparison with:
   ■ other items in the whole report;
   ■ size of related items;
   ■ comparative figure of previous year;
   ■ the amount it was expected to be.

3. Deciding whether to report an item separately because of its nature, e.g. should the fact that the directors have started to sell their shares be disclosed as material? The answer would be influenced by the surrounding circumstances. It might be significant to the shareholders if it is linked with other considerations such as a falling trend in the profits or loss of a major customer or known disagreement amongst the directors.

Relevance is the usefulness of that information for making economic decisions. The usefulness could arise because of the significance of the information for:

■ confirming or correcting past evaluations and assessments;
■ evaluating or assessing the present;
■ predicting the future.

Reliability requires the information to be:

■ a faithful representation of reality, i.e. does it reflect the substance of a transaction and its commercial effect;
■ neutral, i.e. free from deliberate or systematic bias intended to influence decisions;
■ free from material error;
■ complete (within the bounds of materiality);
■ prudent, i.e. in conditions of uncertainty a degree of caution should have been used when making estimates and exercising judgement.

Relevance/reliability trade-off. It has been recognised that stakeholders may require information before the annual report is published. There is, therefore a requirement for companies to produce half yearly and even quarterly reports. Such reports cannot be checked for completeness as thoroughly as the annual reports and it is accepted when determining the relevance and reliability of information to be included in financial statements that one has to make trade off, taking into account the need for timeliness, cost/benefit and completeness.

Activity 14.9 **Conflict between qualities of information**

Relevance and reliability are accorded equal primary status as principal characteristics of information to be included in financial statements. Discuss the possibility of conflict between the two qualities and how such conflict should be resolved.

Comparability requires information to be prepared and presented in a way that it is comparable over time and with those of other similar entities. It is achieved through:

- consistency in the treatment of transactions within each accounting period, from one period to the next and also between different entities;
- disclosure of accounting policies to show that there has been consistent treatment or to allow the stakeholders to take any inconsistency into account when making comparisons.

The Accounting Standards and International Financial Reporting Standards issued by the ASB and IASB contribute to comparability by:

- reducing the options available to different entities when accounting for similar transactions;
- requiring the disclosure of accounting policies and changes in accounting policies.

In order to maintain consistency, the IASB requires the consistent adoption of an *accounting policy* unless there is a good reason for a change in which case the change should be explained.

Understandability is whether the users of financial statements will be able to recognise the significance of the information. This depends on both the preparer of the financial statements and the users themselves. For example:

1. The statutory authorities and the IASB have required the preparers to format the statements in a way that assists understanding, e.g. the Income Statement is required to report income, cost of goods sold, administrative expenses and selling costs and explain any unusual items such as an unusually high level of bad debts.

2. The users are assumed to have a reasonable knowledge of the business, economic activities and accounting and to be willing to study the information with reasonable diligence. However, information on complex matters which need to be included because of its relevance to decision making should not be left out merely because it would be too difficult for certain users to understand.

Faithful representation means that the user can see the commercial reality of the transactions that the entity has entered into. This is not always easy and in recent years the standard setters in the USA and at the IASB have been attempting to agree how financial instruments should be measured and reported, e.g. how to value share options granted to employees and directors.

Neutrality means that the preparers of the financial statements have not presented a biased picture. In recent years the UK government has been accused of spin with a resulting loss of credibility. The accounting profession recognises that it is extremely important that financial statements should remain credible as they are often the basis for investors' decisions. Lack of credibility could have an adverse effect on investment. Investors want the information to be objective, and adherence to the historical cost rule is one of the ways the accountants use to safeguard objectivity. For example, by reporting non-current assets at the cost actually paid, the accountant avoids the subjective judgement involved when assets are valued. We have seen, though, that there are numerous occasions when the accounting process requires subjective judgements to be made. Some such occasions are as follows:

- determining depreciation, when the useful economic life of non-current assets is estimated;
- making allowance for doubtful debts, when the recoverability of the debt is assessed;

■ accruing for unpaid bills, when estimates have to be made because actual amounts are as yet unknown;

■ determining the net realisable value of inventory.

Completeness is required for information to be reliable subject to consideration of materiality and cost. The omission of information can cause the information presented to be biased or even false, e.g. not disclosing that there are likely to be environmental liabilities.

Prudence is the exercise of a degree of caution when conditions are uncertain. The aim is to ensure that income and assets are not over-stated and expense and liabilities are not under-stated. The uncertainties might be of a recurring nature, such as providing for doubtful debts, when too low an estimate would result in the income and assets being over-stated. The uncertainties could also be of an infrequent nature, such as the expected outcome of a legal dispute. In the latter case, although liabilities should not be under-stated, it is not the place of prudence to provide for the worst outcome. For example, if a liability is estimated to be finalised at a figure between £6,000 and £10,000 with the likelihood that it will finally be agreed at £8,500, prudence is not providing for the maximum liability of £10,000 but for the most likely amount of £8,500.

Substance over form requires the substance of a transaction to be reported rather than in accordance with its legal form. For example, if X sells a load of timber to Y for £60,000 subject to an agreement that he has the option to buy it back at an agreed price (say £60,000 plus interest at a specified rate for the period until it is bought back), the transaction is not really a sale but a financing one to borrow that amount and should be accounted for accordingly.

Activity 14.10 **Identification of the defining accounting convention**

You are now familiar with a number of accounting concepts or conventions. Identify which among them would be relevant when deciding on:

a) the value at which inventory is reported on the balance sheet

b) setting up a provision for doubtful debts

c) writing off depreciation of non-current assets

d) whether to capitalise advertising expenses intended to enhance future sales

---

14.9 The elements of financial statements

The effect of transactions and the other events portrayed in the financial statements are known as *elements of financial statements*. The elements directly related to measurement of financial position in the balance sheet are:

1. **Assets.** These are resources controlled by an entity as a result of past transactions or events and from which future economic benefits are expected to flow (see Chapter 16).

2. **Liabilities.** These are present obligations of an entity arising from a past transaction or event the settlement of which is expected to result in an outflow of resources embodying economic benefits (see Chapter 19).

3. **Ownership interest**. This is the residual interest in the assets of an entity after deducting all its liabilities.

The elements directly related to measurement of performance in the Income Statement are:

1. **Income**. The increase in economic benefits during the accounting period in the form of inflows or enhancement of assets or decreases of liabilities that result in increases in equity. Contributions from equity participants are not income.

2. **Expense**. The decrease in economic benefits during the accounting period in the form of outflows or depletions of assets or incurrence of liabilities that result in decreases in equity. Distributions to equity participants are not expenses.

Summary

- There is a range of different stakeholders who have a legitimate interest in financial reports.
- These stakeholders have different areas of interest in a business entity.
- Financial statements are prepared assuming separate entity, accruals, going concern, money measurement and stable value of money.
- Financial statements are prepared adopting working rules of time interval, realisation, historical cost, valuation and non-aggregation.
- Unless capital is maintained, drawing out by the owner of the whole profit would represent in part a repayment of capital invested in the business.
- To report a true and fair view the accounting information included in financial statements should possess qualitative characteristics identified as Materiality, Relevance, Reliability, Comparability, Understandability, Objectivity, Completeness, Prudence and Substance over form.
- The key elements constituting financial statements are assets, liabilities, equity, income and expense.

References

1 Interest in seeking answers to these questions arose when the accounting profession launched its quest for a conceptual framework. The current position in this study is contained in the *Framework for the Preparation and Presentation of Financial Statements* (hereafter referred to as the *Framework*) issued by the International Accounting Standards Board.

2 Companies Act (1985), Sch 4, Pt ii, Para 31, London, The Stationery Office.

3 The diagrammatic presentation is taken from *Statement of Principles of Financial Reporting* (1999), London, Accounting Standards Board.

Suggested answers to activities

14.1 Limitations of financial statements

Traditional financial statements are intended to serve two main purposes. The first is as a vehicle for discharging stewardship. The second is as a basis for making informed economic decisions. On both counts the financial statements are inadequate for the following reasons:

i) The financial statements are only capable of reporting the financial effects of transactions and events. These statements do not communicate non-financial effects (such as staff morale, quality of product lines), equally valuable for assessment of performance and position.
ii) The information contained in financial statements is largely historical and fails to reflect future possibilities that could enhance or impair the entity's performance and financial position and is, therefore, of inadequate significance for decision making.
iii) Since the natural operating cycle of an entity does not always coincide with its accounting periods, the financial statements relating to the accounting periods have necessarily to be prepared on the basis of:
   ■ allocating continuous operations to discrete accounting periods;
   ■ dealing with uncertainties remaining at the end of each period by making assumptions and estimates.
   These introduce an element of conjecture, subjectivity and tentativeness to the performance.

14.2 Economic decisions based on information in financial reports

i) Whether to hold or sell their shares.
ii) Whether to re-appoint or replace the management (i.e. directors).

14.3 Areas of stakeholder interest

The authors suggest that the importance of the different areas to each group of stakeholder can be ranked as Very, Highly or Potentially Important as stated below:

Stakeholders	Stewardship	Profitability	Liquidity	Solvency	National goal	Employee welfare
1. Investors	Very	Very	Highly	Potentially	Potentially	Potentially
2. Lenders	Potentially	Highly	Very	Potentially	Potentially	Potentially
3. Suppliers	Potentially	Highly	Very	Potentially	Potentially	Potentially
4. Employees	Potentially	Highly	Highly	Potentially	Potentially	Potentially

14.4 The going concern assumption

i) Assets are recognised for inclusion in a balance sheet on the basis that the entity will remain ongoing. For example, the pre-paid portion of rent is recognised as an asset on the assumption that the entity will remain ongoing and continue to occupy the premises.
ii) Liabilities are recognised on the basis that the entity will remain in operation. For example, if the entity ceases business and employees lose their jobs, the compensation it may have to pay its employees is not accounted for unless such cessation of business is under contemplation.
iii) Assets are valued on the premise that the entity will continue to operate and at the present scale. For example, assume that machinery of a specialised nature acquired for £500,000 and written down to £250,000 has a realisable value of only £50,000. The lower realisable value is ignored so long as disposal of the machinery is unlikely and the written down value of the machinery is recoverable from its use. Similarly,

the amount realisable on inventory and recoverable from debtors is likely to be lower in a forced realisation on a business ceasing and is not taken into account when preparing annual financial statements.

iv) Liabilities are accounted at the amount that will have to be paid if the business remains ongoing. Any penalties that may arise from settling a loan earlier than the agreed date are ignored.

v) In a balance sheet, assets are classified as non-current and current in accordance with whether they are intended to be realised or used within the next accounting period. Such a classification is valid only on the going concern assumption. In the event of closure of business all assets are for realisation and would fall within a single category. Similarly the balance sheet classification of liabilities as current and non-current depends on the intended period of repayment, if the business remains ongoing. In the event of winding up, the whole classification has to be altered to identify preferential creditors, secured creditors and unsecured ones.

14.5 Business information which money cannot measure

a) Significant business information of interest to those who have a claim for information cannot be accounted for because it is not measurable in terms of money. Such information includes the following:

i) the quality and competence of the entity's employees;

ii) the morale among the staff, their motivation and threat of industrial action;

iii) the quality of the entity's assets and how well they are maintained;

iv) the competitive edge the entity has over its rivals in such form as reputation, location, brand names and past history.

b) Such information, which cannot be measured in terms of money, is communicated by being narrated in financial statements as footnotes or in management or directors' reports.

14.6 Alternative to historical cost accounting

The reluctance to substitute current values for historical cost arises from several factors including the following:

i) The value of an asset or a transaction is subjective and, therefore, could vary according to the thinking and mood of the person doing the valuation.

ii) Value could mean different things. For example, value in use is different from market value. Value in use would vary according to the intended use to which the item is to be put. Market value could itself refer to the value at which the item could be disposed of (realisable value) and the value at which the item could be replaced (the replacement value).

iii) The value cannot be verified (for example during an audit) and that may affect the credibility of the information provided in accounts.

14.7 Realisation rule inhibits performance reporting

Applying the realisation rule, Tessa is able to report a profit because she realised (sold) her investments. Vanessa, on the other hand, cannot account for the holding gain until she realises that gain by selling the investments. Although Vanessa's decision to retain the investments may be wiser, her performance in terms of profit reported is poorer.

Tessa's Balance Sheet	
	£'000
Cash & Bank	60
	60

Vanessa's Balance Sheet	
	£'000
Investments	50
	50

	£'000
Capital	50
Profit	10
	60

	£'000
Capital	50
Profit	0
	50

14.8 IASB'S underlying assumptions

a) The underlying assumptions are (i) accruals ii) going concern.
b) This is because, unless informed otherwise, all stakeholders are expected to assume that transactions and events have been accounted for on accruals basis and that financial statements have been prepared on the assumption that the entity is a going concern.

14.9 Conflict between qualities of information

The following provides some instances of conflict between relevance of information and reliability of information:

i) In order to report the financial performance and position of an entity, information on all its assets and liability would be relevant. Yet one (or more) of these elements may have to be left out of financial statements because of uncertainty as to its existence or measurement.
ii) Waiting for uncertainties to be resolved would imperil the timeliness of information because out-of-date information would be irrelevant for decision making.
iii) Reliability of information demands neutrality as well as prudence, and these two may be mutually conflicting. Neutrality is freedom from deliberate and systematic bias whereas prudence requires a deliberate effort at conservatism when reporting performance.

To sort out such conflicts it has been suggested that:

i) In the event of conflict between relevance and reliability, financial statements should use the most relevant of whichever information is reliable.
ii) The tension between neutrality and prudence should be resolved by finding a balance that ensures that deliberate and systematic understatement of assets or gains and overstatement of liabilities or losses does not occur.

14.10 Identification of the defining accounting convention

Inventory valuation	Time interval	Prudence	Non-aggregation	Consistency
Bad debts allowance	Prudence	Neutrality	Going concern	
Depreciation expense	Prudence	Neutrality	Going concern	Consistency
Advertising expense	Prudence	Neutrality		

Multiple choice questions

Stakeholders and their interests

14.1 Although the primary interest of shareholders of a company will be the discharge of stewardship by the directors and the profitability of their business, they will also be watchful of the company's liquidity levels for the following reasons:

i) Liquidity problems will result in failure to take advantage of profit making opportunities

ii) Faced with liquidity problems the company may not pay dividends

iii) Low liquidity may result in resignation of company directors

iv) If liquidity is low the company may not be able to pay its creditors in time

Which of the above statements are correct?

a	All four	
b	i & ii	
c	i, ii & iv	
d	ii, iii & iv	

14.2 Profitability of a company is one of the main interests of its shareholders because:

i) Higher profit results in shares becoming worth more

ii) Higher profit could result in bigger amounts being paid as dividends

iii) Losses will, in time, erode the capital base and threaten an entity's survival

iv) It is greater prestige to be shareholders in a profitable company

Which of the above statements are correct?

a	All four	
b	i, ii & iii	
c	i, ii & iv	
d	ii, iii & iv	

14.3 Which of the following statements is incorrect?

a) The financial statements are intended only for the use of shareholders and investors

b) Employees of a business will have an interest in both profitability and liquidity levels

c) Banks will be averse to lending to a loss-making company even it is currently very liquid

d) When considering granting credit facilities banks may require more information than in the Annual Report

Accounting concepts

14.4 Accounting concepts must be defined clearly and be understood by both the preparers and users of financial statements for the following reasons:

i) The information in financial statements then becomes more meaningful

ii) It would assist accountants to account for unusual transactions

iii) It would assist standard setters to be consistent in the Financial Reporting Standards they issue

iv) It would improve comparability of financial statements

Which of the above statements are correct?

a	All four	
b	i & ii	
c	i, ii & iii	
d	ii, iii & iv	

14.5 When accounting for transactions and preparing financial statements certain assumptions are made and a number of working rules are complied with. Which of the following would you regard as assumptions rather than working rules:

i) Accruals	ii) Money measurement	iii) Separate entity	
iv) Historical cost	v) Going concern	vi) Non-aggregation	
vii) Prudence	viii) Stable value of money	ix) Consistency	

a	i, ii, iii	
b	i, ii, iii, v, viii	
c	i, v, viii, ix	
d	iii, v, viii, ix	

14.6   Which of the following statements is incorrect?

a) Non-aggregation rule is applied when comparing cost and net realisable value of inventory

b) Non-current assets are depreciated to comply with the matching concept

c) Comparability of financial statements are impaired unless consistency concept is applied

d) A transaction is accounted according to its legal form rather than its commercial substance

14.7   Which accounting concept needs to take precedence when accounting for the cost of advertising which is expected to significantly enhance the sales in future years?

a) Consistency concept

b) Matching concept

c) Prudence concept

d) Neutrality concept

14.8   Which of the following statements is the most appropriate explanation of the prudence concept?

a) Income should not be accounted for until realised in cash

b) Faced with uncertainty an accountant should exercise a degree of caution

c) It is better to understate profit rather than to overstate it

d) It is better to account for expenses even if there is uncertainty as to how much is payable

14.9   In times of rising prices accounting on the basis of the historical cost concept would tend to:

a) Inflate profit and inflate assets

b) Understate profit and understate assets

c) Inflate profits and understate assets

d) Understate profit and inflate assets

14.10 Which of the following is applying the prudence concept?

a) Reporting as an asset the unsold portion of goods purchased for sale

b) Accounting for the personal expenses of the proprietor met by the business as drawings

c) Setting up a provision for receivables not expected to be recovered

d) Accounting for sales although a portion of which is not received by the balance sheet date

14.11 In the financial statements issued by large companies like Imperial Chemical Industries (ICI) the amounts stated are rounded off to the nearest million pounds. The reason for this is:

a) the materiality concept

b) to keep details secret from rival companies

c) to show how big their company is

d) because this is currently fashionable

14.12 An item of information or amount is not separately reported in a financial statement, on account of materiality, if:

a) It accounts for less than 5% of the balance sheet total

b) It would not be significant for economic decisions made by stakeholders

c) It is less than one million pounds

d) Its reporting will assist competitors

14.13 Although income is usually accounted for on accruals concept, dividends proposed by an entity in which shares are held are not accounted for until received. The accounting convention used is:

a) Prudence and consistency

b) Consistency and going concern

c) Realisation and prudence

d) Prudence and substance over form

14.14 The expenses relating to the proprietor and his household should be treated as drawings rather than as business expenses on the basis of which of the following accounting concepts?

a) Matching concept

b) Prudence concept

c) Separate entity concept

d) Substance over form concept

14.15 Identify three of the following accounting concepts as justification for depreciating non-current assets:

i)	Realisation	ii)	Matching	iii)	Neutrality
iv)	Substance over form	v)	Prudence	vi)	Going concern
vii)	Time interval	viii)	Consistency	ix)	Separate entity

a	i, ii, iii
b	ii, iv, v
c	ii, v, vi
d	iv, vii, ix

14.16 To be reliable financial statements must be neutral. This means that when accounting and reporting one has to be objective – avoiding subjective judgement. However, subjective judgement (based on past experience) is necessary in which of the following areas?

i) When estimating the useful economic life of non-current assets

ii) When assessing recoverability of trade receivables

iii) When assessing inflow of future economic benefits

iv) When estimating the extent of obligation to pay when invoice for services has yet to be received

a	i only
b	i and ii
c	i, ii and iii
d	i, ii, iii and iv

14.17 Faced with uncertainty there is a need to exercise prudence. Which of the following would be excessive use of prudence?

a) Non-recoverability of trade receivables is accounted for based on past experience

b) Depreciation is accounted for by estimating the useful economic life of non current assets

c) Future repairs to non-current assets are accounted for at the point the asset is acquired

d) Accrued expenses are accounted for though the related invoices are yet to be received

14.18 Insisting that financial statements should be a faithful representation of transactions and events during an accounting period, an accountant refuses to present the financial statements until invoices relating to all expenses are received. Which of the following desirable qualities may be sacrificed?

a) Prudence

b) Relevance

c) Reliability

d) Neutrality

14.19 A non-current asset, acquired for £240,000 and depreciated by £90,000 is reported in the Balance Sheet at the written down value of £150,000 although, being an item specially manufactured for the business, its realisable value is expected to be only £95,000. Which accounting concept is followed?

a) Prudence

b) Money measurement

c) Going concern

d) Substance over form

14.20 £580 paid for a lap-top computer is written off as an expense rather than capitalised because the business does not capitalise items that cost less than £1,000. This is an application of which concept?

a) Prudence

b) Money measurement

c) Going concern

d) Materiality

14.21 For identifying the value at which inventory is reported on the Balance Sheet, the cost should be compared with net realisable value of each group of interchangeable (fungible) items. This is necessary because of:

a) Prudence concept

b) Non-aggregation rule

c) Going concern concept

d) Realisation concept

14.22 How does the use of historical cost concept under-state assets and over-state profit in times of rising prices?

i)   The assets may be reported in terms of pound sterling of a lower value

ii) Liabilities may be reported in terms of pound sterling of a higher value

iii) Depreciation/cost of sales in the Income Statement fail to reflect current value

iv) Non-current assets may be reported in terms of currency with a higher value

a	i only
b	i and ii
c	ii and iii
d	iii and iv

14.23 Stella in her confectionery business has systematically cultivated a good customer relationship both by showing courtesy and by sending Christmas gifts. She feels that the goodwill she has built up is worth £100,000. Which accounting concept prevents her from reporting goodwill as an asset in her balance sheet?

a) Prudence

b) Money measurement

c) Separate entity

d) Going concern

14.24 A supermarket uses FIFO cost flow assumption when determining the cost of inventory remaining unsold at the year-end. Why is it essential that it should continue with the same practice?

a) This is the practice adopted by everyone in a similar trade

b) So that its performance and position in the year may be compared with those of previous years

c) Otherwise its financial statements would become meaningless

d) So that the cost of any shop-lifting by customers could be identified

Capital maintenance

14.25 Capital maintenance means that:

a) All assets of the business are maintained in an excellent state of repair

b) The money capital at the end of the accounting period is the same as at the beginning

c) The owner has not taken home any of the business assets

d) The non-current assets of the business are maintained in an excellent state of repair

Qualitative characteristics of information in financial statements

14.26 The Framework issued by the IASB suggests that to show a true and fair view the information in financial statements should:

a) Comply with Accounting Standards and possess suggested qualitative characteristics

b) Be an accurate and full record of transactions within each accounting period

c) Not be presented in a way that could mislead users

d) Be prepared on a consistent basis from year to year

14.27 Which of the following statements is incorrect in relation to financial statements?

a) The information included in it should be relevant and reliable

b) It should convey information in a consistent and understandable way

c) When identifying information for inclusion in it subjectivity is not permitted

d) An amount/item may not be reported separately unless it is material for decision making

14.28 Which of the following statements is incorrect in relation to financial statements?

a) A non-current asset should not be reported at a value higher than the amount that it can be sold for

b) A liability should be reported only if there is a present obligation to pay

c) Expenses should be included whether it has been paid for or are yet to be paid for

d) Assets should be reported only if within the control of the entity and future economic benefit is expected

14.29 Besides identifying materiality as the threshold quality, the Framework issued by IASB identifies four others as primary qualitative characteristics that make financial statements useful. Which are these?

i) Substance over form	ii) Relevance	iii) Prudence	a	i, ii, iii, iv
iv) Faithful representation	v) Comparability	vi) Timeliness	b	ii, vii, ix, x
vii) Reliability	viii) Neutrality	ix) Consistency	c	iv, v, vii, xi
x) Understandability	xi) Completeness		d	ii, v, vii, x

14.30 Which of the following qualitative characteristics of information included in financial statements have been identified in the IASB's Framework as desirable for promoting reliability?

i) Faithful representation	ii) Timeliness	iii) Materiality	a	i, v, vi, ix, x
iv) Comparability	v) Prudence	vi) Neutrality	b	ii, iv, v, viii
vii) Substance over form	viii) Relevance	ix) Understandability	c	i, ii, vi, viii
x) Completeness			d	i, v, vi, vii, x

Elements of financial statements

14.31 In terms of the definition of an asset stated in IASB's Framework which of the following would you identify as an asset of a business engaged in inter-continental transport of goods?

i) Lease of premises for five years from the beginning of this year

ii) Amount paid for an advertising contract which is to commence after the year-end

iii) A heavy goods truck intended to be acquired after the year-end

iv) Amount due from a customer in respect of transport work already carried out

a	i and iv	
b	i and ii	
c	i, ii and iii	
d	i, ii and iv	

14.32 Which of the following would be your justification for treating as an asset the amount due from a customer in respect of work already carried out?

i) The customer is within our control because he relies on us for more work

ii) The amount receivable is within our control because we fix the credit terms

iii) The amount receivable represents a future economic benefit expected

iv) The amount receivable arise from (past) work already carried out

a	i only	
b	i and ii	
c	ii, iii & iv	
d	i, ii and iv	

14.33 The IASB's Framework defines a liability as:

a) Amounts a business may have to pay after the balance sheet date

b) Obligations to pay which may arise depending on some future events

c) Unpaid portion of expenses incurred in the current accounting period

d) Present obligations arising from past events which will result in outflow of economic benefit

14.34 The IASB's Framework defines equity interest as:

a) Amount of capital introduced by the owner of the business

b) Opening capital + profit – drawings

c) Residual interest in the assets of an entity after deducting its liabilities

d) What a business owes its owner or owners

Answers to multiple choice questions
14.1: c   14.2: b   14.3: a   14.4: a   14.5: b   14.6: d   14.7: c   14.8: b   14.9: c   14.10: c   14.11: a   14.12: b   14.13: d
14.14: c   14.15: c   14.16: d   14.17: c   14.18: b   14.19: c   14.20: d   14.21: b   14.22: d   14.23: b   14.24: b   14.25: b
14.26: a   14.27: c   14.28: a   14.29: d   14.30: d   14.31: a   14.32: c   14.33: d   14.34: c

Progressive questions

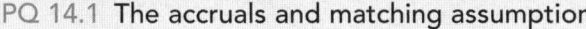

PQ 14.1 The accruals and matching assumption

Susan Pizzy, a young graduate operating as a dealer in computer software, requests your help to finalise the accounts of her shop for the year ended 31st December 20X5. After you completed the task, she writes to you making the following points:

i) The total price paid for software in the year should be regarded as expense. There is no point showing the cost of the unsold portion as an asset in the balance sheet.

ii) She had deliberately avoided paying the last half year's rent and the last quarter's bills for gas and electricity hoping that there would be a corresponding improvement in profit in the first year.

iii) The amount of £36,000 she had received upfront on sub-letting a portion of her shop for three years, at £1,000 per month, should all have been treated as her income for the current year because she has no intention of repaying any portion of it even if the tenant were to leave early.

Required: Draft your response to the points made by Susan.

PQ 14.2 Information needs of a loan creditor

In support of its application for a £60 million loan, Presage plc submitted its Balance Sheets and Cash Flow Statements for the preceding five years. The financier has called also for:

i) the Income Statement for the same period;

ii) the breakup value of the company's freehold premises and machinery;

iii) the corporate plan, the management budgets and cash flow forecasts for the next year.

The Managing Director of Presage is reluctant to provide this information, being of the opinion that:

i) the Income Statement should be of no concern to a financier because the loan together with interest is payable irrespective of the company's performance;

ii) breakup values are irrelevant because the company is expected to remain in operational existence for a long time;

iii) corporate plans, management budgets and cash flow forecasts contain sensitive information and prepared only for internal use and should not be disclosed.

Required: Advise the managing director.

PQ 14.3 The governing accounting concept

When preparing their financial statements for the year ended 31st December 20X6, the following accounting adjustments were made:

i) £16,500 due from a customer was written off as irrecoverable.

ii) 20% of the cost of vehicles was written off as depreciation.

iii) An item of inventory costing £6,000 was written down to its realisable value of £4,500.

iv) School fees paid for the proprietor's son were debited to the Drawings account.

v) £2,500 paid for a photocopying machine was written off (instead of being capitalised).

vi) Insurance paid for the period after the balance sheet date was transferred to a Pre-payments account.

vii) Cost of inventory in hand at the year-end was determined, as usual, on a first in first out basis.

viii) A dividend proposed for the year in respect of shares held in a limited company was not accounted for as income because it had not been received.

Required: Identify the main accounting concepts on the basis of which the above adjustments were made.

PQ 14.4 Conflict among accounting concepts

In the recent past accountants have shown an interest in identifying the concepts which underlie the techniques they use when accounting for transactions. They acknowledge that some among the accounting concepts are fundamental ones but observe also that occasionally there is a conflict between concepts.

Required:

a) Illustrate with a transaction a conflict between the following concepts:
   i)   The matching working rule and the materiality convention;
   ii) The materiality convention and the objectivity convention;
   iii) The matching working rule and the prudence convention;
   iv) The separate entity assumption and the substance over form convention.

b) Explain how you would resolve the conflict, pointing out whether your judgement will be swayed because one of the concepts in conflict is identified as a fundamental one.

PQ 14.5 A question from ACCA

a) Explain clearly the following accounting terms in a manner which an intelligent non-accountant could understand in the context of a profit oriented organisation: (i) expense, (ii) prudence, (iii) objectivity and (iv) matching.

b) Your client has received the following invoice, and has come to you for advice:

From: Marketing Services plc:	£
Agreed monthly fees for general advice – three months to 31. December at £1,000 per month	3,000
Supply of new colour photocopier on 1.10.'5 with five-year guarantee for use by marketing dept	10,000
Deposit paid by us on your behalf for television advertising time in February '6	5,000
Advertising in newspaper from 1 November to 30 November '5 payables in March '6	50,000

Required: Write a letter to your client suggesting, for each of the four items in the invoice, how each item is likely to affect the expenses figure in the accounting year ended 31 December '5. You should explain your suggestions and justify them by reference to accounting conventions.

PQ 14.6 Focus on accounting concepts when preparing financial statements

Norwich Tanners and Curriers (NTC) extracted its year-end trial balance as shown on the right. You are informed as follows:

i) Inventory is ascertained on 5th July 20X6 as £752,000. During the five days after 30th June purchases were £154,000 and sales (made at cost plus a third) were £180,000. The inventory includes £9,000 being the cost of spares bought for repairing the machinery.

ii) Machinery and vehicles are depreciated at 5% and 20% per annum, respectively, using the reducing balance method.

iii) The Insurance account includes £16,000 paid for the year ending on 30th September 20X6.

iv) Interest on the 6% loan, raised in 20X4, and the following items remain unpaid as at 30th June 20X6:

salaries	£32,000
advertising	£18,000
rent	£12,000

v) A trade receivable of £5,000 should be written off and the allowance for doubtful debts adjusted to cover 5% of the amount receivable.

vi) The Lighting and Heating account includes £4,000 paid in respect of the owner's residence, and £500 per week taken by the owner to meet his household expenses is included within other administrative expenses.

Trial balance as at 30th June 20X6	£'000	£'000
Machinery at cost	380	–
Depreciation – machinery	–	180
Motor vehicles at cost	420	–
Depreciation – vehicles	–	200
Inventory – 1st July 20X5	826	–
Salaries	268	–
Insurance	24	–
Telephone & postage	12	–
Sales	–	2,755
Purchases	2,086	–
Advertising	164	–
Motor vehicle maintenance	28	–
Machinery maintenance	46	–
Receivable & payables	485	698
6% loan (repayables 20X9)	–	150
Rent	36	–
Allowance for doubtful debts	–	25
Lighting and heating	29	–
Bank overdraft	–	60
Cash in hand and at bank	16	–
Other admin expenses	198	–
Capital	–	950
	5,018	5,018

Required:
a) The Income Statement for the year ended 30th June 20X6 and the Balance Sheet as at that date.
b) With regard to the adjustments that had to be made in respect of information provided as (i) to (vi), explain the need for these adjustments on the basis of generally accepted accounting concepts.

SECTION 8
ACCOUNTING FOR LIMITED COMPANIES

8

Accounts of limited companies and other organisations

Objectives	By the end of this chapter you should be able to:

By the end of this chapter you should be able to:

▶ Explain what is meant by corporate entity.

▶ Identify the nature of capital invested in companies and the returns available on this capital.

▶ Identify the main changes to company law from the company law review.

▶ Describe the term 'reserves'.

▶ Identify and account for the taxation charge within company accounts.

▶ Prepare the statement of comprehensive income and statement of financial position for companies.

▶ Prepare accounts for clubs and societies.

▶ Identify the differences between the preparation of accounts for companies and charities/public sector.

▶ Explain the difference between a company and a partnership.

▶ Prepare statements of comprehensive income and statements of financial position for a partnership.

The need for companies

In previous chapters we have assumed that the business is that of a sole trader. This is where an individual invests his/her capital in a business and trades with the intention of earning profit that will belong to him/her to do with as he/she chooses. However, this type of business has several drawbacks.

Activity 8.1   Identify two drawbacks of sole trader businesses.

Answer   You should have chosen two from the following list. However, this list is not exhaustive and you may have come up with drawbacks that we have not mentioned. You should be able to explain whether your drawbacks are reasonable.

▶ A sole trader has limited resources available – the capital he/she is able to invest in the business – and limited specialist and management skills.

▶ For a business to grow, more resources are required in terms of capital and expertise.

▶ The sole trader is personally liable for all debts of the business – creditors can claim on the personal assets of the sole trader.

▶ The sole trader business is dependent upon the owner.

Establishing the business as a limited company can overcome all the above drawbacks. Capital resources are available from more than one person, and the company also has easier access to loan funds. Specialist and management skills can be brought into the business by widening the number of owners. A company provides what is known as limited liability to the owners. Ownership can change without there being any effect on the business.

The company

A company has two notions as its basis:

▶ corporate entity

▶ limited liability.

The notion of corporate entity means that several people can band together as owners of a business by investing capital. The business will be a legal entity separate from the owners. It also means that the owners, the investors of capital, can change without the need to change the legal entity of the company.

The notion of limited liability limits the claim on the owners of the business from any of its creditors to the capital these owners invested. It also means that a creditor has to sue the company, not the owners, for payment of any debts due, and these creditors could indeed force the winding up, or liquidation, of the company. There are several hundred thousand companies in the United Kingdom and mainland Europe, many of them large conglomerates such as British Telecom, Guinness, Shell and ICI.

The law in relation to companies in the UK was established by the first Companies Act of 1844, which fused these two notions of corporate entity and limited liability. Any confusion in respect of the two notions was put to rest by the judgment in the case of *Salomon* v *Salomon & Co. Ltd* (1897). The judgment handed down by the House of Lords stated that the company was a separate legal entity distinct from the owners and that creditors could not claim on the personal assets of the owners, only on the assets of the company. Creditors trade with a limited company at their own risk. It is advisable for creditors to investigate the financial stability of a company before they trade with it.

Formation of a company

Further detail in respect of the formation of a company will be found in a company law course, but it is worthwhile identifying the main points here:

▶ All companies must be registered with the Registrar of Companies by the submission of a number of legal documents. This marks the legal birth of a company.

▶ The two most important documents to be filed are the **Memorandum of Association** and the **Articles of Association**.

▶ The Memorandum of Association defines the relationship between the company and any external parties. It also identifies the maximum capital to be invested in the company by the owners, known as the Share Capital. All companies must have at least two shareholders whose names and addresses appear in the memorandum.

▶ The Articles of Association define the rights of shareholders, the rules of operation of the company, and the rights and duties of owners and employees of the company.

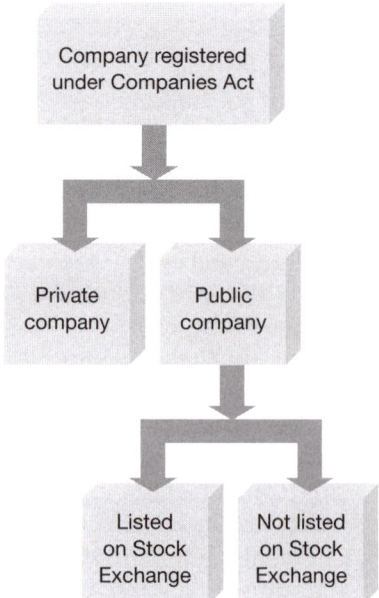

▶ Companies are registered as either public limited companies (plcs) or private companies. Essentially the distinction is that plcs can, if they wish, raise capital by selling shares to the general public. They must have a minimum allotted (i.e. issued to shareholders) share capital of £50,000. Many plcs are quoted on the London Stock Exchange, thus anyone who wants to can become an owner of the company as long as they have the necessary capital to invest. Private companies have restricted ownership. The diagram on the previous page illustrates the type of companies in general that exist.

▶ There must be at least two shareholders in any company but there is no maximum number.

▶ The day-to-day business of the company is generally not carried out by the owners but by directors who are appointed by the owners. The directors report to the owners through the facility of an Annual General Meeting and an Annual Report that incorporates the financial statements.

Company law review in the UK

A review of company law was undertaken during 2001/2 and resulted in a new Companies Act in 2006. This was the most extensive reform of Company Law for nearly 150 years in the UK. As a result of Enron and other corporate scandals across the world, there has been a significant push to require companies to report clearly about their business actions through new legislation. Much of the detail of the review was produced in a steering group report in July 2001 and then in a Government White Paper, *Modernising Company Law*, in July 2002. The objective of the review was to streamline procedures for all companies, especially smaller companies, to make the law clearer, more accessible and responsive to developments. According to the Department of Trade and Industry website on modernising company law, the Company Law Review will:

▶ enable better shareholder engagement,

▶ modernise and de-regulate the law,

▶ give greater clarity to directors on their duties and responsibilities, so that they do not inadvertently fall foul of the law,

▶ facilitate better communications with shareholders,

▶ help speed up decision making, and

▶ deregulate aspects of current law.

All of this should help maintain the UK's position as the best place to set up and run a business.

Company capital

The capital of a company is divided into shares. Investors purchase as many of these as they are able, and want, to buy. For example, a company could be registered with a maximum share capital of 100,000 £1 shares.

The maximum capital of the company would therefore be £100,000 and this would be termed its authorised share capital. A company, not the same one, could also be registered with a share capital of say 50,000 £3 shares – a maximum capital of £150,000. The pound value attached to a share is known as its nominal (or par) value and a company can decide on the nominal value and total number of shares it wishes to issue. The decision will depend on how much capital the company needs to commence its operations. Note that the company does not have to issue all its authorised share capital.

Once a company has made the initial issue of the shares, further trading in these shares can take place in what is known as the share market – for many plcs this is the Stock Exchange. Company shares may well be bought and sold every day on the Stock Exchange, but the company will make no reference to this in the ledger accounts as it is not a transaction between the corporate entity and the buyer, but between the separate shareholder and the buyer. Thus we are differentiating again between the entity of a company and the individual. The company will need to keep a list of who owns shares in it so that it can pay over any return from the trading of the company due to the shareholders. This return paid over to shareholders is known as the **dividend**.

Companies are also able to vary the rights of shareholders within a company by issuing different types of shares. The following activity is concerned with share issues and share transactions.

*A*ctivity 8.2

Obtain a set of company financial statements. This can be done by accessing library facilities, using company websites or by using the Annual Reports Service offered in the *Financial Times* – read the small print at the end of the daily stock exchange listings to see how this is done. Identify the types of shares in issue for your chosen company from the financial statements and notes.

Answer

Your company almost certainly has in issue ordinary shares. These are the most important type of share and are those most commonly traded on the stock exchange. They generally carry voting rights in proportion to the number of shares held. These voting rights give control over the operations of the company to the shareholders through the right to appoint the directors. You should also have been able to identify the dividends paid to ordinary shareholders.

Preference shares may also have been issued by the company. The main feature of preference shares is that they usually carry a specific rate of return to the holder from the company's profits. For example, 5% £1 preference shares would require a payment to the shareholders every year of 5p for every share held. A holder of £10,000 of these preference shares would receive £500.

Preference shares can also be termed cumulative. This means that if the company does not make enough profit in any one year to pay out the amount due to the preference shareholders, it carries over to the next year and accumulates until the company does have enough profit to pay out the amount due – the dividend.

The preference shares may also be *redeemable*, giving the company the right to repay the capital to the preference shareholders at a determined future date.

Shares can also be issued by a company at a value above the nominal value declared in the Memorandum of Association. This is known as issuing shares at a **premium**.

Activity 8.3

Explain why a company may wish to issue shares at a premium.

Answer

A company may wish to raise additional capital. To issue £1 ordinary shares at a price of £1 to new investors would be unfair to the initial investors in the company. The following example illustrates this point.

A company was initially formed by the issue of 100 £1 ordinary shares. The statement of financial position of the company at its formation can be summarised as follows:

Bank	100
Capital 100 £1 ordinary shares	100

The company trades for a number of years, earning profits of £250 in total. Its statement of financial position will then appear as follows:

Assets	350
Capital 100 £1 ordinary shares	100
Profit	250
	350

From this statement of financial position we can conclude that each share now has a book value of £3.50. It is also feasible that if these ordinary shares were traded on the stock exchange they would probably sell at a price in excess of £1. The company at this stage now wishes to raise more capital, £140, so that it can expand by the purchase of further assets. If it issues more £1 ordinary shares at their nominal value then this will be unfair to the original shareholders as the statement of financial position would now be:

Assets	490
Capital 240 £1 ordinary shares	240
Profit	250
	490

Now each share has a book value of £2.04. The original shareholders have lost £1.46 on each share!

To ensure equity (fairness) between old and new shareholders the new shares will be issued at a premium. In this case the shares of £1 nominal value will be issued at £3.50 and the number issued will be 40.

The statement of financial position will now be:

Assets	490
Capital 140 £1 ordinary shares	140
Share premium	100
Profit	250
	490

Now each share has a book value of £3.50.

Note that the premium paid on the shares is entered in a separate ledger account known as share premium.

Activity 8.4

A company is formed with a total authorised (authorised by its inclusion in the Memorandum of Association) share capital of £500,000, consisting of 300,000 £1 ordinary shares and 100,000 5% £2 preference shares. The company wishes to raise £400,000 in capital to start the business. Identify the number of shares of each type it should issue to minimise the preference dividend payment in each of the following circumstances:

1 All shares are to be issued at par.
2 Ordinary shares are to be issued at a premium of 25p and preference shares at a premium of 50p.

Answer

1 300,000 £1 ordinary shares and 50,000 £2 5% preference shares. Preference dividend payment £5,000.
2 300,000 £1 ordinary shares at £1.25 raises £375,000, the further £25,000 required is raised by issuing 10,000 £2 5% preference shares at £2.50. Preference dividend payment £1,000. Issuing the minimum number of preference shares in each case ensures that the preference dividend payment will be minimised. Note that the preference dividend is only calculated on the nominal value of shares issued not the premium.

Rights issues and bonus issues

Companies often make what is termed a rights issue of shares. This is an offer of shares to the existing shareholders that they have a right to purchase at a price below the current market value of the shares. The amount the existing shareholders are allowed to purchase is pro-rata to their existing share holding.

Example 8.1

Alpha plc has in issue one million £1 (nominal value) shares. The current market value of the shares is £3.50. The company proposes a rights issue of one share for every four held at a price of £2.

If all of this rights issue is taken up by the shareholders then the company will issue a further 250,000 shares and will receive £500,000 from the shareholders. The company has benefited in this transaction, as it is a very inexpensive way to raise further

Example 8.1 continued

capital. It does not have to go through all the formalities associated with a full share issue to the public, such as producing what is known as a prospectus. The shareholders benefit, as they are able to buy more shares in the company at a beneficial price and, of course, control of the company remains in their hands. Under a normal issue of shares the existing shareholders could have their control diluted if they did not buy all of the shares issued.

A company can also make a 'bonus issue' of shares to its existing shareholders. As is the case with a sole trader, a company will build up its retained profits over the years and these will appear as a reserve on the statement of financial position. We will talk further about reserves after Activity 8.8.

Example 8.2

Alpha plc's statement of financial position as at 31 March 20X5 shows the following:

Share capital – £1 ordinary shares	500
Retained profits	1,000
	1,500

The company makes a bonus issue of two shares for every one held by the existing shareholders. This means every shareholder receives two free shares for every one held. Note no money changes hands and the cash of the company will not be increased. The statement of financial position after the bonus issue will appear as follows:

Share capital – £1 ordinary shares	1,500
Retained profits	0
	1,500

Once a bonus issue of shares is made, the market value of the shares will fall to reflect the extra number of shares in issue.

Other forms of capital

When considering the business of a sole trader you saw that the owner could increase the funds available in the business not only by investing more money him/herself, but also perhaps by acquiring a loan from a bank. Companies can also raise extra finance in a similar way. However, they are also able to raise loan capital by the issue of **debentures** that can be traded in the market in the same way as a share.

The debenture document sets out the capital value, the interest rate payable, the date the loan is redeemable and any security for the loan. The capital value of the debenture is expressed in nominal value terms, usually in multiples of £100. The interest rate payable on the debenture is set at a fixed percentage of this nominal value. It is important to remember that debentures are loans to the company, not part of its share capital. Because of this, debenture interest is shown as a charge against profits within the statement of comprehensive income, rather than an appropriation of profits. The only difficulty with debentures is that they are often issued at a value above or below nominal value. Thus a £100 debenture could be issued at £99. This means that on issue the cash received by the company will only be £99; that is, the debenture has been issued at a discount of £1. Note, though, that the amount payable by the company on redemption, repayment, of the loan will be £100. In the same way that shares are entered into the company's ledger accounts at nominal value so are the debentures. The question to answer is 'How do we account for the £1 discount on issue?'

Activity 8.5

A company makes an issue of £10,000 6% debentures at £99. Show the entries in the ledger accounts, including cash, to account for this issue.

Answer

The debentures account is used to record the nominal value of the debentures issued as for share capital.

6% DEBENTURES ACCOUNT

		Issue	10,000

CASH ACCOUNT

Debentures	9,900		

The above entries do not maintain duality. A debit of £100 is required to be made somewhere in the ledgers.

This £100 discount on issue can be considered as an expense of making the debenture issue. Therefore we have:

DEBENTURE DISCOUNT ACCOUNT

Issue	100		

Like all other expenses this debenture discount should be written off to the income statement by debiting the income statement.

DEBENTURE DISCOUNT ACCOUNT

Issue	100	Statement of comprehensive income	100

There is also another possibility for the write-off of this discount on issue which is permitted by the Companies Act in the UK and that is to charge it against the share premium account if there is one.

Return on shares and debentures

Any investment is made with the expectation of some form of return. For the sole trader this return was in the form of profits that he/she was free to withdraw from the business. In the same way, the profits of a company belong to the shareholders and they will expect some return on their capital invested. This return is made in the form of a dividend payment. These dividend payments are usually made in two instalments, the interim dividend and the final dividend.

Activity 8.6

From your set of company accounts (see Activity 8.2) identify the interim and final dividend payments made.

Answer

The dividends identified were probably expressed as so many pence per share. For example, if the dividend was declared as 6p per share and there were 100,000 £1 shares in issue, then the total dividend payment made would be £6,000. Note that the dividend is calculated by reference to the nominal value of shares issued.

The interim dividend is generally paid halfway through the financial period and the final dividend, an additional payment, is proposed at the year end. This means that the shareholders will vote at the annual general meeting on the payment of this final dividend as proposed by the directors and, after a vote in favour, the dividend will be paid. Note that this means that all final, proposed, dividends are unpaid at the year end. It has long been UK accounting practice to include this proposed dividend as a current liability in the statement of financial position. However, International Accounting Standards now explicitly state that dividends declared after the statement of financial position date, i.e. proposed dividends, should not be recognised as a liability at the statement of financial position date. This will be a change of accounting practice for all UK companies who report under IASs.

The return made to the debenture holder is in the form of interest at the rate specified on the debenture. In the example at Activity 8.5, the interest payable was 6% on a nominal debenture value of £10,000. Thus the company will be required to pay £600 in interest.

Activity 8.7

Is the interest payable on the debenture an expense of trading for the company?
Is the dividend payable to the shareholders an expense of trading for the company?

Answer

For the debenture interest the answer is yes. This interest is treated in exactly the same way as the interest on a loan for a sole trader, as an expense of trading.

The dividend payable, though, is not an expense. Remember the drawings of a sole trader are not an expense but an extraction of capital invested.

For a company, the dividend payment is shown as a change in equity (which we dealt with in Chapter 2), as the following example demonstrates.

Example 8.3	Alpha Ltd made a net profit before the payment of interest and dividends of £35,000 in year X. There were £10,000 6% debentures in issue and 100,000 £1 ordinary shares in issue at the beginning of year X and retained profits were £20,000. No further issues of shares or debentures were made during the year. The interim dividend declared was 3p per share and the final dividend 4p per share. The interest and dividend payments are shown in the statement of comprehensive income, as follows.

STATEMENT OF COMPREHENSIVE INCOME FOR ALPHA LTD

Profit	35,000
Interest on debentures 6%	600
Net profit	34,400

Statement of changes in equity

	Share capital	Retained profits	Total
Balance at beginning of year	100,000	20,000	120,000
Net profit for the year		34,400	34,400
Interim dividend 3p = 3,000			
Final dividend 4p = 4,000		(7,000)	(7,000)
Balance at end of year	100,000	47,400	147,400

Financing a company

This chapter has shown us so far that a company can raise capital by issuing ordinary shares, preference shares and debentures. There are many different forms of these instruments, e.g. options, warrants, deep discounted bonds, interest rate swaps, but we leave these to later, more detailed, studies of finance and financial management. However, in addition to companies using these various instruments to raise finance they also use bank overdraft facilities and their own earnings, in the form of non-distributed profit, to provide finance. We look at the non-distributed profit in the section on reserves (p. 150)

*A*ctivity 8.8	Pump Ltd, a newly forming company, estimates it will need capital of £1m so that it can remain in business. It estimates its profits per annum before interest payments and dividends as £100,000 in the first year with an estimated 2% increase year on year. It proposes to issue 500,000 50p ordinary shares at a premium of 40p, 220,000 4% £2 preference shares, and to raise the remaining capital it needs from an issue of 3% debentures. Show the capital section of the statement of financial position and the non-current liabilities assuming estimated profit is realised, the statement of changes in equity and the statement of comprehensive income as far as the information provided permits for the first two years of trading. The interim and final dividends for Year 1 are expected to be 2p and 3p, and for Year 2 4p and 5p. Assume the final dividend is paid before the year end.

Answer

STATEMENT OF COMPREHENSIVE INCOME FOR PUMP LTD

	Year 1	Year 2
Profit	100,000	102,000
Interest on debentures 3%	3,300	3,300
Net profit	96,700	98,700

Statement of changes in equity

		Share capital	Share premium	Accounting profits	Total
Balance as at 1.1.Year 1		690,000	200,000		890,000
Profit for Year 1				96,700	96,700
Preference dividend				(17,600)	
Interim dividend	2p			(10,000)	
Final dividend	3p			(15,000)	(42,600)
Balance as at 31.12. Year 1		690,000	200,000	54,100	944,100
Profit for Year 2				98,700	98,700
Preference dividend				(17,600)	
Interim dividend	4p			(20,000)	
Final dividend	5p			(25,000)	(62,600)
Balance as at 31.12. Year 2		690,000	200,000	90,200	980,200

CAPITAL BALANCE SHEET SECTION PUMP LTD

	Year 1	Year 2
Capital 500,000 50p ordinary shares	250,000	250,000
220,000 £2 4% preference shares	440,000	440,000
Share premium account	200,000	200,000
Profit	54,100	90,200
	944,100	980,200
Non-current liabilities		
3% debentures	110,000	110,000

There are several issues to note in the above activity. First, you needed to calculate the amount of debentures issued. Ordinary share raised £450,000 (including the share premium remember, thus 500,000 × 90p), preference shares raised £440,000 (220,000 × £2) and therefore the remaining amount (£1m – 890,000 = £110,000) was required from the debenture issue.

In Year 2, the profit after dividends of £36,100 is in addition to that already accumulated at Year 1, £54,100.

The percentage payable on the preference shares and debentures is applied to the monetary amount whereas the dividend payable is calculated by reference to the number of shares.

Taxation in company accounts

If you look at the statement of comprehensive income (income statement) in your set of company accounts you will notice that there is another item that did not appear in the statement of comprehensive income of a sole trader, and that is **taxation**.

Companies are separate legal taxable entities, unlike a sole trader's business, and are subject to taxation, corporation tax, which will be shown in the statement of comprehensive income. A sole trader does not show taxation in his/her accounts as the taxation authorities view the earnings of the business of the sole trader as personal income and tax accordingly. The calculation of corporation tax is complicated and based on taxable profits, which are not the same as accounting profits. At this level of study you will be given a figure to use as the taxation charge for the year. This tax will not be payable until nine months after the end of the accounting year, so it will be shown as a liability in the statement of financial position (balance sheet), and an expense in the statement of comprehensive income.

Reserves

If you look at the statement of financial position (balance sheet) in your set of company accounts you will notice that the share capital is entered under the heading, Capital and Reserves. **Reserves** that you have met so far consist of accumulated profits of the business, that is, profits that have not been extracted from the business by the shareholders but have been left as further investment, and share premium that was an initial investment by shareholders. These reserves are further classified into capital or revenue reserves. Share premium is an example of a capital reserve, initial capital invested by shareholders. Accumulated profit is an example of a revenue reserve, capital earned from the trading of the business. Another distinction between capital and revenue reserves is that revenue reserves can be distributed in the form of dividends; capital reserves must be retained within the business and cannot be distributed in the form of dividends. This is to protect creditors. Share capital and capital reserves are sometimes known as the creditors' buffer, i.e. the base capital of the company that must not be repaid to shareholders except in very exceptional circumstances.

Another reserve that you might see in your set of accounts is a revaluation reserve. When we considered the non-current assets of a business in our double entry system we tended to record them at historical cost or what the purchaser had paid for them. Look back to Chapter 5 and the details in the Mr Bean examples to revise this. However, there might be circumstances when recording the historical cost or purchase price of the non-current asset does not provide very relevant information to the user of the accounts, as we discussed in Chapter 2.

*A*ctivity 8.9   Identify a circumstance when recording a non-current asset at historical cost might not be the most relevant to the user.

Answer

When the asset has increased in value as the owner has held it due to circumstances outside his/her control. For example, business assets such as land and buildings tend to increase in value in the same way as your house price does. Providing the information on this increase in value is highly relevant, as the owner could if he/she wished sell the asset and increase the business worth. Knowledge of this unrealised, until actual sale, worth is useful both to owners and those who wish to invest in the business as well as other users of accounts.

Common practice has arisen and company law permits us to carry assets at their revalued amount, but we need to know how to account for this increase in value.

Activity 8.10

Company A purchased land in 20X1 for £10,000 for cash. As at 31.12.X5 the company estimates that the land could be sold for £50,000. Identify how this increase in value could be recorded in the company's books (ledgers).

Answer

The land would have been originally recorded in the books at its original purchase price of £10,000. The increase in value the company wishes to reflect is £40,000. This is the amount of the revaluation. Quite simply the fixed asset account of land is shown at £50,000 and the uplift in value, the revaluation, is credited to a revaluation reserve as follows:

LAND ACCOUNT

1.1.X5	Balance b/d	10,000			
31.12.X5	Revaluation reserve	40,000	31.12.X5	Balance c/d	50,000
		50,000			50,000
1.1.X6	Balance b/d	50,000			

REVALUATION ACCOUNT

31.12.X5	Balance c/d	40,000	31.12.X5	Land	40,000
		40,000			40,000
			1.1.X6	Balance b/d	40,000

The revaluation reserve, the £40,000 in the activity above, is shown in the statement of financial position under the capital and reserves section and is a capital un-realised reserve. We will consider revaluation reserves again in Chapter 13.

The following activity brings together various issues that you have come across in your studies so far.

Activity 8.11

The trial balance of Beta Ltd as at 31.12.X5, before adjustment for any of the items listed in the notes, is as follows:

	Dr	Cr
Issued £1 ordinary shares		50,000
Share premium		5,000
Buildings (cost)	55,000	
Fixtures and fittings (cost)	27,000	
Vehicles (cost)	15,000	
Depreciation as at 1.1 X5		
Buildings		3,300
Fixtures and fittings		6,750
Vehicles		5,400
Sales		111,000
Purchases	75,000	
Wages and salaries	12,000	
Other expenses	8,000	
Inventory 1.1.X5	2,500	
6% debentures		30,000
Debenture interest paid	900	
Interim dividend paid	2,000	
Trade receivables and trade payables	28,000	15,000
Accumulated profits 1.1.X5		9,500
Cash	10,550	
	235,950	235,950

The following notes are to be taken into account:

1 Inventory as at 31.12.X5 is £3,400 valued at cost.

2 Depreciation is to be provided for as follows:

  – Buildings 2% per annum straight line

  – Fixtures and fittings 25% straight line

  – Vehicles 20% reducing balance.

3 Corporation tax for the year is estimated at £3,500.

4 Fittings originally costing £2,400 on which depreciation of £1,200 had been provided were sold on 31.12.X5 for £950. No entries have been made in the accounts for the sale nor has any cash been received.

Prepare the statement of comprehensive income, statement of changes in equity and statement of financial position for Beta Ltd for the year ended 31.12.X5.

Answer

BETA LTD
INCOME STATEMENT FOR THE YEAR ENDED 31.12.X5

Sales		111,000
Opening inventory	2,500	
Purchases	75,000	
	77,500	
Closing stock	3,400	74,100
Gross profit		36,900
Wages and salaries	12,000	
Other expenses	8,000	
Debenture interest	1,800	
Depreciation:		
Buildings	1,100	
Fixtures and fittings	6,150	
Vehicles	1,920	9,170
Loss on sale	250	31,220
Profit before tax		5,680
Taxation		3,500
Profit after tax		2,180

BETA LTD
STATEMENT OF CHANGES IN EQUITY

	Share capital	*Share premium*	*Accumulated profits*	*Total*
Balance as at 1.1.X5	50,000	5,000	9,500	64,500
Profit for the year			2,180	2,180
Dividends			(2,000)	(2,000)
Balance as at 31.12.X5	50,000	5,000	9,680	64,680

BETA LTD
BALANCE SHEET AS AT 31.12.X5

	Cost	*Depreciation*	*Net book value*
Non-current assets			
Buildings	55,000	4,400	50,600
Fixtures and fittings	24,600	11,700	12,900
Vehicles	15,000	7,320	7,680
	94,600	23,420	71,180
Current assets			
Inventory		3,400	
Trade receivables		28,000	
Trade receivables (fixtures)		950	
Cash		10,550	
		42,900	

Current liabilities

Trade payables	15,000		
Taxation	3,500		
Debenture interest	900	19,400	23,500
			94,680

Non-current liabilities

6% debentures	30,000
	64,680

Capital and reserves

Ordinary shares of £1	50,000
Share premium	5,000
Accumulated profits	9,680
	64,680

Note that we have used the format non-current assets + (current assets – current liabilities) – non-current liabilities = equity for the statement of financial position in this example.

Format presentation

As you have been looking at your set of company accounts you may have noticed that the presentation of the statement of comprehensive income and statement of financial position are slightly different from the ones we have used so far. The Companies Act UK and the EU Fourth Directive actually specify four types of **format presentation** that can be used for the statement of comprehensive income of a company and two for the statement of financial position. However, the IASs are not as specific as UK law or the EU directives on the format for the statement of comprehensive income and statement of financial position. We will use for our purposes at this level of study simplified versions of the Fourth Directive formats, which also take account of the IAS regulations.

STATEMENT OF COMPREHENSIVE INCOME FOR THE YEAR ENDED 20YZ

Turnover/Revenue		X
Cost of sales		(X)
Gross profit		X
Distribution costs	(X)	
Administration costs	(X)	(X)
Operating profit		X
Income from investments		X
Interest paid and similar charges		(X)
Profit on ordinary activities before tax		X
Tax on ordinary activities		(X)
Profit on ordinary activities after tax		X

Extraordinary charges	X	
Tax	(X)	(X)
Profit for year		X

This presentation of the statement of comprehensive income requires the analysis of expenses under three headings: cost of sales, distribution and administration. Wages and salaries will have to be analysed across these three headings, as will depreciation.

STATEMENT OF FINANCIAL POSITION AS AT 20YZ

ASSETS

Non-current assets

Intangible assets		X
Property, plant and equipment		X
Investments		X
		X

Current assets

Inventory	X	
Trade receivables	X	
Cash at bank and in hand	X	
		X
TOTAL ASSETS		**X**

EQUITY

Capital and reserves

Called up share capital	X	
Share premium account	X	
Revalution reserve	X	
Other reserves	X	
Retained earnings	X	X

Non-current liabilities

Loans		X

Current liabilities

Trade payables	X	
Other	X	X
TOTAL EQUITY AND LIABILITIES		**X**

This format is therefore:

Non-current assets + current assets = equity + non-current liabilities + current liabilities.

This is the format for the statement of financial position recommended by IAS 1 'Presentation of Financial Statements', but remember it is *not required* by IAS 1. You will find that the company accounts you look at will not all be presented in the same format but you should be able to clearly identify the totals for non-current assets, current assets, equity, non-current liabilities and current liabilities and put these together in the various formats of the accounting equation.

You might also have noticed two more statements in your set of accounts in addition to the statement of comprehensive income and statement of financial position: the statement of cash flows (cash flow statement) and the statement of changes in equity. The statement of cash flows we will deal with in Chapter 10 and we will look further at the statement of changes in equity in Chapter 13 (see Chapter 2 also).

Exemplar accounts

We include here for you an exemplar of the presentation of the financial statements. The company we have chosen is Tesco plc and we have summarised the accounts for you.

STATEMENT OF COMPREHENSIVE INCOME YEAR ENDED 23 FEBRUARY 2008

	2008 (£m)	2007 (£m)
Revenue	47,298	42,641
Cost of sales	(43,668)	(39,401)
Pensions adjustment		258
Impairment of the Gerrards Cross site		(35)
Gross profit	3,630	3,463
Administrative expenses	(1,027)	(907)
Profit arising on property related items	188	92
Operating profit	2,791	2,648
Share of post-tax profits of joint ventures and associates	75	106
Profit on sale of investments in associates		25
Finance income	187	90
Finance costs	(250)	(216)
Profit before tax	2,803	2,653
Taxation	(673)	(772)
Profit for the year from continuing operations	2,130	1,881
Profit for the year from discontinued operations		18
Profit for the year	2,130	1.899

STATEMENT OF FINANCIAL POSITION AS AT 23 FEBRUARY 2008

	2008 (£m)	2007 (£m)
Non-current assets		
Goodwill and other intangible assets	2,336	2,045

Property, plant and equipment	19,787	16,976
Investment property	1,112	856
Investments in joint ventures and associates	305	314
Other investments	4	8
Other	320	32
	23,864	20,231
Current assets		
Inventories	2,430	1,931
Trade and other receivables	1,311	1,079
Derivative financial instruments	97	108
Current tax assets	6	8
Short term investments	360	
Cash and cash equivalents	1,788	1,042
	5,992	4,168
Non-current assets classified as held for sale	308	408
	6,300	4,576
Current liabilities		
Trade and other payables	(7,277)	(6,046)
Financial liabilities	(2,527)	(1,640)
Current tax liabilities	(455)	(461)
Provisions	(4)	(4)
	(10,263)	(8,152)
Net current liabilities	(3,963)	(3,576)
Non-current liabilities		
Financial liabilities	(6,294)	(4,545)
Post-employment benefit obligations	(838)	(950)
Other non-current payables	(42)	(29)
Deferred tax liabilities	(802)	(535)
Provisions	(23)	(25)
	(7,999)	(6,084)
NET ASSETS	11,902	10,571
EQUITY		
Share capital	393	397
Share premium	4,511	4,376
Other reserves	40	40
Retained earnings	6,871	5,693
Equity attributable to equity holders	11,815	10,506
Minority interests	87	65
TOTAL EQUITY	11,902	10,571

For the statement of financial position Tesco has used the format:

Non-current assets + (Current assets – Current liabilities) – non-current liabilities = Equity

23,864 + (6,300 – 10,263) – 7,999 = 11,902.

They could just have easily set this out as:

Non-current assets + Current assets = Equity + Non-current liabilities + Current liabilities

23,864 + 6,300 = 11,902 + 7,999 + 10,263

You also should have noted that the previous year's figures are shown on the financial statements to aid comparison between the years. We will return to this comparison in Chapter 12 when we deal with interpretation of financial statements.

We would recommend that you look at several sets of financial statements on the internet. Our suggestions would be:

Adidas at **www.adidas-group.corporate-publications.com**

Shell at **www.annualreview.shell/investor.com**

McDonald's at **www.computershare.com/mcdonalds**

Vodafone at **www.vodafone.com/static/annual_report**

Activity 8.12   Identify the presentational statement of financial position format used by Adidas, Shell, McDonald's and Vodafone in their published financial statements.

Answer   Adidas in its statements for 31 December 2007 uses:

Current assets + Non-current assets = Current liabilities + Non-current liabilities + Equity

This is the format recommended in IAS 1.

Shell in its financial statements for 2007 uses:

Non-current assets +Current assets = Non-current liabilities + Current liabilities + Equity

McDonald's in its financial statements for 31 December 2007 uses:

Current assets + Non-current assets = Current liabilities + Non-current liabilities + Equity

Vodafone in its financial statements for 31 March 2008 uses:

Non-current assets + Current assets = Equity + Non-current liabilities + Current liabilities

---

All of these four are using the format we would recommend to you of Assets = Equity + Liabilities, but you must be able to read financial statements that use any format.

You might also note when you look at the financial statements of real entities that both the company and the group are referred to and often you will have the financial statements for both presented. We will explain the issue of group accounts in Chapter 9.

Other entities

Introduction

We have looked in some detail in this chapter at accounts for companies. There are many other types of organisations/entities that have a need to keep records and prepare information similar to that of companies. We have referred to clubs and societies in Chapter 7, but charities and public sector organisations also need similar information. Statements of comprehensive income and statements of financial position for these types of organisations are prepared using the same principles and concepts as for companies, but of course the Companies Act does not apply to them. Charity accounts have to be prepared in accordance with the Charities Acts and national governments provide detailed requirements for the public sector. We will also look at partnerships and preparation of accounts for them in this section. All these other entities generally use the format of Assets – Liabilities = Capital for their statement of financial position, as this is more useful to them as it gives the figure of working capital.

Clubs and societies

Below, we provide a fully worked example for the preparation of a set of accounts for a club. We advise you to work through this example diligently before you try to answer the question on clubs at the end of the chapter. You will remember that we initially looked at these in Chapter 3.

Example 8.4

The following information is extracted from the records of Mudby Rugby Club for the year ended 31.12.X5:

	1.1.X5	31.12.X5
Bar inventory	16,200	17,860
Creditors for bar purchases	8,600	8,100
Creditors for other expenses	230	1,240

Summary of bank account for the year ended 31.12.X5:

Balance 1.1.X5	16,290	Bar purchases	120,650
Subscriptions received	24,530	Bar wages	15,230
Bar sales	146,320	Other salaries and wages	5,340
Interest on investments	1,230	Rent and rates of club premises	5,670
		General expenses	8,760
		Cost of fittings and furniture	7,680
		Balance 31.12.X5	25,040
	188,370		188,370

Example 8.4
continued

Other information available at the year end is as follows:

▶ Rent and rates have only been paid for three-quarters of the year.

▶ Investments held by the club at 1.1.X5 had several years ago cost £30,750.

▶ Fixtures and fittings held at 1.1.X5 had cost £42,500 on 1.1.X2 and all fixtures and fittings are to be depreciated at 10% on original cost.

Prepare a bar trading account and an income and expenditure account for year ended 31.12.X5 and a statement of financial position as at that date in good form.

A bar trading account simply groups together all the income and expenditure relating to the bar to see if it has been operating at a profit.

BAR TRADING ACCOUNT FOR MUDBY RUGBY CLUB FOR THE YEAR ENDED 31.12.X5

Bar sales		146,320
Opening inventory	16,200	
Bar purchases (120,650 − 8,600 + 8,100)	120,150	
	136,350	
Closing inventory	17,860	118,490
Gross profit on bar		27,830
Bar wages		15,230
Net profit on bar		12,600

INCOME AND EXPENDITURE ACCOUNT FOR THE YEAR ENDED 3.12.X5

Subscriptions		24,530
Bar net profit		12,600
Interest on investments		1,230
		38,360
Other salaries and wages	5,340	
Rent and rates (5,670 + 1,890 for last quarter)	7,560	
General expenses (8,760 − 230 + 1,240)	9,770	
Depreciation of fixtures and fittings		
(10% × 42,500 + 7,680)	5,018	27,688
		10,672

STATEMENT OF FINANCIAL POSITION AS AT 31.12.X5

	Cost	Depreciation	Net book value
Non-current assets			
Fixtures and fittings	50,180	17,768 (W1)	32,412
Investments			30,750
			63,162
Current assets − inventory bar	17,860		
Cash at bank	25,040	42,900	
Current liabilities − rent and rates	1,890		
Creditors other expenses	1,240		

Example 8.4 continued	Bar purchases	8,100	11,230	31,670
				94,832
	Accumulated fund 1.1.X5			84,160 (W2)
	Surplus			10,672
				94,832

W1 total cost value of fixtures and fittings £42,500 + £7,680 = £50,180
Depreciation 10% on £50,180 = £5,018 for Year 31.12.X5
Depreciation at 10% for 3 years on £42,500 = £12,750
Total depreciation £12,750 + £5,018 = £17,768
W2 Net book value 1.1.X5 fixtures and fittings

(£42,500 – £12,750 depreciation)	29,750
Investments	30,750
Inventory	16,200
Bank	16,290
Creditors (£8,600 + £230)	(8,830)
	84,160

Charities

As we stated earlier **charity accounts** have to be prepared in accordance with the charities acts. In this text we do not intend to provide full instruction on the preparation of charity accounts but we have included an exemplar set of financial statements for Oxfam.

STATEMENT OF FINANCIAL POSITION AT 30 APRIL 2007 OXFAM

	2007 (£m)	2006 (£m)
Fixed assets		
Tangible assets	16.6	17.1
Investments	4.4	4.4
	21	21.5
Current assets		
Stocks	1.5	1.6
Trade receivables	20.4	25.5
Cash at bank and in hand	75.6	73.8
	97.5	100.9
Trade payable amounts falling due within one year	(18)	(14)
Net current assets	79.5	86.9
Total assets less current liabilities	100.5	108.4
Trade payable amounts falling due after one year	(1.3)	(2)

Provisions for liabilities and charges	(8.5)	(7.9)
Net assets before pension scheme liabilities	90.7	98.5
Pension scheme liability	(20.1)	(23.3)
Net assets	70.6	75.2
Funds		
General reserve	48.6	47.4
Charitable unrestricted funds	15	19.3
Pension reserves	(20.1)	(23.3)
Endowment funds	2.6	2.6
Restricted funds	24.5	29.2
Total funds	70.6	75.2

SUMMARY INCOME AND EXPENDITURE ACCOUNT 30 APRIL 2007 OXFAM

	2007 (£m)	2006 (£m)
Income	290.7	310.5
Expenditure	297.2	298
(Deficit)/Surplus of income over expenditure before realised losses and gains	(6.5)	12.5
Realised loss on disposal of investment		(0.1)
(Deficit)/surplus of income over expenditure	(6.5)	12.4
Transfers (to)/from other funds		
Transfer from endowment funds		0.2
Transfer (to)/from restricted funds	4.6	(3.5)
Transfer (to)/from unrestricted funds	4.3	0.4
Transfer (to)/from pension funds	(1.2)	(1.4)
General reserves at 30 April 2006	47.4	39.3
General reserves at 30 April 2007	48.6	47.4

Activity 8.13   Identify the differences in the financial statements of Oxfam, the charity, and Tesco, the company.

Answer   Several of the differences are due to the fact that a charity is not set up to make a profit, whereas a company is. Thus the charity uses an income and expenditure account in place of a statement of comprehensive income (profit and loss account). The income and expenditure account of the charity is still prepared using accruals accounting. The (deficit)/surplus on the income and expenditure account is then transferred to the funds of the charity, which are similar to the reserves of a company.

The charity statement of financial position does not show any shares, as of course a charity does not have shareholders. All funds donated to the charity are identified as restricted or unrestricted funds.

The statement of financial position format for the charity is similar to that of a company except the terminology is not in international form, e.g debtors is used not trade receivables, and fixed assets is used not non-current assets.

Public sector

The preparation of accounts for the public sector will depend upon national government legislation and some (although now a minority) will still be prepared using cash accounting instead of accruals accounting. We do not intend to provide further detail on public sector accounting in this text but you will find it useful to look at the final accounts of a public sector organisation in your own country and compare them with the financial statements of a company, charity or club.

Partnerships

Introduction

In Chapters 5, 6 and 7 we dealt primarily with the accounts of a sole trader. However, it is extremely difficult for a sole trader business to grow beyond a certain size. One method of growing a business is to form a partnership, whereby two or more individuals run the business.

Benefits of a partnership

This type of business arrangement has several benefits:

► Capital within the business can be increased as it is injected by each partner.

► Each partner brings their own, often complimentary, skills to the business. For example, one partner may have marketing skills, another financial, and another may be the producer of the items sold.

► Decisions and responsibilities within the business are shared.

► Lenders may be more inclined to provide resources to the business given the increased skills and expertise available from the partners as compared with that of a sole trader.

Like a sole trader, partners are liable to the full extent of their personal assets for the debts of the business unless they form a limited partnership, which rarely occurs.

Partnership Act 1890 UK

Within the UK the law relating to partnerships is still defined by the Partnership Act of 1890, which was only partly updated in 2002. In law there is no maximum to the number of partners permitted within a business. The Act is invoked when no partnership agreement is in place for a business. A partnership agreement is required to identify how the partnership will operate and, in particular, to set down the financial arrangements between partners.

Activity 8.14   Identify financial factors that should be specified within a partnership agreement.

Answer   You should have identified the need for the following financial arrangements:

1 How much capital is to be introduced by each partner.
2 How profits are to be shared between the partners. This will include:

  ▶ Any remuneration payable to a partner for the specific work done
  ▶ The rate at which interest will be paid on capital, if any
  ▶ If drawings are to be permitted and what interest rate will be applied to them, if any
  ▶ How the remaining profit after deductions for partner salaries and interest on capital and addition for interest on drawings have been applied will be divided between the partners.

3 How goodwill should be valued
4 Arrangements covering the retirement or death of a partner
5 Arrangements for the introduction of a new partner.

You may not have identified all of the items that we did in our answer but we hope you at least identified (1) and (2).

Goodwill in partnerships

You probably did not identify this item in Activity 8.14 as we have not dealt with this issue so far. The value of a business, or what it could be sold for, is often greater than the addition of the individual net assets of the business. The difference between the value of a business' separable net assets and what the business could be sold for is known as **goodwill in partnerships**. Goodwill occurs in all businesses, not just partnerships. The sole trader will expect to build up goodwill in his/her business as he/she trades. It is an intangible asset as, unlike other assets such as a building, it cannot be touched. It is also very difficult to value and the only time we can place a reliable measure on it is when a business is sold.

Activity 8.15   Identify means by which a trader could build up goodwill in his/her business

Answer

Basically we need to identify those reasons why a customer would trade with a business. These could be as follows:

- ▶ Good location of the business
- ▶ Established customer base resulting in sales
- ▶ Established reputation or brand (e.g. Virgin or Coca Cola)
- ▶ Licences for sale of particular goods
- ▶ Experienced and customer-focused workforce
- ▶ Existing contracts
- ▶ Trademarks or patents developed.

You may well have identified other issues.

Why do we need to value goodwill in a partnership?

If a partner wishes to retire from a business or a new partner wishes to join then effectively the business is changing in ownership. The retiring partner will wish to ensure that he/she takes from the business his/her share of it, i.e. his/her share of what the business could be sold for. A new partner joining cannot simply be given the net assets of the business, he/she must pay for his/her share, including a share of the goodwill, or the other partners will have given the new partner something for nothing.

Partnership accounts

Partners will contribute capital to start up a business in the same way that a sole trader does. The profit made in the business will belong to the partners and they will share in these profits in a specific ratio. As the partners may well have contributed different amounts of capital and wish to withdraw different amounts then it would be equitable to give and charge interest on these before the remaining profits are allocated. As partners generally work in the business, to maintain equity between partners they will agree appropriate salaries to be paid, but these will be allocated from the profits made. All transactions between the business and the partners, except for the introduction of capital and goodwill transactions, are dealt with through the partners' current accounts. This is to ensure that we maintain a record of the capital contributed by each partner.

The following activity illustrates **partners' capital accounts** and **partners' current accounts**.

*A*ctivity 8.16

Bill and Ben form a partnership on 1 October 20X8. Bill contributes £50,000 in capital and Ben £40,000 in capital to the partnership. They have a partnership agreement that states that profits will be shared in the ratio Bill 60% and Ben 40% after providing for:

- ▶ An annual salary to Ben of £10,000
- ▶ Interest of 4% payable on capital balances at the beginning of the accounting year
- ▶ Interest charged on total drawings for the year at 5%.

▶

Drawings for the accounting year ended 30 September 20X9 were Bill £15,000 and Ben £8,000. Profits for the year before any of the above transactions were £95,000.

Required

Show the transactions in the partners' capital and current accounts for the year ended 30 September 20X9.

Answer

CAPITAL ACCOUNTS

	Bill	Ben		Bill	Ben
30.9.09 Balance c/d	50,000	40,000	1.10.X8 Capital introduced	50,000	40,000
	50,000	40,000		50,000	40,000
			1.10.X9 Balance b/d	50,000	40,000

CURRENT ACCOUNTS

	Bill	Ben		Bill	Ben
Interest on drawings	750	400	Salary		10,000
Drawings	15,000	8,000	Interest on capital	2,000	1,600
30.9.x9 Balance c/d	35,780	36,220	Share of profits (see note below)	49,530	33,020
	51,530	44,620		51,530	44,620
			1.10.09 Balance b/d	35,780	36,220

Note

Profits for the year			95,000
Interest on drawings	Bill	750	
	Ben	400	1,150
			96,150
Salary	Ben		10,000
Interest on capital	Bill	2,000	
	Ben	1,600	3,600
Profit available to share			82,550
60%	Bill	49,530	
40%	Ben	33,020	82,550

This note is usually shown as the profit appropriation account.

Note in the example for Bill and Ben that transactions relating to drawings, salary and interest are dealt with in the current accounts not the capital accounts of the partners.

Activity 8.17

Anne and Sally form a partnership on 1 October 20X8. Anne contributes £80,000 in capital and Sally £60,000 in capital to the partnership. They have a partnership agreement that states that profits will be shared in the ratio Anne 75% and Sally 25% after providing for:

▶ An annual salary to Anne of £10,000 and Sally £20,000
▶ Interest of 4% payable on capital balances at the beginning of the accounting year
▶ Interest charged on total drawings for the year at 5%.

Drawings for the accounting year ended 30 September 20X9 were Anne £15,000 and Sally £5,000. Profits for the year before any of the above transactions were £35,000.

Required
Show the transactions in the partners' capital and current accounts for the year ended 30 September 20X9.

Answer

CAPITAL ACCOUNTS

	Anne	Sally		Anne	Sally
30.9.X9 Balance c/d	80,000	60,000	1.10.X8 Capital introduced	80,000	60,000
	80,000	60,000		80,000	60,000
			1.10.X9 Balance b/d	80,000	60,000

CURRENT ACCOUNTS

	Anne	Sally		Anne	Sally
Interest on drawings	750	250	Salary	10,000	20,000
Drawings	15,000	5,000	Interest on capital	3,200	2,400
Share of loss (see note below)	1,200	400	30.9.X9 Balance c/d	3,750	
30.9.X9 Balance c/d		16,750			
	16,950	22,400		16,950	22,400
1.10.X9 Balance b/d	3,750		1.10.X9 Balance b/d		16,750

Note

Profits for the year			35,000
Interest on drawings:	Anne	750	
	Sally	250	1,000
			34,000
Salary:	Anne	10,000	
	Sally	20,000	
Interest on capital:	Anne	3,200	
	Sally	2,400	35,600
Loss to share:			(1,600)
75% Anne		(1,200)	
25% Sally		(400)	(1,600)

In this partnership, after the transactions for interest on drawings, interest on capital, and salaries there is a loss. This must be shared between the partners in the same ratio that a profit would be. Also in this partnership, because Anne has drawn out more than the total of her salary and net interest then she is overdrawn on her current account.

Retirement of a partner

As we have stated, when a partner retires from a partnership then we must value the goodwill in the partnership and ensure that this is allocated between the partners (in their capital accounts) before the retirement. This is to ensure that the retiring partner extracts his/her correct share from the partnership, i.e. his/her share of what it is 'worth'.

Activity 8.18

A, B and C are in partnership sharing profits in the ratio 5:3:2. As at 30 September 20X8 the balances on the partners' accounts are as follows:

Capital accounts	A	40,000
	B	30,000
	C	38,000
Current accounts	A	12,500
	B	9,600
	C	17,100

A wishes to retire on 30 September 20X8 and at this date the goodwill of the business is valued at £120,000.

Required

Show the partners' accounts immediately after the retirement of A identifying the amount transferred to A's loan account on retirement. After A's retirement profits are to be shared evenly between B and C. Goodwill is to be removed from the books of the partnership after the retirement.

Answer

CAPITAL ACCOUNTS

	A	B	C		A	B	C
Goodwill removed		60,000	60,000	30.9.X8 Balance	40,000	30,000	38,000
Loan account A	100,000			Goodwill	60,000	36,000	24,000
Balance c/d		6,000	2,000				
	100,000	66,000	62,000		100,000	66,000	62,000
				1.10.X8 balance b/d		6,000	2,000

CURRENT ACCOUNTS

	A	B	C		A	B	C
Loan account A	12,500			30.9.X8 Balance	12,500	9,600	17,100
30.9.X8 balance c/d		9,600	17,100				
	12,500	9,600	17,100		12,500	9,600	17,100
				1.10.X8 Balance b/d		9,600	17,100

In total A has left £112,500 on loan to the partnership.

Note in the above accounts that goodwill was brought in, in the old profit share ratios, and removed in the new profit share ratios.

Year-end accounts for a partnership

A partnership will prepare year-end accounts in the same way that a sole trader does. The only difference is that in the partnership there will be an appropriation of profit section in the statement of comprehensive income and/both capital and current accounts to record in the statement of financial position. The following activity involves the preparation of year-end accounts for a partnership and the retirement of a partner.

Activity 8.19

Rod, Harry and James are in partnership sharing profits in the ratio 2:2:1. Interest on drawings is charged at 6% on total drawings for the year and interest on capital is payable on the opening capital balances for the year at 5%. Salaries payable to the partners for a year are Rod £20,000, Harry £15,000 and James £25,000. At the year end 31.12.20X9 Rod wishes to retire. At that date goodwill in the partnership is valued at £100,000 but is not to remain in the books after the retirement of Rod. Rod agrees to leave half of the amount due to him on loan to the partnership. At 31 December 20X9 a loan is taken out with the bank for £65,000. After Rod's retirement Harry and James agree to share profits in the ratio 5:3. The trial balance for the partnership as at 31.12.20X9, before any of the above is accounted for, is as follows:

Trial balance as at 31.12.20X9 for Rod, Harry and James

	Dr	Cr
Sales		517,554
Purchases	256,700	
Stock as at 1 January 20X9	22,300	
Wages	94,000	
Rates and insurance	18,600	
Electricity and gas	9,450	
Vehicle expenses	5,700	

Capital accounts:	Rod		60,000
	Harry		35,000
	James		30,000
Current accounts:	Rod		1,240
	Harry		1,540
	James	650	
Drawings:	Rod	18,600	
	Harry	12,000	
	James	19,000	
Premises		180,000	
Furniture and fittings at cost		12,400	
Vehicles at cost		15,600	
Depreciation premises			
1 January 20X9			9,000
Depreciation furniture and fittings			
1 January 20x9			6,200
Depreciation vehicles			
1 January 20x9			5,616
Trade receivables		1,350	
Trade payables			2,300
Cash at bank		2,100	
		668,450	668,450

Depreciation is to be charged at 10% straight line on fixtures and fittings, 1% straight line on premises and 20% reducing balance on vehicles. There are no accruals and prepayments to take account of. Closing stock at 31 December is valued at £23,400.

Required

Prepare the statement of comprehensive income and statement of financial position of the partnership immediately after the retirement of Rod, clearly showing all transactions in the partners' capital and current accounts.

Answer

The statement of comprehensive income for Rod, Harry and James for the year ended 31 December 20X9 is as follows:

Sales		517,554
Opening stock	22,300	
Purchases	256,700	
	279,000	
Closing stock	23,400	255,600
		261,954
Wages	94,000	
Rates and insurance	18,600	
Electricity and gas	9,450	
Vehicle expenses	5,700	
Depreciation: Premises		
Furniture and fittings		
Vehicles	1,800	
	1,240	
	2,496	
		133,286
		128668
Salaries: Rod	20,000	
Harry	15,000	
James	25,000	
Interest on capital accounts: Rod	3,000	
Harry	1,750	
James	1,500	
Interest charged on drawings: Rod	(1,116)	
Harry	(720)	
James	(1,140)	
Profit share: Rod	26,158	
Harry	26,158	
James	13,078	
		128,668

CAPITAL ACCOUNTS

		Rod	Harry	James			Rod	Harry	James
31.12.X9	Eliminate goodwill		62,500	37,500	1.1.X9	Balance.b/d	60,000	35,000	30,000
31.12.X9	Cash	50,000			31.12.X9	Goodwill introduced	40,000	40,000	20,000
	Loan	50,000							
31.12.X9	Balance c/d		12,500	12,500					
		100,000	75,000	50000			100,000	75,000	50,000
					1.1.X0	Balance/ b/d		12,500	12,500

CAPITAL ACCOUNTS

		Rod	Harry	James			Rod	Harry	James
1.1.X9	Balance b/d			650	1.1.X9	Balance b/d	1,240	1,540	
31.12.X9	Interest on drawings	1,116	720	1,140	31.12.X9	Salaries	20,000	15,000	25,000
31.12.X9	Drawings	18,600	12,000	19,000	31.12.X9	Interest on capital accounts	3,000	1,750	1,500
31.12.09	Rod cash loan	15,341 15,341							
31.12.09	Balance c/d		31,728	18,788	31.12.X9	Share of profits	26,158	26,158	13,078
		50,398	44,448	39,578			50,398	44,448	39,578
					1.1.X0	Balance b/d		31,728	18,788

CASH ACCOUNT

31.12.X9	Balance b/d	2,100	31.12.X9	Cash to Rod	65,341
31.12.X9	Loan from bank	65,000	31.12.X9	Balance c/d	1,759
		67,100			67,100
1.1.X0	Balance b/d	1,759			

STATEMENT OF FINANCIAL POSITION FOR ROD, HARRY AND JAMES AS AT 31 DECEMBER 20X9

	Cost	Depreciation	NBV
Premises	180,000	10,800	169,200
Furniture and fittings	12,400	7,440	4.960
Vehicles	15,600	8,112	7,488
	208,000	26,352	181,648
Stock		23,400	
Trade receivables		1,350	
Cash		1,759	26,509
			208,157
Capital accounts: Harry		12,500	25,000
James		12,500	

Current accounts: Harry	31,728	50,516
James	18,788	
Loan Rod		65,341
Loan bank		65,000
Trade payables		2,300
		208,157

Summary

This chapter has:

▶ introduced you to the accounts of a limited company

▶ identified the concept of legal entity of a company and the differences between a company and a sole trader

▶ noted that the capital of a company is issued in the form of shares

▶ noted that companies are subject to taxation, which is accounted for as a deduction from the profit of the company

▶ identified that companies are required to publish their final accounts, but that the format is only recommended, not specified. However, the preparation of the statement of comprehensive income and statement of financial position of the company require the same techniques as those used for a sole trader

▶ considered the preparation of accounts for clubs and societies, charities and the public sector

▶ introduced you to the concept of partnerships and the preparation of accounts for partnerships.

At the end of this chapter there are several exercises for you that will test your knowledge and understanding of accounting for companies and also the preparation of final accounts in accordance with the specified formats.

Chapter 9 looks at the concept of a group and the preparation of simple group accounts and in Chapter 14 we will look at the preparation of financial statements from incomplete records.

Key terms

limited company	debentures
limited liability	taxation
corporate entity	reserves
Memorandum of Association	format presentation
Articles of Association	charity accounts
annual report	partnerships
shares (share capital)	goodwill in partnerships
dividend	partners' capital accounts
premium	partners' current accounts

Self-assessment questions

1 Answer the following questions for both sole traders and companies:

   (a) Is there any statutory regulation governing them?
   (b) Who owns the business?
   (c) Who manages the business?
   (d) Is the business a separate legal entity?
   (e) Does the business end when its owners change?
   (f) Is taxation an expense of the business?
   (g) How do owners extract profits from the business for their own use?
   (h) Is the business quoted on the stock exchange?

2 The directors of Britton plc wish to raise additional capital. They currently have in issue one million £1 ordinary shares and no long-term loans. What options do they have available to raise extra capital and which would you advise them to choose?

3 The following is an extract from the statement of financial position of Comp plc as at 31.3.X6:

	£m
Ordinary shares £1	20
Share premium account	5
Accumulated profits	12
5% debentures £1	8

   (a) What is the par value of each share?
   (b) What is the book value of each share?
   (c) What is the interest payable per annum on the debentures?
   (d) If the interest rate in the market for debentures similar to those of Comp plc was higher than 5% would the market price of Comp's debentures in the market place be higher or lower than £1?

4 The following trial balance was extracted from the books of Cuddly Toy Ltd as at 31.12.X5.

	Dr (£000)	Cr (£000)
Sales		1,562
Inventory 1.1.X5	660	
Purchases	885	
Land	1,010	
Buildings	980	
Equipment	55	
Vehicles	72	
Depreciation: Premises		390
Equipment		18
Vehicles		25

Trade receivables and payables	180	235
Bank	121	
£1 ordinary shares		900
Share premium		350
Distribution expenses	98	
Administration expenses	24	
Accumulated profits 1.1.X5		185
5% debentures		420
	4,085	4,085

The following information has not yet been accounted for:

▶ Closing inventory 31.12.X5 is valued at £560,000.

▶ Depreciation is to be charged as follows:

– 2% straight line on buildings

– 20% straight line on equipment

– 25% reducing balance on vehicles.

▶ Assets are used as follows:

– buildings: 50% cost of sales, 25% distribution and 25% administration

– equipment: all cost of sales

– vehicles: all distribution.

▶ Taxation to be charged for the year is estimated at £200,000.

▶ An interim dividend has been declared but not yet paid of 6p per share.

Prepare the published income statement, statement of changes in equity and balance sheet for the company as at 31.12.X5.

5 You are required to prepare the statement of comprehensive income for the year ended 31.3.X6 and the statement of financial position as at that date for internal purposes for the following company:

TRIAL BALANCE OF GERRY LTD AS AT 31.3.X6

	Dr	Cr
Ordinary shares £1		100,000
6% preference shares £1		20,000
8% debentures		30,000
Share premium		9,500
Revaluation reserve		10,000
General reserve		12,000
Accumulated profit b/f 1.4.X5		976
Non-current assets (cost £210,000)	191,000	
Inventory 1.4.X5	14,167	
Trade receivables and payables	11,000	7,500
Provision for doubtful debts		324
Bank	9,731	
Purchases and sales	186,000	271,700

▶

Wages and salaries	31,862	
General expenses	15,840	
Debenture interest	1,200	
Preference dividend	1,200	
	462,000	462,000

You are also given the following information:

▶ Inventory 31.3.X6 £23,483.

▶ Depreciation of non-current assets is to be provided at the rate of 10% per annum on cost.

▶ The provision for doubtful debts is to be at 5% of debtors.

▶ £1,200 of debenture interest and £1,437 of general expenses are to be accrued.

▶ £925 of general expenses have been paid in advance.

▶ Provision is to be made for taxation on this year's profits of £9,700.

▶ The directors have decided to increase the general reserve by a further £3,000.

6 The trial balance of Hobo Ltd as at 30.9.X6 was as follows:

	Dr	Cr
Audit fee	1,200	
Bad debts	5,320	
Trade receivables and trade payables	92,360	111,450
Delivery expenses	22,060	
Productive wages	32,300	
Warehouse wages	30,200	
Administrative salaries	15,200	
Purchases and sales	426,500	623,300
Administration expenses	5,600	
Rents administration	12,600	
Inventory 1.10.X5	18,950	
Ordinary 50p shares		100,000
Share premium account		50,000
Accumulated profits 1.10.X5		26,000
Premises	275,000	
Vehicles	18,500	
Equipment	12,000	
Depreciation as at 1.10.X5		
Premises		3,750
Equipment		3,600
Vehicles		6,500
7% debentures		95,000
Bank	51,810	
	1,019,600	1,019,600

The following additional information is available:

▶ Inventory as at 30.9.X6 was valued at £20,650.

▶ Premises and equipment are used at 50% production and 50% distribution, and are to be depreciated at the rate of 1% and 10% straight line respectively.

▶ Vehicles are only used for distribution, and are depreciated at 20% reducing balance.

▶ A provision for bad debts of 5% is to be allowed for.

▶ £500 was prepaid for rent and £600 is owing for production wages as at 30.9.X6.

▶ Taxation for the year is estimated at £22,680.

Prepare the statement of comprehensive income and the statement of financial position for Hobo Ltd as at 30.9.X6 in a form suitable for publication.

7 The trial balance of Burn Ltd. as at 31.12.X9 was as follows:

	Dr	Cr
Purchases and sales	15,260	83,460
Inventory 1.1.X9	6,230	
Trader receivables and payables	8,240	7,210
Production salaries and wages	12,320	
Production expenses	7,210	
Warehouse expenses	950	
Warehouse wages	10,100	
Administration salaries	14,200	
Administration expenses	950	
Ordinary £1 shares		100,000
Share premium account		20,000
Accumulated profits 1.1.X9		62,000
Premises	200,000	
Equipment	50,000	
Vehicles	15,000	
Provision for depreciation: Premises		20,000
Equipment		15,000
Vehicles		6,560
6% Debentures		50,000
Bank	103,520	
Cash	250	
New capital		80,000
	444,230	444,230

The following additional information is available, none of which has been accounted for in the trial balance:

▶ Inventory 31.12.X9 £4,560.

▶ Premises and equipment are used 50% production, 25% distribution and 25% administration and are depreciated at the rate of 2% and 10% respectively.

▶ Vehicles are only used by distribution and are depreciated at 25% reducing balance.

▶ A provision for bad debts of 5% is to be made.

▶ The new capital consists of the issue on 1.12.X9 of 40,000 £1 shares; the ledger clerk did not know how to treat this item in the ledgers.

▶ Tax for the year is estimated at £1,200.

▶ A vehicle, purchased 1.1.X7 for £7,000 was sold on 1.8.X9 for £3,750. The proceeds had been credited to sales.

▶ 5% Debentures were issued on 1.1.X9, par value £10,000, for £9,500. The £9,500 has been credited to accumulated profits 1.1.X9 account.

Prepare the statement of comprehensive income and the statement of financial position for Burn Ltd. as at 31.12.X9 in a form suitable for publication.

8 The trial balance of Black Ltd as at 31 December 20X5 was as follows:

	Dr	Cr
Trade receivables and trade payables	46,800	34,200
Returns inwards	2,450	
Productive wages	74,000	
Distribution expenses	32,870	
Administrative salaries	61,230	
Purchases and sales	321,700	552,600
Office expenses	5,630	
Returns outwards		4,670
Inventory 1.1.X5	22,300	
Ordinary £1 shares		150,000
Debentures 6%		50,000
Accumulated profits 1.1.X5		9,870
Premises	150,000	
Vehicles	85,000	
Equipment	70,000	
Depreciation as at 1.1.X5		
Premises		11,600
Equipment		27,500
Vehicles		29,250
Bank		2,290
	871,980	871,980

The following information is available, none of which has been taken account of in the preparation of the trial balance above:

▶ Inventory as at 31 December 20X5 is valued at £22,000.

▶ Vehicles are primarily used for distribution, buildings equally between production, distribution and administration and equipment equally between production and administration.

▶ Buildings are to be depreciated 1% straight line, equipment 20% straight line and vehicles 25% reducing balance.

▶ Equipment was sold on the 31 December 20X5 for £15,000. This had been credited to sales. The original cost was £20,000 and it had been purchased on 31 December 20X2. No further entries than cash and sales had been made in the books.

▶ Bad debts of £2,600 need writing off and a provision for bad debts at the rate of 5% is to be introduced.

▶ Taxation for the year is estimated at £9,860.

▶ Accruals of £3,500 for administration expense are required and prepayments of £5,600 have been identified within distribution expenses.

▶ The interest on the debentures has not yet been paid.

Prepare the statement of comprehensive income for the year ended 31 December 20X5 and the statement of financial position as at that date in a form suitable for publication.

9 Explain the terms rights issue and bonus issue of shares.

10 Gamma plc has issued share capital of £1,000,000, nominal value of ordinary shares is £2 and accumulated profits of £456,000 as at 31.12.X6. The company proposes to make a rights issue of 2 for 5 existing shares held at a price of £4.25 and a bonus issue of 200,000 ordinary shares. The market value of the shares as at 31.12.X5 is £6.70. Show the capital section of the balance sheet after the two share issues and also identify how many shares a holder of 1,000 shares before the issues will have afterwards.

11 The trial balance of Ria Enterprise for the year ended 31 December 20X0 is as follows:

	Debits	Credits
	£000	£000
Cost of sales	191,700	
Revenue		285,100
Trade receivables (debtors)	18,000	
Trade payables (creditors)		15,700
Operating expenses	39,500	
Rental income from investment properties		1,600
Closing Inventory 31 December 20X0 (note i)	14,000	
Bank interest	1,030	
Preference dividend (full year)	1,330	
Ordinary dividend paid 1 July 20X0	5,340	
Investment property at valuation (note ii)	21,300	
Land and property at valuation (note iii)	84,000	
Plant and equipment at cost (note iv)	48,000	
Plant and equipment accumulated depreciation as at 1 January 20X0		22,400
Revaluation reserve		28,000
Retained earnings as at 1 January 20X0		23,300
Ordinary share capital 25p shares		26,700
10% redeemable preference shares £1		13,300
Bank		8,100
	424,200	424,200

The following notes are applicable:

(i) The inventory (stock) valuation as at 31 December 20X0 included damaged goods valued at £1,070,000. These damaged goods, it is estimated, could be sold for £1,270,000 if £600,000 of remedial work on them were carried out.

(ii) On 31 December 20X0 the investment property was valued at £18m.

(iii) Land and property were revalued to £20m and £64m respectively on 1 January 20X0. The revaluation reserve of £28m represents this revaluation. No further change in valuation has occurred since 1 January 20X0. As at 1 January 20X0 the remaining life of the property was 16 years and property is depreciated on a straight-line basis.

(iv) Plant and equipment is depreciated at 12.5% reducing balance basis.

(v) Depreciation on all non-current assets is charged 50% cost of sales and 50% operating expenses.

(vi) The taxation charge for the year is estimated at £12m.

Prepare the statement of comprehensive income (profit and loss account) for the year ended 31 December 20X0 and the statement of financial position as at that date for Ria.

12 Jacob, Henry and Isaac are in partnership sharing profits in the ratio 3:3:4. Interest on drawings is charged at 5% on total drawings for the year and interest on capital is payable on the opening capital balances for the year at 4%. Salaries payable to the partners for a year are Jacob £30,000, Henry £25,000 and Isaac £33,000. At the year end 31.12.20X0 Jacob wishes to retire. At that date goodwill in the partnership is valued at £250,000 but is not to remain in the books after the retirement of Jacob. Jacob agrees to leave 40% of the amount due to him on loan to the partnership. At 31 December 20X0 a loan is taken out with the bank for £185,000. No entries in respect of this loan have yet been made in the accounts of the partnership. After Jacob's retirement Henry and Isaac agree to share profits in the ratio 2:3. The trial balance for the partnership as at 31.12.20X0, before any of the above is accounted for is as follows:

Trial balance as at 31.12.20X0 Jacob, Henry and Isaac

	Dr	Cr
Sales		623,430
Purchases	323,700	
Stock as at 1 January 20X0	32,300	
Wages	114,000	
Rates and insurance	22,300	
Electricity and gas	19,450	
Vehicle expenses	8,450	
Capital accounts: Jacob		80,000
Henry		65,000
Isaac		60,000
Current accounts: Jacob	980	
Henry		2,880
Isaac	1,450	

Drawings: Jacob	9,600	
Henry	22,000	
Isaac	13,500	
Premises	220,000	
Furniture and fittings at cost	16,400	
Vehicles at cost	32,600	
Depreciation premises 1 January 20X0		28,600
Depreciation furniture and fittings 1 January 20X0		6,560
Depreciation vehicles 1 January 20X0		6,520
Trade receivables	11,870	
Trade payables		12,480
Cash at bank	36,870	
	885,470	885,470

Depreciation is to be charged at 10% straight line on fixtures and fittings, 1% straight line on premises and 20% reducing balance on vehicles. There are no accruals and prepayments to take account of. Closing inventory at 31 December is valued at £34,250.

Prepare the statement of comprehensive income and statement of financial position of the partnership immediately after the retirement of Jacob clearly showing all transaction in the partners' capital and current accounts.

Chapter 7

Published financial statements

Group overview

GUS is a retail and business services group. Its activities comprise general merchandise retailing through Argos Retail Group, information and customer relationship management services through Experian, and luxury goods through a majority shareholding in Burberry Group plc.

Five year summary

Profit by division	2001 £m	2002 £m	2003 £m	2004 £m	2005 £m
Continuing operations:					
Argos Retail Group					
Argos	169	212	241	298	309
Homebase	–	–	2	102	92
Financial Services	(6)	(18)	(13)	(5)	–
Wehkamp	18	19	20	21	20
	181	213	250	416	421
Experian					
Experian North America	156	155	171	180	188
Experian International	61	69	85	102	130
	217	224	256	282	318
Burberry	69	90	117	141	166
Central activities (including GGF and gusco.com)	(3)	(7)	(16)	(20)	(24)
	464	520	607	819	881
Discontinued operations:					
Argos Retail Group	36	42	35	–	–
Lewis	31	31	32	44	55
Property	30	25	26	18	–
	97	98	93	62	55
	561	618	700	881	936
Net interest	(74)	(67)	(58)	(54)	(26)
Profit before amortisation of goodwill, exceptional items and taxation	487	552	642	827	910
Amortisation of goodwill	(92)	(99)	(143)	(193)	(207)
Exceptional items	(85)	(72)	(90)	58	(10)
Profit before taxation	310	380	409	692	693
Tax on profit on ordinary activities	(106)	(122)	(141)	(192)	(221)
Profit after taxation	204	258	268	500	472
Equity minority interests	–	(1)	(17)	(27)	(49)
Profit for the financial year	204	257	251	473	423

Source: GUS Annual Report and Financial Statements 2005, p. 1 and p. 90 (Table).

Discussion points

1 Which activities are the main contributors to the profit of the GUS group?

2 What does the five-year summary tell us about GUS as a group?

Contents

<table>
<tr><td>

Learning outcomes

</td><td>

After reading this chapter you should be able to:

● Explain the key international influences that affect accounting practice in the UK.

● Explain the structure of company reporting as set out in the *Framework* and in UK guidance.

● Explain the main contents of (a) the balance sheet, (b) the income statement (profit and loss account) and (c) the cash flow statement as presented by larger companies.

● Define 'parent company' and 'subsidiary company' and explain how a group is structured.

● Explain the main features of group financial statements.

● Explain the nature of, and reason for, other forms of communication beyond the annual report.

</td></tr>
</table>

7.1 Introduction

It is explained in Chapters 1 and 4 that in the case of sole traders and partnerships the groups of persons who have an interest in the financial statements are limited to the owners themselves, HM Revenue and Customs and organisations such as banks which are asked to provide finance for the company. For limited liability companies the list of potential users widens and the access to internal information becomes restricted. Even the owners of a limited liability company, called the equity holders (shareholders) are not permitted access to the day-to-day records of the company and are treated as being outsiders of (external to) the company they own. The quality and amount of information communicated to these users who are external to the company becomes a matter which is too important to be left entirely to the discretion of the directors running the company.

Chapter 4 outlined the various regulatory authorities which exist to establish the quality and quantity of information to be published by limited liability companies. There are over one million limited liability companies in the UK, although only a few thousand are listed on the Stock Exchange and of these only around 500 have their shares bought and sold regularly. The number of major listed companies, and their importance to the economy in terms of the funds invested in them, means it is appropriate to take them as the benchmark for current practice in external reporting. The practices applied by larger limited liability companies set a good example as a starting point for smaller ones and for organisations that are not limited liability companies, such as charitable trusts or public sector bodies.

In this chapter, and in Chapters 8 to 12, there is mention only of **limited liability companies** because the aim of this book is to provide an understanding of the accounting information published by companies. The more general word **enterprise** (meaning a business activity or commercial project) could be substituted throughout for limited liability company most of what is said in these chapters because the principles and practice described here have a wider application beyond companies, although modifications may be necessary when the needs of the users and the purposes of the enterprise are different from those relevant to a limited liability company.

7.2 International influences

Chapter 3 explained that, since January 2005, two different accounting systems have existed for companies in the UK, depending on the type of company. For the group financial statements of a listed company the accounting system set out by the International Accounting Standards Board (IASB) must be applied. All other companies, and the separate companies in the group, may choose to follow IASB standards but there is no requirement to do so. Companies that do not choose to follow the international accounting standards must continue to follow the rules of UK company law and the UK ASB's accounting standards.

For many years there has been a strong international influence on and from UK accounting practice so the change to international accounting standards in 2005 did not bring many surprises. The UK accounting standard setting body was a founder member of the International Accounting Standards Committee (IASC), set up in 1973, and has been closely involved in its work since that date. In 2001, with an organisational change, the IASC became the IASB but the close similarity between international accounting standards and UK accounting standards continued. The UK ASB has worked continuously towards matching UK standards to IFRS.

Since 1980 the law regulating financial reporting in the UK (now contained in the Companies Act 1985 and related legislation) has reflected its membership of the European Union (EU) and the work of regulators across the EU to harmonise aspects of financial reporting. From 2005 the law governing financial reporting in the UK has been split into two routes. One route is the rule of UK company law influenced by the EU. The other route is the IASB system of accounting as endorsed by the EU.

7.2.1 The European Union

The UK is a member state of the EU and is required to develop its laws so as to harmonise with those of other Member States of the EU. There are two procedures by which the EU influences the accounting practices of UK-based companies.

1 The European Commission, which is the permanent secretariat and staff of the EU, issues a Regulation which overrides national laws and applies to all companies specified in the Regulation.
2 The European Commission issues Directives which are incorporated in national laws of Member States.

The IAS Regulation

In 2002 the European Commission issued the first IAS Regulation. The IAS Regulation is a direct instruction to companies in all Member States. It required that, by 2005, all **listed** companies in the European Union would use IASB standards in preparing their **group** financial statements. This was intended to cause convergence ('bringing together') of accounting practices, and so improve the movement of capital across the stock markets of the EU. The Commission, which prepares and implements the legislation of the European Parliament, has established procedures for giving European approval to each of the IASB Standards. It takes advice from the European Financial Reporting Advisory Group (EFRAG), a team of experts that includes a UK member. The final recommendation to the Commission is made by the Accounting Regulatory Committee, which includes representatives of all Member States. The process of approving IASB standards for use in the EU is called **endorsement**.

Harmonisation through Directives

For many aspects of regulation within the EU, the process of harmonisation starts when a **Directive** is issued by the European Commission, setting out the basic rules which should be followed in each Member State's national laws. For limited liability companies in the UK, two such Directives have been particularly important. These are the Fourth Directive and the Seventh Directive. Together they specify the content of the Companies Act 1985, which was issued in 1985 and amended by a further Act in 1989. One important aspect of Directives is that they specify **formats** for the financial statements (see section 7.3.2) which ensure that all companies produce documents that are similar in appearance and present items in a systematic order. The idea of having standard formats was not a familiar concept in the UK before the Directives became effective in the 1980s, but became accepted during the 1980s and 1990. Having standard formats makes it easier for the reader to find the starting point in reading the financial statements. In later chapters we will see that having standard formats does not solve all the problems of comparability and understandability. For companies that do not apply IFRS these formats continue to apply. For companies using the IFRS there is potentially more flexibility of presentation.

Activity 7.1	*From your general interest reading, or perhaps from your study of law, make a list of other areas of activity in which the UK law is harmonised with that of other countries in the EU.*

7.2.2 IASB

The International Accounting Standards Board (IASB) is an independent body that sets International Financial Reporting Standards (IFRS). It was formed in 2000 as the successor to the International Accounting Standard Committee (IASC) which had been setting International Accounting Standards (IAS) since 1973. These IAS have been adopted by the IASB and will gradually be revised as IFRS. In the meantime the description 'IFRS' is used as a collective name for all forms of international accounting standard, whatever the precise title of the standard.

The IASB's objective is to bring about convergence of national accounting standards and international accounting standards to high-quality solutions. This will help participants in the world's capital markets and other users to make economic decisions.

There are many similarities between the UK accounting standards and the IASB Standards. There are also some differences where the UK standard setter believes a particular approach is justified, or where historical developments have a strong influence. The UK Accounting Standards Board works on projects with the IASB, as do other countries' standard setting bodies, all seeking to develop international convergence.

7.3 Accounting framework

Chapter 1, section 1.3 has explained that the IASB has developed a *Framework* of principles and definitions that are used in setting accounting standards. The UK ASB has also issued a *Statement of Principles*. There are many similarities between these documents because the UK ASB benefited from the earlier work of the IASB. The explanations in this chapter draw mainly on the IASB *Framework*, adding more information where this is needed to understand the separate ideas of the UK ASB.

7.3.1   The primary financial statements

The IASB requires a complete set of financial statements to comprise:[1]

● a balance sheet
● an income statement (showing the profit or loss for the period)
● a statement of changes in equity
● a cash flow statement, and
● notes that summarise the accounting policies and give other explanations.

The IASB also gives general guidance on how to prepare and present the financial statements but stops short of giving precise rules on presentation. There is discretion for companies to present information in a way that best suits the company and those who are likely to use the information.

The UK ASB requires the same four primary statements but with some differences of names. The income statement is called a profit and loss account. The statement of changes in equity is replaced by two items: a statement of total recognised gains and losses and a note of changes in share capital and reserves (explained in Chapter 12 of this book). The Companies Act 1985 sets out formats of financial statements (see section 7.3.2) which give detailed rules on the sequence of information. These formats apply to companies that do *not* follow the IFRS.

A comparison of the primary statements in the IASB and UK ASB systems is shown in Exhibit 7.1.

Exhibit 7.1
Primary statements – IASB and UK ASB compared

IASB system	**UK ASB and company law**
Balance sheet	Balance sheet
Income statement	Profit and loss account
Cash flow statement	Cash flow statement
Statement of changes in equity	
● Statement of recognised income and expense *plus*	● Statement of total recognised gains and losses *plus*
● *Transactions with equity holders (e.g. dividends paid) *plus*	● Reconciliation of movements in shareholders' funds[†]
● *Changes in the retained earnings (accumulated profit or loss) *plus*	
● *Changes in each class of equity and each reserve	
Key: * may be shown on the face of the statement of changes in equity or in notes. [†] Shown with primary statements or in notes	

The IASB's Framework explains that the objective of financial statements is to provide information about the financial position, performance and changes in financial position of an entity that is useful to a wide range of users in making economic decisions.[2]

Financial position

Information about financial position is reported primarily in a balance sheet. It reports economic resources controlled by the company, its financial structure, its liquidity and its solvency. Information about economic resources held by the entity allows users of the information to estimate future cash flows from those resources. Information about

financial structure is useful in predicting future needs for borrowing or for raising new equity finance. Liquidity refers to the availability of cash in the near future after taking account of commitments in the same period. Solvency refers to the availability of cash to meet financial commitments as they fall due. The balance sheet is not a statement of the value of the company because there are limitations in the measurement process and also because not all items which are of value to the company are included in the balance sheet.

Performance

Information about the performance of an entity is primarily provided in an income statement (profit and loss account). Performance is indicated by profitability and changes in profitability. Information about performance is useful in evaluating how well the resources of the entity have been used to generate profit. Statements of financial performance are seen as providing an account of the stewardship of management and also as helping readers to check the accuracy of previous estimates they may have made about the expected outcome of the period.

Changes in financial position

Information about changes in financial position of an entity is useful to help assess the operating, investing and financing activities of the period. It is usually found in a statement of cash flows.

7.3.2   Formats for financial statements

The word **format** means 'shape'. A format for a financial statement sets out the shape of the document. It sets out the items to be reported and the sequence in which they are reported. Section 7.2.1 explains that EU Directives have guided the formats used by UK companies for many years, as set out in company law and UK accounting standards. Since 2005 the group financial statements of listed companies have followed the IASB system of reporting. The IASB system does not specify formats. It does provide some lists of items to be included in financial statements but there is no requirement to present these items in any particular sequence. This means that companies have choices in the shape of their financial statements. This book describes the shapes of financial statements that you are likely to see in company reports but you will need to be flexible in understanding that companies do have choices.

7.3.3   Categories of financial information

The primary financial statements are the core of a much wider range of sources of financial information which users may obtain about a company. The relative position of the primary financial statements is shown in Exhibit 7.2

Activity 7.2   *Write down three items of accompanying information about a company which you feel would be useful in the annual report of a company. Exchange lists with other members of the group and establish the similarities and differences across the group. To what extent would one general set of financial statements with notes and accompanying information meet your collective expectations?*

7.3.4   Notes and accompanying information

The annual report contains the primary financial statements, notes to the financial statements and accompanying information.

Exhibit 7.2
Categories of financial information

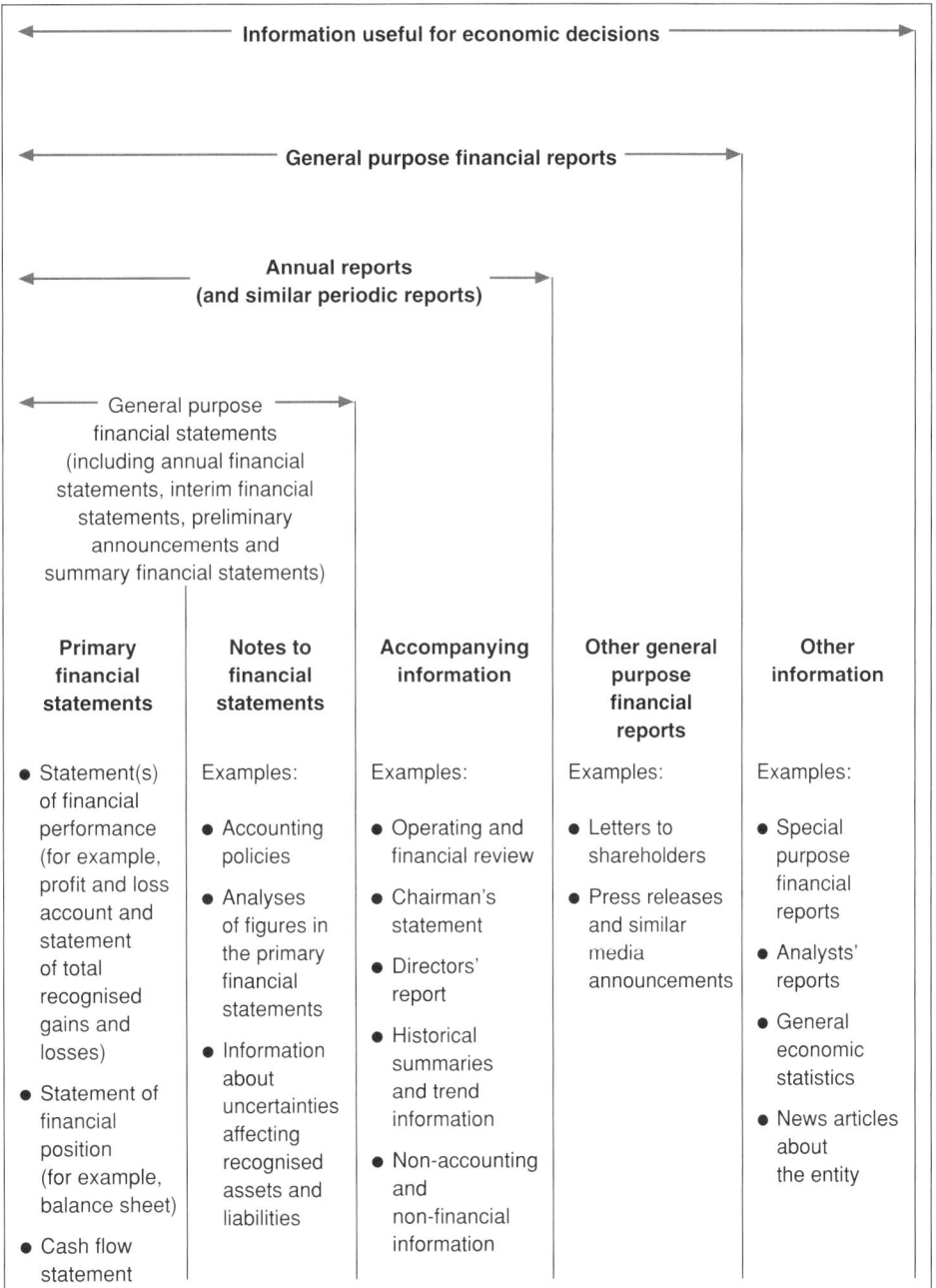

Source: ASB (1999) *Statement of Principles for Financial Reporting*, Accounting Standards Board, Introduction. Reproduced with the permission of the Accounting Standards Board.

Notes to the financial statements

Notes to the financial statements are essential in amplifying and explaining the primary financial statements. They may contain additional information that is relevant to the needs of users about the items in the balance sheet, income statement and cash flow statement. The notes and the primary financial statements form an integrated whole. The wording of the notes is as important as the numbers if ambiguity is to be avoided.

For companies that do not follow the IFRS, many of these notes are required by regulations such as the Companies Act 1985 or relevant UK accounting standards. The ASB also warns that notes to the accounts are not the place to correct or justify a misrepresentation in the primary financial statements. That potential misrepresentation should be dealt with by amending the financial statement to eliminate the problem.

Accompanying information

Accompanying information is any other information additional to the primary financial statements and notes. It could be information which is highly relevant but of lower reliability than the financial statements and notes. It could be information which will only interest a particular group of users. Such accompanying information may not be subject to the audit process which is compulsory for the primary financial statements and notes. The IASB does not give a view on the accompanying information beyond the notes to the financial statements. The view of the UK ASB is that such accompanying information may be very important, one example being the Operating and Financial Review now presented by large companies as management's explanation of the information given in the financial statements (see Chapter 14). Accompanying information may include disclosures of a voluntary or evolutionary nature.

Many annual reports include highlights pages showing amounts, ratios and other calculations that distil a great deal of information into a few key items. The UK ASB agrees that highlights can be useful but warns against focusing attention exclusively on one or two measures. You cannot read about financial statements for long without meeting the phrase 'the bottom line'. That refers to the line in the income statement (profit and loss account) which reports the profit attributable to the equity holders (ordinary shareholders). It may be described as **earnings** for equity holders (ordinary shareholders). When this amount is divided by the number of shares which have been issued by the company it becomes the **earnings per share**. Investors, financial journalists and brokers' analysts have traditionally paid great attention to the earnings per share. The standard setters (both the IASB and the UK ASB) would prefer to discourage this narrow focus and encourage instead a 'building block' approach where the company produces information in such a way that the user of the annual statement can create useful arrangements and combinations of information.

Companies also produce accompanying information for specialised needs. Regulated industries (such as gas, electricity, telecommunications and water) provide supplementary information about their regulated activities. Some companies give non-financial performance indicators (such as speed of answering customer enquiries, or level of customer satisfaction). Graphs, charts, diagrams and even photographs are all ways of providing accompanying information which adds to users' understanding of a document.

7.4 Balance sheet

7.4.1 What items must be reported?

Companies that follow the IASB system of accounting in presenting a balance sheet have choices in the way they present their balance sheet. There is no particular **format** required[3] but some items are listed in the relevant standard as a minimum set of disclosures (see Supplement 7.1 to this chapter). Companies choose the form of layout for items in the balance sheet.

Companies that do not follow the IASB system of accounting must comply with the Companies Act 1985 and the UK accounting standards. The Companies Act 1985 contains more detail of the format that must be used. The details are set out in Supplement 7.2 to this chapter.

7.4.2 What formats are used?

Companies applying the IASB system do not have to follow any particular format but it is likely that any balance sheet you see will resemble one of the three formats described in this section because they will retain some of the traditions of the UK system that has existed for more than 20 years.

Companies that do not apply the IASB system of accounting must follow the requirements of the Companies Act 1985 and the standards of the UK ASB. The Companies Act 1985 permits two different formats of balance sheet, each conforming to the accounting equation but permitting different layouts on the page. The word format means 'shape' so it covers the items to be reported and the sequence in which they are reported. The most commonly used format in the UK is Format 1, which uses the accounting equation to create a vertical format as shown in Exhibit 7.3.

Exhibit 7.3
Vertical format of balance sheet

Assets
minus
Liabilities
equals
Ownership interest

Format 2 uses the accounting equation to create a horizontal format as shown in Exhibit 7.4.

Exhibit 7.4
Horizontal form of balance sheet

		Ownership interest
Assets	equal	plus
		Liabilities

Format 2 is observed more commonly in the financial statements of Continental European countries where the horizontal format is preferred.

Some companies use a variation on Format 2 which stacks the assets on top and the ownership interest and liabilities underneath (see Exhibit 7.5).

Exhibit 7.5
Assets above, ownership interest plus liabilities below

Assets
equals
Ownership interest
plus
Liabilities

When you read a balance sheet you should first of all look at the overall structure to see where the main sections of **assets**, **liabilities** and **ownership interest** are placed. Then you can begin to look at each section in more detail. The process is something like seeing a landscape painting for the first time. You stand back to look at the overall impression of the landscape and the main features first. Then you step forward to look at some of the details in different parts of the painting. Finally if you are very enthusiastic you move in closer and start to examine the details of the texture, brush strokes and shading.

7.4.3 Descriptions in the balance sheet

You will see from the Supplement that the balance sheet formats contain some words you will recognise but also many new words. Non-current assets (fixed assets) are separated from current assets. Current liabilities (due in less than one year) are separated from non-current liabilities (due in more than one year). Some of the items under the Companies Act headings A to J may look rather strange at this stage (particularly A, D, I and J). Do not worry about that at present. If they are appropriate to first-level study they will be explained at some point in this text. If they are not explained, then they are relatively rare in occurrence and the time taken to explain them will outweigh the benefits you would gain from understanding.

The ownership interest is shown at heading K as **capital** and **reserves**. The word **capital** here means the claim which owners have because of the number of shares they own and the word **reserves** means the claim which owners have because the company has created new wealth for them over the years. Various labels are used to describe the nature of that new wealth and how it is created. Some of the new wealth is created because new investors pay more than a specified amount for the shares. Paying more is referred to as paying a **premium**, so this kind of ownership interest is labelled the **share premium**. Some of the new wealth is created because the fixed assets held by the company increase in value and that new valuation is recorded. This kind of owner-ship interest is labelled the **revaluation reserve**. Some of the new wealth is created by making profits through operating activities. This kind of ownership interest is labelled the **retained earnings** reserve.

7.4.4 Subtotals

Subtotals in financial statements help to group information within financial statements into useful sections. There are no rules about the placing of subtotals in either the IASB lists or the Companies Acts formats. Companies have to decide for themselves where to place subtotals and totals in presentation of the list of items in the format. You will need to be flexible in reading balance sheets and using the subtotals provided.

Activity 7.3

Read again the format for the balance sheet. How many of the items there came as no surprise to you? How many looked unfamiliar? Make a note of these and check that you find out about them in later chapters.

7.4.5 Illustration

The remainder of this chapter explores the published financial statements of a hypo-thetical listed company, Safe and Sure plc, which operates in a service industry. There is a parent company called Safe and Sure plc and it owns some subsidiary companies that together make up a 'group'. Buildings and vehicles are the main fixed assets. The Safe and Sure Group sells recycling and cleaning services to customers based on the high reputation of the company's products and name. The Safe and Sure Group follows the IASB system of accounting and has chosen a format that is similar to Format 1 (see Exhibit 7.3).

The following illustration sets out the balance sheet of the Safe and Sure Group plc for Year 7 with comparative amounts alongside for the previous year. The balance sheet is followed by a comment on matters of particular interest.

Safe and Sure Group plc
Consolidated balance sheet at 31 December

	Notes	Year 7 £m	Year 6 £m
Non-current assets			
Intangible assets	1	260.3	237.6
Tangible assets	2	137.5	121.9
Investments	3	2.8	2.0
Taxation recoverable	4	5.9	4.9
		406.5	366.4
Current assets			
Inventories (stocks)	5	26.6	24.3
Amounts receivable (debtors)	6	146.9	134.7
Six-month deposits		2.0	–
Cash and cash equivalents		105.3	90.5
		280.8	249.5
Current liabilities			
Amounts payable (creditors)	7	(159.8)	(157.5)
Bank overdraft	8	(40.1)	(62.6)
		(199.9)	(220.1)
Net current assets		80.9	29.4
Total assets less current liabilities		487.4	395.8
Non-current liabilities			
Amounts payable (creditors)	9	(2.7)	(2.6)
Bank and other borrowings	10	(0.2)	(0.6)
Provisions	11	(20.2)	(22.2)
Net assets		464.3	370.4
Capital and reserves (ownership interest)			
Called-up share capital	12	19.6	19.5
Share premium account	13	8.5	5.5
Revaluation reserve	14	4.6	4.6
Retained earnings	15	431.6	340.8
Equity holders' funds		464.3	370.4

7.4.6 Discussion

The first feature to note is the title, *Consolidated balance sheet*. Companies listed on the Stock Exchange are generally using one name as an umbrella for a group of several companies linked together under one parent. It is thought to be more useful to the shareholders of the parent company to see all the assets controlled by that company within the single financial statement. The word **control** is important here. The parent company owns the other companies. They each own their separate assets. The parent company controls the use of those assets indirectly by controlling the companies it owns. The balance sheet as presented here represents a group where the parent company owns 100% of all the other companies in the group (called its subsidiary undertakings). A similar consolidated balance sheet would be produced if the parent owned less than 100%, provided it had the same element of control. The only additional item would be a **minority interest** in the ownership claim to indicate the proportion of the equity interest in subsidiaries held by shareholders outside the group. The minority interest is also called a **non-controlling interest**.

The second feature to note in the balance sheet as presented is that there are two columns of figures. Companies are required to present the figures for the previous year, in order to provide a basis for comparison.

The balance sheet follows the accounting equation and this company has helpfully set out in the left-hand margin the main elements of the equation. There are some phrases in the balance sheet which you are meeting for the first time but you should not feel intimated by new titles when you can work out what they mean if you think about the ordinary meanings of words.

Intangible assets means assets which may not be touched – they have no physical existence. Examples are the goodwill of a business or the reputation of a branded product.

Tangible non-current (fixed) assets is another phrase which you are seeing here for the first time, but again you can work out the meaning. You know from Chapter 2 what **non-current assets** are and you know that tangible means 'something that may be touched'. So you would not be surprised to find that note 2 to the accounts gives more detail on land and buildings, plant, equipment, vehicles and office equipment.

Investments here means shares in other companies which are not subsidiary undertakings within the group.

The *taxation recoverable* is an amount of tax which has been paid already but may be reclaimed in 18 months' time because of events that have occurred to reduce the tax due, after the tax was paid.

Current assets comprise inventories (stocks), receivables (debtors) and cash. They are set out in order of increasing liquidity. Inventories (stocks) are the least readily convertible into cash while amounts receivable (debtors) are closer to collection of cash. Cash itself is the most liquid asset. The notes to the accounts contain more detailed information. Take as an example note 4, relating to inventories (stocks). It appears as follows:

Note 4	Year 7	Year 6
Inventories (stocks)	£m	£m
Raw materials	6.2	5.4
Work-in-progress	1.9	1.0
Finished products	18.5	17.9
	26.6	24.3

The notes are shown in full in Appendix I at the end of this book. There is a note relating to amounts receivable (debtors), mainly relating to trade receivables (trade debtors). Amounts payable (creditors) has a similar type of note to the balance sheet.

The *non-current liabilities* include long-term borrowings, which are quite low in amount compared with those of many other companies of this size. The provisions relate to future obligations caused by: treating a contaminated site; reorganisation of part of the business; and future tax payable.

That stage of the balance sheet concludes with the net assets, defined as all assets minus all liabilities. Drawing a total at this point is not a requirement of any format, but is used by many companies as the point which creates a pause in the balance sheet before moving on to the ownership interest.

For a company the *ownership interest* is described as *capital and reserves*. The ownership interest in a company is specified in company law as comprising the claim created through the shares owned by the various equity holders (shareholders) and the claim representing additional reserves of wealth accumulated since the company began. That wealth is accumulated by making profits year after year. The claim is reduced when the owners take dividends from the company. (Further information on the reporting of share capital, reserves and dividends is contained in Chapter 12.)

The ownership interest is the part of the balance sheet which causes greatest confusion to most readers. It is purely a statement of a legal claim on the assets after all liabilities have been satisfied. The word *reserves* has no other significance. There is nothing to see, touch, count or hold. To add to the potential confusion, company law delights in finding names for various different kinds of ownership interest. If you are the kind of person who takes a broad-brush view of life you will not worry too much about share premium account, revaluation reserve and retained earnings.

They are all part of accounting terminology which becomes important to a company lawyer when there is a dispute over how much dividend may be declared, but are less important to the investor who says 'How much is my total claim?'

7.5 Income statement (profit and loss account)

7.5.1 What items must be reported?

Companies that follow the IASB system of accounting in presenting an income statement must report the profit or loss for the period. There is no particular format required[4] but some items are listed in the relevant standard as a minimum set of disclosures (see Supplement 7.4 to this chapter). Companies choose the form of layout of the items in the income statement.

Companies that do not follow the IASB system of accounting must comply with the Companies Act 1985 and the UK accounting standards. The Companies Act 1985 contains more detail of the items to be reported and the format that must be used. The details are set out in Supplement 7.3 to this chapter.

7.5.2 What formats are used?

Companies applying the IASB system do not have to follow any particular format but it is likely that any income statement (profit and loss account) you see will resemble one of the formats described in this section because they will retain some of the traditions of the UK system that has existed for more than 20 years.

Companies that do not apply the IASB system of accounting must follow the requirements of the Companies Act 1985 and the standards of the UK ASB. The Companies Act 1985 permits four different formats of profit and loss account but the version most frequently observed in the UK is format 1 (see Supplement 7.4).

7.5.3 Illustration

The published income statements (profit and loss accounts) of most major companies are very similar to the illustration set out here for Safe and Sure plc.

Safe and Sure Group plc
Consolidated income statement (profit and loss account)
for the years ended 31 December

	Notes	Year 7 £m	Year 6 £m
Continuing operations			
Revenue	16	714.6	589.3
Cost of sales	16	(491.0)	(406.3)
Gross profit		223.6	183.0
Distribution costs		(2.2)	(2.5)
Administrative expenses	17	(26.2)	(26.5)
Profit from operations		195.2	154.0
Interest receivable (net)	18	2.3	3.0
Profit before tax	19	197.5	157.0
Tax	20	(62.2)	(52.4)
Profit for the period from continuing operations		135.3	104.6
Discontinued operations			
Loss for the period from discontinued operations	21	(20.5)	(10.0)
Profit for the period attributable to equity holders		114.8	94.6
Earnings per share	22	11.74	9.71

7.5.4   Discussion

The first point to note is the heading. This is a consolidated income statement (profit and loss account) bringing together the results of the activities of all the companies in the group during the year. The individual companies will also produce their own separate profit and loss accounts and these are added together to produce the consolidated picture. Where one company in the group sells items to another in the group, the sale and purchase are matched against each other on consolidation so that the results reported reflect only sales to persons outside the group.

The second point to note is that the income statement (profit and loss account) as presented by the company is more informative than the lists contained in Supplements 7.3 or 7.4 might suggest. That is partly because the company has used subtotals to break up the flow and make it digestible for the reader. One very common subtotal is the **gross profit** calculated as revenue minus the cost of the goods or services sold as revenue.

Starting at the top of the income statement we see that the word *revenue* is used to describe the sales of goods or services. **Revenue** is sometimes described as **turnover** or **sales**. Revenue (turnover) represents sales to third parties outside the group of companies. The **cost of sales** is the total of the costs of materials, labour and overheads which relate closely to earning the sales. The gross profit is sometimes referred to as the **gross margin** and is monitored closely by those who use the financial statements to make a judgement on the operations of the company. Within any industry the gross profit as a percentage of revenue (or turnover, or sales) is expected to be within known limits. If that percentage is low then the company is either underpricing its goods or else taking the market price but failing to control costs. If the percentage is high, then the company is perhaps a market leader which can command higher prices for its output because of its high reputation. However, it might also be seen by customers and competitors as charging too much for its goods or services.

The next item in the profit and loss account is *distribution costs*, which would include the costs of delivering goods to customers. For this company the distribution costs are low because it provides services by contract and does not carry out much distribution work. For many users the trends in an amount are more interesting than the actual amount. They might ask why the amount has decreased. On the other hand, it is not a particularly significant component of the overall picture and the users might show little interest. They would pay more attention to the *administrative expenses*, a collective term for all those costs which have to be incurred in order to keep the business running but which are less closely related to the direct activity of creating revenue (making sales). The directors' salaries, head office costs and general maintenance of buildings and facilities are the kinds of details brought together under this heading. Directors' salaries are always a matter of some fascination and companies are expected to give considerable detail in the notes to the accounts about how much each director is paid and what other benefits are provided.

The *profit from operations* is the end of the first stage of the profit and loss account, where the story of the business operations is complete. The rest of the profit and loss account is concerned with the cost of financing the company.

Interest is paid on loans and received on investments, usually brought together in one net amount which shows, in this case, an excess of interest receivable over interest payable. That suggests a fairly cash-rich company with relatively low levels of borrowing. Next comes the *corporation tax*, which all companies must pay as a percentage of the profit before tax. The percentage is a standard percentage applied to the profit calculated according to the tax rules. Because the tax rules are not identical to the accounting rules, the percentage appears to vary when the reader looks at the profit and loss account. Helpful companies will explain the tax charge in the Operating and Financial Review, as well as providing more detailed notes to the accounts on the tax charge.

That information ends with the profit for the period from continuing operations. Investors or analysts who want to make a forecast of future profits may decide to use this figure as a starting point because the activities will continue. Separately below this line the group shows the results in this period of operations that have been discontinued. Usually operations are discontinued because they are performing poorly so it is no great surprise to see a loss here. The loss is part of the performance of the period but investors can see that the bad news of this operation will not continue in future. Finally the equity holders (ordinary shareholders) see the profit for the period attributable to them.

They do not see here any mention of a reward in the form of a dividend which returns to them some of the wealth created by the company during the period. That information will appear in a statement of changes in equity which is explained in Chapter 12.

4

Accounting for limited companies (1)

Introduction

Most businesses in the UK, except the very smallest, operate in the form of limited companies. More than 2 million limited companies now exist and they account for the majority of UK business activity and employment. The economic significance of this type of business is not confined to the UK; it can be seen in many of the world's developed countries.

In this chapter we consider the nature of limited companies and how they differ from sole proprietorship businesses and partnerships. We examine the ways in which the owners provide finance as well as the rules governing the way in which limited companies must account to their owners and to other interested parties. We shall also see how the financial statements, which were discussed in the previous two chapters, are prepared for this type of business.

Learning outcomes

When you have completed this chapter, you should be able to:

● Discuss the nature of the limited company.

● Explain the role of directors of limited companies.

● Describe the main features of the owners' claim in a limited company.

● Explain how the income statement and balance sheet of a limited company differ in detail from that of sole proprietorships and partnerships.

The main features of limited companies

Legal nature

Let us begin our examination of limited companies by discussing their legal nature. A **limited company** has been described as an artificial person that has been created by law. This means that a company has many of the rights and obligations that 'real' people have. It can, for example, sue or be sued by others and can enter into contracts in its own name. This contrasts sharply with other types of businesses, such as sole proprietorships and partnerships (that is unincorporated businesses), where it is the owner(s) rather than the business that must sue, enter into contracts and so on, because the business has no separate legal identity.

With the rare exceptions of those that are created by Act of Parliament or by Royal Charter, all UK companies are created (or *incorporated*) by registration. To create a company the person or persons (usually known as *promoters*) wishing to create it, fill in a few simple forms and pay a modest registration fee. After having ensured that the necessary formalities have been met, the Registrar of Companies, a government official, enters the name of the new company on the Registry of Companies. Thus, in the UK, companies can be formed very easily and cheaply (for about £100).

Companies may be owned by just one person, but most have more than one owner and some have many owners. The owners are usually known as *members* or *shareholders*. The ownership of a company is normally divided into a number, frequently a large number, of **shares**, each of equal size. Each owner, or shareholder, owns one or more shares in the company. Large companies typically have a very large number of shareholders. For example, at 31 March 2006, BT Group plc, the telecommunications business, had nearly 1.4 million different shareholders.

As a limited company has its own legal identity, it is regarded as being quite separate from those that own and manage it. This fact leads to two important features of the limited company: perpetual life and limited liability. These are explained below.

Just before we leave the topic of the legal separateness of owners and the company, however, it is worth emphasising that this has no connection with the business entity convention of accounting, which we discussed in Chapter 2. This accounting convention applies equally well to all business types, including sole proprietorships and partnerships where there is certainly no legal distinction between the owner(s) and the business.

Perpetual life

A company is normally granted a perpetual existence and so will continue even where an owner of some, or even all, of the shares in the company dies. The shares of the deceased person will simply pass to the beneficiary of his or her estate. The granting of perpetual existence means that the life of a company is quite separate from the lives of those individuals who own or manage it. It is not, therefore, affected by changes in ownership that arise when individuals buy and sell shares in the company.

Though a company may be granted a perpetual existence when it is first formed, it is possible for either the shareholders or the courts to bring this existence to an end. When this is done, the assets of the company are sold off to meet outstanding liabilities. Any surplus arising from the sale will then be used to pay the shareholders.

Shareholders may agree to end the life of a company where it has achieved the purpose for which it was formed or where they feel that the company has no real future. The courts may bring the life of a company to an end where creditors have applied to the courts for this to be done because they have not been paid amounts owing.

Where shareholders agree to end the life of a company, it is referred to as a 'voluntary liquidation'. **Real World 4.1** describes the demise of one company by this method.

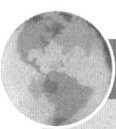

Real World 4.1

'Monotub Industries in a Spin as Founder Gets Titan for £1'   **FT**

Monotub Industries, maker of the Titan washing machine, yesterday passed into corporate history with very little ceremony and with only a whimper of protest from minority shareholders.

At an extraordinary meeting held in a basement room of the group's West End headquarters, shareholders voted to put the company into voluntary liquidation and sell its assets and intellectual property to founder Martin Myerscough for £1. (The shares in the company were at one time worth 650 p each.)

The only significant opposition came from Giuliano Gnagnatti who, along with other shareholders, has seen his investment shrink faster than a wool twin-set on a boil wash.

The not-so-proud owner of 100,000 Monotub shares, Mr Gnagnatti, the managing director of an online retailer . . . described the sale of Monotub as a 'free gift' to Mr Myerscough. This assessment was denied by Ian Green, the chairman of Monotub, who said the closest the beleaguered company had come to a sale was an offer for £60,000 that gave no guarantees against liabilities, which are thought to amount to £750,000.

The quiet passing of the washing machine, eventually dubbed the Titanic, was in strong contrast to its performance in many kitchens.

Originally touted as the 'great white goods hope' of the washing machine industry with its larger capacity and removable drum, the Titan ran into problems when it kept stopping during the spin cycle, causing it to emit a loud bang and leap into the air.

Summing up the demise of the Titan, Mr Green said: 'Clearly the machine had some revolutionary aspects, but you can't get away from the fact that the machine was faulty and should not have been launched with those defects.'

The usually vocal Mr Myerscough, who has promised to pump £250,000 into the company and give Monotub shareholders £4 for every machine sold, refused to comment on his plans for the Titan or reveal who his backers were. But . . . he did say that he intended to 'take the Titan forward'.

Source: Urquhart, Lisa 'Monotub Industries in a Spin as Founder Gets Titan for £1', *Financial Times*, 23 January 2003, FT.com.

Limited liability

Since the company is a legal person in its own right, it must take responsibility for its own debts and losses. This means that once the shareholders have paid what they have agreed to pay for the shares, their obligation to the company, and to the company's creditors, is satisfied. Thus, shareholders can limit their losses to that which they have paid, or agreed to pay, for their shares. This is of great practical importance to potential shareholders, since they know that what they can lose, as part owners of the business, is limited.

Contrast this with the position of sole proprietors or partners. They cannot 'ring fence' assets that they do not want to put into the business. If a sole proprietary or partnership business finds itself in a position where liabilities exceed the business assets, the law gives unsatisfied creditors the right to demand payment out of what the sole proprietor or partner may have regarded as 'non-business' assets. Thus the sole proprietor or partner could lose everything – house, car, the lot. This is because the law sees Jill, the sole proprietor, as being the same as Jill the private individual. The shareholder, by contrast, can lose only the amount committed to that company. Legally, the business operating as a limited company, in which Jack owns shares, is not the same as Jack himself. This is true even if Jack were to own all of the shares in the company.

Real World 4.2 gives an example of a well-known case where the shareholders of a particular company were able to avoid any liability to those that had lost money as a result of dealing with the company.

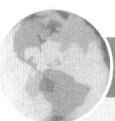

Real World 4.2

Carlton and Granada 1 - Nationwide Football League 0

Two television broadcasting companies, Carlton and Granada, each owned 50 per cent of a separate company, ITV Digital (formerly ON Digital). ITV Digital signed a contract to pay the Nationwide Football League (in effect the three divisions of English football below the Premiership) more than £89 million on both 1 August 2002 and 1 August 2003 for the rights to broadcast football matches over three seasons. ITV Digital was unable to sell enough subscriptions for the broadcasts and collapsed because it was unable to meet its liabilities. The Nationwide Football League tried to force Carlton and Granada (ITV Digital's only shareholders) to meet the ITV Digital's contractual obligations. It was unable to do so because the shareholders could not be held legally liable for the amounts owing.

Carlton and Granada merged into one business in 2003, but at the time of ITV Digital were two independent companies.

Activity 4.1

The fact that shareholders can limit their losses to that which they have paid, or have agreed to pay, for their shares is of great practical importance to potential shareholders.
   Can you think of any practical benefit to a private-sector economy, in general, of this ability of shareholders to limit losses?

Business is a risky venture – in some cases very risky. People with money to invest will usually be happier to do so when they know the limit of their liability. By giving investors limited liability, new businesses are more likely to be formed and existing ones are likely to find it easier to raise more finance. This is good for the private-sector economy and may ultimately lead to the generation of greater wealth for society as a whole.

→   Though **limited liability** has this advantage to the providers of capital (the shareholders), it is not necessarily to the advantage of all others who have a stake in the business, like the Nationwide Football League clubs (see **Real World 4.2**). Limited liability is attractive to shareholders because they can, in effect, walk away from the unpaid debts of the company if their contribution has not been sufficient to meet those debts. This is likely to make any individual, or another business, that is considering entering into a contract, wary of dealing with the limited company. This can be a real problem for smaller, less established companies. Suppliers may insist on cash payment before delivery of goods or the rendering of a service. Alternatively, they may require a personal guarantee from a major shareholder that the debt will be paid before allowing trade credit. In the latter case, the supplier circumvents the company's limited liability status by demanding the personal liability of an individual. Larger, more established companies, on the other hand, tend to have built up the confidence of suppliers.

Legal safeguards

Various safeguards exist to protect individuals and businesses contemplating dealing with a limited company. These include the requirement to indicate limited liability status in the name of the company. By doing this, an alert is issued to prospective suppliers and lenders.

A further safeguard is the restrictions placed on the ability of shareholders to withdraw their investment from the company. These restrictions are designed to prevent shareholders from protecting their own investment and, as a result, leaving lenders and suppliers in an exposed position. We consider this point in more detail later in the chapter.

Finally, limited companies are required to produce annual financial statements (income statement, balance sheet and cash flow statement), and make them publicly available. This means that anyone interested can gain an impression of the financial performance and position of the company. The form and content of these statements are considered in some detail later in the chapter.

Public and private companies

When a company is registered with the Registrar of Companies, it must be registered either as a public or as a private company. The main practical difference between these is that a **public company** can offer its shares for sale to the general public, but a **private company** is restricted from doing so. A public limited company must signal its status to all interested parties by having the words 'public limited company', or its abbreviation 'plc' in its name. For a private limited company, the word 'limited' or 'Ltd' must appear as part of its name.

Private limited companies tend to be smaller businesses where the ownership is divided among relatively few shareholders who are usually fairly close to one another – for example, a family company. Numerically, there are vastly more private limited companies in the UK than there are public ones. Of the 2.1 million UK limited companies now in existence, only 11,500 (representing 0.5 per cent of the total) are public limited companies. Figure 4.1 shows the trend in the numbers of public and private limited companies in recent years.

Since public companies tend to be individually larger, they are often economically more important. In some industry sectors such as banking, insurance, oil refining and grocery retailing they are completely dominant. Although some large private limited companies exist, many are little more than the vehicle through which one-person businesses operate.

| Figure 4.1 | Number of private and public limited companies registered 2001 to 2006 |

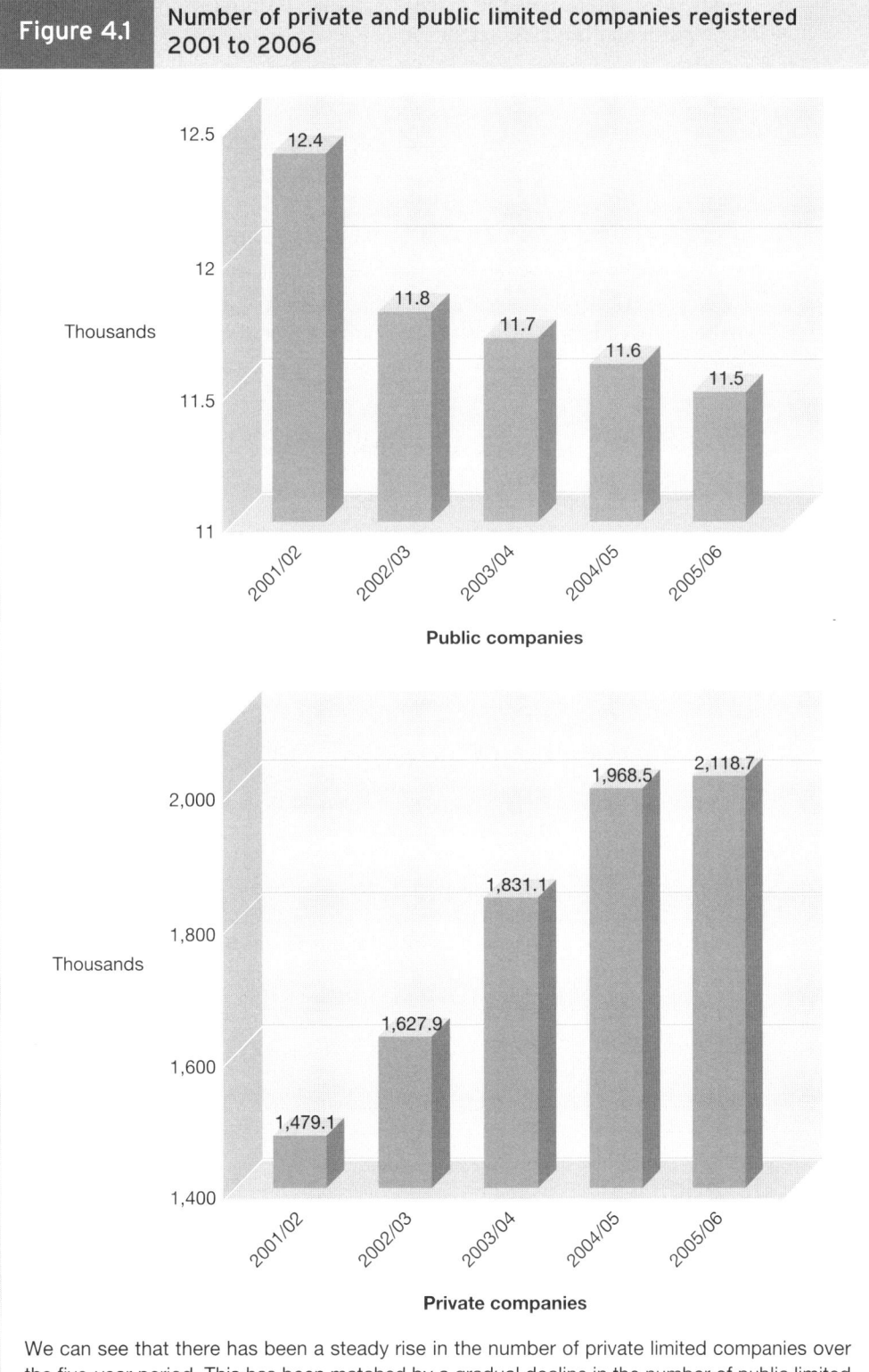

We can see that there has been a steady rise in the number of private limited companies over the five-year period. This has been matched by a gradual decline in the number of public limited companies.

Source: www.companieshouse.gov.uk

Real World 4.3 reveals the extent of market dominance of public limited companies in one particular business sector.

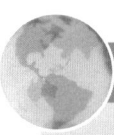

Real World 4.3

A big slice of the market

The grocery sector is dominated by four large players: Tesco, Sainsbury, Morrisons and Asda. The first three are public limited companies and the fourth, Asda, is owned by a large US public company (Wal-Mart). Figure 4.2 shows the share of the grocery market enjoyed by each.

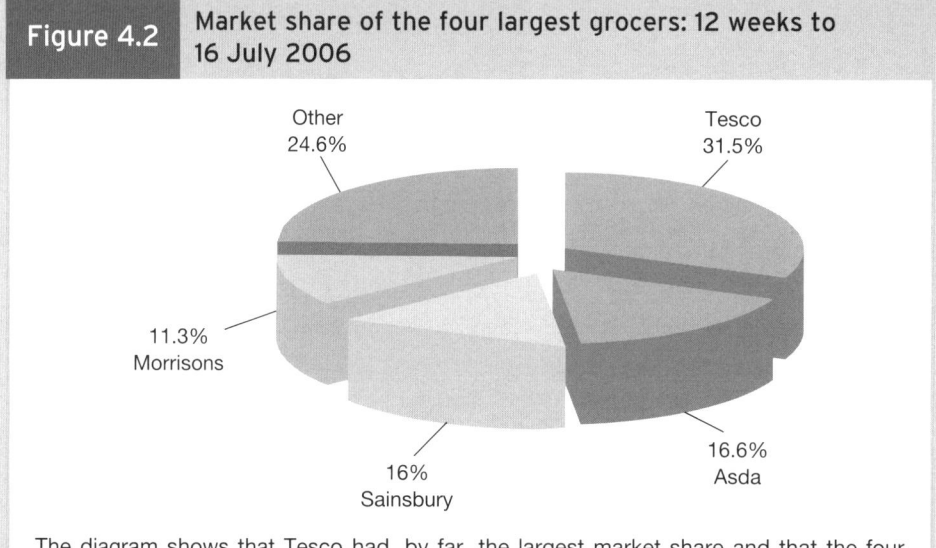

Figure 4.2 Market share of the four largest grocers: 12 weeks to 16 July 2006

The diagram shows that Tesco had, by far, the largest market share and that the four largest grocers, when taken together, had more than 75 per cent of the total market during the period.

Source: sharecast.com, 26 July 2006.

Taxation

Another consequence of the legal separation of the limited company from its owners is that companies must be accountable to the tax authorities for tax on their profits and gains. This leads to the reporting of tax in the financial statements of limited companies. The charge for tax is shown in the income statement (profit and loss account). The tax charge for a particular year is based on that year's profit. Since only 50 per cent of a company's tax liability is due for payment during the year concerned, the other 50 per cent will appear on the end-of-year balance sheet as a short-term liability. This will be illustrated a little later in the chapter. The tax position of companies contrasts with that of sole proprietorships and partnerships, where tax is levied not on the business but on the owner(s). Thus, tax does not impact on the financial statements of unincorporated businesses, but is an individual matter between the owner(s) and the tax authorities.

→   Companies are charged corporation tax on their profits and gains. The percentage rates of tax tend to vary from year to year, but have recently been 30 per cent for larger companies and nineteen per cent for smaller companies. These rates of tax are levied on the company's taxable profit, which is not necessarily the same as the profit shown on the income statement. This is because tax law does not, in every respect, follow the normal accounting rules. Generally, however, the taxable profit and the company's accounting profit are pretty close to one another.

Transferring share ownership – the role of the Stock Exchange

The point has already been made that shares in a company may be transferred from one owner to another. The desire of some shareholders to sell their shares, coupled with the desire of others to buy those shares, has led to the existence of a formal market in which shares can be bought and sold. The London Stock Exchange, and similar organisations around the world, provide a market place in which shares in public companies may be bought and sold. Share prices are determined by the laws of supply and demand, which are, in turn, determined by investors' perceptions of the future economic prospects of the companies concerned. Only the shares of certain companies (*listed* companies) may be traded on the London Stock Exchange. About 1,300 UK companies are listed. This represents only one in about 1,600 of all UK companies (public and private) and about one in nine public limited companies. However, many of these 1,300 listed companies are massive. Nearly all of the 'household name' UK businesses (for example, Tesco, Boots, BT, Cadbury-Schweppes, Vodafone, BP and so on) are listed companies.

Activity 4.2

If, as has been pointed out earlier, the change in ownership of shares does not directly affect the particular company, why do many public companies actively seek to have their shares traded in a recognised market?

The main reason is that investors are generally very reluctant to pledge their money unless they can see some way in which they can turn their investment back into cash. In theory, the shares of a particular company may be very valuable because it has bright prospects. However, unless this value is capable of being turned into cash, the benefit to the shareholders is dubious. After all, we cannot spend shares; we generally need cash.

This means that potential shareholders are much more likely to be prepared to buy new shares from the company (thereby providing the company with new finance) where they can see a way of liquidating their investment (turning it into cash), as and when they wish. Stock exchanges provide the means of liquidation.

Though the buying and selling of 'second-hand' shares does not provide the company with cash, the fact that the buying and selling facility exists will make it easier for the company to raise new share capital when it needs to do so.

Managing a company

A limited company may have legal personality, but it is not a human being capable of making decisions and plans about the business and exercising control over it. People must undertake these management tasks. The most senior level of management of a company is the board of directors.

→ The shareholders elect **directors** (by law there must be at least one director for a private limited company and two for a public limited company) to manage the company on a day-to-day basis on behalf of those shareholders. In a small company, the board may be the only level of management and consist of all of the shareholders. In larger companies, the board may consist of ten or so directors out of many thousands of shareholders. Indeed, directors are not even required to be shareholders. Below the board of directors of the typical large company could be several layers of management comprising thousands of people.

→ In recent years, the issue of **corporate governance** has generated much debate. The term is used to describe the ways in which companies are directed and controlled. The issue of corporate governance is important because, with larger companies, those who own the company (that is, the shareholders) are usually divorced from the day-to-day control of the business. The shareholders employ the directors to manage the company for them. Given this position, it may seem reasonable to assume that the best interests of shareholders will guide the directors' decisions. However, in practice this does not always occur. The directors may be more concerned with pursuing their own interests, such as increasing their pay and 'perks' (such as expensive motor cars, overseas visits and so on) and improving their job security and status. As a result, a conflict can occur between the interests of shareholders and the interests of directors.

The problems and issues associated with corporate governance will be explored in detail in Chapter 10.

Financing limited companies

The owners' claim

The owner's claim of a sole proprietorship is normally encompassed in one figure on the balance sheet, usually labelled 'capital'. With companies, this is usually a little more complicated, though in essence the same broad principles apply. With a company, the owners' claim is divided between shares (for example, the original invest-
→ ment), on the one hand, and **reserves** (that is, profits and gains subsequently made), on the other. There is also the possibility that there will be more than one type of shares and of reserves. Thus, within the basic divisions of share capital and reserves, there might well be further subdivisions. This might seem quite complicated, but we shall shortly consider the reasons for these subdivisions and all should become clearer.
→ The sum of share capital and reserves is commonly known as **equity**.

The basic division

When a company is first formed, those who take steps to form it (the promoters) will decide how much needs to be raised by the potential shareholders to set the company up with the necessary assets to operate. Example 4.1 acts as a basis for illustration.

Example 4.1

A group of friends get together and decide to form a company to operate an office cleaning business. They estimate that the company will need £50,000 to obtain the necessary assets to operate. Between them, they raise the cash, which they use to buy shares in the company, on 31 March 2006, with a **nominal value** (or **par value**) of £1 each.

At this point the balance sheet of the company would be:

Balance sheet as at 31 March 2006

	£
Net assets (all in cash)	50,000
Equity	
Share capital	
50,000 shares of £1 each	50,000

The company now buys the necessary non-current assets (vacuum cleaners and so on) and inventories (cleaning materials) and starts to trade. During the first year, the company makes a profit of £10,000. This, by definition, means that the owners' claim expands by £10,000. During the year, the shareholders (owners) make no drawings of their claim, so at the end of the year the summarised balance sheet looks like this:

Balance sheet as at 31 March 2007

	£
Net assets (various assets less liabilities*)	60,000
Equity	
Share capital	
50,000 shares of £1 each	50,000
Reserves (revenue reserve)	10,000
Total equity	60,000

* We know from Chapter 2 that Assets = Capital (Equity) + Liabilities. This can be rearranged so that Assets – Liabilities = Capital (Equity).

The profit is shown in a reserve, known as a **revenue reserve**, because it arises from generating revenue (making sales). Note that we do not simply merge the profit with the share capital: we must keep the two amounts separate (to satisfy company law). The reason for this is that there is a legal restriction on the maximum drawings of the share-holders' claim (or payment of a **dividend**) that the owners can make. This is defined by the amount of revenue reserves, and so it is helpful to show these separately. We shall look at why there is this restriction, and how it works, a little later in the chapter.

Share capital

Shares represent the basic units of ownership of a business. All companies issue **ordinary shares**. Ordinary shares are often known as *equities*. The nominal value of such shares is at the discretion of the people that start up the company. For example, if the initial capital is to be £50,000, this could be two shares of £25,000 each, 5 million shares of one penny each or any other combination that gives a total of £50,000. Each share must have equal value.

Activity 4.3

The initial capital requirement for a new company is £50,000. There are to be two equal shareholders. Would you advise them to issue two shares of £25,000 each? Why?

Such large denomination shares tend to be unwieldy. Suppose that one of the shareholders wanted to sell his or her shares. S/he would have to find one buyer. If there were shares of smaller denomination, it would be possible to sell part of the shareholding to various potential buyers. Furthermore, it would be possible to sell just part of the holding and retain a part.

In practice, £1 is the normal maximum nominal value for shares. Shares of 25 pence each and 50 pence each are probably the most common.

 Some companies also issue other classes of shares, **preference shares** being the most common. Preference shares guarantee that *if a dividend is paid*, the preference shareholders will be entitled to the first part of it up to a maximum value. This maximum is normally defined as a fixed percentage of the nominal value of the preference shares. If, for example, a company issues 10,000 preference shares of £1 each with a dividend rate of 6 per cent, this means that the preference shareholders are entitled to receive the first £600 (that is, 6 per cent of £10,000) of any dividend that is paid by the company for a year. The excess over £600 goes to the ordinary shareholders. Normally, any undistributed profits and gains also accrue to the ordinary shareholders.

The ordinary shareholders are the primary risk-takers as they are entitled to share in the profits of the company only after other claims have been satisfied, and their potential rewards reflect this risk. There are no upper limits, however, on the amount by which they may benefit. The potential rewards available to ordinary shareholders reflect the risks that they are prepared to take. Since ordinary shareholders take most of the risks, power normally resides in their hands. Usually, only the ordinary shareholders are able to vote on issues that affect the company, such as who the directors should be.

It is open to the company to issue shares of various classes – perhaps with some having unusual and exotic conditions – but in practice it is rare to find other than straightforward ordinary and preference shares. Though a company may have different classes of shares whose holders have different rights, within each class all shares must be treated equally. The rights of the various classes of shareholders, as well as other matters relating to a particular company, are contained in that company's set of rules, known as the 'articles and memorandum of association'. A copy of these rules must be lodged with the Registrar of Companies, who makes it available for inspection by the general public.

Reserves

Reserves are profits and gains that have been made by a company, which still form part of the shareholders' (owners') claim or equity. One reason that past profits and gains may not remain part of equity is that they have been paid out to shareholders (as dividends and so on). Another reason is that reserves will be reduced by the amount of any losses that the company might suffer. In the same way that profits increase equity, losses reduce it.

The shareholders' claim consists of share capital and reserves.

Activity 4.4

Are reserves amounts of cash? Can you think of a reason why this is an odd question?

To deal with the second point first, it is an odd question because reserves are a claim, or part of one, on the assets of the company, whereas cash is an asset. So reserves cannot be cash.

Reserves are classified as either revenue reserves or capital reserves. In Example 4.1 we came across one type of reserve, the revenue reserve. We should recall that this reserve represents the company's retained trading profits and gains on the disposal of non-current assets. It is worth mentioning that retained profits, or earnings as they are often called, represent overwhelmingly the largest source of new finance for UK companies. For most companies they amount to more than share issues and borrowings combined.

→   **Capital reserves** arise for two main reasons:

- issuing shares at above their nominal value (for example, issuing £1 shares at £1.50);
- revaluing (upwards) non-current assets.

Where a company issues shares at above their nominal value, UK law requires that the excess of the issue price over the nominal value be shown separately.

Activity 4.5

Can you think why shares might be issued at above their nominal value? (*Hint*: this would not usually happen when a company is first formed and the initial shares are being issued.)

Once a company has traded and has been successful, the shares would normally be worth more than the nominal value at which they were issued. If additional shares are to be issued to new shareholders to raise finance for further expansion, unless they are issued at a value higher than the nominal value, the new shareholders will be gaining at the expense of the original ones.

Example 4.2 shows how this works.

Example 4.2

Based on future prospects, the net assets of a company are worth £1.5 million. There are currently 1 million ordinary shares in the company, each with a face (nominal) value of £1. The company wishes to raise an additional £0.6 million of cash for expansion and has decided to raise it by issuing new shares. If the shares are issued for £1 each (that is 600,000 shares), the total number of shares will be:

$$1.0 \text{ m} + 0.6 \text{ m} = 1.6 \text{ million}$$

Example 4.2 continued

and their total value will be the value of the existing net assets plus the new injection of cash:

$$£1.5\text{ m} + £0.6\text{ m} = £2.1\text{ million}$$

This means that the value of each share after the new issue will be:

$$£2.1\text{ m}/1.6\text{ m} = £1.3125$$

The current value of each share is:

$$£1.5\text{ m}/1.0\text{ m} = £1.50$$

So the original shareholders will lose:

$$£1.50 - £1.3125 = £0.1875\text{ a share}$$

and the new shareholders will have gained

$$£1.3125 - £1.0 = £0.3125\text{ a share}$$

The new shareholders will, no doubt, be delighted with this outcome; the original ones will not.

Things could be made fair between the two sets of shareholders described in Example 4.2 by issuing the new shares at £1.50 each. In this case it would be necessary to issue 400,000 shares to raise the necessary £0.6 million. £1 a share of the £1.50 is the nominal value and will be included with share capital in the balance sheet (£400,000 in total). The remaining £0.50 is a share premium, which will be shown as a capital reserve known as the **share premium account** (£200,000 in total).

It is not clear why UK company law insists on the distinction between nominal share values and the premium. In some other countries (for example, the United States) with similar laws governing the corporate sector, there is not the necessity of distinguishing between share capital and share premium. Instead, the total value at which shares are issued is shown as one comprehensive figure on the company balance sheet. **Real World 4.4** shows the shareholders' claim of one well-known business.

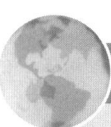

Real World 4.4

How Thorntons is funded

Thorntons plc, the chocolate maker, had the following share capital and reserves as at 24 June 2006:

	£m
Share capital (10 p ordinary shares)	6,724
Share premium account	12,890
Retained earnings	12,340
Total equity	31,954

Note how the nominal share capital figure is nearly half the share premium account figure. This implies that Thorntons has issued shares at higher prices than the 10 p per share nominal value. This reflects its trading success since the company was first formed. Note also how, at balance sheet values, retained earnings (profits) make up nearly 40 per cent of the total for share capital and reserves.

Source: Thorntons plc, Annual Report 2006, p. 22.

Altering the nominal value of shares

The point has already been made that the promoters of a new company may make their own choice of the nominal or par value of the shares. This value need not be permanent. At a later date the shareholders can decide to change it.

Suppose that a company has 1 million ordinary shares of £1 each and a decision is made to change the nominal value of the shares from £1 to £0.50, in other words to halve the value. This would lead the company to issue each shareholder with a new share certificate (the shareholders' evidence of ownership of their shareholding) for exactly twice as many shares, each with half the nominal value. The result would be that each shareholder retains a holding of the same total nominal value. This process is known, not surprisingly, as splitting the shares. The opposite, reducing the number of shares and increasing their nominal value per share to compensate, is known as **consolidating**.

Since each shareholder would be left, after a split or consolidation, with exactly the same proportion of ownership of the company's assets as before, the process should not increase the value of the total shares held.

Activity 4.6

Why might the shareholders want to split their shares in the manner described above?

The answer is probably to avoid individual shares becoming too valuable and making them a bit unwieldy, in the way discussed in the answer to Activity 4.3. If a company trades successfully, the value of each share is likely to rise, and in time could increase to a level that makes them less marketable. Splitting would solve this problem.

Real World 4.5 gives an example of a share split by a large UK company.

Real World 4.5

Share split at Pennon

Pennon Group plc owns South West Water Ltd, the business that provides water and sewerage services to the far south-west of England and Viridor Waste Ltd a waste management business.

In July 2006, Pennon Group plc decided to split its ordinary shares. Each share with a nominal value of 122.1 p was subdivided into three new ordinary shares of 40.7 p per share. This meant that each ordinary shareholder became the owner of three times as many new shares, with each share having a market value of one third of each of the old ones. The reason given by the company was as follows:

> In recent years the price of the company's ordinary shares has risen to the point where they are now one of the most highly priced ordinary shares compared with comparator companies quoted on the London Stock Exchange. It is hoped that the share split will lead to increased market liquidity of the company's shares.

Source: www.pennon-group.co.uk, Investor Information.

Bonus shares

It is always open to a company to take reserves of any kind (irrespective of whether they are capital or revenue) and turn them into share capital. This will involve transferring the desired amount from the reserve concerned to share capital and then distributing the appropriate number of new shares to the existing shareholders. New shares arising from such a conversion are known as **bonus shares**. Issues of bonus shares are quite frequently encountered in practice. Example 4.3 illustrates this aspect of share issues.

Example 4.3

The summary balance sheet of a company is as follows:

Balance sheet as at 31 March 2007

	£
Net assets (various assets less liabilities)	128,000
Equity	
Share capital	
50,000 shares of £1 each	50,000
Reserves	78,000
Total equity	128,000

The company decides that it will issue existing shareholders with one new share for every share currently owned by each shareholder. The balance sheet immediately following this will appear as follows:

Balance sheet as at 31 March 2007

	£
Net assets (various assets less liabilities)	128,000
Equity	
Share capital	
100,000 shares of £1 each (50,000 + 50,000)	100,000
Reserves (78,000 – 50,000)	28,000
Total equity	128,000

We can see that the reserves have decreased by £50,000 and share capital has increased by the same amount. Share certificates for the 50,000 ordinary shares of £1 each that have been created from reserves will be issued to the existing shareholders to complete the transaction.

Activity 4.7

A shareholder of the company in Example 4.3 owned 100 shares before the bonus issue. How will things change for this shareholder as regards the number of shares owned and the value of the shareholding?

The answer should be that the number of shares will double, from 100 to 200. Now the shareholder owns one five-hundredth of the company (that is, 200/100,000). Before the bonus issue, the shareholder also owned one five-hundredth of the company (that is, 100/50,000). The company's assets and liabilities have not changed as a result of the bonus issue and so, logically, one five-hundredth of the value of the company should be identical to what it was before. Thus, each share is worth half as much.

A bonus issue simply takes one part of the owners' claim (part of a reserve) and puts it into another part of the owners' claim (share capital). The transaction has no effect on the company's assets or liabilities, so there is no effect on shareholders' wealth.

Note that a bonus issue is not the same as a share split. A split does not affect the reserves.

Activity 4.8

Can you think of any reasons why a company might want to make a bonus issue if it has no economic consequence?

We think that there are three possible reasons:

● *Share price.* To lower the value of each share without reducing the shareholders' collective or individual wealth. This has a similar effect to share splitting.
● *Shareholder confidence.* To provide the shareholders with a 'feel-good factor'. It is believed that shareholders like bonus issues because it seems to make them better off, though in practice it should not affect their wealth.
● *Lender confidence.* Where reserves arising from operating profits and/or realised gains on the sale of non-current assets are used to make the bonus issue, it has the effect of taking part of that portion of the owners' claim that could be drawn by the shareholders, as drawings (or dividends), and locking it up. The amount transferred becomes part of the permanent capital base of the company. (We shall see, a little later in this chapter, that there are severe restrictions on the extent to which shareholders may make drawings from their claim.) An individual or business contemplating lending money to the company may insist that the dividend payment possibilities are restricted as a condition of making the loan. This point will be explained shortly.

Real World 4.6 provides an example of a bonus share issue.

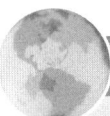

Real World 4.6

Bonus shares

Workspace Group plc provides flexible business accommodation for small and medium-size businesses. In March 2005 it made a 9 for 1 bonus issue of shares following a £15.2 m capitalisation of reserves. The nominal value of a share in the company is 10 p and a total of 151,955,694 new shares was issued. Following the issue, the net asset value per share was divided by 10 so that year-end net asset values were adjusted from £22.40 per share to £2.24 per share.

Source: based on information in 2005 Annual Report and www.workspacegroup.co.uk.

Share capital jargon

Before leaving our detailed discussion of share capital, it might be helpful to clarify some of the jargon relating to shares that is used in company financial statements.

 Share capital that has been issued to shareholders is known as the **issued** (or **allotted**) **share capital**. Sometimes, but not very often, a company may not require shareholders to pay the whole amount that is due to be paid for the shares at the time of issue. This may happen where the company does not need the money all at once.

→ Some money would normally be paid at the time of issue and the company would 'call'
→ for further instalments until the shares were **fully paid**. That part of the total issue price
→ that has been 'called' is known as the **called-up share capital**. That part that has been
→ called and paid is known as the **paid-up share capital**.

Raising share capital

Once the company has made its initial share issue to start business (usually soon after the company is first formed) it may decide to make further issues of new shares. These may be:

● rights issues, that is issues made to existing shareholders, in proportion to their existing shareholding;
● public issues, that is issues made to the general investing public;
● private placings, that is issues made to selected individuals who are usually approached and asked if they would be interested in taking up new shares.

During its lifetime a company may use all three of these approaches to raising funds through issuing new shares (although only public companies can make appeals to the general public).

Borrowings

Most companies borrow money to supplement that raised from share issues and ploughed-back profits. Company borrowing is often on a long-term basis, perhaps on a ten-year contract. Lenders may be banks and other professional providers of loan finance. Many companies raise loan finance in such a way that small investors, including private individuals, are able to lend small amounts. This is particularly the case
→ with the larger, Stock Exchange listed, companies and involves their making a **loan notes issue**, which, though large in total, can be taken up in small slices by individual investors, both private individuals and investing institutions, such as pension funds and insurance companies. In some cases, these slices of loans can be bought and sold through the Stock Exchange. This means that investors do not have to wait the full term of the loan to obtain repayment, but can sell their slice of the loan to another would-be lender at intermediate points in the term of the loan. Loan notes are often
→ known as *loan stock* or **debentures**.

Some of the features of loan notes financing, particularly the possibility that the loan notes may be traded on the Stock Exchange, can lead to a confusion that loan notes are shares by another name. We should be clear that this is not the case. It is the shareholders who own the company and, therefore, who share in its losses and profits. Holders of loan notes lend money to the company under a legally binding contract that normally specifies the rate of interest, the interest payment dates and the date of repayment of the loan itself. Usually, long-term loans are secured on assets of the company.

Long-term financing of companies can be depicted as in Figure 4.3.

It is important to the prosperity and stability of a company that it strikes a suitable balance between finance provided by the shareholders (equity) and from borrowing. This topic will be explored in Chapter 7.

Real World 4.7 shows the long-term borrowings of Rolls-Royce plc, the engine-building business, at 31 December 2005.

| Figure 4.3 | Sources of long-term finance for a typical limited company |

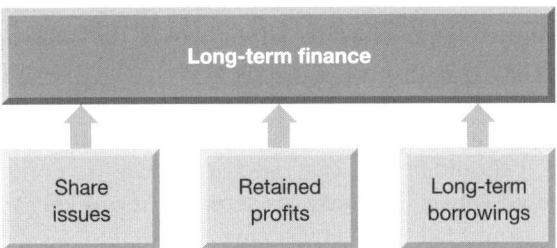

Companies derive their long-term financing needs from three sources: new share issues, retained profit and long-term borrowings. For a typical company, the sum of the first two (jointly known as 'equity finance') exceeds the third. Retained profit usually exceeds either of the other two in terms of the amount of finance raised in most years.

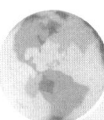

Real World 4.7

Borrowing at Rolls-Royce

The following extract from the annual financial statements of Rolls-Royce plc sets out the sources of the company's long-term borrowing as at 31 December 2005.

	2005 £m
Unsecured	
Bank loans	4
6³⁄₈% Notes 2007	354
7³⁄₈% Notes 2016	200
5.84% Notes 2010	107
6.38% Notes 2013	134
6.55% Notes 2015	49
4¹⁄₂% Notes 2011	524
Other loans 2009 (interest rates nil)	1
Secured	
Bank loans	71
Obligations under finance leases payable:	
Between one and two years	5
Between two and five years	8
After five years	1
	1,458
Repayable	
Between one and two years – by instalments	49
– otherwise	–
Between two and five years – by instalments	11
– otherwise	354
After five years – by instalments	29
– otherwise	1,015
	1,458

Source: Rolls-Royce plc Annual Report and Accounts, 2005, Note 18.

Note the large number of sources from which the company borrows. This is typical of most large companies and probably reflects a desire to exploit all available means of raising finance, each of which may have some advantages and disadvantages. 'Secured' in this context means that the lender would have the right, should Rolls-Royce fail to meet its interest and/or capital repayment obligations, to seize a specified asset of the business (probably some land) and use it to raise the sums involved. Normally, a lender would accept a lower rate of interest where the loan is secured as there is less risk involved. It should be said that whether a loan to a company like Rolls-Royce is secured or unsecured is usually pretty academic. It is unlikely that such a large and profitable company would fail to meet its obligations.

'Finance leases' are, in effect, arrangements where Rolls-Royce needs the use of a non-current asset (such as an item of machinery) and, instead of buying the asset itself, it arranges for a financier to buy the asset. The financier then leases it to the business, probably for the entire economic life of the asset. Though legally it is the financier who owns the asset, from an accounting point of view the essence of the arrangement is that, in effect, Rolls-Royce has borrowed cash from the financier to buy the asset. Thus, the asset appears among the business's non-current assets and the financial obligation to the financier is shown here as long-term borrowing. This is a good example of how accounting tries to report the economic *substance* of a transaction, rather than its strict legal *form*. Finance leasing is a fairly popular means of raising long-term funds.

Withdrawing equity

Companies are legally obliged to distinguish between that part of the shareholders' equity which may be withdrawn and that part which may not. The withdrawable part consists of profits arising from trading and from the disposal of non-current assets. It is represented in the balance sheet by *revenue reserves*.

It is important to appreciate that the total revenue reserves appearing in the balance sheet is rarely the total of all trading profits and profits on disposals of non-current assets generated by the company. This total will normally have been reduced by at least one of the following three factors:

● corporation tax paid on those profits;
● any dividends paid;
● any losses from trading and the disposal of non-current assets.

The non-withdrawable part consists of profits arising from shareholders buying shares in the company and from upward revaluations of assets still held. It is represented in the balance sheet by *share capital and capital reserves*.

The law does not specify how large the non-withdrawable part of a particular company's shareholders' equity should be. However, when seeking to impress prospective lenders and credit suppliers, the larger this part, the better. Those considering doing business with the company must be able to see from the company's balance sheet how large it is.

Activity 4.9

Why are limited companies required to distinguish different parts of their shareholders' claim whereas sole proprietorship and partnership businesses are not?

The reason stems from the limited liability that company shareholders enjoy, but which owners of unincorporated businesses do not. If a sole proprietor or partner withdraws all of the owner's claim, or even an amount in excess of this, the position of the lenders and credit suppliers of the business is not weakened since they can legally enforce their claims against the sole proprietor or partner as an individual. With a limited company, the business and the owners are legally separated and such right to enforce claims against individuals does not exist. To protect the company's lenders and credit suppliers, however, the law insists that the shareholders cannot normally withdraw a specific part of their claim.

Let us now look at another example.

Example 4.4

The summary balance sheet of a company at a particular date is as follows:

Balance sheet

	£
Total assets	43,000
Equity	
Share capital	
20,000 shares of £1 each	20,000
Reserves (revenue)	23,000
Total equity	43,000

A bank has been asked to make a £25,000 long-term loan to the company. If the loan were to be made, the balance sheet immediately following would appear as follows:

Balance Sheet (after the loan)

	£
Total assets (£43,000 + £25,000)	68,000
Equity	
Share capital	
20,000 shares of £1 each	20,000
Reserves (revenue)	23,000
	43,000
Non-current liability	
Borrowings – loan	25,000
Total equity and liabilities	68,000

As things stand, there are assets to a total balance sheet value of £68,000 to meet the bank's claim of £25,000. It would be possible and perfectly legal, however, for the company to pay a dividend (withdraw part of their claim) of £23,000. The balance sheet would then appear as follows:

Example 4.4 continued

Balance Sheet

	£
Total assets (£68,000 – £23,000)	45,000
Equity	
Share capital	
20,000 shares of £1 each	20,000
Reserves (revenue (£23,000 – £23,000))	–
	20,000
Non-current liabilities	
Borrowings – loan	25,000
Total equity and liabilities	45,000

This leaves the bank in a very much weaker position, in that there are now total assets with a balance sheet value of £45,000 to meet a claim of £25,000. Note that the difference between the amount of the borrowings (bank loan) and the total assets equals the capital and reserves total. Thus, the capital and reserves represent a **margin of safety** for lenders and suppliers. The larger the amount of the owners' claim withdrawable by the shareholders, the smaller is the potential margin of safety for lenders and suppliers.

As we have already seen, the law says nothing about how large the margin of safety must be. It is up to each company to decide what is appropriate.

As a practical footnote to Example 4.4, it is worth pointing out that long-term lenders would normally seek to secure a loan against an asset of the company, such as land. This, as we have seen, would give the lender the right to seize the asset concerned, sell it and satisfy the repayment obligation, should the company default.

Activity 4.10

Would you expect a company to pay all of its revenue reserves as a dividend? What factors might be involved with a dividend decision?

It would be rare for a company to pay all of its revenue reserves as a dividend: the fact that it is legally possible does not necessarily make it a good idea. Most companies see ploughed-back profits as a major – usually *the* major – source of new finance. The factors that influence the dividend decision are likely to include:

- the availability of cash to pay a dividend; it would not be illegal to borrow to pay a dividend, but it would be unusual and, possibly, imprudent;
- the needs of the business for finance for new investment;
- the expectations of shareholders concerning the amount of dividends to be paid.

You may have thought of others.

The law states, however, that shareholders cannot, under normal circumstances, withdraw that part of their claim that is represented by shares and capital reserves. This means that potential lenders and credit suppliers know the maximum amount of the shareholders' equity that can be withdrawn. Figure 4.4 shows the important division between that part of the shareholders' equity which can be withdrawn as a dividend and that part which cannot.

Figure 4.4	Availability for dividends of various parts of the shareholders' claim

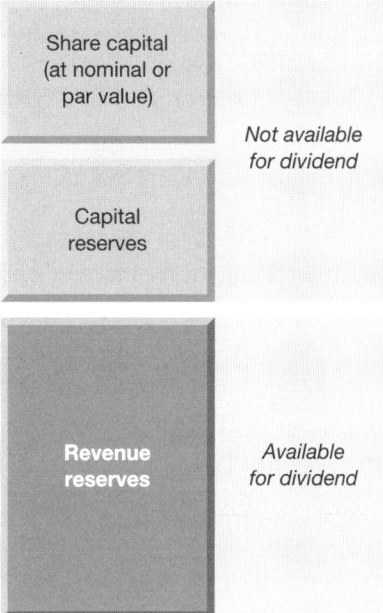

Total equity finance of limited companies consists of share capital, capital reserves and revenue reserves. Only the revenue reserves (which arise from realised profits and gains) can be used to fund a dividend. In other words, the maximum legal dividend is the amount of the revenue reserves.

Earlier in this chapter, the point was made that a potential lender may insist that some revenue reserves are converted to bonus shares (or capitalised) to increase the margin of safety as a condition of granting the loan.

If we refer back to **Real World 4.4**, we can see that Thorntons plc could legally have paid a dividend of £12,340 m on 24 June 2006, which is the amount of its revenue reserves. For several reasons, including the fact that this represented nearly 40 per cent of the balance sheet value of the company's net assets, no such dividend was paid.

Activity 4.11

Can you think of any circumstances where the non-withdrawable part of a company's capital could be reduced, without contravening the law?

It can be reduced as a result of the company sustaining trading losses, or losses on disposal of non-current assets, which exceed the withdrawable amount of shareholders' equity. It cannot be reduced by shareholders making withdrawals.

Though payment of a cash dividend is the standard way for shareholders to withdraw equity from a company, it is not the only way. Provided that certain conditions are met, it is perfectly legal for a company to redeem some of its shares or to buy some of its shares from particular shareholders and cancel them. These conditions are generally not difficult to meet for profitable companies.

The main financial statements

As we might expect, the financial statements of a limited company are, in essence, the same as those of a sole proprietor. There are, however, some differences of detail, and we shall now consider these. Example 4.5 sets out the income statement (profit and loss account) and balance sheet of a limited company:

Example 4.5

Da Silva plc
Income statement for the year ended 31 December 2006

	£m
Revenue	840
Cost of sales	(520)
Gross profit	320
Wages and salaries	(98)
Heat and light	(18)
Rent and rates	(24)
Motor-vehicle expenses	(20)
Insurance	(4)
Printing and stationery	(12)
Depreciation	(45)
Audit fee	(4)
Operating profit	95
Interest payable	(10)
Profit before taxation	85
Taxation	(24)
Profit for the year	61

Balance sheet as at 31 December 2006

	£m
Non-current assets	
Property, plant and equipment	203
Intangible assets	100
	303
Current assets	
Inventories	65
Trade receivables	112
Cash	36
	213
Total assets	516
Equity	
Ordinary shares of £0.50 each	200
Share premium account	30
Other reserves	50
Retained earnings	25
	305
Non-current liabilities	
Borrowings	100
Current liabilities	
Trade payables	99
Taxation	12
	111
Total equity and liabilities	516

Perhaps the most striking thing about these statements is their similarity to those of sole proprietors; the differences are small. Let us now go through and pick up these differences.

The income statement

There are a few features in the income statement that need consideration.

Profit

→ We can see that, following the calculation of **operating profit**, two further measures of profit are shown.

- The first of these is the *profit before taxation*. Interest charges are deducted from the operating profit to derive this figure. In the case of a sole proprietor or partnership business, the income statement would end here.
- The second measure of profit is the *profit for the year*. As the company is a separate legal entity, it is liable to pay tax (known as corporation tax) on the profits generated. (This contrasts with the sole proprietor business where it is the owner rather than the business that is liable for the tax on profits, as we saw earlier in the chapter.) This measure of profit represents the amount that is available for the shareholders.

Audit fee

Companies beyond a certain size are required to have their financial statements audited by an independent firm of accountants, for which a fee is charged. As we shall see in Chapters 5 and 10, the purpose of the audit is to lend credibility to the financial statements. Though it is also open to sole proprietors and partnerships to have their financial statements audited, relatively few do, so this is an expense that is most often seen in the income statement of a company.

The balance sheet

The main points for consideration in the balance sheet are taxation and other reserves.

Taxation

The amount that appears as part of the current liabilities represents 50 per cent of the tax on the profit for the year 2006. It is, therefore, 50 per cent (£12 m) of the charge that appears in the income statement (£24 m); the other 50 per cent (£12 m) will already have been paid. The unpaid 50 per cent will be paid shortly after the balance sheet date. These payment dates are set down by law.

Other reserves

This will include any reserves that are not separately identified on the face of the balance sheet. It may include a *general reserve*, which normally consists of trading profits that have been transferred to this separate reserve for re-investment ('ploughing back') into the operations of the company. In theory, there is no reason to set up a separate reserve for this purpose. The trading profits could remain unallocated and so swell the retained earnings of the company. It is not entirely clear why directors decide to make transfers to general reserves, since the profits concerned remain part of the revenue reserves, and are, therefore, still available for dividend. The most plausible explanation seems to be that directors feel that placing profits in a separate reserve indicates an intention to invest the funds, represented by the reserve, permanently in the company and, therefore, not to use them to pay a dividend. Of course, the retained earnings appearing on the balance sheet is also a reserve, but that fact is not indicated in its title.

Dividends

It has already been mentioned that dividends represent drawings by the shareholders of the company. Dividends are paid out of the revenue reserves of the company and should be deducted from these reserves (usually retained earnings) when preparing the balance sheet. Shareholders are often paid an annual dividend, which may be paid by the company in two parts. An 'interim' dividend may be paid part way through the year and a 'final' dividend shortly after the year end.

Dividends declared by the directors during the year but still unpaid at the year end *may* appear as a liability in the balance sheet. To be recognised as a liability, however, they must be properly authorised before the balance sheet date. This normally means that the dividend must be approved by the shareholders.

Large companies tend to have a clear and consistent policy towards the payment of dividends. Any change in the policy provokes considerable interest and is usually interpreted by shareholders as a signal of the directors' views concerning the future. For example, an increase in dividends may be taken as a signal from the directors' that future prospects are bright: a higher dividend being seen as tangible evidence of their confidence. **Real World 4.8** provides an example of a dividend payment that may well have been interpreted in this way.

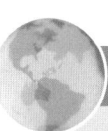

Real World 4.8

'MyTravel Set to Resume Its Dividend' **FT**

MyTravel, the tour operator formerly known as Airtours, has marked a return to financial good health by signalling that it would resume dividend payments for the first time since it fell into financial difficulties in 2001.

The group's improved performance was led by MyTravel's UK business, which has returned to growth after a dismal few years.

The gains in UK performance offset declines at MyTravel's North American operations, which were hit by the effects of Hurricane Wilma.

My Travel came close to collapse four years ago when a series of accounting errors and profit warnings caused the shares to tumble.

But the tour operator has completed a long restructuring, overhauling its management, cutting costs and changing its revenue recognition policies. Yesterday it said that advance bookings for this summer were outperforming the market.

Source: 'MyTravel Set to Resume Its Dividend' FT.com, 14 March 2006.

Self-assessment question 4.1

The summarised balance sheet of Dev Ltd is as follows:

Balance sheet as at 31 December 2006

	£
Net assets (various assets less liabilities)	235,000
Equity	
Share capital: 100,000 shares of £1 each	100,000
Share premium account	30,000
Revaluation reserve	37,000
Retained earnings	68,000
Total equity	235,000

Required:

(a) Without any other transactions occurring at the same time, the company made a one-for-five rights share issue at £2 per share payable in cash. This means that each shareholder was offered one share for every five already held. All shareholders took up their rights. Immediately afterwards, the company made a one-for-two bonus issue. Show the balance sheet immediately following the bonus issue, assuming that the directors wanted to retain the maximum dividend payment potential for the future.

(b) Explain what external influence might cause the directors to choose not to retain the maximum dividend payment possibilities.

(c) Show the balance sheet immediately following the bonus issue, assuming that the directors wanted to retain the *minimum* dividend payment potential for the future.

(d) What is the maximum dividend that could be paid before and after the events described in (a) if the minimum dividend payment potential is achieved?

(e) Lee owns 100 shares in Dev Ltd before the events described in (a). Assuming that the net assets of the company have a value equal to their balance sheet value, show how these events will affect Lee's wealth.

(f) Looking at the original balance sheet of Dev Ltd, shown above, what four things do we know about the company's status and history that are not specifically stated on the balance sheet?

The answer to this question can be found at the back of the book on p. 402.

Summary

The main points of this chapter may be summarised as follows:

The main features of a limited company

- It is an artificial person that has been created by law.

- It has a separate life to its owners and is granted a perpetual existence.

- It must take responsibility for its own debts and losses but its owners are granted limited liability.

- A public company can offer its shares for sale to the public; a private company cannot.

- It is governed by a board of directors, which is elected by the shareholders.

Financing the limited company

- The share capital of a company can be of two main types – ordinary shares and preference shares.
- Ordinary shares (equities) are the main risk-takers and are given voting rights; they form the backbone of the company.
- Preference shares are given a right to a fixed dividend before ordinary shareholders receive a dividend.
- Reserves are profits and gains made by the company and form part of the ordinary shareholders' claim.
- Borrowings provide another major source of finance.

Share issues

- Bonus shares are issued to existing shareholders when part of the reserves of the company is converted into share capital.
- Rights issues give existing shareholders the right to buy new shares in proportion to their existing holding.
- Public issues are made direct to the investing public generally.
- Private placings are share issues to particular investors.
- The shares of public companies may be bought and sold on a recognised Stock Exchange.

Reserves

- Reserves are of two types – revenue reserves and capital reserves.
- Revenue reserves arise from trading profits and from realised profits on the sale of non-current assets.
- Capital reserves arise from the issue of shares above their nominal value or from the upward revaluation of non-current assets.
- Revenue reserves can be withdrawn as dividends by the shareholders whereas capital reserves, normally, cannot.

Financial statements of limited companies

- The financial statements of limited companies are based on the same principles as those of sole proprietorship and partnership businesses. However, there are some differences in detail.
- The income statement has three measures of profit displayed after the gross profit figure: operating profit, net profit before tax and net profit for the year.
- The income statement also shows audit fees and corporation tax on profits for the year.
- Any unpaid tax and unpaid, but authorised, dividends will appear in the balance sheet as current liabilities.
- The share capital plus the reserves will be shown as 'equity'.

Key terms

Limited company	Capital reserves
Shares	Share premium account
Limited liability	Consolidating
Public company	Bonus shares
Private company	Issued share capital
Corporation tax	Fully paid shares
Director	Called-up share capital
Corporate governance	Paid-up share capital
Reserves	Loan notes
Equity	Rights issue
Nominal value	Private placing
Revenue reserve	Debentures
Dividend	Margin of safety
Ordinary shares	Operating profit
Preference shares	

Further reading

If you would like to explore the topics covered in this chapter in more depth, we recommend the following books:

Elliott, B. and Elliott, J. (2006) *Financial Accounting and Reporting*, 11th edn, Financial Times Prentice Hall, Chapters 5–6, 8 and 21–3.

KPMG (2006) *KPMG's Practical Guide to International Financial Reporting Standards*, 3rd edn, Thomson, Section 2.5.

Sutton, T. (2004) *Corporate Financial Accounting and Reporting*, 2nd edn, Financial Times Prentice Hall, Chapters 6 and 12.

Review questions

4.1 How does the liability of a limited company differ from the liability of a real person, in respect of amounts owed to others?

4.2 Some people are about to form a company, as a vehicle through which to run a new business. What are the advantages to them of forming a private limited company rather than a public one?

4.3 What is a reserve? Distinguish between a revenue reserve and a capital reserve.

4.4 What is a preference share? Compare the main features of a preference share with those of:

(a) an ordinary share; and
(b) loan notes.

Exercises

Exercises 4.6 to 4.8 are more advanced than 4.1 to 4.5.

If you wish to try more exercises, visit the students' side of the Companion Website.

4.1 Comment on the following quote:

'Limited companies can set a limit on the amount of debts that they will meet. They tend to have reserves of cash, as well as share capital and they can use these reserves to pay dividends to the shareholders. Many companies have preference as well as ordinary shares. The preference shares give a guaranteed dividend. The shares of many companies can be bought and sold on the Stock Exchange, and shareholders selling their shares can represent a useful source of new capital to the company.'

4.2 Comment on the following quotes:

(a) 'Bonus shares increase the shareholders' wealth because, after the issue, they have more shares, but each one of the same nominal value as they had before.'
(b) 'By law, once shares have been issued at a particular nominal value, they must always be issued at that value in any future share issues.'
(c) 'By law, companies can pay as much as they like by way of dividends on their shares, provided that they have sufficient cash to do so.'
(d) 'Companies do not have to pay tax on their profits because the shareholders have to pay tax on their dividends.'

4.3 Briefly explain each of the following expressions that you have seen in the financial statements of a limited company:

(a) dividend;
(b) audit fee;
(c) share premium account.

4.4 Iqbal Ltd started trading on 1 January 2002. During the first five years of trading, the following occurred:

Year ended 31 December	Trading profit (loss) £	Profit (loss) on sale of non-current assets £	Upward revaluation of non-current assets £
2002	(15,000)	–	–
2003	8,000	–	10,000
2004	15,000	5,000	–
2005	20,000	(6,000)	–
2006	22,000	–	–

Required:
Assume that the company paid the maximum legal dividend each year. Under normal circumstances, how much would each year's dividend be?

4.5 Da Silva plc's outline balance sheet as at a particular date was as follows:

	£m
Net assets (assets less liabilities)	72
Equity	
£1 ordinary shares	40
General reserve	32
	72

The directors made a one-for-four bonus issue, immediately followed by a one-for-four rights issue at a price of £1.80 per share.

Required:
Show the balance sheet of Da Silva plc immediately following the two share issues.

4.6 Presented below is a draft set of simplified financial statements for Pear Limited for the year ended 30 September 2006.

Income statement for the year ended 30 September 2006

	£000
Revenue	1,456
Cost of sales	(768)
Gross profit	688
Salaries	(220)
Depreciation	(249)
Other operating costs	(131)
Operating profit	88
Interest payable	(15)
Profit before taxation	73
Taxation at 30%	(22)
Profit for the year	51

Balance sheet as at 30 September 2006

Non-current assets	
Property, plant and equipment	
Cost	1,570
Depreciation	(690)
	880
Current assets	
Inventories	207
Trade receivables	182
Cash at bank	21
	410
Total assets	1,290
Equity	
Share capital	300
Share premium account	300
Retained earnings at beginning of year	104
Profit for year	51
	755
Non-current liabilities	
Borrowings (10% loan repayable 2009)	300
Current liabilities	
Trade payables	88
Other payables	20
Taxation	22
Borrowings (bank overdraft)	105
	235
Total equity and liabilities	1,290

The following information is available:

(a) Depreciation has not been charged on office equipment with a carrying amount of £100,000. This class of assets is depreciated at 12 per cent a year using the reducing balance method.

(b) A new machine was purchased, on credit, for £30,000 and delivered on 29 September 2006 but has not been included in the financial statements. (Ignore depreciation.)

(c) A sales invoice to the value of £18,000 for September 2006 has been omitted from the financial statements. (The cost of sales figure is stated correctly.)

(d) A dividend of £25,000 had been approved by the shareholders before 30 September 2006, but was unpaid at that date. This is not reflected in the financial statements.

(e) The interest payable on the debenture for the second half-year was not paid until 1 October 2006 and has not been included in the financial statements.

(f) An allowance for receivables is to be made at the level of 2 per cent of receivables.

(g) An invoice for electricity to the value of £2,000 for the quarter ended 30 September 2006 arrived on 4 October and has not been included in the financial statements.

(h) The charge for taxation will have to be amended to take account of the above information. Make the simplifying assumption that tax is payable shortly after the end of the year, at the rate of 30 per cent of the profit before tax.

Required:

Prepare a revised set of financial statements for the year ended 30 September 2006 incorporating the additional information in (a) to (h) above. Note: work to the nearest £1,000.

4.7   Presented below is a draft set of financial statements for Chips Limited.

Chips Limited
Income statement for the year ended 30 June 2006

	£000
Revenue	1,850
Cost of sales	(1,040)
Gross profit	810
Depreciation	(220)
Other operating costs	(375)
Operating profit	215
Interest payable	(35)
Profit before taxation	180
Taxation	(60)
Profit for the year	120

Balance sheet as at 30 June 2006

	Cost £000	Depr'n £000	£000
Non-current assets			
Property, plant and equipment			
Buildings	800	(112)	688
Plant and equipment	650	(367)	283
Motor vehicles	102	(53)	49
	1,552	(532)	1,020
Current assets			
Inventories			950
Trade receivables			420
Cash at bank			16
			1,386
Total assets			2,406
Equity			
Ordinary shares of £1, fully paid			800
Reserves at 1 July 2005			248
Profit for the year			120
			1,168
Non-current liabilities			
Borrowings (Secured 10% loan)			700
Current liabilities			
Trade payables			361
Other payables			117
Taxation			60
			538
Total equity and liabilities			2,406

The following additional information is available:

1 Purchase invoices for goods received on 29 June 2006 amounting to £23,000 have not been included. This means that the cost of sales figure in the income statement has been understated.

2 A motor vehicle costing £8,000 with depreciation amounting to £5,000 was sold on 30 June 2006 for £2,000, paid by cheque. This transaction has not been included in the company's records.

3 No depreciation on motor vehicles has been charged. The annual rate is 20 per cent of cost at the year end.

4 A sale on credit for £16,000 made on 1 July 2006 has been included in the financial statements in error. The cost of sales figure is correct in respect of this item.

5 A half-yearly payment of interest on the secured loan due on 30 June 2006 has not been paid.

6 The tax charge should be 30 per cent of the reported profit before taxation. Assume that it is payable, in full, shortly after the year-end.

Required:

Prepare a revised set of financial statements incorporating the additional information in 1 to 6 above. Note: work to the nearest £1,000.

4.8 Rose Limited operates a small chain of retail shops that sell high-quality teas and coffees. Approximately half of sales are on credit. Abbreviated and unaudited financial statements are given below:

Rose Limited
Income statement for the year ended 31 March 2006

	£000
Revenue	12,080
Cost of sales	(6,282)
Gross profit	5,798
Labour costs	(2,658)
Depreciation	(625)
Other operating costs	(1,003)
Operating profit	1,512
Interest payable	(66)
Net profit before tax	1,446
Taxation	(434)
Net profit for the year	1,012

Balance sheet as at 31 March 2006

	£000
Non-current assets	2,728
Current assets	
Inventories	1,583
Receivables	996
Cash	26
	2,605
Total assets	5,333
Equity	
Share capital (50 p shares, fully paid)	750
Share premium	250
Retained earnings	1,468
	2,468
Non-current liabilities	
Borrowings – Secured loan (2011)	300
Current liabilities	
Trade payables	1,118
Other payables	417
Tax	434
Borrowings – Overdraft	596
	2,565
Total equity and liabilities	5,333

Since the unaudited financial statements for Rose Limited were prepared, the following information has become available:

1 An additional £74,000 of depreciation should have been charged on fixtures and fittings.
2 Invoices for credit sales on 31 March 2006 amounting to £34,000 have not been included; cost of sales is not affected.
3 Allowances for receivables should be provided at a level of 2 per cent of receivables at the year end.
4 Inventories, which had been purchased for £2,000, have been damaged and are unsaleable. This is not reflected in the financial statements.
5 Fixtures and fittings to the value of £16,000 were delivered just before 31 March 2006, but these assets were not included in the financial statements and the purchase invoice had not been processed.
6 Wages for Saturday-only staff, amounting to £1,000, have not been paid for the final Saturday of the year. This is not reflected in the financial statements.
7 Tax is payable at 30 per cent of net profit after tax. Assume that it is payable shortly after the year-end.

Required:

Prepare revised financial statements for Rose Limited for the year ended 31 March 2006, incorporating the information in 1 to 7 above. Note: work to the nearest £1,000.

5

Accounting for limited companies (2)

Introduction

This chapter continues our examination of the financial statements of limited companies. We begin by identifying the legal responsibilities of directors and then go on to discuss the main sources of accounting rules governing published financial statements. Although a detailed consideration of these accounting rules is beyond the scope of this book, the key rules that shape the form and content of the published financial statements are discussed. We also consider the efforts made to ensure that these rules are underpinned by a coherent framework of principles.

The increasing complexity of business and the added demands for information by financial report users have led to the publication of a number of additional financial reports. This chapter considers two of these, namely the segmental financial report and the operating and financial review. These reports aim to provide users with a more complete picture of financial performance and position.

Despite the proliferation of accounting rules and the increasing supply of financial information to users of financial reports, concerns have been expressed over the quality of some of those published reports. This chapter ends by considering some well-publicised accounting scandals and the problem of creative accounting.

Learning outcomes

When you have completed this chapter, you should be able to:

- Describe the responsibilities of directors and auditors concerning the annual financial statements provided to shareholders and others.
- Identify the main sources of regulation affecting the financial statements of limited companies.
- Discuss the framework of principles for accounting.
- Prepare an income statement, balance sheet and statement of changes in equity for a limited company in accordance with international financial reporting standards.

- Explain the purpose of the segmental report and the operating and financial review and describe their main features.

- Discuss the threat posed by creative accounting to the quality of published financial statements.

The directors' duty to account

With most large companies, it is not possible for all shareholders to be involved in the management of the company, nor do most of them wish to be involved. Instead, they appoint directors to act on their behalf. This separation of ownership from day-to-day control creates the need for directors to be accountable for their stewardship (management) of the company's assets. Thus, the law requires that directors:

- maintain appropriate accounting records;
- prepare annual financial statements and a directors' report, and make these available to all shareholders and to the public at large.

The financial statements are made available to the public by submitting a copy to the Companies Registry (Department of Trade and Industry), which allows anyone who wishes to do so to inspect them. In addition, listed companies are required to publish their financial statements on their website.

Activity 5.1

Why does the law require directors to account in this way and who benefits from these requirements?

We thought of the following benefits and beneficiaries:

- *To inform and protect shareholders*. If shareholders do not receive information about the performance and position of their company, they will have problems in appraising their investment. Under these circumstances, they would probably be reluctant to invest and this, in turn, would affect the functioning of the private sector. Any society with a significant private sector needs to encourage equity investment.
- *To inform and protect suppliers of labour, goods, services and finance, particularly those supplying credit (loans) or goods and services on credit*. Individuals and organisations would be reluctant to engage in commercial relationships, such as supplying goods or lending money, where a company does not provide information about its financial health. The fact that a company has limited liability increases the risks involved in dealing with the company. An unwillingness to engage in commercial relationships with limited companies will, once again, affect the functioning of the private sector.
- *To inform and protect society more generally*. Some companies exercise enormous power and influence in society generally, particularly on a geographically local basis. For example, a particular company may be the dominant employer and purchaser of commercial goods and services in a particular town or city. Legislators have tended to take the view that society has the right to information about the company and its activities.

The directors' duty to account is considered in more detail in Chapter 10.

The need for accounting rules

If we accept the need for directors to prepare and publish financial statements, we must also accept the need for a framework of rules concerning how these statements are prepared and presented. Without rules, there is a much greater risk that unscrupulous directors will adopt policies and practices that portray an unrealistic view of financial health. There is also a much greater risk that the financial statements will not be comparable over time or with those of other companies. These risks are likely to undermine the integrity of financial statements in the eyes of users.

Users must, however, be realistic about what can be achieved through regulation. Problems of manipulation and of concealment can still occur even within a highly regulated environment and some examples of both will be considered later in the chapter. The scale of these problems, however, should be reduced. Problems of comparability can also still occur, as accounting is not a precise science. Judgements and estimates must be made when preparing financial statements and these may hinder comparisons. Furthermore, no two companies are identical and the accounting policies adopted may vary between companies for valid reasons.

Sources of accounting rules

In recent years there has been a trend towards the internationalisation of business, which seems set to continue. This trend has led to calls for the international harmonisation of accounting rules to help both users and companies. Harmonisation should help investors and other users of financial statements by making it easier to compare the performance and position of different companies operating in different countries. It should help companies with international operations by reducing the time and cost of producing financial statements: different sets of financial statements would no longer have to be prepared to comply with the rules of different countries.

The International Accounting Standards Board (IASB) is an independent body which is at the forefront of the move towards harmonisation. The Board, which is based in the UK, is dedicated to developing a single set of high quality, global accounting rules that provide transparent and comparable information in financial statements. These rules, which are known as **International Financial Reporting Standards** or International Accounting Standards, deal with key issues such as:

- what information should be disclosed;
- how information should be presented;
- how assets should be valued;
- how profit should be measured.

The overriding requirement for financial statements prepared according to IASB standards is to provide a fair representation of the company's financial position, financial performance and cash flows. There is a presumption that this fair representation will be achieved where the financial statements are drawn up in accordance with the various IASB standards that have been issued.

The authority of the IASB was given a huge boost when the European Commission adopted a regulation requiring nearly all Stock Exchange listed companies of EU member states to prepare their financial statements according to IASB standards for accounting periods commencing on or after 1 January 2005. Although non-listed UK companies are not currently required to adopt IASB standards, they have the option to do so. Many informed observers believe, however, that IASB standards will soon become a requirement for all UK companies.

The EU regulation overrides any laws in force in member states that could either hinder or restrict compliance with IASB standards. The ultimate aim is to achieve a single framework of accounting rules for companies from all member states. The EU recognises that this will only be achieved if individual governments do not add to the requirements imposed by the various IASB standards. Thus, it seems that accounting rules developed within individual EU member countries will eventually disappear. For the time being, however, the EU accepts that the governments of member states may need to impose additional disclosures for some corporate governance matters and regulatory requirements. In the UK, company law requires disclosure relating to various corporate governance issues. There is, for example, a requirement to disclose details of directors' remuneration in the published financial statements, which goes beyond anything required by IASB standards. Furthermore, the Financial Services Authority (FSA), in its role as the UK (Stock Exchange) listing authority, imposes rules on Stock Exchange listed companies. These include the requirement to publish a condensed set of interim (half-year) financial statements in addition to the annual financial statements. (These statements are not required by the IASB, although there is a standard providing guidance on their content and structure.)

Figure 5.1 sets out the main sources of accounting rules for Stock Exchange listed companies discussed above. Whilst company law and the FSA still play an important role, in the longer term, IASB standards seem set to become the sole source of company accounting rules.

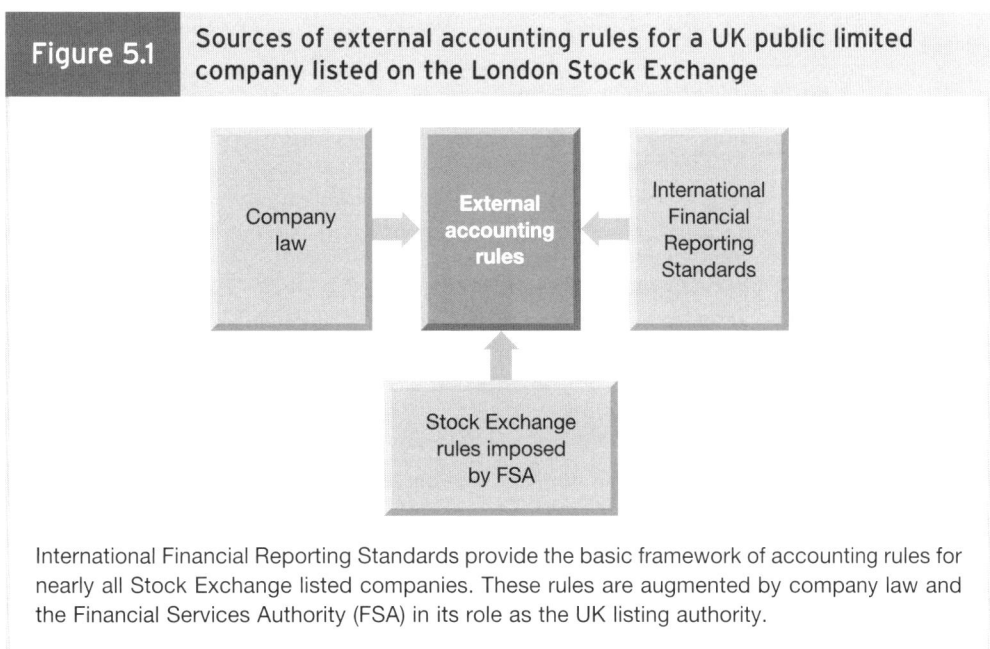

Figure 5.1 **Sources of external accounting rules for a UK public limited company listed on the London Stock Exchange**

International Financial Reporting Standards provide the basic framework of accounting rules for nearly all Stock Exchange listed companies. These rules are augmented by company law and the Financial Services Authority (FSA) in its role as the UK listing authority.

Real World 5.1 provides a list of standards that have been issued, or adopted, by the IASB to give an idea of the range of topics that are covered.

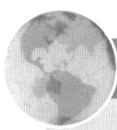

Real World 5.1

International standards

The following is a list of the International Accounting Standards (IASs) or International Financial Reporting Standards (IFRSs) in issue as at 1 August 2007. (The latter term is used for standards issued from 2003 onwards.) Several standards have been issued and subsequently withdrawn, which explains the numerical gaps in sequence. In addition, several have been revised and re-issued.

IAS 1   Presentation of Financial Statements
IAS 2   Inventories
IAS 7   Cash Flow Statements
IAS 8   Accounting Policies, Changes in Accounting Estimates and Errors
IAS 10   Events after the Balance Sheet Date
IAS 11   Construction Contracts
IAS 12   Income Taxes
IAS 14   Segment Reporting
IAS 15   Information Reflecting the Effects of Changing Prices
IAS 16   Property, Plant and Equipment
IAS 17   Leases
IAS 18   Revenue
IAS 19   Employee Benefits
IAS 20   Accounting for Government Grants and Disclosure of Government Assistance
IAS 21   The Effects of Changes in Foreign Exchange Rates
IAS 23   Borrowing Costs
IAS 24   Related Party Disclosures
IAS 26   Accounting and Reporting by Retirement Benefit Plans
IAS 27   Consolidated and Separate Financial Statements
IAS 28   Investments in Associates
IAS 29   Financial Reporting in Hyperinflationary Economies
IAS 31   Interests in Joint Ventures
IAS 32   Financial Instruments: Presentation
IAS 33   Earnings per Share
IAS 34   Interim Financial Reporting
IAS 36   Impairment of Assets
IAS 37   Provisions, Contingent Liabilities and Contingent Assets
IAS 38   Intangible Assets
IAS 39   Financial Instruments: Recognition and Measurement
IAS 40   Investment Property
IAS 41   Agriculture
IFRS 1   First-time Adoption of International Financial Reporting Standards
IFRS 2   Share-based Payment
IFRS 3   Business Combinations
IFRS 4   Insurance Contracts
IFRS 5   Non-current Assets Held For Sale and Discontinued Operations
IFRS 6   Exploration for and Evaluation of Mineral Resources
IFRS 7   Financial Instruments: Disclosures

The IASB has promised a period of stability over the short-term with no new major standards becoming effective until 2009. This should ease the transition to international standards and allow countries to amend their laws where necessary. The IASB, however, has an ambitious agenda and significant changes are likely to occur over the longer term.

Presenting the financial statements

Now that we have gained an impression of the sources of rules affecting limited companies, let us turn our attention to the main rules to be followed in the presentation of financial statements. We shall focus on the IASB rules and, in particular, those contained in IAS 1 *Presentation of Financial Statements*. This standard is very important as it sets out the structure and content of financial statements and the principles to be followed in preparing these statements.

According to IAS 1, the financial statements consist of:

● an income statement;
● a balance sheet;
● a statement of changes in equity;
● a cash flow statement;
● notes on accounting policies and other explanatory notes.

We shall discuss each of these below but, before doing so, we should be clear as to what is the main consideration when preparing these statements.

Fair representation

The overriding requirement is for the financial statements to provide a fair representation of the company's financial position, financial performance and cash flows. There is a presumption that this will be achieved where the financial statements are drawn up in accordance with the various IASB standards that have been issued. It is only in very rare circumstances that compliance with a standard would not result in a fair representation of the financial health of a company.

Activity 5.2

IAS 1 does not say that the overriding requirement is for the financial statements to show a 'correct' or an 'accurate' presentation of financial health. Why, in your opinion, does it not use those words? (*Hint*: think of depreciation of non-current assets.)

Accounting can never really be said to be 'correct' or 'accurate' as these words imply that there is a precise value that any asset, claim, revenue or expense could have. This is simply not true in many, if not most, cases.

Depreciation provides a good example. The annual depreciation expense is based on judgements about the future concerning the expected useful life and residual value. If all relevant factors are taken into account and reasonable judgements are applied, it may be possible to achieve a fair representation of the amount of the cost or fair value of the asset that is consumed for a particular period. However, a precise figure for depreciation for a period cannot be achieved.

Income statement

Although the format of the income statement is not prescribed, IAS 1 sets out the *minimum* information to be presented on the face of income statement. These items include:

- revenue;
- finance costs;
- gains or losses on the sale of assets or settlement of liabilities arising from discontinued operations;
- tax expense; and
- profit or loss.

The standard makes it clear, however, that further items should be shown on the face of the income statement where they are relevant to an understanding of performance. For example, if a business is badly affected by flooding, and inventories are destroyed as a result, the cost of the flood damage should be shown.

As a further aid to understanding, all material expenses must be separately disclosed. However, they need not be shown on the face of the income statement: they can appear in the notes to the financial statements. The sort of material items that may require separate disclosure include:

- write down of inventories to net realisable value;
- write down or disposal of property, plant and equipment;
- disposal of investments;
- restructuring costs;
- discontinuing operations; and
- litigation settlements.

This is not an exhaustive list and, in practice, other material expenses may require separate disclosure.

The standard suggests two possible ways in which expenses can be presented on the face of the income statement. Expenses can be either presented according to their nature, such as depreciation, employee expenses and so on, or according to business functions, such administrative activities and distribution.

So far in this book, expenses have been broadly set out according to their nature. Example 5.1 below, however, shows how expenses may be presented according to business functions.

Example 5.1

Degas plc
Income statement for the year ended 31 May 2007

	£000
Revenue	690
Cost of sales	(330)
Gross profit	360
Distribution costs	(102)
Administrative expenses	(115)
Other expenses	(14)
Operating profit	129
Finance costs	(20)
Profit before tax	109
Taxation	24
Profit for the period	85

The choice between the two ways of presenting expenses should depend on which the directors believe will provide the more relevant and reliable information. The second of these two ways, which is illustrated above, shows how much of the revenue generated was absorbed by particular functions and may provide a better impression of the efficiency of the business. However, it is not always easy to attribute costs to particular functional areas, particularly where facilities and other resources are being shared. If this second approach is adopted, additional information concerning the nature of the expenses, including depreciation charges and employee costs, must also be shown. This is because this kind of information can be useful in predicting future cash flows.

The balance sheet

Again, IAS 1 does not prescribe the format of this financial statement but does set out the *minimum* information that should be presented on the face of the balance sheet. This includes the following:

- property, plant and equipment;
- investment property;
- intangible assets;
- financial assets (such as shares and loan notes of other companies held);
- inventories;
- trade and other receivables;
- cash and cash equivalents;
- trade and other payables;
- provisions;
- financial liabilities (excluding payables and provisions shown above);
- tax liabilities; and
- issued share capital and reserves (equity).

Additional information should be also shown where it is relevant to an understanding of the financial position of the business.

The standard requires that normally a distinction be made on the balance sheet between current assets and non-current assets and between current liabilities and non-current liabilities. However, where a company considers that more reliable and relevant information will be presented by ordering the items according to their liquidity, it is permitted to do this.

The sub-classification of some of the items shown above may be necessary, either to comply with particular standards or because of their size or nature. For example, sub-classifications are required for certain assets such as property, plant and equipment and inventories as well as for provisions and reserves. In addition, details of share capital, such as the number of issued shares, and their par value must also be shown. However, to avoid cluttering up the balance sheet, this additional information can be shown in the notes.

Statement of changes to equity

→ The **statement of changes to equity** aims to help users to understand the changes in share capital and reserves that took place during the period. It reconciles the capital and reserves figures at the beginning of the period with those at the end of the period. This is achieved by showing the effect on the capital and reserves of all revenue and expenses, including gains and losses, as well as the effect of share issues and purchases during the period.

To show the effect on capital and reserves of gains and losses, we first need to understand how they are reported in the financial statements. The general rule is that the income statement should show all *realised* gains and losses for the period. Those gains and losses that remain *unrealised* (because the asset is still held) do not pass through the income statement, but, instead, go directly to a reserve. We saw, in an earlier chapter, an example of an unrealised gain, or loss, which is not passed through the income statement.

Activity 5.3

Can you think of this example?

It is where a business revalues its land and buildings, the gain, or loss, arising is not shown in the income statement. It is transferred to a revaluation reserve, which forms part of the equity. The rule does not just relate to land and buildings, but these types of asset are, in practice, the most common examples of unrealised gains.

Another example of an unrealised gain or loss, which has not been mentioned so far, arises from exchange differences when the results of foreign operations are translated into UK currency. Once again, any gain, or loss, bypasses the income statement and is taken directly to a currency translation reserve. In the statement of changes in equity, we need to take account of *all* gains and losses that have arisen during the period. Thus, movements in the revaluation reserve and currency translation reserve must be identified in addition to realised profits (or losses) reported in the income statement.

To see how a statement of changes in equity may be prepared, let us consider Example 5.2.

Example 5.2

At 1 January 2007 Miro plc had the following equity:

Miro plc

	£m
Share capital (£1 ordinary shares)	100
Revaluation reserve	20
Translation reserve	40
Retained earnings	150
Total equity	310

During 2007, the company made a profit after tax from normal business operations of £42 m and reported a revaluation gain on land and buildings of £120 m. A loss on exchange differences on translating the results of foreign operations of £10 m was also reported. To strengthen its balance sheet, the company issued 50 m new shares during the year at a premium of £0.40. Dividends for the year were £27 m.

The above information for 2007 can be set out in a statement of changes in equity as follows:

Statement of changes in equity for the year ended 31 December 2007

	Share capital £m	Share premium £m	Revaluation reserve £m	Translation reserve £m	Retained earnings £m	Total £m
Balance as at 1 January 2007	100	–	20	40	150	310
Changes in equity for 2007						
Gain on revaluation of properties	–	–	120	–	–	120
Exchange differences on translation of foreign operations	–	–	–	(10)	–	(10)
Net income recognised directly to equity	–	–	120	(10)	–	110
Profit for the period	–	–	–	–	42	42
Total recognised income and expense for the period	–	–	120	(10)	42	152
Dividends	–	–	–	–	(27)	(27)
Issue of share capital	50	20	–	–	–	70
Balance at 31 December 2007	150	20	140	30	165	505

We can see from the example that dividends are shown in the statement of changes in equity and are an appropriation of equity.

Cash flow statement

The cash flow statement tries to help users to assess the ability of a company to generate cash and to assess the company's need for cash. The presentation requirements for this statement are set out in IAS 7 *Cash Flow Statements*, which we shall consider in some detail in Chapter 6.

Explanatory notes

The notes play an important role in helping users to understand the financial statements. They will normally contain the following information:

- a statement that the financial statements comply with relevant IFRSs;
- a summary of the measurement bases used and other significant accounting policies applied (for example, the basis of inventories valuation);
- supporting information relating to items appearing on the income statement, balance sheet, statement of changes in equity or cash flow statement; and
- other disclosures such as future contractual commitments that have not been recognised and management's objectives and policies.

General points

The standard requires that the financial statements be prepared annually, as a minimum. It also requires that comparative figures (that is, the equivalent figures for the immediately preceding period) be provided. The comparative figures enable users to assess the current figure for a particular item against its counterpart for the previous period.

The standard provides support for three key accounting conventions when preparing the financial statements. These are:

● going concern;
● accruals (except for the cash flow statement);
● consistency.

These conventions were covered in Chapters 2 and 3.

To improve the transparency of financial statements, the standard states that:

● offsetting liabilities against assets, or expenses against income, is not allowed. Thus, it is not acceptable, for example, to offset a bank overdraft against a positive bank balance (where the company has both); and
● material items must be shown separately.

The framework of principles

In Chapters 2 and 3, we came across various accounting conventions such as prudence, historic cost, going concern and so on. These conventions were developed as a practical response to particular problems that were confronted when preparing financial statements. They have stood the test of time and are still of value to preparers today. However, they do not provide, and were never designed to provide, a framework of principles to guide the development of financial statements. As we grapple with increasingly complex financial reporting problems, the need to have a sound understanding of *why* we account for things in a particular way becomes more and more pressing. Knowing *why* we account, rather than simply *how* we account, is vitally important if we are to improve the quality of financial statements.

In recent years, much effort has been expended in various countries, including the UK, to develop a clear **framework of principles** that will guide us in the development of accounting. Such a framework should provide clear answers to such fundamental questions as:

● Who are the main users of financial statements?
● What is the purpose of financial statements?
● What qualities should financial information possess?
● What are the main elements of financial statements?
● How should these elements be defined, recognised and measured?

If these questions can be answered, accounting rule makers, such as the IASB, will be in a stronger position to identify best practice and to develop more coherent rules. This should, in turn, increase the credibility of financial reports in the eyes of users. It may even help reduce the possible number of rules, because some issues may be resolved by reference to the application of general principles rather than by the generation of further rules.

The IASB framework

The quest for a framework of accounting principles began in earnest in the 1970s when the Financial Accounting Standards Board (FASB) in the US devoted a very large amount of time and resources to this endeavour. This resulted in a broad framework of principles, which other rule-making bodies, including the IASB, have drawn upon when developing their own frameworks.

The IASB has produced a 'Framework for the Preparation and Presentation of Financial Statements', which begins by discussing the main user groups and their needs. This is well-trodden territory and the various groups and needs identified are broadly in line with those set out in the sections on this topic in Chapter 1. The framework goes on to identify the objective of financial statements, which is:

> to provide information about the financial position, performance and changes in financial position of an enterprise that is useful to a wide range of users in making economic decisions.

This reflects the mainstream view and is very similar to the objective of financial statements that others have developed in recent years.

The IASB framework sets out the qualitative characteristics that make financial statements useful. The main characteristics identified are relevance, reliability, comparability, and understandability, all of which were discussed in Chapter 1. The framework also identifies the main elements of financial statements. These are assets, liabilities, equity, income and expense, and definitions for each element are provided. The definitions adopted hold no surprises and are very similar to those adopted by other rule-making bodies and to those discussed earlier, in Chapters 2 and 3.

The IASB framework identifies different valuation bases in use but does not indicate a preference for a particular valuation method. It simply notes that historic cost is the most widely used method of valuation (although fair values are now increasingly used in international financial reporting standards). Finally, the framework discusses the type of capital base that a business should try to maintain. It includes a discussion of the two main types of capital base – financial capital and physical capital – but, again, expresses no preference as to which should be maintained. The IASB framework does not have the same legal status as an IASB standard. Nevertheless, it offers guidance for dealing with accounting issues, particularly where no relevant accounting standard exists.

Overall, the IASB framework has provoked little debate and the principles and definitions adopted appear to enjoy widespread acceptance. There has been some criticism, mainly from academics, that the framework is really a descriptive document and does not provide theoretical underpinning to the financial statements. There has also been some criticism of the definitions of the elements of the financial statements. However, these criticisms have not sparked any major controversies.

The auditors' role

Shareholders are required to elect a qualified and independent person or, more usually, a firm to act as **auditors**. The auditors' main duty is to make a report as to whether, in their opinion, the financial statements do what they are supposed to do, namely to show a true and fair view of the financial performance, position and cash flows of the company by complying with the relevant accounting rules. To be able to form such an opinion, auditors must scrutinise both the annual financial statements and the evidence upon which they are based. The auditors' opinion must be included with the financial statements sent to the shareholders and to the Registrar of Companies.

The relationship between the shareholders, the directors and the auditors is illustrated in Figure 5.2. This shows that the shareholders elect the directors to act on their behalf, in the day-to-day running of the company. The directors are then required to 'account' to the shareholders on the performance, position and cash flows of the company, on an annual basis. The shareholders also elect auditors, whose role it is to give the shareholders an independent view of the truth and fairness of the financial statements prepared by the directors.

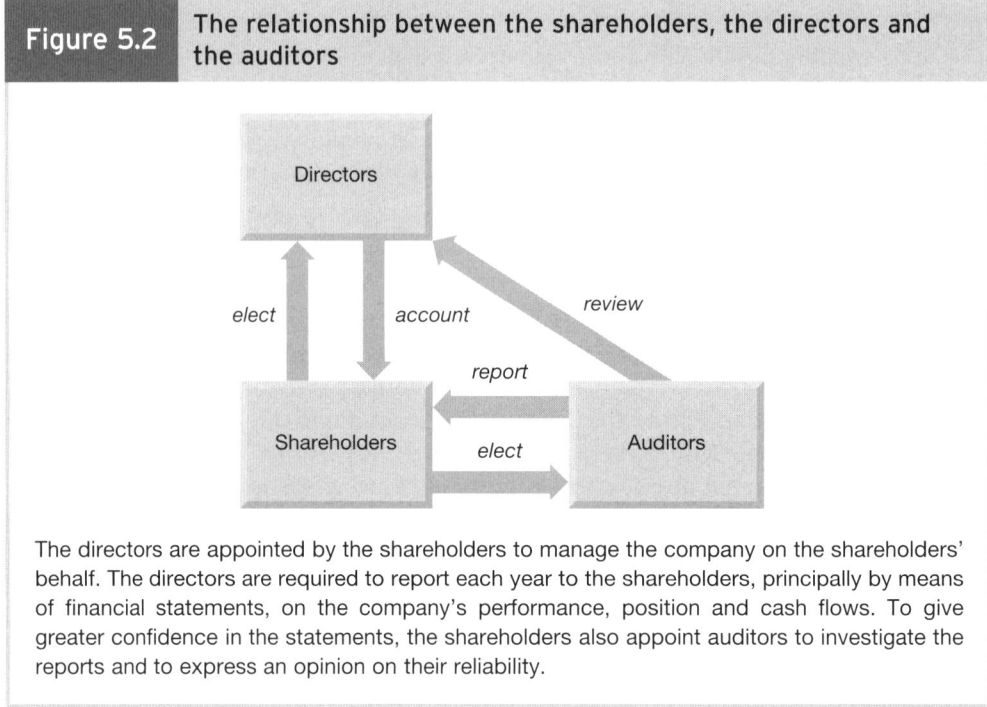

Figure 5.2   The relationship between the shareholders, the directors and the auditors

The directors are appointed by the shareholders to manage the company on the shareholders' behalf. The directors are required to report each year to the shareholders, principally by means of financial statements, on the company's performance, position and cash flows. To give greater confidence in the statements, the shareholders also appoint auditors to investigate the reports and to express an opinion on their reliability.

The role of the auditors and the audit process is considered in more detail in Chapter 10.

Directors' report

In addition to preparing the financial statements, the law requires the directors to prepare an annual report to shareholders and other interested parties. This report contains information of both a financial and a non-financial nature and goes beyond that which is contained in the financial statements. The information disclosed covers a variety of topics including details of share ownership, details of directors and their financial interests in the company, employment policies, and charitable and political donations. The auditors do not carry out an audit of the **directors' report**. However, they will check to see that the information in the report is consistent with that contained within the audited financial statements.

Chapter 21

Accounting for limited companies

In this chapter

We will learn of:
- the merits and de-merits of company formation
- shares and debentures
- financial statements of companies

and will be able to
- account for a share issue
- prepare financial statements of companies both for internal use and for publication

21.1 What is a limited company?

The most common type of business entity in the UK, for any business of reasonable size, is the limited liability company. A business entity acquires limited liability by registering with the Registrar of Companies, a process known as *incorporation*. As part of this process every company is required to file with the Registrar a copy of:

1. *Memorandum of Association* – a document establishing its identity: stating its name, domicile, its objects, limitation of its members' liability and its authorised share capital.

2. *Articles of Association* – which contain internal rules setting out the relationship between the company and its members as well as granting certain powers to its directors.

In the UK limited companies are governed by the Companies Act 2006.

There are many advantages and disadvantages to operating as a limited company rather than carrying on business as a sole trader or in partnership.

21.1.1 Advantages of limited companies

The advantages of operating a business as a limited company include the following:

1. **A greater amount of capital** can be raised because:
   - any number of persons may become *shareholders*;
   - the limitation of liability may prompt more people to contribute capital to even a risky venture;
   - individuals who may not be able to participate in management may contribute capital because, in a company, the management function is delegated to a few chosen persons known as directors.

2. **Delegation of management** to those with appropriate skills and expertise, who are known as *directors*, elected by the shareholders.

3. **Limited liability** is the most sought after attraction. In most other forms of business organisation, if the business fails the owner's personal assets could be at risk if there are insufficient business assets to meet the business liabilities. In a limited company the obligation of each shareholder is normally limited to the amount of capital the shareholder has agreed to contribute.

4. **Legal entity**. What this means is that upon incorporation a company is recognised in law as a person, separate and distinct from the shareholders. Though not endowed with a physical life, in the eyes of the law it is a separate legal person (referred to as body corporate) capable of owning property, entering into contracts, suing and being sued in a court of law and undertaking any legal activity (acting through human agents).

5. **Perpetual succession**. A limited company comes into existence by incorporation. It will continue to exist until its existence is terminated by another legal process known as *liquidation*. While individual shareholders may change, the company continues to exist. In a partnership, on the other hand, the partnership ceases to exist when one of the partners leaves the partnership.

6. **Transferability of shares**. The capital of a company is usually divided into shares. Individuals who own them are known as shareholders, their names and addresses being entered by the Company Secretary in a Share Register. This information is necessary in order to be able to send out notice of meetings and to pay dividends. A shareholder is issued with a share certificate as evidence of their legal title to the share which is transferable if they decide to sell it.

21.1.2 Disadvantages of limited companies

The disadvantages of operating as a limited company include the following:

1. **The need for creditor protection**. While protecting the interest of the shareholders, by granting them limited liability, company law places at risk the interests of those with a claim on the company. This is because, should the company's resources prove insufficient to meet its commitments, those who have a claim on it do not have any recourse to the personal resources of the shareholders or the directors.

2. **Companies are subject to strict legal control**, mainly because of the need to protect (i) the interest of its creditors who are denied recourse to the personal resources of the shareholders and (ii) the interest of the investors who have delegated the management to a few. The legal control includes requirements to:
   - maintain proper accounting records and (subject to exemption of small companies) have the financial statements audited;
   - make regular returns (such as the Annual Return) and file financial statements and a directors' report with the Registrar of Companies;
   - maintain statutory registers such as a Register of Members, Register of Directors and Secretaries and Register of Charges and hold them for public inspection;
   - protect the capital base of the company by, for example, insisting that any distribution to shareholders should be only out of profits determined in accordance with rules prescribed for the purpose.

3. **Publicity**. A significant price a company pays for the many advantages bestowed on it is its inability to protect the confidentiality of information on its performance and

position. Firstly, there is the legal requirement that anyone shall be permitted access to the company's statutory registers. Secondly, all information filed with the Registrar of Companies, including the annual financial statements and reports, is available for anyone's inspection.

4. **Delegation of management to a few has its downside**. Despite the efforts by successive company legislation to safeguard the ownership rights of the shareholders and to compel the directors to discharge adequately their stewardship responsibilities, the powers of the directors are substantial and real. For example, they are usually in control of their own levels of remuneration. The government is not inclined to provide statutory control over directors' remuneration and has favoured voluntary regulation.

   For example, companies are encouraged to comply with the Combined Code on Corporate Governance[1] which recommends that companies should have non-executive directors (i.e. directors who are not full-time employees of the company) and that the non-executive directors should determine the remuneration of the executive directors. The directors are also in control of the rewards paid as *dividends* to shareholders. The shareholders cannot approve dividends at a level higher than that recommended by the directors. No court of law will compel a company to pay a dividend larger than that proposed by directors. This is because there is an assumption that the directors' proposal has taken into account broader strategy issues such as a potential increase in competition or a planned increase in capital expenditure.

21.2 Types of limited companies

Limited companies are of two types:

- *public companies* which identify themselves using the letters plc at the end of their names;
- *private companies* which use the word Ltd as the last part of their name.

A public limited company (plc or PLC) can only start trading if it has a minimum share capital (in the UK[2] this is £50,000 or the Euro equivalent) and is the only form of organisation that may generally issue securities (shares, debentures) to the public. There is no requirement for a public company to have its securities listed on a recognised stock exchange. If it wishes to have its shares listed and be able to offer shares to the public it has to undergo a prolonged in-depth investigation calculated to protect the reputation of the Stock Exchange and the interests of those who buy and sell in it. Public companies listed on a stock exchange are known as *listed companies*. Listed companies are obliged to comply with certain rules, which are known as continuing obligations and which are intended to so regulate the volume and timing of price-sensitive information made available on the company that no-one is given an advantage.

Private companies are not allowed to do some things that public companies can, for example:

1. They are prohibited from asking the public to subscribe for its shares.
2. The transfer of shares from one shareholder to another may be restricted. For example, the Articles of Association may require a shareholder to offer their shares first to the directors of the company if they wish to sell them. This is known as the right of pre-emption.

On the other hand private companies have some concessions that are not available to public companies, as shown below.

Some concessions given to private companies		Public co
Directors	can have one director	at least two
Deliver accounts	within ten months of the year-end	within seven
Retention of records	for at least three years	for six years

21.3 Shares and debentures

A limited company raises long-term finance by issuing *shares* or *debentures*. All companies issue shares known as Ordinary shares. Other varieties of shares may also be issued, one of which is known as Preference shares.

21.3.1 Ordinary shares

An ordinary share is a portion of a company's capital which entitles the owner to certain rights (such as the rights to attend shareholders' meetings, to elect directors and auditors, to approve financial statements and to declare final dividends) and to share in the profits of the company.

21.3.2 Preference shares

Preference shares are so called because they give the right to a dividend before a dividend is paid to the ordinary shareholders. Their dividend, unlike that of the ordinary shareholders, is usually at a fixed percentage and there might be other rights such as the right for their dividend to be cumulative. Preference shares are assumed to be cumulative, irrespective of whether the name expressly confirms this position[3]. This means that the ordinary shareholders cannot be paid a dividend until all arrears (up to and including the current year's preference dividend) are fully discharged.

Preference shares are normally long-term, but not necessarily permanent, capital. For example, the terms of issue might have been that they can be redeemed (i.e. the company takes back the share, paying back the capital and perhaps an additional compensation) by the company at a specified future date.

These shares do not usually have a right to vote at meetings, though exceptionally they might have the right if their dividends are in arrears or there is a possibility that the company will cease trading. If it should cease trading, preference shareholders do not automatically have a prior right to the return of their capital unless this was one of the terms of issue.

21.3.3 Debentures

Debentures (known also as *loan notes* or *bonds*) are a written acknowledgement of debt by a company. The acknowledgement is usually made in a document (known as a debenture deed) which bears the company's seal and states the rate of interest, the nature and type of any security provided and the terms of repayment. Debenture holders, like shareholders, have the right to receive financial statements and, unlike shareholders, have the right to receive interest on their loan whether the company makes a profit or a loss. Like the preference shareholders, they usually have no voting rights unless their interest is not paid or their capital has not been repaid by the agreed date.

Activity 21.1 **Difference between shares and debentures**

Rose Petal has identified a company to invest in and seeks your advice on whether she should invest in that company's shares or debentures.

21.4 Accounting for a share issue

Company law in the UK requires that every share should have a *par value* (also known as nominal value or face value) assigned to the share. In the USA and other countries, shares of no par value are common. Although a committee appointed by the Board of Trade advocated the issue of shares of no par value in the UK[4] to date no action has been taken to allow this.

When issuing its shares, a successful company may fix the price of issue at higher than the share's par value. The extra amount received is known as *share premium*. Upon issuing an ordinary share with a par value of £10, if a company receives £12, company law in the UK requires that the par value alone should be credited to the Share Capital account while the excess is credited to a Share Premium account (see entries in the box on the right).

Dr Cash Book	£12	–
Cr Ordinary Share Capital a/c	–	£10
Cr Share Premium a/c	–	£2

The whole amount received (£12), including the amount recorded in the Share Premium account, is part of the capital contributed by the shareholders and is not available for distribution as dividend. It is permitted[5], however, to use the share premium to pay up new shares for allocation to the shareholders as bonus shares or to write off the expenses of the issue and any commission paid on the issue of the shares.

Activity 21.2 **Accounting for share issue**

Orange plc issued 100,000 ordinary shares of 50p each, at 60p each, fully called up and paid up. £3,000 was incurred as expense on the issue.

Required:
a) Explain the prime entry to account for these transactions.
b) Show how they will be reported on the balance sheet at the year-end.

A company may not always need immediately the full amount of the price at which it issues its shares. For example, a company may issue 10,000 ordinary shares of £1 each at

110p each, but may call for only 80p per share to be paid, and the remainder when it is called for. In this situation, at the point of allotting (i.e. issuing) the shares, only the so far called up value of the shares allotted (i.e. 80p less

Called up capital a/c Dr	£8,000	–
To Ordinary Share Capital a/c	–	£7,000
Share Premium a/c	–	£1,000
Being allotment of 10,000 shares of £1 each, at 110p each, 70p called up		

10p premium on each share) is credited to the Share Capital account. The journal entry recording the allotment is as shown above on the right. If we assume that £7,800 is received by the balance sheet date, the amount received is posted from the Cash Book to the credit of the Called Up Capital account, which would then report £200 as yet to be received. This is shown on the balance sheet as an asset.

Activity 21.3 Accounting for issue of shares partly called up

Pink plc issued 100,000 ordinary shares of 50p each, at 60p each, 40p called. By the year-end it had received £32,000 from the issue and has incurred £2,000 as expense on issue.

Required: Set out the journal entry accounting for the share issue and show how they will be reported on the balance sheet at the year-end.

Clue: The amount called up (40p) on each share includes the premium (10p). Hence, the called up value of each share at the point of allotment is only 30p.

At any point in time only the called up value of the number of shares in issue at that point is reported in the Share Capital account. Assuming that a company which has issued 10,000 shares of £1 each, 70p called up at the time of issue, makes the remaining call of 30p per share, the call when made is accounted for as shown on the right. The Share Capital account reports by then the fully called up value (£1 each) of 10,000 ordinary shares in issue.

Final call a/c Dr	£3,000	–
To Ordinary Share Capital a/c	–	£3,000
Being a final call of 30p each made on 10,000 ordinary shares		

We learned in Chapter 10 that a Trade Receivables Control account held the total of the amounts due from customers and that the Trade Receivables Ledger held the individual customer accounts. It is a similar position with the Share Capital account which, like the Control account, records the called up value of the shares of that class in issue. Particulars of the individual shareholdings are kept in a share register on a memorandum basis (i.e. outside double entry accounting system).

Once the shares have been issued there is no further entry in the financial records of the company. If the shares are sold, the company has no financial interest and only needs to have the particulars of the new shareholder to enter in the share register (often referred to as the Register of Members).

For example, let us assume that Jane, who was allotted 300 shares, sells them to Jackie at a price far in excess of the issue price. No entries will be made in the company's books of account relating to this transfer. The particulars of the number of shares transferred from Jane to Jackie are recorded in the share register (which is not a book of account). No part of the money paid by Jackie to Jane reaches the company.

> ### Activity 21.4 **Accounting for share transfers between shareholders**
>
> Beige plc has in issue 100 million shares of £1 each, 70p called up, and issued at 10p premium. Miriam, who has received an allotment of 5,000 shares from Beige plc, sold her entire holding to Michael at 220p per share.
>
> Required:
> a) Set out how the shares in issue will be reported on the Balance Sheet of Beige plc.
> b) Explain how the shares sold by Miriam will be accounted for in the books of Beige plc.
> c) If Beige plc goes into liquidation and its resources prove inadequate to meet its liabilities, how much more will Michael be obliged to pay in respect of the shares he bought from Miriam?

21.5 Financial statements of companies for internal use

The financial statements (i.e. Income Statement and Balance Sheet) of companies, prepared for the internal use of the board of directors, will be no different from the financial statements prepared in Chapter 4 except for the following matters which relate only to companies:

1. **Taxation**. Companies are required to pay tax (known as *corporation tax* in the UK) on the profit made in each accounting period. The estimated tax on the year's profit (assumed as £24,000) is accounted for by debiting a Tax (expense) account and crediting a Tax (liability) account. The tax expense is deducted from the profit at the bottom of the Income Statement to arrive at the profit after tax which is available for distribution to the shareholders as dividend or re-investment within the company. The liability is reported in the Balance Sheet under current liabilities.

Taxation (expense) account					Taxation (liability) account		
	£						£
Taxation a/c	24					Taxation a/c	24

Tax has to be estimated at the date the balance sheet is prepared. The amount needs to be agreed with the tax authorities and the final amount of tax is often different from the original estimate. If the estimate was too low we say that there has been an under-provision and in the Income Statement of the following year the amount under-provided is added to the tax estimated for that year. The amount of tax expense reported on the Income Statement would therefore include the estimated amount of that year's tax plus the amount previously under-provided or, in rare circumstances, less any amount over-provided previously.

2. **Interim dividends paid** are posted from the Cash Book to a Dividend account, which is shown as a deduction, not in the Income Statement, but in a separate portion of the Income Statement known as the *statement of changes in equity* (see Section 21.7 below).

3. **Final dividends proposed** need to be disclosed only as a note. It cannot be accounted for because, until it is declared, it would not qualify to be regarded as a liability. As we have seen (in Chapter 19) to be regarded as a liability it must be an obligation arising

from a past event. The obligating event, in the case of final dividend, is a resolution of the shareholders, which may be expected at their next meeting. Remember, however, that the directors have the power to declare (not just propose) any number of interim dividends. Dividends *declared* are accounted for by debiting a Dividend (expense) account and crediting a Dividend (liability) account, as shown below:

Dividend (expense) account					Dividend (liability) account	
	£					£
Dividend a/c	200				Dividend a/c	200

4. **Preference dividends** need to be accounted for, irrespective of whether the directors have proposed their payment, if any ordinary dividend has been paid. This is because preference shares have a priority right. The preference dividend is accounted for by debiting an expense account and crediting a liability account, as shown below.

Preference Dividend (expense) account					Preference Dividend (liability) account	
	£					£
Preference Dividend a/c	1,000				Preference Dividend a/c	1,000

The expense (unlike in the case of ordinary dividend) is always included in the Income Statement. The point of inclusion depends on whether the preference shares qualify to be regarded as part of the company's capital or, if they are of the redeemable variety[6], need to be reported on the balance sheet as a non-current liability.

If the preference shares qualify to be regarded as part of the company's capital, the preference dividend is shown on the Income Statement, as a deduction from profit after taxation. If, on the other hand, the preference shares are regarded as a non-current liability, then the preference dividend, being equivalent to interest paid, is shown on the Income Statement before deducting taxation.

21.6 Grouping of expenses by function

When preparing the Income Statements of companies, rather than randomly listing the operating expenses, it is usual to group them under meaningful functional headings. We are familiar already with the concept of cost of sales and that it includes all expenses on placing the goods sold in the condition in which and the location from which they are sold. Other operating expenses are classified as distribution costs or administrative expenses.

1. **Distribution costs** typically include:
   - warehousing expenses such as warehouse rent, wages and other remuneration of warehousing staff, depreciation, repairs and maintenance of equipment used in this activity;
   - sale promotion costs such as advertising, sale promotion expenses, commission and other remuneration to sales staff, and arguably bad debts (i.e. assuming it arose from bad selling).
   - Delivery to customer costs such as carriage outwards, depreciation, repair and maintenance of vehicles, and remuneration of staff engaged on this activity.

2. **Administrative expenses** typically include:
   - expenses of administering the company such as staff salary and other forms of remuneration, stationery, telephone, postage (unless incurred for delivery), depreciation of equipment used for this activity, bank charges;
   - cost of premises such as rent, rates, depreciation of building (unless used for production/selling activity), lighting and heating;
   - cost of checking on the administration, such as audit fees;
   - cost of administrative failure, such as from loss of goods, bad debts (if it arises from inadequacy of credit management), fines and penalties, development cost written off.

21.7 Statement of changes in equity

The word *equity* is used to indicate an element of risk. Normally, ordinary shares are referred to as equity shares because they are entitled to the residual portion of a company's profit, after all priority claims (such as those of preference shares and debentures) are met.

Once the profit after tax has been calculated in the Income Statement, the directors have to decide how much to distribute to the shareholders and how much to retain. The profit that is retained from year to year is known as *accumulated profit* or *retained earnings* and forms part of the company's *reserves*. A reserve is any profit retained within the company.

IAS 1 *Presentation of financial statements*[7] requires that the movement of retained earnings in each accounting period should be traced in a *statement of changes in equity* as on the right.

Note that the statement starts with the accumulated balance of retained earnings brought forward from prior years, adds the profit after tax from the Income Statement and deducts the dividend paid in the year to ordinary shareholders (only), ending with the amount of retained earnings carried forward to next year. That amount (£482) is reported on the balance sheet as part of the capital and reserves.

Statement of changes in equity	
Retained earnings b/f	£428
Profit for the year after tax	£84
Dividend paid	(£30)
Retained earnings c/f	£482

IAS 8 *Accounting policies, changes in accounting estimates and errors*[8] permits two items to be shown as adjustments from the amount of retained earnings brought forward from prior years (hence included in the statement of changes in equity, rather than in the year's Income Statement). These two items are (a) any corrections of prior period errors and (b) the retrospective portion of the effect of any changes in accounting policy.

1. **Correction of prior period errors** are material omissions or mis-statements in previous financial statements. These errors are corrected retrospectively by adjusting the balance brought forward from those years. For example, a material loss arising from a fraud in the previous year, neither detected nor accounted for when the financial statements of that year were prepared, will be reported, in this year's statement of changes in equity as a deduction from retained earnings brought forward.

2. **Retrospective effect of adjustments arising from a change of accounting policy** is another item which should be reported in the statement of changes in equity. For illustration, let us assume that a building acquired at a cost of £500,000, six years prior to commencement of the current one, has not been depreciated and that it is now decided to depreciate the building using the straight-line method over an estimated life of 50 years. A change of policy (such as this one regarding the measurement of the cost that needs to be

expensed) has to be given retrospective effect[7] (i.e. from the date the asset was acquired). Depreciation would amount to £10,000 (£500,000/50 years) per year. The backlog depreciation (i.e. the portion relating to previous six years) of £60,000 is deducted in the statement of changes in equity from the retained earnings brought forward whereas the current year's expense (£10,000) is included, under the appropriate heading in the Income Statement.

Activity 21.5 Financial statements for internal use

The year-end trial balance of Azure plc has been extracted as shown on the right. You are informed as follows:

i) The cost of inventory as at 31st December 20X8 was £328,000.

ii) Rent has been agreed at £2,000 per month.

iii) Salaries (£18,000) and audit fees (estimated at £10,000) remain unpaid as at 31.12.20X8.

iv) A trade debt of £5,000 should be written off and the Allowance for doubtful debts adjusted to cover 5% of remaining debts.

v) Non-current assets are to be depreciated at 20% per annum using the reducing balance method.

vi) Income Tax on the year's profit is estimated at £29,000.

vii) Directors have proposed a final dividend for 20X8 of 3p per ordinary share.

Required: Prepare for internal use

a) The Income Statement for the year ended 31st December 20X8, grouping the expenses, as appropriate, under the following headings:
   i) administrative expenses
   ii) distribution cost.
b) The Statement of changes in equity.
c) The Balance Sheet as at that date.

Trial Balance as at 31st December 20X8		
	£'000	£'000
Non-current assets at cost	840	
Accum depn – 31.12.20X7	–	190
Directors' fees	18	–
2007 final dividend paid	45	–
Inventory – 31st Dec. 20X7	294	
Sales	–	4,154
Rent	30	–
Salaries	312	–
Receivables & payables	505	380
20X8 interim dividend paid	36	–
Retained profit b/f	–	214
Advertising	74	–
Allowance for doubtful debts	–	17
Carriage outwards	19	–
Other admin expenses	192	–
6% Preference shares of £1	–	200
8% Debentures (issued 20X2)	–	50
Interest paid on debenture	2	–
Ordinary shares of 50p each	–	400
Share Premium a/c	–	40
Purchases	3,244	–
Cash & bank balance	34	–
	5,645	5,645

21.8 Financial statements of companies for publication

The financial statements for publication means those that are prepared to be (i) sent out to every shareholder and debenture holder and (ii) filed with the Registrar of Companies so that anyone interested could, for a fee, have access to them. When financial statements are prepared for publication care needs to be exercised with regard to their format and the disclosures required.

21.8.1 The format of presentation of the Income Statement

The financial statements should be presented in one of the acceptable formats. For the Income Statement IAS 1[6] allows companies a choice between two formats. Format 1 analyses expenses by their function, e.g. cost of sales, distribution costs and administrative expenses. Format 2 analyses expenses according to their nature, e.g. inventories and staff costs. The Income Statements would appear as follows:

Format 1

Income Statement for the year . . .	
	£
Revenue	2,400
Cost of sales	(1,580)
Gross profit	820
Other operating income	30
Distribution costs	(142)
Admin expenses	(498)
Profit from operations	210
Finance costs	(12)
Profit before tax	198
Income tax expense	(39)
Profit after tax	159

Format 2

Income Statement for the year . . .	
	£
Revenue	2,400
Other operating income	30
Changes in inventories	(11)
Raw materials used	(1,454)
Staff costs	(560)
Depreciation	(195)
Profit from operations	210
Finance costs	(12)
Profit before tax	198
Income tax expense	(39)
Profit after tax	159

Note that after identifying the profit from operations the presentation in both formats is identical.

21.8.2 The format of presentation of the Balance Sheet

The Balance sheet could be presented as a two-sided report with the equity and liabilities listed on one side and the assets on the other with a clear distinction between non-current and current assets and liabilities. An alternative is to use a vertical format. There is choice as to the sequence of items in the vertical format. For example, on the format illustrated in IAS 1, current liabilities are stated on the Capital and liability section of the balance sheet. The alternative of showing the current liabilities as a deduction from current assets, on the asset section of the balance sheet, as is common in the UK, is also permitted.

21.8.3 Disclosure of minimum required information

Companies have to strike a balance between publishing too much information (disclosing sensitive particulars to rivals) and failing to disclose what is required under the company law and various Accounting Standards. Examples of items required to be disclosed by the Companies Act and those required to be disclosed *separately* by IAS 1 are listed below:

Disclosures required under UK company law	Separate disclosures required under IAS 1
1. Turnover (sales) with segmental breakdown 2. Depreciation 3. Directors' emoluments (specified details) 4. Audit fees and expenses 5. Number of employees with break-down 6. Employee remuneration 7. Exceptional items	1. Impairment loss 2. Loss/gain on asset disposal 3. Long term investment disposal gain/loss 4. Discontinued operations 5. Litigation settlements 6. Reversal of provisions

Note: disclosures required by company law may be in notes whereas the disclosures required by International Standards may be required to be shown on the face of the published financial statements. For example, when a business discontinues an operation (i.e. abandons or disposes one of its major lines of business) the income and expenses relating to it need to be specifically identified on the Income Statement. This is important as stakeholders need to be aware that a corresponding profit or loss will not arise in the future.

Activity 21.6 Financial Statements for publication (format 1)

Magnolia plc buys processed leather to make vanity bags for sale. Their year-end trial balance has been extracted as shown on the right. You are informed as follows:

i) The cost of year-end inventory was £504,000.

ii) On 1st April 20X3 £400,000 was paid to acquire an established brand name which was amortised using the straight-line method, anticipating a commercial life of ten years. A market survey carried out on 1st April 20X7, however, reveals that the discounted present value of the income from that brand, on that date, was £100,000 and that the brand's commercial value may be exploited for only two more years from that date.

iii) Expenses need adjustment as follows:

	Accruals	Pre-payments
Heating/lighting	£11,000	–
Rent & rates	–	£12,000
Wages & salaries	£42,000	–

iv) A machine, acquired for £60,000 and written down down to £44,000 by 1st April 20X7, was sold on that date for £29,000.

v) Buildings are depreciated at 2% per annum using the straight-line method and assuming that a third of the cost of land and building relates to land, which is not depreciated; machinery and equipment are depreciated at 30% and 20% per annum, respectively, using the reducing balance method.

Trial Balance as at 31st March 20X8

	£'000	£'000
Land & building	1,800	–
Machinery	840	–
Office equipment	320	–
Accum depn – 31.3.20X7		
Building	–	360
Machinery	–	416
Office equipment	–	70
Brand name	240	–
Inventory – 31.3.20X7	349	–
Heating & lighting	29	–
8% Loan notes	–	200
Investments	180	–
Carriage inwards	34	–
Retained earnings	–	748
Salaries	298	–
Machine maintenance	31	–
Postage & stationery	18	–
6% Preference shares	–	400
Ordinary shares – 20p	–	1,000
Share Premium a/c	–	30
Interest on loan notes	8	–
Disposal of machinery	–	29
Rent & rates	282	–
Purchases & sales	2,148	3,617
Interim dividend paid	50	–
Receivables/payables	410	349
Cash and bank	27	–
Dividend received	–	20
Advertising	149	–
Carriage outwards	26	–
	7,239	7,239

vi) Apart from those that may be properly allocated, the following expenses should be apportioned as:

	Cost of sales	Admin exp	Distrib cost
Salaries	40%	50%	10%
Rent & rates	40%	30%	30%

vii) 6% preference shares are redeemable at par in 2010; loan notes were issued in 20X6.

viii) Income tax on the year's profit is estimated at £58,000.

Required: Prepare for publication an Income Statement for the year ended 31st March 20X8, using format 1 as illustrated in IAS 1 and the Balance Sheet as at that date.

Clue:
i)   Do not disclose any more information than the minimum.
ii) Focus on correctly classifying operating expenses by their function.

Activity 21.7 **Financial Statements for publication (format 2)**

Set out the Income Statement of Magnolia plc (Activity 21.6) using format 2 as illustrated in IAS 1.

21.9 Issue of bonus shares

Bonus shares (known also as scrip issue) means issuing more shares free (i.e. without any charge) by a company to its ordinary shareholders. Such a step may be taken, for example, when a company wishes to:

1. Prepare the market for a new share issue for cash.

2. Reward existing shareholders without having to deplete its cash resources by paying a dividend.

3. Bring the issued capital of the company (i.e. the portion of the capital held as shares by the shareholders) more in line with the amount of its capital and reserves.

21.9.1 Accounting for a bonus issue

If a company with an issued share capital of 10,000 shares of £1 each decides to make a bonus issue of one for every five, the issue of 2,000 shares (i.e. 10,000 × 1/5) bonus shares is accounted for as shown below:

Dr Bonus Issue a/c	£2,000	
Cr Share Capital a/c		£2,000

Dr Share Premium a/c	£2,000	
Cr Bonus Issue a/c		£2,000

The bonus shares are preferably charged against the balance in the Share Premium account as this account may be applied only for limited purposes (see Section 21.4) and the opportunity to use the account should be taken when it arises.

21.10 Rights issue of shares

A company may permit its shareholders a right to acquire from it (i.e. not from the market) additional shares at a privileged price – i.e. a price lower than the one at which it is currently sold on the stock market (but not lower than its par value). Such rights, when granted, need to be restricted. Otherwise shareholders might abuse such rights, buying as many shares as possible at the privileged price and disposing of them at the market price.

21.10.1 Accounting for a rights issue

Assume that a company with an issued capital of 100,000 ordinary shares of £1 each allows its shareholders the right to buy one for every five shares held (observe the restriction of the right by limiting it to one for five) at a price of 120p each whereas the market rate is 150p each (observe the privileged price). If all the shareholders exercise the right (as they probably would) the amount received (20,000 shares @ 120p each = £24,000) will be posted from the Cash Book to the credit of Share Capital account (20,000 @ the par value of £1 each = £20,000) and the excess to the Share Premium account (20,000 @ 20p each = £4,000).

Activity 21.8 Accounting for a bonus issue and rights issue

Olive plc made a bonus issue of one for every 15 shares on 31st March and a rights issue, three months later, of one for every four shares at 120p each. The market price on that date was 150p each. Shown on the right is an extract from the year-end trial balance, without accounting for the bonus issue and after posting the amount received on the rights issue from the Cash Book to a Suspense account.

Trial Balance as at . . .		
	£'000	£'000
Ordinary shares of £1	–	300
Share Premium a/c	–	28
Suspense a/c	–	96

Required: Show how the transactions will be reported on the company's year-end balance sheet, assuming that the directors wish to write off the cost of bonus issue against Share Premium account balance.

21.11 Statement of changes in equity – an extended version

A company may opt[5] to publish an extended version of the statement of changes in equity, including within it changes resulting from all transactions with shareholders, i.e. changes in share capital, share premium, as well as every class of reserves. To illustrate let us assume the reserves position of a company is as stated in the boxes shown below:

Reserves balances at beginning of year	Changes in reserves during year
£24,000 in the Share Premium account £30,000 in revaluation reserve £54,000 in retained earnings	1. Profit after tax £39,400; dividend paid £12,000 2. Premium on share issue £3,000 3. Revaluation surplus arising in the year £15,000 £500 of revaluation surplus is realised[a]

a) Revaluation surplus is regarded as realised and will need to be transferred to retained earnings either when the corresponding asset is disposed of or, annually, to the extent that the depreciation of the revalued asset is more than the depreciation would have been on the basis of the asset's historical cost (see Section 17.7.7, paragraph 2).

The extended version of this company's statement of changes in equity is as follows:

Statement of changes in equity for the year ended . . .	Share premium	Revaluation reserve	Retained earnings	Total
Balance b/f	£24,000	£30,000	£54,000	£108,000
Share issue	£3,000	–	–	£3,000
Non-current assets	–	£15,000	–	£15,000
Transfer – additional depreciation	–	(£500)	£500	–
Profit for the year after tax	–	–	£39,400	£39,400
Dividend paid (to ordinary shares)	–	–	(£12,000)	(£12,000)
Balance c/f	£27,000	£44,500	£81,900	£153,400

An additional column, built in to the statement, could trace any changes in Share Capital as well.

Activity 21.9 Statement of changes in equity

On the right is the capital and reserves section of Crimson plc's balance sheet as at 30th June 20X8. During the year ending on that date the following transactions took place:

	£
Ordinary shares – £1	360,000
Share Premium a/c	29,500
Revaluation reserve	84,000
Retained earnings	128,200

i) A bonus issue of one for three was made in July 20X7.

ii) A cash issue of 60,000 ordinary shares of £1 each was made on 1st September 20X7, at 180p per share, incurring £1,500 as expenses. The expenses were written off against the Share Premium account.

iii) Land and buildings were revalued again, identifying a surplus of £20,000, which was placed in the revaluation reserve. Additional depreciation of buildings, because it was based on current values rather than historical cost, was £8,000 in the year. The transfer has been made.

iv) Profit after tax in the year was £39,200, out of which an ordinary dividend of £10,000 was paid on 3rd January 20X8.

Required: Statement of changes in equity showing the movements in all reserves.

Clue: The amounts reported on the balance sheet are year-end ones. It is necessary to work backwards from these amounts, e.g. the value of ordinary shares at year-end (£360,000) includes £60,000 issued in the year. The shares in issue prior to that (£300,000) include the bonus of one for three. The number of shares in issue prior to the bonus needs to be worked out as 300,000 × ¾ = 225,000 shares.

Summary

■ Most businesses of any significant size in the UK are limited liability companies

■ Operating as a limited company brings many advantages as well as some disadvantages

■ Limited companies can be of two types – public (plc) and private (Ltd)

■ Limited companies raise finance by issuing shares and debentures and such issues need to be accounted for

■ Financial statements must be prepared both for internal use and for publication

References

1 *The Combined Code on Corporate Governance*, 2006, London, Financial Reporting Council.

2 Companies Act (2006), Section 762, London, The Stationery Office.

3 *Henry v Great Northern Railway Company* (1857), 1 De G and J 606.

4 The Gedge Committee Report, 1954, Gedge Committee, Cmd 9112, London, HMSO, http://www.bopcris.ac.uk/bopall/ref9192.html

5 The Companies Act (2006), Section 610, London, The Stationery Office.

6 IAS 32 *Financial instruments: disclosure and presentation*, revised 2003, effective 1.1.2005, London, International Accounting Standards Board.

7 IAS 1 *Presentation of financial statements*, revised 2003, effective 1.1.2005, London, International Accounting Standards Board.

8 IAS 8 *Accounting policies, changes in accounting estimates and errors*, revised 2003, effective 1.1.2005, London, International Accounting Standards Board.

Suggested answers to activities

21.1 Difference between shares and debentures

1. **Status**. The shareholder is a member with rights (such as invitation to participate in shareholders' meetings, elect directors, appoint auditors, receive financial statements), whereas the debenture-holder is only a creditor of the company.

2. **Rewards**. Shareholders are entitled to a dividend only if the company makes distributable profit, as defined by company law, and the amount is paid or proposed by directors and, in the case of final dividend, approved by the shareholders, whereas debenture-holders are entitled to receive interest for each year, irrespective of whether the company makes a profit.

3. **Security**. Debenture-holders may, depending on the terms agreed when they were issued, have a fixed or floating mortgage on the company's assets, so that, in case of need, they may have recourse to these assets to recover their capital plus interest up to that date, whereas the shareholders have no such protection.

4. **In a liquidation of company**. Debenture-holders will rank with creditors (and may even have the added advantage of claiming their dues from any asset on which they are secured), whereas the shareholders may or may not get any return of what they are owed, depending on whether the amounts realised from the company's assets is sufficient to pay for the expenses of liquidation (including the liquidator's remuneration) and to repay the claims of outsiders.

21.2 Accounting for share issue

a) Prime entry:
   (i) £60,000 received on share issue is posted from the Cash Book to the credit of the Share Capital account (£50,000) and the Share Premium account (£10,000).
   (ii) £3,000 expenses on share issue is posted from the Cash Book to the debit of the Share Premium account.

b)

Balance Sheet extract	
	£
Capital and reserves:	
Ordinary shares of 50p each	50,000
Share Premium a/c	7,000

21.3 Accounting for issue of shares partly called up

a) Journal entry:

		£	£
Called up capital	Dr	£40,000	–
To Share Capital a/c		–	£30,000
Share Premium a/c		–	£10,000
Being allotment of 100,000 ordinary shares of 50p each, at 60p, 40p called			

b) Balance sheet extract:

	£	£
Current assets:		
Called up capital not received		8,000
Capital and reserves:		
Ordinary shares of 50p each 40p called up	30,000	
Share Premium a/c	8,000	

21.4 Accounting for share transfers between shareholders

a) Balance Sheet extract:

	£'000
Ordinary shares of £1	60,000
Share Premium a/c	10,000

b) No entries in books of account of Beige plc. share register alone needs to be amended.

c) Michael needs to pay for 5,000 shares × 40p remaining call not yet made = £2,000.

21.5 Financial statements for internal use

Income Statement for the year ended 31 Dec. 20X8

	£	£'000
Sales		4,154
Inventory – 1.1	294	
Purchases	3,244	
Inventory – 31.12	(328)	(3,210)
Gross profit		944
Distribution costs:		
Advertising	74	
Bad debts[a]	13	
Carriage outward	19	(106)
Admin expenses:		
Directors' fees	18	
Salaries[b]	330	
Rent[c]	24	
Audit fees	10	
Depreciation[d]	130	
Other expenses	192	(704)
Finance cost[e]		(4)
Profit before tax		130
Taxation		(29)
Profit after tax		101
Preference dividend[f]		(12)
Retained profit		89

Balance Sheet as at 31 Dec. 20X8

	£'000	£'000	£'000
Non-current assets	840	(320)	520
Current assets:			
Inventory		328	
Trade receivables	500		
Allowance for doubtful debts	(25)	475	
Pre-paid rent		6	
Cash & bank		34	843
			1,363

	£'000	£'000
Capital and reserves:		
Ordinary shares of 50p	400	
6% Preference shares of £1[f]	200	
Share Premium a/c	40	
Retained earnings	222	862
Non-current liabilities:		
8% Debentures		50
Current liabilities:		
Trade payables	380	
Accrued salary	18	
Audit fees payable	10	
Preference dividend	12	
Interest accrued[f]	2	
Taxation	29	451
		1,363

Movement of equity

	£'000
Retained profit b/f	214
Profit after tax for 20X8	89
2007 Final dividend paid[g]	(45)
20X8 Interim dividend[g]	(36)
Retained profit c/f	222

Notes: Final dividend proposed on ordinary shares for 20X8 is £24,000.[h]

Notes:
a) Bad debts: 5 + 25 – 17 = £13
b) Salaries: 312 + 18 = £330
c) Rent: 30 – 6 pre-paid = £24
d) Depn: 20% of (840 – 190) = £130
e) Finance cost: 8% of 50 = £4
f) Preference dividend calculated at 6% of £200,000, needs to be accounted for, because they have priority over the ordinary shares. Preference shares, not being redeemable, are regarded as equity (as per IAS 32). Therefore the preference shares are reported on the balance sheet as part of equity and the dividend is shown as a deduction from profit after taxation.
g) Final dividend (on ordinary shares) for 20X7 paid in 20X8 as well as the interim dividend paid in 20X8 are both shown as deductions in the movement of equity.
h) Final dividend for 20X8, yet to be declared, is only disclosed as a note, calculated as: 400,000/50p each = 800,000 shares @ 3p = £24,000.

21.6 Financial statements for publication (format 1)

Income Statement for the year ended 31 March 20X8

	£'000
Sales revenue	3,617
Cost of sales[a]	(2,416)
Gross profit	1,201
Distribution costs[b]	(340)
Admin expenses[c]	(383)
Profit from operation	478
Disposal of machine[d]	(15)
Impairment of brand[e]	(140)
Dividend received	20
Finance cost	(16)
Preference dividend[f]	(24)
Profit before taxation	303
Taxation	(58)
Profit after taxation	245

Movement of equity

	£'000
Balance b/f	748
Profit for the year	245
Interim dividend	(50)
Balance c/f	943

Balance Sheet as at 31 March 20X8

	£'000	£'000	£'000
Non-current assets:			
Land & buildings	1,800	(384)	1,416
Machinery	780	(514)	266
Equipment	320	(120)	200
Brand name			50
Investments			180
Current assets:			
Inventory		504	
Trade receivables		410	
Pre-payments		12	
Cash and bank balance		27	953
			3,065

	£'000	£'000
Capital and reserves:		
Ordinary shares of £1	1,000	
Share Premium a/c	30	
Retained earnings	943	1,973
Non-current liabilities:		
6% Preference shares[g]	400	
8% Loan notes	200	600
Current liabilities:		
Trade payables	349	
Accrued expenses[g]	61	
Taxation	58	
Preference dividend	24	492
		3,065

Notes:
Functional grouping of operating expenses:

a) Cost of sales:

Opening inventory	£349
Purchases	£2,148
Depn of machinery[h]	£114
Salaries (40% of 340)	£136
Rent & rates (40% of 270)	£108
Carriage inwards	£34
Machine maintenance	£31
Closing inventory	(£504)
	£2,416

b) Distribution cost:

Salaries (10% of 340)	£34
Rent & rates (30% of 270)	£81
Advertising	£149
Carriage outwards	£26
Amortisation of brand[i]	£50
	£340

c) Administrative expenses:

Salaries (50% of 340)	£170
Depn – building #[j]	£24
Rent & rates (30% of 270)	£81
Heat & lighting #	£40
Postage & stationery	£18
Depn – equipment #[k]	£50
	£383

\# These allocations are based on assumptions.

d) Machinery Disposal account:

	£'000		£'000
Machinery	60	Proceeds	29
		Accum depn	16
		Loss	15
	60		60

e) Impairment of brand: £240 – recoverable 100 = £140
f) Being redeemable preference shares are regarded as a non-current liability (per IAS 32). Accordingly, the preference dividend is reported on the Income Statement before deducting taxation.
g) Accrued expenses: heating 11 + salaries 42 + interest 8 = £61
h) Depn of machinery: 30% of ((840 – 60) – (416 – 16)) = £114
i) Amortisation of brand name: £100/2 years = £50
   Branding is a sale promotion exercise. Therefore the amortisation of brand is grouped with distribution cost.

j)

Cost of land and building	1,800
Cost of land	(600)
Cost of building	1,200

k) Depn of equipment: 20% of (320 – 70) = £50

21.7 Financial statements for publication (format 2)

Income Statement for the year ended 31.3.20X8	
	£'000
Sales revenue	3,617
Changes in inventory[a]	155
Raw material consumed[b]	(2,148)
Staff costs[c]	(340)
Depreciation & amortisaton[d]	(238)
Other operating expenses[e]	(568)
Profit from operations[f]	478
Disposal of machinery	(15)
Impairment of brand	(140)
Dividend received	20
Finance costs	(16)
Preference dividend	(24)
Profit before taxation	303
Taxation	(58)
Profit after taxation	245

Notes:
a) Changes in inventory: the difference between opening and closing inventory – since the closing inventory is larger the difference is added.
b) Raw material is purchases, unless any raw materials remain unused.
c) Staff costs: £340,000 without classifying by function.
d) Depn: machine (114), building (24), equipment (50) and amortisation of brand (50) = £238,000.
e) Other operating expenses: rent & rates (270), carriage in (34), machine maintenance (31), advertising (149), carriage outwards (26), heating & lighting (40) and postage and stationery (18) = £568,000.
f) Profit from operation is identical on both formats and the remainder of the presentation is the same.

21.8 Accounting for a bonus issue and rights issue

Workings:

Balance Sheet as at . . .	
	£'000
Capital & reserves:	
Ordinary shares	400
Share Premium a/c	24

Ordinary Share Capital account

	£'000		£'000
		Balance b/f	300
		Bonus issue	20
		Suspense a/c	80

Share Premium account

	£'000		£'000
Bonus issue	20	Balance b/f	28
Balance c/d	24	Suspense a/c	16

21.9 Statement of changes in equity

Changes in equity for the year ended 30.6.20X8	Share premium	Revaluation reserve	Retained earnings	Total
Balance b/f[a]	£58,000	£72,000	£91,000	£221,000
Share issue[b]	£48,000	–	–	£48,000
Expenses of issue	(£1,500)	–	–	(£1,500)
Bonus issue[c]	(£75,000)	–	–	(£75,000)
Land & buildings[d]	–	£20,000	–	£20,000
Transfer – depreciation[e]	–	(£8,000)	£8,000	–
Profit after tax	–	–	£39,200	£39,200
Dividend paid	–	–	(£10,000)	(£10,000)
Balance c/f	£29,500	£84,000	£128,200	£241,700

Notes:
a) All these amounts are the balancing ones in each account, starting with the balances carried down at the end.
b) 60,000 shares had been issued at a premium of 80p each = £48,000.
c) Bonus issue is one third of 225,000.
d) Surplus arising from revaluation during the year of land and buildings.
e) Revaluation Reserve is deemed to be realised and is transferred.

Multiple choice questions

Limited companies

21.1 Which of the following will *not* be the most compelling reason for investing in a limited company rather than in a partnership?

a) Limitation of liability

b) Absence of confidentiality of information on its performance and position

c) Divorce of management from ownership

d) Perpetual succession

21.2 Which one or more of the following would you consider to be among the disadvantages of forming a limited company?

a) Legal control and stringent requirements that have to be complied with

b) The need to entrust control and decisions to a few directors

c) Restrictions on return of capital if in excess of company's requirements

d) The ease with which the share of ownership could be disposed of

w	a, b, & c
x	b, c & d
y	a, c & d
z	c & d

21.3 Which of the following statements contained in the Articles of Association of Caves would identify it as a private limited company rather than a public limited company?

a) The liability of each member is limited

b) The company shall have not less than two directors, each holding office for five years

c) To qualify for election as a director a member shall own not less than 1,000 shares

d) A member shall not transfer the shares to another without offering it first to the directors

21.4 As at 31st March 20X8 M plc has in issue 100 million ordinary shares of £1 each, 80p called up. On that day Terry paid 120p per share to buy 4,000 ordinary shares from Lester. In the event M plc becomes insolvent and is unable to meet in full its debts, what is the maximum Terry may be required to pay from his personal resources?

a	Nothing
b	£800
c	£4,000
d	£2,000

Shares and debentures

21.5 Which of the following statements is incorrect?

a) In a company liquidation preference shares are always entitled to priority return of capital

b) Normally preference shares have no votes at meetings of shareholders

c) Preference shares are always cumulative, even if the name does not confirm the position

d) Preference shares have priority right to receive dividend

21.6 Which of the following statements is correct?

a) Ordinary shareholders could be paid dividend even when a company does not make profit

b) Debenture holders are not entitled to receive interest in a year when the company makes an operating loss

c) Preference shareholders will get a dividend only when ordinary shares receive them too

d) Preference shares and debentures have priority right for a reward over ordinary shares

Share issue

21.7 Paragraph 5 of a company's Memorandum of Association states that the share capital of the company shall consist of one million shares of £1 each. £1,000,000 referred to here is known as:

a) The authorised capital of the company

b) The issued capital of the company

c) The paid up capital of the company

d) The intended share capital of the company

21.8 £120,000 recorded in the Cash Book, upon issuing 100,000 ordinary shares of £1 each, should be credited to which account or accounts?

a) To a Suspense account

b) To the Share Capital account

c) £100,000 to the Share Capital account and £20,000 to the Share Premium account

d) To the Share Premium account

21.9 £360,000, being the proceeds of issuing 600,000 ordinary shares of 50p each, has been posted from the Cash Book to the credit of the Share Capital account. Which of the following journal entries is needed to correct the error?

a) debit Cash account £360,000, credit Share Capital account £300,000, credit Share Premium account £60,000

b) debit Suspense account £360,000, credit Share Capital account £300,000, credit Share Premium account £60,000

c) debit Share Capital account £300,000, credit Share Premium account £360,000

d) debit Share Capital account £60,000, credit Share Premium £60,000

21.10 X plc offered for issue ten million ordinary shares of £1 each at 120p per share. Applications were received, however, for only eight million shares and the directors proceeded to allot the shares applied for. Expenses of the issue amounted to £3,000. X plc availed itself of section 610 of the Companies Act, 2006. What will be the balance in the Share Premium account after these transactions are accounted for?

a	£2,000,000	
b	£1,600,000	
c	£1,597,000	
d	£1,997,000	

21.11 Y plc issued 800,000 ordinary shares of 20p each at 25p each. At the point of issue all shares were fully called up. However, by the year-end £15,000 due on the share issue was yet to be received. What will be the amount reported as balance in the company's Share Capital account?

a	£200,000	
b	£160,000	
c	£145,000	
d	£185,000	

21.12 £15,000 still to be received at the year-end out of the total amount receivable from a company's share issue should be reported when preparing that company's financial statements as:

a	An income in the Income Statement	
b	An asset on the balance sheet	
c	A loss on the Income Statement	
d	A liability on the balance sheet	

21.13 The balance appearing on the Ordinary Share Capital account at any point of time is:

a) The authorised capital of the company

b) The issued capital of the company

c) The paid up capital of the company

d) The so far called up value of the number of its shares already in issue

21.14 Z plc allotted one million shares of 50p each, as 35p called up per share, requiring an immediate payment of 45p per share. Accounting entries to record the allotment are:

a) debit Share allotment £450,000, credit Share Capital £350,000, credit Share Premium £100,000

b) debit Share Capital £350,000, debit Share Premium £100,000, credit Cash £450,000

c) debit Share allotment £350,000, credit Share Capital £250,000, credit Share Premium £100,000

d) debit Share allotment £500,000, credit Share Capital £400,000, credit Share Premium £100,000

21.15 For which one or more of the following reasons could a balance in the share premium be applied?

a) To issue bonus shares

b) For distribution to shareholders as dividend

c) To write down the value of assets, particularly when they are impaired

d) To write off expenses of issuing shares or debentures

w	a & b
x	b & c
y	a & d
z	c & d

21.16 For which one or more of the following reasons does company law attempt to protect the balance in the Share Premium account by restricting how it may be applied?

a) It is part of the capital actually contributed by the shareholders

b) It should be protected from erosion as part of the creditor's buffer

c) It is not realised in cash

d) It is immoral to allow a company to make profit by trading on its own shares

w	a & b
x	b & c
y	a & d
z	c & d

21.17 During the year a company used the balance it had in its Share Premium account for all of the following purposes. Identify the one not permitted by company law.

a) Write off commission expense on the issue of shares

b) Write off the cost of issuing bonus shares

c) Write off goodwill acquired when another business was bought as a going concern

d) Write off expenses of issuing shares

21.18 The directors of a company are considering the use of a large balance in the Share Premium account for the purposes listed below. Which among these planned actions is/are not legally permitted?

a) Write off accumulated losses of prior years

b) Write down the value of non-current assets to their recoverable amounts

c) Distribute as dividends

d) Cancel the calls yet to be made on the shareholders in respect of shares issued

w	a, b & c
x	b, c & d
y	a, c & d
z	All four

21.19 A company was able to acquire a land with a market value of £6 million by issuing four million ordinary shares of £1 each. When accounting for the acquisition of land and the issue of shares, how much should be credited to the Share Premium account?

a	£6,000,000
b	£2,000,000
c	£4,000,000
d	£10,000,000

21.20 Q plc allotted ten million of its ordinary shares of £1 each, quoted in the market at 180p each, to acquire P Ltd as an ongoing business. The tangible assets of P Ltd had a market value on this date of £15 million. How much has Q plc paid to acquire P Ltd's goodwill?

a	£10,000,000
b	£15,000,000
c	£18,000,000
d	£3,000,000

Bonus issue/rights issue

21.21 Which of the following actions, when taken by a company, will not change the balance it has on its Share Capital account?

a) Make a fresh issue of shares for cash

b) Make a rights issue of shares

c) Receive from the shareholders the calls which were in arrears

d) Make a call on the partly called up shares already in issue

21.22 To raise additional finance a company offered its existing shareholders two ordinary shares of 50p each, for every five held by them, at a discounted price of 80p each. This is known as:

a) Bonus issue of shares

b) Share option

c) Rights issue of shares

d) Scrip issue of shares

21.23 At commencement of a year X plc had in issue 500,000 ordinary shares of £1 each fully called up, and a balance of £90,000 in the Share Premium account. During the year they made a bonus issue of three for every 20 shares, using the balance in the Share Premium account and, thereafter, a rights issue of one for every five shares at 180p each. What will be the balances, by the year-end, in the company's Share Capital account and Share Premium account?

	Share Capital	Share Premium
a	£630,000	£149,000
b	£714,000	£15,000
c	£690,000	£107,000
d	£500,000	£90,000

21.24 Which of the following will be the effect when a company makes a bonus issue of two for every five ordinary shares?

a) The liquidity of the company will improve

b) The company will have more capital employed (meaning total assets)

c) Capital and reserves of the company will increase

d) The items making up the capital and reserves will change in amount

21.25 Which one or more of the following will be the effect when a company makes a rights issue of one for every three ordinary shares?

a) The company will have more investments

b) The company's liquidity will improve

c) The company's capital and reserves will increase

d) The company's share premium balance may remain unchanged or increase

w	a, b & c
x	b, c & d
y	a, c & d
z	All four

21.26 The capital and reserves of a company appear as shown on the right. On this day the directors of the company resolve to make a bonus issue of one for every five ordinary shares, using up to maximum profits not available for distribution. Which of the following entries is correct?

Ordinary shares of 50p	£800,000
Share Premium account	£120,000
Retained earnings	£195,500

a) debit Share Premium account £160,000, credit Share Capital account £160,000

b) debit Share Premium account £120,000, credit Share Capital account £120,000

c) debit Retained earnings £160,000, credit Share Capital account £160,000

d) debit Share Premium £120,000, debit Retained earnings £40,000, credit Share Capital £160,000

21.27 The capital and reserves of a company appear as shown on the right. On this day the directors of the company resolve to make a bonus issue of one for every five ordinary shares, for the purpose of enlarging the capital base of the company. Which of the following entries is correct?

Ordinary shares of 50p	£800,000
Share Premium account	£120,000
Retained earnings	£195,500

a) debit Share Premium account £160,000, credit Share Capital account £160,000

b) debit Share Premium account £120,000, credit Share Capital account £120,000

c) debit Retained earnings £160,000, credit Share Capital account £160,000

d) debit Share Premium account £120,000, debit Retained earnings £40,000, credit Share Capital £160,000

21.28 N plc, with an issued capital of £500,000 in ordinary shares of 20p each, made a rights issue of one for every ten. All rights were taken up. £75,000 received on the issue has been posted from the Cash Book £50,000 to the credit of Share Capital account and the remainder to the credit of a Suspense account. Which of the following journal entries is needed to correct the error?

a) debit Suspense account £25,000, credit Share Premium account £25,000

b) debit Bank account £75,000, credit Share Capital account £50,000 and credit Suspense account £25,000

c) debit Share Premium account £25,000, credit Suspense account £25,000

d) debit Suspense account £25,000, debit Share Capital account £50,000 and credit Bank account £75,000

Financial statements of companies

21.29 The year-end trial balance of Quin plc reports £400,000 8% loan notes (issued 20X4) and £16,000 as interest paid. In this regard identify the amounts to be reported as expense in the Income Statement for the year ended 31.12.20X8 and as current liabilities on the balance sheet.

	Interest expense	Current liability	
a	£16,000	£32,000	
b	£32,000	£32,000	
c	£32,000	£16,000	
d	£48,000	£16,000	

21.30 Epsilon plc had in issue £400,000 6% debentures as at 31st March 20X7 and on 31st December redeemed £300,000 of these debentures at 10% premium. Interest on debentures was paid annually in arrears on 31st December. No debentures were issued newly. Calculate the interest expense in the year to 31st March 20X8.

a	£6,000	
b	£32,500	
c	£19,500	
d	£24,000	

21.31 Clinton plc depreciates machinery at 30% per annum using the reducing balance method and time apportioning for the nearest months of usage. As at 31.12.20X7 machinery costing £720,000 was reported on the balance sheet at £485,600. A machine acquired for £120,000 on 1st July 20X6 was sold on 30th September 20X8 for £54,000. With regard to machinery, identify the items that would appear in their Income Statement for the year ended 31st December 20X8.

	Depreciation	Disposal gain/loss	
a	£140,325	£1,335 loss	
b	£176,325	£17,400 loss	
c	£125,745	£1,335 loss	
d	£140,325	£17,400 loss	

21.32 The commercial exploitation of a product commenced on 1st January 20X6. The development cost relating to that product, amortised over five years from that date using the sum of the year's digits method, was reported as £360,000 as at 31st December 20X7. What is the amortisation in the year ended 31st December 20X8?

a	£120,000	
b	£180,000	
c	£72,000	
d	£96,000	

21.33 Rocky plc, engaged in retailing consumer durables, received £30,000 as dividend from the investments it holds in other companies. This should be reported in current year's financial statements as:

a) Addition to retained earnings brought forward in the statement of changes in equity

b) As an income after identifying profit from operations in the Income Statement

c) As a deduction from administration expenses in the Income Statement

d) As addition to capital and reserves total in the balance sheet

21.34 A debit balance appearing on the trial balance as taxation has been identified as the under-provision for tax relating to the previous year's profit. This amount should be included in the current year's financial statements of a company as

a) Part of administrative expenses in the Income Statement

b) Part of the tax expense reported in the current year's Income Statement

c) A deduction from the sub-total of capital and reserves on the balance sheet

d) A deduction from retained earnings brought forward in the movement of equity

21.35 The year-end trial balance of Aroma plc reports a debit balance of £4,800 described as taxation. It is explained that this amount represents an under-provision for previous year's taxation. Taxation on current year's profit has been estimated at £72,800. Identify the amount of taxation expense to be included in the current year's Income Statement and the current liabilities to be shown on the corresponding balance sheet.

	Tax expense	Tax liability	
a	£72,800	£68,000	
b	£68,000	£72,800	
c	£72,800	£77,600	
d	£77,600	£72,800	

21.36 The year-end trial balance of Flavour plc reports a credit balance of £1,500 described as taxation. It is explained that this amount represents an over-provision for previous year's taxation. Taxation on the current year's profit has been estimated at £58,200. Identify the amount of taxation expense to be included in the current year's Income Statement and the current liabilities to be shown on the corresponding balance sheet.

	Tax expense	Tax liability	
a	£58,200	£59,700	
b	£59,700	£58,200	
c	£56,700	£58,200	
d	£58,200	£58,200	

21.37 Current year's depreciation charge relating to equipment used for designing products should be included as an expense in the current year's Income Statement, within which of the headings stated on the right?

a	Within administrative expenses	
b	Within distribution cost	
c	Within cost of sales	
d	Within other operating expenses	

21.38 A company had to pay £15 million in respect of customers' claims for injuries suffered from goods manufactured and sold in the previous year. When preparing the financial statements for the previous year the company was not aware of nor did they provide for these damages. How should the company report the amount paid?

a) In the current year's Income Statement, describing it as an extraordinary item

b) In the statement of changes in equity as a deduction from balance brought forward

c) In the current year's Income Statement, included as part of administration expenses

d) On the balance sheet as a deduction from the total of capital and reserves

21.39 The cost of dividend payable on redeemable preference shares should be included:

a) As a deduction in the statement of movement of equity

b) In the Income Statement as a deduction prior to identifying profit from operations

c) In the Income Statement before identifying the profit before tax

d) In the Income Statement after identifying profit after tax

21.40 Which of the following would you not include within the heading capital and reserves in a company balance sheet?

a) Revaluation reserve

b) Share Premium account

c) Preference shares

d) Dividend declared

21.41 To enable stakeholders to make informed decisions, which of the following needs to be reported separately, preferably on the face of the published Income Statement, assuming the amounts are material?

a) Amount written off as impairment loss of a non-current asset

b) Profit relating to an activity which has been discontinued in the year

c) Loss on disposal of machinery

d) Reversal (no longer needed) of a provision for a customer's claim for damages

w	b and c	
x	a, b & d	
y	a, c & d	
z	All four	

21.42 Which one or more of the following would you report as a liability on a company balance sheet?

a) Redeemable preference shares

b) Retained earnings

c) Dividend declared

d) Loan notes

w	a, b and c	
x	b, c & d	
y	a, c & d	
z	All four	

21.43 Which one or more of the following items will be included in the statement of changes in equity for the year ended 30th September 20X8?

a) Preference dividend paid

b) Ordinary dividend declared

c) Backlog depreciation arising because of a change of policy

d) Gain on revaluation of a non-current asset

w	a and b	
x	b and c	
y	a, c & d	
z	b, c and d	

21.44 The share capital account of the company reports a balance of £500,000 reporting ordinary shares of 20p each. Directors have declared an interim dividend of 5p per share. What is the amount of the dividend to be accounted for?

a	£125,000	
b	£25,000	
c	£50,000	
d	£75,000	

21.45 The following are particulars of dividends proposed, declared and paid to ordinary shareholders:

i) January 20X8: Paid £30,000 as second interim for 2007, declared in December 2007.

ii) April 20X8: Paid £90,000 final for 2007, proposed in December 2007, declared in March 20X8.

iii) August 20X8 : Paid £45,000 first interim for 20X8.

iv) December 20X8: Declared £20,000 second interim for 20X8.

v) December 20X8: Proposed £120,000 final for 20X8.

vi) January 20X9: Paid £20,000 second interim for 20X8.

What is the dividend to be shown in the equity statement and the Balance Sheet for the year ending 31st December 20X8?

	Equity statement	Balance Sheet	
a	£305,000	£140,000	
b	£155,000	£50,000	
c	£185,000	£50,000	
d	£155,000	£20,000	

21.46 When preparing the financial statements for the year a company has included the following in the statement of changes in equity. Identify the incorrect one:

a) Ordinary dividend paid

b) Preference dividend paid

c) Correction of prior period error

d) Backlog adjustment arising from a change of policy

21.47 Development cost account appearing on the year-end trial balance includes research expenses of £312,500. £280,000 of this amount had been incurred in prior years. Which of the following is the correct accounting entry for correcting this error?

a) debit Research Expenses account £312,000, credit Development Cost account £312,000

b) debit Income Statement £32,500, debit statement of changes in equity £280,000 and credit Development Cost account £312,500

c) debit Income Statement £312,500, credit Development Cost account £312,500

d) debit statement of changes in equity £312,500, credit Development Cost account £312,500

21.48 Which one or more of the following is a company obliged to disclose when preparing financial statements for publication?

a) Depreciation written off

b) Particulars as well as the impact of any change in accounting policy

c) Authorised capital of the company

d) Final dividend proposed

w	a, b & c	
x	a, c & d	
y	b, c & d	
z	All four	

Answers to multiple choice questions

21.1: b   21.2: w   21.3: d   21.4: b   21.5: a   21.6: d   21.7: a   21.8: c   21.9: d   21.10: c   21.11: b   21.12: b
21.13: d   21.14: a   21.15: y   21.16: w   21.17: c   21.18: z   21.19: b   21.20: d   21.21: c   21.22: c   21.23: c
21.24: d   21.25: x   21.26: d   21.27: c   21.28: a   21.29: c   21.30: c   21.31: a   21.32: b   21.33: b   21.34: b
21.35: d   21.36: c   21.37: c   21.38: b   21.39: c   21.40: d   21.41: z   21.42: y   21.43: x   21.44: a   21.45: d
21.46: b   21.47: b   21.48: z

SECTION 9
CASH FLOW STATEMENTS

Chapter 22

Cash Flow Statements

In this chapter

We will learn:
- of the need for focusing on cash availability
- why information in a Cash Flow Statement is more reliable than those in other financial statements

and will be able to:
- prepare a Cash Flow Statement and
- interpret the information it conveys

22.1 Why a business should focus on its cash resources

The *performance* of a business entity is usually gauged in terms of its profit-generating ability. Experience teaches, however, that its *survival* could depend on its cash-generating ability.

To exploit opportunities and to meet its bills as they fall due, the business has to generate the necessary cash – ensuring that the amounts and timing match the needs. On the face of it, it would appear that a company making profit would necessarily have correspondingly more cash. Such an expectation would be met if the additional profit did not get tied up in additional inventory, receivables and non-current assets. An entity making profit but unable to find cash when necessary could face problems such as the following:

1. Failure to settle accounts on time could lead to suppliers stopping supplies and other suppliers refusing or limiting credit. Continuing failure could ultimately lead to liquidation.

2. Lost opportunities for making profit because of inability to find the cash outlay, e.g. for buying new assets or investing in a lucrative new line of business.

3. Enforced borrowing on unfavourable terms to pay its trade or other payables.

As the availability of cash is so important for its survival, it is usual for a business to prepare and keep updating cash projections (i.e. forecasts). A company that usually settles its debts, say at weekly intervals, may prepare its projections of expected cash inflows and outflows on a weekly basis. This gives forewarning of any cash shortfall allowing the company to take timely remedial action, e.g. by delaying payment of some debts or arranging for an overdraft. Such projections are available only for internal use of the company's management.

Those external to the business have to rely on the Cash Flow Statement that accompanies the annual Income Statement and Balance Sheet. Their estimate of future cash flow is, therefore, based on the past year's cash flow. The expectation is that information on the cash flows in the past year would provide a basis for assessing the company's liquidity, solvency and financial adaptability. This is the reason for the insistence that annual reports published by companies should include its Cash Flow Statement.[1]

22.2 Preparation of a Cash Flow Statement

A Cash Flow Statement is one, presented in the format prescribed in IAS 7 *Cash flow statements*, summarising cash inflows (i.e. receipts) and outflows (i.e. payments) during the year. The information for the cash inflows and outflows is derived from the information appearing in the Income Statement and the opening and closing balance sheets.

In many ways, the approach is similar to the approach we followed when preparing financial statements from incomplete records in Chapter 20. For example, if trade receivables (appearing in the opening balance sheet) was £3,000 and credit sales for the year (reported in the Income Statement) is £9,000, the total amount receivable by the year-end would be £12,000 if we assumed that no cash had been received from customers. If, however, the closing balance sheet reports trade receivables as £4,000, then the cash inflow (received) during the year should be the difference of £8,000.

Identifying cash flows in an exercise or examination question is helped if we remember the four rules that we applied in Chapter 20, namely:

1. There are two classes of account, assets and expenses, that have debit balances and two classes, liabilities and income, that have credit balances.

2. Unless it has been stated to the contrary always assume that:
   - purchases and sales of goods are on credit terms;
   - acquisition/disposal of assets are on cash terms.

3. When less than full information has been provided adopt the crossword puzzle mentality – i.e.:
   - identify how many letters (amounts) are needed to complete the word (account);
   - make a guess only after all clues (information) provided have been fully used up.

4. Take good care to identify whether the information provided is:
   - a payment or expense, i.e. the amount paid (cash outflow) or the whole amount payable for the period (expense);
   - a receipt or income, i.e. the amount received (cash inflow) or the whole amount receivable for the period (income).

For example, if the information provided is that £11,000 has been paid as rent (note that what is referred to is payment rather than expense) and that £1,000 more is payable for the year, the expense for the year could be identified as £12,000. On the other hand, if the information provided is that rent per month has been agreed at £1,000, making an expense of £12,000 for the year, and that £1,000 of it remains unpaid at the year-end, the cash outflow could be identified as £11,000.

Activity 22.1 Income and expense items with period-end adjustments reversed

Income/expense for the year ended 31.12.20X8		As at 1.1.20X8		As at 31.12.20X8	
	£'000		£'000		£'000
Sales	1,680	Trade receivables	245	Trade receivables	368
Purchases	1,246	Trade payables	246	Trade payables	296
Rent	60	Pre-paid rent	15	Accrued rent	10
Salaries	246	Accrued salary	32	Accrued salary	46

Required: Calculate the cash inflow/outflow during the year ended 31.12.20X8.

22.3 Format of a Cash Flow Statement

The cash flow information, if presented in an account format, would be no more than a summarised Cash account as follows:

Cash account

	£		£
Balance b/f	34	Purchases[a]	514
Sales[a]	852	Rent[a]	11
Disposal of asset[b]	14	Furniture[b]	140
Share capital[c]	50	Salary[a]	58
		Tax[a]	29
		Loan repaid[c]	25
		Interest[a]	9
		Balance c/d	164
	950		950
Balance b/d	164		

The Cash Flow Statement presents the same information in a statement format identifying the net cash inflow for the year as £130 (difference between the £34 in hand at the beginning of the year and the £164 at the end). The statement contains an explanation for the net cash flow by reporting individual sources of inflows and reasons for outflows. It does this by reporting flows under three headings – cash flow from operating activities, cash flow from investing activities and cash flow from financing activities.

If we look at the Cash account shown above, the items marked with the superscript [a] are revenue items (i.e. income or expense items). In the Cash Flow Statement, all these items are listed as *Cash flows from operating activities*. Items marked [b] and [c] are all items of a capital nature (i.e. those related to items on the balance sheet). In a Cash Flow Statement the items marked [b] are listed under the heading *Cash flows from investing activities* and items marked [c] are listed under the heading *Cash flows from financing activities*.

Cash Flow Statement for the year ended xxx		
	£	£
Cash flow from operating activity:		
Sales	852	
Purchases	(514)	
Rent	(11)	
Salary	(58)	
Interest	(9)	
Tax	(29)	231
Cash flow from investing activity:		
Furniture	(140)	
Disposal of asset	14	(126)
Cash flow from financing activity:		
Share capital	50	
Loan repayment	(25)	25
Net increase in cash in the year		130
Cash at commencement of year		34
Cash at end of the year		164

Notes:
i) cash outflows are identified by stating the amounts within brackets;
ii) the statement ends by reconciling the cash inflow (outflow) with the opening and closing cash balances.

Activity 22.2 Cash flow using the direct method

Saddle plc has supplied you with copies of its Balance Sheets and Income Statement as follows:

Balance Sheet as at 31 December		
	20X7	20X8
	£'000	£'000
Non-current assets	540	720
Accum depn	(145)	(190)
	395	530
Investments	115	140
Current assets:		
Inventories	315	418
Trade receivables	412	438
Cash & Bank	48	51
	1,285	1,577

Income Statement for the year ended 31.12.20X8	
	£'000
Sales revenue	2,460
Cost of sales	(1,780)
Gross profit	680
Operating expenses	(424)
Operating profit	256
Interest	(24)
Profit before tax	232
Taxation	(48)
Profit after tax	184

	£'000	£'000
Capital & reserves:		
Ordinary shares – £1	600	800
Share premium	40	55
Accumulated profit	217	311
	857	1,166
Non-current liabilities:		
12% Loan note	250	200
Current liabilities:		
Trade payables	139	166
Taxation	39	45
	1,285	1,577

Movement in equity	£'000
Accumulated profit b/f	217
Profit after tax	184
Dividend paid	(90)
Accumulated profit c/f	311

Required: Prepare Saddle plc's Cash Flow Statement for the year ended 31st December 20X8.

22.4 Why operating profit does not equal cash inflow

If a trader's sales are all on a cash basis, the amount of sales in a year should be equal to the amount of cash inflow in that year. Again, if the trader buys only to replace his sales (i.e. carries no inventory) and buys strictly on a cash basis, we would expect his cash position in the year to have improved by the amount of his gross profit in the year. Finally, if all expenses are paid for immediately (i.e. no accruals) and no expenses (such as depreciation) are incurred that do not involve a corresponding cash outflow, we would expect the cash position to have improved by the amount of operating profit.

In Activity 22.2 Saddle plc reports an operating profit of £256,000, whereas its cash inflow in the year from operating activity (see box on the right for working) is only £199,000. One reason for this is that depreciation amounting to £45,000 (being difference between £145,000 and £190,000 reported on the two balance sheets), although an operating expense, would not have involved any cash outflow in the current year. Besides,

	£'000
Inflow from sales	2,434
Outflow on purchases	(1,856)
Outflow on expenses	(379)
Net cash inflow	199

the additional cash generated by operating activity would be tied up in additional inventory (£315,000 increased to £418,000) of £103,000 and additional trade receivables (£412,000 increased to £438,000) of £26,000; although part of these increases was made possible by the increase of trade payables (from £139,000 to £166,000) by £27,000.

A reconciliation statement such as the one set out on the left would add credibility to the information stated on the Cash Flow Statement. Amortisation of an intangible asset is another expense which, like depreciation, does not involve immediate cash outflow but would reduce operating profit.

Reconciliation of operating profit with cash flow	£'000
Operating profit	256
Depreciation	45
Inventory increase	(103)
Receivables increase	(26)
Payables increase	27
Cash flow	199

22.5 Cash Flow Statement using the indirect method

The Cash Flow Statement illustrated in Section 22.3 above identifies individually:

1. the cash inflow from sales;
2. the cash outflow on purchases;
3. the cash outflow on each operating expense such as rent, salary, stationery, advertising and so on.

Such a presentation is known as the *direct method*. Most companies are reluctant to disclose cash flow information in such detail. Instead they opt to present the cash flow on the *indirect method*, as illustrated on the right. This method arrives at the amount of cash generated from operations (£199) by including the reconciliation of operating profit within the cash flow statement.

Note that apart from the manner of arriving at the amount of cash generated from operations, there is no difference between the direct and indirect methods of presenting the cash flow statement.

Note also that in both methods all revenue items (including interest, dividend and tax) are stated within the heading 'Cash flow from operating activities'. IAS 7 permits the alternative of including:

Cash Flow Statement for the year ended 31.12.20X8		
	£'000	£'000
Cash flow from operating activities:		
Operating profit	256	
Depreciation	45	
Inventory increase	(103)	
Receivables increase	(26)	
Payables increase	27	
Cash generated from operations		199
Interest		(24)
Dividend paid		(90)
Tax paid		(42)
		43
Cash flow from investing activities:		
Non-current asset	(180)	
Investments	(25)	(205)
Cash flow from financing activities:		
Share capital	200	
Share Premium account	15	
Loan note repaid	(50)	165
Net increase in cash in the year		3
Cash – 31.12.20X7		48
Cash – 31.12.20X8		51

- interest paid within the heading 'Cash flow from financing activities' on the premise that interest is a cost of raising finance;

- interest received and dividend received within the heading 'Cash flow from investing activities', on the premise that these are returns on investments made in other companies.

Note that in Activity 22.3, because the Income Statement has not been given, it is necessary to work back from the end of year accumulated profit to arrive at the operating profit.

Activity 22.3 Cash flow statement using the indirect method

The balance sheets of Paddles plc are shown on the right. You are informed as follows:

i)   There were no disposals of non-current assets in the year.

ii) A dividend of £30,000 was paid in October 20X8.

iii) Debenture interest of £36,000 has been paid in the year.

iv) Corporation tax, estimated at £82,000 has been accounted for.

Required:

a) A cash flow statement for the year ended 31st December 20X8.

b) Make three comments on the Information provided by the Cash Flow Statement.

Clue: Unless the full Income Statement (with information on sales and cost of sales) is provided it is impossible to prepare the Cash Flow Statement using the direct method.

Balance sheets as at 31 December				
		20X7		20X8
	£'000	£'000	£'000	£'000
Non current assets:	720		820	
Accum depn	(242)	478	(258)	562
Investments		180		240
Current assets:				
Inventory	590		407	
Trade receivables	332		392	
Cash & bank balance	11	933	4	803
		1,591		1,605

	£'000	£'000	£'000	£'000
Equity & reserves:				
Ordinary shares of £1	350		500	
Share Premium a/c	75		115	
Accumulated profit	137	562	254	869
Non-current liabilities:				
12% Debentures		400		150
Current liabilities:				
Trade payables	478		418	
Accrued expenses	64		72	
Taxation	87	629	96	586
		1,591		1,605

22.6 Cash flow from asset disposal

Upon disposal of any non-current asset the cash flow improves by the amount of the proceeds received (less any expenses involved). The gain or loss on disposal does not affect the cash flow. However, when arriving at the cash flow on the indirect method, starting with the figure of operating profit, care needs to be taken to ensure that any disposal gain or loss is not included within the figure of operating profit. For example, if a vehicle acquired for £20,000 and depreciated by £8,000, is sold for £15,000, note that:

1. Cash flow improves by the proceeds of £15,000.

2. The operating profit may include the gain on disposal of £3,000.

3. If we assumed a profit from operations of say £100,000, including within it the gain on the vehicle disposal of £3,000, the operating profit used in the reconciliation should, therefore, be reduced to £97,000 (i.e. after excluding the disposal gain). Unless this is done, the gain (of £3,000) would be double counted.

Activity 22.4 Focus on asset disposal

During the year ended 30th June 20X8 Middle plc sold for £78,000 a machine acquired for £200,000 and written down to £52,000. You are provided with an extract of the company's performance in the year as shown on the right. The non-current assets have been depreciated in the year by £28,000 and working capital changes in the year were as stated below on the left. Tax liability reported as at 30th June 20X7 was £39,000 and as at 30th June 20X8 was £52,000.

Operating profit	£284,000
Interest paid	(£24,000)
Profit before tax	£260,000
Taxation	(£50,000)
Profit after tax	£210,000
Dividend paid	(£40,000)

Inventory increased by	£18,000
Receivables decreased by	£30,000
Payables increased by	£21,000
Accrued expenses increased by	£4,000

Required: Identify the amount of cash generated from operations in the year.

Clue: The gain on machine disposal of £26,000 is included within the amount of £284,000 reported as operating profit.

22.7 Cash and cash equivalents

The requirement of IAS 7 is that the Cash Flow Statement should trace the movements within the year not only of cash but also of what are known as *cash equivalents*. IAS 7 defines cash equivalents as short-term highly liquid investments (such as bank deposits) that are readily convertible to known amounts of cash and which are subject to insignificant changes in value. The implication is that when identifying the amount of cash and cash equivalent on any date:

1. We should include any bank balance as well as amounts held in a deposit account provided, *at the date of making the deposit*, there was only a short maturity date of three months or less.

2. We should not include any investments in equity shares because these are not readily convertible to a known amount of cash (their price could change from day to day) and it cannot be said that they are subject to only an insignificant risk of change in value.

3. We should also include (as an offset) any bank overdraft (but not bank loan).

Activity 22.5 Identifying the amount of cash and cash equivalent

In each of the following independent cases identify the total cash inflow or outflow during the year.

	Scenario A		Scenario B		Scenario C	
	30.6.20X7	30.6.20X8	30.6.20X7	30.6.20X8	30.6.20X7	30.6.20X8
Cash in hand	£640	£850	£1,400	£800	£400	£250
Bank current account	£11,200	£24,800	£11,200	–	–	–
Bank overdraft	–	–	–	£4,500	£8,900	£5,400
Bank loan	£30,000	£24,000	£30,000	£24,000	£30,000	£24,000
Bank deposit (three months)	–	–	£2,800	–	£2,000	£3,000
Bank deposit (four months)	–	–	£3,000	£2,000	–	£5,000
Equity investments	£12,000	£15,800	£9,200	£11,400	£15,500	£19,200

Activity 22.6 Cash Flow Statement involving asset disposal

Shown on the right are the balance sheets of Saddle plc. You are informed as follows:

i) A vehicle which cost £72,000 was sold in the year for £54,000.

ii) Expenses written off in the year includes the following:
Depreciation £64,000
Investments written off £20,000

iii) £17,000 was received as dividend in the year.

iv) A part of the debentures were redeemed on 1st January 20X8 at a premium of 25% and the premium paid was written off against the balance in the Share Premium account.

v) Corporation tax on the profits earned in 20X8 has been accounted for at £92,000.

vi) £25,000 has been paid as dividend.

Required: Prepare the Cash Flow Statement for the year ended 31st December 20X8.

Balance Sheets as at 31 December				
	20X7		20X8	
	£'000	£'000	£'000	£'000
Non-current assets:	760		920	
Accum depn	(288)	472	(318)	602
Investments		186		214
Current assets:				
Inventory	596		397	
Trade receivables	332		392	
Cash & bank balance	5	933	0	789
		1,591		1,605

	£'000	£'000	£'000	£'000
Equity & reserves:				
Ordinary shares of £1	350		500	
Share Premium a/c	75		125	
Accumulated profit	137	562	294	919
Non-current liabilities:				
12% Debentures		400		100
Current liabilities:				
Trade payables	478		396	
Accrued expenses	64		72	
Taxation	87		96	
Bank overdraft	0	629	22	586
		1,591		1,605

22.8 Usefulness of the Cash Flow Statement

Research[2] shows that more than half of Britain's small businesses collapse because of cash-flow problems. There are many reasons for such problems, including:

1. **Marketing problems**, e.g. tougher market conditions, failure to focus on a specific market because of poor research, failure to adapt the product to meet customer needs and failure to carry out in-depth market research.

2. **Financial problems**, e.g. the business is unsure how much it owes and how much it is owed, failure to control cash by carrying too much inventory, paying suppliers too promptly and allowing customers too long to pay, bad debts, under-capitalisation (this means that the asset base may be inadequate for the level of operation), a lack of working

capital, borrowings being increased just to keep the business running, failure to pay taxes, failure to control costs ruthlessly, personal extravagance and fraud.

3. **Staff problems,** e.g. failure to build a team that is compatible and has the skills to finance, produce, sell and market, bad labour relations, poor management.

It is claimed that a Cash Flow Statement is not only very useful but also is better than an Income Statement when assessing the performance of a company. The reasons given to support this claim are as follows:

1. Cash is the lifeblood of a business entity: its scarcity (i) affects performance because opportunities for making profit may be missed and because finances may have to be raised at penal rate, (ii) affects the ability to meet bills as they fall due and thereby miss discounts, alienating suppliers and other payables and (iii) may even jeopardise its survival.

2. Cash flow is easy to understand and is significant when investment decisions are made.

3. Information in a Cash Flow Statement is objective, whereas the performance as reported in an Income Statement depends, for its accuracy on: (i) choice of accounting policies such as the valuation model adopted, (ii) estimates made on matters such as useful economic life and scrap value of assets and (iii) accounting procedures adopted such as choice of depreciation method and the cost flow assumptions when valuing closing inventory.

4. Information in Cash Flow Statement is less susceptible to manipulation. It is not affected by schemes such as off-balance sheet financing and creative accounting.

Summary

- In running a business it is essential to focus on the availability of cash.
- A Cash Flow Statement should be prepared in IAS 7 format with three headings and the flow of cash and cash equivalents must be traced in each accounting period.
- Focusing on cash is at least as important than focusing on performance, if not more so.

References

1. IAS 7 *Cash flow statements*, 1992, effective 1.1.1994, London, International Accounting Standards Board.

2. http://www.insolvencyhelpline.co.uk/ltd-companies/htm

Suggested answers to activities

22.1 Income and expense items with period-end adjustments reversed

Trade Receivables account (asset)				Trade Payables account (liability)			
	£'000		£'000		£'000		£'000
Balance b/f	245	Cash[a]	1,557	Cash[a]	1,196	Balance b/f	246
Sales	1,680	Balance c/d	368	Balance c/d	296	Purchases	1,246
	1,925		1,925		1,492		1,492
Balance b/d	368					Balance b/d	296

Rent account (expense)

	£'000		£'000
Balance b/f	15		
Cash[a]	35	Income	
Balance c/d	10	Statement	60
	60		60

Salaries account (expense)

	£'000		£'000
Cash[a]	232	Balance b/f	32
		Income	
Balance c/d	46	Statement	246
	278		278
		Balance b/d	46

Note:
a) Balancing figure, in each account.

22.2 Cash flow using the direct method

Cash Flow Statement for the year ended 31.12.20X8

	£'000	£'000
Operating activity:		
Sales		2,434
Purchases		(1,856)
Expenses		(379)
Interest		(24)
Dividend paid		(90)
Tax paid		(42)
		43
Investing activity:		
Non-current asset	(180)	
Investments	(25)	(205)
Financing activity:		
Share capital	200	
Share premium	15	
Loan note	(50)	165
Cash inflow in the year		3
Cash – 31.12.20X7		48
Cash – 31.12.20X8		51

Workings:

Non-current asset account

	£'000		£'000
Balance b/f	540		
Cash[a]	180	Balance c/d	720
	720		720
Balance b/d	720		

Accumulated depreciation account

	£'000		£'000
		Balance	145
Balance c/d	190	Depreciation[a]	45
	190		190
		Balance b/d	190

Investments account

	£'000		£'000
Balance b/f	115		
Cash[a]	25	Balance c/d	140
	140		140
Balance b/d	140		

Expenses account

	£'000		£'000
Depreciation[b]	45	Income	
Cash[a]	379	Statement	424
	424		424

Trade Receivables account

	£'000		£'000
Balance	412	Cash[a]	2,434
Sales	2,460	Balance c/d	438
	2,872		2,872
Balance	438		

Trade Payables account

	£'000		£'000
Cash[a]	1,856	Balance b/f	139
Balance c/d	166	Purchases[b]	1,883
	2,022		2,022
		Balance b/d	166

Cost of Sales

	£'000		
Inventory	315		
Purchases[a]	1,883		
Inventory	(418)		
	1,780		

Share Capital account

	£'000		£'000
		Balance b/f	600
Balance c/d	800	Cash[a]	200
	800		800
		Balance b/d	800

Share Premium account

	£'000		£'000
		Balance b/f	40
Balance c/d	55	Cash[a]	15
	55		55
		Balance b/d	55

Tax (expense) account

	£'000		£'000
Tax (L)	48	Income statement	48
	48		48

Tax (liability) account

	£'000		£'000
Cash[a]	42	Balance b/f	39
Balance c/d	45	Tax (exp)	48
	87		87
		Balance b/d	45

Notes:
a) Balancing figures in each account.
b) A figure derived from another account.

22.3 Cash Flow Statement using the indirect method

Cash Flow Statement for the year ended 31.12 20X8		
	£'000	£'000
Operating activities:		
Operating profit[b]	265	
Depreciation[c]	16	
Inventory decrease[k]	183	
Receivables increase[l]	(60)	
Payables decrease[m]	(60)	
Accruals increase[n]	8	
	352	
Interest paid	(36)	
Tax paid[d]	(73)	
Dividend paid[j]	(30)	213
Investing activities:		
Non-current assets[e]	(100)	
Investments[f]	(60)	(160)
Financing activities:		
Share capital[g]	150	
Share premium[h]	40	
Debenture redeemed[i]	(250)	(60)
Net decrease in cash in 20X8		(7)
Cash – 31.12.20X7		11
Cash – 31.12.20X8		4

Comments on the cash flow:

1. The cash flow from operating activities in the year (£352,000) is more than adequate to service loan capital (£36,000), share capital (£30,000) and pay tax (£73,000) leaving a surplus to improve its working capital.

2. By investing more in non-current assets (£100,000) and investments (£60,000) the company increases its asset base and so increases its future earning power.

3. The company is progressively replacing its loan capital with equity capital.

Notes:

a) The balancing figures in each account.

b) **Income Statement**

	£'000
Operating profit[a]	265
Interest paid[o]	(36)
Profit before tax	229
Taxation	(82)
Profit after tax	147

Movement of equity:

	£'000
Balance b/f	137
Profit after tax	147
Dividend paid[j]	(30)
Balance c/f	254

c) **Accumulated Depreciation account**

	£'000		£'000
		Balance b/f	242
Balance c/d	258	Depreciation[a]	16
	258		258
		Balance b/d	258

d) **Taxation (liability) account**

	£'000		£'000
Cash[a]	73	Balance b/f	87
Balance c/d	96	Tax (expense)	82
	169		169
		Balance b/d	96

e) **Non-current Asset account**

	£'000		£'000
Balance b/f	720		
Cash[a]	100	Balance c/d	820
	820		820
Balance b/d	820		

f) **Investments account**

	£'000		£'000
Balance b/f	180		
Cash[a]	60	Balance c/d	240
	240		240
Balance b/d	240		

g) **Share Capital account**

	£'000		£'000
		Balance b/f	350
Balance c/d	500	Cash[a]	150
	500		500
		Balance b/d	500

h) **Share Premium account**

	£'000		£'000
		Balance b/f	75
Balance c/d	115	Cash[a]	40
	115		115
		Balance b/d	115

i) **12% Debentures account**

	£'000		£'000
Cash[a]	250	Balance b/f	400
Balance c/d	150		
	400		400
		Balance b/d	150

j) Dividend paid = (30)
k) Inventory: 590 – 407 = (£183)
l) Trade receivables: 332 – 392 = £60
m) Trade payables: 478 – 418 = (£60)
n) Accruals: 64 – 72 = £8

22.4 Focus on asset disposal

Operating activities:	
	£'000
Operating profit	284
Gain on disposal[a]	(26)
Depreciation[b]	28
Inventory increase[c]	(18)
Receivables decrease[d]	30
Payables increase[e]	21
Accruals increase[e]	4
	323
Interest paid	(24)
Tax paid[f]	(37)
Dividend paid	(40)
Cash generated	222

Notes:

a) The gain of £26,000 is included within £78,000 received as proceeds on disposal. The whole of the proceeds will be reported as an inflow of cash generated by the investing activities. Therefore unless the gain (which is included within the operating profit) is removed, there will be a double counting of £26,000.

b) Depn, though an expense deducted when the operating profit was arrived at, does not involve a cash outflow in the current year.

c) Inventory increase ties up cash.

d) Decrease in trade receivables releases cash.

e) Increases in trade payables as well as accruals release cash.

f)

Taxation (liability) account			
	£'000		£'000
Cash paid	37	Balance b/f	39
Balance c/d	52	Tax (exp)	50
	89		89
		Balance b/d	52

22.5 Identifying the amount of cash and cash equivalent

	Scenario A	
Opening:	640 + 11,200	£11,840
Closing:	850 + 24,800	£25,650
	Cash inflow	£13,810

	Scenario B	
Opening:	1,400 + 11,200 + 2,800	£15,400
Closing:	800 − 4,500	(£3,700)
	Cash outflow	£19,100

	Scenario C	
Opening:	400 − 8,900 + 2,000	(£6,500)
Closing:	250 − 5,400 + 3,000	(£2,150)
	Cash inflow	£4,350

22.6 Cash Flow Statement using the indirect method

Cash Flow Statement for the year ended 31.12.20X6		
	£'000	£'000
Operating activity:		
Operating profit[a]	241	
Depn	64	
Investment w/off	20	
Inventory decrease	199	
Receivables increase	(60)	
Payables decrease	(82)	
Accruals increase	8	390
Dividend received		17
Dividend paid		(25)
Tax paid		(83)
		299
Investing activity:		
Non-current asset	(232)	
Disposal of asset	54	
Investments	(48)	(226)
Financing activity:		
Share capital	150	
Share premium	125	
Debenture redemption	(375)	(100)
Cash outflow in the year		(27)
Cash & cash equivalent – 20X5		5
Cash & cash equivalent – 20X6		(22)

Workings:

Income Statement	
	£'000
Operating profit	241
Disposal of asset	16
Dividend received	17
Profit before tax	274
Tax	(92)
Profit after tax[b]	182

Movement of equity	
	£'000
Balance b/f	137
Profit after tax[a]	182
Dividend paid	(25)
Balance c/f	294

Non-current assets account

	£'000		£'000
Balance b/f	760	Disposal	72
Cash[a]	232	Balance c/d	920
	992		992
Balance b/d	920		

Accumulated Depreciation account

	£'000		£'000
Disposal[a]	34	Balance b/f	288
Balance c/d	318	Depn	64
	352		352
		Balance b/d	318

Investment account

	£'000		£'000
Balance b/f	186	Write off	20
Cash[a]	48	Balance c/d	214
	234		234
Balance b/d	214		

Debenture Redemption account

	£'000		£'000
Cash[a]	375	Debentures	300
		Share Premium	75
	375		375

Disposal of Non-current asset

	£'000		£'000
Non-current asset	72	Accum depn[b]	34
Gain[a]	16	Cash	54

Share Premium account

	£'000		£'000
Debenture redemption	75	Balance b/f	75
Balance c/d	125	Cash[a]	125
	200		200
		Balance b/d	125

Taxation (liability) account

	£'000		£'000
Cash[a]	83	Balance b/f	87
Balance c/d	96	Tax (exp)	92
	179		179
		Balance b/d	96

Notes:
a) Balancing figure in each account.
b) Use of the figure derived in another account.

Multiple choice questions

The concept

22.1 Which of the following statement(s) are correct with regard to preparation of Cash Flow Statements?

a) Cash Flow Statement is less objective than an Income Statement

b) Cash Flow Statement is a forecast of the cash flows a company expects in the next year

c) If receipts in a year exceed payments the difference is identified as net cash inflow

d) IAS 7 requires the Cash Flow Statements to be prepared under three headings

w	a & b
x	b & c
y	a & d
z	c & d

Identification of cash inflow from sales

22.2 A company's Balance sheets report its trade receivables as shown on the right. In each of the following independent scenarios, identify the cash inflow from sales in the year ended 30th June 20X8.

As at 1st July 20X7	£498,500
As at 30th June 20X8	£525,400

a) Its sales were £720,800

x	£720,000
y	£693,900
z	£746,900

b) Its sales were £988,400 and return inwards £18,200

x	£693,100
y	£979,700
z	£943,300

c) Its sales were £920,400, return inwards £5,500, discount allowed £7,800, and discount reversed £900

x	£881,100
y	£879,300
z	£890,300

d) Its opening inventory was £328,400, purchases £752,800, closing inventory £412,200 and it effects its sales at prices calculated to yield a gross profit ratio of 25%.

x	£809,350
y	£865,100
z	£642,100

Identification of cash outflow on purchases

22.3 Particulars of a company's inventory are stated on the right. Identify the company's cash outflow relating to purchases, in each of the following independent scenarios.

As at 1st January 20X7	£218,400
As at 31st December 20X7	£244,600

a) Its purchases were £540,200, and its trade payables £118,400 on 31st December 20X6 and £286,400 a year later

x	£372,200
y	£398,400
z	£708,200

b) Its purchases in the year and returns outwards were £712,800 and £35,600, respectively, while trade payables were £392,600 on 1st January 20X7 and £388,500 on 31st December 20X7

x	£673,100
y	£681,300
z	£707,500

c) Its sales in the year ended 31st December 20X7, made at prices calculated to yield a gross profit ratio of 20%, were £720,000 while its trade payables were £294,200 on 31 December 20X6 and £282,800 on 31st December 20X7

x	£885,100	
y	£879,300	
z	£613,600	

d) Its sales in the year ended 31st December 20X7, made at prices calculated to yield a profit margin of a fourth of cost, were £988,400 while its trade payables were £294,800 on 31st December 20X7 and £312,400 a year earlier

x	£799,320	
y	£834,520	
z	£785,100	

e) During the year to 31st December 20X7 its sales made at cost plus a fifth were £850,200, its carriage inwards was £12,400 and its trade payables were £324,800 on 31st December 20X6 and £298,500 on 31st December 20X7

x	£720,260	
y	£748,600	
z	£761,000	

Identification of cash outflows on operating expenses

22.4 Rent on business premises have been agreed at £3,000 per month. £9,000 rent had been pre-paid at commencement of the year; while two months rent were in arrears by the year end. Identify the cash outflow on rent.

a	£36,000	
b	£21,000	
c	£39,000	
d	£51,000	

22.5 As at the beginning of the year £112,500 was owed to the advertising agent. His bill for the current year was for £827,200, but this includes £30,000 for future television advertising which needs to be paid only next year. However, £49,800 is owed to the agent as at the year-end for services already performed in the current year. Identify the cash outflow in the current year.

a	£734,500	
b	£889,900	
c	£859,900	
d	£764,500	

22.6 Operating expenses for the year amounted to £826,400. Accrued operating expenses were £42,400 at the beginning of the year and £58,900 at the year-end. Depreciation of non-current assets for the year was £112,400. Identify the cash outflow on operating expenses in the year.

a	£922,300	
b	£730,500	
c	£809,900	
d	£697,500	

22.7 Operating expenses for the year amounting to £752,400 include depreciation of £98,400, amortisation of development cost of £35,000 and directors' emoluments of £80,000. Pre-paid operating expenses were £32,400 at the beginning of the year while £72,500 remains accrued at the year-end. Identify the cash outflow.

a	£514,100	
b	£434,100	
c	£647,500	
d	£581,500	

Identification of cash outflow on non-operating expenses

22.8 A company had £400,000 8% loan notes in issue on 1st January 20X7 and repaid £150,000 of it by 30th September. Interest in arrears was £8,000 on 1st January 20X7 and £5,000 on 31st December 20X7. Identify the cash outflow in respect of interest during the year ended 31st December 20X7.

a	£32,000	
b	£24,000	
c	£26,000	
d	£20,000	

22.9 On 1st April 20X7, a company had in issue £300,000 6% loan notes and redeemed a third of these on 30th June 20X7 paying a premium of 10%. It pays interest on loan notes half yearly in arrears on 30th June and 31st December. Identify the cash outflow in respect of interest during the year ended 31st March 20X8.

a	£13,500	
b	£15,000	
c	£18,000	
d	£16,500	

Identification of cash inflow from operating income

22.10 A business owns seven flats rented out to staff at £500 per month. All flats were tenanted during the year. As at 1st January 21 months' rent was in arrears and as at 31st December 14 months' rent was in arrears. Identify the cash inflow during the year ended 31st December.

a	£45,500	
b	£42,000	
c	£24,500	
d	£38,500	

22.11 Interest income of a company was £39,400 during the year ended 31st March 20X8. Interest receivable was £9,400 as at 31st March 20X7 and £10,500 by 31st March 20X8. Identify the cash inflow from interest during the year.

a	£39,400	
b	£38,300	
c	£40,500	
d	£28,900	

Identification of cash flows from acquisition and disposal of non-current assets:

22.12 As at 1st April 20X7 a business owned non-current assets costing £420,000 written down by that date to £284,400. Depreciation for the year was £54,000. Year-end Balance Sheet reports non-current assets at a written down value of £582,400. Identify the cash outflow on acquiring non-current assets in the year.

a	£39,400	
b	£38,300	
c	£40,500	
d	£28,900	

22.13 Non-current assets of a company were reported on its balance sheets as shown on the right. Identify the cash outflow on acquisition and inflow from disposal in each of the following independent scenarios:

	30.6 20X7	30.6 20X8
Cost	£640,000	£580,200
Accum depn	£(112,800)	£(164,200)

a) A machine acquired for £120,000 and depreciated by £32,400 was sold in the year for £68,000.

	Outflow on acquisition	Inflow upon disposal	
x	£60,200	£68,000	
y	None	£19,600	
z	£59,800	£48,400	

b) A machine acquired for £150,000 was sold at a loss of £38,400. Depreciation written off in the year was £72,500.

x	£150,000	£111,600	
y	£90,200	£90,500	
z	£59,800	£167,300	

c) Computer equipment acquired for £90,000 was sold at a gain of £12,800. Depreciation written off for the year was £82,400 and disposal expenses were £3,000.

x	£30,200	£71,800	
y	£59,800	£46,200	
z	£30,200	£74,800	

d) Computer equipment acquired for £30,000 and written down to £18,000 was traded in for another, the difference of £15,000 being paid in cash. A vehicle which cost £88,000 was sold at a loss of £12,400. Depreciation written off in the year was £129,800.

x	£25,200	£2,800	
y	£40,200	£9,200	
z	£40,200	£12,800	

Identification of cash flows from/on shares and loans

22.14 The balances in the Share Capital account, Share Premium account and 8% Loan Notes account are stated on the right. Identify the cash inflow from share issue and outflow on redemption of loan notes in each of the following independent scenarios:

	31.3 20X7	31.3 20X8
Share capital	£400,000	£700,000
Share premium	£36,000	£74,000
8% Loan notes	£500,000	£200,000

a) Loan notes were redeemed at 10% premium and the premium paid was written off against the balance in the Share Premium account.

	Inflow on Share issue	Outflow on redemption	
x	£300,000	£300,000	
y	£368,000	£330,000	
z	£368,000	£300,000	

b) Loan notes were redeemed at 25% premium. Premium on redeeming the loan notes and £2,000 expenses of issuing shares were written off against the Share Premium account.

x	£415,000	£375,000	
y	£411,000	£300,000	
z	£300,000	£375,000	

c) Loan notes were redeemed at 10% premium and the premium on redemption was written off against the balance in the Share Premium account. A bonus issue of one for every four shares was made, prior to the cash issue, writing off the cost against the balance in the Share Premium account.

x	£368,000	£330,000	
y	£468,000	£300,000	
z	£200,000	£330,000	

d) Besides redeeming the loan notes at 10% premium, the company made a bonus issue of one for every five shares, and a rights issue of one ordinary share of £1 each for every four held after the bonus issue at 120p per share. Thereafter the company made an issue of shares for cash, incurring £3,000 as expense on share issue, and £2,000 as expenses on redeeming the loan notes. The company applies the balance in the Share Premium account for reasons permitted by company law.

x	£300,000	£330,000	
y	£229,000	£300,000	
z	£373,000	£332,000	

Preparation of Cash Flow Statement on the direct method

22.15 Which of the following items will appear on a Cash Flow Statement prepared on the direct method?

a) Depreciation
b) Bad debts
c) Receipts from customers
d) Payments to suppliers
e) Dividend received
f) Dividend paid
g) Revaluation gain
h) Proceeds of share issue
i) Bonus issue of shares
j) Current year tax yet to be paid

w	a, c, d, e, g, h	
x	b, c, e, f, h, i	
y	c, d, e, f, i, j	
z	c, d, e, f, h	

22.16 When the Cash Flow Statement is presented on the direct method which of the following items will be listed under the heading 'cash flow from operating activities'?

a) Operating expenses	f) Dividend proposed
b) Depreciation	g) Tax paid
c) Cash paid for purchases	h) Proceeds on disposal of non-current asset
d) Interest paid	i) Interest received
e) Dividend received	j) Gain on disposal of non-current assets

w	a, c, d, e, g, h, i
x	a, b, c, f, h, j
y	a, c, d, f, g, h
z	a, b, c, g, h, i

22.17 Bearing in mind that IAS 7 permits an alternative classification of a few items when presenting Cash Flow Statements, which of the following cash flow items may be reported under the heading 'cash flow from investing activities'?

a) Acquisition of non-current assets	e) Interest received
b) Gain on disposal of non-current assets	f) Dividend received
c) Interest paid	g) Dividend paid
d) Proceeds of disposal of non current assets	h) Tax paid

w	a, c, e, f, g
x	a, d, e, f
y	a, c, e, f, g
z	b, c, e, f, h

22.18 Bearing in mind that IAS 7 permits an alternative classification of a few items when presenting Cash Flow Statements, which of the following cash flow items may be reported under the heading 'cash flow from financing activities'?

a) Amount paid to redeem long-term loans	e) Interest paid
b) Dividend received	f) Bonus issue of shares
c) Gain on revaluation of non-current assets	g) Rights issue of shares
d) Proceeds of issuing own shares	h) Dividend paid

w	a, d, f, g, h
x	a, b, c, f, g, h
y	a, c, d, f, g
z	a, d, e, g

22.19 Which of the following items will never appear in a Cash Flow Statement?

a) Gain on disposal of non-current assets	e) Dividend proposed
b) Tax on current year's profit	f) Bonus issue of shares
c) Proceeds on disposal of non-current asset	g) Rights issue of shares
d) Gain on revaluation of non-current assets	h) Dividend paid

w	a, b, d, e, f
x	a, b, c, f, g, h
y	a, c, d, f, g
z	a, c, d, e, f, g

Preparation of Cash Flow Statement on the indirect method

22.20 Which of the following statements is correct in relation to preparation of a Cash Flow Statement?

a) The amount reported as cash generated by operating activity will differ depending on whether the Cash Flow Statement is prepared on direct or indirect method

b) Using the indirect method of preparing Cash Flow Statement, depreciation is added because depreciation generates cash

c) A Revaluation Gain will appear as a cash inflow

d) Gain on disposal of an asset is shown as a source of cash inflow

w	None
x	a only
y	b & c
z	c & d

22.21 Which of the following items will appear on a cash flow statement prepared on the indirect method?

a) Depreciation	f) Dividend paid
b) Bad debts	g) Revaluation gain
c) Receipts from customers	h) Proceeds of share issue
d) Dividend proposed	i) Bonus issue of shares
e) Dividend received	j) Current year tax yet to be paid

w	a, c, d, e, h
x	a, e, f, h
y	c, d, e, f, j
z	c, d, e, f, h

22.22   Cash generated from operating activities has been wrongly identified as £950 as shown below on the left. Which of the following corrections need to be made to identify the cash flow?

Operating profit	£948
Depreciation	(£32)
Inventory increase	£42
Receivables decrease	£21
Payables increase	(£29)
Cash inflow	£950

a) Depreciation should have been added

b) Inventory increased should have been deducted

c) Receivables decrease should have been deducted

d) Payables increase should have been added

Correct answers are	
w	a and b
x	a, c and d
y	b, c and d
z	a, b and d

22.23   Which of the following statements is correct with regard to calculation of cash generated by operating activities, when using the indirect method?

a) Increase in the amount of interest remaining unpaid should be added

b) Depreciation and amortisation of intangibles should be added

c) Loss of asset disposal should not be deducted from operating profit

d) Increase in inventory should be deducted

w	a and b
x	b and c
y	b, c and d
z	a, c and d

22.24   Operating profit, after deducting loss on asset disposal of £34,000 and depreciation amounting to £58,000, has been reported as £842,500. Changes in working capital items in the year were as shown on the left. Calculate the cash generated by operating activity for inclusion in a Cash Flow Statement prepared using the indirect method.

Inventory increased by	£21,000
Receivables decreased by	£54,500
Payables decreased by	£12,500
Accruals increased by	£8,200

a	£929,700
b	£896,200
c	£842,500
d	£963,700

22.25   A machine acquired for £360,000 and depreciated by £210,000 was sold in the year for £180,000. Operating profit for the year, reported as £980,000, includes the gain on disposal of the machine. Ignoring depreciation and changes in working capital items, the amounts to be included in a Cash Flow Statement prepared on the indirect method would be:

Cash flow from:		
	Disposal	Operating profit
a	£120,000	£950,000
b	£90,000	£980,000
c	£180,000	£980,000
d	£180,000	£950,000

Answers to multiple choice questions
22.1: z   22.2a: y   22.2b: z   22.2c: x   22.2d: y   22.3a: x   22.3b: y   22.3c: z   22.3d: y   22.3e: y   22.4: b   22.5: c
22.6: d   22.7: a   22.8: a   22.9: b   22.10: a   22.11: b   22.12: c   22.13a: x   22.13b: y   22.13c: z   22.13d: y
22.14a: y   22.14b: x   22.14c: x   22.14d: z   22.15: z   22.16: w   22.17: x   22.18: z   22.19: w   22.20: w   22.21: x
22.22: z   22.23: y   22.24: d   22.25: d

Progressive questions

PQ 22.1 Cash Flow Statement on both direct and indirect methods

Balance sheets of Pilchard Ltd are given below:

Balance Sheet as at 31st March				
	20X7		20X8	
	£'000	£'000	£'000	£'000
Non-current asset		780		940
Accum depn		(240)		(320)
		540		620
Current assets:				
Inventory	324		396	
Trade receivables	438		412	
Cash & bank	12	774	3	811
		1,314		1,431

	£'000	£'000	£'000	£'000
Ordinary shares of £1		600		750
Share Premium a/c		100		120
Retained earnings		74		90
		774		960
Non-current liabilities:				
6% Loan notes		200		150
Current liabilities:				
Trade payables	298		265	
Taxation	42		45	
Bank overdraft	–	340	11	321
		1,314		1,431

You are informed as follows:

i) Extracts from the Income Statement for the year ended 31 March 20X8 are shown on the right.

	£'000
Operating profit	103
Interest	(12)
	91
Taxation	(45)
Profit after tax	46

ii) There were no acquisitions or disposals of non-current assets during the year.

iii) Loan notes were redeemed at 30% premium on 31 March 20X8 and the premium written off against share premium.

Required:

a) Prepare the Cash Flow Statement for the year ended 31 March 20X8 using the indirect method.

b) Prepare the Cash Flow Statement using the direct method on the basis of the following additional information:
   i) Sales in the year were £840,000.
   ii) Purchases in the year were £620,000.

Clue: The cash balance at the beginning of the year was £12,000 whereas the cash and cash equivalent (i.e. cash taken together with the overdraft) by the end of the year was (£3,000 – £11,000 overdraft) £8,000 negative. Thus there has been an outflow of £20,000.

PQ 22.2 A basic cash flow statement on the indirect method

The Balance Sheets of Fixem plc are stated on the right. You are informed as follows:

a) Non-current assets acquired for $120,000 and written down to $60,000 were sold during the year for $90,000.

b) Depreciation amounting to $74,000 has been written off in the year.

c) Payments made in the year include:
   Interest on loan notes: $16,000
   Dividends: $20,000

d) Tax on the profits earned in the year ended 31st December 20X7 has been estimated at $48,000.

Required: A cash flow statement for the year ended 31 December 20X7 in accordance with the format prescribed by IAS 7.

Balance Sheets as at 31 December				
	20X7		20X6	
	$'000	$'000	$'000	$'000
Non-current assets		540		480
Current assets:				
Inventory	320		365	
Trade receivables	286		298	
Cash & bank	34	640	27	690
		1,180		1,170
	$'000	$'000	$'000	$'000
Share capital	500		400	
Share premium	60		40	
Retained earnings	227	787	120	560
Non-current liabilities:				
8% Loan notes		100		300
Current liabilities:				
Trade payables	245		275	
Taxation	48	293	35	310
		1,180		1,170

PQ 22.3 CAT paper 6 – June 2005

The information shown below has been extracted from the financial statements of Snowdrop Ltd:

Balance Sheet as at 31 May		
	2005	2004
	$'000	$'000
Non-current asset	4,600	2,700
Inventory	580	500
Trade receivables	360	230
Bank	0	170
	5,540	3,600

Equity & reserves:	$'000	$'000
Ordinary shares	3,500	2,370
Share Premium a/c	300	150
Retained earnings	1,052	470
	4,852	2,990
Non-current liabilities:		
10% Loan note	0	100
Current liabilities:		
Trade payables	450	365
Taxation	180	145
Bank overdraft	58	0
	5,540	3,600

Additional information:

i) Income Statement for the year ended 31 May 2005 shows as stated on the right.

ii) $270,000 was paid as dividend.

iii) Depreciation written off $700,000.

iv) During the year non-current assets with a net book value of $200,000 was sold for $180,000.

	$'000
Operating profit	1,042
Interest payables	(10)
Profit before tax	1,032
Tax	(180)
Profit for the year	852

Required:

a) A Cash Flow Statement for the year ended 31 May 2005 using the indirect method.

b) Comment on the financial position of Snowdrop as shown by the Cash Flow Statement you have prepared.

c) Briefly state some of the ways in which companies could manipulate their year-end cash position.

PQ 22.4 ACCA paper 1.1 – June 2005

The following information is available for Sioux, a limited liability company:

Balance Sheet as at 31.12	2004 $'000	2004 $'000	2003 $'000	2003 $'000
Non-current assets:				
Cost or valuation		11,000		8,000
Accumulated depreciation		(5,600)		(4,800)
Net book value		5,400		3,200
Current assets:				
Inventories	3,400		3,800	
Receivables	3,800		2,900	
Cash at bank	400	7,600	100	6,800
		13,000		10,000

	2004 $'000	2004 $'000	2003 $'000	2003 $'000
Equity & liabilities:				
Ordinary share capital	1,000		1,000	
Revaluation reserve	1,500		1,000	
Retained earnings	3,100	5,600	2,200	4,200
Non-current liabilities:				
10% Loan notes		3,000		2,000
Current liabilities:				
Trade payables	3,700		3,200	
Income tax	700	4,400	600	3,800
		13,000		10,000

Summarised Income Statement for the year ended 31 December 2004	$'000
Profit from operations	2,650
Finance cost (loan note interest)	(300)
	2,350
Income tax expenses	(700)
Net profit for the period	1,650

Notes:

i) During the year non-current assets which cost $800,000, with a net book value of $350,000, were sold for $500,000.

ii) The revaluation surplus arose from the revaluation of some land that was not being depreciated.

iii) The 2003 income tax liability was settled at the amount provided for at 31 Dec. 2003.

iv) The additional loan notes were issued on 1 January 2004. Interest was paid on 30 June and 31 December 2004.

v) Dividends paid during the year amounted to $750,000.

Required: Prepare the Cash Flow Statement for the year ended 31 December 2004.

PQ 22.5 Interpretation of information in a cash flow statement

Dynamic plc reports a bank overdraft of £13,000 as at 31 December 20X7 whereas, a year prior to that date it reported a favourable bank balance of £10,000. Directors of the company are unable to appreciate fully the information contained in the Cash Flow Statement presented to them by their finance personnel. They have requested you to:

a) Advise them on whether depreciation expense is featuring in the Cash Flow statement because it is a source of cash.
b) Explain how a loss made on disposal of a non current asset could be included as a source of cash inflow.
c) Comment on whether the liquidity of the company has become worse in the year, taking into consideration the cash outflow of £23,000 and the bank overdraft the year has ended with along with the fact that current liabilities as at 31 December 20X7 amount to £312,000.

Cash Flow Statement year ended 31 December 20X7		
	£'000	£'000
Operating activity:		
Operating profit	540	
Depreciation	62	
Loss on asset disposal	30	
	632	
Inventory increase	(12)	
Receivables increase	(18)	
Payables increase	10	
Interest paid	(40)	
Tax paid	(35)	
Dividend paid	(20)	517
Investing activity:		
Property, plant & equip	(340)	
Asset disposal proceeds	40	
Investments	(50)	(350)
Financing activity:		
12% Loan Notes	(400)	
6% Loan Notes	100	
Share issue	110	(190)
Cash outflow		(23)
Cash & cash equivalent – 31.12.X6		10
Cash & cash equivalent – 31.12.X7		(13)

PQ 22.6 A question from CIMA

Income Statement for the year ended 30 September 1998	£'000
Sales revenue	8,000
Cost of sales	(4,500)
Gross profit	3,500
Other expenses	(1,000)
Interest	(14)
Profit before taxation	2,486
Taxation	(800)
Dividends	(700)
Retained profit	986
Retained earnings b/f	4,400
Retained earnings c/f	5,386

Balance Sheet as at 30 September

	1998		1997	
	£'000	£'000	£'000	£'000
Non-current assets		8,100		6,800
Current assets:				
Inventories	800		600	
Receivables	670		620	
Bank	80		300	
Current liabilities:				
Trade payables	(420)		(340)	
Dividend declared	(400)		(360)	
Taxation	(635)	95	(595)	225
		8,195		7,025
Long-term loans		(1,200)		(1,400)
		6,995		5,625

	£'000	£'000
Share capital	1,100	1,000
Share premium	509	225
Retained earnings	5,386	4,400
	6,995	5,625

During the year the company acquired non-current assets costing £1,900,000. Non-current assets which had a net book value of £310,000 were sold for £80,000.

Required: Prepare a Cash Flow Statement for year ended 30.9.1998.

Chapter 13

Cash flow statements

Objectives

After studying this chapter carefully, you should be able to:

- explain the reasons for publishing cash flow statements;

- describe the main elements of a cash flow statement in accordance with IAS 7;

- explain and illustrate the direct and indirect methods for deriving cash flows from operating activities;

- prepare simple cash flow statements from given data, consistent with IAS 7;

- comment on the meaning of the numbers in simple cash flow statements.

13.1 Introduction

We briefly explored the idea of cash flow statements at the end of Chapter 2 and in Section 6.3. As a reminder, try the following activity.

Activity 13.A Why are cash flow statements an important element in annual published financial statements, and how do the IASB's rules and national laws based on the EU Fourth Directive influence their content and presentation?

Feedback The simple answer to why cash flow statements are important is that adequate liquidity and the availability of cash are vital to the successful operation of a business entity. The income statement and balance sheet do not provide adequate information about these factors, because the accrual basis of accounting is focused on revenues and expenses. Thus the matching principle relates earnings with consumption, not receipts with payments, and a business may be profitable but at the same time have severe cash shortages. Cash flow statements, which are not based on the accruals convention, focus on cash movements over the reporting period and therefore facilitate prediction of possible or likely cash movements in the future.

The EU Fourth Directive makes no mention of cash flow statements. This is a function of its origins, as discussed in Part 1 of this book, in an era before such statements were common. Thus, most national laws within the EU are also silent on this matter. The IASB, on the other hand, has issued IAS 7 (*Cash Flow Statements*). This, or national standards like it, are the basis for most practice internationally.

Why it matters *It is important to remember that the traditional accounting process involves uncertainty. Not only is profit determination complex but it is also potentially misleading. In any accounting year, there will be a mixture of complete and incomplete transactions. Transactions are complete when they have led to a final cash settlement and these transactions cause few profit-measurement difficulties. Considerable problems arise, however, in dealing with the many incomplete transactions. For these, the profit can only be estimated by valuing assets and liabilities at the balance sheet date or by using the accruals concept, whereby revenue and costs are matched with one another so far as possible and dealt with in the income statement of the period to which they relate.*

A statement that focuses on changes in cash and other liquid assets rather than on profits has two potential benefits. First, it provides different and additional information on movements and changes in net liquid assets, which assists appraisal of an entity's progress and prospects; and, second, it provides information that is generally more objective (though not necessarily more useful) than that contained in the income statement.

Activity 13.B Opinion has varied sharply in the last three decades on exactly what aspect of 'liquidity' should best be focused on in published financial statements. Consider the two balance sheet extracts from A Co., as shown in Table 13.1, which focus on working capital, i.e. on net current assets.

Table 13.1 **Balance sheet extracts for A Co.**

	000s 31.12.X1	000s 31.12.X2
Inventory	4,600	4,300
Accounts receivable	1,300	2,600
Cash and bank	2,500	1,200
	8,400	8,100
Accounts payable	7,900	6,500
Working capital	500	1,600

Identify the change in position.

Feedback If we look solely at cash, we could state that A had experienced a decrease in cash of 1,300,000 over the year. On the other hand, looking at working capital (or net current assets) indicates an increase of 1,100,000 over the year. It is debatable which figure the users of financial statements should have regard to when taking decisions. If the company expects to have to pay its creditors quickly, then the decrease in cash might be alarming. Otherwise, assuming that the debtors will pay, the liquidity has improved.

Up to the end of the 1980s practice was generally focused on working capital, i.e. on the current assets and current liabilities. The original IAS 7, before a revision in 1992, reflected this preference, referring to funds flow rather than to cash flow. Now, however, the focus is much more closely on cash. More strictly, it is changes in both cash and cash equivalents, i.e. those items that are so liquid as to be 'nearly cash' (see below), that are analysed.

IAS 7 is uncompromising in that it applies to all entities. It requires that a cash flow statement is presented as an integral part of all sets of financial statements, unlike for example FRS 1 in the UK, which exempts small companies and parent's unconsolidated statements.

13.2 An outline of the IAS 7 approach

Statements prepared following IAS 7 distinguish cash flows under three headings: operating activities, investing activities and financing activities. The standard defines these as follows:

■ *Operating activities* are the principal revenue-producing activities of the entity, and other activities that are not investing or financing activities.
■ *Investing activities* are the acquisition and disposal of long-term assets and other investments not included in cash equivalents.
■ *Financing activities* are activities that result in changes in the size and composition of the equity capital and borrowings of the entity.

The concept of cash equivalents requires further clarification:

Cash equivalents are held for the purpose of meeting short-term cash commitments rather than for investment or other purposes. For an investment to qualify as a cash equivalent it must be readily convertible to a known amount of cash and be subject to an insignificant risk of changes in value. Thus, an investment normally qualifies as a cash equivalent only when it has a short maturity of, say, three months or less from the date of acquisition (IAS 7, para. 7).

The last sentence of this quotation shows the IASC (the IASB's predecessor) desperately trying to write a 'principle' rather than a 'rule'. The result is a lack of clarity. This might mean that entities from other countries that report under IFRS may interpret the definition differently, in accordance with local cultures and characteristics. For example, bank borrowings are generally considered to be financing activities. However, in some cases, bank overdrafts that are repayable on demand form an integral part of an entity's cash management. In these circumstances, bank overdrafts are included as a component of cash and cash equivalents.

It should not be assumed that 'cash and cash equivalents' are interpreted identically in different countries. For example, in the United States the definition of cash equivalents is similar to that in IFRS (except that 'say, three months' becomes a 90-day limit), but under US GAAP the changes in the balances of overdrafts are classified as financing cash flows rather than being included within cash and cash equivalents. Under the UK standard, cash is defined as cash in hand and deposits receivable on demand (up to 24 hours' notice), less overdrafts repayable on demand. Cash equivalents are not included in the total to be reconciled to, but are dealt with under other headings.

Cash flows from operating activities are primarily derived from the principal revenue-producing activities of the entity. Therefore, they generally result from the transactions and other events that enter into the determination of net profit or loss. However, all cash flows from the sale of productive non-current assets, such as plant, are cash flows from investing activities.

It follows from the above, of course, that the nature of the business, i.e. of the principal revenue-producing activities, may differ significantly from one business to another, in which case the implications of apparently similar transactions may also differ. For example, an entity may hold securities and loans for dealing or trading purposes, in which case they are similar to inventory acquired specifically for resale. Therefore, cash flows arising from the purchase and sale of dealing or trading securities are classified as operating activities. Similarly, cash advances and loans made by financial institutions such as banks are usually classified as operating activities since they relate to the main revenue-producing activity of that entity.

The definitions of operating, investing and financing activities given earlier make it clear that any principal revenue-producing activity that is not a financing or investing activity, as defined, is automatically an operating activity.

Investing activities consist essentially of cash payments to acquire, and cash receipts from the eventual disposal of, property, plant and equipment and other long-term productive assets. Financing activities are those relating to the size of the equity capital, whether by capital inflow or capital repayment, or to borrowings (other than any short-term borrowings accepted as cash equivalents). Note that interest paid and dividends paid could be interpreted as either operating or as financing activities. Similarly, interest and dividends received could be treated as either operating or investing. Taxes paid are generally to be shown as operating flows.

13.3 Reporting cash flows from operating activities

Entities are allowed to use either of two methods to analyse and report cash flows from operating activities. These are:

(a) the direct method, whereby major classes of gross cash receipts and gross cash payments are disclosed; or
(b) the indirect method, whereby net profit or loss is adjusted for the effects of transactions of a non-cash nature, for any deferrals or accruals of past or future operating cash receipts or payments, and for items of income or expense associated with investing or financing cash flows.

IAS 7 encourages entities to report cash flows from operating activities using the direct method, but this is not a requirement. The indirect method takes reported net profit and removes non-cash items included in the calculation of that profit figure. The indirect method thus undoes the effects of the accrual basis. The direct method, in contrast, amounts to an analysis of the cash records. Therefore, the direct method provides information that may be useful in estimating future cash flows and that is not available under the indirect method.

The differences between the methods are best shown by example. Table 13.2 shows the typical headings that might be seen in a direct calculation of operating cash flows. Table 13.3 shows the headings for an indirect calculation.

Table 13.2 **Illustration of calculation of cash flow from operating activities by the direct method**

Item	€
Cash received from customers	144,750
Cash paid to suppliers and employees	(137,600)
Cash dividend received from associate	900
Other operating cash receipts	10,000
Interest paid in cash	(5,200)
Taxes paid	(4,500)
Net cash from operating activities	8,350

A comparison of the two tables makes it clear that the indirect method is at the same time more complicated for the reader, and less informative in terms of actual cash flows, than the direct method. As noted above, IAS 7 encourages – but does not require – the use of the direct method, and the same applies in US GAAP. However, the UK standard requires the indirect method, on the grounds that the benefits to users of the direct method are outweighed by the costs of preparing it, and that consistent practice is desirable. In practice, the indirect method seems generally widely used in IFRS or US practice, and the next section examines this method in more detail.

Table 13.3 **Illustration of calculation of cash flow from operating activities by the indirect method**

Item	€	€
Net income		8,000
Adjustments to reconcile net income to net cash provided by operating activities:		
Depreciation and amortization	8,600	
Provisions for doubtful accounts receivable	750	
Provision for deferred income taxes	1,000	
Undistributed earnings of associate	(2,100)	
Gain on sale of equipment	(2,500)	
Payment received on instalment sale of product	2,500	
Changes in operating assets and liabilities:		
Increase in accounts receivable	(7,750)	
Increase in inventory	(4,000)	
Increase in accounts payable	3,850	
Total adjustments to net income		350
Net cash from operating activities		8,350

13.4 The preparation of cash flow statements

A cash flow statement prepared by the indirect method is in essence a reconciliation between the opening and closing cash and cash equivalents of the accounting period. A convenient way to begin is to determine the differences between opening and closing balance sheets. These differences can then be analysed and presented in the desired format, segregating the inflows from the outflows.

Table 13.4 shows summarized balance sheets for the years X1 and X2, and columns for difference, outflow and inflow.

Activity 13.C

Complete the blank columns in Table 13.4. Some of the items are more straightforward than others. Remember that depreciation is an expense, but not a cash movement. However, the depreciation for the year will have reduced the retained profits.

Table 13.4 **Balance sheet differences: (1) basic information**

Item	X1	X2	Difference	Outflow	Inflow
Fixed assets – cost	94	140	+46		
less depreciation	(22)	(30)	−8		
Inventory	12	16	+4		
Receivables	18	40	+22		
Cash	10	4	−6		
	112	170			
Share capital	70	76	+6		
Retained profits	24	30	+6		
Debentures	0	20	+20		
Payables	18	44	+26		
	112	170			

Feedback The result should be as shown in Table 13.5.

Table 13.5 Balance sheet differences: (2) inflows and outflows

Item	X1	X2	Difference	Outflow	Inflow
Fixed assets – cost	94	140	+46	46	
less depreciation	(22)	(30)	−8		8
Inventory	12	16	+4	4	
Receivables	18	40	+22	22	
Cash	10	4	−6		6
	112	170			
Share capital	70	76	+6		6
Retained profits	24	30	+6		6
Debentures	0	20	+20		20
Payables	18	44	+26		26
	112	170		72	72

It is important that the logic of Table 13.5 is fully understood. Fixed assets have increased, i.e. money has been spent on buying new ones. This clearly represents a cash outflow. The argument concerning depreciation is rather more complicated. Depreciation is merely the allocation of cost over different accounting periods and, of itself, involves no cash flows at all. However, the depreciation charge for the year (of 8 in our example) will have been deducted from the profit for the year, and the net cash inflow from operating will therefore be understated by this non-cash-flow-related charge. It is in this sense that the depreciation charge for the year has the effect of increasing the calculated cash inflows.

As regards the inventory difference, the money tied up in closing inventory has increased by 4, and so an outflow of 4 has been necessary to finance this extra amount. With debtors, the entity is owed 22 more than before, i.e. it has received 22 less than a constant debtors figure would indicate – again having the effect of an outflow (strictly, perhaps, a negative inflow). The reduction in the cash balance of 6 is the balancing number.

The remaining items are fairly straightforward. Share capital has increased, by the sale of shares creating a cash inflow. Annual profits will in principle cause net cash inflows. The issue of debentures clearly creates a cash inflow of the amount borrowed. An increase in creditors, of 26, is equivalent to borrowing money of this amount, and so it represents a cause of cash increase.

Several simplifying assumptions have been made in this example. It is assumed that no fixed assets have been sold, and that there are no dividends or taxation paid. However, such issues could be dealt with using the logic of the previous paragraphs (see Activity 13.G later).

The next stage is to arrange the inflow and outflow figures in a more helpful way. This should be consistent with the layout headings of IAS 7, i.e.

- cash flows from operating activities;
- cash flows from investing activities;
- cash flows from financing activities;
- net change in cash or cash equivalents (simplified here to 'cash').

Figure 13.1 **Cash flow statement derived from Table 13.5**

Cash flows from operating activities:		
net profit		6
add back depreciation		8
		14
changes in current items:		
increase in inventory		(4)
increase in debtors		(22)
increase in creditors		26
net cash flow from operations		14
Cash flows from investing activities:		
purchase of fixed assets		(46)
Cash flows from financing activities:		
issue of share capital	6	
issue of debentures	20	
net cash flow from financing		26
Net change in cash (14 − 46 + 26)		(6)
Cash at beginning of year		10
Cash at end of year		4
Cash reduction		(6)

This leads to a statement as in Figure 13.1.

So the reduction in cash of 6 is made more understandable. A major cash outflow for fixed assets of 46 has been partly financed by new long-term money of 26, and partly by the effects of daily operations of 14, meaning that cash was reduced on balance by 6.

Activity 13.D

Assuming that the debentures were issued on 1 January of a particular year and that interest was paid on 31 December, redraft the 'net cash flow from operations' entry of the cash flow statement in Figure 13.1 using the direct method, given that the balance sheets are as shown in Table 13.5 and the income statements are as in Figure 13.2.

Figure 13.2 **Income statements (example)**

	Year to 31 Dec X1		Year to 31 Dec X2	
Sales		150		250
Opening inventory	8		12	
Purchases	104		180	
	112		192	
Closing inventory	12		16	
Cost of sales		100		176
Gross profit		50		74
Wages and salaries	28		42	
Depreciation	4		8	
Debenture interest	–		2	
Other expenses	14		16	
		46		68
Retained profit for the year		4		6

Feedback Net cash flow is as set out in Table 13.6.

Table 13.6 **Net cash flow (example)**

Cash receipts from sales in X2 (250 + 18 − 40)	228
Cash paid to suppliers and employers [(180 + 18 − 44) + 42 + 16]	(212)
Cash generated from operations	16
Cash interest paid	(2)
Net cash flow	14

The figure for cash receipts and cash paid to suppliers are the income statement entries adjusted for the change in debtors and the change in creditors respectively.

Now try Activity 13.E for yourself.

Activity 13.E The balance sheet of AN Co. for the year-ended 31 March 20X2 is as shown in Figure 13.3. Prepare the cash flow statement for the year ended 31 March 20X2 using the indirect method, given that no fixed assets were sold during the year, and given that the increase in debentures took place on 1 April 20X1.

Figure 13.3 **Balance sheets for AN Co.**

	20X1 (€000s)	20X2 (€000s)
Fixed assets	160	230
less depreciation	44	60
	116	170
Current assets		
Inventory	20	25
Debtors	18	15
Cash	21	27
	59	67
Creditors payable within one year		
Creditors	21	27
Taxation	12	16
Dividend	18	20
	51	63
Net current assets	8	4
Creditors payable after one year		
Debentures (10 per cent interest)	30	32
Net assets	94	142
Represented by		
Ordinary share capital of €1 shares	27	33
Share premium account	24	30
Retained profits	43	79
	94	142

Feedback The cash flow statement derived from Figure 13.3 would look like that shown in Figure 13.4.

Figure 13.4 **Cash flow statement derived from Figure 13.3**

	€000
Operating profit:	
Increase in retained profits	36.0
Add interest on loans	3.2
Taxation	16.0
Dividend	20.0
	75.2
Net cash inflow from operations is:	
Operating profit	75.2
Depreciation	16.0
Increase in inventory	(5.0)
Decrease in debtors	3.0
Increase in creditors	6.0
Interest paid	(3.2)
Taxes paid	(12.0)
	80.0
We therefore have:	
Cash inflow from operating activities	80.0
Cash flows from investing activities:	
Purchase of fixed assets	(70.0)
Cash flows from financing activities:	
Issue of new shares (6 + 6)	12
Dividends paid	(18)
Issue of new debentures	2
	(4.0)
Net cash flows	6.0
Opening cash balance	21.0
Closing cash balance	27.0
Increase in cash	6.0

Activity 13.F   Comment on the implications for AN Co. of the statement prepared in Activity 13.E.

Feedback   The broad picture is that cash inflows arise from operations (80) and from new long-term funding (12 + 2). Cash outflows arise from investment in fixed assets (70) and the payment of dividends (18). Most of the new long-term investment has therefore been financed out of the proceeds of day-to-day operations.

A common complication is that some fixed assets are likely to have been sold in the year, as in the next activity.

Activity 13.G   All the information in Activity 13.E, as given in Figure 13.4, still stands except that, additionally, fixed assets originally costing €40,000, with accumulated depreciation of €15,000, have been sold during the year ended 31 March 20X2 for €26,000. Prepare a cash flow statement in the proper format that takes account of this additional information.

Feedback First of all we need to consider the effects of the new information. The amount spent on new fixed assets can be found:

Opening balance at cost + new cost − old cost = closing balance at cost.

Hence, in our example:

160,000 + new cost − 40,000 = 230,000,

and outflow on new fixed assets is therefore 110,000 to ensure a balance in the equation. Similarly for the depreciation figures in the balance sheet:

44,000 + annual charge − 15,000 = 60,000,

and so the annual charge is 31,000.

The resulting cash flow statement would look like that shown in Figure 13.5.

Figure 13.5 **Cash flow statement for Activity 13.G**

		€000
Operating profit:		
Increase in retained profits		36.0
Add interest on loans		3.2
Taxation		16.0
Dividend		20.0
		75.2
Net cash inflow:		
Operating profit		75.2
Depreciation		31.0
Profit on disposal		(1.0)
Increase in inventory		(5.0)
Decrease in debtors		3.0
Increase in creditors		6.0
Interest paid		(3.2)
Taxes paid		(12.0)
		94.0
Result		
Cash inflow from operating activities		94
Cash flows from investing activities:		
Purchase of fixed assets	(110)	
Disposal of fixed assets	26	
		(84)
Cash flows from financing activities:		
Issue of new shares (6 + 6)	12	
Dividends paid	(18)	
Issue of new debentures	2	
		(4)
Net cash flows		6
Opening cash balance		21
Closing cash balance		27
Increase in cash		6

It is important to interpret cash flow statements in the context of the particular entity, and taking a reasonably long-term view. Borrowing, which will tend to lead to negative figures in the cash flow statement, may be a good thing as long as an excessively high leverage ratio is avoided and as long as long-term profitability is enhanced. Some entities may be structured so as to provide much of their cash needs through a positive cash flow from operations. Different industries may have different typical cash flow structures. For example, large retailers – especially if they buy on credit and sell for cash – may have large positive operating cash flows. Capital-intensive industries may have a greater tendency to raise external finance.

13.5 A real example

In practice, and in the context of consolidated financial statements, published cash flow statements can be rather more complicated. We present in Figure 13.6 (on p. 261) the consolidated statement of cash flows for Bayer for the financial year ended 31 December 2008, prepared in accordance with IAS 7.

Study Figure 13.6 carefully. You should be able to explain the rationale behind the movements in Figure 13.6 in the same way as we have done it for you in relation to Table 13.5.

Summary

- Cash flow statements provide a different focus from the income statement and balance sheet, giving important insights into cash and liquidity changes and trends.

- Cash flow statements are not always required by law; but they are virtually universal, for listed companies, and are required by national regulation in many countries. IAS 7 has had a major influence in this area.

- IAS 7 requires four major sections in a cash flow statement:
  - cash flows from operating activities;
  - cash flows from investing activities;
  - cash flows from financing activities;
  - net change in cash or cash equivalents.

- Cash flows from operating activities may be prepared using either the direct or the indirect method. In practice the indirect method generally predominates.

- Practice in the usage and interpretation of cash flow statements is required.

 References and research

The key reference is IAS 7, *Cash Flow Statements*.

Some specific suggestions for reading are as follows:

- G. Gebhardt and A. Heilmann, 'Compliance with German and International Accounting Standards in Germany: Evidence from cash flow statements', *The Economics and Politics of Accounting – International Perspectives on Trends, Policy and Practice* (C. Leuz, D. Pfaff and A. Hopwood, chapter 4.2), Oxford University Press, 2004.
- C. Yap, 'Users' perceptions of the need for cash flow statements – Australian evidence', *European Accounting Review*, Vol. 6, No. 4, 1997.

Figure 13.6 **Bayer Group consolidated statement of cash flows**

	2008 € million
Income from continuing operations after taxes	1,720
Income taxes	636
Non-operating result	1,188
Income taxes paid or accrued	(812)
Depreciation and amortization	2,722
Change in pension provisions	(292)
(Gains) losses on retirements of noncurrent assets	(75)
Non-cash effects of the remeasurement of acquired assets (inventory work-down)	208
Gross cash flow	**5,295**
Decrease (increase) in inventories	(692)
Decrease (increase) in trade accounts receivable	(134)
(Decrease) increase in trade accounts payable	(36)
Changes in other working capital, other non-cash items	(825)
Net cash provided by (used in) operating activities (net cash flow), continuing operations	**3,608**
Net cash provided by (used in) operating activities (net cash flow), discontinued operations	–
Net cash provided by (used in) operating activities (net cash flow) (total)	**3,608**
Cash outflows for additions to property, plant, equipment and intangible assets	(1,759)
Cash inflows from sales of property, plant, equipment and other assets	167
Cash inflows from (outflows for) divestitures	(41)
Cash inflows from (outflows for) noncurrent financial assets	(390)
Cash outflows for acquisitions less acquired cash	(1,617)
Interest and dividends received	553
Cash inflows from (outflows for) current financial assets	(2)
Net cash provided by (used in) investing activities (total)	**(3,089)**
Capital contributions	–
Dividend payments and withholding tax on dividends	(1,126)
Issuances of debt	2,277
Retirements of debt	(752)
Interest paid	(1,272)
Net cash provided by (used in) financing activities (total)	**(873)**
Change in cash and cash equivalents due to business activities (total)	**(354)**
Cash and cash equivalents at beginning of year	**2,531**
Change in cash and cash equivalents due to changes in scope of consolidation	3
Change in cash and cash equivalents due to exchange rate movements	(86)
Cash and cash equivalents at end of year	**2,094**

Source: Adapted from Bayer Annual Report 2008, p. 132.

❓ EXERCISES

Feedback on the first two of these exercises is given in Appendix D.

13.1 'Expenses and revenues are subjective; cash flows are facts. Therefore cash flow statements cannot mislead.' Discuss.

13.2 Study Figure 13.6 in the chapter. Write a short report on Bayer's management of its cash flows over the period reported.

13.3 The balance sheet of Dot Co. for the year ended 31 December 20X2, together with comparative figures for the previous year, is shown in Figure 13.7 (all figures €000).

Figure 13.7 **Balance sheet for Dot Co.**

	20X1		20X2	
Fixed assets		180		270
Less depreciation		(56)		(90)
		124		180
Current assets				
Inventory	42		50	
Debtors	33		40	
Cash	11		–	
		86		90
Creditors payable within one year				
Trade and operating creditors	(24)		(33)	
Taxation	(17)		(19)	
Dividend	(26)		(28)	
Bank overdraft	–		(10)	
		(67)		(90)
Net current assets		19		–
Net assets		143		180
Represented by				
Ordinary share capital €1 shares		20		25
Share premium account		8		10
Retained profits		55		65
Shareholders' fund		83		100
Debentures (15 per cent interest)		60		80
Capital employed		143		180

You are informed that there were no sales of fixed assets during 20X2, and that new shares and debentures issued in 20X2 were issued on 1 January.

Calculate operating profit and net cash flow from operations, and prepare a cash flow statement for the year 20X2, consistent with IAS 1, as far as the available information permits. Comment on the implications of the statement.

13.4 Repeat Exercise 13.3, but this time work on the assumption that fixed assets that had originally cost €30,000, with accumulated depreciation of €12,000, had been sold during the year ended 31 December 20X2 for €11,000.

SECTION 10
INTERPRETATION OF FINANCIAL STATEMENTS

Chapter 23

Accounting ratios and interpretation of financial statements

In this chapter

We will learn of:

- accounting ratios as a tool of analysis
- method of calculating and interpreting the ratios
- the limitations of accounting ratios

and will be able to:

- calculate accounting ratios and interpret the information in financial statements of a company

23.1 The need to interpret financial statements

Financial statements, together with non-financial ones (such as the Chairman's review, Directors' Report and Operational and Financial Review) communicate information to meet the users' need to make sensible economic decisions. As the financial statements are prepared from the accounting records, users need to be confident that these are authentic, accurate and complete. Assuming that they are, many users need help in understanding the statements and accountants often prepare reports interpreting the data. When doing so they rely heavily on what are known as accounting ratios.

23.2 What is an accounting ratio?

An *accounting ratio* merely compares one amount in a financial statement with another in the hope of drawing meaningful conclusions from the relationship. There are four alternative formats in which the relationship could be expressed, for example, as:

1. *A pure ratio*   – e.g. A and B share profits in the ratio 2:1, respectively.
2. *A fraction*   – e.g. This year's profit is a half of last year's profit.
3. *A percentage form* – e.g. This year's profit is 50% of last year's.
4. *Times*   – e.g. Inventory turns over five times in the year.

It would be futile to trace the relationship between two amounts unless we expect there to be a meaningful relationship between them. The format chosen to report the relationship is the one regarded as most appropriate to communicate the relationship. For example, if we assume that sales in a year were £100 and the gross profit £25, the relationship between them is usually communicated at (25/100 × 100 =) as 25%. This is known as the *gross profit ratio*.

A ratio on its own would not be significant, unless whether it is good, bad or normal could be established by comparing it with something we refer to as a comparator. There are three comparisons that can be helpful. These are comparisons with:

1. **Ratios of previous periods**. This is known as *inter-temporal comparison* and aims to establish trends and assess whether the trend is in the correct direction (i.e. improving).

2. **Forecast ratios**. The relationship that management had expected when preparing forecasts and budgets.

3. **Ratios of similar businesses**. This is known as *inter-firm comparison*.

A change in the relationship needs careful interpretation. It is tempting to jump to conclusions too quickly, e.g. the gross profit % has fallen compared with the previous year even though the sales have increased, therefore performance has worsened. Such a change should prompt further enquiry. This might indicate that far from being a cause for alarm, the lower gross profit ratio may have been deliberately intended to expand the customer base or to eliminate a rival.

Activity 23.1 Interpreting a change in ratio

A company's sales have decreased and yet its year-end trade receivables have increased. Suggest possible reasons for the change in relationship between sales and receivables.

23.3 The need to focus the interpretation

One of the first things that an accountant does before interpreting the financial information is to identify the interests and priorities of the person wanting the report. For example, is it for the company's owners, the management or creditors such as the bank and suppliers? Establishing this is important because the interests and priorities of each could be different. For example, perhaps:

1. The priority of the shareholders could well be the profitability of the business, how much it has grown and how much they can expect as a dividend.

2. The priority of management could be continuation of employment and how their bonuses will be affected.

3. The priority of a creditor could be liquidity, i.e. the ability to pay what is owed on time.

Notwithstanding the individual priorities, all may have a common interest in the following three areas:

1. **Profitability**. The financial performance in the short term is important to the shareholders because dividend decisions tend to be based on the current year's profits. Financial performance in the longer term is also important to creditors as falling profits and losses could not only reduce its liquidity but also threaten its going concern status.

2. **Liquidity**. The entity's ability to meet its bills and exploit opportunities depends on whether it can find ready cash when needed.

3. **Stewardship**. i.e., the management performance, bearing in mind their fiduciary relationship with the shareholders who have entrusted them with the management.

Let us illustrate the calculation of accounting ratios by reference to the financial statements of an imaginary company Oldy plc.

Income Statement for the year ended 31 December 20X8	£'000
Sales revenue	34,800
Cost of sales	(22,400)
Gross profit	12,400
Operating expenses	(7,850)
Operating profit	4,550
Unusual items	(200)
Dividend received	30
Interest paid	(40)
Profit before tax	4,340
Taxation	(890)
Profit after tax	3,450
Preference dividend	(60)
Retained profit	3,390

Balance Sheet as at 31 December	20X7		20X8	
	£'000	£'000	£'000	£'000
Non-current assets:				
Property, plant & equipment	35,800		37,400	
Accumulated depreciation	(8,240)	27,560	(9,280)	28,120
Development cost		320		510
Investments		390		825
Current assets:				
Inventory	1,840		2,848	
Trade receivables	2,680		3,262	
Cash & bank	110	4,630	140	6,250
		32,900		35,705

	£'000	£'000	£'000	£'000
Capital & reserves:				
Ordinary shares of 50p each	10,000		12,000	
6% Preference shares of £1	1,000		1,000	
Retained earnings	18,302	29,302	19,692	32,692
Non-current liabilities:				
8% Loan notes	500		500	
Deferred tax	42	542	54	554
Current liabilities:				
Trade payables	2,180		1,607	
Accrued expenses	128		94	
Taxation	748	3,056	758	2,459
		32,900		35,705

Change in equity	£'000
Balance b/f	18,302
Retained earnings	3,390
Dividend paid	(2,000)
Balance c/f	19,692

Other information:
1. Oldy's shares are listed on 31 December 20X8 at 180p.
2. Oldy issued 4,000,000 ordinary shares of 50p each on 1st April 20X8.

23.4 Profitability ratios

Shareholders invest in a company to obtain dividends and capital growth in the value of their shares. As they have alternative opportunities to invest their capital they want to know each year whether it is better to keep their shares rather than selling and investing in another company. One of the things they consider when making this decision is the relative return their company is making on the assets under their control compared to other companies. The ratios they use for this are the return on capital employed (*ROCE*) relating the profit before interest and tax (PBIT) to the average capital employed and return on equity (*ROE*). We will consider each of these.

23.4.1 Return on Capital Employed (ROCE): also known as the primary ratio

$\dfrac{\text{Profit before interest \& tax}}{\text{Average capital employed}} \times 100$	$\dfrac{£4,380^{a}}{£31,545^{b}} \times 100 = 13.9\%$

a) $4,340 + 40 = £4,380$.   b) $[(29,302 + 542) + (32,692 + 554)]/2 = £31,545$.

ROCE enables comparison with alternative investment opportunities, e.g. a low ROCE might even suggest that investing in a fixed bank deposit is a better alternative.

This ratio is also of use to the management when making financing or investing decisions. For example, if deciding whether to borrow additional funds the interest rate would be compared with the ROCE – if Oldy's ROCE were, say, 7%, it would not make sense to borrow funds at an interest rate of 8% per annum. When considering the management of the business assets, decisions such as the evaluation of acquisitions, disposals or starting or disposing of particular lines of business activity should also take into account the effect on the ROCE. For example, an activity might be profitable and yet the overall ROCE might be improved by disposing of it.

Care required when interpreting

Any ratio prompts further enquiry. A low ROCE might reflect *over-capitalisation*, i.e. the profits are not commensurate with the amount of capital invested. The question is whether this can be improved and, if so, how. One answer is to consider how the ROCE is made up.

Make-up of ROCE

ROCE is the product of net profit ratio and asset turnover ratio. For example, assuming that the information relating to a company is as stated on the right, the net profit ratio ($80/800 \times 100$) is 10% and the asset turnover ($800/500$) 1.6

Sales	£800
Net profit	£80
Capital employed	£500

times. The ROCE is $10\% \times 1.6$ times = 16%. What this means is that ROCE of a company can be improved by (i) improving net profit ratio by reducing costs or (ii) improving the asset turnover by reducing the amount of assets or increasing the sales. Further enquiry is needed to establish if all or any of these solutions is achievable.

A high ROCE may suggest *over-trading*, i.e. the company is trying to achieve business levels far in excess of what its asset base could support. If the high level of activity is likely to be capable of being maintained, then a request to the shareholders, perhaps by way of a rights issue, for additional funds could be the way forward. The ROCE can also be affected by a company's accounting policies, e.g. an upwards revaluation of the non-current assets would affect the ROCE adversely. Shareholders are also concerned with the amount of finance that has been borrowed by a company. This affects the return achieved for the shareholders, known as the return on equity (ROE).

23.4.2 Return on Equity (ROE)

This return differs from ROCE in that the profit figure used is the profit before tax, i.e. after the interest expenses have been deducted, comparison is with the equity part of the capital employed in the business (i.e. without prior charge capital such as Preference shares, Loan notes and Deferred tax). It is calculated as follows:

$\dfrac{\text{Profit before tax}}{\text{Average equity capital \& reserves}} \times 100$	$\dfrac{£4,340}{£29,997^a} \times 100 = 14.5\%$

a) $[(10,000 + 18,302) + (12,000 + 19,692)]/2 = £29,997$.

ROE will be better than ROCE to the extent that the earning ability of the company (as reflected by 13.9% ROCE) is more than the amount at which it rewards prior charge capital (such as preference shares 6% and loan notes 8%). The ROE ratio is useful for assessing the justification for retaining equity in the company and for using non-equity capital (6% after tax) and borrowed capital (8% before tax).

The ROE like ROCE can be affected by a company's accounting policies, e.g. an upwards revaluation of the non-current assets would affect the ROE adversely with the revaluation amount being included within the reserves.

23.4.3 Gross Profit Ratio

This ratio reflects the company's trading policy. It is calculated as follows:

Gross profit/sales $\times$ 100	$£12,400/£34,800 \times 100 = 35.6\%$

This ratio does not necessarily reflect a company's profit making ability. A company with a low GP ratio and a large sales revenue (such as a supermarket) could well be far more profitable than another dealing, say, in designer clothing with a higher gross profit percentage.

The percentage does not depend on the sales volume but on the relationship between two factors, namely, the cost price per unit and the selling price per unit. If a company is able to determine its selling price, then factors such as the prices charged by competitors and the amount it can spend on advertising have an influence. On the cost side, factors such as obtaining inventory from cheaper sources can reduce cost per unit and improve the gross profit percentage.

The gross profit ratio is a useful tool, used by auditors and tax authorities, to establish the acceptability of accounting information, e.g. each type of business has a typical gross profit % which is seen as a norm and enquiries would be made if the company's percentage was significantly different from the norm. This particularly applies to cash-based businesses where accounting systems may be less effective with a higher potential for concealing cash from sales which would be reflected in a lower gross profit %.

Variations in gross profit %

There can be a number of reasons for a variation in the GP ratio over time. These include:

1. **Commercial reasons:**
   - changes in the sale price;
   - changes in cost of goods sold;
   - changes in the *sales mix* (the variation in the mix of more profitable lines and less profitable ones);

2. **Management failings:**
   - inadequacy of controls, which results in pilferage by staff and shoplifting by customers;
   - failing to ensure that goods accounted for as opening inventory or purchases are also accounted for, either within sales or stated as closing inventory;
   - inaccuracies in inventory-taking;
   - inaccuracies in pricing the items remaining unsold;

3. **Manipulations:**
   - overstating or understating the quantity of closing inventory;
   - overstating or understating the price used to calculate closing inventory;
   - inflating sales by the owner introducing cash and describing it as sales revenue;
   - understating the purchases by concealing invoices from suppliers.

23.4.4 Operating profit margin (often referred to as the net profit ratio)

The profit figure used in this ratio is arrived at by deducting the operating expenses from the gross profit.

$\dfrac{\text{Operating profit}}{\text{Sales}} \times 100$	$\dfrac{£4,550}{£34,800} \times 100 = 13.1\%$

This ratio does not tell us whether one company is superior in profitability to another. Whether it is satisfactory depends on factors such as those stated in relation to the GP ratio. As with the gross profit % there are industry norms. For example, the normal profit margin in a manufacturing industry is between 8 and 10%; and in a high-volume low-margin activity like food retailing it is around 3%. A higher ratio than the industry norm will attract competition and cannot be maintained unless there are barriers to entry in such forms as need for significant initial capital, protection from patents or other special features.

A higher profit margin in identical circumstances may result from a higher gross profit % which we have discussed above. It could also indicate good cost control over the operating expenses. In order to ascertain which, the next step would be to compare each of the operating expenses as a % of sales with the ratios of previous years and other companies. The net profit ratio is useful when forecasting future profit trends when applied to predicted sales.

Activity 23.2 Possible reasons for a fall in gross profit ratio

Tarrant Electronic report their gross profit for the year, along with comparative figures, arrived at as shown on the right.

Required:
a) Identify the gross profit ratios.
b) Explain possible reasons for the change in relationship between sales (which increased) and the gross profit (which decreased).

Year ended 30th June	20X8		20X7	
	£'000	£'000	£'000	£'000
Sales		884		876
Inventory	128		116	
Purchases	726		652	
Inventory	(164)	(690)	(128)	(640)
Gross profit		194		236

Activity 23.3 Assessment of comparative profitability

Salmon Ltd and Tuna Ltd are both retailers of ready-made garments. Salmon aims at the more expensive end of the market, Tuna at the cheaper end. The financial statements of both companies are shown below:

Income Statement for the year ended 31.12.20X8		
	Salmon	Tuna
	£'000	£'000
Sales revenue	2,840	18,460
Cost of sales	(1,988)	(16,712)
Gross profit	852	1,748
Distribution costs	(184)	(216)
Admin expenses	(429)	(426)
Operating profit	239	1,106
Interest	(40)	–
Profit before tax	199	1,106
Taxation	(39)	(220)
Profit after tax	160	886
Includes depreciation	142	96

Balance Sheet as at 31 December 20X8		
	Salmon	Tuna
	£'000	£'000
Non-current assets	3,200	1,840
Accum depn	(648)	(484)
	2,552	1,356
Inventory	548	414
Trade receivables	346	28
Cash & bank	34	12
	3,480	1,810
	£'000	£'000
Ordinary shares of £1	2,000	900
Retained earnings	669	354
8% Loan notes	500	–
Trade payables	266	328
Taxation	45	228
	3,480	1,810

Required: Comment on the comparative profitability of both companies, on the basis of calculating four relevant accounting ratios.

23.5 Ratios to assess liquidity

Liquidity is the entity's ability to muster liquid resources (i.e. cash) as and when needed to exploit opportunities and meet bills as they fall due. Liquidity is usually evaluated by an overall ratio supported by ratios for the individual current assets and current liabilities.

23.5.1 Current or working capital ratio

The overall ratio is known as the *current* or *working capital ratio*. It compares the current assets with the current liabilities. It has been customary to think (not quite correctly) that if a business has current assets double the amount of its current liabilities then, in an emergency, it would be possible to settle the current liabilities in full if only 50% of the current assets are realised in cash. It is calculated as follows:

$\dfrac{\text{Current assets}}{\text{Current liabilities}}$	$\dfrac{£6,250}{£2,459} = 2.5 \text{ times}^{a}$

a) It is always expressed as a times cover. As a rule of thumb a ratio of two or more has been customarily regarded as satisfactory.

This traditional rule that to be satisfactory current assets should be double the size of the current liabilities may not be appropriate in all circumstances. For example it depends on:

1. **Type of business.** A supermarket operates with negative working capital, whereas a business engaged in long-term contracts requires much larger current ratio.

   Type of product. Inventory might be kept low if it is a fashion item with the risk of rapid obsolescence.

   Type of customers. Whether customers take the full credit period or respond to the offer of cash discount and pay early.

2. **Relations with banks and availability of overdraft facilities.** If it is known that an overdraft facility is available there is less need to hold cash in hand to meet future liabilities.

Care required when interpreting

A low ratio does not necessarily indicate a problem. It could be low because the industry norm is low, for example a supermarket making its purchases on one month's credit. If we assume that a month's purchase amounts to, say, £300 million, on the balance sheet the current liabilities reported will invariably be in excess of that amount, whereas the current assets will be much smaller. The resources the supermarket uses to settle the current liabilities in the month following the balance sheet date would not be the ones reported in the form of current assets on that date. The resources needed will be generated by purchases made in the days following the balance sheet date and the sale of those items within a few days. It could be low because there has been investment in non-current assets to expand the operational base – however, if so, the risk of overtrading should be considered. What is significant, in the case of Oldy plc, is that the ratio has improved from 1.5 to 2.5 times within a year. This reflects better management of working capital.

23.5.2 Individual asset and liability ratios

These measure in days how long it takes for the business to convert its inventory and receivables into cash in order to assess how many days it would take to find the cash to discharge its current liabilities. The customary ratios used for evaluating liquidity of a business are the *liquidity* (or *acid test* or *quick ratio*), *inventory days, trade receivable days, trade payable days* and the *cash flow ratio*. We will consider each of these as follows:

23.5.2.1 Liquidity ratio or acid test ratio or (as is it sometimes known) quick ratio

Inventory is left out of the equation on the premise that (i) it is the least liquid of current assets (arguably) and (ii) in a going concern scenario inventory needs to remain on the shelf and hence the ability to meet current liabilities must be gauged without relying on liquidating the inventory. It is calculated as follows:

$\dfrac{\text{Current asset} - \text{inventory}}{\text{Current liabilities}}$	$\dfrac{£6,250 - £2,848}{£2,459} = 1.4 \text{ times}^{a}$

a) It is always expressed as times cover. As a rule of thumb a ratio of one or more is regarded as satisfactory.

23.5.2.2 Inventory days

This assesses how many days it would take for goods held in inventory to be realised in cash. It is calculated as follows:

$\dfrac{\text{Inventory (year-end)}}{\text{Purchases}^{a}} \times 365 \text{ days}$	$\dfrac{\text{£2,848}}{\text{£23,408}} \times 365 = 44.4 \text{ days}$

a) Purchases in the year has been calculated as $22,400 + 2,848 - 1,840 = £23,408$.

Whether the ratio would be regarded as satisfactory depends on the type of product. For example, the number of Inventory days for designer clothing may be expected to be substantially more than those for products with short shelf lives.

23.5.2.3 Trade receivables days/receivable collection period

This ratio shows the relationship between trade receivables and sales. It is used to assess how many days it takes on average to collect trade receivables and is calculated as follows:

$\dfrac{\text{Year-end receivables}}{\text{Sales in the year}^{a}} \times 365$	$\dfrac{\text{£3,262}}{\text{£34,800}} \times 365 = 34 \text{ days}$

a) We assume that all sales are made on credit terms.

Whether the ratio is satisfactory depends on the credit days permitted to customers. If Oldy is a retailer, selling, as is usual, on one month credit terms, the ratio of 34 days would be satisfactory.

23.5.2.4 Trade payables days/payables payment period

This ratio is used to assess how many days it takes on average to settle trade payables. It is calculated as follows:

$\dfrac{\text{Year-end payables}}{\text{Purchases in the year}^{a}} \times 365 \text{ days}$	$\dfrac{\text{£1,607}}{\text{£23,408}^{b}} \times 365 = 25 \text{ days}$

a) We assume that all purchases were made on credit terms.
b) Purchases in the year has been calculated as $22,400 + 2,848 - 1,840 = £23,408$.

Whether the ratio is satisfactory depends on the credit terms agreed with the suppliers. If supplies are purchased on one month's credit terms, the ratio of 25 days means that Oldy is not exceeding the credit period. However, by paying earlier than 30 days Oldy is not taking full advantage of the credit made available by the suppliers.

23.5.2.5 Cash flow ratio

$\dfrac{\text{Operating profit + depreciation}^{a}}{\text{Current liabilities}}$	$\dfrac{\text{£4,550 + £1,040}^{b}}{\text{£2,459}} = 2.3 \text{ times}$

a) Depreciation and similar expenses not involving cash outflow in the current year are added back.
b) Depreciation is calculated on the basis of accumulated depreciation figures as: $9,280 - 8,240 = 1,040$.

This ratio compares the company's cash generating ability with its current liabilities. The cash generating ability is the operating profit plus items of expense such as depreciation (which do not involve a cash outflow). Oldy has sufficient cash generating ability in a year to meet its current liabilities 2.3 times over.

Activity 23.4 **Evaluation of liquidity**

Refer back to Activity 22.3 for information on Salmon and Tuna. You are further informed as follows:

As at 31 Dec.20X7		
	Salmon	Tuna
	£'000	£'000
Inventory	472	328
Trade receivables	298	32
Cash and bank	52	39
Trade payables	217	294
Taxation	38	198

i) Their balance sheets as at 31 December 20X7 includes items shown on the left.
ii) In 20X8 depreciation written off was £142,000 by Salmon and £96,000 by Tuna
iii) In the year ended 31 December 20X7:

	Salmon	Tuna
	£'000	£'000
Sales	2,140	17,200
Purchases	1,680	14,900
Depreciation	122	78
Operating profit	218	994

Required: Comment on the liquidity of both companies making inter-temporal as well as inter-firm comparisons based on not less than six sets of accounting ratios.

23.6 Ratios to measure operating performance

The performing efficiency of business is gauged by calculating how hard it uses its available resources. If a business with a capital base of £100,000 is able to achieve a sales level of ten times that amount (i.e. capital is turned around ten times) it is considered to be more efficient than another achieving comparatively lower levels of asset turnover. Similarly, by calculating the turnover ratio for the amount of inventory carried, the satisfactoriness of purchasing management can be evaluated. The efficiency of credit management can be evaluated by calculating the *receivables turnover ratio* and the *payables turnover ratio*. These performance ratios are calculated as follows:

23.6.1 Asset turnover

The rate of turnover is calculated as follows:

$\dfrac{\text{Sales for the year}}{\text{Average capital employed in the year}}$	$\dfrac{£34,800}{£31,545^a} = 1.1 \text{ times}^b$

a) Capital employed as at a particular day may be found by either adding together the non-current assets and the current assets less current liabilities or, as done below, by deducting current liabilities from the total assets:

$$[(32,900 - 3,056) + (35,705 - 2,459)]/2 = £31,545$$

b) Asset turnover ratio is always expressed as a times cover.

There is no norm to be regarded as the ideal, but inter-temporal and inter-company comparisons would be made. If the times cover appears by comparison to be excessively high it could be a good sign that the business is highly efficient at generating sales; alternatively it could indicate over-trading (i.e. trying to do too much business with too little capital).

One example could be attempting to maintain revenue levels without keeping the asset base modernised and up to date. This would result from the depreciated written down value falling each year with an apparent increase in the rate of asset turnover.

In such a case, there could be further analysis to identify the *non-current asset turnover ratio* and the *current asset turnover ratio*. If the operational asset base were being run down, the non-current turnover ratio (sales/book value of the non-current assets) would be higher – to establish which of the non-current assets was being run down it would be necessary to refer to the non-current asset schedule appearing in a note to the balance sheet. As we have seen when we considered ROCE, company A could prove more profitable than company B, by improving its asset turnover, even if the net profit margin remains identical for both.

Non-financial ratios

Many business entities go even further when they calculate physical ratios such as:

a) sales per square metre of selling space;

b) sales per sales staff.

23.6.2 Inventory turnover

This ratio identifies the number of times the inventory has been turned around (i.e., sold and replaced). An increase in this ratio indicates improvement in the buying function with the focus on buying only those goods that can be quickly sold. It is calculated as follows:

$\dfrac{\text{Cost of sales}}{\text{Average inventory}}$	$\dfrac{£22,400}{(1,840 + 2,848)/2} = 9.6 \text{ times}$

The more frequent the turnaround the greater is the profit, not only because there is a profit margin at each cycle, but also because of the decrease in capital tied up in inventory, storage costs and insurance as well as loss from obsolescence.

Care required when interpreting

The inventory turnover ratio will differ in accordance with whether the entity is a wholesaler, retailer, exporter, importer, trader or manufacturer having regard to how long the manufacturing process takes. For example, the ratio has by necessity to be high in businesses such as bakery, dairy and any that deal with perishables or products with a limited sell by date.

The inventory turnover ratio is usually exaggerated because entities tend to fix their accounting period to end when their inventory holdings are at the lowest, e.g. a farmer when the crops have been harvested and sold.

The inventory turnover ratio is also susceptible to manipulations by such means as deliberately running down the inventory by postponing re-ordering, conducting heavily discounted sales before the year-end and undertaking an aggressive write down of inventory.

23.6.3 Trade receivables turnover

$\dfrac{\text{Credit Sales}}{\text{Average receivable}}$	$\dfrac{£34,800}{(2,680 + 3,262)/2} = 11.7 \text{ times}$

Although a business may sell goods on credit in an effort to promote sales, it remains conscious that amounts tied up in trade receivables are unproductive. That is why it sets a credit period and endeavours to enforce it. The measure of its success in this endeavour is the trade receivables collection period. Whether the ratio is satisfactory can only be judged in accordance with the nature of the business, the type of product it sells, the kind of customers it has, the credit terms on offer by competitors, the length of credit offered by the business, whether the business offers discounts for prompt payment, and so on. A high turnover rate is generally better because it means that less of the amounts generated by credit sales remain tied up in trade receivables. However, care is needed that the pressure to increase the rate of turnover does not adversely affect the level of sales. A low turnover rate can be an indication of poor credit management.

Importance of sound credit management

It is important to monitor the collection period on a regular basis.

It was reported, for example [http://www.prnewswire.co.uk/cgi/news/release?id=169387] that 4,818 companies failed during the first quarter of 2006 and of the 34 industries surveyed by Experian, 22 recorded an increase in business failures in the first quarter of 2006, e.g. food retailing was up by 52% and motor traders up by 68%. Businesses need, therefore, to be vigilant to the threat of insolvency and maintain sound credit management by carrying out regular checks on both new and existing customers to reduce the risk of bad debts and failure.

23.6.4 Trade payables turnover

$\dfrac{\text{Credit purchases}}{\text{Average payables}}$	$\dfrac{£22,400 + £2,848 - £1,840}{(£2,180 + £1,607)/2} = \dfrac{£23,408}{£1,894} = 12.4 \text{ times}$

a) Cost of sales + closing inventory minus opening inventory would provide the figure of purchases.

A business would aim at the lowest possible ratio, without alienating the creditors, because liquid resources would then be available for alternative uses.

There are, of course, other ways of assessing superior performance of one business over another, for example, physical facilities available (in the form of floor space, staff numbers, retail outlets and so on) to achieve particular levels of sales and profits could be taken into account to identify the better performer.

Activity 23.5 An assessment of operational efficiency

Income Statement for the year ended 30th June 20X7	
	£'000
Sales revenue	16,425
Cost of sales	(9,855)
Gross profit	6,570
Expenses	(3,942)
Net profit	2,628

Mackeral plc's capital employed as at 30th June 20X7 is £7.5 million. Summary of their Income Statement appears on the left. Directors expect that their performance next year will be as shown below on the right and that the year-end capital employed will be £9.0m.

Required:
Assuming that their expectations material-

Income Statement for the year ended 30th June 20X8	
	£'000
Sales revenue	21,600
Cost of sales	(12,960)
Gross profit	8,640
Expenses	(5,076)
Net profit	3,564

ise, (a) calculate for each of the two years the ROCE, identifying how much of improvement arises from asset turnover and how much from improvement in net profit margin and (b) explain how exactly the directors are planning to improve the company profitability.

23.7 | Level of risk to equity shareholders

Many companies finance their activities by raising both share and loan capital. If a company obtains loan finance it is said to be geared. A company is said to be highly geared if the loan capital is more than 50% of its total capital employed. The level of gearing is expressed as a *gearing ratio* or *debt equity ratio*.

23.7.1 Gearing (or leverage) ratio

This ratio focuses on the proportion of capital employed provided by non-equity (or prior charge) capital, i.e. including preference shares and debentures.

$\dfrac{\text{Prior charge capital}}{\text{Total capital employed}} \times 100$	$\dfrac{£1,000 + £500}{£32,692 + £554} \times 100 = 4.5\%$

Oldy plc is geared, but to be regarded as highly geared the ratio should exceed 50%.

Companies may plan to borrow if they have investment opportunities offering a ROCE which exceeds the rate of interest on fixed interest (prior charge) capital. If this results in high gearing, it is not necessarily detrimental so long as the company continues to be able to service the debt. If, however, there is any prospect of fall in profit, high gearing could be detrimental to equity holders because a fall in profit would have a more than proportionate impact on the amount of profit available to equity holders.

23.7.2 Debt equity ratio

The debt equity ratio is merely an alternative formula expressing the level of gearing:

$\dfrac{\text{Prior charge capital}}{\text{Equity capital (including reserves)}} \times 100$	$\dfrac{£1,000 + £500}{£12,000 + £19,692} \times 100 = 4.7\%$

Activity 23.6 How high gearing affects equity

	£'000
Ordinary shares	4,000
6% Preference shares	3,000
Reserves	500
	7,500
8% Loan notes	5,000
	12,500

Extract from Sardine plc's Income Statement for the year ended 30th September 20X8 is shown on the right and relevant portion of its balance sheet as at 30.9.20X8 is shown on the left. Assume that tax is calculated at 20% of profit.

Income Statement for the year ended 30.9.20X8	
	£'000
Operating profit	945
Interest on loan	(400)
Profit before tax	545
Income tax	(80)
Profit after tax	465
Preference dividend	(180)
Retained profit	285

Required:
a) Calculate the extent of the company's capital gearing.
b) Identify how high gearing affects equity shareholders by working out the percentage fall in the retained profits (available for ordinary shares) if there is a 20% fall in operating profit.

23.8 Share market ratios

If a company is one listed on a stock exchange, when making decisions such as whether to hold the shares, buy more, or dispose of existing holdings, investors consider the following accounting ratios.

23.8.1 Earnings per share (EPS)

Every company listed on any stock exchange is required to publish a figure of EPS in the hope that it will assist the investor in making an estimate of what each equity share in the company may be able to earn.

$$\frac{\text{Profit after tax} - \text{preference dividend}}{\text{Weighted average number of ordinary shares}} \times 100 \qquad \frac{£3,450 - £60}{£23,000^{a}} \times 100 = 14.7\text{p}$$

a) Since four million shares had been issued on 1st April 20X8, the weighted average number of shares in issue in the year would be (20,000 shares × 3/12 months) + (24,000 shares × 9/12 months) = 23,000 shares.

Activity 23.7 Earnings per share

	£'000
Ordinary shares of 50p each	900
6% Preference shares	100
Share Premium account	120
Retained earnings	90
	1,210

Equity and reserves portion of Sardine plc's Balance sheet as at 31st December 20X8 is shown on the left and an extract from the Income Statement ending on that date is shown on the right. 300,000 ordinary shares of 50p each have been issued on 1st May 20X8. No dividends were paid in the year.

	£'000
Operating profit	158
Interest	(30)
Profit before tax	128
Taxation	(25)
Profit after tax	103

Required: Earnings per share.

Clue: If after issuing 300,000 shares there are 1,800,000 (900,000/50p) ordinary shares in issue, then in the four months to 1st May 20X8 1,500,000 ordinary shares would have been in issue.

23.8.2 Price earnings ratio (PE ratio)

The PE ratio calculates how many years earnings are represented by the share price. By comparing the market price of each share with that share's earning power (EPS) an attempt is made to gauge the confidence the market has in that company. A high PE ratio reflects a high level of market confidence that there will be a growth in the share price. Usually the PE ratio of a high-quality blue chip may be 15 or more, whereas the PE ratio of companies without market appeal may be eight or even less. The market appeal of a company would depend on a number of factors some of which are identified in the box on the right.

Factors that usually affect price earnings ratio:

1. Overall mood of share market
2. Prospects within the industry
3. The company's own history
4. Market's view of the company's prospects
5. Volume of shares being traded at any time

Market price per share $\dfrac{\text{Market price per share}}{\text{Earnings per share}}$	$\dfrac{180\text{p}}{14.7\text{p}} = 12.2$ times

23.8.3 Dividend cover

Dividend cover measures the ability of the company to pay dividends at the current level:

$\dfrac{\text{Earnings per share}}{\text{Dividend per share}}$	$\dfrac{14.7\text{p}}{8.3^{\text{a}}} = 1.8$ times

a) £2,000/24,000 shares = 8.3p per share (assuming a dividend of £2,000).

What this means is that earnings are 1.8 times the amount of dividend paid. It is an important ratio to consider if a company's earnings are volatile. The 1.8 tells us that the company will be able to maintain dividends at current levels, unless the earnings fall by more than 40%.

23.8.4 Dividend yield

Dividend yield is based on the dividend declared and the share price quoted on the Stock Exchange. The ratio expresses the dividend as a percentage of the share price.

$\dfrac{\text{Dividend per share}}{\text{Price per share}} \times 100$	$\dfrac{8.3\text{p}}{180\text{p}} \times 100 = 4.6\%$

It is used to compare the annual return on the amount invested in the share with the returns that may be expected from other similar investments.

23.8.5 Earnings yield

Since the dividend a company pays depends on the directors' dividend policy, a more meaningful comparison of the return from investing in the shares could be by identifying an earnings yield by expressing the earnings per share (rather than the dividend per share) as a percentage of the market price of each share.

$\dfrac{\text{Earnings per share}}{\text{Price per share}} \times 100$	$\dfrac{14.7\text{p}}{180\text{p}} \times 100 = 8.2\%$

23.8.6 Interest cover

This ratio is useful for providers of loan capital (rather than equity capital). It measures the possible impact of a fall in profit levels on the interest payments.

$\dfrac{\text{Profit before interest \& tax}}{\text{Interest expense}} \times 100$	$\dfrac{£4,340 + £40}{£40} \times 100 = 110$ times

Activity 23.8 **Investors' dilemma**

Gloria seeks your opinion on whether she should invest in ordinary shares of Minnow plc or Mullet plc. Shares of both companies have a par value of £1 and she has provided you with the information stated on the right.

Required: What advice would you give her?

	Minnow	Mullet
Earnings per share	18p	24p
Market price per share	252p	192p
Dividend paid per share	5p	15p

23.9 Limitations of accounting ratios

23.9.1 Ratios indicate symptoms

Accounting ratios are to the accountant what physical symptoms are to the doctor. A reading from a thermometer or a blood pressure gauge would in itself have no significance unless the medical practitioner is able to expertly interpret the reading. The relationship traced by an accounting ratio is only a symptom. Other corroboration might be required. This can take the form of:

1. Other ratios, e.g. if asset turnover is rising quickly calculate the non-current asset ratio and the current asset ratio to see if there has been a reduction in either. Then explore further, e.g. if the current asset turnover is rising, look at the individual current asset turnover rates.

2. Additional explanations from the company if to do so would be to their benefit (say to obtain a bank loan) or may be legally obliged to as is the case with the auditors and tax authorities.

3. Alternative sources of information such as from credit agency reports, bank references, comments in trade press and so on.

Be wary

Every effort must be made to identify possible bias. For example, an owner of a business proposing to sell it may be tempted to inflate the gross profit, e.g. by recording fictitious sales. Similarly, managers interested in a management buyout may be tempted to deflate the gross profit in order to be able to buy the business at a lower price.

23.9.2 Ratios need comparators to be meaningful

A ratio, in isolation, would be of little use, unless the ratio has a norm with which it can be compared or a standard against which it can be judged. The relationship traced by a ratio would be meaningful only in comparison with:

1. what the relationships were in the past;

2. what relationships were aimed at when the business established its budget;

3. what relationship competitors and others achieve in the same industry.

Comparative information may be obtained from membership of a trade association where members submit their financial data in a standardised format. The association prepares an inter-firm comparison report which compares each member's performance with the other members, whilst maintaining each firm's anonymity. A typical inter-firm comparison report calculates the company's own ratios and a quartile analysis of all members so a company can see how it compares with the average in the industry.

23.9.3 Ratios are no more than red flags

The ratios are simply red flags that should raise questions. They do not supply the answers. The accounting ratios are incapable of providing answers to the numerous questions raised by the users of accounting reports. All that they can do is to provide a basis for comparison and to indicate trends. For example, we learnt that the ROCE of Oldy plc for the year is

13.9%. This does not tell us what the potential yield could have been in the circumstances of the business or how best such a yield could have been achieved.

23.9.4 Knowledge of a business's commercial thinking is essential

A relationship traced by a ratio would be meaningless unless it is interpreted in the light of the circumstances of the business involved. For example, a business may have built up high inventory levels, resulting in poorer inventory turnover ratio as well as deterioration of the liquidity ratio with the resulting increase in trade payables. A negative reason might have been that it was unable to sell its stock; a positive reason might have been that it was a deliberate move either to launch a significant sales push or in anticipation of a rise in the price of its purchases.

An interpretation of accounting ratios, without full awareness of the attendant circumstances, may well lead to false conclusions and inappropriate decisions. We have seen that the symptoms revealed by the same set of ratios are capable of several, sometimes conflicting, interpretations. For example, significantly high inventory turnover ratio and receivable turnover ratios may well be interpreted as signs respectively, of super efficiency and effective credit control. What these ratios may mask is that the entity is losing business because of inadequate inventory levels to meet customer needs and that customers are being alienated by an overly severe credit policy.

23.9.5 Trends are vital

Much more important than a relationship currently existing is the trend in relationships. These can be significant as a basis for predicting future financial position and performance.

23.9.6 Ratios must be applied to comparable companies

Inter-firm comparison would be meaningless unless the companies being compared:

- are of a similar nature, e.g. manufacturer, wholesaler or retailer;
- have adopted identical accounting policies on all matters such as asset valuation, depreciation, inventory cost flow assumptions, deferral of development costs, deferral of borrowing costs;
- are engaged in similar business practices on matters like buying/leasing assets, dealing in consignment goods, debt factoring;
- are financed with similar levels of gearing.

23.9.7 Inflation distorts ratios

The size of the capital employed in a company will depend on the price levels prevailing when most of its non-current assets were acquired. For example, given the steadily rising price levels, a company which acquired its assets in the recent past may well appear to have a larger asset operating base than another which acquired its assets at an earlier date, merely because the latter acquired its assets when the value of money was higher.

23.9.8 Year-end figures on a Balance Sheet are not always representative

Most companies choose as their year-end a date when inventory levels are at the lowest. As a result inventory turnover levels reported using the year-end inventory figure could be overstated.

23.9.9 Ratios can be deliberately manipulated

This can take the form of window dressing, e.g. sending customers faulty goods at the year-end and treating them as sales knowing that they will be returned in the following financial period.

23.10 | Interpreting financial information by other means

There are, of course, alternative ways of placing the information in a financial statement in proper perspective. These include the following two forms:

1. Graphical representations, such as pie charts and bar charts, can be used to portray the comparative sizes of each item in (say), an Income Statement.

2. Component percentages can be used to equate the focal point of attention in a financial statement to 100 and then to express all other significant figures in that statement as percentages of that figure.

Income Statement for the year ended 31.12.20X8	
	£'000
Sales revenue	950
Cost of sales	(665)
Gross profit	285
Admin expenses	(152)
Distribution cost	(56)
Interest	(12)
Profit for the year	65

For example, if information in the Income Statement shown on the left, is to be presented as component percentages, sales revenue will be equated to 100 and the whole of the information in it presented as shown on the right.

Income Statement for the year ended 31.12.20X8	
	£'000
Sales revenue	100%
Cost of sales	(70)%
Gross profit	30%
Admin expenses	(16)%
Distribution cost	(6)%
Interest	(1)%
Profit for the year	7%

Any individual expense classification may be expressed as a percentage of sales. The classification of costs may be by function (e.g. distribution cost, administrative expenses) or by type of expense (e.g. advertising, carriage outwards).

An expense ratio is useful, first, for establishing whether the particular cost has remained in line with changes in sales. Second, an entity bent on improving profitability may wish to review each class of expenditure with a view to pruning them if possible. A first step in this effort is to establish the relative size of each expense classification by expressing it as a percentage of the sales.

Some of the steps an entity may consider as part of pruning its expenses include reducing:

■ establishment expenses – by moving the head office from a city centre to a less expensive location;

■ administration expenses – by downsizing and making middle managers redundant;

■ selling expenses – by cutting the advertising expenditure or rates of sales commission;

■ distribution costs – by using carriers instead of operating the entity's own delivery fleet;

■ financial costs – by renegotiating the terms of a loan and replacing it with a loan at a lower rate of interest.

Summary

- Accounting ratios are the main tools of analysis used for interpreting information in the financial statements.
- Accounting ratios trace, in one of four different forms, the relationship between two amounts reported in financial statements with a view to drawing conclusions from that relationship and from movements in that relationship.
- Accounting ratios are only useful as signals identifying symptoms which need proper diagnosis, interpretation and appropriate action.

Suggested answers to activities

23.1 Interpreting a change in ratio

The adverse change in relationship between sales and trade receivables could have arisen because of any one or more of the following reasons:

1. **Commercial reasons:**
   - the credit terms allowed by competitors in the industry may have changed;
   - because of keener competition in the market, extended credit may be the only way to survive;
   - because of a change in customer base, the new customers may be ones who could negotiate better credit terms;
   - extension of credit period may be a strategy to survive in a declining market;
   - the company may have taken debt indemnity insurance and hence willing to extend credit period.
2. **Financial reasons:** with improvement in liquidity position there could have been a decision to extend credit period.
3. **Administrative reasons** such as breakdown in credit control.

23.2 Possible reasons for a fall in gross profit ratio

a)

Gross profit ratio
20X8   £194,000/£884,000 × 100 = 21.9%
20X7   £236,000/£876,000 × 100 = 26.9%

b) Possible reasons for fall in gross profit ratio:
  i) **Commercial reasons:**
   - market price for the product has fallen;
   - costs (purchase price, processing costs, carriage inwards, freight duty) and so on have increased and they could not be passed on to customer by increasing sale price;
   - an adverse variation in sales mix, i.e. more is sold of less profitable items.
  ii) **Accounting errors:**
   - not establishing the correct cutoff to ensure that all goods accounted for as opening inventory and purchases are included within closing inventory unless they have been sold;
   - error in inventory taking, such as failing to include some items in the count or overlooking items in bonded warehouse or with customers on sale or return basis;
   - error in ascribing cost to the items listed on the stock sheet.
  iii) **Failure of internal controls:**
   - pilferage of goods by staff, shoplifting by customers, failure to account for goods removed by owner.
  iv) Manipulation of accounts calculated to deliberately understate the entity's performance.

23.3 Assessment of comparative profitability

	Salmon £'000		Tuna £'000	
1. Gross profit ratio	$852/2{,}840 \times 100$	30%	$1{,}748/18{,}460 \times 100$	9.5%
2. Net profit ratio	$239/2{,}840 \times 100$	8.4%	$1{,}106/18{,}460 \times 100$	6%
3. ROCE	$239/3{,}169^{a} \times 100$	7.5%	$1{,}106/1{,}254^{b} \times 100$	88.2%
4. ROE	$199/2{,}669 \times 100$	7.5%	$1{,}106/1{,}254 \times 100$	88.2%

a) $2{,}000 + 669 + 500 = 3{,}169$ b) $900 + 354 = 1{,}254$

Comments:

1. Catering for customers at the upper end of the market, Salmon Ltd is able to fix its sale prices high, earning a gross profit ratio of 30%, whereas Tuna Ltd's gross profit ratio is only 9.5% because its trading policy is higher turnover with lower margins.

2. Higher gross profit ratio is reflected in higher net profit ratio as well for Salmon – 8.4% compared to 6%. However, as we shall see when considering operating efficiency, Salmon incurs a higher proportion of its earnings on administration and distribution expenses.

3. The ROCE identifies Tuna (88.2%) as far more profitable than Salmon which earns only 7.5%, calling into question whether it is justified in borrowing loan notes at 8%. Although considering the type of customers it caters for it has to maintain a better selling environment, with consequent capital cost, there arises a suspicion as to whether it is over capitalised. On the other hand Tuna could be over-trading.

4. Salmon's ROE is lower than ROCE because it services loan notes at a rate (8%) higher than what it earns (7.5%). In the absence of any prior charge capital Tuna's ROE is the same as its ROCE.

23.4 Evaluation of liquidity

	Salmon . . .				Tuna . . .			
	20X7 £'000		20X8 £'000		20X7 £'000		20X8 £'000	
Current ratio	$822/255$	3.2 times	$928/311$	3 times	$399/492$	0.8 times	$454/556$	0.8 times
Liquidity ratio	$350/255$	1.2 times	$380/311$	1.4 times	$71/492$	0.14 times	$40/556$	0.07 times
Inventory days	$472/1{,}680 \times 365$	102.5 days	$548/2{,}064 \times 365$	96.9 days	$328/14{,}900 \times 365$	8 days	$414/16{,}798 \times 365$	8.9 days
Receivable days	$298/2{,}140 \times 365$	50.8 days	$346/2{,}840 \times 365$	44.5 days	$32/17{,}200 \times 365$	0.7 days	$28/18{,}460 \times 365$	0.5 days
Payables days	$217/1{,}680 \times 365$	47.1 days	$266/2{,}064 \times 365$	47 days	$294/14{,}900 \times 365$	7.2 days	$328/16{,}798 \times 365$	7.1 days
Cash flow ratio	$218 + 122/255$	1.3 times	$239 + 142/311$	1.2 times	$994 + 78/492$	2.2 times	$1{,}106 + 96/556$	2.2 times

Comments:

1. Although dealing in the same product (ready-made garments) the companies cannot be compared because:
   - They are operating in two diverse markets – Salmon is at the upper end where convenience and facilities matter more than the price, whereas Tuna operates at the opposite extreme, pruning down profit margins and focusing on sales volume.
   - Their trading practices are obviously different – Salmon buys probably on one month's credit and sells also on similar terms, whereas Tuna is selling mostly on cash terms and buying predominantly on cash terms.

2. Considering the trading practices, the normal rule of thumb is probably applicable to Salmon, and it is faring well under that rule. Current ratio at 3 is well above the ratio of 2 regarded as comfortable and is being maintained at that level over the two years. Similarly, the liquidity ratio at 1.2, maintained at the same level over the two years, compares well with one regarded as ideal.

   If we assume, as is normal in the retail trade, that its customers have been allowed 30 days' credit, the control over receivables (credit management) is not satisfactory, although the trend is improving because the receivable days have fallen from over 50 days to 44.5 days. Payables days remain at 47. This may not be a satisfactory position unless six weeks' credit period has been agreed with suppliers.

   Inventory is being held for more than three months. Although the inventory days too are improving the position is still not satisfactory if we bear in mind that (i) demand for ready-made garments could be volatile, changing as it would with fashion trends and (ii) there is a cost attaching to holding high inventory in the form of storage costs, insurance and risks of obsolescence. However, those to whom Salmon owes money need not be too concerned with its liquidity position because it continues to generate sufficient cash every year (as seen from the cash flow ratio) to settle its owings 1.2 times.

3. It is evident that the trading practices of Tuna are such (doing business mainly on cash terms and focusing more on quick turnover than high margins) that the normal rule of thumb would not apply to it. Hence there need not be any concern that its current ratio is so much below 2 and the liquidity ratio so much below 1. Its cash generating ability continues to cover its current liabilities by more than twice. It takes only 8–9 days to convert its inventory into cash. Its receivables days and payables days, though not quite meaningful in the context of its trading practices, show that cash is collected from its sales within less than a day and payables do not remain unpaid for more than 7 days, over the 2 year period.

23.5 An assessment of operational efficiency

a)

	Year to June 20X7 £'000		Year to June 20X8 £'000	
ROCE	2,628/7,500 × 100	35%	3,564/9,000 × 100	39.6%
Net profit ratio	2,628/16,425 × 100	16%	3,564/21,600 × 100	16.5%
Asset turnover	16,425/7,500	2.19 times	21,600/9,000	2.4 times

ROCE is the product of net profit ratio × asset turnover:

16% × 2.19 times = 35%	16.5% × 2.4 times = 39.6%

b) How directors plan to achieve improved profitability:
   i) By pruning down operating expenses (as seen in the workings below) while gross profit remains constant at 40% of sales, the operating expenses are reduced from 24% to 23.5% of sales.
   ii) By making the company's assets work harder: improving asset turnover from 2.19 times to 2.4 times.

Workings:	2007	2008
GP ratio	6,570/16,425 × 100 = 40%	8,640/21,600 × 100 = 40%
Operating expenses to sales	3,942/16,425 × 100 = 24%	5,076/21,600 × 100 = 23.5%

23.6 How high gearing affects equity shareholders

a) Capital gearing expresses prior charge capital (i.e. preference shares and loan notes) as a percentage of total capital employed: 5,000 + 3,000/12,500 × 100 = 64% (highly geared).

b) 20% fall in operating profit will reduce the retained profit (available to ordinary shareholders) to £104,800 (as shown on the right). That is a fall of (285 − 104.8) = £180,200 or, expressed as a percentage (180,200/285,000 × 100) = 63.2%. Thus the amount available for ordinary shareholders would suffer by a more than proportionate impact whenever there is a decrease in profit, in a highly geared company.

	£'000
Operating profit	756
Interest on loan	(400)
Profit before tax	356
Taxation @ 20%	(71.2)
Profit after tax	284.8
Preference dividend	(180)
Retained profit	104.8

23.7 Earnings per share

Weighted average number of shares in issue in 20X8		
		£'000
1.1 to 1.5	1,500,000 × 4/12 months	500
1.5 to 31.12	1,800,000 × 8/12 months	1,200
		1,700

	£'000
Profit after tax	103
Preference dividend	(6)
Available for ordinary shares	97

Earnings per share:

£97,000/1,700,000 shares × 100 = 5.7p

23.8 Investors' dilemma

Ratios:

	Minnow £'000		Mullet £'000	
Price earnings ratio	252/18	14	192/24	8
Dividend yield	5/252 × 100	2%	15/192 × 100	7.8%
Earnings yield	18/252 × 100	7.1%	24/192 × 100	12.5%
Dividend cover	18/5	3.6 times	24/15	1.6 times

Comments:

1. Although dividend yield is low (2% compared to Mullet's 7.8%) and earnings yield (at 7.1%) is not substantially more than the market rate on bank fixed deposits, if Gloria is aiming at long-term investment she should invest in Minnow plc for the following reasons:
   - PE ratio at 14 is almost as high as what could be expected on blue chip companies.
   - High PE ratio reflects the market confidence in the company and such confidence is usually translated into more demand for shares in that company and, therefore, further increase in its share price, opening the door for making capital gains whenever these shares are disposed of.
   - Minnow's policy is obviously to plough back profits into further expansion of its activities rather than paying out as dividend.
   - Given the high dividend cover (3.6 times) even in the unlikely event of a fall in profits Minnow will be able to maintain its current levels of dividend payment.

2. On the other hand, if Gloria is to retire from work and seeks an investment capable of providing an income, she is advised to invest in Mullet plc because the dividend yield from it is almost 8% per annum and the earnings yield a very attractive 12.5% per annum. She must remember, however, that a fall in Mullet's profits will impair its capacity to maintain dividends at current levels.

Multiple choice questions

The concept

23.1 Which of the following statements is correct?

a) An accounting ratio should always be expressed as a percentage

b) An accounting ratio compares two amounts appearing on the balance sheet

c) An accounting ratio traces the relations between two amounts in financial statements

d) An accounting ratio may be expressed in one of four alternative forms

w	a & b	
x	a & c	
y	b & c	
z	c & d	

Gross profit ratio

23.2 Sales in the year ending 31st March 20X8 were £43,200. Identify the gross profit ratio, as a percentage, in each of the following independent situations:

a) Gross profit for the year was £5,400

x	20%	
y	12.5%	
z	25%	

b) Goods are sold throughout the year at a price fixed at cost plus a third

x	25%	
y	20%	
z	10%	

c) Opening inventory, purchases, carriage inwards and closing inventory were £4,400, £21,400, £1,200 and £5,400, respectively

x	40%	
y	33%	
z	50%	

23.3 Which of the following conclusions could be drawn if the gross profit ratio falls from 25% to 18%?

a) There has been a deliberate change in trading policy

b) There has been a mistake in counting or valuing closing inventory

c) There has been an increase in costs which could not be passed on to the customers

d) There has been shoplifting by customers or pilferage by staff not accounted for

w	a & b	
x	a, b & c	
y	b, c & d	
z	All four	

23.4 Which one or more of the following will reduce a company's gross profit ratio?

a) Increasing profit margins added to cost

b) Omission from closing inventory of items with customers on a sale or return basis

c) Inability to pass on increasing cost of purchases to customers

d) During rising prices, valuing closing inventory using LIFO instead of FIFO

w	a & b	
x	a, b & c	
y	b, c & d	
z	c & d	

23.5 Which one of the following will reduce a company's gross profit ratio, when sales are increasing?

a) Decision to increase the quantity of inventory held

b) Increase in advertising costs and expenses of delivering goods to customers

c) Decision to extend the credit period allowed to customers

d) Adverse change in the sales mix, i.e. lower sales of more profitable lines

w	b	
x	c	
y	a	
z	d	

23.6 Which one of the following could cause a significant increase in a company's gross profit ratio?

a) Loss of goods by customer shoplifting or pilferage by staff

b) Inclusion in closing inventory of goods for which invoices have yet to be received

c) Increase in the sales volume

d) Failure to account for goods removed for own use by the proprietors

w	a	
x	b	
y	c	
z	d	

Return on capital employed ratio (ROCE) and return on equity ratio (ROE)

23.7 Which of the following ratios is known as the primary ratio?

a) Earnings per share

b) Return on capital employed ratio

c) Price earnings ratio

d) Liquidity ratio

23.8 As at 31st March 20X8 a listed company had no loan notes in issue and its capital employed was £3.9 million. Shown on the right are summaries of the liability side of its balance sheet as at 31st March 20X9 and its Income Statement for the year ended on that date. Which of the following is the correct calculation of its ROCE and ROE ratio?

	£'000
Ordinary shares	2,500
Share premium	150
Reserves	1,450
	4,100
9% Loan notes	400
Current liabilities	1,500
	6,000

	£'000
Operating profit	746
Interest on loan	(36)
Profit before tax	710
Taxation	(150)
Profit after tax	560
Dividend paid	(120)
Retained profit	440

	ROCE		ROE	
a	£710/£4,000 × 100 =	17.75%	£440/£4,000 × 100 =	11%
b	£746/£4,200 × 100 =	17.76%	£710/£4,000 × 100 =	17.75%
c	£746/£4,000 × 100 =	18.65%	£710/£4,100 × 100 =	17.32%
d	£746/£4,200 × 100 =	17.74%	£710/£4,100 × 100 =	17.32%

Working capital ratio and liquidity ratio

23.9 In which line of business would you expect the working capital ratio to be higher:

a) Supermarket

b) Dealer in white goods such as refrigerators, washing machines and cookers

c) Construction industry

d) Retailer

23.10 A company's balance sheet as at 31st March 20X9 reports its current assets and current liabilities as shown on the right. Which of the following is the correct calculation of the company's working capital ratio and liquidity ratio?

Current assets:	£'000	Current liabilities:	£'000
Inventory	548	Trade payables	392
Trade receivables	486	Accrued expense	48
Pre-payments	12	Taxation	118
Cash and bank	32	Dividend declared	60

	Working capital ratio			Liquidity ratio	
a	(548 + 486 + 12 + 32)/(392 + 48 + 118 + 60)	1.7	(486 + 12 + 32)/(392 + 48 + 118 + 60)	.9	
b	(486 + 12 + 32)/(392 + 48 + 118 + 60) × 100	86%	(548 + 486 + 12 + 32)/(392 + 118 + 60)	1.9	
c	(548 + 486 + 12 + 32)/(392 + 48 + 118)	1.9	(486 + 12 + 32)/(392 + 48 + 118 + 60)	.9	
d	(486 + 12 + 32)/(392 + 48 + 118 + 60)	.9	(548 + 12 + 32)/(392 + 48 + 118 + 60)	1.0	

Inventory days

23.11   Prichard's sales in the year ended 31st December 20X8 were £390,000. The sales produced a gross profit ratio of 30%.

a) If the cost of inventory on 31st December 20X7 was £78,000 and that of 31st December 20X8 was £96,000, what are the inventory days?

x	128 days	
y	109 days	
z	120 days	

b) If Prichard reports his inventory days as 90, and the cost of closing inventory as £54,000, what would have been the cost of his opening inventory?

x	£108,000	
y	£135,000	
z	£54,000	

c) What will be Prichard's sales in 20X9, if he always sets his sale prices to produce a gross profit ratio of 20% and reports his opening inventory as £54,000, purchases as £292,000 and inventory days as 60?

x	£298,000	
y	£357,600	
z	£372,500	

23.12   a) What consequence will you expect if the inventory days are reduced from 78 to 64?

i)   Profitability of the business will improve

ii) Liquidity of the business will improve

iii) Operational efficiency of the business will improve

x	i only	
y	i & ii	
z	i, ii & iii	

b) In which one or more of the following circumstances will it not be sensible to reduce inventory days?

i)   when the business is already suffering cash shortage

ii) when the business is unable to meet demand for its products

iii) when suppliers are already pressing for payment of overdue bills

x	i & ii	
y	ii only	
z	iii only	

Trade receivable days

23.13   Afford Mills is in business as a textiles wholesaler. Sales in the year ended 30th June 20X8 were £365,000 and Afford allows its customers 45 days' credit, with sales taking place consistently throughout the year.

a) If, following a 25% increase in sales in the year ended 30th June 20X9, there is an increase in the amount of trade receivables, the increase in receivables will need to be funded by:

i)   obtaining more credit from suppliers

ii) retaining more profit within the business

iii) introducing additional capital

x	i & ii	
y	i, ii & iii	
z	ii & iii	

b) It is not sensible for Afford Mills to reduce the credit period allowed to its customers to less than 45 days when:

i) competitors allow 45 days

ii) business is short of cash

iii) Afford is attempting to increase its sales

x	ii & iii	
y	i & ii	
z	i & iii	

c) It is not sensible for Afford Mills to extend the credit period allowed to customers to more than 45 days when:

i) the business has cash flow problems

ii) the business is unable to meet the customers' demand for more goods

iii) the customers are not buying as much as they did earlier

x	i & iii	
y	ii & iii	
z	i & ii	

23.14 Marlin's wholesale reported its sales in the year ended 30th June 20X8 as £511,000.

a) If her trade receivables on 30th June 20X8 were £63,000, calculate her receivable days.

x	60 days	
y	45 days	
z	30 days	

b) If her receivable days are calculated to be 63 days, ascertain her trade receivables as at 30th June 20X8.

x	£126,400	
y	£321,930	
z	£88,200	

c) If, in the year ended 30th June 20X9, the sales are expected to increase by 20%, while receivable days remain 63, ascertain the trade receivables as at 30 June 20X9.

x	£105,840	
y	£88,200	
z	£3,552,667	

d) If her sales in the year ended 30th June 20X9 are expected to be 10% lower than those in the previous year and if one sixth of these sales remain outstanding at that year-end, ascertain the receivable days.

x	54 days	
y	61 days	
z	45 days	

Trade payable days

23.15 A business would attempt to negotiate extended credit period from its suppliers if:

a) It experiences cash flow problems

b) It wishes to negotiate better trade discounts

c) It wishes to extend credit period allowed to its customers

d) It wishes to earn more cash discounts

x	a & c	
y	b, c & d	
z	b & d	

23.16 A business should endeavour to reduce its payables days if:

a) It breaches credit period allowed by suppliers

b) It wishes to improve its sales

c) It wishes to reduce bad debts

d) It has cash surplus to its needs

w	a & b	
x	b & c	
y	a & d	
z	c & d	

23.17   A fall in trade payables days may signal:

a) A reduction in profitability

b) An improvement in liquidity

c) Worsening operational efficiency

23.18   In respect of the year ended 31st December 20X8 Hussain reports his purchases as £624,000 and his trade payables at the year-end as £114,000. His payables days would be:

a	94 days	
b	67 days	
c	48 days	

23.19   In respect of the year ended 31st March 20X9 Akbar reports his purchases as £578,160 and his trade payables days as 54 days. Ascertain his trade payables as at 31st March 20X9.

a	£92,400	
b	£85,536	
c	£72,840	

23.20   Which of the following may be expected to improve a company's liquidity?

a) Increase of the inventory days

b) Reduction of trade payables days

c) Reduction of trade receivables days

d) Repayment of loan notes

Cash flow ratio

23.21   Your advice is sought by a bank which is considering a request for a substantial overdraft facility from Fairways, a supermarket with sales outlets spread throughout the UK. The operating profit of Fairways for the year ended 30th June 20X8 was £4,428,500, after writing off £84,500 as depreciation. Shown on the right are items reported on Fairways' balance sheet as at the year-end. Which one of the following accounting ratios will you draw to the bank's attention when recommending or not recommending the overdraft?

	£'000
Inventory	324
Trade receivables	16
Cash and bank	12
Current liabilities	842

a	Net current liabilities	£352,000 – £842,000	£490,000	
b	Current ratio	£352,000/£842,000	0.41	
c	Liquidity ratio	£28,000/£842,000	0.03	
d	Cash flow ratio	£4,428,500 + £84,500/£842,000	5.4 times	

Operating efficiency

23.22   In which line of business would you expect the stock turnover ratio to be higher?

a) Supermarket

b) Dealer in white goods such as refrigerators, washing machines and cookers

c) Construction industry

d) Greengrocer

23.23   A company reports its net profit ratio as 5.4% and its total asset turnover as 7 times. Which of those stated on the right is the correct calculation of the company's ROCE?

a	5.4/7 = 0.7%	
b	5.4 × 7 = 37.8%	
c	5.4 + 7 = 12.4	

23.24 A company's sales in the year ended 31st March 20X9 were £948,200 and its operating profit £182,750. Its assets and liabilities at the year-end were as stated on the right. Which of the following is the correct calculation of the asset turnover and current asset turnover?

	£'000
Non-current assets	417,500
Current assets	298,400
Current liabilities	154,200

	Total asset turnover		Current asset turnover	
a	£561,700/£948,200 × 100	59.2%	£144,200/£948,200 × 100	15.2%
b	£948,200/£561,700	1.7 times	£948,200/£144,200	6.6 times
c	£715,900/£948,200 × 100	75.5%	£298,400/£928,200 × 100	32.1%
d	£948,200/£715,900	1.3 times	£928,200/£298,400	3.1 times

23.25 During the year ended 30th June 20X9 a company's sales were £498,400. As at 30th June 20X8 the cost of its inventory was £98,200 and its trade payables £124,600. Identify its inventory turnover ratio in each of the following independent scenarios.

a) Its purchases in the year ending 30th June 20X9 were £392,400 and the cost of year-end inventory £112,400.

w	3.7 times
x	26.8%
y	3.5 times
z	28.0%

b) As at 30th June 20X9 its cost of inventory was £74,200 and trade payables £114,800, while it paid £294,800 to its suppliers during the year ended 30th June 20X9.

w	3.1 times
x	32.4%
y	3.3 times
z	27.9%

c) As at 30th June 20X9 the cost of its inventory was £148,200 and throughout the year it sold its goods at consistent prices calculated at cost plus 25%.

w	3.2 times
x	3.0 times
y	27.50%
z	3.6 times

23.26 Which of the following changes in accounting ratios would please a company management concerned with cash flow problems in their company?

a) Increase in gross profit ratio
b) Increase in inventory turnover
c) Decrease in payables turnover without obtaining extended credit period from suppliers
d) Decrease in trade receivables turnover

Capital gearing

23.27 Which of the following steps will result in lowering the capital gearing of a company?

a) Paying dividends to its shareholders
b) Making a bonus issue of shares to ordinary shareholders
c) Making a rights issue of ordinary shares
d) Issuing loan notes with a long redemption date

23.28 Which of the following statements is/are correct?

a) It is always bad to invest in a highly geared company

b) Redemption of long-term loans will reduce a company's gearing

c) Paying dividends to its shareholders will increase its capital gearing

d) If loan notes form less than 5% of a company's capital employed it is not geared

w	b only	
x	a & b	
y	b & c	
z	b & d	

23.29 A listed company's capital employed as at 31st December 20X8 was £8,000,000. This amount includes the items shown on the right. Which capital gearing calculation shown below would you accept as correct?

	£'000
8% Loan notes	500
6% Preference shares	2,000

a) £500,000/£8,000,000 × 100 = 6.25%

b) £500,000 + £2,000,000/£8,000,000 × 100 = 31.25%

c) £2,000,000/£8,000,000 × 100 = 25%

d) £8,000,000 − £500,000 − £2,000,000/£8,000,000 × 100 = 68.75%

Stock market ratios

23.30

	£'000
Operating profit	5,000
Interest paid	(80)
Profit before tax	4,920
Taxation	(994)
Profit after tax	3,926

Extract from a listed company's Income Statement for the year ended 30th June 20X9 is shown on the left. The issued share capital of the company consisting of ordinary shares of 50p each is reported in the year-end balance sheet as £5 million, while the same balance sheet reports 8% loan notes at £1 million. Calculate the earnings per share of this company for the year ended 30th June 20X9 in each of the following independent scenarios:

a) During the year ended 30th June 20X9 the company did not pay any dividend or issue any shares

w	98.4p	
x	39.3p	
y	39.3%	
z	50p	

b) The company has also in issue £500,000 6% preference shares but, during the year ended 30th June 20X9, no shares have been issued nor dividend paid

w	39.3p	
x	39p	
y	97.8p	
z	77.9p	

c) The company has also in issue £500,000 6% preference shares which, as at 30th June 20X8, were in arrears for three years' dividend. During the year ended 30th June 20X9 no shares were issued nor any dividend paid

w	39.3p	
x	39p	
y	97.8p	
z	77.9p	

d) The company made an issue of 2 million ordinary shares of 50p each on 1st April 20X9 at 70p each and paid a dividend of 3p per share on 29th June 20X9

w	60.4p	
x	46.2p	
y	39.3p	
z	39p	

23.31 Four companies in the same line of business and with identical trading practices and accounting policies, report their earnings per share as shown on the left. Which of these companies would you say is the most profitable one?

Equity shares in issue		EPS
W plc	4 million ordinary shares of £1 each	21p
X plc	20 million ordinary shares of 50p each	12p
Y plc	200 million ordinary shares of 20p each	5p
Z plc	500 million ordinary shares of 10p each	3p

a	W plc
b	X plc
c	Y plc
d	Z plc

23.32 Information relating to Bamby plc is stated on the left. Identify the correct share market ratios from those stated on the right.

Earnings per share	24p
Market price per share	192p
Dividend per share	8p

	PE ratio	Dividend yield	Earnings yield
a	8	4.2%	12.5%
b	12.4%	33.3%	8
c	8	24	33.3%

Answers to multiple choice questions

23.1: c   23.2a: y   23.2b: x   23.2c: z   23.3: z   23.4: y   23.5: d   23.6: b   23.7: b   23.8: b   23.9: c   23.10: a   23.11a: z
23.11b: x   23.11c: z   23.12a: z   23.12b: y   23.13a: y   23.13b: z   23.13c: z   23.14a: y   23.14b: z   23.14c: x   23.14d: y
23.15: x   23.16: y   23.17: b   23.18: b   23.19: b   23.20: c   23.21: d   23.22: d   23.23: b   23.24: d   23.25a: w   23.25b: y
23.25c: z   23.26: b   23.27: c   23.28: y   23.29: b   23.30a: x   23.30b: x   23.30c: x   23.30d: x   23.31: d   23.32: a

Progressive questions

PQ 23.1 A basic interpretation of financial statements

Small Fry's business submits to you the following financial statements:

Income Statement for the year ended 31.12.20X8

	£	£
Sales		625,000
Inventory – 31.12.20X7	54,500	
Purchases	415,000	
Depreciation – machinery	18,000	
Inventory – 31.12.20X8	(62,500)	
Cost of sales		(425,000)
Gross profit		200,000
Admin expenses		(118,000)
Distribution costs		(48,000)
Interest on loan		(9,000)
Profit for the year		25,000

Balance Sheet as at 31.12.20X8

Non-current assets:	Cost	Accum depn	£
Machinery	180,000	(45,000)	135,000
Motor vehicles	27,000	(12,000)	15,000
			150,000
Current assets:			
Inventory		62,500	
Trade receivables		31,250	
Cash & bank		6,250	100,000
			250,000

	£	£
Capital	100,000	
Profit for the year	25,000	125,000
Loan notes		75,000
Trade payables		50,000
		250,000

Required: Assess (a) the profitability, (b) the liquidity and (c) the operational efficiency of this business, calculating not less than two ratios on which you will base your assessment.

PQ 23.2 CAT paper 6 – December 2005

Aber and Cromby are two retail businesses in the leisurewear market. Your manager has asked you to review the performance of both businesses from the financial statements which are provided below:

Income Statements for the year to 31 October 2005	Aber	Cromby
	$'000	$'000
Revenue	5,500	7,200
Cost of sales	(4,400)	(5,040)
Gross profit	1,100	2,160
Expenses	(610)	(1,685)
Profit from operations	490	475
Finance cost	(15)	(15)
Profit before tax	475	460
Tax	(200)	(180)
Net profit	275	280

Balance Sheets as at 31st October 2005	Aber		Cromby	
	$'000	$'000	$'000	$'000
Non-current assets		3,750		7,200
Inventory	125		360	
Trade receivables	500		190	
Bank	30	655	0	550
		4,405		7,750

	Aber		Cromby	
	$'000	$'000	$'000	$'000
Equity & reserves:				
Ordinary shares of $1		3,000		7,000
Reserves		1,080		410
		4,080		7,410
Non-current liabilities:				
Loan notes		75		110
Current liabilities:				
Trade payables	200		205	
Tax	50		20	
Overdraft	0	250	5	230
		4,405		7,750

Required:
a) Calculate the following ratios for each:
   i)   gross profit percentage;
   ii) return on capital employed;
   iii) earnings per share;
b) Comment on the performance of each as indicated by each of the ratios.
c) Explain the limitations of using ratios as the basis for analysing performance.

PQ 23.3 ACCA paper 1.1 – June 2003

Extracts from the financial statements of Apillon for the year ended 31 March 20X2 and 20X3 are given on the right.

Note:
a) Sales revenue includes cash sale of $300,000 in 20X2 and $100,000 in 20X3.

Required:
a) Calculate the following for each of the two years:
   i) current ratio;
   ii) quick ratio (acid test);

Income Statement for the year ended 31 March	20X2		20X3	
	$'000	$'000	$'000	$'000
Sales revenue (note a)		3,100		3,800
Opening inventory	360		540	
Purchases	2,080		2,580	
Closing inventory	(540)	(1,900)	(720)	(2,400)
Gross profit		1,200		1,400
Expenses		(900)		(1,100)
Net profit		300		300

iii) inventory turnover period
(use closing inventory);
iv) average period of credit
allowed to customers;
v) average period of credit
taken from suppliers.
b) Make four brief comments on
the changes in the position of
the company as revealed by the
changes in these ratios and/or in
the given figures from the financial
statements.

Balance Sheet as at 31 March				
	20X2		20X3	
	$'000	$'000	$'000	$'000
Current assets:				
Inventory	540		720	
Trade receivables	450	990	700	1,420
Current liabilities:				
Trade payables	410		690	
Bank overdraft	20	430	170	860

PQ 23.4 CAT paper 6 – December 2004

Nicola is thinking of investing in a limited liability company called Tressven. She has asked for your help to calculate some ratios she needs to decide whether or not to invest. She has given you the summarised financial statements of Tressven which are shown on the right.

Income Statement for the year ended 31.10.2004	
	$'000
Sales revenue	23,420
Cost of sales	–8,245
Gross profit	15,175
Expenses	–2,460
Operating profit	12,715
Finance costs	–50
Profit before tax	12,665
Income tax	–1,515
Net profit	11,150

Balance sheet as at 31 October 2004		
	$'000	$'000
Non-current assets		31,000
Current assets:		
Inventory	1,450	
Trade receivables	2,500	
Cash	50	4,000
		35,000
	$'000	$'000
Capital & reserves:		
Ordinary shares $.50		25,000
Reserves		7,520
		32,520
Current liabilities:		
Trade payables	860	
Tax	620	1,480
Loan notes		1,000
		35,000

Additional information:

i) During the year Tressven paid $10 million dividends.

ii) The market share price of Tressven is £1.50.

iii) Tressven's major competitor is a company called Hilladay which has the ratios stated on the right:

Dividend per share	10 cents
Dividend cover	5 times
Earnings per share	20 cents
Price earnings ratio	13.4
Dividend/equity ratio	15%
Interest cover	100 times

Required:
a) Calculate the ratios which have been calculated for Hilladay.
b) Comment on Tressven's ratios.

PQ 23.5 Progress of an entity from one year to the next

The summarised financial statements of Burstow Ltd are stated below:

Balance Sheet as at 30th September					Income Statement for the year to 30th September		
20X7			**20X8**		**20X7**		**20X8**
£			£		£		£
	Non-current assets:				386,400	Sales	764,200
70,000	Premises		150,000		29,600	Inventory – 1.10	51,200
65,000	Plant and equipment		162,000		310,720	Purchases	682,400
135,000			312,000		(51,200)	Inventory – 30.9	(85,300)
	Current assets:				(289,120)	Cost of sales	(648,300)
51,200	Inventory		85,300		97,280	Gross profit	115,900
29,700	Trade receivables		55,700		(43,400)	Admin expenses	(37,650)
15,600	Cash & bank		3,500		(14,680)	Distribution costs	(24,650)
96,500			144,500		–	Interest	(7,000)
231,500			456,500		39,200	Profit before tax	46,600
£			£		(4,600)	Taxation	(20,000)
100,000	Share capital £1 each		120,000		34,600		26,600
25,000	Share Premium account		30,000				
36,000	Retained earnings		50,600				
161,000			200,600				
	Non-current liabilities						
–	7% Loan notes		100,000				
	Current liabilities:						
52,300	Trade payables		131,100				
18,200	Taxation		24,800				
231,500			456,500				

Required: Comment on
a) the operational performance
b) the profitability
c) the liquidity
d) the capital structure of Burstow Ltd, supporting your answer with relevant accounting ratios.

PQ 23.6 Return on Capital Employed

Stated below are particulars with regard to six different companies 'a' to 'f'. Each of these companies has borrowed £2,500 at 8% interest per annum. Fill the blanks with appropriate figures

	Sales	Net profit after interest	Interest on loan notes	Capital employed	Net profit ratio	Total asset turnover	Return on capital employed
a)	£10,000	£800	£200	£5,000	?	?	?
b)	£15,000	?	£200	£8,000	12%	?	?
c)	£10,000	?	£200	?	5%	?	20%
d)	?	£800	£200	?	?	4	20%
e)	?	?	£200	£10,000	10%	4	?
f)	£20,000	?	£200	?	?	4	10%

PQ 23.7 Interpretation from an investor's focus

William commenced business on 1st April 20X0 using as initial capital an amount provided by his mother. The accounts for the first two years of business have been prepared as follows:

Income Statement for the year ended 31st March		
	20X7	20X8
	£	£
Sales	70,000	98,000
Cost of sales	(42,000)	(63,000)
Gross profit	28,000	35,000
Overheads – Variable	(14,000)	(24,500)
– Fixed	(8,400)	(11,200)
Net profit (loss)	5,600	(700)

Balance Sheet as at:			
	1.4.20X6	31.3.20X7	31.3.20X8
	£	£	£
Non-current asset	49,000	49,000	56,000
Current assets:			
Inventories	3,500	7,500	4,000
Trade receivables	–	9,700	16,800
Bank balance	9,100	2,400	–
Current liabilities:			
Trade payables	(2,100)	(3,500)	(9,600)
Bank overdraft	–	–	(2,800)
Capital employed	59,500	65,100	64,400

In an effort to persuade his mother to lend him a further amount, William points out that:

i)   The sales in the second year were 40% more than that in the first and the sales next year will probably be around £150,000.

ii) The net loss in the second year results from the increase in fixed costs because of renting larger premises to allow for the anticipated expansion in sales.

iii) A cash injection is urgently needed to maintain the business at the intended scale. Currently the business is unable to comply with the suppliers' term of one month's credit and the inventory levels are inadequate to meet customer demand.

The bank overdraft has not been negotiated. The mother's concern, however is that William is capable of earning around £7,000 per year if he finds paid employment and she herself could earn 8% per year on her savings.

Required: Your advice is sought by William's mother.

PQ 23.8 Working Capital cycle

The financial statements of a trader include the information stated on the right. Inventory as at 31 December 20X6 was £37,240. Assume that all sales were on credit terms.

Income Statement for the year ended 31 December 20X7	
Sales	£396,400
Cost of sales	£214,840

Balance Sheet as at 31 December 20X7	
Inventory	£42,820
Trade receivables	£32,960
Trade payables	£38,440

Required:

a) How would you measure the working capital cycle of a trader?

b) Calculate the working capital of the trader on the basis of information provided.

c) Explain why a business should endeavour to keep its working capital cycle as short as possible.

PQ 23.9 Preparing financial statements from accounting ratios

The following information is available for the period ended 31 May 20X9:

i)   Working capital at 31 May 20X9 was £11,500.

ii) Drawings during the year were £3,000.

iii) Depreciation of non-current assets during the year @ 10% on cost was £1,500. No new non-current assets were acquired during the period.

iv) Assume that inventory and trade payables remained constant throughout the year.

v)   General expenses (without depreciation) was 25% of sales.

vi) The following ratios applied:
     Acid test ratio was 1.25 times; Current ratio was 1.5 times; Total asset turnover was 2 times
     Inventory turnover: 5 times; Trade Receivables turnover: 8 times

Required:

Prepare an Income Statement for the year ended 31 May 20X9 and a Balance Sheet as at that date (show all calculations).

Chapter 13

Ratio analysis

Five year summary

	2005 £'000	2004 £'000	2003* £'000	2002 £'000	2001* £'000
Consolidated profit and loss account					
Turnover – continuing operations	187,704	178,746	167,095	163,800	159,921
Profit before interest	10,520	9,584	9,444	10,410	10,148
Net interest payable	(2,366)	(2,578)	(3,049)	(3,296)	(4,063)
Profit before taxation	8,154	7,006	6,395	7,114	6,085
Taxation	(2,584)	(2,037)	(1,972)	238	(1,570)
Profit after taxation	5,570	4,969	4,423	7,352	4,515
Dividends	(4,460)	(4,426)	(4,422)	(4,435)	(4,490)
Retained profit	1,110	543	1	2,917	25

	2005 £'000	2004 £'000	2003 £'000	2002 £'000	2001 £'000
Group balance sheet and key ratios					
Net assets	42,728	41,406	41,668	43,015	40,097
Net borrowings	(18,843)	(15,930)	(19,191)	(28,139)	(36,299)
Net debt	(29,171)	(25,996)	(28,864)	(37,193)	(44,515)
Gearing ratio	68.3%	62.8%	69.3%	86.5%	111.0%
Additions to fixed assets	11,204	10,359	6,813	5,379	6,142
Basic earnings per share (excluding exceptional items)	8.6p	7.6p	6.8p	11.2p	6.8p
Dividends per share	6.80p	6.80p	6.80p	6.80p	6.80p
Net assets per share	64.1p	62.2p	62.5p	64.6p	60.2p
Number of outlets – continuing operations					
Own stores	369	378	389	395	400
Franchises	216	203	198	181	163

Dividends and shareholder returns

Basic earnings per share have increased by 11.9% from 7.64p per share to 8.55p per share. Despite the increase in profits, the level of dividend cover remains low and, therefore, the Directors are recommending that the fully year dividend per share should remain at 6.80p per share which means that a final dividend of 4.85p per share will be paid in November.

Source: Thorntons plc Annual Report 2005, pp. 43, 5.

Discussion points

1 What does the reader learn from the ratios and performance measures presented by the company?

2 What major ratios are not shown in this summary?

Learning outcomes

After reading this chapter you should be able to:

- Define, calculate and interpret ratios that help analyse and understand (a) performance for investors, (b) management performance, (c) liquidity and working capital, and (d) gearing.
- Explain investors' views of the balance of risk and return, and the risks of investing in a geared company when profits are fluctuating.
- Explain how the pyramid of ratios helps integrate interpretation.
- Describe the uses and limitations of ratio analysis.
- Carry out a practical exercise of calculating and interpreting ratios.

13.1 Introduction

Ratios are widely used as a tool in the interpretation of financial statements. The ratios selected and the use of the resulting information depend on the needs of the person using the information. What investors really want to do is choose the best moment to sell shares when the share price is at its highest. To choose that best moment, the investors will monitor the company's performance. Bankers lending to the company will also monitor performance, and look for indicators of solvency and ability to repay interest and capital.

Many users will rely on others to monitor ratios on their behalf. Employees will look to their advisers, perhaps union officials, to monitor performance. Small private investors with limited resources will rely heavily on articles in the financial sections of newspapers. Professional fund managers will look to their own research resources and may also make use of the analysts' reports prepared by the brokers who act for the fund managers in buying and selling shares. Each broker's analyst seeks as much information as possible about a company so that he or she can sell information which is of better quality than that of any other broker's analyst. There is fierce competition to be a highly rated analyst because that brings business to the broking firm and high rewards for the analyst.

In monitoring performance the expert analysts and fund managers will use ratios rather than absolute amounts. A figure of £100m for sales (revenue) means nothing in isolation. The reader who knows that last year's sales (revenue) amounted to £90m sees immediately an increase of 11.1%. The reader who knows that fixed (non-current) assets remained constant at £75m knows that the fixed (non-current) assets this year have earned their value in sales (revenue) 1.33 times ($100/75 = 1.33$) whereas last year they earned their value in sales (revenue) 1.2 times ($90/75 = 1.2$). Ratios show changes in relationships of figures which start to create a story and start to generate questions. They do not provide answers.

The fund managers and analysts all have their own systems for calculating ratios and some keep these a carefully guarded secret so that each may hopefully see an important clue before the next person does so. That means there is no standard system of ratio analysis. There are, however, several which are used frequently. A selection of these will be used here as a basic framework for analysis. As you start to read more about company accounts you will find other ratios used but you should discover that those are largely refinements of the structure presented here.

13.2 A note on terminology

Ratio analysis is not a standardised exercise. It is often taught in finance courses and management accounting courses as well as in financial accounting courses. Businesses use ratios to describe their own performance. There is a tendency towards creating ratios that suit the purpose and towards using descriptions that are personal choices of the presenter. This chapter gives commonly used names for ratios (such as 'gross profit percentage') and links these to the terminology of the IASB system of accounting by using additional descriptions in brackets. For example, the title 'gross profit percentage' is used as a name for a ratio and it is defined as follows:

$$\frac{\text{Gross profit}}{\text{Sales (revenue)}} \times 100\%$$

In the denominator of this ratio the word 'sales' describes the activity that creates gross profit; the additional word (revenue) in brackets reminds you that the information will be found in financial statements under 'revenue'. Similarly 'fixed assets (non-current assets)' uses the commonly established words 'fixed assets' with the addition of (non-current assets) in brackets to remind you of where the information will be found in the balance sheet.

13.3 Systematic approach to ratio analysis

A systematic approach to ratio analysis seeks to establish a broad picture first of all, and then break that broad picture down until there are thumbnail sketches of interesting areas. Four key headings commonly encountered in ratio analysis are:

1 *Investor ratios.* Ratios in this category provide some measure of how the price of a share in the stock market compares to key indicators of the performance of the company.

2 *Analysis of management performance.* Ratios in this category indicate how well the company is being run in terms of using assets to generate sales (revenue) and how effective it is in controlling costs and producing profit based on goods and services sold.

3 *Liquidity and current assets.* The management of cash and current assets and the preservation of an adequate, but not excessive, level of liquidity is an essential feature of business survival especially in difficult economic circumstances.

4 *Gearing (referred to in American texts as 'leverage').* Gearing is a measure of the extent to which there is financial risk indicated in the balance sheet and in the profit and loss account (see section 13.4 on risk and return). Financial risk means the risk associated with having to pay interest and having an obligation to repay a loan.

In the following sections key ratios for each of these aspects of a systematic analysis are specified by the name of the ratio and the definition in words. Below each definition there is a brief discussion of the meaning and interpretation of the ratio.

13.3.1   Investor ratios

Investors who buy shares in a company want to be able to compare the benefit from the investment with the amount they have paid, or intend to pay, for their shares. There are two measures of benefit to the investors. One is the profit of the period (usually given the name **earnings** when referring to the profit available for equity holders (ordinary shareholders)). The other is the **dividend** which is an amount of cash that is paid to the shareholders. Profit indicates wealth created by the business. That wealth may be accumulated in the business or else paid out in the form of dividend. Four ratios are presented with a comment on each.

Earnings per share	$\dfrac{\text{Profit after tax for ordinary equity holders}}{\text{Number of issued ordinary shares}}$

Comment. **Earnings per share** is the most frequently quoted measure of company performance and progress. The percentage change from year to year should be monitored for the trend. Criticisms are that this strong focus on annual earnings may cause 'short-termism' among investors and among company managers. The IASB and the UK ASB would like to turn the attention of preparers and users of accounts away from reliance on earnings per share as a single performance measure, but the earnings per share remains a strong feature of comments on company results.

Price–earnings ratio	$\dfrac{\text{Share price}}{\text{Earnings per share}}$

Comment. The **price–earnings ratio** (often abbreviated to 'p/e ratio') compares the amount invested in one share with the earnings per share. It may be interpreted as the number of years for which the currently reported profit is represented by the current share price. The p/e ratio reflects the market's confidence in future prospects of the company. The higher the ratio, the longer is the period for which the market believes the current level of earnings may be sustained.

In order to gain some feeling for the relative magnitude of the p/e ratio of any individual company, it should be compared with the average p/e ratio for the industry, given daily in the *Financial Times*. The p/e ratio is quite commonly used as a key item of input information in investment decisions or recommendations.

Dividend per share	$\dfrac{\text{Dividend of the period}}{\text{Number of issued ordinary shares}}$

Comment. The **dividend per share** is one of the key measures announced by the company at the end of the financial year (and sometimes as an interim dividend during the year as well). Shareholders immediately know how much to expect in total dividend, depending on the number of shares held. The figure of dividend per share is the cash amount paid by the company. It may or may not be subject to tax in the hands of the recipient, depending on whether or not the recipient is a taxpayer.

The dividend of the period is equal to any interim dividend paid plus the final recommended dividend (see section 12.7). To find the recommended dividend you will have to look beyond the financial statements. The Directors' Report will contain a note on the recommended dividend which is to be paid to shareholders following their agreement at the annual general meeting. There may also be a description of the recommended dividend in the Chairman's Statement, or a Highlights Statement, or the Operating and Financial Review (OFR).

Dividend cover (payout ratio)	$\dfrac{\text{Earnings per share}}{\text{Dividend per share}}$

Comment. Companies need cash to enable them to pay dividends. For most companies the profits of the business must generate that cash. So the dividend decision could be regarded as a two-stage question. The first part is, 'Have we made sufficient profits?' and the second stage is, 'Has that profit generated cash which is not needed for reinvestment in fixed or current assets?' The **dividend cover** helps in answering the first of these questions. It shows the number of times the dividend has been covered by the profits (earnings) of this year. It could be said that the higher the dividend cover, the 'safer' is the dividend. On the other hand, it could be argued that a high dividend cover means that the company is keeping new wealth to itself, perhaps to be used in buying new assets, rather than dividing it among the shareholders.

The dividend policy of the company is a major decision for the board of directors. Many companies like to keep to a 'target' dividend cover with only minor fluctuations from one year to the next. The evidence from finance research is that company managers have two targets, one being the stability of the dividend cover but the other being a desire to see the dividend per share increase, or at least remain stationary, rather than decrease. Dividends are thought to carry a signal to the market of the strength and stability of the company.

Dividend yield	$\dfrac{\text{Dividend per share}}{\text{Share price}} \times 100\%$

Comment. The **dividend yield** is a very simple ratio comparing dividend per share with the current market price of a share. It indicates the relationship between what the investor can expect to receive from the shares and the amount which is invested in the shares. Many investors need income from investments and the dividend yield is an important factor in their decision to invest in, or remain in, a company. It has to be noted that dividends are not the only benefit from share ownership. Section 13.4 on risk and return presents a formula for return (yield) which takes into account the growth in share price as well as the dividend paid. Investors buy shares in expectation of an increase in the share price. The directors of many companies would take the view that the dividend yield should be adequate to provide an investment income, but it is the wealth arising from retained profits that is used for investment in new assets which in turn generate growth in future profits.

13.3.2   Analysis of management performance

Management of a business is primarily a function requiring **stewardship**, meaning careful use of resources for the benefit of the owners. There are two central questions to test this use of resources:

1 How well did the management make use of the investment in assets to create sales (revenue)?
2 How carefully did the management control costs so as to maximise the profit derived from the sales (revenue)?

Return on shareholders' equity	$\dfrac{\text{Profit after tax for ordinary equity holders}}{\text{Share capital + Reserves}} \times 100\%$

Comment. A key measure of success, from the viewpoint of shareholders, is the success of the company in using the funds provided by shareholders to generate profit. That profit will provide new wealth to cover their **dividend** and to finance future expansion of the business. The **return on shareholders' equity** is therefore a measure of company performance from the shareholders' perspective. It is essential in this calculation to use the profit for ordinary equity holders, which is the profit after interest charges and after tax. The formula uses the phrase **equity holders** which will probably be the wording that you see in the financial statements. It has the same meaning as **ordinary shareholders**.

Return on capital employed	$\dfrac{\text{Operating profit (before interest and tax)}}{\text{Total assets – Current liabilities}} \times 100\%$

Return on capital employed	$\dfrac{\text{Operating profit (before interest and tax)}}{\text{Ordinary share capital + reserves + long-term loans}} \times 100\%$

Comment. **Return on capital employed** (ROCE) is a broader measure than return on shareholders' equity. ROCE measures the performance of a company as a whole in using all sources of long-term finance. Profit before interest and tax is used in the numerator as a measure of operating results. It is sometime called 'earnings before interest and tax' and is abbreviated to EBIT. Return on capital employed is often seen as a measure of management efficiency. The denominator can be written in two ways, as shown in the alternative formulae. Think about the accounting equation and rearrange it to read:

$$\text{Total assets – current liabilities = Ordinary share capital plus}$$
$$\text{reserves plus long-term loans}$$

The ratio is a measure of how well the long-term finance is being used to generate operating profits.

Return on total assets	$\dfrac{\text{Operating profit (before interest and tax)}}{\text{Total assets}} \times 100\%$

Comment. Calculating the **return on total assets** is another variation on measuring how well the assets of the business are used to generate operating profit before deducting interest and tax.

Operating profit as % of sales (revenue)	$\dfrac{\text{Operating profit (before interest and tax)}}{\text{Sales (revenue)}} \times 100\%$

Comment. The ratio of operating profit as a percentage of sales (revenue) is also referred to as the **operating margin**. The aim of many successful business managers is to make the margin as high as possible. The margin reflects the degree of competitiveness in the market, the economic situation, the ability to differentiate products and the ability to control expenses. At the end of this section it is shown that companies are not obliged to seek high **margins**. Some cannot, because of strong competitive factors. Yet they still make a satisfactory return on capital employed by making efficient use of the equipment held as fixed (non-current) assets.

Gross profit percentage	$\dfrac{\text{Gross profit}}{\text{Sales (revenue)}} \times 100\%$

Comment. The gross profit as a percentage of sales (revenue) is also referred to as the **gross margin**. It has been seen in earlier chapters that the gross profit is equal to sales (revenue) minus all cost of sales. That gross profit may be compared with sales (revenue) as shown above. The gross profit percentage concentrates on costs of making goods and services ready for sale. Small changes in this ratio can be highly significant. There tends to be a view that there is a 'normal' value for the industry or for the product that may be used as a benchmark against which to measure a company's performance.

Because it is such a sensitive measure, many companies try to keep secret from their competitors and customers the detailed breakdown of gross profit for each product line or area of activity. Companies do not want to give competitors any clues on how much to undercut prices and do not want to give customers a chance to complain about excessive profits.

Total assets usage	$\dfrac{\text{Sales (revenue)}}{\text{Total assets}} \times 100\%$

Comment. **Total assets usage** indicates how well a company has used its fixed and current assets to generate sales (revenue). Such a ratio is probably most useful as an indication of trends over a period of years. There is no particular value which is too high or too low but a sudden change would prompt the observer to ask questions.

Fixed assets (non-current assets) usage	$\dfrac{\text{Sales (revenue)}}{\text{Fixed assets (non-current assets)}} \times 100\%$

Comment. **Fixed assets usage** is a similar measure of usage, but one which concentrates on the productive capacity as measured by fixed assets, indicates how successful the company is in generating sales (revenue) from fixed assets (non-current assets). The ratio may be interpreted as showing how many £s of sales (revenue) have been generated by each £ of fixed assets.

13.3.3 Liquidity and working capital

Liquidity is a word which refers to the availability of cash in the near future after taking account of immediate financial commitments. Cash in the near future will be available from bank deposits, cash released by sale of stocks and cash collected from customers. Immediate financial commitments are shown in current liabilities. The first ratio of liquidity is therefore a simple comparison of current assets with current liabilities.

Current ratio	Current assets:Current liabilities

Comment. If the current assets amount to £20m and the current liabilities amount to £10m the company is said, in words, to have 'a current ratio of 2 to 1'. Some commentators abbreviate this by saying 'the current ratio is 2'. Mathematically that is incorrect wording but the listener is expected to know that the words 'to 1' have been omitted from the end of the sentence.

The current ratio indicates the extent to which short-term assets are available to meet short-term liabilities. A current ratio of 2:1 is regarded, broadly speaking, as being a reasonable order of magnitude. As with other ratios, there is no 'best' answer for any particular company and it is the trend in this ratio which is more important. If the ratio is worsening over time, and especially if it falls to less than 1:1, the observer would look closely at the cash flow. A company can survive provided it can meet its obligations as they fall due. Some companies therefore operate on a very tight current ratio because they are able to plan the timing of inflows and outflows of cash quite precisely.

Companies which generate cash on a daily basis, such as retail stores, can therefore operate on a lower current ratio. Manufacturing businesses which have to hold substantial stocks would operate on a higher current ratio.

Acid test	Current assets minus inventories (stock):Current liabilities

Comment. In a crisis, where short-term creditors are demanding payment, the possibility of selling stocks (inventories) to raise cash may be unrealistic. The **acid test** takes a closer look at the liquid assets of the current ratio, omitting the stocks (inventories). For many companies this ratio is less than 1:1 because it is unlikely that all creditors will require payment at the same time. As with the current ratio, an understanding of the acid test has to be supported by an understanding of the pattern of cash flows. Analysts in particular will often ask companies about the peak borrowing requirements of the year and the timing of that peak in relation to cash inflows.

Stock holding period (inventories holding period)	$\dfrac{\text{Average inventories (stock) held}}{\text{Cost of sales}} \times 365$

Comment. The **stock holding period** (inventories holding period) measures the average period during which stocks (inventories) of goods are held before being sold or used in the operations of the business. It is usually expressed in days, which is why the figure of 365 appears in the formula. If months are preferred, then the figure 12 should be substituted for the figure 365. One point of view is that the shorter the period, the better. An opposite point of view is that too short a period may create a greater risk of finding that the business is short of a stock item.

In calculating the stock holding period it is preferable to use the average of the stock (inventories) held at the start of the year and the stock (inventories) held at the end of the year. Some analysts use only the year-end figure if the start-of-year figure is not available. Whatever variation is used, it is important to be consistent from one time period to the next.

Customers (trade debtors) collection period	$\dfrac{\text{Trade receivables (trade debtors)}}{\text{Credit sales (revenue)}} \times 365$

Comment. The **customers'** (trade debtors') **collection period** measures the average period of credit allowed to credit customers. An increase in this measure would indicate that a company is building up cash flow problems, although an attempt to decrease the period of credit allowed might deter customers and cause them to seek a competitor who gives a longer period of credit. It is important to be aware of the normal credit period for the industry. Some companies offer discount for prompt payment. Any offer of discount should weigh the cost of the discount against the benefit of earlier receipt of cash from customers. When you are looking for information in the annual report of companies using the IASB system you will probably have to start on the face of the balance sheet with the heading 'trade and other receivables' and then read the corresponding Note to the balance sheet to find the amount of trade receivables. If you are looking at the balance sheet of a company that does not use the IASB system you will have to find the Note to the balance sheet that gives detailed information about trade debtors.

Suppliers (trade creditors) payment period	$\dfrac{\text{Trade payables (trade creditors)}}{\text{Credit purchases}} \times 365$

Comment. The **suppliers'** (trade creditors') **payment period** measures the average period of credit taken from suppliers of goods and services. An increase in this measure could indicate that the supplier has allowed a longer period to pay. It could also indicate that the company is taking longer to pay, perhaps because of cash flow problems. If payment is delayed then the company may lose discounts available for prompt payments. A reputation for being a slow payer could make it more difficult to obtain supplies in future. Some large companies have gained a reputation for delaying payment to smaller suppliers. Company law now requires company directors to make a statement of policy in relation to creditor payment.

Companies do not usually report **purchases** directly, so the figure must be calculated as follows:

$$\text{Purchases} = \text{Cost of goods sold} + \text{Closing stock} - \text{Opening stock}$$

Analysts often use **cost of goods** sold rather than calculate purchases, arguing that stock levels are broadly similar at corresponding period-ends.

Working capital cycle	Stock (inventories) holding period PLUS Customers (trade debtors) collection period MINUS Suppliers (trade creditors) payment period

Comment. You saw in Chapter 9 (Exhibit 9.1) the **working capital cycle** whereby stocks (inventories) are purchased on credit, then sold to customers who eventually pay cash. The cash is used to pay suppliers and the cycle starts again. We can now put some timings into the diagram. The working capital represents the long-term finance needed to cover current assets that are not matched by current liabilities. The longer the total of the stock holding period and customer collection period, compared to the suppliers payment period, the greater the need for working capital to be financed long term.

13.3.4 Gearing

The term **gearing** is used to describe the mix of loan finance and equity finance in a company. It is more properly called **financial gearing** and in American texts is called **leverage**. There are two main approaches to measuring gearing. The first looks at the balance sheet and the second looks at the profit and loss account.

Debt/equity ratio	$\dfrac{\text{Long-term liabilities plus Preference share capital*}}{\text{Equity share capital} + \text{reserves}} \times 100\%$

* where preference share capital is in existence

Comment. From the balance sheet perspective the **gearing** measure considers the relative proportions of long-term (non-current) loans and equity in the long-term financing of the business. The precise meaning of long-term liabilities will vary from one company to the next. It is intended to cover the loans taken out with the aim of making them a permanent part of the company's financing policy. As they come due for repayment, they are replaced by further long-term finance. The starting point is the loans (but not the provisions) contained in the section headed *non-current liabilities*. However the accounting rules require separate reporting of loans due for repayment within one year, reported as current liabilities. It is necessary to look in the *current liabilities* for bank loans that are becoming due for repayment. In some companies the bank overdraft is a semi-permanent feature and so is included in this ratio calculation.

Preference share capital is included in the numerator because it has the characteristics of debt finance even although it is not classed as debt in company law. The preference shareholders have the first right to dividend, before the ordinary shareholders receive any dividend. This is why they are called 'preference' shares. The amount of the dividend is usually fixed as a percentage of nominal value of shares. The amount repaid to preference shareholders on maturity is the amount of the share capital only. They do not normally take a share of accumulated profits.

Different industries have different average levels, depending on the types of assets held and the stability or otherwise of the stream of profits. A low gearing percentage indicates a low exposure to financial risk because it means that there will be little difficulty in paying loan interest and repaying the loans as they fall due. A high gearing percentage indicates a high exposure to financial risk because it means that there are interest charges to be met and a requirement to repay the loans on the due date.

Interest cover	$\dfrac{\text{Operating profit (before interest and tax)}}{\text{Interest}}$

Comment. The importance of being able to meet interest payments on borrowed funds is emphasised by measuring gearing in terms of the profit and loss account. If the profit generated before interest and tax is sufficient to give high cover for the interest charges, then it is unlikely that the company is overcommitting itself in its borrowing. If the interest cover is falling or is low, then there may be increasing cause for concern.

Activity 13.1

Write down the name of each ratio given in this section. Close the book and test your knowledge by writing down the formula for each ratio. Then write one sentence for each ratio which explains its purpose. Be sure that you know each ratio and understand its purpose before you proceed with the rest of the chapter.

13.4 Investors' views on risk and return

Uncertainty about the future means that all investments contain an element of risk. For investors who are averse to risk, there is a fear of income falling below an acceptable level and a fear of losing the capital invested in the company. Given a choice between two investments offering the same expected return, risk-averse investors will choose the least risky investment.

13.4.1   Return

The word **return** has many meanings but for an investor the basic question is, 'What have I gained from owning these shares?' One simple formula which answers that question is:

$$\frac{(Market\ price\ of\ share\ today - Price\ paid\ for\ share) + Dividends\ received}{Price\ paid\ for\ share} \times 100\%$$

Investors in a company which is in a low-risk industry may be willing to accept a low rate of return. Investors in a company which is in a high-risk industry will be seeking a higher rate of return to compensate for the additional risk they take.

Research has shown that share prices react very rapidly to any item of information which is sufficiently important to affect investors' decisions. This phenomenon is sometimes referred to as the **efficient markets hypothesis**, which is a statement that share prices react immediately to make allowance for each new item of information made available. The annual results of a listed company are announced through the Stock Exchange by means of a document called a **preliminary announcement**, issued approximately two months after the accounting year-end. The annual report then goes to the printers and is distributed to shareholders about three months after the related year-end.

When investors evaluate share price by calculating return, they take the most up-to-date price available.

13.4.2   Risk

There are two main types of risk: operating risk and financial risk.

Operating risk exists where there are factors which could cause sales (revenue) to fluctuate or cause costs to increase. Companies are particularly vulnerable to operating risk when they have a relatively high level of fixed operating costs. These fixed costs are incurred independently of the level of activity. If sales (revenue) fall, or the direct costs of sales increase, the fixed costs become a greater burden on profit.

Financial risk exists where the company has loan finance, especially long-term loan finance where the company cannot relinquish its commitment. Loan finance carries an obligation to pay interest charges and these create a problem similar to the fixed costs problem. If the sales (revenue) are strong and the direct costs of sales are well under control, then interest charges will not be a problem. If sales (revenue) fall, or the direct costs of sales rise, then a company may find that it does not have the cash resources to meet the interest payments as they fall due. Repaying the loan could become an even greater worry.

Both operating risk and financial risk are important to the company's shareholders because they have the residual claim on assets after all liabilities are met. If the company's assets are growing then these risks will not pose a problem but if the business becomes slack then the combination of high fixed operating costs and high interest charges could be disastrous. As a rule of thumb, investors look for low financial risk in companies which have high operating risk and, conversely, will tolerate a higher level of financial risk where there is relatively low operating risk.

The terms **operating gearing** and **financial gearing** are frequently used to describe the extent of operating risk and financial risk. (Financial gearing has been explained in the previous section.) In terms of the profit and loss account they are defined as follows:

Operating gearing	$\dfrac{\text{Profit before fixed operating costs}}{\text{Fixed operating costs}}$

Financial gearing	$\dfrac{\text{Profit before interest charges}}{\text{Interest charges}}$

In analysis of published accounting information, it is not possible to estimate the operating gearing because detailed information on fixed costs is not provided. Thus the term **gearing** is applied only in measuring financial gearing. Despite the lack of published information, professional investors will be aware of the importance of operating gearing and will try to understand as much as possible about the cost structure of the company and of the industry. The next section illustrates the benefits to shareholders of having gearing present when operating profits are rising and the risks when operating profits are falling.

13.4.3 Impact of gearing when profits are fluctuating

In a situation of fluctuating profits the presence of a fixed charge, such as an interest payment, will cause the profit for ordinary shareholders to fluctuate by a greater percentage. Exhibit 13.1 sets out data to illustrate this fluctuation. Company X has no gearing but company Y has loan finance in its capital structure.

Exhibit 13.1
Data to illustrate the effect of gearing on profits for ordinary shareholders

	X plc £m	Y plc £m
Summary balance sheet		
Total assets minus current liabilities	1,000	1,000
Ordinary shares (£1 nominal value per share)	1,000	500
Loan stock (10% per annum)	–	500
	1,000	1,000
Expected level of profit		
Operating profit	100	100
Interest	–	(50)
Net profit for ordinary shareholders (A)	100	50

Exhibit 13.2 uses the data to ask 'what happens to earnings per share if there is an increase or a decrease in operating profit?'

Exhibit 13.2
Fluctuations in profit

(a) Effect of 20% decrease in operating profit		
Operating profit	80	80
Interest		(50)
Net profit for ordinary shareholders (B)	80	30
Percentage decrease of (B) on (A)	20%	40%
(b) Effect of 20% increase in operating profit		
Operating profit	120	120
Interest	–	(50)
Net profit for ordinary shareholders (C)	120	70
Percentage increase of (C) on (A)	20%	40%

The conclusion to be drawn from Exhibit 13.2, panels (a) and (b), is that a 20% increase or decrease in operating profit causes a corresponding 20% increase or decrease in profit for ordinary shareholders in the ungeared company but a 40% increase or decrease in profit for ordinary shareholders in the geared company. It would appear preferable to be a shareholder in a geared company when profits are rising but to be a shareholder in an ungeared company when profits are falling.

13.5 Pyramid of ratios

The various ratios which contribute to the analysis of management performance may be thought of as forming a pyramid, as in Exhibit 13.3.

Exhibit 13.3
Pyramid of ratios for analysis of management performance

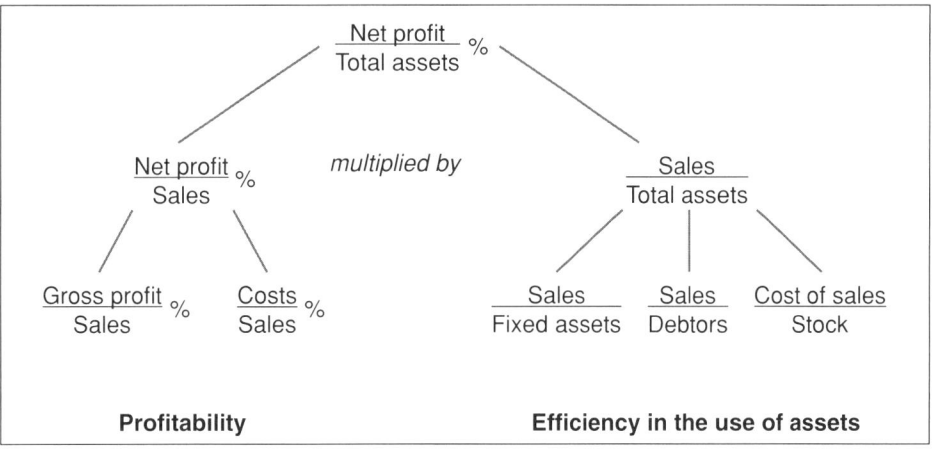

At the apex is the **return on capital employed** (measuring capital employed here as total assets). As the pyramid spreads out there are more detailed explanations of how the pyramid is built up. Net profit as a percentage of total assets has two components. One is the net profit as a percentage of sales (revenue) and the other is sales (revenue) as a multiple of total assets. Multiply these two together and you return to the net profit as a percentage of total assets. This relationship indicates that there could be two quite different types of business, both of which may be highly successful. One business trades on low margins, charging prices which look highly competitive, and succeeds by having a high level of sales (revenue) so that the assets are being used very effectively. The other business trades on high margins and sells goods or services less frequently. You could contrast the discount furniture store on the outskirts of town, where the car park is always full and the prices are unbeatable, with the old-world charm of the retail furnisher in the town centre whose prices look high but which attracts customers preferring extra service and attention. Both businesses are able to earn sufficient return on total assets to satisfy the owners.

The pyramid then spreads out into two areas: profitability and efficiency in the use of assets. The relationships here are additive – each component explains a little of the profitability of sales (revenue) or the efficiency in the use of assets. The pyramid is a useful tool of detective work to trace the cause of a change in return on capital employed.

13.6   Use and limitations of ratio analysis

The important feature of ratios is that they indicate trends and deviations from expected patterns. Ratios taken in isolation for a single company or a single period of time are of limited usefulness. The first requirement is to find a benchmark against which to compare ratios calculated for one period only.

13.6.1   Evaluating ratios by comparison

The comparison could be made with any or all of the following:

- the company's prior expectations of the outcome
- external observers' prior expectations of the outcome
- ratios based on previous years' figures for this company
- ratios calculated from this year's figures for other companies
- ratios calculated from previous years' figures for other companies
- industry averages published by commercial organisations.

The company's prior expectations are set out in a budget which is usually kept confidential. It is therefore unlikely that the user of the financial statements will have access to such a high-quality source of comparison. External observers may also have prior expectations. Professional analysts make forecasts of profits to help them or their clients in making investment decisions. The forecasts may be sent to clients of professional advisers, by way of investment advice bulletins. There are directories which publish such forecasts.

In the absence of information based on expectations, the user of the annual report may have to rely on the past as a possible predictor of the future, or on comparisons with other companies and industry norms. Professional investment advisers will collect data from annual reports and calculate ratios in their preferred manner. Advisory services will process the information and sell the results in the form of directories, on-line search facilities or CD-ROM with regular updates. One of the most widely used sources of ratio analysis of company accounts is Datastream, available in many colleges and universities and also used commercially. Organisations such as Reuters publish regular analyses of company information but usually charge a commercial fee. Newspapers and weekly journals such as the *Financial Times* and the *Investors Chronicle* are yet another source of information which will include ratios.

It could be argued that companies should themselves publish the norms against which their own particular results may be compared, but most would claim that their business is unique and no comparisons would be entirely valid.

13.6.2   Limitations

No two companies are exactly alike in the nature of their operations. Comparisons must make allowances for differences in the types of business or the relative weighting of different types of business. Many companies operate in more than one industry so that comparison with industry norms has to be treated with care.

Accounting numbers are used in ratio analysis and it has been a theme of the preceding chapters that accounting numbers may be affected by different accounting policies. The most common causes of variation due to accounting policy differences lie in depreciation and stock valuation, both of which are highly subjective.

Ratios are primarily a starting point from which to identify further questions to ask about the present position and future directions of the operations and the financing of a company. They do not provide answers in themselves.

13.7 Worked example of ratio analysis

In the following worked example, information is provided about a company buying and selling television and video equipment. Data are given for the current year in the first pair of columns and there are comparative figures for the previous year in the second pair of columns. Ratios are calculated for the two years as an indication of trends. Tentative comments are provided as to the possible interpretation of the resulting figures.

13.7.1 Financial statements to be analysed

Peter (Television) plc
Profit and loss account
for the year ended 31 December Year 2

	Year 2		Year 1	
	£m	£m	£m	£m
Revenue		720		600
Cost of sales		(432)		(348)
Gross profit		288		252
Distribution costs	(72)		(54)	
Administrative expenses	(87)		(81)	
		(159)		(135)
Operating profit		129		117
Interest payable		(24)		(24)
Profit before taxation		105		93
Taxation		(42)		(37)
Profit for the period for ordinary equity holders		63		56

Balance sheet as at 31 December Year 2

	£m	£m	£m	£m
Non-current (fixed) assets:				
Land and buildings		600		615
Plant and equipment		555		503
		1,155		1,118
Current assets:				
Inventories (stock)	115		82	
Trade receivables (debtors)	89		61	
Prepayments	10		9	
Bank	6		46	
	220		198	
Current liabilities:				
Trade payables (creditors)	(45)		(30)	
Taxation	(21)		(19)	
Accruals	(29)		(25)	
	(95)		(74)	
Net current assets		125		124
		1,280		1,242
6% debentures		(400)		(400)
		880		842
Ordinary shares of £1 each		500		500
Retained earnings		380		342
Share capital and reserves		880		842

Extract from directors' report

The directors propose a dividend of 6.0 pence per share in respect of Year 2 (Year 1: 5.0 pence), amounting to £30m in total (Year 1: £25m).

Notes to the financial statements: Reconciliation of movements in equity

	£m
Share capital and reserves at the end of year 1	842
Less dividend paid in respect of year 1	(25)
Add profit for year 2	63
Share capital and reserves at the end of year 2	880

13.7.2   Share price information

When investors evaluate share price, they take the most up-to-date price available. However, for the exercise of comparing financial ratios it is useful to take the share prices immediately after the preliminary announcement at the end of February or beginning of March, representing the market's opinion when the accounting information has not become too much out of date.

Market price at 1 March Year 2	202 pence
Market price at 1 March Year 3	277 pence

13.7.3   Presenting the ratio calculations

Because there are so many variations on the methods of calculating ratios in accounting, it is extremely important to practise a useful and informative layout. That must include, at a minimum:

- the name of each ratio
- the formula in words
- the workings to show how the formula has been applied
- the value of the ratio
- a narrative comment.

Exhibits 13.4 to 13.7 present this information in a set of ratio calculations for Peter (Television) plc, each exhibit covering one of the main headings explained earlier. The calculations are given first for the more recent year, Year 2, followed by the comparative figures for Year 1. A commentary is provided for each exhibit.

Activity 13.2

Use the ratios explained in section 13.6 to carry out a full analysis of the Year 2 column of the accounts of Peter (Television) plc. Prepare your analysis before you read Exhibits 13.4 to 13.7. When you have finished, compare your analysis with the ratios calculated. Where your answers differ, be sure that you understand whether it is due to an arithmetic error or a more fundamental point. Keep a note of your score of the number of items calculated correctly.

Then go back to Year 1 and repeat the exercise. Hopefully your score of correct items will have increased.

Exhibit 13.4
Investor ratios

Ratio	Definition in words	Year 2		Year 1	
		Workings	Result	Workings	Result
Earnings per share	$\dfrac{\text{Profit after tax for ordinary equity holders}}{\text{Number of issued ordinary shares}}$	$\dfrac{63}{500}$	12.6 pence	$\dfrac{56}{500}$	11.2 pence
Price earnings ratio	$\dfrac{\text{Share price}}{\text{Earnings per share}}$	$\dfrac{277}{12.6}$	22	$\dfrac{202}{11.2}$	18
Dividend per share	$\dfrac{\text{Dividend of the period}}{\text{Number of issued ordinary shares}}$	$\dfrac{30}{500}$	6.0 pence	$\dfrac{25}{500}$	5.0 pence
Dividend cover (payout ratio)	$\dfrac{\text{Earnings per share}}{\text{Dividend per share}}$	$\dfrac{12.6}{6.0}$	2.1 times	$\dfrac{11.2}{5.0}$	2.24 times
Dividend yield	$\dfrac{\text{Dividend per share}}{\text{Share price}} \times 100$	$\dfrac{6.0}{277} \times 100\%$	2.17%	$\dfrac{5.0}{202} \times 100\%$	2.48%

Comment: Earnings per share increased over the period, indicating an improved profit performance for shareholders. The price earnings ratio rose, indicating greater confidence in the stock market about the sustainability of this new level of profit. The dividend cover has fallen marginally, but is still more than twice covered. This marginal decrease in dividend cover is caused by increasing the dividend per share from 5 pence to 6 pence. The dividend yield has fallen, despite the increased dividend per share, because the market price has risen. The fall in yield may not be significant if it reflects a general trend in the market where, possibly, all shares have risen in price over the year. To say anything more about these ratios requires comparative figures for the industry and for the market as a whole. Both types of data would be found in the *Financial Times*.

Exhibit 13.5
Analysis of management performance

Ratio	Definition in words	Year 2		Year 1	
		Workings	Result	Workings	Result
Return on shareholders' equity	$\dfrac{\text{Profit after tax for ordinary equity holders}}{\text{Share capital + Reserves}} \times 100\%$	$\dfrac{63}{880} \times 100\%$	7.2%	$\dfrac{56}{842} \times 100\%$	6.7%
Return on capital employed	$\dfrac{\text{Operating profit (before interest and tax)}}{\text{(Total assets − Current liabilities)}} \times 100\%$	$\dfrac{129}{1{,}280} \times 100\%$	10.1%	$\dfrac{117}{1{,}242} \times 100\%$	9.4%
Operating profit on sales (revenue)	$\dfrac{\text{Operating profit (before interest and tax)}}{\text{Sales (revenue)}} \times 100\%$	$\dfrac{129}{720} \times 100\%$	17.9%	$\dfrac{117}{600} \times 100\%$	19.5%
Gross profit percentage	$\dfrac{\text{Gross profit}}{\text{Sales (revenue)}} \times 100\%$	$\dfrac{288}{720} \times 100\%$	40%	$\dfrac{252}{600} \times 100\%$	42%
Total assets usage	$\dfrac{\text{Sales (revenue)}}{\text{Total assets}} \times 100\%$	$\dfrac{720}{(1{,}155 + 220)}$	0.52 times	$\dfrac{600}{(1{,}118 + 198)}$	0.46 times
Fixed assets (non-current assets) usage	$\dfrac{\text{Sales (revenue)}}{\text{Fixed assets (non-current assets)}} \times 100\%$	$\dfrac{720}{1{,}155}$	0.62 times	$\dfrac{600}{1{,}118}$	0.54 times

Comment: The return on shareholders' equity and the return on capital employed both show an improvement on the previous year. This is due to an improvement in the use of assets (total assets and fixed assets) which more than offsets a fall in the operating profit as a percentage of sales (revenue). The gross profit percentage fell by a similar amount, which suggests that the price charged for goods and services is not keeping pace with increases in costs. The company should look carefully at either increasing prices or attempting to control costs of goods sold more effectively.

Exhibit 13.6
Liquidity and working capital

Ratio	Definition in words	Year 2		Year 1	
		Workings	Result	Workings	Result
Current ratio	Current assets:Current liabilities	220:95	2.3:1	198:74	2.7:1
Acid test	(Current assets – Inventories):Current liabilities	(220 – 115):95	1.11:1	(198 – 82):74	1.11:1
Stock holding period (inventories holding period)	$\dfrac{\text{Average inventories (stock) held}}{\text{Cost of sales}} \times 365$	$\dfrac{(115 + 82)/2}{432} \times 365$	83.2 days	$\dfrac{(*82 + 82)/2}{348} \times 365$	86 days
Customers' (trade debtors') collection period	$\dfrac{\text{Trade receivables (trade debtors)}}{\text{Credit sales (revenue)}} \times 365$	$\dfrac{89}{720} \times 365$	45.1 days	$\dfrac{61}{600} \times 365$	37.1 days
Suppliers' (trade creditors') payment period	$\dfrac{\text{Trade payables (trade creditors)}}{\text{Credit purchases}} \times 365$	$\dfrac{45}{432 + 115 - 82} \times 365$	35.3 days	$\dfrac{30}{348 + 82 - *82} \times 365$	31.5 days

Note: *Assuming the opening inventories are the same as the closing inventories.

Comment: The current ratio has fallen over the period while the acid test ratio remains constant. The ratios appear relatively high and are probably still within acceptable ranges (although this needs to be confirmed by comparison with industry norms). One cause of the relatively high current ratio at the start and end of the period appears to be in the combination of stock holding period and customers collection period compared to the suppliers payment period. The period of credit taken by customers has increased and this should be investigated as a matter of urgency. There is a marginal decrease in the stock holding period but it remains relatively long, compared to the creditors payment period. The acid test remains similar because there is an increase in the number of customer days for payment and a similar increase in the number of supplier days for payment.

Exhibit 13.7
Gearing (leverage)

Ratio	Definition in words	Year 2		Year 1	
		Workings	Result	Workings	Result
Debt/equity ratio	$\dfrac{\text{Long-term liabilities plus Preference share capital}}{\text{Equity share capital + reserves}} \times 100\%$	$\dfrac{400}{880} \times 100\%$	45.5%	$\dfrac{400}{842} \times 100\%$	47.5%
Interest cover	$\dfrac{\text{Operating profit (before interest and tax)}}{\text{Interest}}$	$\dfrac{129}{24}$	5.38 times	$\dfrac{117}{24}$	4.88 times

Comment: Gearing in the balance sheet has remained almost constant and the interest cover has increased marginally. The relative stability of the position indicates that there is probably no cause for concern but the ratios should be compared with those for similar companies in the industry.

13.8 Linking ratios to the cash flow statement

In Chapter 7 the cash flow statement of a company was illustrated and discussed. Any ratio analysis which seeks to interpret liquidity, management performance or financial structure should be related to the information provided by the cash flow statement. Ratios give a measure of position at a particular point in time while the cash flow statement gives some understanding of the movements in cash and cash-related items.

The operating cash flow will be explained by a note showing the movements in working capital and these may usefully be linked to changes in the rate of movement of stock or the period of credit allowed to customers and taken from suppliers. The ratio will give the change in terms of number of days, while the cash flow statement will indicate the overall impact on liquid resources.

If the efficiency in the use of fixed assets appears to have fallen, it may be that new assets were acquired during the year which, at the balance sheet date, were not fully effective in generating sales. That acquisition will appear in the cash flow statement. If the gearing has changed, the impact on cash flow will be revealed in the cash flow statement.

Activity 13.3   *Read again the sections of Chapters 3, 4 and 7 on cash flow statements. What is the purpose of the cash flow statement? What are the main headings? Which ratios may be used in conjunction with the cash flow statement to help understand the financial position of the company?*

13.8.1 Explanation of a cash flow statement

The cash flow statement in Exhibit 13.8 is calculated from the balance sheets and profit and loss account of Peter (Television) plc (see section 13.6). It is presented using headings similar to those of Safe and Sure in Chapter 7. The headings are taken from the international accounting standard IAS 7.

In Chapters 3, 5 and 6 you saw simple cash flow statements prepared using the information entered in the cash column of a spreadsheet. Those were examples of what is called the **direct method** of preparing a cash flow statement because the figures came directly from the cash column of the transaction spreadsheet. The cash flow statement in Exhibit 13.8 is said to be prepared using the **indirect method** because it takes an indirect route of starting with an accruals-based profit figure and then making adjustments to arrive at the cash figure. Consider each line in turn.

One purpose of the cash flow statement is to answer the question, 'Why do we have a cash problem despite making an operating profit?' We saw in Exhibit 3.7 of Chapter 3 that profit and cash flow can be different because the cash generated in making a profit is spent in various ways. The cash flow statement emphasises ways in which cash has come into, or moved out of, the company. So we start with profit before taxation of £129m.

Depreciation is an expense in the profit and loss account which represents cost being shared across accounting periods. There is no cash flow and so there should be no deduction for this item. To correct the position, depreciation of £50m is 'added back' as an adjustment to the accounting profit.

Next we consider how changes in working capital have affected cash flow. Looking first at current assets, we find that the inventories (stocks) have increased from £82m to £115m. Allowing inventories (stocks) to increase has reduced the cash available for other purposes. Trade receivables (debtors) have increased from £61 to £89. This means the cash is flowing less fast and so cash is reducing. Prepayments have increased

Exhibit 13.8
Cash flow statement

Peter (Television) plc
Cash flow statement
for the year ended 31 December Year 2

Notes: Assume depreciation charge for year is £50m.
No non-current (fixed) assets were sold.

[The words and figures printed in italics are not normally shown in published cash flow statements – they are to help you with interpretation.]

	£m	£m
Cash flows from operating activities		
Profit before taxation		129
Adjustment for items not involving a flow of cash:		
Depreciation		50
		179
Increase in inventories (stocks) *(115 – 82)*	33	
Increase in trade receivables (debtors) *(89 – 61)*	28	
Increase in prepayments *(10 – 9)*	1	
Reduction in cash due to increases in current assets	62	
Increase in trade payables (creditors) *(45 – 30)*	(15)	
Increase in accruals *(29 – 25)*	(4)	
Increase in cash due to increases in liabilities	(19)	
Reduction in cash due to working capital changes		(43)
Cash generated from operations		136
Interest paid		(24)
Taxes paid *(42 +19 – 21)*		(40)
Net cash inflow from operating activities		72
Cash flows from investing activities		
Capital expenditure *(1,155 – 1,118 + 50)*		(87)
		(15)
Cash flows from financing activities		
Equity dividends paid *(dividend proposed at end of Year 1)*		(25)
Decrease in cash		(40)
Check in balance sheet Decrease in bank (46 – 6) = 40		

---

from £9m to £10m. This is also using up cash. In total the increases in current assets have used up £62m of the cash generated in making profit.

Looking next at current liabilities, we see that trade payables (creditors) have increased from £30m to £45m. If payables (creditors) are increasing, it means they are not being paid. This helps cash flow by not spending it. Accruals have increased by £4m, again helping cash flow by not making a payment. It is not a good idea to help cash flow indefinitely by not paying creditors, but where stocks and debtors are expanding to use up cash flow, it is helpful if current liabilities are expanding in a similar way to hold back cash flow.

Interest paid is taken from the profit and loss account as £24m. There is no liability for unpaid interest at either the start of end of the period so the amount in the profit and loss account must equal the amount paid.

The taxation payment involves more calculation. Cash has been required to meet the liability of £19m remaining in the Year 1 balance sheet, and also to pay half of the tax expense of Year 2, which is £21m. The calculation is: tax expense of the year as shown in the income statement (profit and loss account), minus liability at the end of the year (balance sheet), plus liability at the start of the year (balance sheet).

Capital expenditure is calculated by comparing the book values at the beginning and end of the year and adjusting for changes during the year. We are told there were no sales of fixed assets so any increase must represent an addition. The balance started at £1,118m, fell by £50m for depreciation, increased by the unknown figure for additions, and finished at £1,155m. The missing figure is calculated as £87m.

The dividend paid during year 2 was the dividend proposed at the end of Year 1. If you look back to section 13.7.1, you will see the dividend paid as an entry in the 'reconciliation of movements on equity'.

Finally the right-hand column of the cash flow statement is added and produces a figure of £40m which is then checked against the balance sheet figures. This shows that cash has fallen from £46m to £6m and so the calculation is confirmed as being correct.

13.8.2 Analyst's commentary

Here is the comment made by one analyst in a briefing note to clients.

Despite making a profit before taxation of £129,000, the cash balances of the company have decreased by £40,000 during the year.

The cash generated by operating profit is calculated by adding back depreciation of £50,000 because this is an accounting expense which does not involve an outflow of cash. The resulting cash flow of £179,000 was eroded by allowing current assets to increase by more than the increase in current liabilities. This suggests that we should ask questions about the rate of usage of inventories (stocks) and the period of credit allowed to credit customers (debtors). Our analysis [see section 13.7] shows that the inventories (stocks) holding period reduced marginally from 86 to 83 days, which is not unexpected in the industry. The period of credit taken from suppliers increased by 4 days but the customers collection period increased by 8 days. Our attention should focus on the control of credit customers to look for any weaknesses of credit control and a potential risk of bad debts.

After paying interest charges and taxation the company was still in cash surplus at £72,000 but swung into cash deficit through capital expenditure of £87,000. Taking in the dividend payment of £25,000 the positive cash flow of £72,000 changed to a negative cash flow of £40,000.

We take the view that in the short run it is reasonable to run down cash balances in this way. The company probably had excessive liquidity at the end of Year 1. However if there is to be a further major investment in fixed assets we would want to see long-term finance being raised, either through a share issue or through a new long-term loan.

13.8.3 EBITDA

EBITDA stands for earnings before interest, taxation, depreciation and amortisation. It is increasingly used by analysts as an approximate measure of cash flow because it removes the non-cash expenses of depreciation and amortisation from profit. Instead of a price–earnings multiple based on earnings per share, the analyst will relate share price to EBITDA. The reason appears to be a desire to get away from the subjectivity of accruals-based profit and closer to cash flow as something objectively measured.

13.8.4 Free cash flow

'Free cash flow' is a phrase that you may encounter in company reports, particularly in the narrative discussions by the chief executive and the finance director. It is a term that is used differently by different people and so you have to read it in the setting where it is used. A common theme is to say, 'We have calculated our operating cash flow and allowed for investment in working capital and we have deducted the amount of cash invested in capital expenditure.' How much cash does that leave free to pay dividends or to invest in new ideas for expansion?

Following this theme, the calculation of free cash flows generally start with the net cash flow generated from operations (operating cash flow after tax) and then deducts the capital expenditure of the period. This leaves an amount of 'free' cash (in the sense of 'freely available' for future planning). The free cash is available to pay dividends to shareholders and to pay for further investment to expand the business. Directors have to decide their priorities and allocate the cash accordingly. If the free cash flow is a negative figure then the company will need to borrow to pay dividends or finance expansion.

13.9 Summary

The main areas of ratio analysis explained in this chapter are:

- investor ratios (summarised in Exhibit 13.4)
- analysis of management performance (summarised in Exhibit 13.5)
- liquidity and working capital (summarised in Exhibit 13.6)
- gearing (summarised in Exhibit 13.7).

Section 13.8 explains how the interpretation of ratios may be linked to an understanding of cash flows.

It is essential to treat ratio analysis with great caution and to understand the basis of calculation and the nature of the data used. For that reason the illustrations have been set out in detail using a layout that allows you to demonstrate your knowledge of the formula, your ability to collect data for calculation, and the result of that calculation which can then be interpreted. In this chapter all the information has been made available to you as and when you required it. In Chapter 14 we move on to consider published financial statements where more exploration may be required to find the most useful information.

The general principles explained in this chapter can be applied to the annual report of any profit-seeking business. The precise formulae may require adaptation to suit particular national characteristics. However international comparison requires great caution. Accounting policies and practices are not yet harmonised entirely. If the underlying data are not comparable then neither are the ratios.

The key is to ask first, 'What value do we expect for this ratio?' Then calculate the ratio and seek an interpretation of the similarity or difference.

QUESTIONS

The Questions section of each chapter has three types of question. 'Test your understanding' questions to help you review your reading are in the 'A' series of questions. You will find the answers to these by reading and thinking about the material in the book. 'Application' questions to test your ability to apply technical skills are in the 'B' series of questions. Questions requiring you to show skills in problem solving and evaluation are in the 'C' series of questions. A letter [S] indicates that there is a solution at the end of the book.

A   Test your understanding

A13.1 Which ratios provide information on performance for investors? (Section 13.3.1)

A13.2 Which ratios provide information on management performance? (Section 13.3.2)

A13.3 Which ratios provide information on liquidity and working capital? (Section 13.3.3)

A13.4 Which ratios provide information on gearing? (Section 13.3.4)

A13.5 What is the view of investors on risk and return? (Section 13.4)

A13.6 Why is financial gearing riskier for a company which has fluctuating profits? (Section 13.4.3)

A13.7 Explain the use of the pyramid of ratios in analysis of performance. (Section 13.5)

A13.8 What are the limitations of ratio analysis? (Section 13.6)

B   Application

B13.1 [S]
The following financial statements relate to Hope plc:

**Income statement (profit and loss account)
for the year ended 30 June Year 4**

	£000s	£000s
Revenue		6,200
Cost of sales		(2,750)
Gross profit		3,450
Administration and selling expenses		(2,194)
Operating profit		1,256
Debenture interest		(84)
Profit before taxation		1,172
Taxation		(480)
Profit for equity holder		692

The directors have recommended a dividend of 36.7 pence per share in respect of Year 4, to be paid following approval at the next annual general meeting.

Balance sheet as at 30 June Year 4

	£000s	£000s	£000s
Non-current (fixed assets) net of depreciation			1,750
Current assets:			
Stocks and work-in-progress	620		
Trade receivables (debtors)	1,540		
Cash	200	2,360	
less: Current liabilities:			
Trade payables (creditors)	(300)		
Other creditors and accruals	(940)	(1,240)	
Net current assets			1,120
Total assets *less* current liabilities			2,870
Non-current liabilities			
6% debentures			(1,400)
Total net assets			1,470
Share capital and reserves			
Issued share capital:			
900,000 ordinary shares of 50p nominal value			450
Retained earnings			1,020
			1,470

Required

(a) Calculate ratios which measure:
   (i)   liquidity and the use of working capital;
   (ii) management performance; and
   (iii) gearing.

(b) Explain how each ratio would help in understanding the financial position and results of the company.

(c) The market price is currently 1,100 pence per share. Calculate ratios which are useful to investors.

B13.2

The following financial statements relate to Charity plc:

Profit and loss account for year ended 30 September Year 4

	£000s	£000s
Revenue		2,480
Cost of sales		(1,100)
Gross profit		1,380
Administration and selling expenses		(678)
Operating profit		702
Debenture interest		(31)
Profit before taxation		671
Taxation		(154)
Profit for equity holders		517

Note: The directors have recommended a dividend of 11.4 pence per share in total in respect of Year 4, to be paid following approval at the next annual general meeting.

Balance sheet as at 30 September Year 4

	£000s	£000s	£000s
Non-current assets, net of depreciation			785
Current assets:			
Inventories (stocks)	341		
Trade receivables (debtors)	801		
Cash	110	1,252	
less: Current liabilities			
Trade payables (creditors)	(90)		
Other payable and accruals	(654)	(744)	
Net current assets			508
Total assets *less* current liabilities			1,293
Non-current liabilities			
7% debentures			(440)
Total net assets			853
Share capital and reserves			
Issued share capital			
(1,360,000 ordinary shares of 25p nominal value)			340
Retained earnings			513
			853

Required

(a) Calculate ratios which measure:
   (i)   liquidity and the use of working capital;
   (ii) management performance; and
   (iii) gearing.

(b) Explain how each ratio would help in understanding the financial position and results of the company.

(c) The market price of one share is 800 pence. Calculate ratios which will be of interest to investors.

C Problem solving and evaluation

C14.1

Carry out a ratio analysis of Safe and Sure plc, using the financial statements set out in Appendix I (at the end of this book) and applying the method of analysis set out in section 13.6. Making a comparison of Year 7 with Year 6, write a short commentary on each ratio separately and then summarise the overall themes emerging from the ratios. Assume a share price of 260 pence is applicable at 31 December Year 7 and a share price of 210 pence is applicable at 31 December Year 6.

Section 11
Recent Developments in Financial Reporting

Narrative reporting

A business, particularly a large business, may have extremely complex organisational arrangements, financing methods and operating characteristics. To portray financial performance and position faithfully, the published financial statements must reflect this complexity. As a result, these statements may well be difficult to understand and to interpret. To help users gain a clearer picture, a narrative report may be produced to accompany the financial statements. This report will provide a commentary on the business and its financial results.

The UK Accounting Standards Board (ASB) has issued a reporting statement (RS1), mainly aimed at listed companies, for an **operating and financial review** (OFR). The OFR is a narrative report which aims to provide a balanced and comprehensive examination of:

- the performance of the business during the year and its position at the end of the year;
- the key trends and factors affecting performance and position during the year as well as those which are likely to affect future performance and position.

The OFR is meant to reflect the directors' views of the business and should complement as well as supplement the financial statements.

Activity 5.5

What are the main characteristics concerning quality that information contained within the OFR should possess? (*Hint*: think back to Chapter 1.)

To be useful, the information should contain the characteristics for accounting information in general, which we identified in Chapter 1. Thus, the information should be relevant, understandable, reliable and comparable. The fact that we are dealing with narrative information does not alter the need for these characteristics to be present.

A further requirement of the OFR is comprehensiveness. This means that it should include all significant information that will help assess business performance. Thus, information that places the business in an unfavourable light should not be omitted.

The OFR framework

The framework for an OFR, rests on the disclosure of four key elements of a business. Each of these elements is discussed below.

1. The nature of the business

This element will include a description of the environment within which the business operates. It is a potentially wide area and may include a commentary on products sold, business processes, business structure, and competitive position. A commentary on the legal, economic and social environment may also be included.

The objectives of the business and the strategy adopted to achieve those objectives should also be discussed. Real World 5.2 below reveals how one well-known business describes in its OFR the strategy that has been adopted.

 ## Real World 5.2

Tesco's strategy

The 2006 annual report of Tesco plc includes a 17-page OFR, which provides a lot of information about its business and its financial results. The strategy of the business is described in the OFR as follows:

> Tesco has a well-established and consistent strategy for growth, which is strengthening the core business and driving our expansion into new markets. This four-part strategy was laid down in 1997 and it has been the foundation of Tesco's success in recent years. Its objectives are:
>
> - to grow the core business;
> - to become a successful international retailer;
> - to be as strong in non-food as in food; and
> - to develop retailing services – such as Tesco Personal Finance, Telecoms and tesco.com.

Source: 2006 Annual Report Tesco plc, p. 1.

Key performance indicators (KPIs) used by the directors to assess whether the strategy is effective should be included in the OFR. These KPIs quantify the factors that are critical to the success of the business and are often a mixture of financial and non-financial measures. Key financial measures may relate to sales revenue growth, profit, total shareholder return, dividends and so on. Key non-financial measures may relate to market share, employee satisfaction, product quality, supplier satisfaction and so on.

2. Business performance

This element will examine the development and performance of the business for both the year under review and the future. It should include any factors affecting performance, such as changes in market conditions or the launch of new products or services. It should also examine trends and factors that may affect future prospects. **Real World 5.3** provides an extract from Tesco's OFR, which describes plans that have potentially a significant effect on future prospects.

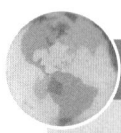

Real World 5.3

Foreign parts

In line with the strategy mentioned above, Tesco plc has become increasingly international in its focus. Future growth in international activities is planned to be significant, as stated in the following extract from Tesco's 2006 OFR:

> At the end of February (2006), our international operations were trading from 814 stores, including 341 hypermarkets, with a total of 32.8 m sq. ft. of selling space. Almost 56% of Group sales area is now in International . . . We plan to open 396 new stores in the current year (2006/2007), adding 6.6 m sq. ft. of selling area.

Source: 2006 Annual Report Tesco plc, p. 8.

3. Resources, risks and relationships

The OFR should describe the resources of the business and how they are managed. The resources identified should include any items not reflected in the balance sheet. These items will, of course, vary between businesses but may include corporate reputation, patents, trademarks, brand names, market position and the quality of employees.

The OFR should also include a description of the main risks and uncertainties facing the business and the ways in which the directors deal with them. **Real World 5.4** reveals how Tesco plc comments on one important risk in its OFR.

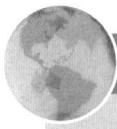

Real World 5.4

Risky business

In its 2006 OFR, Tesco plc identifies more than twenty forms of risk that the business must consider. These cover a wide range and include competition, financial, environmental, product safety, terrorism and currency risks. The risk posed by competitors is described as follows:

> The retail industry is highly competitive. The Group competes with a wide variety of retailers of varying sizes, and faces increased competition from UK retailers, as well as international operators, here

and overseas. Failure to compete with competitors on areas including price, product range, quality and service could have an adverse effect on the Group's financial results.

We aim to have a broad appeal in price, range and store format in a way that allows us to compete in different markets. We track performance against a range of measures that customers tell us are critical to their shopping trip experience. We constantly monitor customer perceptions of ourselves and our competitors to ensure that we can respond quickly if we need to.

Source: 2006 Annual Report Tesco plc, p. 14.

This element also requires a commentary on key relationships with stakeholders, apart from shareholders, that may affect the performance of the business and its value. The stakeholders may include customers, suppliers, employees, contractors, lenders as well as other businesses with which the business has strategic alliances. Real World 5.5 reveals how, in the 2006 OFR, Tesco plc describes the relationship with its customers.

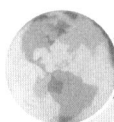

Real World 5.5

Every little helps

Our customers have told us what they want from an 'every little helps' shopping trip and this year 12,000 of them attended our Customer Question Times to offer ideas on how we can improve. Clubcard also helps us to understand what our customers want, whilst allowing us to thank them for shopping with us – this year we gave away £320 m in Clubcard vouchers.

We don't always get it right but we try to make their shopping trip as easy as possible, reduce prices where we can to help them spend less and give them the convenience of shopping where and when they want – in small stores, large stores or on-line.

Source: 2006 Annual Report Tesco plc, p. 14.

4. Financial position

This final element of the OFR framework should describe events that have influenced the financial position of the business during the year and those that are likely to affect the business in the future. It should also include a discussion of the capital structure, cash flows and liquidity of the company. Real World 5.6 reveals how Tesco plc comments on its cash flows.

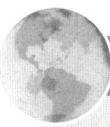

Real World 5.6

Tesco's cash

Tesco's 2006 OFR contains the following comment concerning its cash flows.

The Group generated net cash of £165 m during the year, benefiting from strong cash flow from operating activities of £3.4 bn and the net proceeds of £346 m from our property joint venture with Concensus. Within this, £239 m of cash was released from working capital, which was £199 m lower than last year. This was mainly due to a smaller rise in trade creditors (payables) than last year (last year's increase was exceptionally large and the change in International year end reduced trade creditors), higher non-food stocks (linked to global sourcing) and increased debtors (resulting from advance rent on new leasehold stores in Korea).

Source: 2006 Annual Report Tesco plc, p. 4.

This final element should also comment on the treasury policy of the business. Treasury policy is concerned with such matters as managing cash, obtaining finance and managing relationships with financial institutions. Possible areas for discussion may include major financing transactions and the effects of interest charges or interest rate changes on current or future results. Real World 5.7 shows how Tesco plc comments on major new funding arrangements during the year and its debt position at the end of the year in its 2006 OFR.

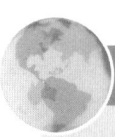

Real World 5.7

Funding Tesco

Tesco plc finances its operations by a combination of retained profits, share issues, leases and borrowing of different forms. The 2006 OFR includes the following:

> New funding of £529 m was arranged during the year, including a net £484 m from property joint ventures and £45 m from medium-term notes (MTNs). We renewed our €10 bn MTN programme on 28 February 2006. At the year end, net debt was £4.5 bn (last year £3.9 bn) and the average debt maturity was six years (last year eight years).

Source: 2006 Annual Report Tesco plc, p. 16.

The Business Review and RS1

Recent legislation requires all companies (except small companies) to include a Business Review as part of the Directors Report. This is a narrative report, which for listed companies in particular, covers much of the ground discussed above. As the form that a Business Review should take is not clearly specified, directors of larger companies are likely to look to RS1 for guidance.

Summary financial statements

We saw earlier that the directors must provide each shareholder with a copy of the annual financial statements. For large companies, these financial statements can be extremely detailed and complicated: along with the accompanying notes they may extend over many pages. It is possible, however, for the directors to provide a summarised version of the full financial statements as an alternative. The main advantages of providing summarised financial statements are that:

● many shareholders do not wish to receive the full version, because they may not have the time, interest or skill necessary to be able to gain much from it;
● directors could improve their communication with their shareholders by providing something closer to the needs of many shareholders;
● reproducing and posting copies of the full version is expensive and a waste of resources where particular shareholders do not wish to receive it.

Many large companies send all of their private shareholders a copy of the summary financial statements, with a clear message that the full versions are available on request. The full version is, however, required for filing with the Registrar of Companies.

Creative accounting

Despite the proliferation of accounting rules and the independent checks that are imposed, concerns over the quality of published financial statements surface from time to time. Some directors apply particular accounting policies or structure particular transactions in such a way as to portray a picture of financial health that is in line with what they would like users to see rather than what is a true and fair view of financial position and performance. This practice is referred to as **creative accounting** and it poses a major problem for accounting rule makers and for society generally.

Activity 5.6

Why might the directors of a company engage in creative accounting?

There are many reasons and these include:

- to get around restrictions (for example, to report sufficient profit to pay a dividend);
- to avoid government action (for example, the taxation of excessive profits);
- to hide poor management decisions;
- to achieve sales revenue or profit targets, thereby ensuring that performance bonuses are paid to the directors;
- to attract new share capital or loan capital by showing a healthy financial position;
- to satisfy the demands of major investors concerning levels of return.

Creative accounting methods

The ways in which unscrupulous directors can manipulate the financial statements are many and varied. However, they usually involve adopting unorthodox practices for reporting key elements of the financial statements such as revenue, expenses, assets and liabilities. They may also involve the use of complicated or obscure transactions in an attempt to hide the underlying economic reality. The manipulation carried out may be designed to 'bend' the rules or may be designed to break the rules. Below we consider some of the more important ways in which rules may be bent or broken.

Overstating revenue

Some creative accounting methods are designed to overstate the revenue for a period. These methods often involve the early recognition of sales revenue or the reporting of sales transactions that have no real substance. **Real World 5.8** below, which is an extract from an article that appeared in *The Times*, provides examples of both types of revenue manipulation.

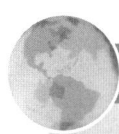

Real World 5.8

Overstating revenue

Hollow swaps: telecoms companies sell useless fibre optic capacity to each other in order to generate revenues on their income statements. Example: Global Crossing.

Channel stuffing: a company floods the market with more products than its distributors can sell, artificially boosting its sales. SSL, the condom maker, shifted £60 million in excess inventories on to trade customers. Also known as 'trade loading'.

Round tripping: also known as 'in-and-out trading'. Used to notorious effect by Enron. Two or more traders buy and sell energy among themselves for the same price and at the same time. Inflates trading volumes and makes participants appear to be doing more business than they really are.

Pre-dispatching: goods such as carpets are marked as 'sold' as soon as an order is placed . . . This inflates sales and profits.

Note that some of the techniques used, such as round tripping, may inflate the sales revenue for a period but will not inflate reported profits. Nevertheless, this may still benefit the business. Sales revenue growth has become an important yardstick of performance for some investors and can affect the value they place on the business.

Source: (2002) 'Dirty Laundry: How Companies Fudge the Numbers', *The Times* Business, 22 September.

The manipulation of revenue has been at the heart of many of the accounting scandals recently exposed. Given its critical role in the measurement of performance, this is, perhaps, not surprising. **Real World 5.9** provides an example of the impact of the early recognition of revenue on the financial results of one well-known business.

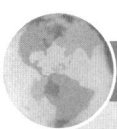

Real World 5.9

Not to be copied

One case of overstating revenue is alleged to have been carried out by the Xerox Corporation, a large US company and a leading player in the photocopying business. It is alleged that the company brought forward revenues in order to improve reported profits as its fortunes declined in the late 1990s. These revenues related to copier equipment sales, particularly in Latin America. To correct for the overstatement of revenues, Xerox had to restate its equipment sales revenue figures for a five-year period. The result was a reversal in reported revenues of a staggering $6.4 billion, although $5.1 billion was reallocated to other revenues as a result. This restatement was one of the largest in US corporate history.

In June 2002 the company paid a fine of $10 m but denied any wrongdoing.

Sources: based on information in (2003) 'Can't Tell the Scandals without a Scorecard', *The Wall Street Journal Europe*, October, p. A5; 'Xerox Acts to Put Itself on a Firmer Footing', FT.com, 28 June 2002.

Massaging expenses

Some creative accounting methods focus on the manipulation of expenses. Those expenses that rely on directors' estimates of the future or their choice of accounting policy are particularly vulnerable to manipulation.

Activity 5.7

Can you identify the kind of expenses where the directors make estimates or choices in the ways described?

These include certain expenses that we discussed in Chapter 3, such as:

● depreciation of property, plant and equipment;
● amortisation of intangible assets, such as goodwill;
● inventory costing methods; and
● allowances for receivables.

By changing estimates about the future (for example, the useful life or residual value of an asset), or by changing accounting policies (for example, switching from FIFO to AVCO), it may be possible to derive an expense figure, and consequently a profit figure, that suits the directors.

The incorrect capitalisation of expenses may also be used as a means of manipulation. This involves treating expenses as if they were amounts incurred to acquire or develop non-current assets, rather than amounts consumed during the period. Businesses that build their own assets are often best placed to undertake this form of malpractice.

Activity 5.8

What would be the effect on the profits and total assets of a business of incorrectly capitalising expenses?

Both would be artificially inflated. Reported profits would increase because expenses would be reduced. Total assets would be increased because the expenses would be incorrectly treated as non-current assets.

Real World 5.10 provides an example of one business that capitalised expenses on a huge scale.

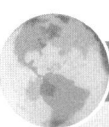 ## Real World 5.10

Sorry – wrong numbers

One particularly notorious case of capitalising expenses is alleged to have occurred in the financial statements of WorldCom (now renamed MCI). This company, which is a large US telecommunications business, is alleged to have overstated profits by treating certain operating expenses, such as basic network maintenance, as capital expenditure. This happened over a fifteen-month period during 2001 and 2002. To correct for this over-statement, profits had to be reduced by a massive $3.8 bn.

Source: based on two personal views on WorldCom: FT.com site, 27 June 2002.

Concealing 'bad news'

Some creative accounting methods focus on the concealment of losses or liabilities. The financial statements can look much healthier if these can somehow be eliminated.

One way of doing this is to create a 'separate' entity that will take over the losses or liabilities.

Real World 5.11 describes how one large business concealed losses and liabilities.

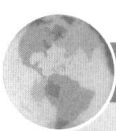

Real World 5.11

For a very special purpose

Perhaps the most well-known case of concealment of losses and liabilities concerned the Enron Corporation. This was a large US energy business that used 'special purpose entities' (SPEs) as a means of concealment. SPEs were used by Enron to rid itself of problem assets that were falling in value, such as its broadband operations. In addition, liabilities were transferred to these entities to help Enron's balance sheet look healthier. The company had to keep its gearing ratios (the relationship between borrowing and equity) within particular limits to satisfy credit-rating agencies and SPEs were used to achieve this. The SPEs used for concealment purposes were not independent of the company and should have been consolidated in the balance sheet of Enron, along with their losses and liabilities.

When these, and other accounting irregularities, were discovered in 2001, there was a restatement of Enron's financial performance and position to reflect the consolidation of the SPEs, which had previously been omitted. As a result of this restatement, the company recognised $591 m in losses over the preceding four years and an additional $628 m worth of liabilities at the end of 2000.

The company collapsed at the end of 2001.

Source: Thomas, C. W. (2002) 'The Rise and Fall of Enron', *Journal of Accountancy*, 194(3), April. This article represents the opinion of the author and necessarily that of the Texas Society of Certified Public Accountants.

Overstating assets

Finally, creative accounting may involve the overstatement of asset values. This may involve revaluing the assets, using figures that are higher than their fair market values. It may also involve the capitalising of costs that should have been written off as expenses, as described earlier.

Real World 5.12 describes how one large business went much further by reporting assets that simply did not exist.

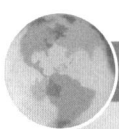

Real World 5.12

When things go sour

Parmalat, a large, family-controlled, Italian dairy-and-food business, announced in December 2003 that a bank account held in the Cayman Islands did not, as had been previously reported, have a balance of $3.95 billion. The fake balance turned out to be part of a web of deception: it had simply been 'invented' in order to help offset more than $16 billion of outstanding borrowings. According to Italian prosecutors, the business had borrowed heavily on the strength of fictitious sales revenues.

A Cayman Islands subsidiary, which was supposed to hold the fake bank balance, engaged in fictitious trading in an attempt to conceal the true nature of the deception. This included the supply of 300,000 tones of milk powder from a fake Singapore-based business to a Cuban business through the subsidiary.

Source: Based on information in 'How it all went so sour' P. Gumbel *Time Europe Magazine* 21 November 2004.

Checking for creative accounting

When examining the financial statements of a business, a number of checks may be carried out on the financial statements to help gain a 'feel' for their reliability. These can include checks to see whether:

● the reported profits are significantly higher than the operating cash flows for the period, which may suggest that profits have been overstated;
● the corporation tax charge is low in relation to reported profits, which may suggest, again, that profits are overstated, although there may be other, more innocent explanations;
● the valuation methods used for assets held are based on historic cost or fair values, and if the latter approach has been used why and how the fair values were determined;
● there have been any changes in accounting policies over the period, particularly in key areas such as revenue recognition, inventories valuation and depreciation;
● the accounting policies adopted are in line with those adopted by the rest of the industry;
● the auditors' report gives a 'clean bill of health' to the financial statements; and
● the 'small print', that is the notes to the financial statements, is not being used to hide significant events or changes.

Real World 5.13 describes the emphasis that one analyst places on this last check.

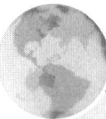

Real World 5.13

Taking note   **FT**

Alistair Hodgson, investment manager at private client stockbroker Pilling and Co says:

> I almost look at the notes more than I look at the main figures at first. The notes tend to hold the key to anything that looks strange. I look to pick out things that the auditor has told the company to declare – the kind of thing they might not want to declare, but they have got to do so in order to make the accounts honest.

Source: 'It Pays to Read Between the Lines', FT.com, 17 September 2005.

Some further checks may be carried out to provide confirmation of positive financial health. These may include checks to see whether:

● the business is paying increased dividends;
● the directors are buying shares in the business.

Although the various checks described are useful, they cannot be used to guarantee the reliability of the financial statements. Some creative accounting practices may be very deeply seated and may go undetected for years.

Creative accounting and economic growth

A few years ago there was a wave of creative accounting scandals, particularly in the USA, but also in Europe; however, it seems that this wave has now subsided. The quality of financial statements is improving and, it is to be hoped, trust among investors and others is being restored. As a result of the actions taken by various regulatory bodies and by accounting rule makers, creative accounting has become a more risky and difficult process for those who attempt it. However, it will never disappear completely and a further wave of creative accounting scandals may occur in the future.

The recent wave coincided with a period of strong economic growth, and during good economic times, investors and auditors become less vigilant. Thus, the opportunity to manipulate the figures becomes easier. We must not, therefore, become too complacent. Things may change again when we next experience a period of strong growth.

Summary

The main points of this chapter may be summarised as follows:

The directors' have a duty to:
- Maintain appropriate accounting records.
- Prepare and publish financial statements and a directors' report.

Accounting rules are necessary to:
- Avoid unacceptable accounting practices.
- Improve the comparability of financial statements.

Accounting rules
- The International Accounting Standards Board (IASB) has become an important source of rules.
- Company law and the London Stock Exchange are also a source of rules for UK companies.

Presenting financial statements
- IAS 1 sets out the structure and content of financial statements.
- It identifies five financial statements – the income statement, balance sheet, statement of changes in equity, cash flow statement and explanatory notes.
- The overriding consideration is to provide a fair representation of the financial health of a company and this will normally be achieved by adherence to relevant IASB standards.
- IAS 1 identifies information to be shown in the various financial statements.
- It also identifies some of the principles to be followed in preparing the statements.

Framework of principles
- This helps to underpin accounting rules.
- The IASB framework identifies and discusses, the users of financial statements, the objective of financial statements, the qualitative characteristics of financial statements, the elements of financial statements, different valuation bases, and different capital maintenance bases.
- The IASB framework draws on earlier work by other rule-making bodies.

Other statutory reports
- The auditors' report provides an opinion by an independent auditor concerning whether the financial statements provide a true and fair view of the financial health of a business.

- The directors' report contains information of a financial and a non-financial nature, which goes beyond that contained in the financial statements.

Additional financial reports

- Segmental reports disaggregate information on the financial statements to help achieve a better understanding of financial health.
- Companies can be segmented according to products or services and according to geographical operations.
- An IASB standard requires certain information relating to each segment to be shown.
- Identifying a segment and allocating costs between segments can raise problems.
- An operating and financial review (OFR) discusses the nature and objectives of the business, the development and performance of the business both in the period and in the future, the resources, risks and key relationships of the business and the financial position of the business both during the period and in the future.
- In the UK, the ASB has issued a reporting standard on the preparation of an OFR.
- Summary financial statements are available to investors who do not require the full set of financial statements.

Creative accounting

- Despite the accounting rules in place there have been examples of creative accounting by directors.
- This involves using accounting practices to show what the directors would like users to see rather than what is a fair representation of reality.
- There are various checks that can be carried out to the financial statements to see whether creative accounting practices may have been used.

 Key terms

International Financial Reporting
  standards
Statement of changes to equity
Framework of principles
Auditor
Directors' report

Segmental financial report
Transfer price
Operating and financial review (OFR)
Summary financial statements
Creative accounting

CHAPTER 31

Sustainability – environmental and social reporting

31.1 Introduction

The main purpose of this chapter is to provide an overview of the impact of sustainability on financial reporting.

Objectives

By the end of the chapter, you should be able to:

- discuss the evolution of sustainability reporting including:
  - triple bottom line reporting
  - the connected framework
  - IFAC Sustainability Framework
  - the accountant's role in a capitalist society;
- Discuss the evolution of environmental reporting in the annual report:
  - European Commission initiatives
  - United Nations initiatives
  - US initiatives
  - Self-regulation schemes
  - economic consequences
  - environmental audit;
- discuss the evolution of social accounting in the annual report:
  - the corporate report
  - corporate social reporting;
- need for comparative data:
  - Global Reporting Initiative
  - benchmarking.

31.2 How financial reporting has evolved to embrace sustainability reporting

Primary stakeholders

When corporate bodies were first created the primary stakeholders were the shareholders who had invested the capital and it was seen as the directors' responsibility to maximise their return by way of dividends and capital growth. This view was promoted by Milton Friedman[1] writing that:

few trends would so thoroughly undermine the very foundations of our free society as the acceptance by corporate officials of a social responsibility other than to make as much money for their shareholders as they possibly can.

It follows from this that directors were accountable to the shareholders who in turn should hold them to account. The Friedman approach offers protection for shareholders provided they actually do exercise their ability to hold directors accountable. However, it does not have regard to the interests of any other group affected by a company's decisions, such as consumers, employees or communities impacted upon by a company's operations unless there is a financial benefit to the company.

Other stakeholders

Since Friedman's writing in the 1960s companies have been under pressure to be account-able to a growing number of stakeholders. The pressure can be seen to come from

- Europe, e.g. the limiting and charging for landfill waste;
- national legislation, e.g. the Companies Act 2006 requirement that the business review in the Directors' Report must include information about:
  - environmental matters (including the impact of the company's business on the environment),
  - the company's employees, and
  - social and community issues.

Companies are now expected to act responsibly in their relationships with other stake-holders who have a legitimate interest in the business. Although there was a fear within companies that their financial performance would be damaged if public costs and other stakeholder interests were taken into account, societal pressure has grown since the 1990s. The following is a quote from The World Business Council for Sustainable Development:[2]

> CSR is the continuing commitment by business to behave ethically and contribute to economic development while improving the quality of life of the workforce and their families as well as of the local community and society at large.

There are three interesting points to highlight in this quotation. The first is the reference to behave ethically, the second is the acknowledgement that a company has an economic objective and the third is the extension to improve the quality of life of other stakeholders which includes environmental and social impacts.

As far back as 1975 there have been various initiatives such as the corporate report pro-posing the disclosure of additional information, such as employment and value added reports. External corporate reporting has been evolving from the simple financial reporting of profits and losses, assets and liabilities to, for example, the inclusion of information on govern-ance (e.g. disclosure of directors remuneration), as well as non-financial information such as environmental and social policies.

The concept of the triple bottom line was to integrate the reporting of economic, environ-mental and social impacts to recognise wider stakeholder interests.

31.3 The Triple Bottom Line (TBL)

TBL was a concept developed in the 1990s[3] under which financial, social and environmental performance were to be reported within the annual report. Economic performance was already highly developed, e.g. return on investment, gearing and liquidity ratios. The fact of reporting social and environmental impacts provided an incentive for a company to identify and establish performance indicators.

Environmental impacts were identified in relation, amongst other things, to waste, emissions and energy. Social impacts were identified in relation, amongst other things, to employment and human rights issues.

However, sustainability reporting is evolving and the author of TPL writes[4] that:

> In sum, the TBL agenda as most people would currently understand it is only the beginning. A much more comprehensive approach will be needed that involves a wide range of stakeholders and coordinates across many areas of government policy, including tax policy, technology policy, economic development policy, labour policy, security policy, corporate reporting policy and so on. Developing this comprehensive approach to sustainable development and environmental protection will be a central governance challenge – and, even more critically, a market challenge – in the 21st century.

31.4 The Connected Reporting Framework

The Accounting for Sustainability project[5] has developed a Connected Reporting Framework which will:

> help provide clearer, more consistent and comparable information for use both within an organisation and externally. The new Connected Reporting Framework developed by the Project explains how all areas of organisational performance can be presented in a connected way, reflecting the organisation's strategy and the way it is managed.

The principles which underlie the new Framework are:

- sustainability issues should be clearly linked to the organisation's overall strategy;
- sustainability and more conventional financial information should be presented together so that a more complete and balanced picture of the organisation's performance is given; and
- there should be consistency in presentation to aid comparability between years and organisations.

The Connected Reporting Framework has the following five key elements

1 An explanation of how sustainability is connected to the overall operational strategy of the organisation and the provision of sustainability targets.

2 Five key environmental indicators, which all organizations should consider reporting, being: polluting emissions, energy use, water use, waste and significant use of other finite resources

3 Other key sustainability information should be given where the business or operation has material impacts.

4 The inclusion of industry benchmarks, when available, for key performance indicators, to aid performance appraisal.

5 The up-stream and down-stream impact of the organisation's products and services: the sustainability impacts of its suppliers and of the use of its products or services by customers and consumers.

31.4.1 The Connected Reporting Framework illustrated

The following is an extract from the 2007 Aviva plc Annual Report:

> Working with the Accounting for Sustainability project, Aviva is helping define a new reporting standard for sustainable business and a tool-kit to embed sustainable decision making. The table . . . (*see below for extract*) demonstrates some of the measures in the sustainability model. We continue to work towards internalising the cost of carbon and demonstrating how environmental impacts of the business can be brought into our reporting and accounting process:

	Key indicators	
Greenhouse gas Emissions	**Waste**	**Resource usage**
CO$_2$ emissions *Other significant emissions*	*Hazardous and* *non-hazardous waste* *Conservation investment*	*Water* *Energy intensity* *Paper usage*
	Direct company impacts **Cash flow performance**	
CO$_2$ emissions Total cost of offsetting 100% of our global CO$_2$ emissions in 2007 is approximately £909,000. We incur up to a 2% premium for zero emission / renewable electricity compared to fossil fuels.	Total disposal cost for hazardous and non hazardous waste in the UK was £464,000 in 2007 (**2006: £585,000**) which includes UK landfill tax at circa £80 per tonne.	The operating cost of water usage was £938,000 in 2007 (2006: £670,000)

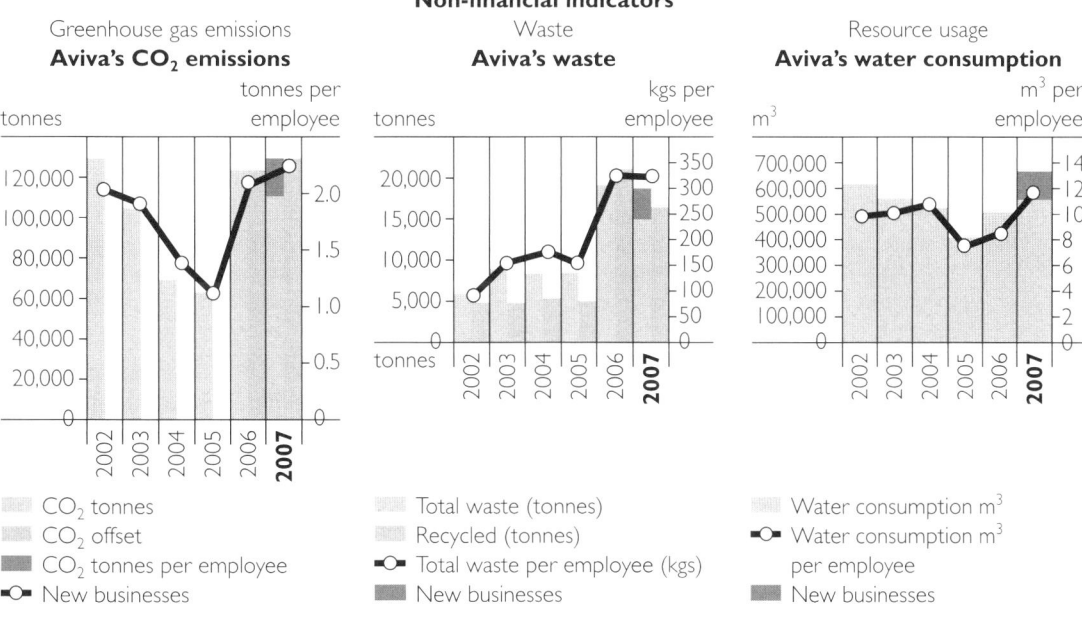

Non-financial indicators

| Greenhouse gas emissions
Aviva's CO$_2$ emissions | Waste
Aviva's waste | Resource usage
Aviva's water consumption |

CO$_2$ tonnes
CO$_2$ offset
CO$_2$ tonnes per employee
New businesses

Total waste (tonnes)
Recycled (tonnes)
Total waste per employee (kgs)
New businesses

Water consumption m^3
Water consumption m^3 per employee
New businesses

Commentary on our performance, strategy and targets

Greenhouse gas emissions	Waste	Resource usage
In 2007, our total CO_2 emissions increased, mainly due to the inclusion of emissions data from our new business in Aviva USA, Aviva Global Services, Sri Lanka and Russia. From our existing businesses, emissions have shown an 11% decrease, by 13,555 tonnes reflecting significant focus on energy efficiency and resourcing renewable energy.	In 2007, the total volume of waste decreased and the total amount recycled increased. Plastic wrap from the Auto Windscreens operation is now being recycled – 70 tonnes per year with a value of £135 per tonne.	There is limited scope for the retro-fitting of latest technologies in water usage reduction in washrooms. However, where possible we take advantage of such technologies.

	Industry Benchmark Information	
Greenhouse gas emissions	Waste	Resource usage
• Carbon Disclosure Project CDP 5. 'Best in class' • Innovest ranking 'AAA'. • BREEAM minimum ranking 'Good' for new build and refurbishment.	200 kg of waste per employee per year. Recycling rate of 60–70% (BRE Office toolkit).	7.7 m³ per employee per year. (National Water Demand Management Centre).

31.5 IFAC Sustainability Framework[6]

The Framework indicates that the successful management of a sustainable organisation requires attention to four perspectives. These perspectives are: business strategy, internal management, financial investors and other stakeholders.

As far as accountants are concerned, in an organisation a business strategy perspective would typically be taken by finance directors, an internal management perspective by management accountants and financial controllers, and a financial investors'/other stakeholders' perspective by accountants preparing and auditing the published financial statements.

31.5.1 The Framework's four perspectives

Taking a perspective means being aware of needs and concerns in relation to sustainability. For example, the importance attached to the control of carbon emissions by other stakeholders influences the priority given to it by management. This might also have to be reconciled with the business strategy perspective which could be that funds are being diverted away from productive capital investment. Taking a perspective means being aware, communicating effectively and influencing behaviour within an organisation.

Figure 31.1 is an extract from the Framework summarising the four perspectives.

Figure 31.1 The four perspectives

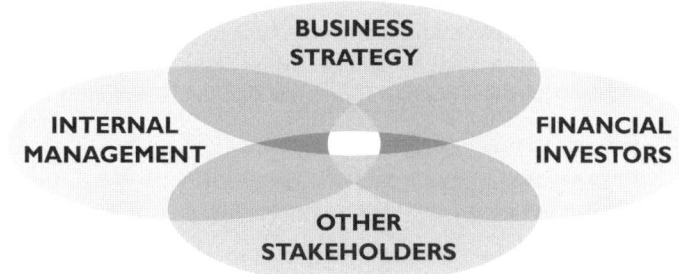

Part A: Business strategy perspective – taking a strategic approach

The Framework emphasises the importance of adopting a strategic approach, so that sustainable development is a part of strategic discussions, objectives, goals and targets, and is integrated with governance and accountability arrangements and risk management. Only by taking a business strategy approach can organisations make sustainable development a part of doing business.

Part B: Internal management perspective – making it happen

In many organisations, (a) enhancing performance evaluation and measurement, (b) changing behaviours, and (c) introducing sustainability and environmental accounting as an extension of existing accounting/information systems to accommodate organisational plans for sustainable development, can be a challenge for organisations, and can take time to achieve. Therefore, this perspective also includes advice on how organisations can achieve relatively simple quick wins to improve energy efficiency and reduce waste, that can help them improve environmental performance while reducing their costs, all in a relatively short time frame.

Part C: Financial investors' perspective – telling the story to investors

The Framework offers advice on both incorporating environmental and other sustainability issues into financial statements in a way that supports an organisation's stewardship role and enhanced reporting to investors in financial reporting, including narrative reporting using management commentary.

Part D: Other stakeholders' perspective – wider transparency

The final perspective considers an evolving part of sustainable development that builds on the development of stakeholder relationships (covered in the business strategy perspective) to improve transparency and non-financial reporting against a broader set of expectations. Such reporting commonly takes the form of separate sustainability or corporate social responsibility (CSR) reports that may be based on *de facto* standards, such as those from the Global Reporting Initiative (GRI). This perspective also includes sustainability assurance, to help to improve credibility and trust.

   The proposals in the triple bottom line, the Connected Reporting Framework and the Sustainability Framework are voluntary proposals for best practice.

31.5.2 Why is the qualitative information voluntary?

It is voluntary in recognition of the fact that market and political pressures exist; that each company balances the perceived costs (e.g. competitive disadvantage) and the perceived benefits of voluntary disclosure (e.g. improved investor appeal) in determining the extent of its voluntary disclosures.[7]

Companies have traditionally been ranked according to various criteria, e.g. their ability to maximise their shareholders' wealth or return on capital employed or EPS growth rates. However, there is a philosophical view that holds that a company:

> possesses a role in society because society finds it useful that it should do so . . . [It] cannot expect to find itself fully acceptable to society if it single-mindedly pursues its major objective without regard for the range of consequences of its actions.[8]

This means that a company is permitted to seek its private objectives subject to legal, social and ethical boundaries. This takes accounting beyond the traditional framework of reporting monetary transactions that are of interest primarily to the shareholders.

31.6 The accountant's role in a capitalist industrial society

In a capitalist, industrial society, production requires the raising and efficient use of capital largely through joint stock companies. These operate within a legal framework which grants them limited liability subject to certain obligations. The obligations include **capital maintenance provisions** to protect creditors (e.g. restriction on distributable profits) and **disclosure provisions** to protect shareholders (e.g. the publication of annual reports).

The state issues statutes to ensure there is effective control of the capital market; the degree of intervention depends on the party in power. Accountants issue standards to ensure there is reliable information to the owners to support an orderly capital market. Both the state and the accountancy profession have directed their major efforts towards servicing the needs of capital. This has influenced the nature of the legislation, e.g. removing obligations that are perceived to make a company uncompetitive, and the nature of the accounting standards, e.g. concentrating on earnings and monetary values.

However, production and distribution involve complex social relationships between private ownership of property and wage labour[9] and other stakeholders. This raises the question of the role of accountants. Should their primary concern be to serve the interests of the share-holders, or the interests of management, or to focus on equity issues and social welfare?[10]

Prior to the formation in the UK of the ASB, the profession identified with management and it was not unusual to allow information to be reported to suit management. If management were unhappy with a standard, they were able to frustrate or delay its implementation, as with deferred tax. Often, reported results bore little resemblance to the commercial substance of the underlying transactions.

The ASB has concentrated on making reports reflect the substance of a transaction. It has developed a conceptual framework for financial reporting to underpin its reporting standards and criteria has been defined for the recognition of assets, liabilities, income and expense.

The ASB did not produce mandatory requirements for narrative or qualitative disclosures – the operating and financial review (OFR) was voluntary (now the business review in the directors' report). However, the fact that it proposed the publication of an OFR was an import-ant in itself because it recognised that there was a need for narrative disclosure, even where this was not capable of audit verification.

31.7 The accountant's changing role

Accountants now make positive contributions to sustainability management by their respons-ible roles in systems and external reporting. They are responsible for the financial systems which provide the raw data for strategic planning, the management of risk, the measurement and reporting of performance and the allocation. For example, they identify environmental costs to measure and report on the efficiency of energy costs and social costs such as the cost of staff turnover and absenteeism.

Sustainability information reported to investors and other stakeholders needs to be based on sound systems of accounting, internal control and be externally assured. Professional accountants provide the expertise for the design and operation of systems and external auditors are increasingly providing an assurance capability.

Accountants have a central role in finance from which they are able to encourage a sustainability culture within an organisation by raising sustainability as a consideration when making decisions. This can be at an operating level as when they identify environmental or social costs or at a strategic level when capital investment decisions are being made.

31.8 Sustainability – environmental reporting

There has been a growing concern since the early 1990s that insufficient attention has been given to the impact of current commercial activities on future generations. This has led to the need for sustainable development which meets the needs of the present without compromising the ability of future generations to meet their own needs.

Why have companies become sensitive to the environmental concerns of stakeholders other than their shareholders? This has been a reaction to pressure from a variety of stakeholders ranging from the government to local communities and from environmental groups to individual consumers and individual investors.

We will now look at the development of environmental reporting.

31.9 Environmental information in the annual accounts

Much of the environmental information falls outside the expertise of the accountant, so why was it included in the annual report? The annual report had already become the accepted vehicle for providing shareholders with information on matters of social interest such as charitable donations and this extended to present qualitative information such as a statement of company policy.

However, in addition to recognising the concerns of other stakeholders companies also began to realise that there could be adverse financial implications for their capacity to raise funds.

Potential individual investors

The government in *This Common Inheritance*[11] indicated that shareholders could seek information about environmental practices from companies that they invest in and make their views known.

Potential corporate investors

Acquisitive companies needed to be aware of contingent liabilities,[12] which can be enormous. In the USA the potential cost of clearing up past industrially hazardous sites has been estimated at $675 billion. Even in relation to individual companies the scale of the contingency can be large, as in the Love Canal case. In this case a housing project was built at Love Canal in Upper New York State on a site that until the 1950s had been used by the Hooker Chemicals Corporation for dumping a chemical waste containing dioxin. Occidental, which had acquired Hooker Chemicals, was judged liable for the costs of clean-up of more than $260 million.[13] Existing shareholders and the share price would also be affected by these increased costs.

There is recognition that there is a wider interest than short-term profits.

31.10 Background to companies' reporting practices

Some companies have independently instituted comprehensive environmental management systems but many have not. There has been a tendency initially for companies to target the area that they considered to be the most sensitive and to treat it rather as a PR exercise or damage limitation. There was a concern that resources devoted to achieving environmental benefits would merely increase costs and companies made a point of referring to cost benefits to justify their outlay as in the following extract from the Scottish Power 1994 Annual Report:

> The company is committed to meeting or bettering increasingly stringent environmental controls for electricity generation and is developing new technologies and plant which can achieve significant benefits at realistic cost. At Longannet Power Station, more than £24 million is being invested in low Nox burners, which produce fewer nitrous oxides, and in renewing equipment to reduce dust from flue gases . . . This process is expected to be environmentally superior and lower in costs than alternative technologies.

This was quite understandable as it had been estimated that the enforcement of stringent environmental controls to reduce pollution could have substantial cost implications estimated at £15 billion for Britain in 1991.[14]

Companies were reactive and concentrated on satisfying statutory obligations or explaining their treatment of what they perceived to be the major environmental concern affecting their company. For example, in the case of Pearson, a major publishing company, a major concern was the use for printing of renewable resources and their 1993 Annual Report they included the following:

> One aspect of our company's environmental responsibilities is to keep their purchasing policies under review. Pearson's most significant purchase is paper. Our publishing companies between them buy some 180,000 tonnes of paper a year . . . Pearson makes certain that it buys paper only from responsibly managed forests and avoids paper bleached with chlorinated organic compounds where possible . . .

By 2007 Pearson published a CSR report, *Our Business and Society*, which included the following extract on the environment:

> The environmental considerations relating to the purchase of paper continue to be a priority for us . . . Pearson has further developed its responsible paper sourcing practice. As part of an action plan on responsible paper sourcing agreed with the WWF UK Forest & Trade Network, we established a database on the environmental characteristics of the paper we purchase. We have also met a number of our key suppliers and manufacturers of paper and some NGOs to discuss and review environmental issues including certification and increasing the recycled content in the paper we use in our books.

Although this was an *ad hoc* approach to environmental reporting it did not mean that significant benefits were not achieved. The following extract from the 2001 Annual Report of the Body Shop indicates the level of benefit:

At the Body Shop, we have made a significant commitment to reducing our CO_2 impact by switching electricity supply at both our Littlehampton sites and all UK company-owned shops to a renewable source. This initiative, together with our 15% investment in Bryn Titli wind farm, means that we offset an estimated 48% of electricity, gas and road freight used for all our UK operations including company-owned shops in the last financial year.

In some jurisdictions there have been mandatory requirements. In the USA, e.g. the Securities and Exchange Commission requires companies to disclose:

(a) the material effects of complying or failing to comply with environmental requirements on the capital expenditures, earnings and competitive position of the registrant and its subsidiaries;

(b) pending environmental legal proceedings or proceedings known to be contemplated, which meet any of three qualifying conditions: (1) materiality, (2) 10% of current assets, or (3) monetary sanctions; and

(c) environmental contingencies that may reasonably have material impact on net sales, revenue, or income from continuing operations.

A typical disclosure of amounts appears in the following extract from the Bayer Schering Pharma AG 2006 Annual Report:

We have spent substantial amounts on environmental protection and safety measures up to now, and anticipate having to spend similar sums in 2007 and subsequent years. In 2006, our operating and maintenance costs in the field of environmental protection and safety totaled €59m (2005: €65m). Our capital expenditure on environmental protection projects and other ecologically beneficial projects totaled €4m (2005: €5m).

31.11 European Commission recommendations for disclosures in annual accounts

In May 2001 the European Commission issued a *Recommendation on the Recognition, Measurement and Disclosure of Environmental Issues in the Annual Accounts and Annual Reports of Companies*.[15]

The Commission view was that there were two problems. The first was that there was a lack of explicit rules, which meant that any one or all of the different stakeholder groups, e.g. investors, regulatory authorities, financial analysts and the public in general, could feel that the disclosures were insufficient or unreliable; the second was that there was a low level of voluntary disclosure, even in sectors where there was significant impact on the environment.

31.11.1 Lack of explicit rules

The lack of harmonised guidelines has meant that investors have been unable to compare companies or to adequately assess environmental risks affecting the financial position of the company. Whilst recognising that there are existing financial reporting standards on the disclosure of provisions and contingent liabilities and that companies in environmentally sensitive sectors are producing stand-alone environmental reports, the Commission was of the opinion that there is a justified need to facilitate further harmonisation on what to disclose in the annual accounts.

As mentioned above, the cost of collecting and reporting is frequently perceived to be a deterrent and the Recommendation intends to avoid unjustified burdensome obligations. It also proposes that Recommendations should be within existing European Directives, e.g. the Fourth and Seventh Directives.

31.11.2 Stakeholder groups' information needs

All groups require relevant disclosures that are consistent and comparable – particularly disclosure in the notes to the accounts relating to environmental expenditures either charged to the profit and loss account or capitalised including fines and penalties for non-compliance and compensation payments.

31.11.3 Key points relating to recognition, measurement and disclosure

The approach to recognition and measurement is a restatement of current financial reporting requirements with some additional illustrations and explanations. The disclosures are fuller than currently met within annual accounts.

Recognition and measurement

For the recognition of environmental liabilities the criteria are the same as for IAS 37 *Provisions, Contingent Liabilities and Contingent Assets* e.g. requirement for probable outflow of resources, reliable estimate of costs and recognition of liability at the date operations commence if relating to site restoration.

For the capitalisation of environmental expenditure the criteria to recognise as an asset apply, e.g. it produces future economic benefits. There are also detailed proposals relating to environmental expenditure which improves the future benefits from another asset and to asset impairment.

Disclosures

Disclosure is recommended if the issues are material to either the financial performance or financial position. Detailed proposals in relation to environmental protection are for the disclosure of:

● the policies that have been adopted and reference to any certification such as EMAS (see section 31.12.2 below);

● the improvements made in key areas with physical data if possible, e.g. on emissions;

● progress implementing mandatory requirements;

● environmental performance measures, e.g. trends for percentage of recycled packaging;

● reference to any separate environmental report produced.

There are, in addition, detailed cross-references to the requirements of the Fourth and Seventh Directives, e.g. description of valuation methods applied and additional disclosures, e.g. if there are long-term dismantling costs, the accounting policy and, if the company gradually builds up a provision, the amount of the full provision required.

31.12 Evolution of stand-alone environmental reports

There is a steady growth in the rate at which environmental reports are being produced. The rate is faster where there are clear risks such as paper, chemicals, oil and gas, and pharmaceuticals.

In some jurisdictions such as Denmark, the Netherlands, Norway and Sweden, there is legislation requiring environmental statements from environmentally sensitive industries either in their financial statements or in a stand-alone report; in other countries, voluntary disclosures are proposed.

The following is an extract relating to a Danish experience where most companies now produce separate CSR reports (www.sustainabilityreporting.eu/denmark/index.htm):

> Most Danish companies now publish separate CSR reports, independent of their statutory annual reporting. In recent years, more companies have started integrating their financial and non-financial data into the same report, for instance by adding a section on non-financial data at the end of the report. The companies preparing the best reports, however, are those which grasp the connection between the non-financial data and their business. As a result, these companies have fully integrated non-financial data with financial data in the report. In doing this, the companies clearly demonstrate their full understanding of the value of reporting on non-financial data. *They demonstrate that the data are being used as a serious management and communication tool and that they are able to link CSR to business strategy.* However, as statutory reports do not necessarily reach all stakeholders. These companies also make use of a number of other communication channels to report on their CSR work. When we consider the future focus on climate change, the companies' desire to adapt their reporting to their future stakeholders, the Danish Government's pressure on Danish companies to integrate CSR in their business strategy, and the need for cost cuts owing to the current crisis, we are convinced that the trend will be that more Danish companies begin to employ completely integrated reporting.

When considering inclusion of CSR reporting in the annual report, one of the problems has been the volume of data. Companies are overcoming this by issuing summary CSR reports in hard copy and uploading the full CSR report onto their websites. The following is an extract relating to experience in the Netherlands (www.sustainabilityreporting.eu/netherlands/index.htm):

> In the Netherlands, various companies are aiming for further integration of the CSR information into their annual reports. Companies are increasingly using the Internet in order to reduce the size of their CSR reports. They publish hard copy summary reports, with the full versions available on the Internet.

> Attention is also being given to the increasing use of non-financial information:

> In the Netherlands, from 2006, health insurance became an entirely private activity. As a result, health insurance companies have certain responsibilities towards their clients. To monitor this process, these companies have to publish mandatory CSR reports to the health insurance authority. CSR reporting by health insurance companies to their stakeholders has consequently increased. Government departments (ministry, province, municipality) also have to provide information on their performance in relation to their policy plans.
>
> This includes both financial and non-financial performance indicators and will also lead to an increase in reporting. Amsterdam has already published its first CSR report.

CSR is also being progressively introduced into academic programmes. For example, the Erasmus University Rotterdam has started a one-year postgraduate course on CSR Management & CSR Auditing, which includes one module on CSR Reporting.

In Chapter 30 we discussed the development of corporate governance and the concentration was on the accountability of the board to the shareholders for their strategic control of the assets and their responsibility to act in the best interest of the shareholders. The effectiveness of their control would be assessed in financial terms by reference to ratios such as ROCE, ROI, growth rate of EPS, earnings and dividend yield.

In the early stages of environmental, social and now sustainability reporting the emphasis was on reporting to other stakeholders. This was extended by the concept of the triple bottom line and it is interesting to see that sustainability and corporate governance are potentially merging as companies see that the two do not have separate audiences. Shareholders and stakeholders are both beginning to look at both aspects. The following is an extract relating to Swedish experience (www.sustainabilityreporting.eu/sweden/index.htm):

> During the last year newspapers, television and other media have reported more than ever before on climate change and supply chain related issues. The media interest in corporate responsibility and the need for change and transparency has an even longer tradition. The manner in which these trends will have an impact on the further development of sustainability reporting is, of course, an interesting question. We are at a turning point in reporting on sustainability. The Accounting Modernisation Directive implemented in the Swedish Annual Accounts Act may help companies to focus their reporting on non-financial risks. Some companies are already integrating their efforts on sustainability and corporate social responsibility with their work on corporate governance. Interesting to note is the fact that some companies' governance reports include information on sustainability. There is a call for transparent non-financial reporting from the financial community. Last but not least, the Swedish Government's requirements on reporting sustainability will pave the way for GRI reporting also in the public sector.

There has been a growing pressure for CSR information to be subject to assurance reports to give stakeholders the same confidence as they have obtained from the audit reports on financial statements. The following is an extract relating to a UK experience (www.sustainabilityreporting.eu/uk/index.htm):

> The challenges facing companies are:
>
> ● starting assurance engagements using the updated, 2008 version of the AA1000AS;
> ● improving the standards of assurance statements (as in previous years), including: more detailed commentary on methodology and recommendations in the statement; and focusing more on the materiality, completeness and responsiveness principles rather than just simply checking accuracy of information;
> ● providing an organisational response to the assurance engagement in the report, including how any recommendations will be put into place; and
> ● dealing with the mandatory reporting on carbon emissions according to the requirements of the Climate Change Bill.

There is progress being made at varying rates around the world. One of the stimuli has been the environmental, social and sustainability award schemes. One of the earliest of the award schemes was that of the ACCA.

31.12.1 The ACCA award schemes

In 2000 the ACCA commemorated ten years of progress in environmental reporting. After these ten years the ACCA established in 2002 a new structure for the UK awards to reflect the ever-increasing public awareness of the environmental, social and economic impacts of business. The ACCA Award scheme was restructured in 2001 under the title 'The ACCA

Awards for Sustainability Reporting'. There are three different award categories: the ACCA UK Environmental Reporting Awards, the ACCA Social Reporting Awards and a new category, the ACCA Sustainability Reporting Awards. Details of Award winners can be found on the ACCA website.

These schemes have given environmental reporting a high profile and contributed greatly to the present quality of reports. The schemes now take place in a number of countries and regions. These include Hong Kong, Malaysia, Singapore, South Africa, Sri Lanka, Europe and North America.

The following is an extract relating to the Singapore awards (www.accaglobal.com/singapore/publicinterest/sustainability/sustainability).

Singapore Awards for Sustainability Reporting

ACCA is pleased to announce the launch of the ACCA Singapore Awards for Sustainability Reporting 2008. Formerly known as the Singapore Environmental and Social Reporting Awards (SESRA), the awards which are now into its seventh year are endorsed by the National Environment Agency and supported by the Singapore Environment Council and TüV SüD PSB. Joining the list of supporting organisations this year is Singapore Compact for CSR.

ACCA Singapore invites organisations of all sizes and sectors to submit their application into the awards. The closing date for entries is 31 March 2009. The Awards ceremony will be held in June 2009.

The aim of the awards is to promote transparency and give recognition to those organisations which report and disclose environmental, social and full sustainability information. The awards also provide a platform to raise awareness of corporate transparency issues.

ACCA has promoted sustainability reporting for more than a decade since the introduction of the environmental reporting awards in 1991 in the United Kingdom. ACCA is involved in reporting awards around the world in Europe, Africa, North America and the Asia Pacific region.

Any organisation of any size or industry sector; be it private or public with operations in Singapore can enter into the awards.

The entries are reviewed by a judging panel comprising of experts within the field of environmental and sustainability reporting. At the core of the judging criteria are completeness, credibility and communication.

This year ACCA will be giving out awards in the following categories; Environmental Reporting, Social Reporting and the newly added category of Sustainability reporting. In addition to the main awards and commendations, ACCA Singapore will also be introducing new awards for 'First Time Reporter'. The introduction of the new awards is to encourage greater participation and to acknowledge a wider range of efforts that organisations have taken towards enhancing sustainability and transparency.

The criteria that each scheme sets can vary and reflect local interests. For example, the Hong Kong awards for 2008 were in the following categories:

Best Sustainability Report	CLP Holdings Limited
Runner Up – Best Sustainability Report	Swire Pacific Limited
Commendation For Excellent Communication Using The Internet	MTR Corporation
Commendation For Demonstration Of Integrity In Reporting	Gammon Construction Limited
Commendation For Addressing Sectoral Issues	The China Navigation Company Limited

Encouragement has been actively given to SME reporting. For example, in 2000, at the Europe-wide level, the European Environmental Reporting Awards (EERA), in which entries are selected from the winners of national schemes organised by EU Member States, selected four winners:

- Overall winner: Shell International (UK),
- Best first-time reporter: Acquedotto Pugliese (Italy),
- Best SME reporter: Obermurtaler Brauereigenossenschaft (Austria),
- Best sustainability report: Novo Nordisk (Denmark).

The judges commented on strengths, and in respect of the best SME reporter listed:

- its comprehensive reporting on corporate performance including five-year trend data for various indicators and quantified targets;
- an analysis of the environmental impact arising from the product development activity;
- detailed description of supplier audits;
- disclosure of internal audit procedures and results; and
- evidence of environmental interest including obtaining EMAS registration (the first site to do this in Austria).

SMEs continue to be encouraged to develop CSR reporting.

In the UK the ACCA awards again looked carefully at assurance and reported (www.accaglobal.com/uk/publicinterest/sustainability/):

- All the shortlisted companies for the 2008 ACCA UK Sustainability Reporting Awards have some form of external assurance of their reports, including the small and medium-sized enterprises (SMEs), but the scope and approach varies widely between reports.
- Many assurance statements continue to lack concrete recommendations from the assurance provider, meaning that they do not provide the reader with a clear account of the outcomes of the engagement. Assurance was picked up by the 2008 judges as being a general weakness, both in terms of the assurance statement itself and the organisational response to the assurance engagement's outcomes.
- As in previous years, non-accounting assurance providers tend to use the AccountAbility AA1000 Assurance Standard (sometimes in combination with the ISAE300) and Big 4 accounting firms are encouraged to use the ISAE3000.
- UK organisations (as well as those elsewhere in Europe) will have to start using the new version of AA1000AS, launched in October 2008, from 2009 onwards.
- There continues to be a wider scope of assurance processes than the traditional assurance statement approach. For example, the inclusion of an external stakeholder assurance panel (as demonstrated by Shell's report) and different 'niche' assurance providers for different areas of the business/reporting (as demonstrated by De Beers' sustainability report).

31.13 International charters and guidelines

There have been a number of international and national summits, charters and recommendations issued. In some jurisdictions such as Denmark, the Netherlands, Norway and

Sweden, there is now legislation requiring environmental statements from environmentally sensitive industries either in their financial statements or in a stand-alone report; in other countries, voluntary disclosures are proposed. Below are brief descriptions of just some of the voluntary disclosures proposed by the United Nations, Europe and the USA, and of some self-regulation schemes in which companies can elect to participate.

31.13.1 United Nations

At the United Nations we can see that the United Nations Environment Programme (UNEP)[16] has made major impacts, e.g. it was the driving force behind the 1987 Montreal Protocol on Substances that Deplete the Ozone Layer whereby industrialised countries ceased production and consumption of a significant proportion of all ozone-depleting substances in 1996. It is estimated that 1.5 million cases of melanoma skin cancer due to the sun's UV-B radiation will be averted by the year 2060 as a result of the Protocol. It has had similar success as the leading force for the sound global management of hazardous chemicals and the protection of the world's biological diversity by forging the Convention on Biological Diversity. It is innovative in its approach, e.g. entering into a partnership agreement with the International Olympic Committee (IOC) in 1995 as a result of which the environment now figures as the third pillar of Olympism, along with sport and culture, in the IOC's Charter. UNEP has initiated the development of environmental guidelines for sports federations and countries bidding for the Olympic Games.

UNEP is actively concerned with climate change. As a science-based organisation it is able to make available better and more relevant scientific information on climate change impacts to developing country decision-makers. UNEP states that 'it will help improve capacity to use this information for policy purposes, as well as providing scientific, legal and institutional support to developing country negotiators and their institutions so that they can meaningfully contribute to a strengthened international regime on climate change'.

31.13.2 Europe

In Europe the Eco-Management and Audit Scheme (EMAS)[17] was adopted by the European Council on 29 June 1993, allowing voluntary participation in an environmental management scheme. Its aim is to promote continuous environmental performance improvements of activities by committing organisations to evaluating and improving their own environmental performance.

The main elements of the current EMAS regulations include:

● making environmental statements more transparent;
● the involvement of employees in the implementation of EMAS; and
● a more thorough consideration of indirect effects including capital investments, administrative and planning decisions and procurement procedures.

Companies that participate in the scheme are required to adopt an environmental policy containing the following key commitments:

● compliance with all relevant environmental legislation;
● prevention of pollution; and
● achieving continuous improvements in environmental performance.

The procedure is for an initial environmental review to be undertaken and an environmental programme and environmental management system established for the organisation.

Verification is seen as an important element and environmental audits, covering all activities at the organisation concerned, must be conducted within an audit cycle of no longer than three years. On completion of the initial environmental review and subsequent audits or audit cycles a public environmental statement is produced.

An organisation's environmental statement will include the following key elements:

- a clear description of the organisation, and its activities, products and services;
- the organisation's environmental policy and a brief description of the environmental management system;
- a description of all the significant direct and indirect environmental aspects of the organisation and an explanation of the nature of the impacts as related to these aspects;
- a description of the environmental objectives and targets in relation to the significant environmental aspects and impacts;
- a summary of the organisation's year-by-year environmental performance data which may include pollution emissions, waste generation, consumption of raw materials, energy use, water management and noise;
- other factors regarding environmental performance including performance against legal provisions; and
- the name and accreditation number of the environmental verifier, the date of validation and deadline for submission of the next statement.

The following extract from the Schering 2000 Annual Report indicates the persuasive influence of schemes such as EMAS:

We aim at achieving the ISO 14001 certification or the Eco Management and Audit Scheme (EMAS) validation for all production sites. We have begun to integrate the existing management systems for quality, safety and environmental protection, and to organise throughout the Group. This Integrated Management System (IMS) is based on International Standard ISO 9000 (for quality) as well as ISO 14001 and EMAS (for environmental protection).

31.13.3 The USA

In the USA the Environmental Accounting Project began in 1992 to encourage companies to adopt environmental accounting techniques which would make environmental costs more apparent to managers and, therefore, make them more controllable. It was thought that this could result in three positive outcomes namely, the significant reduction of environmental costs, the gaining of competitive advantage and the improvement of environmental performance with the initial concern being to reduce pollution.

31.14 Self-regulation schemes

There are a number of examples of self-regulatory codes of conduct from institutions, e.g. The International Chamber of Commerce (ICC),[18] The International Organization for Standardization (ISO), and bodies representing particular industries, e.g. the European Chemical Industry Council (CEFIC).[19] We will describe briefly the ICC Charter and ISO standards.

31.14.1 The International Chamber of Commerce (ICC)

The ICC launched **the Business Charter for Sustainable Development** in 1991 to help business around the world improve its environmental performance relating to health, safety and product stewardship. The Charter set out sixteen Principles which include:

- *Policy statements* – such as giving environmental management high corporate priority; aiming to integrate environmental policies and practices as an essential element of management; continuing to improve corporate policies performance; advising customers, distributors and the public in the safe use, transportation, storage and disposal of products provided; promoting the adoption of these principles by contractors acting on behalf of the enterprise; developing products that have no undue environmental impact and are efficient in their consumption of energy and natural resources, and that can be recycled, reused, or disposed of safely; fostering openness and dialogue with employees and the public, anticipating and responding to their concerns about the potential hazards and impacts of operations, products, wastes or services; and measuring environmental performance.

- *Financially quantifiable practices* – such as employee education; assessment of environmental impacts before starting a new activity or decommissioning; conduct or support of research on the environmental impacts of raw materials, products, processes, emissions and wastes associated with the enterprise and on the means of minimising such adverse impacts; modification of the manufacture, marketing or use of products or services to prevent serious or irreversible environmental degradation.

The following extract from the Nestlé 2000 Environment Progress Report is a good example of a company that has applied the ICC approach and is proactive in seeking improvements:

> Message from CEO
>
> I am pleased about the clear progress in a number of key areas, including a significant decline in the amounts of water and energy used to bring each kilo of Nestlé product into your home, and a similar reduction in factors which potentially affect global warming. However, we are never completely satisfied with our current performance, and are committed to further environmental improvements.
>
> We try to remain sensitive to the environmental concerns of our consumers and the public as a whole. . . . we have pledged our allegiance to *The Business Charter for Sustainable Development* of the International Chamber of Commerce, and we are committed to being a leader in environmental performance.

In 2007 Nestlé published its *Creating Shared Value Report* (see http://www.nestle.com/csv). This profiles Nestlé's global efforts to increase the delivery of high-quality, nutritious food products that add to consumers' health and well-being. The report also profiles Nestlé's ongoing commitment to develop nutritious, popularly positioned products that are affordable and accessible to consumers at the base of the global economic pyramid.

The following is an extract from the Nestlé CSV Report:

> Nestlé is committed to reporting its performance openly. In 2008, we published our first global report on Creating Shared Value. It is a first step towards providing evidence that the successful creation of long-term shareholder value is dependent also on the creation of value for society.
>
> We first explored the concept of Creating Shared Value in our 2005 report, 'The Nestlé concept of corporate social responsibility', which focused on our Latin American operations . . . Since then, in conjunction with our business areas and advisers including SustainAbility and AccountAbility, we have identified and assessed critical issues, developed global performance indicators and engaged stakeholders in debate.

In order to provide assurance to stakeholders over Nestlé Creating Shared Value reporting, an external auditor Bureau Veritas has been engaged. For more information read the full Bureau Veritas Assurance Statement.

Nestlé is also among the first food companies to join the Global Reporting Initiative multi-stakeholder programme to develop global reporting standards and indicators on sustainability in the food industry.

31.14.2 The International Organization for Standardization (ISO)

ISO is a non-governmental organisation established in 1947, and comprises a worldwide federation of national standards with the aim of establishing international standards to reduce barriers to international trade. Its standards, including environmental standards, are voluntary and companies may elect to join in order to obtain ISO certification.

One group of standards, the ISO 14000 series, is intended to encourage organisations to systematically assess the environmental impacts of their activities through a common approach to environmental management systems. Within the group, the ISO 14001 standard states the requirements for establishing an EMS and companies must satisfy its requirements in order to qualify for ISO certification.

What benefits arise from implementation of ISO 14001?

Those who support the ISO approach consider that there are a number of positive advantages, such as:

- **Top-level management become involved** – they are required to define an overall policy and, in addition, they recognise significant financial considerations from certification, e.g. customers might in the future prefer to deal with ISO compliant companies, insurance premiums might be lower and there is the potential to reduce costs by greater production efficiency.
- **Environmental management** – ISO 14001 establishes a framework for a systematic approach to environmental management which can identify inefficiencies that were not apparent beforehand resulting in operational cost savings and reduced environmental liabilities. We have seen above, for example, that Nestlé reduced its energy consumption by 20%.
- **A framework for continual improvements is established** – there is a requirement for continual improvement of the management system.

What criticisms are there of a compliance approach?

Compliance approaches which set out criteria such as a commitment to minimise environmental impact can allow companies to set low objectives for improvement and report these as achievements with little confidence that there has been significant environmental benefit.

31.15 Economic consequences of environmental reporting

There can be internal and external favourable economic consequences for companies. They can achieve cost reductions and become more attractive to potential investors.

31.15.1 Cost reductions

It has been reported that the discipline of measuring these risks can yield valuable management information with DuPont, for example, reporting that since it began measuring and reporting on the environmental impact of its activities, its annual environmental costs dropped from a high of US$1 billion in 1993 to $560 million in 1999.

31.15.2 Investors

Investors are gradually beginning to require information on a company's policy and programmes for environmental compliance and performance in order to assess the risk to earnings and statement of financial position. One would expect that the more transparent these are the less volatile the share prices will be which could be beneficial for both the investor and the company. This will be a fruitful field for research as environmental reporting evolves with more consistent, comparable, relevant and reliable numbers and narrative disclosures.

This has also given rise to Socially Responsible Investing (SRI) which considers both the investor's financial needs and the investee company's impact on society to an extent that in 1999 over US$2,000 billion in assets were invested in 'ethical' investment funds. In the UK there is pressure from bodies such as the Association of British Insurers for institutional investors to take SRI principles into account. Investors are also able to refer to indices such as the Dow Jones Sustainability Indices and the FTSE4Good Index.

Dow Jones Sustainability Indices

The Dow Jones Sustainability Indices were begun in 1999 and were the first global indices tracking the financial performance of the leading sustainability-driven companies worldwide.

FTSE4Good Index Series

The FTSE4Good Index Series provides potential investors with a measure of the performance of companies that meet globally recognised corporate responsibility standards. FTSE4Good is helpful as a basis for socially responsible investment and as a benchmark for tracking the performance of socially responsible investment portfolios.

However, research carried out by Trucost and commissioned by the Environment Agency (www.environment-agency.gov.uk/business) into quantitative disclosures found that direct links between management of environmental risks and shareholder value are almost non-existent, with only 11% of FTSE 350 making a link between the environment and some aspect of their financial performance and only 5% explicitly linking it to shareholder value.

31.16 Summary on environmental reporting

Environmental reporting is in a state of evolution ranging from *ad hoc* comments in the annual report to a more systematic approach in the annual report to stand-alone environmental reports.

Environmental investment is no longer seen as an additional cost but as an essential part of being a good corporate citizen and environmental reports are seen as necessary in communicating with stakeholders to address their environmental concerns.

Companies are realising that it is their corporate responsibility to achieve sustainable development whereby they meet the needs of the present without compromising the ability of future generations to meet their own needs. Economic growth is important for shareholders and other stakeholders alike in that it provides the conditions in which protection of the environment can best be achieved, and environmental protection, in balance with other human goals, is necessary to achieve growth that is sustainable.

However, there is still a long way to go and the EU's Sixth Action Programme 'Environment 2010: Our Future, Our Choice'[20] recognises that effective steps have not been taken by all member states to implement EC environmental directives and there is weak ownership of environmental objectives by stakeholders. The programme focuses on four major areas for action – climate change, health and the environment, nature and biodiversity, and natural resource management – and emphasises how important it is that all stakeholders should be involved to achieve more environmentally friendly forms of production and consumption as well as integration into all aspects of our life such as transport, energy and agriculture.

As with the other environmental reporting initiatives discussed above and the corporate governance approach we have seen with the Hampel Report and the OFR, the programme concentrates on setting general objectives rather than quantified targets apart from the targets relating to climate change where there is the EU's 8% emission reduction target for 2008–12 under the Kyoto Protocol. This is a sensible way to progress with an opportunity for best practice to evolve.

However, significant improvements are still required, with research indicating that although the majority of FTSE All Share companies discuss their interaction with the environment in their Annual Report and Accounts, the vast majority lack depth, rigour or quantification.

31.17 Environmental auditing: international initiatives

The need for environmental auditors has grown side by side with the growth of environmental reporting. This is prompted by the need for investors to be confident that the information is reliable and relevant. There have been various initiatives around the world and we will briefly refer to examples from Canada, the USA and Europe.

Canada

The Canadian Environmental Auditing Association (CEAA) was founded in 1991 to encourage the development of environmental auditing and the improvement of environmental management through environmental auditor certification and the application of environmental auditing ethics, principles and standards. It is a multidisciplinary organisation whose international membership base now includes environmental managers, ISO 14001 registration auditors, EMS consultants, corporate environmental auditors, engineers, chemists, government employees, accountants and lawyers. The CEAA is now accredited by the Standards Council of Canada as a certifying body for EMS Auditors.[21]

USA

The Registrar Accreditation Board (RAB)[22] was established in 1989 by the American Society for Quality to provide accreditation services for ISO 9000 Quality Management Systems (QMS) registrars.

In 1991, the American National Standards Institute (ANSI) and RAB joined forces to establish the American National Accreditation Program for Registrars of Quality Systems.

In 1996, with the release of new ISO 14000 Environmental Management Systems (EMS) standards, the ANSI-RAB National Accreditation Program (NAP) was formed covering the accreditation of QMS and EMS registrars as well as accreditation of course providers offering QMS and EMS auditor training courses. Certification programmes for both EMS and QMS auditors are now operated solely by RAB.

RAB exists to serve the conformity assessment needs of business and industry, registrars, course providers and individual auditors.

Since 1999 the European Federation of Accountants (FEE) Sustainability Working Party (formerly Environmental) has been active in the project Providing Assurance on Environmental Reports[23] and is actively participating with other organisations and collaborating on projects such as GRI Sustainability Guidelines which are discussed further in section 31.23 below.

31.18 The activities involved in an environmental audit

There are many activities commonly seen in practice. These can be grouped into those assessing the *current position* and those evaluating decisions affecting the *future*.

31.18.1 Assessing the current position

The assessment embraces physical, systems and staff appraisal.

- Physical appraisal is carried out by means of:
  - **site inspections**;
  - **scientific testing** to sample and test substances including air samples;
  - **off-site testing and inspections** to examine the organisation's impact on its immediate surroundings; after all, the company's responsibility does not stop at the boundary fence.
- Systems appraisal is carried out by means of:
  - **systems inspections** to review the stated systems of management and control in respect of environmental issues;
  - **operational reviews** to review actual practices when compared to the stated systems;
  - **compliance audits for certification schemes**.
- Staff appraisal is carried out by means of:
  - **awareness tests for staff** to test, by questionnaire, the basic knowledge of all levels of staff of the systems and practices currently used by the organisation. This will highlight any areas of weakness.

31.18.2 Assessing the future

The assessment embraces planning and design processes and preparedness for emergencies.

- Planning and design appraisal is carried out by means of:
  - **review of planning procedures** to ensure that environmental factors are considered in the planning processes adopted by the organisation;
  - **design reviews** to examine the basic design processes of the organisation (if applicable) to ensure that environmental issues are addressed at the design stage so the organisation can avoid problems rather than have to solve them when they happen.
- Preparedness for emergencies is appraised by means of:
  - **review of emergency procedures** to assess the organisation's preparedness for specific, predictable emergencies;
  - **review of crisis plans** to review the organisation's general approach to crisis management with the audit covering such topics as the formation of **crisis management teams** and resource availability.

31.18.3 The environmental audit report

We can see from the above that an environmental audit may be wide-ranging in its scope and time-consuming, particularly when auditing a major organisation. A typical report could include:

- Current practice
  - a comprehensive review and comment on current operational practices.
- List of action required
  - areas of **immediate concern** which the organisation needs to address as a matter of urgency;
  - areas for improvement over a set period of time.
- Qualitative assessment
  - a **statement of risk** as seen by the audit team based on an overview of the whole situation with a qualitative assessment of the level of environmental risk being faced by the organisation.
- An action plan
  - a **schedule of improvement** may also be produced which gives a timetable and series of stages for the organisation to follow in improving its environmental performance.
- Encouraging good practice
  - a positive statement of 'good practice' may be included. This has a dual value in that it is a motivational tool for management and an educational tool to foster staff awareness of what constitutes 'good practice'.

31.18.4 What is the status of an environmental audit report?

Legal position

There is no legal obligation to carry out an environmental audit or to inform outside parties of any critical findings when such an audit is carried out. The reports are usually regarded as 'confidential' even when carried out by external auditors who provide the service as an 'optional extra' which is offered to the organisation for an additional fee.

Public interest

There is a strong case for requiring both environmental audits and the publication of the resultant reports. Requiring reports to be put into the public domain would encourage transparency in the process and avoid accusations of secrecy. However, this 'public interest' argument has been heard before in accounting and has met with some resistance in the guise of commercial sensitivity.

Mandatory position

The lack of legal obligation could be regarded as a crucial weakness of the environmental audit process as there could be a major danger to the environment which remains 'secret' until after the crisis when it is then too late. The responsible organisation will of course inform all appropriate parties of any revealed risk but it would be foolhardy to assume that all organisations are responsible. The ASB has become involved with potential liability for the company in its consideration of provisions. Whilst this is only viewing it from the viewpoint of the shareholder, it may well be the only pragmatic way forward at present.

31.18.5 Experience in the USA

The increasing importance of environmental accounting can be seen in the USA in the work of the United States Environmental Protection Agency (EPA) and its Environmental Accounting Project (EAP) which has been operating since 1992.

In this large project the EPA attempts to identify the currently 'hidden' societal costs faced by organisations. These costs are those which an organisation incurs in its interaction with the environment and which in theory are totally avoidable. By identifying these costs, the organisation is motivated to address them and by implication make every attempt to reduce them, thus improving the environment.

The EPA has a very impressive website, which can be found at the following address: www.epa.gov/epahome/aboutepa/htm. Here the basic ideas and concepts governing the EPA's study of environmental accounting are set out.

The work of the EPA has also been of a more practical nature in helping organisations address environmental issues from an environmental viewpoint. A brief review of three such cases may help explain the proactive approach to environmental accounting, which goes beyond traditional reporting.

A. The Chrysler Corporation (a major vehicle manufacturer) was faced with a problem with the use of mercury switches in its electrical systems on vehicles. Mercury is dangerous to use and is very dangerous as a waste product when the vehicle is scrapped. The company had always resisted the use of non-mercury switches on pure cost terms.

However, during the EPA project, by looking at the environmental cost it was seen that non-mercury switches actually made a saving of $0.11 per unit. The company on an annual basis would make an $18,000 annual saving on one plant alone by this component change.

B. Amoco Corporation (a major oil company) needed to identify the cost of complying with environmental protection regulations and used one of its refineries in Yorktown, Virginia, as an experimental site. From an analysis of the financial accounts it was found that environmental costs represented 21.9% of the non-crude cost of the product (crude oil being the major cost).

This figure was six times the level previously assumed to be the environmental cost of production. The realisation of the scale of the cost led to changes in managerial policies and practices.

C. Majestic Metals Inc. of Denver, Colorado, had a problem with pollution caused by its paint-spraying machinery and practices. Through an environmental accounting exercise, the company decided to use high-volume, low-pressure (HVLP) sprayers and this reduced the cost of environmental damage (as shown by fines and rectification costs) by $40,000 per year. From a capital investment appraisal viewpoint the project gave a positive NPV over eight years of $140,000, an internal rate of return (IRR) of 906% and a discounted payback of 0.12 years – an impressive range of results in any terms.

The EPA's website has many more cases showing the impact of an environmental accounting approach.

31.19 Concept of social accounting

This is a difficult place to start because there are so many definitions of social accounting[24] – the main points are that it includes non-financial as well as financial information and addresses the needs of stakeholders other than the shareholders. Stakeholders can be broken down into three categories:

- **internal stakeholders** – managers and workers;
- **external stakeholders** – shareholders, creditors, banks and debtors;
- **related stakeholders** – society as represented by national and local government and the increasing role of pressure groups such as Amnesty International and Greenpeace.

31.19.1 Reporting at corporate level

Prior to 1975, social accounting was viewed as being in the domain of the **economist** and concerned with national income and related issues. In 1975, *The Corporate Report* gave a different definition:

> the reporting of those costs and benefits, which may or may not be quantifiable in money terms, arising from economic activities and subsequently borne or received by the community at large or particular groups not holding a direct relationship with the reporting entity.[25]

This is probably the best working definition of the topic and it establishes the first element of the social accounting concept, namely **reporting at a corporate level** and interpreting corporate in its widest sense as including all organisations of economic significance regardless of the type of organisation or the nature of ownership.

31.19.2 Accountability

The effect of the redefinition by *The Corporate Report* was to introduce the second element of our social accounting concept: accountability. The national income view was only of interest to economists and could not be related to individual company performance – *The Corporate Report* changed that. Social accounting moved into the accountants' domain and it should be the aim of accountants to learn how accountability might be achieved and to define a model against which to judge their own efforts and the efforts of others.[26]

31.19.3 Comprehensive coverage

The annual report is concerned mainly with monetary amounts or clarifying monetary issues. Despite the ASB identifying employees and the public within the user groups,[27] no standards have been issued that deal specifically with reporting to employees or the public.

Instead, the ASB prefers to assume that financial statements that meet the needs of investors will meet most of the needs of other users.[28] For all practical purposes, it disassociates itself from the needs of non-investor users by assuming that there will be more specific information that they may obtain in their dealings with the enterprise.[29]

The information needs of different categories, e.g. employees and the public, need not be identical. The provision of information of particular interest to the public has been referred to as **public interest accounting**,[30] but there is a danger that, whilst valid as an approach, it could act as a constraint on matters that might be of legitimate interest to the employee user group. For example, safety issues at a particular location might be of little interest to the public at large but of immense concern to an employee exposed to work-related radiation or asbestos. The term 'social accounting' as defined by *The Corporate Report* is seen as embracing all interests, even those of a small group.

Equally, the information needs within a category, say employees, can differ according to the level of the employees. One study identified that different levels of employee ranked the information provided about the employer differently, e.g. lower-level employees rated safety information highest, whereas higher-level employees rated organisation information highest.[31] There were also differences in opinion about the need for additional information, with the majority of lower-level but minority of higher-level employees agreeing that the social report should also contain information on corporate environmental effects.[32]

The need for social accounting to cope with both inter-group and intra-group differences was also identified in a Swedish study.[33]

31.19.4 Independent review

The degree of credibility accorded a particular piece of information is influenced by factors such as whether it is historical or deals with the future; whether appropriate techniques exist for obtaining it; whether its source causes particular concern about deliberate or unintentional bias towards a company view; whether past experience has been that the information was reasonably complete and balanced; and, finally, the extent of independent verification.[34]

Given that social accounting is complex and technically underdeveloped, that it deals with subjective areas or future events, and that it is reported on a selective basis within a report prepared by the management, it is understandable that its credibility will be called into question. Questions will be raised as to why particular items were included or omitted – after all, it is not that unusual for companies to want to hide unfavourable developments.

31.20 Background to social accounting

A brief consideration of the history of social accounting in the UK could be helpful in putting the subject into context. *The Corporate Report* (1975) was the starting point for the whole issue. This was at a time when there was the general dissatisfaction with the quality of financial reporting which had resulted in the creation of a standard-setting regulatory body (the Accounting Standards Steering Committee) and additional statutory provisions, e.g. Companies Act provisions relating to directors.

The Corporate Report was a discussion paper issued by the ASSC which represented the first UK conceptual framework. Its approach was to identify users and their information needs. It identified seven groups of user, which included employees and the public, and their information needs. However, although it identified that there were common areas of interest among the seven groups, such as assessing liquidity and evaluating management performance, it concluded that a single set of general-purpose accounts would not satisfy each group – a different conclusion from that stated by the ASB in 1991, as discussed above.[35] The conclusions reached in *The Corporate Report* were influenced by the findings of a survey of the chairmen of the 300 largest UK listed companies. They indicated a trend towards acceptance of multiple responsibilities towards groups affected by corporate decision-making and their interest as stakeholders.[36]

It was proposed in *The Corporate Report* that there should be additional reports to satisfy the needs of the other stakeholders. These included a statement of corporate objectives, a statement of future prospects, an employment report and a value added statement.

Statement of corporate objectives

Would this be the place for social accounting to start? Would this be the place for vested interests to be represented so that agreed objectives take account of the views of all stakeholders and not merely the management and, indirectly, the shareholders? At present, social accounting appears as a series of add-ons, e.g. a little on charity donations, a little on disabled recruitment policy. Corporate objectives or the mission statement are often seen as something to be handed down; could they assume a different role?

The employment report

The need for an employment report was founded on the belief that there is a trust relationship between employers and employees and an economic relationship between employment prospects and the welfare of the community. The intention was that such a report should contain statistical information relating to such matters as numbers, reasons for change, training time and costs, age and sex distribution, and health and safety.

Statement of future prospects

There has always been resistance to publishing information focusing on the future. The arguments raised against it have included competitive disadvantage and the possibility of misinterpretation because the data relate to the future and are therefore uncertain.

The writers of *The Corporate Report* nevertheless considered it appropriate to publish information on future employment and capital investment levels that could have a direct impact on employees and the local community.

Value added reports

A value added report was intended to give a different focus from the profit and loss account with its emphasis on the bottom line earnings figure. It was intended to demonstrate the interdependence of profits and payments to employees, shareholders, the government and the company via inward investment. It reflected the mood picked up from the survey of chairmen that distributable profit could no longer be regarded as the sole or prime indicator of company performance.[37]

The value added statement became a well-known reporting mechanism to measure how effectively an organisation utilised its resources and added value to its raw materials to turn them into saleable goods. Figure 31.2 is an example of a value added statement.

Several advantages have been claimed for these reports, including improving employee attitudes by reflecting a broader view of companies' objectives and responsibilities.[38]

There have also been criticisms, e.g. they are merely a restatement of information that appears in the annual report; they only report data capable of being reported in monetary terms; and the individual elements of societal benefit are limited to the traditional ones of shareholders, employees and the government, with others such as society and the consumers ignored.

There was also criticism that there was no standard so that expenditures could be aggregated or calculated to disclose a misleading picture, e.g. the inclusion of PAYE tax and welfare payments made to the government in the employee classification so that wages were shown gross whereas distributions to shareholders were shown net of tax. The effect of both was to overstate the apparent employee share and understate the government and shareholders' share.[39]

In the years immediately following the publication of *The Corporate Report*, companies published value added statements on a voluntary basis but their importance has declined. There was a move away from industrial democracy and the standard-setting regulators did not make the publication of value added statements mandatory.

Figure 31.2 Barloworld Limited value added statement for year ended 30 September 2004

R million	2004	%	2003	%
Revenue	36,673		34,603	
Paid to suppliers for materials and services	26,184		25,486	
Value added	10,489		9,117	
Income from investments*	287		274	
Total wealth created	10,776		9,391	
Wealth distribution				
Salaries, wages and other benefits (note 1)	5,993	56	5,450	58
Providers of capital	1,298	12	1,512	16
Finance cost	468		531	
Dividends paid to Barloworld Ltd shareholders	626		736	
Dividends paid to outside shareholders in subsidiaries	204		245	
Government (note 2)	1,059	10	809	9
Reinvested in group to maintain and develop operations	2,426	22	1,620	17
Depreciation	1,535		1,226	
Retained profit	814		415	
Deferred taxation	77		(21)	
	10,776	100	9,391	100
Value added ratios				
Number of employees (30 September)	25,233		22,749	
Turnover per employee (Rand)#	1,528,615		1,506,410	
Wealth created per employee (Rand)#	449,168		406,086	

Notes:

1. Salaries, wages and other benefits

Salaries, wages, overtime payments, commissions, bonuses and allowances	4,483		4,385	
Employer contributions+	1,150		1,065	
	5,593		5,450	

2. Central and local government

Current taxation	828		637	
Regional Services Council levels	39		33	
Rates and taxes paid to local authorities	62		54	
Customs duties, import surcharges and excise taxes	122		76	
Skills development levy	13		11	
South African withholding taxation			2	
Cash grants and cash subsidies granted by the government	(5)		(4)	
Gross contribution to central and local government	1,059		809	

* Includes interest received, dividend income and share of associate companies and joint ventures retained profit.

Based on average number of employees.

+ In respect of pension funds, retirement annuities, provident funds, medical aid and insurance.

31.20.1 Why *The Corporate Report* was not implemented

The Corporate Report's proposals for additional reports have not been implemented. There are a number of views as to why this was so. There is a view that the business community, despite the results of the chairmen survey, were concerned about the possibility of their reporting responsibility being extended through the report's concept of public accountability and welcomed the release of the Sandilands Report on inflation accounting which overshadowed *The Corporate Report*. There is a view that *The Corporate Report* fell short of making a significant contribution 'by virtue of its failure to select the accounting models appropriate to the informational needs of the individual user groups which it had identified'.[40]

However, the most likely reason for it not being fully implemented was the change of government. The Labour government produced a Green Paper in 1976, *Aims and Scope of Company Reports*, which endorsed much of *The Corporate Report* concept. The reaction from the business community and the Stock Exchange was hostile to any move away from the traditional stewardship concept with its obligations only to shareholders. The CBI view was that other users could ask for information, but that was no reason for companies to be required to provide it.[41] In the event, there was a change of government and the Green Paper sank without trace.

The new government supported the view of Milton Friedman, who wrote in 1962 that 'few trends could so . . . undermine the very foundations of our free society as the acceptance by corporate officials of a social responsibility other than to make as much money . . . as possible'.

Many responsible members of the business community pressed for change,[42] but the mid 1980s saw a decline in the commercial support for social accounting, as profit, dividends and growth superseded all other social goals in business. The movement continued but advocates were regarded at best as well-meaning radicals and at worst as dangerous politicised activists devoted to the destruction of the capitalist system.

By the early 1990s, interest was appearing in the commercial sector but from a free market rather than regulatory viewpoint. The thought was that socially responsible policies need not mean lower profits – in fact, quite the opposite. Given this change in perception, companies began to embrace social accounting concepts – suddenly accountants were able to make a contribution, e.g. evaluating the profit implication of crèche facilities for working mothers being provided by the employer rather than the state. There was also a growth within society in general of a socially responsible point of view which even extended to share investment decisions with the marketing of ethically sound investments.

31.21 Corporate social responsibility

Companies are increasingly recognising the importance of adopting a social, ethical and environmentally responsible approach to business activity and entering into dialogue with all groups of stakeholders. We have discussed the environmentally responsible approach above – the socially responsible approach includes a wide range of activities including the companies' dealings in the marketplace, the workplace, and the community, and in the field of human rights.

Reporting is slowly evolving from simply reporting the amount of charitable donations in the annual report to including additional activities which the company considers to be of key interest. The reporting might be brief but it gives an attractive picture of a company's social responsibility. For example, the 2001 Kingfisher Annual Report has a brief two-page section for social responsibility in which it gives information on:

- environmental issues, e.g. a commitment to sustainable forestry, winning the Business in the Environment award for energy saving; and

- social issues, e.g. from training young unemployed people to recycling electrical goods; making charitable donations that supported the Woolworth Kids First, You Can Do It and Green Grants schemes; and winning a Business in the Community award for Innovation relating to its work forming partnerships with local disability organisations.

We can see from this that community involvement can take many forms, e.g. charitable donations, gifts in kind, employee volunteering initiatives, staff secondments, and sustainable and mutually beneficial partnerships with community and voluntary organisations active in a variety of fields including education, training, regeneration, employment and homelessness.

The approach to CSR is becoming increasingly formalised with the setting up of committees reporting to the Board and more comprehensive CSR Reports.

Committees reporting to the Board

The 2004 Kingfisher Annual Report described the role of the Social Responsibility Committee whose purpose is to review progress in fulfilling the Social Responsibility Plan, including monitoring the resources required to support the Plan and ensuring that actions taken maximise the opportunity to meet the expectations of key Group stakeholders and emerging corporate governance standards (e.g. investor surveys, Turnbull, Business in the Community Survey). The seniority of the Committee members is an indication that it has significant influence in advising the board and ensuring the Plan is delivered.

CSR Reports

The following is an extract from the CSR Report accompanying the Marks & Spencer 2004 Annual Report:

What Corporate Social Responsibility means to us
Marks & Spencer has a strong tradition of CSR . . . Our founders believed that building good relationships with employees, suppliers and wider society was the best guarantee of long-term success . . . Managing CSR well will allow us to identify potential risks to the Company and respond to areas of performance where we fall behind . . . it also means we can identify opportunities to differentiate ourselves from our competitors. CSR can help us to draw shoppers to our stores, attract and retain the best staff, make us a partner of choice with suppliers and create value for our shareholders.

Their approach is built around three Principles, namely **Products, People and Places**, and a framework developed by their Board-level CSR Committee during 2002 with a detailed statement for each Principle. For example, the **Principle for Places** reads as follows:

Help make our communities good places in which to live and work
We recognise our obligations to the communities in which we trade. We were founding members of Business in the Community . . . Our relationship with communities is interdependent. Successful retailing requires economically healthy and sustainable communities . . . we provide employment and products and services and often become an important part of the fabric of the high street. We place much emphasis on our stores, their location, design, construction and activities. A 'Store of the Future' project has helped to improve the environmental standards we use to locate, build and refurbish them. Day-to-day operations are managed

within an overall compliance system that includes emergency planning, energy and water usage, health and safety, waste disposal, recycling, recovery of shopping trolleys and donations of unsold food to charities . . . We are also active in a wider sense . . . A recent development is our growing co-operation with suppliers and business partners in community programmes.

31.22 Need for comparative data

There is evidence[43] that environmental performance could be given a higher priority when analysts assess a company if there were comparable data by sector on a company's level of corporate responsibility.

We will consider two approaches that have taken place to satisfy this need for comparable data: benchmarking and comprehensive guidelines.

31.22.1 Benchmarking

There are a number of benchmarking schemes and we will consider two by way of illustration – these are the London Benchmarking Group, established in 1994, and the Impact on Society, established in December 2001.

The London Benchmarking Group[44]

The Group started in 1994 and consists of companies which join in order to measure and report their involvement in the community, which is a key part of any corporate social responsibility programme, and which have a tool to assist them effectively to assess and target their community programmes. Organisations such as Deloitte & Touche, British Airways and Lloyds TSB are members.

The scheme is concerned with corporate community involvement. It identifies three categories into which different forms of community involvement can be classified, namely, charity donations, social or community investment and commercial initiatives, and includes only contributions made over and above those that result from the basic business operations.

It uses an input/output model, putting a monetary value on the 'input' costs which include contributions made in cash, in time or in kind, together with full cost of staff involved; and collecting 'output' data on the community benefit, e.g. number who benefited, leveraged resources and benefit accruing to the business.

Impact on Society[45]

This is a website created in 2001 which provides free access to corporate social responsibility information from leading companies. It is the first time a common set of indicators against which companies can be measured has been provided, offering insight into areas such as the environment, the workplace, the community in which the company operates, the marketplace and human rights. The information ranges from relatively easy-to-measure numeric data, such as water usage, through to more complex, often perception-based information, e.g. from employee surveys. The information is then summarised into clear company profiles and can be compared and contrasted according to a range of parameters, such as specific indicators or industry sectors.

The site provides **qualitative** information for each company with key indicators as shown in Figure 31.3. It also provides quantitative information as a percentage, absolute cash value or physical volume.

Figure 31.3 Impact on Society key indicators

Indicator area	Indicators reported against
Marketplace	Advertising complaints upheld; upheld cases of anti-competitive behaviour; customer satisfaction levels; average time to pay bills to suppliers; customer retention; customer complaints about products and services; provision for customers with special needs.
Environment	Overall energy consumption; water usage; quantity of waste produced by weight; upheld cases of prosecution for environmental offences; CO_2/greenhouse gas emissions; percentage of waste recycled; environmental impact; benefits or costs of company's core products and services; environmental impact over the supply chain.
Workplace	Workforce profile by race, gender, disability and age; number of legal non-compliances with health and safety and equal opportunities legislation; upheld cases of corrupt or unprofessional behaviour; staff turnover; value of staff training, perception measures of the company by its employees; absenteeism rates; pay and conditions compared to local equivalent average; work profile compared to local community profile.
Community	Cash value of support as percentage of pre-tax profits; estimated combined value of staff company time; gifts in kind and management time; leverage of other resources; perception measure of company as a good neighbour.
Human rights	Existence of confidential grievance procedures for staff; proportion of suppliers or partners screened for human rights compliance; proportion of suppliers or partners meeting company's own standards on human rights; perception by staff and local community of company's performance on human rights; wage rates.

An illustration of the scheme applied to Marks & Spencer for human rights and the environment is as follows:

Human rights

Particularly applicable to countries with operations or suppliers in developing countries.

The issues measured under human rights largely apply to companies who operate in, or buy from suppliers in, developing countries. What does or does not constitute a human right is always under some debate. However, the Universal Declaration of Human Rights is a main reference point. Before they can report that they definitely fall outside the scope of this section, companies need to answer a 'gatekeeper' question. Unless they can answer that they are definitely not exposed to human rights issues, they need to do more research and report against this indicator area.

The human rights indicators are being developed further: in consultation with non-governmental organisations and businesses engaged in human rights issues. While some companies have chosen to report, others await more fully developed indicators in this area.

Environment

Use of recycled material

Percentage of material used from recycled sources

Non-weight bearing food product cardboard packaging

Recycled cardboard
2000   60%
1999   50%
1998   25%

Many types of packaging use recycled materials as a matter of course, e.g. glass bottles, tin cans and transport boxes. Where we believe that the use of recycled materials is the best environmental option and that we are able to achieve improvements we set targets. We have been working to increase our use of recycled cardboard (made from at least 50% post-consumer waste) for all our non-weight bearing food product packaging.

31.23 International initiatives towards triple bottom line reporting

There are no mandatory standards for sustainability reporting but there are Sustainability Reporting Guidelines which were issued in 2000 by the Global Reporting Initiative Steering Committee on which a number of international organisations are represented including ACCA, the Institute of Social and Ethical Accountability, the New Economics Foundation and SustainAbility Ltd from the UK.

31.23.1 The Global Reporting Initiative (GRI)

The GRI has a mission to develop global sustainability reporting guidelines for voluntary use by organisations reporting on the three linked elements of sustainability, namely, the economic, environmental and social dimensions of their activities, products and services.

Economic dimension

This includes financial and non-financial information on R&D expenditure, investment in the workforce, current staff expenditure and outputs in terms of labour productivity.

Environmental dimension

This includes any adverse impact on air, water, land, biodiversity and human health by an organisation's production processes, products and services.

Social dimension

This includes information on health and safety and recognition of rights, e.g. human rights for both employees and outsourced employees.

31.23.2 How will the guidelines assist organisations?

The aim is to assist organisations to report information that complements existing reporting standards and is consistent, comparable and easy to understand so that:

● Parties contemplating a relationship such as assessing investment risk, obtaining goods or services or entering into any other commercial partnership arrangement will have available to them a clear picture of the human and ecological impact of the business so that they can make an informed decision.

● Management have the means to develop information systems to provide the basis for monitoring performance, making inter-company comparisons and reporting to stakeholders.

31.23.3 What information should appear in an ideal GRI report?

There are six parts to the ideal GRI report:

1 CEO statement – describing key elements of the report.

2 A profile – providing an overview of the organisation and the scope of the report (it could for example be dealing only with environmental information) which sets the context for the next four parts.

3 Executive summary and key indicators – to assist stakeholders to assess trends and make inter-company comparisons.

4 Vision and strategy – a statement of the vision for the future and how that integrates economic, environmental and social performance.

5 Policies, organisation and systems – an overview of the governance and management systems to implement this vision with a discussion of how stakeholders have been engaged. This reflects the GRI view that the report should not be made in isolation but there should have been appropriate inputs from stakeholders.

6 Performance review.

   The GRI issued Draft Sustainability Reporting Guidelines in 2006 (www.grig3.org/guide-lines/overviewg.html). The Guidelines consist of principles for defining report content and ensuring the quality of reported information as well as standard disclosures comprising performance indicators and other disclosure items. There is also detailed guidance to assist users in applying the Guidelines in the form of technical protocols that are being developed on indicator measurement, e.g. specific indicators for energy use, child labour and health and safety.

31.23.4 How are GRI reports to be verified?

CSR Reports are now able to be verified by independent, competent and impartial external assurance providers. The assurance providers now have a standard – the AA1000 Assurance Standard (www.accountability.org.uk) to provide a framework for their work. This Standard was launched in 2003 to address the need for a single approach to deal effectively with the qualitative as well as quantitative data that makes up sustainability performance plus the systems that underpin the data and performance. It is designed to complement the GRI Reporting Guidelines and other standardised or company-specific approaches to disclosure. It requires reports against three Assurance Principles which are Materiality, Completeness and Responsiveness, as well as statements as to how conclusions were reached and on the independence of the assurance providers.

As an example, in the 2004 Annual Report of O_2 Ernst & Young, who were the assurance providers, stated that they were forming a conclusion on matters such as (a) Materiality – whether O_2 had provided a balanced representation of material issues concerning O_2's corporate responsibility performance, (b) Completeness – whether O_2 had complete information on which to base a judgement of what was material for inclusion in the Report, and (c) Responsiveness – whether O_2 had responded to stakeholder concerns. They also explained what they did to form their conclusions:

What we did to form our conclusions
There are currently no statutory requirements in the UK in relation to the independent review of corporate responsibility reports. The AA1000 Assurance Standard sets out principles for social and environmental report assurance. We have been asked by O_2 to set out our conclusions by reference to the assurance principles described in the AA1000 Assurance Standard.

31.23.5 Will there be any impact on matters that are currently disclosed?

There may be an overlap with existing disclosures in the OFR and there is also a pressure for additional information to permit a greater understanding of future risks, e.g. the GRI acknowledges that in financial reporting terms a going concern is one that is considered to be financially viable for at least the next financial year but seeks additional information such as:

- The extent to which significant internal and external operational, financial, compliance, and other risks are identified and assessed on an ongoing basis. Significant risks may, for example, include those related to market, credit, liquidity, technological, legal, health, safety, environmental and reputation issues.

- The likely impact of prospective legislation, e.g. product, environmental, fiscal or employee-related.

31.23.6 The nature of the accountant's involvement

There will be inputs from accountants in each of the three elements with a greater degree of quantification at present for the economic and environmental dimensions. For example:
The economic dimension may require economic indicators such as:

- profit: segmental gross margin, net profit, EBIT, return on average capital employed;
- intangible assets: ratio of market valuation to book value;
- investments: human capital, R&D, debt/equity ratio;
- wages and benefits: totals by country;
- labour productivity: levels and changes by job category;
- community development: jobs by type and country showing absolute figures and net change;
- suppliers: value of goods and services outsourced, performance in meeting credit terms.

The environmental dimension may require environmental indicators such as:

- products and services: major issues, e.g. disposal of waste, packaging practices, percentage of product reclaimed after use;
- suppliers: supplier issues identified through stakeholder consultation, e.g. forest stewardship;
- travel: objectives and targets, e.g. product distribution, fleet operation, quantitative estimates of miles travelled by transport type.

Social dimensions may require social indicators such as:

- quality of management: employee retention rates, ratio of jobs offered to jobs accepted, ranking as an employer in surveys;
- health and safety: reportable cases, lost days, absentee rate, investment per worker in injury prevention;
- wages and benefits: ratio of lowest wage to local cost of living, health and pension benefits provided;
- training and education: ratio of training budget to annual operating cost, programmes to encourage worker participation in decision making;
- freedom of association: grievance procedures in place, number and types of legal action concerning anti-union practices.

Summary

Sustainability is now recognised as having three elements. These are the economic, environmental and social. It is recognised that advances in environmental and social improvement are dependent on the existence of an economically viable organisation.

As environmental and social reporting evolves there are proposals being made to harmonise the content and disclosure. This can be seen with the publication of the triple bottom line, the Connected Framework and the IFAC Sustainability Framework.

In addition there are benchmark schemes which allow stakeholders to compare corporate social reports and evaluate an individual company's performance. The management systems that are being developed within companies should result in data that are consistent and reliable and capable of external verification. The benchmarking systems should assist in both identifying best practice and establishing relevant performance indicators.

Corporate social reporting is coming of age. Initially there were fears that it would add to costs and there are present concerns that it is diverting too much of a finance director's attention away from commercial and stragetic planning. However, it is becoming generally recognised that a company's reputation and its attractiveness to potential investors are influenced by a company's behaviour and attitude to corporate governance and sustainability.

Companies are reacting positively to the need to be good corporate citizens and it is interesting to see the developments around the world where sustainability, good corporate governance and strategic planning are merging into an integrated system. This will take time but companies are taking up the challenge to be transparent and innovative in their financial reporting. Award schemes are encouraging the spread of best practice. Companies are integrating their non-financial narrative and using the Internet to get their message out to a wider public.

The time has passed since corporate governance, sustainabilty, environmental and social reporting were seen purely as a PR exercise.

REVIEW QUESTIONS

1 Discuss the relevance of corporate social reports to an existing and potential investor.

2 Obtain a copy of the environmental report of a company that has taken part in the ACCA Awards for Sustainability Reporting and critically discuss from an investor's and public interest viewpoint.

3 'Charters and guidelines help make reports reliable but inhibit innovation and reduce their relevance.' Discuss.

4 Discuss the implications of the Global Reporting Initiative for the accountancy profession.

5 Discuss *The Corporate Report*'s relevance to modern business; identify changes that would improve current reporting practice and the conditions necessary for such changes to become mandatory.

6 (a) Explain the term 'stakeholders' in a corporate context.

   (b) 'Social accounting recognises all *Corporate Report* users as stakeholders.' Discuss.

7 Discuss the value added concept, giving examples, and ways to improve the statement.

8 Outline the arguments for and against a greater role for the audit function in corporate social reporting.

9 (a) 'Human assets are incapable of being valued.' Discuss.

(b) Football clubs have followed various policies in the way in which they include players within their accounts. For example, some clubs capitalise players, as shown by a 1992 Touche Ross survey:[46]

Club	Value	Basis	Which players
	£m		
Tottenham Hotspur	9.8	Cost	Those purchased
Sheffield United	8.7	Manager's valuation	Whole squad
Portsmouth	7.0	Directors' valuation	Whole squad
Derby County	6.5	Cost	Those purchased

Other clubs disclose squad value in notes to the accounts or in the directors' report:

Manchester United	24.0	Independent valuation
Charlton Athletic	4.1	Directors' valuation
Millwall	11.0	Manager's valuation

Discuss arguments for and against capitalising players as assets. Explain the effect on the profit and loss account if players are not capitalised.

10 (a) Examine the recent financial press to identify examples of a failure to meet information needs in respect of an area of public interest.

(b) Obtain a set of accounts from a public listed company and assess the success in meeting the needs of the traditional users. Repeat the process for non-traditional users and discuss how you could improve the situation (i) marginally, (ii) significantly.

11 Discuss the impact of the following groups on the accounting profession:

(a) Environmental groups;

(b) Customers;

(c) Workforce;

(d) Ethical investors.

12 Nissan, the Japanese car company, decided that 'any environmentalism should pay for itself and for every penny you spend you must save a penny. You can spend as many pennies as you like as long as other environmental actions save an equal number.'[47] Discuss the significance of this for each of the stakeholders.

13 (a) 'Accounting should contribute to the protection of the environment.' Discuss whether this is a proper role for accounting and outline ways in which it could.

(b) Outline, with reasons, your ideas for an environmental report for a company of your choice.

(c) Discuss the arguments against the adoption of environmental accounting.

14 (a) Obtain the annual reports of companies that claim to be environmentally aware and assess whether these reports and accounts reflect the claim. The various oil, chemical and pharmaceutical companies are useful for this.

(b) Look at your own organisation/institution, outline the possible environmental issues and discuss how these could or should be disclosed in the annual report.

EXERCISES

An extract from the solution is provided in the Appendix at the end of the text for exercises marked with an asterisk (*).

* **Question 1**

The following information relates to the Plus Factors Group plc for the years to 30 September 20X8 and 20X9:

	Notes	20X9 £000	20X8 £000
Associated company share of profit		10.9	10.7
Auditors' remuneration		12.2	11.9
Payables for materials			
At beginning of year		1,109.1	987.2
At end of year		1,244.2	1,109.1
Receivables			
At beginning of year		1,422.0	1,305.0
At end of year		1,601.0	1,422.0
11% debentures	1	500.0	600.0
Depreciation		113.7	98.4
Employee benefits paid		109.9	68.4
Hire of plant, machinery and vehicles	2	66.5	367.3
Materials paid for in year		3,622.9	2,971.4
Minority interest in profit of the year		167.2	144.1
Other overheads incurred		1,012.4	738.3
Pensions and pension contributions paid		319.8	222.2
Profit before taxation		1,437.4	1,156.4
Provision for corporation tax		464.7	527.9
Salaries and wages		1,763.8	1,863.0
Sales	3	9,905.6	8,694.1
Shares at nominal value			
Ordinary at 25p each fully paid	4	2,500.0	2,000.0
7% preference at £1 each fully paid	4	500.0	200.0
Inventories of materials			
Beginning of year		804.1	689.7
End of year		837.8	804.1

Ordinary dividends were declared as follows:

Interim   1.12 pence per share (20X8, 1.67p)
Final   3.57 pence per share (20X8, 2.61p)
Average number of employees was 196 (20X8, 201)

Notes:

1   £300,000 of debentures were redeemed at par on 31 March 20X9 and £200,000 new debentures at the same rate of interest were issued at £98 for each £100 nominal value on the same date. The new debentures are due to be redeemed in five years' time.

2   This is the amount for inclusion in the statement of comprehensive income.

3   All the groups' sales are subject to value added tax at 15% and the figures given include such tax. All other figures are exclusive of value added tax. This VAT rate has been increased to 17.5% and may be subject to future changes, but for the purposes of this question the theory and workings remain the same irrespective of the rate.

4   All shares have been in issue throughout the year.

The statement of value added is available for 20X8 and the 20X9 statement needs to be completed.

	Workings	£000	
Turnover	1	7,560.1	
Less: Bought-in materials and services	2	4,096.4	
Value added by group		3,463.7	
Share of profits of associated company		10.7	
		3,474.4	
Applied in the following ways			
To pay employees	3	2,153.6	62.0%
To pay providers of capital	4	566.5	16.3%
To pay government		527.9	15.2%
To provide for maintenance and expansion of assets	5	226.4	6.50%
		3,474.4	100.0%

Workings

1 *Turnover*

Sales inclusive of VAT	8,694.1
VAT at 15%	1,134.0
	7,560.1

2 *Bought-in materials and services*

Cost of materials	
Creditors at end of year	1,109.1
Add: Payments in year	2,971.4
	4,080.5
Less: Payables at beginning of year	987.2
Materials purchased in year	3,093.3
Add: Opening inventory	689.7
Less: Closing inventory	(804.1)
Materials used	2,978.9
Add: Cost of bought-in services	
Auditors' remuneration	11.9
Hire of plant, machinery and vehicles	367.3
Other overheads	738.3
	4,096.4

	£000
3 *To pay employees*	
Benefits paid	68.4
Pensions and pension contributions	222.2
Salaries and wages	1,863.0
	2,153.6
4 *To pay providers of capital*	
Debenture interest	
11% of £600,000	66.0
Dividends	
Preference 20X8 7% of £200,000	14.0
Ordinary 20X8 8 million shares at 4.28p	342.4
Minority interest	144.1
	566.5
5 *To provide for maintenance and expansion of assets*	
Profit before tax	1,156.4
Less:	
tax	(527.9)
minority interest	(144.1)
dividends	(356.4)
Retained profits	128.0
Depreciation	98.4
	226.4

Required:

(a) Prepare a statement of value added for the year to 30 September 20X9. Include a percentage breakdown of the distribution of value added.

(b) Produce ratios related to employees' interests based on the statement in (a) and explain how they might be of use.

(c) Explain briefly what the difficulties are of measuring and reporting financial information in the form of a statement of value added.

Question 2

David Mark is a sole trader who owns and operates supermarkets in each of three villages near Ousby. He has drafted his own accounts for the year ended 31 May 20X4 for each of the branches. They are as follows:

	Arton		Blendale		Clifearn	
	£	£	£	£	£	£
Sales		910,800		673,200		382,800
Cost of sales		633,100		504,900		287,100
Gross profit		277,700		168,300		95,700
Less: Expenses:						
David Mark's salary	10,560		10,560		10,560	
Other salaries and wages	143,220		97,020		78,540	
Rent			19,800			
Rates	8,920		5,780		2,865	
Advertising	2,640		2,640		2,640	
Delivery van expenses	5,280		5,280		5,280	
General expenses	11,220		3,300		1,188	
Telephone	2,640		1,980		1,584	
Wrapping materials	7,920		3,960		2,640	
Depreciation:						
Fixtures	8,220		4,260		2,940	
Vehicle	3,000	203,620	3,000	157,580	3,000	111,237
Net profit/(loss)		74,080		10,720		(15,537)

The figures for the year ended 31 May 20X4 follow the pattern of recent years. Because of this, David Mark is proposing to close the Clifearn supermarket immediately.

David Mark employs 12 full-time and 20 part-time staff. His recruitment policy is based on employing one extra part-time assistant for every £30,000 increase in branch sales. His staff deployment at the moment is as follows:

	Arton	Blendale	Clifearn
Full-time staff (including managers)	6	4	2
Part-time staff	8	6	6

Peter Gaskin, the manager of the Clifearn supermarket, asks David to give him another year to make the supermarket profitable. Peter has calculated that he must cover £125,500 expenses out of his gross profit in the year ended 31 May 20X5 in order to move into profitability. His calculations include extra staff costs and all other extra costs.

Additional information:

1 General advertising for the business as a whole is controlled by David Mark. This costs £3,960 per annum. Each manager spends a further £1,320 advertising his own supermarket locally.

2 The delivery vehicle is used for deliveries from the Arton supermarket only.

3 David Mark has a central telephone switchboard which costs £1,584 rental per annum. Each supermarket is charged for all calls actually made. For the year ended 31 May 20X4 these amounted to:

Arton	£2,112
Blendale	£1,452
Clifearn	£1,056

Required:

(a) A report addressed to David Mark advising him whether to close Clifearn supermarket. Your report should include a detailed financial statement based on the results for the year ended 31 May 20X4 relating to the Clifearn branch.

(b) Calculate the increased turnover and extra staff needed if Peter's suggestion is implemented.

(c) Comment on the social implications for the residents of Clifearn if (i) David Mark closes the supermarket, (ii) Peter Gaskin's recommendation is undertaken.

* Question 3

(a) You are required to prepare a value added statement to be included in the corporate report of Hythe plc for the year ended 31 December 20X6, including the comparatives for 20X5, using the information given below:

	20X6	20X5
	£000	£000
Non-current assets (net book value)	3,725	3,594
Trade receivables	870	769
Trade payables	530	448
14% debentures	1,200	1,080
6% preference shares	400	400
Ordinary shares (£1 each)	3,200	3,200
Sales	5,124	4,604
Materials consumed	2,934	2,482
Wages	607	598
Depreciation	155	144
Fuel consumed	290	242
Hire of plant and machinery	41	38
Salaries	203	198
Auditors' remuneration	10	8
Corporation tax provision	402	393
Ordinary share dividend	9p	8p
Number of employees	40	42

(b) Although value added statements were recommended by *The Corporate Report*, as yet there is no accounting standard related to them. Explain what a value added statement is and provide reasons as to why you think it has not yet become mandatory to produce such a statement as a component of current financial statements either through a Financial Reporting Standard or company law.

Question 4

Gettry Doffit plc is an international company with worldwide turnover of £26 million. The activities of the company include the breaking down and disposal of noxious chemicals at a specialised plant in the remote Scottish countryside. During the preparation of the financial statements for the year ended 31 March 20X5, it was discovered that:

1 Quantities of chemicals for disposals on site at the year-end included:

(A) Axylotl peroxide 40,000 gallons

(B) Pterodactyl chlorate 35 tons

Chemical A is disposed of for a South Korean company, which was invoiced for 170 million won on 30 January 20X5, for payment in 120 days. It is estimated that the costs of disposal will not exceed £75,000. £60,000 of costs have been incurred at the year-end.

Chemical B is disposed of for a British company on a standard contract for 'cost of disposal plus 35%', one month after processing. At the year-end the chemical has been broken down into harmless by-products at a cost of £77,000. The by-products, which belong to Gettry Doffit plc, are worth £2,500.

2 To cover against exchange risks, the company entered into two forward contracts on 30 January 20X5:

No. 03067 Sell 170 million won at 1,950 won = £1: 31 May 20X5
No. 03068 Buy $70,000 at $1.60 = £1: 31 May 20X5

Actual sterling exchange rates were:

	won	$
30 January 20X5	1,900	1.70
31 March 20X5	2,000	1.38
30 April 20X5 (today)	2,100	1.80

The company often purchases a standard chemical used in processing from a North American company, and the dollars will be applied towards this purpose.

3 The company entered into a contract to import a specialised chemical used in the breaking down of magnesium perambulate from a Nigerian company which demanded the raising of an irrevocable letter of credit for £65,000 to cover 130 tons of the chemical. By 31 March 20X5 bills of lading for 60 tons had been received and paid for under the letter of credit. It now appears that the total needed for the requirements of Gettry Doffit plc for the foreseeable future is only 90 tons.

4 On 16 October 20X4 Gettry Doffit plc entered into a joint venture as partners with Dumpet Andrunn plc to process perfidious recalcitrant (PR) at the Gettry Doffit plc site using Dumpet Andrunn plc's technology. Unfortunately, a spillage at the site on 15 April 20X5 has led to claims being filed against the two companies for £12 million. A public inquiry has been set up, to assess the cause of the accident and to determine liability, which the finance director of Gettry Doffit plc fears will be, at the very least, £3 million.

Required:
Discuss how these matters should be reflected in the financial statements of Gettry Doffit plc as on and for the year ended 31 March 20X5.

Question 5

Examine the EPA's website (www.epa.gov/epahome/aboutepa.htm) and prepare one of the cases as a presentation to the group showing clearly how environmental accounting was used and the results of the exercise.

Question 6

The following items have been extracted from the accounts:

	2005 (€m)	2004 (€m)
Other income	844	980
Cost of materials	25,694	24,467
Financial income	−188	54
Depreciation/amortisation	4,207	3,589
Providers of finance	1,351	1,059
Retained	1,815	1,823
Revenues	46,656	44,335
Government	1,590	1,794
Other expenses	4,925	5,093
Shareholders	424	419
Employees	7,306	7,125

Required:

(a) Prepare a Value Added Statement showing % for each year and % change

(b) Draft a note for inclusion in the Annual Report commenting on the Statement you have prepared.

References

1 M. Friedman, *Capitalism and Freedom*, University of Chicago Press, 1962, p. 133.
2 www.wbcsd.org/templates/TemplateWBCSD5/layout.asp?type=p&MenuId=MTE0OQ
3 J. Elkington, *Cannibals With Forks: The Triple Bottom Line of 21st Century Business*, Capstone, 1997.
4 www.johnelkington.com/TBL-elkington-chapter.pdf.
5 www.sustainabilityatwork.org.uk/strategy/report/0.
6 web.ifac.org/sustainability-framework/ip-introduction.
7 S.J. Gray and C.B. Roberts, *Voluntary Information Disclosure and the British Multinationals: Corporate Perceptions of Costs and Benefits, International Pressures for Accounting Change*, Prentice Hall, 1989, p. 117.
8 AICPA, *The Measurement of Corporate Social Performance*, 1977, p. 4.
9 C. Lehman, *Accounting's Changing Roles in Social Conflict*, Markus Weiner Publishing, 1992, p. 64.
10 *Ibid.*, p. 17.
11 *This Common Inheritance*, Government White Paper, 1990.
12 KPMG Peat Marwick McLintock, *Environmental Considerations in Acquiring*, Corporate Finance Briefing, 17 May 1991.
13 M. Jones, 'The cost of cleaning up', *Certified Accountant*, May 1995, p. 47.
14 M. Campanale, 'Cost or opportunity', *Certified Accountant*, November 1991, p. 32.
15 See http://www.iasplus.com/resource/0105euroenv.pdf
16 See www.unep.org
17 See http://ec.europa.eu/environment/emas/index_en.htm
18 See www.iccwbo.org
19 See www.cefic.be/
20 See http://ec.europa.eu/environment/newprg/
21 See www.ceaa-acve.ca/aboutus.htm

22 See www.rabnet.com/
23 See www.fee.be/issues/other.htm#Sustainability
24 M.R. Matthews and M.H.B. Perera, *Accounting Theory and Development*, Chapman and Hall, 1991, p. 350.
25 Accounting Standards Steering Committee, *The Corporate Report*, 1975.
26 R. Gray, D. Owen and K. Maunders, *Corporate Social Reporting*, Prentice Hall, 1987, p. 75.
27 ASB, *Statement of Principles: The Objective of Financial Statements*, 1991, para. 9.
28 *Ibid.*, para. 10.
29 *Ibid.*, para. 11.
30 F. Okcabol and A. Tinker, 'The market for positive theory: deconstructing the theory for excuses', *Advances in Public Interest Accounting*, vol. 3, 1990.
31 H. Sebreuder, 'Employees and the corporate social report: the Dutch case', in S.J. Gray (ed.), *International Accounting and Transnational Decisions*, Butterworth, 1983, p. 287.
32 *Ibid.*, p. 289.
33 *Ibid.*, p. 287.
34 AICPA, *op. cit.*, p. 243.
35 *Statement of Principles, op. cit.*
36 R. Gray, D. Owen and K. Maunders, *op. cit.*, p. 44.
37 *Ibid.*
38 S.J. Gray and K.T. Maunders, *Value Added Reporting: Uses and Measurement*, ACCA, 1980; B. Underwood and P.J. Taylor, *Accounting Theory and Policy Making*, Heinemann, 1985, p. 298.
39 *Ibid.*, p. 174.
40 M. Davies, R. Patterson and A. Wilson, *UK GAAP* (4th edition), Ernst & Young, 1994, p. 71.
41 R. Gray, D. Owen and K. Maunders, *op. cit.*, p. 48.
42 R.W. Perks and R.H. Gray, 'Corporate social reporting – an analysis of objectives', *British Accounting Review*, 1978, vol. 10(2), pp. 43–59.
43 Business in the Environment, *Investing in the Future*, May 2001.
44 See www.lbg-online.net/
45 See www.iosreporting.org
46 R. Bruce, *The Independent*, 25 October 1993, p. 29.
47 M. Brown, 'Greening the bottom line', *Management Today*, July 1995, p. 73.

Bibliography

The following references have been helpful for students carrying out assignments in the developing areas of environmental and social reporting:

Association of British Insurers, *Investing in Social Responsibility – Risks and Opportunities*, London: Association of British Insurers, 2001.
C.A. Adams, W.-Y. Hill and C.B. Roberts, 'Corporate social reporting practices in Western Europe: legitimating corporate behaviour?', *British Accounting Review*, vol. 30, no. 1, 1998, pp. 1–22.
C.C. Adams, A. Coutts and G. Harte, 'Corporate equal opportunities (non-) disclosure', *British Accounting Review*, vol. 27, no. 2, 1995, pp. 87–108.
P. Bartram, 'Go green, not into the red', *Accountancy Age*, 31 October 2002, p. 15.
J. Bebbington, 'Sustainable development: a review of the international development business and accounting literature', *Accounting Forum*, vol. 25, no. 2, 2001, pp. 128–157.
J. Bebbington and I. Thomson, 'Commentary on: Some thoughts on social and environmental accounting education', *Accounting Education: An international journal*, vol. 10, no. 4, 2001, pp. 353-355.
F. Birkin, P. Edwards and D. Woodward, 'Some Evidence on Executives' Views of Corporate Social Responsibility', *British Accounting Review*, vol. 33, 2001, pp. 357–397.
J.H. Blokdijk and F. Drieenhuizen, 'The environment and the audit profession – a Dutch research study', *The European Accounting Review*, December 1992, pp. 437–443.

K. Bondy, D. Matten and J. Moon, 'The adoption of voluntary codes of conduct in MNCs – a three countries comparative study', *Business and Society Review*, vol. 109, no. 4, 2004, pp. 449–478.

K. Bondy, D. Matten and J. Moon, 'Codes of conduct as a tool for sustainable governance in MNCs', in S. Benn and D. Dunphy (eds.) *Corporate Governance and Sustainability: Challenges for Theory and Practice*, Routledge, 2006.

W. Chapple and J. Moon, 'Corporate social responsibility (CSR) in Asia: a seven country study of CSR website reporting', *Business and Society*, vol. 44, no. 4, 2005, pp. 115–136.

Commission of the European Communities, *Commission Recommendation of 30 May 2001 on the Recognition, Measurement and Disclosure of Environmental Issues in the Annual Accounts and Annual Reports of Companies*, Luxembourg: OOPEC, 2001.

'Corporate social responsibility', Guidance for the Financial Services Sector, www.abi.org.uk

A. Crane, D. Matten and J. Moon, *Corporations and Citizenship*, UK, Cambridge University Press, 2006.

D. Crowther, *Social and Environmental Accounting*, Harlow: Financial Times Prentice Hall, 2000, p. 109 (Financial Times Executive Briefings), ISBN: 0273650920.

Deloitte & Touche, *Accounting for Carbon under the UK Emissions Trading Scheme – Discussion Paper*, London: Deloitte & Touche, 2002.

C. Evans, 'Sustainability: the bottom line', *Accountancy*, vol. 131, no. 1313, January 2003, p. 16.

R. Gray, J. Bebbington, D. Walters and M. Houldin (eds.), *Accounting for the Environment*, Paul Chapman Publishing, 1993.

R. Gray, D. Owen and C. Adams, *Accounting and Accountability: Changes and Challenges in Corporate Social and Environmental Reporting*, Prentice Hall, 1996.

R. Gray, J. Bebbington and M. Houldin, *Accounting for the Environment* (2nd edition), London: Sage Publications, 2001.

D. Hawkins, *Corporate Social Responsibility: Balancing Tomorrow's Sustainability and Today's Profitability*, Palgrave MacMillan, 2006.

A. Henriques and J. Richardson, *The Triple Bottom Line: does it all add up?*, Earthscan, 2004.

R. Howes, *Environmental Cost Accounting: An introduction and practical guide*, London: CIMA, 2002.

M.J. Jones, 'Accounting for biodiversity', *British Accounting Review*, vol. 28, no. 4, 1996, pp. 281–304.

B. O'Dwyer, *The State of Corporate Environmental Reporting in Ireland*, London: Certified. Accountants Educational Trust for the Association of Chartered Certified Accountants, 2001, p. 47 (Research Report 69).

D. Owen (ed.), *Green Reporting: Accountancy and the Challenge of the Nineties*, Thompson Business Press, 1992.

L.S. Paine, *Value Shift – why companies must merge social and financial imperatives to achieve superior performance*, New York: McGraw-Hill, 2002.

PricewaterhouseCoopers, *The Politics of Responsible Business – a survey of political and business opinion on corporate social responsibility*, London: PricewaterhouseCoopers in association with the Industry and Parliament Trust, 2001.

J. Rayner and W. Raven (eds.), *Corporate Social Responsibility Monitor*, London: Gee, 2002, 1 vol., looseleaf, updated.

R. Roslender and J.R. Dyson, 'Accounting for the worth of employees: a new look at an old problem', *British Accounting Review*, vol. 24, no. 4, 1992, pp. 311–330.

C.A. Tilt, 'Environmental policies of major companies: Australian evidence', *British Accounting Review*, vol. 29, no. 4, 1997, pp. 367–394.

T. Tinker and T. Puxy, *Policing Accounting Knowledge: The Market for Excuses Affair*, Paul Chapman Publishing, 1995.

J.S. Toms, *Environmental Management, Environmental Accounting and Financial Performance*, London: Chartered Institute of Management Accountants, 2000.

Ethics for accountants

32.1 Introduction

The main purpose of this chapter is to describe the use of ethical codes in business and in the accounting profession.

> ### Objectives
>
> By the end of the chapter, you should be able to:
>
> - discuss the nature of business ethics;
> - describe two approaches to the design of ethical codes;
> - discuss the role of ethics in business;
> - discuss ethical issues raised for accountants;
> - discuss the growth of voluntary standards.

32.2 What do we mean by 'ethics'?

The issue of ethics is at the very centre of all societies. Every society, such as a nation, must operate according to some ethical guidelines, however idiosyncratic or singular they may seem to outsiders – without such guidelines the society would lapse into anarchy and eventual collapse. This also applies to sub-societies, e.g. a family, a group of friends or even a business organisation, and in this chapter we introduce the student of accounting to the basics of ethics as they could be applied to business.

In any study a good starting point is the production of a working definition of the issue under consideration. The *Oxford English Dictionary* has one of the more accessible definitions of ethics. It states four possible views of ethics:

> Ethics can be defined as (i) the science of morals; (ii) moral principles; (iii) a philosophy **or (iv) a code**.

In this chapter we will adopt the fourth definition of ethics as **an ethical code**, i.e. we will concentrate on the bureaucratic view of how to operate ethics in practice. The other three views are more properly the domain of philosophers as they are really concerned with what ethics should be.

32.3 The nature of business ethics

Business ethics refers to the relationship of a business to three significant 'environments' or 'levels'. Each business seeks for a harmonisation (or even a compromise) between the three levels of ethics which are traditionally viewed as follows:

1 The macro level

The macro ethical guidelines applied to a business in the national and international context are usually the result of political, cultural, legal and religious pressures.

2 The organisational level

The organisational ethical guidelines are the ethics specific to an organisation. In many texts they are referred to as 'corporate social responsibility'. The guidelines may be of long duration, e.g. the ethics of the original founders of the organisation (such as the Co-operative Wholesale Movement or the John Lewis Partnership) or short duration, e.g. the ethical beliefs of the current senior managers of the business and of the current trading partners in the industrial sector within which the organisation operates. For example, is it ethical for a large business to delay paying small business suppliers to preserve their own cash flow and possibly lead to the insolvency of the supplier?

It is not, however, a question of large versus small. The Code of Ethics recommended by the Institute of Business Ethics for SMEs[1] states 'Stick to your agreed terms of payment' as one of the practical rules for good business conduct.

3 The individual level

Individual ethical guidelines or personal ethics refers to the ethics of each individual in the organisation. These are naturally the result of a much more varied set of influences or pressures. As an individual each of us 'enjoys' a series of ethical pressures or influences including the following:

● parents – the first and, according to many authors, the most crucial influence on our ethical guidelines;

● family – the *extended* family which is common in Eastern societies (aunts, uncles, grand-parents and so on) can have a significant impact on personal ethics; the *nuclear* family which is more common in Western societies (just parent(s) and siblings) can be equally as important but more narrowly focused;

● social group – the ethics of our 'class' (either actual or aspirational) can be a major influence;

● peer group – the ethics of our 'equals' (again either actual or aspirational) can be another major influence;

● religion – ethics based in religion are more important in some cultures, e.g. Islamic societies have some detailed ethics demanded of believers as well as major guidelines for business ethics. However, even in supposedly secular cultures, individuals are influenced by religious ethics;

● culture – this is also a very effective formulator of an individual's ethics;

● professional – when an individual becomes part of a professional body then they are subject to the ethics of the professional body.

How do professional ethics differ from those arising from parents and peers?

The essential difference is that the ethics handbook which governs the behaviour of all staff in an organisation are more likely to be formally codified. A code of behaviour may be written as a formal Statement of Professional Ethics or subsumed within the staff. The fact that the Code is formally specified means that it is capable of being policed with information systems in place to assist monitoring and enforcement.

Harmonisation

We have seen above that 'business' has a complex 'web' of relationships with various parties each operating with their own ethics guidelines. The task of the business is therefore to ensure effective operations whilst meeting the various ethical demands of all interested parties.

32.4 Ethical codes for businesses

There are two approaches to defining an ethical code, namely, the positivist and normative approaches.

32.4.1 The rationale for the positivist approach

This places emphasis on the preparation of a formal, written ethical code for the guidance of all employees within an organisation. Such an approach is to be expected as, in all control models, it is considered to be essential to have a fixed, rigid standard against which to measure performance. Any ambiguities of performance measurement can lead to disputes and confusion. This is especially true with ethics as the term has a variety of meanings and constructs within the mind of each individual. It is, therefore, hardly surprising that a business tries to produce a 'hard copy' of ethics for the use of all interested parties.

Diageo, for example, has a Conduct (CoBC), which is a code of conduct and ethics applicable to all directors and employees of the company containing specific provisions relating to compliance with legal and regulatory requirements, conflicts of interest, maintenance of accurate records and the reporting of financial information in an accurate and timely manner.

The Company has also, in addition, adopted a Code of Ethics[2] specifically for its Chief Executive Officer (CEO), Chief Financial Officer (CFO) and Other Senior Financial Officers. This includes, amongst other requirements:

Honest and ethical conduct

The Senior Officers owe a duty to the Company to advance the Company's business interests when the opportunity to do so arises . . . prohibited from taking a business opportunity that is discovered through the use of corporate property, information or position, unless the Company has already been offered the opportunity and turned it down . . . prohibited from using corporate property, information or position for personal gain from competing with the Company . . . who intend to make use of Company property or services in a manner not solely for the benefit of the Company should consult beforehand with the Chairman of the Audit Committee . . . must maintain the confidentiality of all information so entrusted to them, except when disclosure is authorized or legally mandated . . . should protect the Company's assets and ensure their efficient use . . . only for legitimate business purposes.

The Diageo Board of Directors shall determine, or appoint the Diageo Audit Committee to determine, appropriate actions to be taken in the event of violations of the CoBC or of this Code of Ethics by any Senior Officers, such determinations to be reported back to the Board in a timely fashion. Such actions shall be reasonably designed to deter wrongdoing and to promote accountability for adherence to the CoBC and to this Code of Ethics.

There are many examples of ethical codes in practice and for further study reference can be made to companies listed on the Institute of Business Ethics website (www.ibe.org.uk, examples.html).

The limitations of the positivist approach

Key arguments against the positivist approach of written codes can be summarised as follows:

- **Status of the source**: the source, or who writes the code of ethics, can be a crucial question with the risk that ethical codes could be imposed on a business against the 'natural' beliefs of its employees. This is always a key danger in multinational companies where the management in the parent country may impose ethical beliefs on subsidiaries in other countries which are contrary to the cultural or religious beliefs of the host country.

- **Flexibility**: it is a well-known axiom that rules once in place do tend to have an existence well beyond their appointed time and this could cause serious ethical problems. It is important that there are procedures in place determining how written codes may be changed to meet changing beliefs and customs.

- **Comprehensiveness**: it is questionable whether one written code can cover all the possible issues raised under ethics. It is a weakness of all codified rules that they tend to apply only to known or, at least, anticipated situations. As discussed under flexibility, procedures are required to cope with totally new and unexpected situations – ethical issues often fall into this category and new situations and potential conflicts are always arising which limits the effectiveness of a written code.

The support given by professional bodies in the designing of ethical codes

There are excellent support facilities available. For example, the Chartered Association of Certified Accountants website (www.accaglobal.com) makes a toolkit available for accountants who might be involved with designing a Code of Ethics. The site also provides an overview which considers matters such as why ethics are important, links to other related sites, e.g. the Center for Ethics and Business from Loyola Marymount University in Los Angeles with a quiz to establish one's ethical style (www.ethicsandbusiness.org) – see below for more details – and a toolkit (www.ethics.org) to assist in the design of a Code of Ethics.

32.4.2 The rationale for the normative approach

The alternative approach is to adopt a more 'normative' ethical stance where a philosophy is developed for the business following a theoretical, religious or pragmatic approach as follows:

The theoretical approach

A business may take any one of the many theoretical stances on ethics. It is not the purpose of the chapter to go into detail but typically the business could adopt any philosophy including:

- **Utilitarianism**, as propounded by Jeremy Bentham (1748–1832) or John Stuart Mill (1806–1873), where individual happiness is balanced against the needs of society.

- **Deontological philosophy**, as propounded by Immanuel Kant (1724–1804), revised by David Hare (b. 1919), which is a philosophy based upon perceived absolutes of 'right', 'wrong' and 'duty'.

- **Marxism and post-Marxism,** based on the ideas of Karl Marx (1818–1883) and the post-marxists such as Herbert Marcuse (1898–1979), Roland Barthes (1915–1980) and Michel Foucault (1926–1984). Their views are of importance in multi-national situations and look at the imposition of ethics based upon economic power.

- **Postmodernism,** put forward by those such as A.J. Ayer (1910–1989), Jean-François Lyotard (1924–1998) and Jacques Derrida (b. 1930), has a particular resonance for business by offering an almost 'free market' approach to ethics.

- **Social philosophy,** with the work of John Rawls (b. 1921) and Alasdair MacIntyre (b. 1929), who adopt a more community-centred approach.

There are many theorists whose views can be explored for a deeper understanding of the approach.

The religious approach

This approach is applied when business ethics are formulated on some basic religious foundation, e.g. Judeo-Christian or Islamic or Hindu or Buddhist or Jainist.

The pragmatic approach

This is the approach where a business simply addresses each ethical problem as it arises and solves such problems by committee – the establishment of ethical committees is common-place in many large organisations.

There are, however, difficulties with the approach which can be summarised as:

- Inefficiency: this is a very time-consuming process and some issues are urgent and need a swift solution.

- Inconsistency: the approach can, over time, lead to inconsistencies and apparent changes of approach which can be embarrassing and confusing.

- Theoretical underpinning: there is the question of who is qualified to sit on such committees, which can be a major question for a business. In some hospitals in the USA philosophers are employed by hospitals to help medical staff address key ethical issues on a case-by-case basis. These philosophers, however, will operate from one of the theoretical standpoints highlighted above.

The impact of an individual's ethical style on choice of approach

There is an interesting quiz that identifies an individual's ethical style which is available on the Center for Ethics and Business website (www.ethicsandbusiness.org). It identifies two major ethical styles for recognising and resolving ethical dilemmas, namely, an ethic of justice and an ethic of care.

An ethic of justice

People who follow this style value impersonal principles, like justice, fairness, equality or authority which can be applied to all equally without exception. The advantage of this approach is that it attempts to make logical, impartial decisions but these might be seen by others to be too legalistic, inflexible and uncaring with a concern not to set precedents.

An ethic of care

People who follow this style value an equitable approach. The advantage of this approach is that it attempts to make subjective *ad hoc* decisions that take account of the individual specific circumstances but these might be seen by others to be too arbitrary and take no account of the precedent that might be set.

Thus the 'normative' approach, whilst being sound in concept, does raise enormous practical difficulties for business. This explains the reliance on written codes, which despite their drawbacks are at least accessible and in many ways 'reliable'.

32.5 The background to business ethics

A brief survey of the recent history of business ethics may prove useful at this point in our study.

The separatist view

In classical economic theory the business has only one purpose, as typified by the following précis of the ideas of Milton Friedman:

> Managers should single-mindedly pursue only one goal: the maximisation of profit for the benefit of shareholders. The invisible hand of the market then guarantees their actions contribute to social welfare in the best possible way.

This view of ethics is often referred to as the 'separatist view' and assumes that the business will conform to some ethical standard because of the combined influence of the law (via governmental pressure) and the (almost magical) powers of 'market forces'. Thus it assumes that businesses will behave ethically because it makes sound business sense to do so!

The integration view

The alternative view, proposed by Jeurissen in his Sankt Gallen lecture, is known as the 'integration view'. This view recognises the impact of law and market forces but also gives the organisation a duty or responsibility to respond and reflect the views of the moral community within which it operates. In other words the business may well have a wider social responsibility with objectives broader than simply profit maximisation.

Thus society allows the business the freedom to operate on 'market lines' provided that the 'public' can rely upon the integrity of the management to operate for the wider benefit of society in the long term. It is the conditional nature of the freedom that makes business ethics important.

Promotion of business ethics

At an institute level, the Chair of the Institute of Business Ethics, Neville Cooper put the issue with remarkable clarity in 1987 when he said:

> Our conviction is that, essentially, industry and commerce are highly ethical undertakings. The ethical demands on us . . . are to run them supremely efficiently, responsibly and with clear moral standards.[3]

At a corporate level, the chairman of a major UK food company in referring to his company's code of ethics said:

> . . . business ethics are not negotiable – a well founded reputation for scrupulous dealing is itself a priceless company asset and the most important single factor in our success is faithful adherence to our beliefs.

Management commitment to business ethics

This view of business ethics has its spiritual home in the development of codes of behaviour formulated in the USA since the 1960s and imported into Britain in the 1980s. Research carried out by the Institute of Business Ethics in 1987 in respect of the 300 largest UK companies did support this view, where the replies received did show ethics being taken seriously by senior management. Many ethical statements were shown to be published in the annual accounts and report documents produced by these companies. This research supported other surveys, especially that carried out by the journal *International Management* in 1982.

Well-known failures to follow acceptable ethical practices

The importance of business ethics is also, sadly, reinforced by a series of high-profile scandals caused by an obvious lack of business ethics. There are many examples including BCCI and the activities of the late Robert Maxwell with the Mirror Group of companies.

The issue of public confidence in business integrity is at the key of the continued acceptance of the freedom to operate within a market economy. It was as a result of such scandals that the Institute of Business Ethics was formed in 1987 to

> . . . clarify ethical issues in business, to propose positive solutions to problems and to establish common ground with people of goodwill of all faiths.

This, voluntary, organisation has been attempting to spread the issue of ethics and ethical behaviour across all business enterprises both nationally and internationally.

Concerns about ethical standards still exist

In 2003 a new guide *Developing a Code of Business Ethics* was published by the Institute of Business Ethics (IBE) accompanied by a comment by the guide's author (www.ibe.org.uk) that business should be shocked to find how low they score in the trustworthiness stakes with 60% of people not trusting business leaders to tell the truth. The IBE view is that the existence of a Code provides the criteria against which business decisions can be measured and that, without it, ethical dilemmas may be hard to identify – making the point as an example that it is too easy, when trying to win contracts, or simply dealing with suppliers or customers, to take decisions that may not stand critical assessment when the heat of the immediate pressure is off.

UK commitment to self-regulation

The self-regulation approach is a feature of the business culture of the UK. The work of the Cadbury Committee (1991, updated in 1992) helped the issue of corporate governance and managerial behaviour and the Greenbury Report (1995), which looked in detail at the issue of directors' remuneration packages, included an ethical view of such, again reflecting the usual UK approach. The Hampel Report (1998) reinforced the voluntary, self-regulatory nature of such views of business ethics.

Thus the issue of business ethics is seen to be a key feature of business success but ethics are (in the view of business) best 'enforced' on a voluntary basis.

32.6 The role of ethics in modern business

When considering the issues raised under business ethics a useful starting point is to examine the areas covered by the Ethical Codes published by the various organisations which indicate the key areas of concern.

32.6.1 Conflicts of interest

These are always issues of concern as management must be concerned with the benefit of the organisation and they must not put personal gain ahead of the gain for the organisation. Where there is a possibility of conflict, the usual practice is for the manager (including directors) to declare an interest to their fellow managers who can then assess the actions of the manager in such a light. Ideally the manager should withdraw from taking decisions where they may gain personally, but this may not always be practical. The awarding of contracts, employment of relatives and share dealings are all areas of concern here.

Public perceptions

The manager needs to not only be behaving ethically but also to be **seen** to be behaving ethically. Recent issues in Parliament have highlighted the dangers of conflicts of interest and how even innocent conflicts can be seen to have a more sinister, ulterior motive. The whole issue of **insider dealing** has recently caused problems in respect of share options for directors and their actions in taking up the options at advantageous times.

32.6.2 Gifts

The practice of giving and receiving gifts in business has always been a very fine ethical question. Ideally gifts should not be seen as an inducement to promote business in a manner which is less than open and honest. However, gifts are often intended as a sign of goodwill and respect and have no other motive than this. The issue becomes even more cloudy when we consider corporate hospitality, e.g. are tickets for the Football World Cup given to potential customers a legitimate gift? An apparently innocent social event could be seen to have sinister overtones in the 'cold light of day'.

There is a normal, human need to show respect and the giving and receiving of gifts is a key part of this. Japan for example is an illustration of cultural ethical differences where gifts are commonplace in business. In most businesses the key factor is scale. Small, low-value gifts (diaries, low cost pens, etc.) are not perceived as a threat to ethical behaviour but high-value gifts are not acceptable.

This is the policy set out in the PSA Peugeot Citroen 2003 Code of Ethics:

> Employees act with integrity and honesty in their dealings with customers and suppliers, refraining from directly or indirectly soliciting gifts and refusing to accept gifts of any significant value.

The issue also applies to the payment of 'bribes' to encourage business, totally unacceptable in the eyes of most managers but common practice in many countries and industries (e.g. the defence industry). Thus, ethically no bribes (however named) should be paid or received. This is made clear in the following extract from Associated British Foods 2005 Annual Report

> Bribery – we will not condone the offering or receiving of bribes or other such facilitating payments to any person or entity for the purpose of obtaining or retaining business or influencing political decisions.

There is a growing concern over the use of gifts of cash, goods or services in relation to governmental officials. Such officials, by the very nature of their work, must be above reproach in respect of ethical behaviour. Unfortunately these officials are often very poorly paid and thus the temptation is great.

Commercial organisations must have very precise codes for dealing with governmental officials. These codes must cover the relationship with the official before, during and after the main business has been carried out. This is to prevent the temptation of payment paid later, even after the official has left government service, since the suspicion will always remain of unfair treatment.

32.6.3 Confidentiality

The business has secrets which could have commercial value if revealed, so the manager is required to maintain confidentiality. A common policy is that set out in the PSA Peugeot Citroen 2003 Code of Ethics:

> Employees of PSA Peugeot Citroen member companies must not divulge confidential business information to outsiders or to other Group employees who are not authorised to have such information. Employees refrain directly or indirectly using privileged information obtained in their jobs for personal gain.

This does, however, itself raise a keen ethical point: what should the manager do if the organisation is carrying out an illegal or immoral act? In most codes of practice, published by organisations and professional bodies, secrecy must be maintained but there is, surely, a wider social element of the individual's duty to society? It is here that **whistle-blowing** starts to be a possible course of action. This involves the employee in informing an outside agency of the organisation's unacceptable behaviour. Most organisations would regard this as 'gross misconduct' and would dismiss the employee even though the employee was acting with the highest of motives.

Governments have seen the danger to individuals of this and have taken steps to prevent the victimisation of employees who whistle-blow. The UK and US governments are taking a lead in this approach. In the USA many organisations have **whistle-blowing hotlines** where employees can tell about unethical behaviour in confidence; in the UK there are professional organisations who provide this service to their members. An interesting approach to whistle-blowing can be seen in the work of the charity Public Concern at Work. They outline the process and protection offered to whistle-blowers on their website: www.pcaw.demon.co.uk.

32.6.4 Products and processes

It is becoming a recognised fact of business that society expects certain standards in respect of processes of production and products, and businesses could face severe censure if these standards are broken.

Processes
The environment is a major topic of concern so businesses have to be 'green' in their products and processes; this is very apparent in the oil industry.

Products
The product can also be an issue; for instance tobacco products cause major issues of concern for much of society. An additional example was the sale of 'alco-pops', the alcoholic drink in an apparent 'soft drink' form.

Selling practices
Selling practices can also cause concern as instanced by the concern voiced over the sale of baby milk substitute products in the Third World. Changes in marketing practices were demanded and were forthcoming because of ethical concerns.

The following is an extract from the GlaxoSmithKline statement on business ethics relating to products and selling practices:

Business ethics
Our products are important to the health of people around the world, so it is particularly important that we operate to high ethical standards, act responsibly and comply with the law.

The sale and promotion of pharmaceutical products is highly regulated by governments and medical agencies. We are aware of the sensitivity and concerns regarding the marketing of medicines and we are absolutely committed to high ethical standards. We have developed marketing codes and policies and provide training to guide sales representatives, to ensure that they behave ethically and comply with the law.

32.6.5 Employment practices

The treatment of employees is also a major ethical concern for business; businesses need to be seen to be fair to their workers. This means looking, for example, at the status of women, ethnic minorities, older employees and disabled people within the workplace.

It also covers the employment of children, a very sensitive issue as evidenced by the recent court case of a major high street retailer taking legal action against a TV programme for suggesting they **knowingly** bought products from manufacturers overseas who employed child labour. Thus the ethics of an organisation in this area is a matter of interest to society.

Most business organisations of any size will take action to address these very real areas of societal concern within their formal, written, ethical code. It is here that the main ethical effort in business is concentrated.

32.7 International Accreditation Programme

An international accreditation programme is available to companies through Social Accountability International (SAI).

Social Accountability International

SAI is a US-based, non-profit organisation (www.cepaa.org) dedicated to the development, implementation and oversight of voluntary verifiable social accountability standards to improve workplace conditions. It convenes key stakeholders to develop consensus-based voluntary standards and accredits qualified organisations to verify compliance.

In 1996, SAI convened an international multi-stakeholder Advisory Board which developed Social Accountability 8000 (SA 8000), a voluntary standard for workplaces based on ILO (International Labour Organization) and other human rights conventions with independent verification.

SA 8000 is a way for retailers, brand companies, suppliers and other organisations to maintain just and decent working conditions throughout the supply chain. It is based on international workplace norms in the ILO conventions and the UN's Universal Declaration of Human Rights and the Convention on Rights of the Child. It includes, e.g. a standard for compensation which reads as follows:

Compensation: Wages paid for a standard work week must meet the legal and industry standards and be sufficient to meet the basic need of workers and their families; no disciplinary deductions.

There are also standards relating to child labour, forced labour; health and safety; freedom of association and right to collective bargaining; discrimination; discipline; working hours and management systems. For further information refer to www.sa-intl.org.

32.8 The role of professional accounting ethics

Within the UK the various professional accounting bodies do provide their members with very detailed ethical guidelines. Accountants both in practice and in businesses are required to follow these guidelines in their normal patterns of work and can be punished individually for breaches of these professional codes of ethics. There are, however, two distinct approaches to ethics, one for the accountant in practice and another for those within business.

32.8.1 Accountants in practice

The accountant in practice has a considerable body of ethical support to work from, particularly if he/she is a member of one of the various Chartered Accountancy bodies.

These bodies (for England and Wales, Scotland and Ireland) publish guidelines covering key areas of accounting work and behaviour such as

- their relationship with the client;
- the type of work they can do for the client;
- the way to safeguard independence;
- the standards of behaviour expected of accountants;
- the manner of dealing with conflicts of interest;
- the way in which they will behave in given situations such as takeovers, insolvencies and so on;
- the nature and type of advice they can give clients.

In 2002 following the recommendations of the Co-ordinating Group on Audit and Accounting Issues, the Accountancy Foundation, which had been set up in 1999 as a self-regulatory body, was replaced by extending the powers of the Financial Reporting Council. The new structure is shown in Figure 32.1.

Figure 32.1 New structure of the FRC

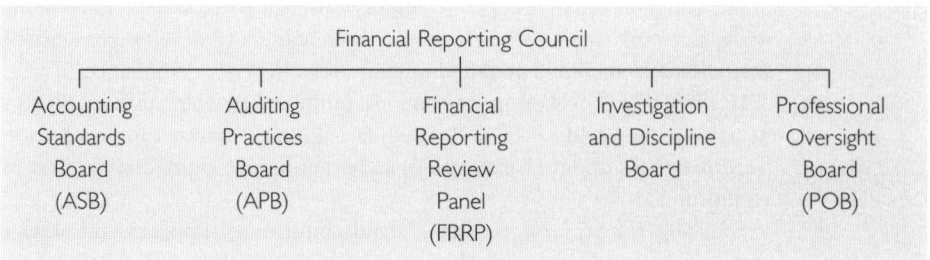

The ASB will continue to be responsible for accounting standards; the APB will be responsible for standards for audit integrity, independence and objectivity previously set by the professional bodies; the FRRP will become more proactive in investigating possible departures from standards; the Investigation and Discipline Board provides an independent hearing for those disciplinary cases where there is a public interest; the Professional Oversight Board (POB) will oversee ethical standards.

The intention has been to put in place a regime (supplemented by the Higgs and Smith Reports) that will maintain public confidence that there is sound corporate governance, that the financial reports give a fair view and the audit process is effective to avoid the prospect of the large-scale accounting frauds that have occurred in the USA.

The POB has recommended that the profession should share experience of dealing with ethical issues or fraud through greater use of 'real-life' case studies as part of training. The professional bodies have responded and included ethics within their examination syllabi. For example, the ACCA in its Paper P1, *Professional Accountant*, covers personal and professional ethics, ethical frameworks and professional values, as applied in the context of the accountant's duties and as a guide to appropriate professional behaviour and conduct in a variety of situations. In addition, as part of their ethical development, students will be required to complete a two-hour online training module, developed by ACCA. This will give students exposure to a range of real-life ethical case studies and will require them to reflect on their own ethical behaviour and values. Students will be expected to complete the ethics module before commencing their Professional level studies.

Alongside the developments in the professional examination system, there has been a growing increase in the coverage of corporate social responsibility and sustainability reporting in academic teaching programmes. There have been various approaches, such as designing separate modules within an undergraduate programme, as at Nottingham University Business School, to embedding CSR within syllabi, as at Waikato, where the Dean states: 'In contrast with the traditional university approach of creating a centre to study sustainability, the Waikato Management School embraces sustainability at the heart of our activities. We see sustainability as central to the future of business' (www.mngt.waikato.ac.nz).

As well as coverage in the teaching programmes there has also been a growing pressure from academics for more academic research challenging the managerialist perspective in the post-Enron era.

32.8.2 Accountants in business

The accountant working within business has a different set of problems due to the dual position as an employee and a professional accountant. There is a potential clash of issues where the interests of the business could be at odds with professional standards.

The various professional bodies approach things in different ways. For example, the ICAEW established the Industrial Members Advisory Committee on Ethics (IMACE) in the late 1970s to give specific advice to members with ethical problems in business. This is supported by a strong local support network as well as a national helpline for the guidance of accountants. At the moment IMACE is dealing with 200 to 300 problems per year but this is more a reflection of the numbers of chartered accountants in business than a reflection on the lack of ethical problems. A survey[4] carried out by the Board of Chartered Accountants in Business indicated that 11% of members had put their jobs on the line over ethical issues.

The type of problem raised is a good indication of the ethical issues raised for accountants in business. They include:

- requests by employers to manipulate tax returns;
- requests to produce figures to mislead shareholders;
- requests to conceal information;
- requests to manipulate overhead absorption rates to extort more income from customers (an occurrence in the defence industries);

- requests to authorise and conceal bribes to buyers and agents, a common request in some exporting businesses;
- requests to produce misleading projected figures to obtain additional finance;
- requests to conceal improper expense claims put in by senior managers;
- requests to over- or undervalue assets;
- requests to misreport figures in respect of government grants;
- requests for information which could lead to charges of 'insider dealing';
- requests to redefine bad debts as 'good' or vice versa.

These issues are also reflected by the other professional bodies, the Chartered Association of Certified Accountants (ACCA), the Chartered Institute of Management Accountants (CIMA) and the Chartered Institute of Public Finance and Accountancy (CIPFA). The last of these organisations has added problems in that there is an overt political dimension to many decisions taken as its members are working in local government and the concept of 'value for money' is becoming a key feature of their work. Cases in respect of local councils in Westminster and Doncaster have demonstrated the ethical difficulties encountered by CIPFA members in carrying out their duties within their very singular environment.

The accountant in business has this problem of dual ethical structures; they are professionals but they are also employees and on a surprising number of occasions there is a conflict between the two roles on ethical issues. The solution of this conflict causes many problems for the accountant who is left with only three possible solutions, namely:

1 Take some action either by informing a superior (letting them take some action) or by whistle-blowing to an outside agency such as the professional body, the police, the media or whatever. This may well cause the accountant some personal problems and is difficult if the superior is the 'guilty party'.

2 Resign on principle and leave the organisation with personal and professional ethics intact but with a possibly damaged career.

3 Ignore the action and hope someone else notices the unethical behaviour and takes the appropriate action.

All accountants may have to face these choices at some time during their career and it is a test of character which choice is made. The choice itself may well be a function of the individual's own ethical background influenced by the factors mentioned earlier.

32.9 National and international regulation

It is likely that there will be an increase in formal regulation as the search for greater transparency and ethical business behaviour continues.

32.9.1 National regulation

Money laundering – overview
There are various estimates of the scale of money laundering ranging up to over 2% of global gross domestic product. Certain businesses are identified as being more prone to money laundering, e.g. import/export companies and cash businesses such as antiques and art dealers, auction houses, casinos and garages. However, the avenues are becoming more and more sophisticated with methods varying between countries, e.g. in the UK there is the

increasing use of smaller non-bank institutions whereas in Spain it includes cross-border carrying of cash, money-changing at bureaux de change and investment in real estate.

Money laundering – implications for accountants

In 1997 the APB in the UK issued Practice Note 12 *Money Laundering* which required auditors to take the possibility of money laundering into account when carrying out their audit and to report to the appropriate authority if they become aware of suspected laundering.

In 1999 there was also guidance from the professional accounting bodies, e.g. *Money Laundering: Guidance Notes for Chartered Accountants* issued by the Institute of Chartered Accountants which deal with the statute law, regulations and professional requirements in relation to the avoidance, recognition and reporting of money laundering.

Since that date, there has been an intensification of efforts to control it in the EU and the UK prompted by terrorist implications and the determination to target criminal activities. For example:

- In 2001 the EU Parliament approved a New Money Laundering Directive (effective from June 2003) which stipulated that accountants are included in existing legislation requiring suspicious activities to be reported.

- In 2002 the UK Parliament passed the Proceeds of Crime Act under which the Assets Recovery Agency (www.assetsrecovery.gov.uk/) began operations in February 2003 with opportunities for accountants to be employed as financial investigators to follow often complex financial arrangements in order to link the proceeds of crime to extant assets.

- In 2006 changes were made to anti-money laundering law which meant that accountants providing privileged services to clients were treated in the same way as lawyers and were not required to report suspicions to the National Criminal Intelligence Service.

Whistle-blowing – defined

Some disclosures which may be embarrassing to senior management may also be a statutory obligation, e.g. in the UK an accountant or internal auditor has the same legal duty to report to external authorities suspicions of terrorism or money laundering as any other employee. This means that there is an implicit authorisation by management. By whistle-blowing, we mean the unauthorised disclosure, in good faith, of serious information relating to questionable practices, where disclosure is perceived to be in the public interest. Such information can be extremely varied: e.g. a financial accountant may be reporting the managing director of a subsidiary company for materially padding his expenses, or an internal auditor may be disclosing audit findings.

Whistle-blowing – proportionate response

Because every whistle-blowing situation is different there is no right answer and any response needs to be proportionate. What is proportionate will of course reflect the potential whistle-blower's own value system, e.g. deciding what he ought to do if there was a dangerous product defect which management considered too expensive to rectify and were concealing or a theft of funds or over-optimistic projections.

Whistle-blowing – protection

In the UK the Public Interest Disclosure Act came into force in 1999 protecting whistle-blowers who raised genuine concerns about malpractice from dismissal and victimisation in order to promote the public interest. The scope of malpractice is wide-ranging, including, e.g. the covering up of a suspected crime, a civil offence such as negligence, a miscarriage of justice, and health and safety or environmental risks.

Whistle-blowing – policies

Companies should have in place a policy which gives clear guidance to employees on the appropriate internal procedures to follow if there is a suspected malpractice. Employees, including accountants and internal auditors, are expected to follow these procedures as well as acting professionally and in accordance with their own professional code.

The following is an extract from Associated British Foods 2005 Annual Report:

> Associated British Foods plc encourages an open culture in all its dealings between employees and people with whom it comes in contact. Effective and honest communication is essential if malpractice and wrongdoing is to be effectively dealt with. The procedure below provides guidelines for individuals who feel they need to raise certain issues to Associated British Foods plc or their own employing subsidiary, in confidence ('WHISTLEBLOWING'), and is designed to protect those raising a genuine concern from any detriment, in line with the Public Interests Disclosures Act 1998 . . .
>
> Usually concerns about issues at work can be easily resolved. However, when the concerns are about breaches of the law or regulations; serious misconduct by another person; health and safety matters or financial malpractice it can be more difficult to know what to do. Individuals who have a reasonable belief that malpractice is occurring have a responsibility to speak out, in the confidence that they are supported by the Company.

However, although the whistle-blowing policies might have been followed and the accountants protected by the provisions of the Public Interest Disclosure Act, it could result in a breakdown of trust making their position untenable; this means that a whistle-blower might be well advised to have an alternative position in mind.

Breach of confidentiality

Auditors are protected from the risk of liability for breach of confidence provided that:

(a) disclosure is made in the public interest;

(b) disclosure is made to a proper authority;

(c) there is no malice motivating the disclosure.

32.9.2 International regulation

The OECD drew up a new anti-bribery convention making it a criminal offence for business executives to bribe foreign officials. The implication for accountants is that companies will have to ensure that financial statements do not omit or falsify cases involving bribery and prohibit the establishment of off-the-books accounts for the purpose of bribing foreign public officials or of hiding the bribery. The convention has been ratified by major trading nations including the UK, USA, Japan and Germany. The pressure for the OECD convention came initially from the USA where there was already anti-bribery legislation and then from multinational companies which were finding that some government officials were demanding not 1% but up to 30% of contract prices to award contracts; this not only made it far more difficult to conceal but was seen to be hitting the bottom line too hard. The convention had commercial support and has been ratified by major trading nations including the UK, USA, Japan and Germany. In the UK, the Anti-Terrorism, Crime and Security Act 2001 has extended the common law relating to bribery of UK officials to include the bribery of foreign officials.

Events with the European Commission have highlighted the potential for ethical issues and the inevitability of whistle-blowing as being a logical step in the absence of an effective internal process for dealing with ethical issues. In this case, the whole Commission resigned due to the ethical malpractice of a few, brought to light by the public revelation of a whistle-blower in the accounting function.

UK regulation

In 2001 the government took action to outlaw bribery by UK nationals and companies, even in circumstances where the acts took place overseas, measures which go beyond the requirements of the Convention. In 2004 the OECD carried out a favourable examination of the UK's progress in implementing the OECD Bribery Charter and commended it for other aspects of the anti-bribery framework such as employee whistleblower protection, the ability of the tax authorities to make spontaneous disclosures of suspicious information to law enforcement agencies and the support the government has provided to a number of private sector and civil society anti-corruption initiatives, including Transparency International's Business Principles on Countering Bribery, the International Business Leaders' Forum, the Commonwealth Business Council and the Extractive Industries Transparency Initiative conference.

32.10 The role of the accountant as guardian of business ethics

There is therefore an established need for business ethics, but the question arises: who can police the organisation for ethical breaches? This is a crucial question as any set of rules is only as effective as its enforcement mechanism allows it to be.

There needs to be some sort of 'ethical guardian' who can police the code of ethics within an organisation to bring out any unethical practices and ensure that corrective action is taken as appropriate.

There are 'ethics committees' in some organisations which act as a court to judge ethical breaches, but in themselves they are only part of the guardian function.

It is therefore a possible function of an accountant's role to be the guardian of ethics within a business because the following attributes are possessed by the accountant:

● skill – the accountant is trained in the establishment and management of control systems and ethics is simply another layer of control;

● stewardship – the accountant already acts as the steward of the shareholders' interests and the function is similar when discussing ethics;

● rule orientation – the accountant is a trained follower of rules and is accomplished at ensuring others obey stated rules and regulations;

● judgement – ethics requires the application of fine judgement, an attribute common in many accountants;

● professionalism – the accountant is one of the main professionals working within businesses and the attributes of a professional are essential to make judgements on ethical breaches.

32.10.1 The role of the accountant in practice

This could well prove to be a new area of responsibility for accountants in both practice and business and it is not without precedent. The work, for example, of the Audit Commission in the public sector is perhaps an indication of the future role of accountants in practice. The Commission does make judgements on the traditional accounting areas but it is also looking at other more subjective measures of performance within public sector organisations and perhaps this is a growth area, especially as the demand by society for more accountability in business becomes more powerful and politically impossible to ignore.

32.10.2 The role of the accountant in business

The accountant within business could also be seeing a growth in the ethical policing role as internal auditors take on the role of assessing the performance of managers as to their adherence to the ethical code of the organisation. This is already partially happening as conflicts of interest are often highlighted by internal audits and comments raised on managerial practices. This is after all a traditional role for accountants, ensuring that the various codes of practice of the organisation are followed. The level of adherence to an ethical code is but another assessment for the accountant to undertake.

Implications for training

If, as is likely, the accountant has a role in the future as 'ethical guardian', additional training will be necessary. This should be done at a very early stage, as in the USA, where accountants wishing to be Certified Public Accountants (CPAs) are required to pass formal exams on ethical practices and procedures before they are allowed the privilege of working in practice. Failure in these exams prevents the prospective accountant from practising in the business environment.

32.11 Growth of voluntary standards

Social, environmental and ethical reporting is at an early stage but it is receiving increasing attention from industry and commerce with the growing recognition that long-term shareholder value cannot be achieved without acknowledging responsibility to wider stakeholder groups.[5] There has already been stakeholder pressure for management to balance the interests of investors, employees, suppliers, customers and the public. Finally, industry, commerce and stakeholders are moving towards a common goal which is to provide innovative reports. However, this requires a commitment from the directors, who are the ones who control the information, and an acceptance of the fact that it is not appropriate to produce only favourable comments. This has now been recognised by some of our major companies, e.g. BT's 1999 Social Report.

The Institute of Social and Ethical Accountability was founded in 1996 as an international membership organisation, based in the UK. In November 1999 the institute launched a world first international processing standard, AA 1000, enabling organisations to build quality into their existing and developing social and ethical management systems. The standard defines how companies should report on issues such as pollution and labour issues. Its objective is to encourage a collaborative approach, with inputs from stakeholders including interest and pressure groups. Two major concerns that have been voiced are:

● Companies should not see consultation with a wide range of stakeholders as an excuse to avoid their responsibility for dealing with adverse social and environmental effects.

● Credibility will only be achieved if there is an independent audit and there could be a risk of ineffectual auditing.

AA 1000 addresses the latter point by setting out criteria for the social and ethical auditor, namely:

- integrity,
- objectivity and independence,
- professional competence,
- professional behaviour exercising rigour, judgement and clear communication,
- confidentiality,
- due care to stakeholders.[6]

AA 1000 will provide a consistent measure of performance and a uniform basis for reporting but the institute recognises that this is a dynamic field and plans to keep the standard under constant review. In this it resembles the ASB policy of revisiting FRSs when there has been experience and feedback from stakeholders and management.

32.11.1 IFAC Code of Ethics for Professional Accountants – revised June 2005

The International Federation of Accountants (IFAC) believes that the accountancy profession worldwide endeavours to achieve a number of common objectives and to observe certain fundamental principles. It recognises that due to national differences of culture, language, legal and social systems, the task of preparing, implementing and enforcing detailed ethical requirements is primarily that of the member bodies in each country. IFAC sees its role as establishing an international code of ethics for professional accountants as a foundation for national codes covering ethical requirements applying to all professional accountants, professional accountants in public practice and employed professional accountants.

We have already discussed the code as it relates to auditors in Chapter 30 and now consider the broader aspects relating to the profession in general.

Characteristics of a profession include:

- mastery of a particular intellectual skill, acquired by training and education;
- adherence by its members to a common code of values and conduct;
- maintaining an objective outlook;
- acceptance of a responsibility to the public consisting of clients, credit grantors, governments, employers, employees, investors, the business and financial community, and others who rely on the objectivity and integrity of professional accountants to maintain the orderly functioning of commerce.

Conflicts of interest

A code setting out ethical requirements is required because accountants may find that conflicts arise between their duties of loyalty to an employer, to the profession and to society as well as their own self-interest. It should be implicit in any such code that a professional accountant's responsibility to satisfy the needs of an individual client or employer is not paramount and satisfying public interest is also important, e.g.:

- financial institutions and investors rely on the integrity of independently audited financial statements when making loan and investment decisions;

- financial executives contribute to the efficient and effective use of the organisation's resources;
- internal auditors provide assurance about a sound internal control system which enhances the reliability of the external financial information of the employer;
- tax experts help to establish confidence and efficiency in, and the fair application of, the tax system.

Fundamental principles

Professional accountants should carry out their work with

- *integrity* – being straightforward and honest;
- *objectivity* – acting fairly and not allowing prejudice or bias, conflict of interest or influence of others to override objectivity;
- *professional competence* – applying up-to-date technical and professional standards;
- *confidentiality* – respecting the confidentiality of information acquired during the course of performing professional services.

32.11.2 National response in the UK

In 2003 the final report from the government's Co-ordinating Group on Auditing and Accounting Issues required auditors to comply with the Auditing Practice Board's Ethical Standards on auditor independence, rather than those of the professional accountancy bodies. The APB issued its Consultation Paper *Draft Ethical Standards for Auditors* in November 2003, issued as a standard in December 2004 and revised in April 2008.

How have professional bodies responded to the APB Ethics Standard 2004?

There are five Ethical standards issued in December 2004. These are:

- ES 1 – Integrity, objectivity and independence,
- ES 2 – Financial, business, employment and personal relationships,
- ES 3 – Long association with the audit engagement,
- ES 4 – Fees, remuneration and evaluation policies, litigation, gifts and hospitality, and
- ES 5 – Non-audit services provided to audit clients.

The ASB approach in the Standards has been to set down rules to ensure that auditors are perceived by stakeholders to be independent. This approach has been criticised by the professional audit institutes who favour the IFAC principle-based approach described above.

Following their issue there was concern expressed by the auditing institutes that the Standards restrict a number of activities previously permitted to be carried out by practitioners for their clients such as auditors undertaking accounting work for audit clients who do not have knowledgeable management. The Standards also placed restrictions on fee concentration that would significantly affect businesses' choice of practitioners by prohibiting the audit of any client that would constitute more than 10% of practice income.

Another concern expressed was that the Standards were not appropriate for smaller entities and various exemptions are set out in the ASB's Provisions for Small Entities, such as being permitted to provide non-audit services provided there is a discussion of objectivity and independence issues with those concerned with corporate governance.

32.12 Conflict between Codes and Targets

On the one hand we see companies developing Codes of Ethical Conduct whilst on the other hand we see some of these same companies developing Management by Objectives which set staff unachievable targets and create pressures that lead to unethical behaviour. Where this occurs there is the risk that an unhealthy corporate climate may develop resulting in the manipulation of accounting figures and unethical behaviour.

There is a view[7] that there is a need to create an ethical climate that transcends a compliance approach to ethics and focuses instead on fostering socially harmonious relationships. An interesting article[8] proceeds to make the argument that the recent accounting scandals may be as much a reflection of a deficient corporate climate, with its concentration on setting unrealistic targets and promoting competition between the staff, as of individual moral failures of managers.

Summary

In this chapter we have attempted to explain how business ethics has adopted the definition of ethics as **an ethical code** in order to have a mechanism that (a) makes the ethical expectations of the business clear to staff and other stakeholders and (b) allows performance to be monitored. Although ethics are often perceived as a qualitative or philosophical matter, there is a public expectation and demand for quantitative measures – after all, we live in the age of performance criteria and league tables!

Accountability requires that a report should be made to relevant parties if the monitoring provides evidence that there has been a breach of the code. The relevant party would depend on the nature of the breach, e.g. petty dishonesty by junior staff might be reported to the immediate line manager, fraud by senior managers reported to the audit committee and material misrepresentation of the profit reported to the shareholders.

The accountant is heavily involved with ethical issues as a member of society, as a member of a professional body with a formal code of ethics and as a member and/or employee of a business. The prevalence of the self-regulation ethos in the UK also supports directors delegating to the accountant responsibility for ethical policing.

Accountants' expertise in designing systems and measuring compliance leaves them in a strong position to undertake the monitoring of the ethical code and, as with all control systems, there will be a continuing need to balance costs and benefits. It would, for example, be uneconomic to require all staff to take a truth test to support every expense claim that was lodged!

It is interesting to note that the Auditing Practices Board is actively considering an approach to the government to provide auditors with greater powers in relation to fraud. Given that companies might be reluctant to increase the fees paid to auditors, there might well be a case for state funding for monitoring that is a form of ethical policing. One attraction of this might be that there would be pressure from the government to formulate an ethical code. It is a strength of the self-regulatory ethos that best practice trickles down but it can trickle mighty slowly!

REVIEW QUESTIONS

1 Outline **three** areas where ethics and ethical behaviour are of importance to business.

2 Discuss the role of the accounting profession in the issue of ethics.

3 How might a company develop a code of ethics for its own use?

4 Outline the advantages and disadvantages of a written code of ethics.

5 (a) Obtain an ethical statement from:
   (i) a commercial organisation;
   (ii) a charitable organisation.
   (b) Review each statement for content and style.
   (c) Compare each of the two statements and highlight any areas of difference which, in your view, reflect the different nature of the two organisations.

6 In each of the following scenarios outline the ethical problem and suggest ways in which the organisation may solve the problem and prevent its reoccurrence.
   (a) A director's wife uses his company car for shopping.
   (b) Groceries bought for personal use are included on a director's company credit card.
   (c) The director is sent overseas on business with a business air ticket but he converts it to two economy class tickets and takes his wife with him.
   (d) A director negotiates a contract for management consultancy services but it is later revealed that her husband is a director of the management consultancy company.
   (e) The director of a company hires her son for some holiday work within the company but does not mention the fact to her fellow directors.
   (f) You are the accountant to a small engineering company and you have been approached by the Chairman to authorise the payment of a fee to an overseas government employee in the hope that a large contract will be awarded.
   (g) Your company has had some production problems which have resulted in some electrical goods being faulty (possibly dangerous) but all production is being dispatched to customers regardless of condition.
   (h) Your company is about to sign a contract with a repressive regime in South America for equipment which **could** have a military use. Your own government has given you no advice on this matter.
   (i) Your company is in financial difficulties and a large contract has just been gained in partnership with an overseas supplier who employs children as young as seven years old on their production line. The children are the only wage earners for their families and there is no welfare available in the country where they live.
   (j) You are the accountant in a large manufacturing company and you have been approached by the manufacturing director to prepare a capital investment proposal for a new production line. After your calculations the project meets **none** of the criteria necessary to allow the project to proceed but the director instructs you to change the financial forecast figures to ensure the proposal is approved.
   (k) Review the last week's newspapers and select **three** examples of failures of business ethics and justify your choice of examples.
   (l) At the year-end, goods are dispatched although not tested in order to improve the current year's sales figures. The management fully expect returns to be made but not within the period prior to the auditor signing the accounts.

7 Select one philosophical viewpoint of ethics and prepare a single A4 piece of paper with a set of notes summarising the viewpoint.

8 With your researches produced for Question 7 discuss how this viewpoint may be applied to a **named** business of your choice to help develop appropriate ethics for this business.

9 'The management of a listed company has a fiduciary duty to act in the best interest of the shareholders and it would be unethical for them to act in the interest of other shareholders if this did not maximise the existing earnings per share.' Discuss.

10 The financial director of a listed company makes many decisions which are informed by statute, e.g. the Companies Act and the Public Interest Disclosure Act, and by mandatory pronouncements by, e.g. the ASB, the APB and his professional accounting body. What guidance is available when there is a need for an ethical decision which does not contravene statutory or mandatory demands – how can there be confidence that the decision is right?

11 An approach has been made to the Board to support a takeover bid where the offer price exceeds the current market capitalisation.
   (a) Discuss situations where you consider it (i) ethical to recommend the offer to shareholders and (ii) unethical; and
   (b) Discuss whether an aggrieved shareholder should be able to obtain relief from the court if the decision was unethical.

12 The finance director has been carrying out some sensitivity analysis and produced figures that show that the return on capital employed could be improved if the company were to downsize, make existing staff redundant and replace them with lower-paid temporary staff. The current return on capital employed and PE ratio exceed the industry average but the change of policy would take the company into the top quartile with a favourable impact on the directors' performance targets and bonuses. This is a common commercial practice. Discuss whether there is an ethical problem in (a) the company pursuing such a policy; (b) the finance director submitting such a proposal; and (c) the finance director failing to submit such a proposal.

13 Discuss the following:
   (a) Why an accountant should be involved with designing or monitoring ethical codes.
   (b) What additional training this would require.
   (b) How an accountant could become an effective 'guardian of business ethics'.

14 Confidentiality means that an accountant in business has a loyalty to the business which employs him/her which is greater than any commitment to a professional code of ethics. Discuss.

15 Lord Borrie QC has said[9] of the Public Interest Disclosure Bill that came into force in July 1999 that the new law would encourage people to recognise and identify with the wider public interest, not just their own private position and it will reassure them that if they act reasonably to protect the legitimate interest of others, the law will not stand idly by should they be vilified or victimised. Confidentiality should only be breached, however, if there is a statutory obligation to do so. Discuss.

16 The following is an extract from a *European Accounting Review*[10] article:

> on the teaching front, there is a pressing need to challenge more robustly the tenets of modern day business, and specifically accounting, education which have elevated the principles of property rights and narrow self-interest above broader values of community and ethics.

Discuss how such a challenge might impact on accounting education.

17 The International Association for Accounting Education and Research states that: 'The Professional ethics should pervade the teaching of accounting' (www.iaaer.org). Discuss how this can be achieved on an undergraduate accounting degree.

References

1 www.ibe.org.uk/smes.html
2 www.diageo.com/NR/rdonlyres/3E090C4A-D792-4319-8246-7E57678DD231/48910/CodeofEthics_07_v5.pdf
3 Simon Webley, *Company Philosophies and Codes of Business Ethics*, Institute of Business Ethics (1988).
4 'Dispute resolution', *Accountancy*, May 1998, p. 99.
5 Andrew Bolger, *Financial Times*, 2 July 1998, p. 10.
6 www.accountability21.net.
7 T. Morris, *If Aristotle Ran General Motors*, Henry Holt and Company, New York, N.Y., 1997, pp. 118–145.
8 J.F. Castellano, K. Rosenweig and H.P. Roehm, 'How Corporate Culture Impacts Unethical Distortion of Financial Numbers', *Management Accounting Quarterly*, Summer 2004, vol. 5, no 4.
9 W. Raven, 'Social auditing', *Internal Auditor*, February 2000, p. 8.
10 D. Owen, 'CSR after Enron: a role for the academic accounting profession?', *European Accounting Review*, vol. 14, no. 2, 2005.

Bibliography

C.A. Adams, *The Nature and Processes of Corporate Reporting on Ethical Issues*, London: CIMA, 1999.
C. Adams and N. Kuasirikun, 'A comparative analysis of corporate reporting on ethical issues by UK and German chemical and pharmaceutical companies', *European Accounting Review*, vol. 9, no. 1, 2000, pp. 53–79.
T. Cannon, *Corporate Responsibilty: A Textbook on Business Ethics, Governance, Environment: Roles and Responsiblities*, Pitman, 1994.
A. Chatzidakis, S. Hibbert and A. Smith, 'Ethically concerned, yet unethically behaved: towards an updated understanding of consumer's (un)ethical decision making', *Advances in Consumer Research*, vol. 32, pp. 693–698.
H. Collins and E. Wray-Bliss, 'Discriminating ethics', *Human Relations*, 2005.
A. Crane and D. Matten, 'Questioning the domain of the business ethics curriculum', *Journal of Business Ethics*, vol. 54, no. 4, 2004, pp. 357–369.
I.A. Davies and A. Crane, 'Ethical decision-making in the fair trade companies', *Journal of Business Ethics*, vol. 45, no. 1/2, 2003, pp. 79–92.
J. Donaldson, *Key Issues in Business Ethics?*, Academic Press, 1989.
Trevor Gambling and Rifaat Ahmed Abdel Karim, *Business and Accounting Ethics in Islam*, Mansell, 1991.
V. Henderson, *What's Ethical in Business?*, McGraw Hill, 1992.
Institute of Applied Professional Ethics – www.cats.ohiou.edu/ethics.
International Business Ethics Institute – www.business-ethics.org.
Jack Maurice, *Accounting Ethics*, Pitman Publishing, 1996.
Marcia P. Miceli and Janet P. Near, *Blowing the Whistle: The Organizational and Legal Implications for Companies and Employees*, Lexington Books, 1992.
D. Matten and A. Crane, 'What is stakeholder democracy? Perspectives and Issues', *Business Ethics: A European Review*, vol. 14, no. 1, 2005, pp. 6–13.
Peter Pratley, *The Essence of Business Ethics*, Prentice Hall, 1995.
William Shaw and Vincent Barry, *Moral Issues in Business* (7th edition), Wadsworth, 1998.
M. Velasquez, *Business Ethics: Concepts and Cases*, Prentice Hall, 1992.
Simon Webley, *Codes of Ethics and International Business*, Institute of Business Ethics, 1997.

Index